CAMBRIDGE STUDIES IN MUSIC

GENERAL EDITORS: JOHN STEVENS AND PETER LE HURAY

Words and Music in the Middle Ages

CAMBRIDGE STUDIES IN MUSIC

GENERAL EDITORS: JOHN STEVENS AND PETER LE HURAY

Volumes in the series include:

Music and poetry in the early Tudor court
JOHN STEVENS

Music and theatre from Poliziano to Monteverdi
NINO PIRROTTA

Music and patronage in sixteenth-century Mantua
IAIN FENLON

Patrons and musicians of the English Renaissance
DAVID PRICE

Music and the Reformation in England 1549–1660
PETER LE HURAY

The music of the English parish church
NICHOLAS TEMPERLEY

The organ music of J. S. Bach
Volume I: Preludes, toccatas, fantasias, fugues, etc.
Volume II: Works based on chorales
Volume III: A background
PETER WILLIAMS

Mendelssohn's musical education
R. LARRY TODD

The musical language of Berlioz
JULIAN RUSHTON

Musical life in Biedermeier Vienna
ALICE M. HANSON

'S'onques nuls hom': Crusade song from British Library MS Harl.
3775 fol. 14r

WORDS AND MUSIC IN THE MIDDLE AGES

SONG, NARRATIVE, DANCE AND DRAMA, 1050–1350

JOHN STEVENS

*Professor of Medieval and Renaissance English
in the University of Cambridge
and President of Magdalene College*

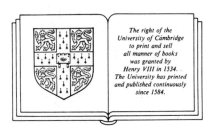

*The right of the
University of Cambridge
to print and sell
all manner of books
was granted by
Henry VIII in 1534.
The University has printed
and published continuously
since 1584.*

CAMBRIDGE UNIVERSITY PRESS

CAMBRIDGE

NEW YORK   NEW ROCHELLE

MELBOURNE   SYDNEY

Published by the Press Syndicate of the University of Cambridge
The Pitt Building, Trumpington Street, Cambridge CB2 1RP
32 East 57th Street, New York, NY 10022, USA
10 Stamford Road, Oakleigh, Melbourne 3166, Australia

First published 1986
Reprinted 1988

Printed in Great Britain at the University Press, Cambridge

British Library cataloguing in publication data
Stevens, John, 1921–
Words and music in the Middle Ages : song
narrative, dance and drama, 1050–1350. –
(Cambridge studies in music)
1. Vocal music – Europe – History and criticism
I. Title
784'.094   ML1402

Library of Congress cataloguing in publication data
Stevens, John, 1921–
Words and music in the Middle Ages.
(Cambridge studies in music)
Bibliography.
Includes index.
1. Music – 500–1400 – History and criticism.
2. Poetry – Medieval – History and criticism.
3. Drama – Medieval – History and criticism.   4. Music
and literature.   I. Title.   II. Series.
ML172.S86   1986   784'.09'02   85–25496

ISBN 0 521 24507 9 hard covers
ISBN 0 521 33904 9 paperback

The music examples are drawn by John Stevens

'Sounds pass quickly away but numbers remain.'

Ignoto

'There is, I am persuaded, a world of profound mathematics in this matter of music: indeed, no one could doubt that.'

Gerard Manley Hopkins

'No art is more enveloped in dark diallect then Musick is, all which Impedimenta I would have Removed, that the access to the art and practise may be more Recomendable and Inviting.'

Roger North

For Karl

CONTENTS

Part II: Relations of speech, action, emotion and meaning

PREFACE

During the long time that I have been working towards, if not always directly on, this book, I have incurred more debts of gratitude than I can possibly repay. Its questions have been the theme of many a *dulce colloquium*. At appropriate places below I name some at least of those whose expertise has saved me from particular error or omission. In this Preface I should like to mention those whose help has been of longer standing and wider import.

Chief amongst them is Karl Reichl, who in the course of innumerable conversations over the years, in England and in Germany, has given me the benefit of his wide-ranging knowledge of lyric and narrative in literatures and languages almost too numerous to mention. At a later stage he not only read the whole manuscript and contributed valuable comments but also offered solutions for various cruxes and checked the vernacular translations (an act of quixotic goodwill). I am grateful to my daughter Deborah for her inspired choice of husband and for her forbearance in letting him fulfil all the duties of a son-in-law. Another old friend, Margaret Bent, also read large sections of the completed manuscript; her sceptical but always warm-hearted comments made me do much re-thinking and re-writing, especially of Part III. I doubt whether even now I will have met her exacting standards; but I am deeply grateful to her for being an intellectual presence. Peter le Huray also, my co-editor in this series, was generous enough to read the text as a whole at an early stage and to comment and encourage. Arthur Taylor, after a lifetime spent in removing howlers from schoolboys' Latin, took up the task again out of the kindness of his heart; elegancies as well as accuracies in the translations are often due to him. Other colleagues to whom I am grateful include Richard Axton, Patrick Boyde, Peter Dronke, Peter Rickard and the late Leslie Topsfield.

One of the great pleasures of having research students is the way they so quickly become one's teachers and advisers. Amongst these I must thank Jennifer Fellows, who has plied me with bibliographical information and given much other assistance; Susan Rankin, for reading and commenting on several chapters as well as allowing me to use her completed dissertation; and Janthia Yearley, for the same kind offices and the same generosity in scholarship. During the last two years others have ungrudgingly taken on more menial tasks and earned my thanks – Simon Lavery, Ann Buckley and Mary O'Neill. My wife, Charlotte, has not only helped in similar drudgery but devoted many hours to preventing my working books from falling to pieces, binding them with more elegance than some deserved.

But music, and its study, is a vain and empty pursuit unless it is submitted sometimes to the judgment of the ear. In this respect too I have been lucky in persuading my friends John Pritchard, Judith Nelson and Poppy Holden to sing for me on various occasions. To hear what a skilful performer can do with a suggested style of interpretation is often an education as well as a delight. Likewise I must acknowledge a pervasive debt to Mary Berry. To the Schola Gregoriana and to her inspiring direction of it since 1975, I owe almost all my experience of plainchant and of ecclesiastical drama in their living setting, the liturgy of the Church – the culminating point of many companionable Cambridge weekends.

I have incurred many debts at the University Press – especially to Rosemary Dooley for kindly enquiries, patient prodding and acts of friendship over many years; but also to her successor as editor, Penny Souster, who has handled the last tangle of problems with inexhaustible goodwill. Eric van Tassel's subediting sets his authors impossible standards of meticulousness and clarity (I am both grateful and sad to think that mine was his last book before he departed for Princeton). Many librarians, too, have been kind to me, but none more continuously so than Richard Andrewes of the Pendlebury Library, inheriting the late Charles Cudworth's tolerance of wayward but well-meaning borrowers. Derek Williams and his staff in the Anderson Room of the Cambridge University Library have never failed in cheerfulness and resource, even whilst the room seemed to be falling about their ears. I have moreover to thank the British Academy for two research grants which enabled me to study in libraries abroad; and my College for timely leave.

Finally, this book is, for its author, a record of friendship and its sub-text one of *dilecta familiaritas*. To all those, named and unnamed, who have helped to make a book about music an experience of *armonia*, I express my heartfelt thanks.

J.S.

Magdalene College
August 1985

NOTE TO THE READER

Terms

I have tried not to use technical terms when more common ones would serve. Nevertheless there are inevitably a number of terms both musical and literary which may not be familiar to all. For the reader's convenience these are listed in the Glossary.

Metrical and musical symbols

I use 'p' (paroxytone) and 'pp' (proparoxytone) according to the common practice of Latinists to describe the accent at the end of a line. Thus, '7p' means a line of seven syllables accented on the last but one; '7pp' the same, accentuated on the last but two. In referring to French and Italian lines, however, I use a superscript '˘' to indicate a line with an extra weak syllable at the end. Thus '10˘' means a line of *eleven* syllables of which the last is unstressed.

The standard system is used for indicating pitches by letters. Starting from the bass: *G-B*, *c-b*, *c′* (middle c)-*b′*, *c″-b″*.

Musical examples

The musical examples, most of which are taken from the MSS or facsimiles, are transcriptions rather than editions; I have occasionally made small emendations without noting them, more particularly in the literary texts on the basis of standard editions. In many of the examples a standardized representation of the original notation has been provided above the stave.

References

References in the notes to books and articles are by author's name and, if more than one work is referred to, by name and date. In the case of multi-volume works only the first date is given. Fuller details will be found in the Bibliography. French chanson titles are frequently followed by R in brackets with a number; the reference is to *Raynauds Bibliographie des altfranzösischen Liedes* in Hans Spanke's revised edition (1955). For the principal manuscripts I have used titles which are listed on p. 512 under 'Sources', and referred to by a numbered reference (e.g. Source 19). Abbreviations of periodicals, series and works of reference are listed on pp. xvi–xvii; for other abbreviations, consult the Bibliography.

ABBREVIATIONS

(★ indicates full details in the Bibliography)

AcM	*Acta Musicologica*
AH	★*Analecta Hymnica*
AMw	*Archiv für Musikwissenschaft*
AnnM	*Annales Musicologiques*
Archiv	*Archiv für das Studium der neueren Sprachen und Literaturen*
CCM	*Cahiers de civilisation médiévale*
CFMA	Les classiques français du moyen âge
CMM	Corpus Mensurabilis Musicae
CSM	Corpus scriptorum de musica
EBM	★*Early Bodleian Music*
EEH	★*Early English Harmony*
EETS	Early English Text Society
EM	*Early Music*
HDM	★*Harvard Dictionary of Music*
HMT	*Handwörterbuch der musikalischen Terminologie*
Index	★*The Index of Middle English Verse*
JAMS	*Journal of the American Musicological Society*
JEGP	*Journal of English and Germanic Philology*
JMT	*Journal of Music Theory*
JPMMS	*Journal of the Plainsong and Mediaeval Music Society*
KJb	*Kirchenmusikalisches Jahrbuch*
LU	★*Liber Usualis*
MÆ	*Medium Ævum*
MD	*Musica Disciplina*
MGG	*Die Musik in Geschichte und Gegenwart*, ed. F. Blume, 16 vols. (Kassel 1949–79)
ML	*Music and Letters*
MLWL	*Revised Medieval Latin Word-List* (London, 1965)
MMMA	Monumenta Monodica Medii Aevi
MP	*Modern Philology*
MQ	*Musical Quarterly*
MR	*Music Review*
MSD	Musicological Studies and Documents, general ed. A. Carapetyan
New Grove	★*The New Grove Dictionary of Music and Musicians*

NOHM	★*The New Oxford History of Music*
ODCC	★*Oxford Dictionary of the Christian Church*
PL	*Patrologiae Cursus Completus . . . Series Latina*
PMFC	★*Polyphonic Music of the Fourteenth Century*
PMLA	Publications of the Modern Language Association
PMMS	Plainsong and Mediaeval Music Society
PRMA	*Proceedings of the Royal Musical Association*
R	*Raynauds Bibliographie*
RBM	*Revue Belge de Musicologie*
RdM	*Revue de musicologie*
RILM	*Répertoire International de la Littérature Musicale*
RIM	*Rivista italiana di musicologia*
RISM	Répertoire International des Sources Musicales
RMA	Royal Musical Association
SATF	Société des Anciens Textes Français
SiMG	*Sammelbände der Internationalen Musikgesellschaft*
SinP	*Studies in Philology*
TLF	Textes littéraires français
ZfdA	*Zeitschrift für deutsches Altertum*
ZfdP	*Zeitschrift für deutsche Philologie*
ZffSL	*Zeitschrift für französische Sprache und Literatur*
ZfrP	*Zeitschrift für romanische Philologie*
ZMw	*Zeitschrift für Musikwissenschaft*

'Ut quid iubes': *versus* from Paris,
Bibliothèque Nationale, MS lat. 1154 fol. 131v

INTRODUCTION

English songs – that is, songs with English words – are few and far between in the early Middle Ages; only a score survive from the three centuries that followed the Norman Conquest, and they are scattered in a variety of sources.[1] On their own they form a woefully inadequate basis for any serious study of words and music in the period up to Chaucer. This small and fragmented repertoire can easily be extended to about a hundred songs by taking into account songs with French and Latin texts, some found in the same manuscripts, others not. That the 'songs of England' might be a more rewarding basis for study than 'English songs' seems obvious indeed, if only because French and Latin were more important languages for the educated; the surprise is only that no one up to the present has undertaken it. In a subsequent volume I hope to present these 'songs of England' in a modern transcription, together with an account of the sources in which they are found and an examination of the relations between music and poetry in them.

The present volume has taken a different direction. The 'songs of England' seemed insufficient, especially on the vernacular side, to provide answers to the questions which needed asking. This determined me to attempt to understand the European traditions to which the insular songs were clearly indebted. Here the opposite problem arose. Instead of insufficiency, a superabundance of material – songs in Provençal, northern French, German, Italian and Spanish, to say nothing of a huge and varied Latin repertoire – thousands of items in all. Here certain limitations would be necessary.

The decision to limit the study to monophonic song resulted in the first instance from an accident of exploration, though a natural one. The enquiry had to start somewhere, and since most of the songs of England survived with only one line of music, it seemed sensible to take this type of art-song as the starting-place. However, what began as a decision of convenience soon became one of scholarly conviction, personal inclination and, in due course, sheer practical necessity. The conviction arose from a growing sense that an understanding of medieval song was bound to be based, if it was to be true to

---

[1] Dobson and Harrison, *Medieval English Songs* (1979), print twenty of which about half are monophonic; it is impossible to be precise because the borderline between polyphony and monophony is blurred (e.g. 'Angelus ad virginem' appears in various forms).

the facts, on an understanding of melody. (The truth of this has been splendidly demonstrated for church music by Frank Harrison in his *Music in Medieval Britain* (1958), which traces the growth of liturgical polyphony from Gregorian chant.)

The primacy of melody is a thing which Oriental peoples may find easier to grasp than Westerners. One current European description of melody is as 'the surface of harmony' – a phrase which shows how far we have moved from the conceptions of the Middle Ages. Medieval writers have, in fact, no word for 'harmony' in our sense. They have terms, of course, to describe concordant and discordant intervals, such as *diatessaron* (a fourth) and *diapente* (a fifth), borrowed from Greek theory. But they have no word to describe the temporal structure established by a progression of related chords, which is the primary meaning we give to the term 'harmony'. It is not until the late fifteenth century that we find the word *harmonia* used to describe chords in the modern sense (Gafurius, 1496: 'harmonia . . . conficitur ex acuto, gravi et medio sono'), and not until the early eighteenth century that harmony was formally recognized as a structural element in music.[2] The word 'harmony', in its Latin and vernacular forms, means to the Middle Ages in general something quite different. The word is constantly in their mouths, and refers to the proportional harmoniousness of *melody*.

The distinction between monophonic and polyphonic music is superficially obvious, but it proves quite difficult to maintain under scrutiny. The development of polyphony itself is not, in the earlier centuries at least, a harmonic study but a study of the way one melody is combined with another or with others. And linear conceptions continued to dominate music until the end of the Middle Ages. Moreover, scores of monophonic songs occur as melodies in polyphonic pieces, especially in *conductus* and motet. To take an example, the principal melody of the *conductus* 'Procurans odium' (2 or 3 voc.) occurs in another *conductus* of the same type from the repertoire of Notre Dame in Paris, 'Purgator criminum' (3 voc.) and also as a well-known trouvère chanson, Blondel de Nesle's 'Amour dont sui espris' (R1545).[3] The melody appears again as a religious song (R1546) celebrating the miracles of the Virgin, in the collection by Gautier de Coinci (d. 1236).[4] The inter-relation of monophonic and polyphonic is complex; and, clearly, the distinction between monophony and polyphony can never be a hard-and-fast one in this period.[5] And yet there is a distinction. It would certainly be anachronistic and misleading to talk of 'harmonizations' of Blondel's melody 'Amour dont sui

[2] Apel, 'Harmony' in *HDM*. See also Dahlhaus, 'Harmony' in *New Grove*: he rightly bases his account of medieval theory on the concept of *musica harmonica* but does not mention the other medieval concept – of a melodic *harmonia* (balance and proportion).

[3] For the reference R1545 and all similar references in the text, see the List of Abbreviations. Terms such as *conductus* and *discantus* are briefly defined in the Glossary.

[4] Full details of the whole complex in Chailley's study of Gautier de Coinci (1959), 52–4.

[5] This is further argued in an interesting article by E. H. Sanders, 'Consonance and Rhythm in the Organum of the 12th and 13th centuries', *JAMS* 33 (1980) 264.

espris' (assuming it is Blondel's). Nevertheless, something has happened when a melody is used polyphonically, given a *discantus* or a counterpoint, and the listener must take account of it. The dynamic and the tonality of the melody are no longer entirely, or even primarily, determined by linear relations but by 'vertical' ones. Since only a limited number of concords are admissible for use, especially at cadences, the main melody is framed in a set of 'vertical' relationships which are certainly harmonic in a rudimentary way. Such a frame may give a new power to the melody but deprives it of fluidity and flexibility.

The largest and finest monument of melodic art in the European heritage is, beyond any doubt whatsoever, the traditional song of the Catholic Church – ecclesiastical chant or plainsong. It was the music *par excellence* of the liturgy; indeed, for most of the Middle Ages in most churches, the exclusive music. We should not let our traditional engagement, natural and rewarding though it may be, with the growth of polyphony and harmony delude us into believing that the period with which we are concerned, *c.* 1100–1350, was a period in which polyphony was widespread or was as important as it now seems to be to us. As Frank Harrison has written,[6]

Plainsong was an integral part of the Christian liturgies from the beginning of their history. Polyphony, on the other hand, gained a place in the liturgy by its ability to lend ceremonial distinction to the performance of the established plainsong. Its function, therefore, was analogous to that of the many other forms of ceremonial by which the more significant parts of the ritual were distinguished from the less significant . . .

Plainsong was the basic stuff of liturgical music; polyphony was a ceremonial ornament. One reason why it could not be widespread is that it demanded the services of skilled and literate solo singers. Polyphony, it has to be remembered, was not synonymous with choral singing. The *chorus*, i.e. the monks or secular clergy 'in choir', sang the chant, not music in parts. The surviving European manuscripts of liturgical chant are numbered in their thousands, a perpetual witness to the unquestioned predominance of melody as the song of the Church.

The total corpus of early-medieval melodies is huge. Apart from the inheritance of traditional chant, two adjacent, and overlapping, repertoires are important: (i) the newly composed ecclesiastical chants of the ninth to the thirteenth centuries, many of which have verse texts – tropes, sequences ('proses'), rhymed offices, *conductus*; (ii) the melodies of the liturgical drama, in so far as they were not taken from the official liturgy. Some part of these repertoires is 'para-liturgical' – associated with the liturgy but not prescribed. But there are also (iii) non-liturgical Latin songs, variously called *versus*, *conductus*, *cantus*, *cantiones*, *planctus* etc., contained in manuscripts associated especially with St Martial at Limoges and, later, with Notre Dame in Paris. In

[6] Harrison (1958), 104.

addition each major European vernacular produced song-melodies which have survived. The earliest repertoire is that of the troubadours starting in the early twelfth century; it is written in Provençal, the *langue d'oc*, but was not confined to the area of present-day Provence. The largest is that of their equivalents in the north of France, the trouvères, written in the *langue d'oïl*. Neither of these excludes religious songs, but they are primarily courtly. Associated with the trouvère repertoire but distinguishable from it is the phenomenon of the *refrains*, short snatches of courtly verse with tuneful melodies forming the material of dance-song. In France composers of note continued to cultivate the art of melody alongside the new polyphony well into the fourteenth century. Two of especial note are Jehan de Lescurel (d. 1304) and Guillaume de Machaut (d. 1377). The surviving songs of Italy and Spain are almost entirely religious: the popular *laude spirituali* of Italy, connected with the growth of Franciscanism in the thirteenth century; and the somewhat more courtly *cantigas de Santa María* of Spain, also thirteenth-century. The German sources contain the songs of the Minnesinger, from the thirteenth century onwards, and a few *Geisslerlieder* (penitential songs) of the fourteenth century. The melodic art of the Meistersinger, as of the popular composers of the French noël, lies in the fifteenth and sixteenth centuries.

Faced with such a wealth of melody, two limitations seemed essential – one geographical, the other chronological. A natural geographical limitation suggested itself. I have chosen to deal mainly with northern France, the cultural area to which the greater part of Britain belonged. To a degree we find hard to imagine, the Norman civilization had permeated and overlaid, though it never obliterated, the 'old English' culture. French and Latin were its linguistic instruments. Both had their special domains – Latin in the liturgy of the Church and in the higher learning, French in courtly and aristocratic life; but both were generally useful and used – in business, in administration, in diplomacy, in ceremony, and, not least, in entertainment. Latin as well as French was a living, *spoken* language, and a natural vehicle for verse, wit, story and song.

However, I have not confined myself strictly to the Norman area or to the wider realm of the *langue d'oïl*. For instance, in the chapter on narrative as a musical genre it seemed desirable not to exclude German poems; this was partly because the linguistic kinship between German and English was bound to be illuminating (Latin and French have no important traditions of alliterative verse, for instance), partly because the chapter aims to bring together for the first time in English, or I believe in any language, a comprehensive range of the material necessary for understanding the problems of musical narrative. Similarly, in discussing the chansons of the trouvères I have made more than occasional use of troubadour song, for it was with the troubadours that vernacular courtly song in all its sophistication began. Furthermore, I have relied deeply on Dante, if only because in the *De Vulgari Eloquentia* and in passages elsewhere he speaks more penetratingly about the whole enterprise of vernacular song, Provençal, Northern French and Italian, than any other medieval writer. I have strayed towards the south on other occasions, too, as for instance by describing a Padua Annunciation ceremony at the beginning of the chapters on drama. But I hope never to have done so without making the reader aware of it – and never when it might mislead.

The chronological bounds of the study are defined roughly as *c.* 1050 to *c.* 1350, by which time art-song became more and more cultivated as a polyphonic form. But I have not regarded the bounds as sacrosanct. There was seldom any temptation to go beyond the fourteenth century; but in several parts of the book I have gone backwards in time, to before the Conquest, because the nature of the argument or of the materials demanded it. For instance, it would be hardly practicable to discuss such theoretical concepts as the difference between *ritmus* and *metrum* without grounding them in earlier writers. Moreover, the appeal to the past was a favourite medieval procedure. Reverence for past masters, the *auctores* who wielded *auctoritas* (the very terms are revealing), meant that everything each one said could, and indeed should, be reconciled with everything else. So, in treating Boethius and Bede as in an important sense contemporary masters, we are entering into an essential element of the thought we wish to understand. My reasons, however, for allowing pre-Conquest material into discussions of sequence and *planctus* and of the liturgical drama are more purely practical; it seemed helpful, and for the most part unavoidable, if the object was not to be falsified.

The decisions to limit the scope of this book to monophonic music, to the period *c.* 1050–*c.* 1350, and to the French-speaking area of northern Europe were all, for the reasons given, easier to take than to carry out to the letter. A further limitation proved even harder to observe than these. I was clear from the start that I wished to centre the investigation in what might in a very loose sense be called 'secular' song; but the inadequacy of the term was only too evident. 'Vernacular' would be even more misleading. The single word that comes nearest to defining the corpus of melody is 'non-liturgical', but even that is not very satisfactory. I have, in fact, interpreted 'song' widely enough to include, for instance, the liturgical drama, much of which is not merely associated with the liturgy but deeply embedded in it. The Latin *conductus*, too, with its strong festive affiliations, is often part of a liturgy, or at least a 'para-liturgy' – on New Year's Day (*in festo circumcisionis*) for example.[7] Finally, I have devoted one complete chapter, though with a strong sense of my own temerity in doing so, to considering some aspects of Gregorian chant itself, since the relationship of words and music in the chant must be of fundamental interest and has often been misrepresented.

Such, roughly, is the material scope of the book; and, despite the self-imposed limitations, its breadth is bound to have led to some superficialities. This risk seemed to me, however, worth taking. Indeed, it had to be taken in

---

[7] The term 'para-liturgical' is discussed in chapter 3 p. 80.

order to achieve the wider aims. The principal of these was to examine the
relations between words and music. There has never been, to my knowledge,
anything approaching a general study of words and music in this period,
though German scholars such as Hans Spanke and Ewald Jammers have made
many signal contributions towards one.[8] Yet the need for such a study seems
evident, since anyone who is interested in medieval songs and lyrics, whether
as scholar or performer, makes assumptions about the way melodies and
poems are related to each other. These assumptions are not of trivial importance, especially in this early period, and often determine the very questions
which can be asked as well as the answers that can be given. For instance, if
you believe that composers in all ages must inevitably respond to the sounds
of individual words, you are not likely to question the view that the chansons
of the trouvères are fit for declamation. And, if you hold that view, other
consequences follow. What I have tried to do above all is to examine the
ready-made and often unconscious assumptions that we all have and to
discover what questions need to be asked. In the event I have, I am aware,
raised more problems than I have been able to solve, and have uncovered some
areas of general and not merely personal ignorance.

There is, of course, not one relationship between words and music requiring definition but several. Indeed, to demonstrate multiplicity seemed in itself
worthwhile. For this reason the book proceeds by a series of separate studies,
each devoted to a different part or aspect of early monody – the courtly
chanson; Latin song; sequence and *lai*; dance-song in French and Latin; and so
on. In several of the individual chapters I found myself considerably hampered
by the absence of any succinct published account of the *material* I wished to
study – not simply in English but in any language. This was particularly the
case with narrative, as already mentioned, and with dance-song, but it applies
also to the Latin *lai*, to the *planctus* and, one could say, to the whole area of
Latin monophonic song.

Surprising as it might seem, there is no substantial account in English of the
'secular' melodic tradition; and even the compendious and lucid chapter by Sir
Jack Westrup in the *New Oxford History of Music* is now many years out of
date.[9] It is true that the non-liturgical monophonic music of the period is
briefly discussed in the various standard histories which have appeared since
then, but it is usually tucked away in a corner and rarely treated with the fresh

---

[8] See Bibliography, especially Spanke (1936) and Jammers (1963).
[9] To the works cited in the text (Stäblein (1975), van der Werf (1972), Westrup in *NOHM* II)
should be added, from general histories of medieval music, Reese (1940) and Hoppin (1978)
for their comparatively generously allotted space. Gérold's *La Musique au moyen âge* (1932),
moreover, deserves special mention for its lucid and comprehensive coverage of the
monophonic repertory (in some 250 pp) and its fine selection of examples. A. Machabey's
'Introduction à la lyrique musicale romane' (1959) is also useful. Amongst the more literary
introductions to medieval European lyric Dronke's *Medieval Lyric* (1968, rev. 1978) with
extensive bibliographies and several musical illustrations is outstanding for its balance
between the particular and the general.

interest which it deserves. In a word, the phenomenon of melody outside the central chant traditions is felt, if not stated, to be peripheral. We still live with the unfortunate legacy of generations of historians for whom the 'evolution of polyphony' was the all-important event to which the whole musical creation moved, even though evolutionary conceptions of art are now discredited and interest in exotic musics is much more lively and appreciative.

So the second aim of the book became to provide a conspectus of the art of melody in northern Europe, *c.* 1050–1350. It is only a conspectus at best and not the systematic account which is needed; the descriptions are subsidiary to the main argument. Nevertheless it seemed necessary to do something in a descriptive way to help not only literary readers but also musicians to find their bearings in one of the least frequented bits of artistic countryside in the European scene. I have been greatly helped in compiling my 'guide' by the timely publication of *The New Grove*. This magnificent all-round lantern has illuminated many dark corners for me; but it does not, of course, in itself provide the needed 'guide', and its coverage of the monophonic material is distinctly uneven. Readers of German with a good musical knowledge are now catered for by the magisterial work of Bruno Stäblein, *Schriftbild der einstimmigen Musik* (1975), to which I am myself deeply indebted; it covers the whole field, liturgical and non-liturgical.

The study of the trouvère tradition, it should be added, has been made much easier of late by the publication (in the series Monumenta Monodica Medii Aevi, inaugurated by Stäblein), of the first two volumes devoted to non-liturgical monody; they contain virtually all the versions of all the melodies of eleven trouvères, edited by Hendrik van der Werf. The editor's earlier general study, *The Chansons of the Troubadours and Trouvères* (1972), is also by far the best recent description in English of the courtly repertoire; I have found myself obliged to differ from van der Werf on a number of crucial issues, but this has not diminished my gratitude for the stimulus his book provides.

It is natural and right that someone who has spent a good number of years working on what might seem a specialized topic should ask himself and explain to others why in his view it is not a 'mere specialism'. There are several reasons why the diverse and changing relations of music and poetry never cease to fascinate and have seemed to justify expenditure of time and labour. But the principal reason is that they compel one to ask central questions about what might, for want of a better term, be called the 'aesthetic' of the age. To consider the relationship – or what in some cases seems like a non-relationship – between a poem and its melody is to find oneself meditating on the 'meaning', for contemporaries, of the sounds they heard, including the sound of poetry when read. In this instance I have found the meditation fruitful – or like to think I have – first for the new insights it has given me into the particular examples of song or chant or poem analysed in each chapter – the *carole*, for example, the recitation of the *Passion*, saints' lives, the plays of St Nicholas, *planctus* and *lai*. In some cases the word 'insight' may be too positive; what I

have achieved may look like a deeper, more complex sense of enigma.
Secondly, setting the particular gains and enriching riddles on one side, I
found myself increasingly interested in the bearing of certain general concepts
– those of 'number', *musica*, *ritmus*, *harmonia*, *modulatio*, for instance – on the
problem of interpretation, especially rhythmic interpretation.

As a result my third and final aim in this volume became to try to throw new
light if I could on this vexed problem. To anyone with a serious interest in the
songs of the Middle Ages one question is centrally absorbing – what was the
rhythmic relationship of words and melody in monophony? It is absorbing
because of its practical import for editors and performers; absorbing intellectually, because its consideration demands a close acquaintance with the techniques of the two arts – a substantial demand in itself; and absorbing imaginatively because at root it is, as I have hinted, not purely a technical but an
aesthetic question. Its solution is dependent on the way people felt about music
and about poetry in the twelfth and thirteenth centuries. If it could be solved,
we should have taken a great step forward in understanding; and even if it
cannot, the endeavour to reach a solution – or, at least, formulate a hypothesis
– in an open-minded spirit must be educative and illuminating.

The hypothesis I shall put forward in the last chapters of the book is that of
an approximate equality of syllables, and consequently of notes or note-
groups, for that major part of the repertoire which is in my view unmeasured.
The isosyllabic hypothesis is not a new one in itself; a number of scholars have
advocated it, even adopted it for their transcriptions in the course of this
century – notably the Italians Ugo Sesini, Giuseppe Vecchi and Raffaello
Monterosso. The positive case for it has, however, never been fully argued;
nor, I believe, has the right emphasis yet been put upon the unique way it can
represent the relationship between the words and the melody. The case rests
on historical and aesthetic grounds as well as on technical ones and requires the
careful interpretation of a wide variety of evidence, musical and theoretical,
on the issue of rhythm and metre. This is why I have chosen to place my
discussion of it at the end. The musical transcriptions in the text of the chapters
which precede it are mostly 'neutral' and unmeasured. The analyses also are,
as far as may be, independent of any particular rhythmic interpretation and
have, I think, a validity of their own.

Finally, there are two particular omissions from the present study which
call for comment. I do not discuss, except incidentally, the new French
monophonic art of the fourteenth century – the songs of Jehan de l'Escurel
and, much more important, Guillaume de Machaut. One reason for the
omission will, I think, become evident to the reader. The intricate rhythmic
patterns of Machaut's monophonic *lais* and lesser forms (exemplified in the
Remede de Fortune) represent a new departure. The novelty of their 'measure' is
specified in elaborate but unambiguous mensural notation. Although there
are many features which link Machaut to the centuries-old art of melody, he
is, to my mind at least, even here the proponent of an *ars nova* the fascination of

which may have motivated the rhythmic revisers of whom I speak in chapter
13 (see especially section 11).[10]

There is a second considered omission: I have not discussed 'the
instrumental assumption', as it might be called. Performances of monophonic
song on the concert platform and in the recording studio have generally been
and still are accompanied by instruments. In the early days the attempts were
cautious and dull. More recently a 'thousand twangling instruments' have
hummed about our ears. The results – especially the rococo-like virtuosity of
recent ensembles – have often been impressive and incline one to forget that
there is questionable historical warrant for the practice. In crudest form the
unspoken argument has been as follows: 'Medieval literature and art contain
thousands of references to, and depictions of, instruments and players. The
musical sources of the period contain hundreds of songs without any performance instructions whatever. Therefore the songs were accompanied by the
instruments.' But were they? The question needs thorough scholarly
investigation.[11] Such an investigation will have to take into account the
likelihood that different genres obeyed different rules. The performance of
lais, for example, is often described as taking place with instrumental support.
Concerning the performance of chansons there is, on the other hand, a
weighty silence; neither manuscript illuminations in the chansonniers, nor the
texts of the songs, nor the regulations of the puys seem to have anything to say
about this. This unanswered question is of real musical importance; there
could be as great a difference between the performances, varied as they are, to
which we are accustomed and those of the Middle Ages (which may also have
varied) as between Gregorian chant as it was romantically performed in the
nineteenth century and the style which Guido of Arezzo was trying to teach in
the eleventh.

[10] Another reason for omitting Machaut is that he has been the subject of intensive study over
the years, has been admirably edited and often performed in versions unquestionably more
authentic than those we hear of earlier medieval songs.
[11] The first issue of the *Basler Jahrbuch für historische Musikpraxis* (1977) was entirely devoted to
problems of the performance of monophonic song, with special attention to the relevance of
non-European traditions. The volume is full of interest, but it seems to me symptomatic of
the present situation that Thomas Binkley's 55-page article is based entirely on the unquestioned 'instrumental assumption'.

PART I
NUMBER IN MUSIC AND VERSE

I

THE COURTLY CHANSON

The sixth and last book of St Augustine's *De Musica* is entitled 'Deus numerorum aeternorum fons et origo' and describes 'the ascent from rhythm in sense to the immortal rhythm which is truth'. The account is highly theological and speculative, and if one had not read the five books which precede it one might be forgiven for not realizing that it forms the peroration of what seems at first sight to be an elementary treatise on Latin quantitative metre.[1] The all-embracing, metaphysical nature of the concept of *musica* is one to which I shall return in chapter 11, 'Music and meaning', where I discuss the relationship between music in our modern sense and words regarded not simply as sounds but as having 'meaning' and referring to things other than themselves. Our concern in the present chapter is with an aspect of *musica* which is indeed metaphysical but also of direct practical import – number.

By suggesting that 'number' is an aspect of *musica*, I may already have inverted the proper order of things. It would be truer to say that 'number' (the Latin *numerus*, translating Greek *rhythmos*) is the fundamental reality; *musica* is the theory of its realization in sounds. Thus, Plotinus (A.D. 205–70):

Number exists before objects which are described by number. The variety of sense objects merely recalls to the soul the notion of number.[2]

Or the encyclopedist Isidore of Seville (flor. *c.* 600):

Sine musica nulla disciplina potest esse perfecta

Without music no branch of learning can be complete.[3]

To some extent it is a matter of terminology. There are many instances of the term *musica* being used in the same fundamental sense as 'number' is here.

---

[1] The *De Musica libri sex* is in *Oeuvres de Saint Augustin*, ed. Finnaert and Thonnard, 1st series, VII. (Paris 1947.) A convenient synopsis is by W. F. Jackson Knight, *St Augustine's De Musica* (1949). It is Augustine's only educational treatise (A.D. *c.* 387–9).

[2] Plotinus, VI.6.4.20–4. For Greek text, see P. Henry and H.-R. Schwyzer, *Plotini Opera*, tom. III, Enneas VI (Brussels and Leiden 1973). I thank Henry Chadwick for tracing this text.

[3] Isidore, *Etymologies*, III ch. xvi ed. W. M. Lindsay (Oxford 1911). See Strunk, 94, for this excerpt in transln.

Musicam nosse nihil aliud nisi cunctarum rerum ordinem scire.[4]

To understand music is nothing other than to have knowledge of the ordering of the universe.

However, in the present chapter it is 'number' in its various senses and implications that will be pursued.[5]

1   Number symbolism and numerical disposition

Numerus, 'number', has several different meanings in the Middle Ages and beyond. It means, of course, the numbers of arithmetic in the ordinary mathematical sense. It means proportion and order, since these are what numbers properly describe; 3 - 9 - 81 - 243 is a set of proportions which could describe a building or a piece of music. It means, as applied to the arts of sound in time, rhythm; Pope can still say in 1711, 'I lisped in numbers for the numbers came.' More metaphorically, 'number' is a term to describe all relationships of harmony and proportion between moving bodies or in man between 'the various sensible, intellectual and moral qualities'.[6] Some idea of the richness of the concept of number, as well as of the difficulty of making firm distinctions between its various meanings, can be gained from a passage aptly chosen by D. W. Robertson out of St Augustine's *De Musica*, which describes a wood-carver at work:

Thus the artisan, by means of the rational numbers which are in his art, is able to produce the corporal [i.e. 'kinesthetic'] numbers that are implicit in the habitual action of his craft. He can by means of these corporal numbers produce overt numbers, those by which he moves his members and to which are relevant the numbers governing

---

[4] Cited de Bruyne, III.231, from Thomas of York (thirteenth century), referring to Trismegistus in the *Sapientiale*.

[5] On number and number symbolism in the Middle Ages and earlier, see Hopper (1938); Butler (1970); Otto von Simson, *The Gothic Cathedral* (1956), especially on numbers in architecture; and the series of three articles in *Viator* 6 (1975) by C. W. Jones (literature), R. L. Crocker (music) and W. Horn (art), with further refs. De Bruyne, *Etudes d'esthétique médiévale* (1946), is rich in original texts, omitted from the abridgement transl. E. B. Hennessy, *The Esthetics of the Middle Ages* (New York 1969). Number symbolism in medieval literature is discussed with bibliographical references by Reiss (1970). The 'immense mathematical refinement' behind Boethius's *De Musica* is made clear in Chadwick, *Boethius: the Consolations of Music, Logic, Theology and Philosophy* (1981); see especially chapter II, on the liberal arts. I am grateful also to Gillian Evans for help and advice, especially on medieval arithmetics. See also Robertson *passim*; and the seminal study by Curtius (Excursus XV on numerical composition). References to recent, and not so recent, work by musicologists on number and proportion in polyphonic music, mostly of the fifteenth and sixteenth centuries, will be found in the footnotes to Brian Trowell's paper 'Proportion in the Music of Dunstable', *PRMA* 105 (1978–9) 100–1. *New Grove* has no articles on number or on numerology as such. See also note 62 below.

[6] Robertson (1953), 114, n. 109.

intervals of time. He can, further, by means of these overt numbers, produce in wood visible forms rendered numerous by the intervals carved in it.[7]

The passage is part of the argument to prove that 'the immortal rhythm which is truth' manifests itself in all the Creator's works.

Number-theory has been given quite a lot of attention in the last thirty or forty years, and most readers of medieval poetry, if not yet most listeners to medieval music, have an idea what it is about. Unfortunately, it is still often regarded as one of the curious aberrations of 'the medieval mind'; and the over-enthusiastic application of its data to vernacular literature by some scholars has perhaps hardened our natural modern resistance to its imaginative truth. So I hope to be forgiven for taking the reader over some familiar ground before suggesting how number is applicable to the object of the present study, medieval song.

One important distinction is necessary at the outset. Number *symbolism* must not be confused with numerical *disposition*. The philosophers of number symbolism use their analysis of numbers to give us information which is not itself numerical, as for instance in this early interpretation of the 318 men whom Abraham circumcised:

'And Abraham circumcised 10, and 8, and 300 men of his household.' What, then, was the knowledge given to him in this? Learn the 18 first and then the 300. The 10 and 8 are thus denoted. Ten by I, and 8 by H. You have [the initials of the name of] Jesus. And because the cross was to express the grace [of our redemption] by the letter T, he says also '300'. *No one else has been admitted by me to a more excellent piece of knowledge than this, but I know that ye are worthy.*[8]

The information is put forward as esoteric; it is, in fact, arrived at, as to I and H, by gematria, a fairly simply code whereby figures stand for letters of the alphabet. The Greek *Tau* signifying 300 is also a symbol, because of its shape, of the Cross. This was also numerologically satisfying since 300 is 3 (the Godhead, the first 'real' number etc.) × 100 (symbolizing totality).[9]

To give symbolic meaning to number was not an invention of the Middle Ages, nor of the early Christian Church. Vincent Hopper's wide-ranging study opens with an account of number symbolism in various primitive or pre-Christian societies. As an example of the richness of association and of archetypal similarity between cultures I quote his account of the number 10.

---

[7] Transl. Robertson, 115, from VI.xvii. 57 (ed. Finnaert and Thonnard, p. 472): 'An vero faber potest rationabilibus numeris qui sunt in arte ejus, sensuales numeros qui sunt in consuetu-dine ejus operari; et sensualibus numeris progressores illes quibus membra in operando movet, ad quos jam intervalla temporum pertinet, et his rursus formas visibiles de ligno fabricari, locorum intervallis numerosas.'

[8] Cited by Hopper, 75, from Barnabas, Epistle IX (see Ante-Nicene Christian Library, i (1867); Hopper's italics). Barnabas was probably a Christian in Alexandria (A.D. 70–100).

[9] Butler, 3: three points 'could enclose a triangle, the first plane figure visible to sense, and thus the first *real* number'. See also Hopper, 41. On *Tau*, see Hopper, 76.

With the use of a decimal system, it follows naturally that 10, symbol of the entire method of numeration, becomes an important number. In its earliest appearances it is a number of finality or completeness, as in higher ranges are 100 and 1,000. In the Babylonian spring festival (3500–1900 B.C.) the tenth day was marked by a procession of *all* the gods. In the flood legend of the same people, 10 kings, intimating 10 ages, are named as preceding the flood. Sargon recognizes 10 gods as guardians of the city. The Rigveda (1200–800 B.C.) is made up of 10 books of hymns celebrating the 10 Vedic gods. Herodotus was struck by the 10 divisions of Athens, the tenth paid for ransom (the Hebrew tithe), and the chorus of ten for each god in Aeginetan worship. By extension of 10, the Egyptians, according to the same writer, gave 100 days as the time for the rising of the Nile.[10]

It could be said that with 10 (completeness, finality, perfection), as with 2 (representing diversity, opposition, antithesis) and 3 (which stands for ' "all" (beginning, middle and end) . . . best (superlative), . . . holy (triads of gods)', we are indeed dealing with archetypes, the fundamental numerical 'images' of the human mind.[11]

The number symbolism of the Middle Ages builds on such basic patterns as these its huge, ramifying, mind-dazzling structures. But medieval philosophers and poets were not their own numerical architects; their structures were to plans drawn up from two sources – the Pythagorean school of Greek philosophy and the writings of the early Fathers on the 'numbers' of the Bible.[12]

The standard guide to the exposition of the Bible, the *Glossa Ordinaria*, interweaves numerology with other symbolic interpretation, a perfectly normal procedure.[13] I quote from a translation of the gloss on the passage in Genesis (vi. 14–16) in which God commands Noah to build an ark: 'Make thee an ark of planed timbers: rooms shalt thou make in the ark and shalt smear it within and without with pitch . . .'

Noah built the ark of incorruptible timbers as Christ built the Church with men who were going to live for eternity, and the Church floats above the waters of tribulation just as the Ark floats on the waves. The ark is made up of squared timbers; so the Church, made up of saints whose life is firm and ready for all good works, resembles squared timbers that stand firm at every point. The timbers are fixed together with pitch inside and outside, so that this compact unity may symbolize charitable patience, the virtue which prevents the Church from being so disturbed by those within or without as to depart from brotherly concord. For pitch is the hottest and strongest form of glue and it symbolizes the fervour of charity and its strength for

[10] Hopper, 10.   [11] Hopper, 11.
[12] On Pythagoras, consult B. Münxelhaus, *Pythagoras Musicus. Zur Rezeption der pythagoreischen Musiktheorie als quadrivialer Wissenschaft in lateinischen Mittelalter* (Bonn–Bad Godesberg 1976).
[13] The *Glossa Ordinaria*, compiled largely by Anselm of Laon (d. 1117) and his followers, 'contains a hotch potch of material drawn from the writings of the early Church Fathers' (*The Cambridge History of the Bible*, II: *The West from the Fathers to the Reformation*, ed. G. W. H. Lampe (Cambridge 1962), ch. 7 ('The People's Bible', by R. L. P. Milburn), pp. 294–5).

holding together a society which endures all things. Now the fact that the ark is six times as long as it is broad and ten times as long as it is deep presents an exact likeness with the human body in which Christ was made manifest. For the length of a body from the crown of the head to the sole of the foot is six times the breadth, that is to say from one side to the other, and it is ten times its height, that is the measurement from the back to the belly. Then, the broad expanse of fifty cubits symbolizes the manner in which the heart expands under the influence of that love which the Holy Ghost inspires, as the apostle said: 'the love of God hath been shed forth in our hearts'. For it was on the fiftieth day after the Resurrection that Christ sent forth the Holy Spirit which expanded the hearts of the faithful. Now a length of three hundred cubits amounts to six times fifty, and in the same way the whole extent of time falls into six ages, in which Christ was proclaimed without ceasing: in the fifth he is the subject of prophecy, while in the sixth he is openly proclaimed in the Gospel.[14]

Number *symbolism* is not my principal concern in this chapter, though there will be occasion to return to it later. The other branch of number philosophy is more important – numerical *disposition*. By numerical disposition I mean the use of numbers (or their discovery, since numbers are the ultimate reality) for their own sake, not for any collateral truth they may reveal. There is a beauty in numbers, as there is in music, which needs no justification; it exists to be contemplated, to be enjoyed. One does not need to be much of a mathematician to take pleasure in the number 5 which when squared or cubed always reproduces itself; or in the series of the 'perfect' numbers, 6 (= 1 + 2 + 3), 28 (= 1 + 2 + 4 + 7 + 14) and so on; or in the fact that 'the progression of the odd numbers from the monad always produces squares' (i.e. 1 + 3 = 4; 4 + 5 = 9; 9 + 7 = 16; 16 + 9 = 25 etc.).[15] Another perfection of 6 is that it represents the area of the right-angled triangle with sides 3, 4, 5. The so-called 'triangular' numbers, also, fascinated the Pythagoreans, whose number theory lies behind so much of the medieval: they 'discovered that the sum of any number of successive arithmetical terms (beginning with 1) forms a triangle: 1 = ., + 2 = .·., + 3 = .·.·. , and so on'.[16] The triangular number most reverenced was the next in series .·.·. , the tetraktys, the basis of 'the legendary oath of the Pythagoreans', because it consists of 10 digits, and 10 was the first 'boundary' of number.[17] Naturally there are reasons, often many reasons, why any particular number is regarded as significant; but the important thing for us to understand is that *all* numbers and their relations have significance whether the human mind can grasp it or not. To quote the

---

[14] *Ibid.*, 295.
[15] Hopper, 42. A 'perfect' number is 'one whose divisors add up to the number itself' (Hopper, 37), e.g. 6 = 1×2×3 *and* 1+2+3.
[16] Hopper, 37.
[17] Hopper, 42.

introduction to the *Arithmetic* of Nicomachus (first century A.D.) which formed the basis of all medieval arithmetics:

All that has by nature with systematic method been arranged in the universe seems both in part and as a whole to have been determined and ordered in accordance with number, by the forethought and the mind of him that created all things; for the pattern was fixed, like a preliminary sketch, by the domination of number pre-existent in the mind of the world-creating God, number conceptual only and immaterial in every way...[18]

To deal with numbers, then, in all their immateriality is not simply to play intellectual games but to gain insight into the Mind which created all things 'by number, weight and measure'. To 'dispose' numbers in the structure of a building, of a treatise, of a piece of music, was in a sense to imitate God's own work of creation, or at least to rejoice practically in a skill which must bring the user closer to the underlying purposes of God in his Universe. 'Numerus est qui cuncta disponit' (Cassiodorus).[19]

   Number disposition soon impinges upon geometry, as the mention of 'triangular' and 'square' numbers has shown. 'The geometric approach to mathematics provided a link (other than astrological) between abstract number and concrete reality. It is by numbers, said Philolaus, that things become known... As the number 3 is the most fundamental representation of surface, so from the number 4 the first solid is produced.'[20] At some time in the Pythagorean era someone (the Middle Ages were sure it was Pythagoras himself) discovered the way numbers were disposed to make musical sounds. 'Pythagoras' discovered what every young violinist soon re-discovers – that if you stop a string in the middle, the half-string sounds a note precisely one octave higher. The ratio 2:3 produces a fifth, 3:4 a fourth, 8:9 a tone, and so on into the obscurer ratios. Medieval manuscripts frequently depict Pythagoras inventing the musical scale either by working in a smithy with hammers of various weights or by plucking a monochord (i.e. a single string). A particularly splendid miniature from a Canterbury manuscript of the mid twelfth century, now in Cambridge University Library, shows Pythagoras weighing hammers and plucking a monochord both at the same time.[21] He is in company with the other great authors (*auctores*, authorities) Boethius, Plato and, appropriately, the arithmetician Nicomachus. The importance of having the mathematical basis of music established from the very earliest times cannot be exaggerated. No one could doubt that music and number were connected in their very essence.

[18] Nicomachus of Gerasa, *Introduction to Arithmetic*, English transl. Martin Luther D'Ooge (New York 1926), 189 (opening of ch. 6). The original Greek text is ed. Ricardus Hoche, *Nicomachi Geraseni Pythagorei Introductionis Arithmeticae Libri ii* (Leipzig 1866). See also Chadwick (1981), 71ff: Nicomachus and Boethius.
[19] Cassiodorus's *Arithmetic* is discussed by de Bruyne, I, ch. 2, 40–2.
[20] Hopper, 34–5.
[21] Cambridge UL MS I.i.3, fol. 61v, reproduced by Smits van Waesberghe in his book on musical education (1969), pl. 8 (p. 57).

II Number disposition and poetic theory

The *numerus* that 'disposes all things' inevitably disposes poetry and music, not just in a general metaphysical way but in particular detail, as I hope to show. Dante, as usual, makes a good starting-point: not only is he the poet who more magnificently than any other demonstrates the art of number in action, in the *Divine Comedy*, but he also talks about it in relation to his own poetry (in the *Convivio*) and to that of the troubadours. So on the one hand he constructs his great poem to contain 100 cantos (a number of totality and completion), and on the other he can argue in the *De Vulgari Eloquentia* that lines containing an odd number of syllables (9 excepted) are superior to those in evens (this is because even numbers are subject to odd numbers as women to men and matter to form). The *Divine Comedy* abounds in number symbolism; but it is Dante's interest in number disposition, irrespective of significance, which particularly commands our attention.[22]

The maker of a good *canzone* will be indebted to three of the seven liberal arts – grammar, rhetoric and music.[23]

O uomini, che vedere non potete la sentenza di questa
canzone, non la rifiutate però; ma ponete mente la
sua bellezza, ch'è grande sì per construzione, la quale
si pertiene a li gramatici, sì per l'ordine del sermone, che
si pertiene a li rettorici, sì per lo numero de le sue
parti, che si pertiene a li musici.

You people who cannot see the meaning of this canzone, do not reject it nevertheless; but set your minds on its beauty, which is great because of its structure (the grammarians' concern), because of the order of its language (which is the rhetoricians' concern), and because of the 'number' of its constituent parts (which is the musicians' concern).

It is noteworthy that all three types of expert engage themselves with order, and this points to Dante's central explicit concern in poetry – craftsmanship. Kenelm Foster and Patrick Boyde, in their admirable Introduction to *Dante's Lyric Poetry* (1966), write that

in general, the stress, when Dante is discussing poetry, falls on form and structure, in particular on sound-structure. And this . . . means that the poet has an overriding concern with beauty. He is a maker of beautiful objects; not *only* this, but very definitely this. His motive in 'making' is what we should now call aesthetic.[24]

[22] Dante's number symbolism is discussed by Hopper, ch. 7 ('The Beauty of Order: Dante'). See also the references given by Reiss, n. 18; only one is later than Hopper's study. More recently, see 'Numero' in *Enciclopedia Dantesca*, IV.87. As to odd numbers, 'They say there is divinity in odd numbers . . .' (*Merry Wives*, V.i.3).

[23] Dante, *Convivio* II.xi.9. All quotations from Dante's works follow the *Le opere di Dante*, ed. Barbi (see Bibliography).

[24] Foster and Boyde, introd. p. xviii.

It is in the *De Vulgari Eloquentia* (*c.* 1305) that Dante most clearly states the technical consequences of his emphasis on 'numbers' (*numeri* are the special province of the *musicus*, the expert in sound) and on *armonia*.[25] *Armonia* (harmoniousness, concord) is one of his favourite concepts:

armonizantes verba opera sua cantiones vocant . . . cantio nil aliud esse videtur quam actio completa dictantis verba modulationi armonizata (II.viii.5–6)

when they construct a verbal harmony, they call their works songs . . . A song is evidently nothing other than the completed action of one who artistically puts words together into a harmonious whole.[26]

He has just said that those who 'harmonize' words, in his sense, make songs, whether they have music with them or not; poems are, amongst other things, musical constructs in words. But a song in the fullest sense is 'the completed action of one who artistically puts words together into a harmonious whole' – harmonious, that is, in itself and ready for the other harmony of music.

Elsewhere in the *De Vulgari* Dante propounds another definition of *poesis*:

nichil aliud est quam fictio rethorica musicaque poita (II.iv.2)[27]

A recent rendering is: 'a product of imagination expressed with the aid of rhetoric and music'.[28] The meaning of the word *musica* and the place of poetry as itself a manifestation of *musica* in its wider sense will be discussed in a later chapter. At this stage it only has to be emphasized that poetry, verse-making, is an art of 'music' in the wide medieval sense:

the general drift, without doubt, of Dante's scattered allusions to the art of poetry is towards identifying its specific element with music, taking this term in the special sense which it has in this context – the art of treating words as items in an aural harmony.[29]

[25] The concept of *armonia* is further discussed below, chapters 11 and 12. Dante's general attitude to music is the subject of my article 'Dante and music' (1968a). Monterosso, 'Musica e poesia' (1965), is most valuable. See also his article 'Musica' in *Enciclopedia Dantesca* (Rome 1971), and the article 'Dante' in *New Grove* (Boyde). The standard edition of the *De Vulgari* is by Marigo (1957); it has Italian transl. and detailed commentary. The most recent edition is by P. V. Mengaldo, in Vulgares Eloquentes 3, vol. I: *Introduzione e testo* (Padua 1968), with no translation or commentary; English transl. by A. G. Ferrers Howell (1890; repr. 1973); and by S. Purcell, *Dante: Literature in the Vernacular* (Manchester 1981). The *Convivio* is transl. into English by W. W. Jackson (Oxford 1909).

[26] Marigo translates *modulationi* as 'per una modulazione' (p. 237) and glosses it 'in modo che possano ricevere un accompagnamento musicale'. The crux is whether *modulatio* here refers to a musical melody, as he concludes, or to a verbal *armonia*, as I believe ('harmonious whole'). The term *accompagnamento* is in any case unsatisfactory.

[27] Transl. Ferrers Howell, 55. The reading is disputed: Foster and Boyde read *poita*; *Le opere di Dante* reads *posita*.

[28] Foster and Boyde, introd. p. xvii.

[29] *Ibid.* The Latin term *musica* is only rarely precisely equivalent to modern English 'music'. Frequent medieval meanings are 'the theory of music', 'harmoniousness of sound in any medium', and 'metaphorical music (e.g. of the heavens)'. See below, chapter 11:1.

To what extent, we must now ask, is this 'aural harmony' (*armonia* in Dante's terminology) bound up with the theory and practice of number? His most compendious definition, in the *De Vulgari*, of the technique of song-writing runs:

Tota igitur ars cantionis circa tria videtur consistere: primo, circa cantus divisionem; secundo, circa partium habitudinem; tertio, circa numerum carminum et sillabarum. De rithimo vero mentionem non facimus, quia de propria cantionis arte non est . . . Si quid autem rithimi servare interest huius quod est ars, illud comprehenditur ibi cum dicimus 'partium habitudinem'. Quare sic colligere possimus ex predictis diffinientes, et dicere, stantiam esse sub certo cantu et habitudine, limitatam carminum et sillabarum compagem. (II.ix.4–6)

The whole art of song, therefore, is seen to consist in three things: first, the basic structure of the stanza; second, the proportioning of the parts; third, harmoniousness ('number') of lines and syllables. We make no mention of rhyme because it does not properly belong to the art of song . . . If it is of import to pay heed to whatever in this rhyming qualifies as art, that is considered when we speak of 'proportioning of the parts'. So we can, from what has been said above, draw together our definitions and say that a stanza has a fixed 'music' [? verbal as well as melodic] and numerical proportion, being a bounded structure of lines and syllables.[30]

These three techniques which have to be studied in the composition of the perfect highly wrought stanza are, as Dante restates them:

(i) *cantus divisionem*, the formal structure of the stanza, divided AA–B into *frons* (with two *pedes*), and a *cauda* (the latter part), 'sub certo cantu' – i.e. so as to establish a unique (?) 'music'. Or perhaps *certo* means 'fixed', 'clearly defined'? Marigo, in his commentary, allows the possibility of 'una melodia già composta', i.e. of a *contra-factum*; but Monterosso discounts it.[31] Dante seems to be calling for a clearly defined sound-pattern – but it is not at all certain that he is thinking of actual music. He may have the verbal text solely, or the melody, or both in mind.

(ii) *partium habitudinem*, the harmonious putting-together, or proportioning, of lines and rhymes, as appears from chapter xi: 'contextum carminum et rithimorum relationem'. Marigo refers to Boethius's use of *habitudo* in his *De Arithmetica*, 40, for *proporzione numerica*; Monterosso adds an apt reference to his *De Musica*, ii.20, also.[32] Dante observes that this aspect of stanza-making is the one which requires the highest art.

(iii) *numerum carminum et sillabarum*, the 'harmony' of lines and syllables. Three lines have the prerogative of being used frequently – the lines of eleven, seven and five syllables.

From this Dantean idealization of a single stanza it seems clear that Dante had in mind some 'abstract', some Idea of an *armonia* for each poem/song,

---

[30] *Rithimus* (*rhythmus, ritmus* etc.), which here means rhyme, normally refers to the syllable-counting (often accentual and later often rhymed, also) tradition of medieval Latin verse. See below, chapter 12:1 for main discussion. Dante, *De Vulgari* II.xii, observes that you can have a stanza *sine rithimo* (without rhyme) or with *eundem rithimum* all through.

[31] Ed. Marigo, 243; Monterosso (1965), 91.

[32] Ed. Marigo; Monterosso (1965), 92.

which was not closely dependent on the nature of *individual* words or phrases, either as meanings or as sounds. Thus, in his discussion there are several striking omissions, but one in particular: Dante nowhere makes a distinction between the speech-rhythm of the line – that is, the actual sounds the words make when spoken – and its metre – that is, the assumed norm or basic underlying pattern. Such a distinction, and the tension that would arise from the conception of *two* sound-patterns, did not, I suggest, exist for medieval poets.[33] Dante's discussion of verse seems to rest entirely on a numerical basis.

Dante is not alone in this. It would be difficult to over-estimate the significance of the extraordinary emphasis twelfth- and thirteenth-century vernacular poets laid on the precise numbering of syllables and on the proper handling of rhyme. The significance, as I have said, lies in the concept of 'harmoniousness', *armonia* – not mere euphony but a positive balanced structural accord in sound. Paul Zumthor sums up the courtly poet's ideal when he observes that the only aesthetic philosophy the Middle Ages could understand was that of *musica*.[34] Rhymes and syllable-counting – these are what the theorists agree on and insist on. The number of theorists is not great, and the earliest treatments of vernacular poetry come from the south of Europe in the thirteenth and early fourteenth centuries. Most of them are late codifications. But the song-tradition they codify was not dead. This was, indeed, the period in which the big chansonniers were being compiled. And, as we shall see, the theory is substantiated absolutely by the songs themselves. Besides Dante, the encyclopedist Brunetto Latini, Antonio da Tempo, and the authors of the huge *Las Leys d'Amors* belong to this time; and they speak with a unanimous voice.

The earliest, Brunetto Latini (?1230–94), writing in French for a European public, gives advice, in his *Li Livres dou Tresor*, which is short and to the point:[35]

ki bien voudra rimoier, il li covient a conter toutes les sillabes de ses dis . . .

If you wish to write good poetry, you must count all the syllables in your poems.

The other requirement of a poet as craftsman is that he should handle his rhyme correctly and make sure that the verbal accent of the rhyme-word falls

---

[33] The matter needs more investigation. I discuss it (1982) as a problem of English poetry. Dragonetti, 499ff., distinguishes 'rhythme métrique' and 'rhythme de tension' in trouvère poetry for reasons that I cannot accept; he states that 'toute structure rhythmique introduit un conflit ou une entente entre deux ordres temporels' (501) but produces no medieval evidence to support his view. It does not accord with the theorists cited below, chapters 11 and 12. See also the pragmatic analyses below (e.g. chapter 15, note 10) and in Stevens (1974–5), 16–17 and Fig. 1.

[34] Zumthor, *Langues et techniques*, 221.

[35] Brunetto Latini (ed. Carmody), 327. It is the most comprehensive and original of the vernacular encyclopedias. Long extracts in A. Pauphilet, ed., *Jeux et Sapience du Moyen Age* (Bibliothèque de la Pléiade, Paris, 1951). The quotation comes from Bk III, 'Ci commence li livres de bone parleure'.

in the right place. This is, perhaps, the only context in which the intrinsic sound of a word is mentioned as significant.

Antonio da Tempo completed his treatise *Delle rime volgari trattato* in 1332. After retailing the three kinds of writing according to the rhetoricians – *prosaicum, metricum* (measured, i.e. quantitative) and *rithmicum* (unmeasured, 'syllabic' verse) – Antonio then gives the accepted definition, *secundum grammaticos*, of a poem in the *ritmus* tradition:[36]

consonans paritas syllabarum certo numero comprehensarum

A harmonious equality of syllables held together by a fixed 'number' (number, proportion)

This same definition applies, he says, to vernacular poems of every kind (*in quolibet vulgari rithimo*) except *frottole*. What does Antonio mean by *consonans paritas*, 'harmonious equality'? He cannot mean that all lines are of the same length, because later he says that in *rithimi* you usually have either eleven or seven syllables per line.[37] *Consonans* must have its literal, physical meaning (Quintilian often uses it of verbal harmony); for *paritas* the simplest and most obvious meaning could well be the right one – 'parity' of syllables may consist in temporal equality. In any case – and this is the most important point – the form of the poem/song comprises a fixed number of syllables. Neither this theorist nor any other speaks of 'feet' in relation to verse of this kind. The concept of feet (iambic, trochaic etc.) belongs to the tradition of quantitative verse, the *musica metrica* of tradition. The distinction between the two major rhythmical traditions is of prime importance, and I shall revert to it in chapter 12.

Antonio da Tempo is a comparatively late authority, and one sign of this is that he interests himself in a repertory of poems having a distinctly fourteenth-century flavour – the *sonettus, ballata, mandrialis* (madrigal), *motus confectus* (*frottola*). But that he is concerned with traditional principles of 'syllabism' is evident from all his comments: he says of the sonnet, for example,[38]

si sonettus in huiusmodi rithimis non contingeret ad rectum numerum syllabarum, nunquam bene sonaret auribus audientium secundum musicos et cantores.

If a sonnet, amongst 'rhythmic' poems of this kind, did not achieve the correct number of syllables, it would never sound well, according to musicians and singers, in the ears of those who heard it.

The ideal is apparently upheld on practical grounds (by the *cantor*) and on theoretical (by the *musicus*), if the traditional contrast is intended between speculative and practising musicians.

[36] Antonio da Tempo (ed. Grion), 71. I am grateful to Patrick Boyde for drawing my attention to this treatise. Grion (*ibid.*, 10) dates its compilation 1329–32.

[37] Ed. Grion, 82: 'omnes rithimi ut plurimum compilantur ex versibus undenariis et septenariis'.

[38] *Ibid.*, 74. Antonio da Tempo is, of course, no later than Dante; they both see themselves as the inheritors of a living tradition.

Las Leys d'Amors from Toulouse, is of about the same date, the first half of the fourteenth century, but differs from the treatise just discussed in being concerned essentially with a tradition of verse-making that stretched back two centuries. It has been called 'the funeral oration' of troubadour poetry; the 'laws' 'revêtaient d'un air de noblesse et d'élégance ce qui était déjà du passé; elles codifiaient la décadence'.[39] There are other treatises on *la dreicha maniera de trobar* from about 1300, but they are shorter.[40] *Las Leys* is a big work and was attached to a big enterprise. Its ponderousness sorts curiously with its expressed aim: to praise and to preserve *gay saber*, joyous knowledge – the blending of the art of love with the love of art.

The treatise, *Las Leys d'Amors*, resulted from the meetings of the *puy* of Toulouse – the 'sobregaya companhia dels vii Trobadors de Tolosa'. Like the *puy* at Arras it was a more or less official municipal 'school' of poetry and song. Of the seven founders of *la Consistoire du Gai Savoir* only one was an aristocrat. For their first meeting in 1324 they sent out invitations to all the poets of the *langue d'oc*: they have a splendid place at their disposal where new poems are sung nearly every Sunday. At the 1324 *concours* Arnaut Vidal was awarded the Flower of the Violette d'Or and in the same year became Docteur en Gaie Science. It was decided that their proceedings should be codified, and Guilhem Molinier, a good lawyer, was entrusted with the task. 'Trobars es far noel dictat. en romans fi: be compassat' (courtly composition consists of making a new poem, in the pure vernacular and well 'compassed'): so wrote Molinier in definition. *Compassat* is a key term and refers to the formal shape of the composition, which must be precisely kept. The rules require 'a new composition [*dictat*], *measured in syllables*, rhymed; sometimes in several stanzas, sometimes in one single':

. . . noel dictat. compassat per sillabas. am rims. et alcunas vetz am coblas motas. et alqunas vetz ab una cobla solamen. E deu hom en aytals dictatz seguir ornat . aytal cum mostron aquestas nostras leys damors. Encaras aytals dictatz deu hom far am bels motz . e plazens . clars . acordans . am bona et am certa sentensa . oz am belas e am plazens methaforas . don hom puesca trayre bo sen.

---

[39] There are two prose redactions of the first version of *Las Leys*: one, in three books (ed. J. Anglade, Bibliothèque méridionale, Toulouse 1920); the second, in five (ed. M. Gatien-Arnoult (1841–3)). Extracts from the latter are printed and translated by R. Nelli and R. Lavaud in *Les troubadours*, II: *Le trésor poétique de l'Occitanie* (Bibliothèque Européenne, 1966); the quotation in the text is from their useful introduction, p. 613. A third redaction in verse is entitled *Flors del gay saber* (unpublished MS in Barcelona). A fourth redaction (in prose) is ed. J. B. Noulet, A. Jeanroy and J. Anglade, *Las Leys d'Amors*, 4 vols. (Toulouse 1919–20); see Anglade's commentary, IV.17–27. The whole complex position of MSS and editions is lucidly set out in *Dictionnaire des lettres françaises*. N. Zaslaw, in *Current Musicology* 25 (1978) 99–120, relates *Las Leys* to the musical scene in fourteenth-century Provence.

[40] These diverse grammatical works in the vernacular (mostly thirteenth-century) are edited and described by H. Marshall, *The Razos de Trobar* (1972). The treatises are largely grammatical, sometimes 'antiquarian'. The only one to mention music is the anonymous *Doctrina de compondre dictats*, which Marshall argues is by Jofre de Foixa. The comments are 'generally limited to a judgment as to whether a new or a borrowed tune is appropriate' (Introduction, p. xciv). The treatise is 'a characteristic product of the decadence of troubadour poetry'.

One should in such compositions employ the ornaments [?figures of rhetoric] which display our existing laws of love: moreover they must be expressed in words that are beautiful, pleasant, pure; the words must harmonize and put forward either a proper and clear literal meaning or attractive metaphors from which a proper meaning can be drawn.[41]

Again, we find great emphasis on 'accord' and harmoniousness; the technical aspects of importance are syllabic construction and rhyme: no *romans* or *dictatz* belongs to this science 'unless it is properly measured and set in rhyme, and unless it has a fixed number of syllables'.[42] The concept of the metrical foot never appears, even though some considerable attention is given later in the treatise – an unusual feature, this – to the actual sounds of words, that is to *accen* and to *temps* (duration).[43]

   From these none-too-numerous writers on vernacular poetry much can be learnt. Musical theorists, on the other hand, have little to say about 'number' in the sense that we have been considering it – that is, as a term to describe both the arithmetical and the harmonious dimensions of songs composed on syllabic principles.[44] The main reason for this is that the more practical treatises are in the earlier period primarily concerned with plainchant and in the later with polyphony; they are not concerned with secular song to any significant degree. The interests of their authors lie in the domain of *musica harmonica* – a branch of *musica* distinct from *musica metrica* and *musica rhythmica*; it deals with pitched sounds, scales, concords etc. There are also, of course, many discussions of the metaphysics of sound. *Musica* (as chapter 11:1 will show) is an all-embracing term, and one cannot always be immediately sure whether a writer who uses the word is talking about what we call music, or about the 'music of speech' in verse or prose, or about acoustical theory, or about a metaphorical harmony of gesture, of dance or of the movement of the spheres.

III   Number: the texts

Writings on the subject of vernacular song are, we have seen, much concerned with 'number' both as an arithmetical and as a broader concept – of

---

[41] Gatien-Arnoult, 1.8–9 (text and modern French transln.).

[42] Gatien-Arnoult, 1.12–13: 'non est degus [proper] romans ni degu dictatz: si non es be conpassatz e mes per rimas. o de sillabas non havia cert compas'. It is evident from this context that *compas* refers to the 'compass' of a poem/song established by counting syllables.

[43] The most interesting thing about the definition of *accens* (*Las Leys*, Gatien-Arnoult, 1.58–9) is that the author relates it to speech-sound, produced in reading or orating(?) (*can melodies, quom fay legen o pronuncian*), and contrasts this to the sound of musical melody (song), which is not at all the same and as a rule does not observe accent (*non ges del can de musica, quar aquel regularmen no te, ni garda accen*). His example to prove this is the respond 'Benedicta venerabilis' – which is slightly unexpected and puzzling. Are we to assume that all song is subsumed under plainchant? I think this is probably so.

[44] See Seidel, 'Rhythmus/Numerus' (1980) in *HMT*, espec. sect. 11 (p. 15): 'In der Musiktheorie des Mittelalters sind die Termini "Rhythmus" und "Metrum" peripher.'

proportion, balance and harmony. The authors write as practitioners, at least of verse, perhaps also of music. And it is with the practice of 'number' in song that the rest of this chapter will deal. I shall attempt chiefly to describe the application of number to the chanson.

The high courtly chanson, to give it its northern French name (Provençal *canso*; Italian *canzone*; Latin *cantio*), is the principal song-form of the twelfth and thirteenth centuries.[45] The great majority of the entries in the formally written chansonniers of the late thirteenth century are of chansons.[46] There are some differences, naturally, between the songs of the troubadours and the songs of the trouvères, and these emerge from close study. There is more individuality in troubadour art. But chanson and *canso* belong, with other common genres, to the same great tradition; their poet–composers shared the same ideals and pursued a common aesthetic.

As an example of the troubadour *canso* we may take 'Can l'erba fresch' e.lh folha par', by Bernart de Ventadorn, who was active in the second half of the twelfth century.[47]

[45] The present chapter does not attempt to 'cover' the troubadour-trouvère repertoire in all its variety but concentrates on the high-style courtly *canso*/chanson. A wider picture will emerge in due course, in particular from chapter 14 where the other genres are discussed. The substantial article in *New Grove*, 'Troubadours and Trouvères' (Stevens and Karp), gives an all-round view of both repertoires (see note 56 below for the trouvères), dealing with social status; courtly ideals and courtly love (*fin'amors*); origins; genres, themes, motifs; literary styles and techniques; manuscript sources; modality (tonality); musical-poetical forms; rhythmic interpretation. The art. contains lengthy bibliography, plates and musical examples. Van der Werf (1972) gives the most up-to-date account in English of the troubadours and trouvères, but Stäblein (1975), espec. pp. 76–90 should also be consulted. See, too, Jammers (1963), anthology with introduction – weighted naturally towards German song, and Jammers (1975) devoted to the monophonic repertoire as a whole.

Texts of some 2600 troubadour poems (in Provençal) survive; roughly a tenth of them have their melodies. These are best studied in de la Cuesta's edition (1979) of the whole musical repertoire with diplomatic representation of the neumes above an unmeasured melodic transcription. Another edition of the complete repertoire appeared as this book went to press, too late for me to take account of it: van der Werf and Bond, ed., *The Extant Troubadour Melodies*. De la Cuesta replaces Gennrich, *Nachlass* (1958–65), always unsatisfactory to use because of the absence of verbal texts and its compressed presentation. All known troubadours are listed in Pillet and Carstens' bibliography (1933) and their poems, with individual sources, given alphabetically beneath each name. Corpus of texts printed in de Riquer (1975) with Spanish transln, without music.

Amongst introductory books of a general nature, that of Davenson (1961 rev. 1971) is especially attractive; see also Aubry (1909, English transln 1914) and Beck (1908) and (1910). All these have musical examples. The anthologies of Press (1971) and Goldin (1973) have parallel texts and English translations. That of Pierre Bec, *Anthologie des troubadours* (Paris 1979) has texts, notes, French translations and a musical appendix (by Gérard Le Vot). Van der Werf (1972) prints four troubadour and eleven trouvère chansons. Accessible anthologies of the melodies have been edited by F. Gennrich, *Troubadours, Trouvères, Minne- und Meistergesang* (1951; English transln 1960); Maillard (1967a). Other melodies in the appropriate sections of the *Oxford Anthology* (1977).

Dronke's wide-ranging two-volume study (1965a) provides an incomparable literary context. Other literary studies such as Topsfield (1975), a study of ten individual poets, and L. Paterson, *Troubadours and Eloquence* (Oxford 1975) contribute through their stylistic

Ex. 1

Cant	l'er-	ba	fres-	q'l	fuel-	ha	par.	
2 el	fuelh	s'es-	pan-	dis	pel	ver-	ian.	
3 el	ros-	sin-	hol	au-	tet	e	clar.	
4 aus-	sa	sa	uoiz	en	dreg	son	chan.	
5 ioi	ay	de	lui.	e	ioi	ai	de	la	flor.
6 ioi	ai	de	mi.	e	de	mi-	dons	ma-	ior.
7 de	to-	tas	partz	soi	de	ioi	claus	e	senh.
8 mas	ilh	es	iois.	que	totz	los	au-	tres	uens.

comments to an understanding of the completed songs, words-and-music. Metrical analyses of 885 songs can be found in Frank, *Repertoire* (1953–7).

Musical studies are less securely based, partly because of the unsatisfactory nature of the sources, partly because of the intractability of the rhythmic problem, and partly because there is as yet no agreed mode of analysis. The uncertainties are succinctly expounded by Karp, art. cit. 'Troubadours and Trouvères §III, 2: Music, modality'. Van der Werf (1972) ch. 4 'Melodic characteristics' discusses the function of recitation formulas, 'step-wise structures', etc – the terminology is borrowed from Curt Sachs, *The Wellsprings of Music* (The Hague 1962), structural tones and 'scales'. See also Gushee's art. on analysis and compositional process in *Forum Musicologicum* 3 (1982) 165. One thing is evident – the traditional terms of chant-analysis (based on the modes) are even less adequate for the description of troubadour (and trouvère) melodies than they are to the chant itself. See, however, the subtler analyses of Stäblein (1975), 86, who emphasizes the stylistic kinship between the high-style *canso* and Gregorian *Stilideal*, and his 'Zur Stilistik der Troubadour-Melodien' in *AcM* 38 (1966) 27, which examines a range of troubadour melodies.

(Continued overleaf)

1   Can l'erba fresch' e.lh folha par
      e la flors boton' el verjan,
      e.l rossinhols autet e clar
      leva sa votz e mou so chan,
    joi ai de lui, e joi ai de la flor
    e joi de me e de midons major;
    daus totas partz sui de joi claus e
        sens,
    mas sel es jois que totz autres jois
        vens.

2   Ai las! com mor de cossirar!
      que manhtas vetz en cossir tan:
      lairo m'en poirian portar,
      que re no sabria que.s fan.
    per Deu, Amors! be.m trobas
        vensedor:
    ab paucs d'amics e ses autre senhor.
    car una vetz tan midons no destrens
    abans qu'eu fos del dezirer estens?

3   Meravilh me com posc durar
      que no.lh demostre mo talan.
      can eu vei midons ni l'esgar,
      li seu bel olh tan be l'estan:
    per pauc me tenh car eu vas leis no
        cor.
    si feira eu, si no fos per paor,
    c'anc no vi, cors melhs talhatz ni
        depens
    ad ops d'amar sia tan greus ni lens.

4   Tan am midons e la tenh car,
      e tan la dopt' e la reblan
      c'anc de me no.lh auzei parlar,
      ni re no.lh quer ni re no.lh man.
    pero ilh sap mo mal e ma dolor,
    e can li plai, mi fai ben et onor,
    e can li plai, eu m'en sofert ab mens,
    per so c'a leis no.n avenha blastens.

5   S'eu saubes la gen enchantar,
      mei enemic foran efan,
      que ja us no saubra triar
      ni dir re que.ns tornes a dan.
    adoncs sai eu que vira la gensor
    e sos bels olhs e sa frescha color,
    e baizera.lh la bocha en totz sens,
    si que d'un mes i paregra lo sens.

6   Be la volgra sola trobar,
      que dormis, o.n fezes semblan,
      per qu'e.lh embles un doutz
        baizar,
      pus no valh tan qu'eu lo.lh deman.
    per Deu, domna, pauc esplecham
        d'amor!
    vai s'en lo tems, e perdem lo melhor!
    parlar degram ab cubertz entresens,
    e, pus no.ns val arditz, valgues nos
        gens!

    The musical sources of troubadour song (see *New Grove* art. 'Sources, MS' §III, 3) are few and late. One principal MS, Paris BN fr. 22543 [troubadour MS R], is described briefly in the list of Sources below; it is early fourteenth century and full of musical gaps. The other most important chansonnier, Milan, Biblioteca Ambrosiana R 71 sup. [troubadour MS G] is ed. Sesini (1942) with poor facsimiles, isosyllabic but metrical transcriptions (see chapter 12 note 2 below) and still valuable introduction.

[46] See below, chapter 14:1.

[47] 'Can l'erba fresch' e.lh folha par.' The text edited by Carl Appel (1915), no. 39 (p. 219), is based on eleven MSS. The music survives only in Paris BN fr. 22543 (Source 32), *c.* 1300. Facsimile of fol. *R* 57v in Appel's edition, pl. XIX, with metrical analysis of edited text; and neutral transcription of the song with text of *R* on pp. 37–8 of Appel's article on the melodies (1934). I give melody and text from *R*, followed by the complete edited text (from Appel) with translation by Press, 79. Another, slightly more colloquial, translation is in Goldin, 136. The melody can also be studied in de la Cuesta's edition (1979), no. 15 (p. 145). See also the detailed analytical study of eighteen songs by G. Scherner van Ortmerssen, *Die Text-Melodiestruktur in den Liedern des Bernart de Ventadorn*, Forschungen zur romanischen Philologie 21 (Münster 1973). Texts of twenty of Bernart's songs, without their music, are most recently published by de Riquer with full bibliography and modern Spanish translations: 'Can l'erba' is no. 68 (p. 412).

7   Be deuri'om domna blasmar,   *Envoi*: Messatger, vai, e no m'en prezes
      can trop vai son amic tarzan,   mens,
      que lonja paraula d'amar   s'eu del anar vas midons sui
      es grans enois e par d'enjan,   temens.
    c'amar pot om e far semblan alhor,
    e gen mentir lai on non a autor.
    bona domna, ab sol c'amar mi dens,
    ja per mentir eu no serai atens.

1   When the fresh grass and the leaf appears, and the flower blossoms on the bough,
    and the nightingale raises high and clear its voice and pours out its song, joy I have
    for it, and joy for the flower, and joy for myself and for my lady yet more: on all
    sides I am bound and circled by joy, but that is joy which all other joys
    overwhelms.

2   Alas, how I die of deep thought! For many a time I am so deep in thought that
    robbers could carry me off and I'd know naught of what they do. By God, love,
    you find me indeed easy to conquer, with few friends and no other lord! Why did
    you but once not constrain my lady, before I was consumed by desire?

3   I marvel how I can endure not to reveal to her my longing. When I see my lady and
    behold her, her lovely eyes so well become her that I can scarce hold back from
    running towards her. So would I, were it not for fear, for I never saw person more
    well-shaped and fashioned for love to be yet so slow and reluctant.

4   I love my lady so much and hold her dear, I fear her so much and respect her, that I
    never dared speak to her of myself, nor seek I anything, nor ask I anything of her.
    Yet she's aware of my pain and my sorrow, and when it pleases her she does me
    honour and good, and when it pleases her I am content with less, so that from it
    there might come to her no reproach.

5   If I could enchant people, my enemies would be children, so that not one could
    ever spy out or say anything that might do us harm. Then I know that I would see
    the most noble one, and her fair eyes and her fresh complexion; and I would cover
    her mouth with kisses so that for a month the mark would show.

6   Well would I like to find her alone while she slept or pretended to, that I might steal
    from her a sweet kiss, since I'm not so worthy as to ask it of her. By God, lady,
    little of love do we achieve! Time goes by and we lose the best of it; we should
    speak with secret signs and, since boldness avails us not, may guile avail us!

7   A man should indeed blame his lady when too much she goes putting him off; for
    long talk of loving is most tedious and equal to deceit. For one can love and make a
    pretence elsewhere, and smoothly lie there where there's no sure proof. Good
    lady, if only you deign to love me, I will never be tainted by lies.

E. Messenger go, and do not esteem me less if I'm afraid of going to my lady.

    Bernart's song rehearses many of the commonplaces (I use the word in a
neutral, non-derogatory sense) of courtly love-poetry in a most attractive

form. Using the opening formula of literally hundreds of medieval songs, the
poet describes the delights of spring – fresh grass and leaf, and the nightingale
warbling. These joys unite with his own *joie de vivre* and with the joy that he
has in his lady. 'Daus totas partz sui de joi claus e sens'; but the joy that comes
from her exceeds all others. It is no accident that the word *joi* rings through the
first stanza – 'joi ai de lui, e joi ai de la flor', and so on. *Joi, joie*, which can only
partially be represented by the English equivalent, is a central concept in the
courtly experience. It is what the song tries to define. In the remainder of the
poem the singer tells of the intensity of his love, though not without some
humour at his own expense: he wishes he could cast spells on their 'enemies'
and turn them into children; he'd like to cover his lady's face with kisses so
passionate that the prints would last for a month; his love-trances are so deep
that brigands could carry him off without his noticing it. (The playful self-
mockery reminds us of Chaucer's *To Rosemounde*.)

  Amongst the conventional fictions so elegantly handled here are those of
the unattainable lady; of her unimpeachable reputation, which must not be
tarnished; of a hostile world of spies around them, anxious to think and say the
worst; of the lover's fantasy of joys stolen whilst his sweetheart sleeps; of a
God of Love who commands his only allegiance. We may call them 'fictions'
in this and in most cases, since they are repeated over and over again in
different forms and have little claim to be recognized as 'real' experiences. The
joi of *fin' amors* is not generally a matter of strongly individualized feeling; the
individuality of the poem lies in the success with which the shared ideal is
re-created. Bernart is highly successful.[48]

  Courtly ideals centred, as is well known, upon this conception of love
which, although not new in the twelfth century and not confined to the
countries of western Europe, certainly acquired a new importance in courtly
and aristocratic circles at this period.[49] The phenomenon is often called
'courtly love', a term invented by nineteenth-century scholars; the common
medieval terms such as *fin' amors* (refined love) or Chaucer's 'gentil lovyng'
are more revealing. Refinement, *gentilesse*, is the essence of this courtly
experience – or, rather, of this complex of courtly experiences. The
refinement springs, or is at least claimed to spring, from the *joi* of being a
worthy lover; and the discipline of this *joi* is *mesura* (moderation, measure) –

[48] For a recent account of Bernart as poet, see Topsfield, ch. 4. Facts about his life are few: 'he
addressed love songs to Eleanor of Aquitaine and may have been present at the coronation of
Henry II and Eleanor in Westminster Abbey in 1154' (p. 112). He is 'the first troubadour
who uses these commonplaces of love extensively'. Dronke (1968), 121–2, stresses Bernart's
seductive casuistry in this song.
[49] See Stevens and Karp, 'Troubadours and trouvères' in *New Grove*. The first part of the article
includes a brief summary (pp. 190–1) of theories about courtly love and its origins. Dronke
(1965a), ch. 1, gives a necessary corrective to the traditional view of a completely novel and
narrowly localized experience. See also E. T. Donaldson, 'The Myth of Courtly Love' in his
Speaking of Chaucer (London 1970); and Stevens *Medieval Romance* (London 1973), ch. 2,
'Idealisms of Love'.

'in love's joy I hold and direct my mouth, my eyes, my heart, my under-standing', as Bernart himself says.[50]

But what, you may ask, has this to do with 'number'? First, the song 'Can l'erba fresch'' is numerically disposed in a completely tidy and unambiguous manner. Each stanza consists of four lines of 8 syllables followed by four lines of 10, making 72 syllables in all. This number is repeated precisely for each subsequent stanza. There are seven stanzas, which brings the total count to 504, plus a two-line *envoi* = 524. Whether a poet's choice of a total number also has a symbolic significance is a question to be taken up later. Extending the sense of 'number' to include pattern, we find in Bernart's song one of the more taxing uses of rhyme, though it is common enough in the troubadour repertoire: it consists of the repetition of the same rhyme-scheme *and sounds*, but with different rhyme-words, in each stanza. This means, for instance, that in the poem as a whole he needs fourteen rhymes on -*ar*, fourteen on -*an*, and so on. (He does not, however, altogether avoid the repetition of the same word in rhyme: *mens* occurs twice (4.7; envoi.1) and, in accord with general medieval practice, homonyms may be rhymed (*sens/sens*: 5.7–8).) This use of the same rhyme-sound throughout the *canso* was known as *coblas unissonans* (*cobla*, Fr. *couplet*, is the term for 'stanza').[51] Various other schemes can be readily identified: one is the same as that just described, except that some end-words of the first stanza do not find their rhyming 'answer' within that stanza but wait to be answered in the second or subsequent stanzas; another has repetition of the same rhyme-scheme but with the sounds changing every two or three stanzas (*coblas doblas, coblas ternas*); a third has repetition of the same rhymes but with a different scheme in each stanza (this is uncommon). A high peak of metrical virtuosity is reached in the sestina (Arnaut Daniel's 'Lo ferm voler' is the first and most famous): the rhyme-*words* of the first stanza (*intra, ongla, arma, verga, oncle, cambra*) are repeated in a different, and calculated, order in each of the stanzas 2–5; the three-line *tornada* contains all the six rhyme-words. Other links between stanzas contributing to the 'numerositie' of a whole poem may be made by such devices as: *coblas capfinidas* (the last line of one stanza is linked verbally with the first line of the next); *coblas capcaudadas* (a variety of the preceding, depending on the rhyme-word); and *coblas retrogradas* (the rhyme-words or rhyme-sounds of one stanza are inverted in the next). It only remains to add that the sound patterns are not, of course, restricted to rhyme, as (to take an obvious example) the elaborate play on the word *joi* in stanza 1 shows. This is a 'figure of sound' often mentioned by the rhetoricians.

All this is somewhat technical. But technicalities are necessary to describe

---

[50] 'Qu'en joi d'amor ai et enten / la boche e.ls olhs e.l cor e.l sen' (Appel (1915), no. xv, strophe 1); Press, 66–7.

[51] Bernart's technical virtuosity is discussed by Nichols and Galm in their edition (1962), closely based on Appel's: see introd., 17ff, where the terms are explained and illustrated. The volume includes translations but no music.

the self-conscious craftsmanship that went into the realization of 'number' in troubadour verse. The metrical ingenuity of the troubadour and trouvère poets is truly amazing. On the basis of Istvan Frank's *Répertoire métrique* the corpus of troubadour poems alone contains approximately 1,575 separate and distinguishable metrical schemes, of which some 1,200 were used only once.[52] Much care went into the creation of Bernart's verbal *armonia*; and, though this is still speculative, it seems as if the deliberate exploitation of varying dialect forms may have contributed.[53]

IV   Number: the melodies

It is time now to turn to the music of Bernart's 'Can l'erba fresch'' and to see whether there is a comparable realization of the 'number' principle there also. We can start once more with simple arithmetic: the melody contains precisely the same number of notes or note-groups as the poem has syllables. There is a high prevalence, in fact, in this melody of single notes: lines 5 and 6 consist entirely of singles; lines 2 and 3 have one note-group each. But whether a syllable is matched by a single note or two or more notes in ligature (i.e.

bound together visually, as at 1.4 ⬥ is immaterial;[54] the stanza has 72

units of musical sound, corresponding to the 72 syllables of the text. The simple arithmetical correspondence extends also to the line. The poetic unit of the line is marked off by rhyme, and almost invariably by syntactical or speech-phrase pause as well – one notes how often the modern editor will put punctuation at the end of a line. The musical phrase, similarly, marks the end of the line with a cadence or semi-cadence. This is usually at lower pitch than the phrase which it concludes. In 'Can l'erba' only line 2 holds the cadence up in the air, as it were, in order to lead smoothly on into the next line. The sense of correspondence between poetic line and melodic phrase is an abiding feature of *chanson/canso* style. The *canso* often (and the trouvère chanson almost always) provides another frame of arithmetical correspondence: it is normal for a *canso* to be in the form A A B, where A is a unit of two lines (the *pes* of Dante's analysis) repeated (making a *frons* of four lines) and B a unit of from three or four to about eight lines (constituting the *cauda*). The musical structure normally follows this form A A B: that is to say, the two metrically identical *pedes* (A A) of the first section are also melodically identical – phrases 3 and 4 echo phrases 1 and 2. The *cauda* (B) uses, for the most part, new material. In 'Can l'erba', however, the composer, whether Bernart or another, has not followed this increasingly standard plan. Instead he has devised a scheme of

---

[52] The figures are reported by van der Werf (1972), 63, as supplied to him by Professor Bruce Beatie.

[53] Nichols and Galm, introd., 16.

[54] A citation in the form '1.4' means 'line 1, note (or note-group) 4'. The oblique part of the ligature represents two separate notes, not a slide.

his own which may be represented $ABCA^1/DDEF$. Both the near-repetition of line 1 in line 4 and the doubling of the D melody are quite unusual.[55]

This, however, is the moment to stress that once the simple basic requirements of syllable, line and (normally) AAB structure have been met, the music creates its own pattern, an *armonia* that is completely independent of the sense or sound of the text. (The matching of the parallel lines 5 and 6, with their anaphora 'ioi ay de . . ./ioi ai de . . .' with identical music is a striking exception to the rule.) The *armonia* of the melody is built up from two or three identifiable motifs – the ascending major third *fga* (1.1–3), and the descending minor third *gfe*, which seems to centre on its middle term, *f*, in lines 5 and 6, before taking on a more dynamic meaning in line 7, to be supplanted by the minor third on *d* in the last line. (The notes of the 'Phrygian' third *efg* do again occur here, but the weighting of the line is heavily towards a *d* tonality and the *d* cadence (see 8.1–2, 7, 8, 10, all *ds*).) It is important – especially since such an analysis as this gives a static impression, as of a machine that is not working – to realize that such a melody as this is fluid and dynamic; its *armonia* exists in a temporal dimension, it *moves*. Only performance can fully convey it. I will simply comment that the energy of its movement is created by rise and fall both within the line-unit and within the stanza as a whole. One way of viewing it – hearing it, rather – is as an arch of melody stretching from line 1 to line 4 (the melody of each phrase is compassed within a fifth, but the ranges contrast – the climactic point is in 3.1–4) followed by the 'holding' pair (5–6) and rounded off with a less emphatically arched melody (opening and closing) of 7 and 8. The musical 'rhyme' of the final cadence (cf. 1.6–8 and 4.6–8) gives a satisfying sense of closure.

There are several other things which might be observed about Bernart's 'Can l'erba fresch'' – the predominantly stepwise movement of the melody, the placing of the melismas, the varying of the cadence figures, their tonal implications, and so on. These are all features of the 'moving *armonia*' which I have sketched. But they are not confined to Bernart de Ventadorn's songs nor to the troubadour repertory as such. They are found also in the *grans chans* of the trouvères.[56] It is to a late trouvère that I shall now turn to establish the

---

[55] It is noteworthy that he, like all other song-writers, nevertheless respects the integrity of the *frons* (the first main section) as a whole. Lack of precise melodic parallelism is found elsewhere (cf. Thibaut's 'L'autre jour en mon dormant' (R339)).

[56] The trouvères have left a larger legacy than the troubadours: some 2,130 poems are listed in the standard bibliography by Raynaud (rev. Spanke 1955), and at least two-thirds of these have melodies, often surviving in variant versions in up to ten or more manuscripts. Sometimes a text has more than one melody, and occasionally the reverse is true. The gap in time between the composition of the chansons and their being copied into the surviving chansonniers is less than with the troubadours (see note 45) but is often as much as a century. It is striking that of the seventeen chansonniers described by David Fallows in *New Grove* 'Sources, MS' §III, 4, the medieval provenance is not known in a single instance.

(Continued overleaf)

essential continuity of the *canso*/chanson tradition. Adam de la Halle's 'D'amourous cuer voel canter' (R833) was written a century or more later.[57] The first two stanzas run:

1 D'amourous cuer voel canter
    por avoir aïe:
   n'os autrement reclamer
    celi ki m'oblie,
   dont ne me porroie oster
   comment c'on m'ait assali,
   moy voelle ou non a ami,
    tant l'ai encierie
   et tant m'i sont abieli
    li penser.

2 Tant est sage pour blasmer
    celui qui folie,
   tant biele pour esgarder
    ke, cose c'on die,
   ne m'en porroit desevrer.
   Comment metroie en oubli
   si grant valor que je di,
    male gent haïe
   ki a tort m'en volés si
   destorner?

My loving heart makes me want to sing, to get help. I dare not call otherwise for the attention of my lady who has forgotten me. From her I couldn't drag myself away, however much I were attacked [for loving her]; whether she wants me for a friend or not, so much have I cherished her and so pleasing are the thoughts [of love] to me. (2) She is so wise in reproof of him who acts foolishly, and so beautiful to look at, that nothing anyone says could ever part me from her. How could I come to forget such marvellous personal worth as I am describing – you hateful and wicked people, who wrongly are thus determined to deflect me [from loving].

[57] Marshall, no. 1 (p. 35). Adam de la Halle (le Bossu) (*c.* 1245/50–?1286; or, according to some, – after 1306). For biographical summaries, see Falck, art. in *New Grove*, and Marshall, introd., 1–2. One of the last generation of trouvères, he was active in Arras but spent some time in Paris and served under Robert II, Count of Artois in Italy, where Robert had been sent to the aid of Charles d'Anjou. Adam also composed polyphonic rondeaux and motets; *Robin et Marion*, a dramatic *pastourelle–bergerie*; and a *chanson de geste* (not completed), *Roi de Sezile*. The thirty-six courtly chanson-texts are excellently edited by Marshall (1971) from trouvère MS *P* (BN fr. 847) which I have used also for Ex. 2. Coussemaker's edition (1872) contains texts and melodies (modern square notation, unmeasured) of thirty-four chansons with the other musical works. Wilkins's (1967) contains all Adam's music, but the promise of a full critical edition is not altogether substantiated – the melodies are transcribed from a single MS (Source 34) in modal rhythm, and variants are not recorded. The melodies are best studied in van der Werf (1979) (see note 45 above). In 'Manuscript Presentation' (1981) I attempt to set out some of the criteria which an edition of the chansons should meet and describe their principal sources.

   Five chansonniers are available in facsimile (see list of Sources, nos. 2; 26; 28; 29; 31). In some cases transcriptions in modal rhythm are provided. Study of the melodies best begins with the parallel versions now available for eleven trouvères in *MMMA* vols XI–XII (Van der Werf 1977, 1979). To the anthologies listed (note 45 above) should be added Rosenberg and Tischler (1981) containing over 200 texts, and their melodies (modally transcribed) when surviving. This useful collection (with excellent bibliography) presents, unfortunately, a somewhat unbalanced picture of the trouvère repertoire properly so called (see ch. 14:1 below).
   Works of especial interest for words-and-music are Chailley's study (1959) of *contrafacta* in Gautier de Coinci; Dragonetti (1960) on trouvère poetic techniques; Mölk and Wolfzettel (1972), a metrical analysis of the repertoire; and Räkel (1977) on *contrafacta* as evidence about the transmission of the melodies.

This chanson survives in seven manuscripts, and in five of these it comes first in what (with some variations) appears to be a sort of standard order for Adam de la Halle's songs. The Arras chansonnier presents it in a particularly interesting way.[58] The elaborate initial D which starts the section contains a miniature: a tonsured clerk sits at a writing-desk with a pen in one hand and what might be a scraper in the other. He seems to be copying – making a book? The inference of this choice of illustration might be that the chansons are indeed to be regarded as works of considered literary (and musical?) art. The principal source of Adam's works, on the other hand, trouvère MS *W* (Source 34), gives a different slant on the chansons. The miniature, roughly 3″ × 3″, shows two men sitting at a bench; the one on the viewer's right, with his legs crossed, holds up a paper on which the words 'Damoureus cuer voel cant[er]' are just visible. To our right is an audience of seven persons, two of them apparently women. Here the emphasis is evidently on the performance of the chansons (reading? singing?) as a public act. (We may note in passing that there is no sign of any musical instrument.)

In this, the first of his thirty-six chansons, the poet asserts again and again his unshakeable fidelity to his lady, whom it appears he has only seen once. How could he forget such 'valor' (intrinsic personal worth)? Some hateful people ('male gent haïe') want him to give her up. But he will be patient and undemanding. Hope bears him up, together with her 'valor': those who enjoy her society learn the true meaning of *cortoisie*. Adam's chanson quite lacks the witty elegance of Bernart de Ventadorn's, but we can easily recognize the same conventions – the unhappy but resolute service in love; the hostility of those around them; the *joie* of love ('joieuse vie', 5.2); the uplifting nature of the experience. As J. H. Marshall, Adam's most recent literary editor, writes,[59]

These songs are songs about love, rather than love songs in any Romantic sense. More than celebrations of the physical and moral qualities of a shadowy beloved, they are celebrations of the idea and nature of love itself.

With regard to the question of 'number' in its various meanings we find that 'D'amourous cuer' meets our expectations as fully as 'Can l'erba fresch''. As a metrical structure it is indeed well wrought. The ten lines of each stanza are of three varying syllabic lengths – 7, 5 (with weak ending), 3 – adding up to 60 (63) syllables in each stanza. Each stanza has three rhymes, and these are repeated precisely, so that the whole poem of 60 lines has only these three rhyme-sounds (*coblas unissonans*, again).[60] Whatever we may think of his 'message', Adam certainly has an impressive, craftsmanlike control over his 'medium'. His medium may indeed turn out, to an unusual degree, to be

---

[58] Chansonnier d'Arras (Arras Bibl. municipale 657): see Source 2.
[59] Marshall (1971), introd., 3.
[60] The metrical structure of 'D'amourous cuer' is not unique. Cf. R685, 'Ains ne vi grant hardement' by Richart de Fournival.

his message; the fabric of 'numbers', to be at least as important as the tissue of courtly commonplaces that he hangs on it. It is, moreover, very tempting to see something more in the numbers of Adam's song than was apparent in Bernart's. The number disposition seems to make deliberate play with sixes and threes. On the assumption, unproven, that the 'weak' syllables ending lines 2, 4 and 8 do not count, there are 60 syllables in each stanza and 60 lines in the poem; there are six stanzas containing only three rhymes in all; there are three different line-lengths in each stanza; and there are three syllables in each last line. On the contrary assumption about weak endings, there would be 63 syllables per stanza. But to compensate for the lost 'beauty' of a double 60 we could count in each stanza three lines of 6 syllables each. These number correspondences seem to me too marked to be coincidental. A certain amount of work has been done recently on number, the 'arithmetical principle', in German medieval poetry, by Hatto and others.[61] This work has been criticized, strangely, by some for emphasizing 'numerical structure at the expense of numerical signification' (the terms imply the same distinction as the one I have made above between numerical disposition and numerical symbolism). But numerical structure or disposition, as I have already said, may surely exist in and for itself; and the title of one of Hatto's articles, 'The Beauty of Numbers', precisely hits off what, I think, we should feel about such a chanson as 'D'amourous cuer'.[62]

We are of course bound to ask in particular cases whether the numbers used have a meaning. This is not the same as asking whether they could be given one. It suffices to say that the Middle Ages could allegorize anything from Ovid's *Metamorphoses* to the building of a boat, *after the event*. To say, therefore, that the numbers 3, 6 and 10 had significance, as indeed they did, for medieval thinkers is to say nothing specific and individual about the chanson 'D'amourous cuer'. Numbers are 'certain good' and do not have to be justified. However, even the concept of number disposition needs careful handling; not all assertions about number pattern are certainly right. It will be worthwhile, I think, to digress for a moment from Adam de la Halle to consider the much-admired chansons of another trouvère, Thibaut de Champagne, roi de Navarre (1201–53).[63]

The Germanists have tended to argue that a Minnesinger before he started to write a song thought of a good round number and worked his poem out to

---

[61] See Reiss, 172–3, n. 19–20, for bibliography.

[62] A. T. Hatto, 'On the Beauty of Numbers in Wolfram's Dawn-songs', *MLR* 45 (1950) 181. His arguments are unfortunately vitiated by the concept of the 'bar' rather than of the syllable as the unit. The 'bar', as we understand it, is not appropriately applied to medieval monophonic song. See also Hatto and R. J. Taylor, 'Recent Work on the Arithmetical Principle in Medieval Poetry', *MLR* 46 (1951) 396.

[63] Thibaut IV, Count of Champagne and Brie, King of Navarre. For biography and musical analysis, see Karp, 'Thibaut IV' in *New Grove*. The standard edition of the poems is by Wallensköld (1925); for the melodies of his chansons, see van der Werf (1979), 3–311. To judge from what survives, Thibaut wrote more songs than any other trouvère.

fit it. The numerical analysis of a small selection of Thibaut's chansons
suggests at first sight that he may have done something similar:

'Seignor, sachies' (R6):	7 syll. × 10 lines = 70 syll.	
'Poine d'amours' (R106):	10 × 6: 60	
	7 × 2: 14	
	6 × 1: 6	= 80
'Pour conforter' (R237):	7 × 4: 28	
	3 × 2: 6	
	4 × 1: 4	= 38
'De tous maus n'est' (R275):	7 × 7	= 49
'Dieus est ensi conme est li pelicans' (R273):	10 × 10	= 100

and so on. The next five chansons by Thibaut in Raynaud's catalogue have
respectively 80 (R315), 80 (R324), 70 (R335), 50 (R339) and 75 (R342) syllables.
Plausible though the theory may be, there are some obvious objections to be
made to it. First, if you are writing a decasyllabic stanza – that is, a stanza in
which all the lines have 10 syllables – you cannot fail to end up with a round
number. Five out of ten of the chansons mentioned are so constructed. But
secondly, what in any case *is* a 'round' number? The number 49, being the
square of 7, has obvious claims to be regarded as an excellent number to work
with (R275 above). And, for all we know, the number 38 (R237 above) may
have had some especial meaning for Thibaut. So, the validity of a round
number can never, I think, be self-evident; it requires substantiation in one of
two ways. Either it must be shown to be meaningful in relation to the subject
of the poem, as for instance if a poem on the five wounds of Christ were
written in five stanzas of 5 lines each; or it must be worked out, 'played' with,
in the poem itself, in the way that I believe Adam de la Halle plays with 6 in
'D'amourous cuer'.

Amongst Thibaut's chansons there are at least three which stand out as
candidates for special numerical status: 'Dieus est ensi conme est li pelicans'
(R273) with 100 syllables per stanza; 'Ausi com l'unicorne sui' (R2075) with 72;
and 'Du tres douç nom a la vierge Marie' (R1181) with 80. They stand out
because they combine these 'round' numbers with promising subject matter.
The first is one of Thibaut's rare religious songs and takes as its subject the
traditional image of God/Christ feeding sinners with his own blood in the
same way as the pelican was thought to feed her young.[64] Ten lines of 10
syllables in each line would seem a promising enough start for a poem about
God's dealings with Man (Hugo of St Victor found that 10 represented
'rectitude in faith' and 100 'amplitude in charity');[65] but in order to be sure that
the choice of number was meaningful we would expect to find something
made of it, and this something I have not been able to detect. 'Ausi com
l'unicorne sui', a rather unusual poem (in the allegorical style that became

---

[64] Text ed. Wallensköld, chanson 56 (p. 194).
[65] Hopper, 100–1.

more fashionable later on), makes some play with threes – Love's prison has three special features (pillars of Desire, gates of Pleasant Sight, chains of Good Hope) and is guarded by three watchmen (*trois portiers*); but it is written in 8-syllable lines, has four rhyme-sounds in each stanza, and has five stanzas.[66] Admittedly, there are nine lines to each stanza and in the first they fall syntactically into three groups of 3. But taken as a whole the evidence is not persuasive. Finally, the chanson to the Virgin:

> Du tres douz nom a la Virge Marie
> vous espondrai cinq letres plainement . . .

The poet promises to expound the five letters of the Virgin's sweet name M-A-R-I-A, and he does so stanza by stanza. Apart from the fact of there being five stanzas (the conventional number in any case for a courtly chanson) there seems to be no sign of number play at all, either in symbolism or by disposition.[67] The chanson is written in eight-line stanzas of 10 syllables to a line, with three rhymes to a stanza and a three-line envoi.

This brief excursus into Thibaut's chansons is, of course, a mere preliminary; the question requires the thorough analysis of some two thousand poems. But first results do not encourage the belief that 'number', which is the organizing principle, both practically and ideally, of *la grande chanson courtoise*, necessarily seeks expression in overt arithmetical play, symbolic or otherwise. It exists for its own sake.

We may return now to Adam de la Halle's chanson 'D'amourous cuer' and consider its music. The melody seems to me an example of an 'harmonious' artefact perfectly capable of standing on its own. Adam, of course, accepts the conventional structural 'controls' of *chanson*-form already described: the musical phrase coincides with the line-length; a 'weak' ending in the words (*a-i-ĕ, ob-li-ĕ*) is respected in the melody; the number of notes and note-groups (in ligature) coincides precisely with the number of syllables (60+3) in the stanza; the overall form A A B is mirrored in the musical form. These restraints apart, the musician (in this case certainly Adam himself) was free to exercise his own fine invention. He does not have to echo the rhyme-scheme in his melody: he does not have to (and apparently never does) reproduce the sounds of individual words or phrases or their stresses – which vary continuously in any case from stanza to stanza.[68] Still less is he concerned with the meaning of the words, individually or as a totality. His sole business is to create an *armonia* which will run alongside the verse, self-sufficient, a beautiful object in its own right.

[66] The song is named by Johannes de Grocheo as a type of the *cantus coronatus* (see below, chapter 12, note 52). Text ed. Wallensköld, chanson 24 (p. 111), from fifteen MSS.

[67] This, despite the fact that the poet has a playful approach. His exposition depends partly on sound-play. For instance, M is to be pronounced *ah-me = ames*. See strophe 1, lines 3–4: 'La premiere est M, qui senefie / que les *ames* en sont fors de torment' (Wallensköld, chanson 57 (p. 200)).

[68] See below, chapter 15, note 10.

Ex. 2

There are innumerable ways of creating such an *armonia*, and each song has to be analysed as a thing in itself. The shape of 'D'amourous cuer' relies on a balance between a high point and a low point which are stated in the first phrase and its answer. This is repeated as phrases 3 and 4. The first four phrases all oscillate around *f*, *g* and *a* at the cadence: the first and third turn upwards in an 'open' form; the second and fourth turn downwards to a 'close'. Line 5, which begins the long second section (the *cauda*), moves indecisively in this same narrow range, twice repeating the opening phrase of the song but transposed down a fourth. Line 5 moves smoothly into line 6 which reasserts the high *cdc* position before coming to rest on *f*, lightly chiming with the cadences of lines 2 and 4. The *b* flat at the beginning of line 7 is significant; it signals a lower hexachord and a shift of tonal centre as it moves snakewise down to low *c*. Line 8 tries a lift, as it were, echoing 6 a fourth lower, but falls back again to *c*. Line 9 contains another echo, and a minor climax before leading with an 'open' cadence into the last phrase of all, of four notes *cc(d)d* which precisely repeat the opening four notes of the song.

It is again not easy to put this kind of analysis into words – into words, at least, that will convey the imaginative and intricate musical design which this melody so patently has. In the last resort we have to feel it *as music*. It is a flowing pattern in which various kinds of 'numbers' are musically realized – in actual numbers of notes and note-groups, and in proportions, balances, echoes; it is, to repeat, an *armonia*. One thing, I hope, is clear: this is not a negligent art, nor indeed a negligible one. It is necessary to insist on this, since the author of the only substantial account in English of troubadour and trouvère song states an oppposite point of view.[69] He complains of the composers paying 'little attention to the form of the melody' and of their 'lack of interest in small details of the melody' as well as in 'correspondence between form and melody'.[70] He writes:

Considering the care with which the troubadours and trouvères designed the form of their poems and considering the agreement among the manuscripts regarding rhyme and stanzaic form one would expect the authors, composers and scribes to pay equal attention to detail regarding the musical form. But the manuscripts make it abundantly clear that the form of the poem must have been of far greater interest to everybody involved than the form of the melody. Convention and lack of sophistication in the form of the melody are typical, while originality and attention for detail are exceptional.[71]

The ground of van der Werf's dissatisfaction evidently lies to some degree in the relationship of the melody to the poem. To this we shall return (see chapter 15, below). At this stage I wish only to take issue with his deprecation of the music *per se*. Are the charges which he brings against the melodies true?

It may be admitted in the first place that the sources which we have do, on the whole, agree less wholeheartedly on the details of the melody than on

[69] Hendrik van der Werf (1972).

[70] Van der Werf, 64–5, cited in Stevens (1974), 18, with comment.

[71] Van der Werf, 63. James A. Winn, *Unsuspected Eloquence* (New Haven 1981), 81ff, unfortunately repeats this misconceived notion. A more borderline case should however be mentioned here – the minor chanson-genre of *jeu-parti* (sung debate). As B. Brumana has pointed out, the *jeu-parti* repertoire contains an unusually high proportion of alternative melodies ('Le musiche nei *jeux-partis* francesi', unpublished Ph.D. dissertation, Perugia 1969–70). The genre requires perhaps an 'unbalanced' attention to the wit of the argument, with a consequent diminution of musical interest. Further on the *jeu-parti*, see M. F. Stewart in *AcM* 51 (1979) 86–107.

those of the text, and that sometimes there can be wide divergence.[72] There are various comments, however, to be made on this, for it certainly does not follow necessarily either that the melodies were a purely secondary concern or that they lacked art. Major variations can be explained by the peculiar circumstances of a 'mixed' transmission, part oral, part written.[73] Minor variations may have arisen from legitimate creative play with the melody by an individual performer, or an inventive musical scribe.

The existence of several manuscripts without music and, equally, of several manuscripts with 'blank' songs (songs with staves ruled for music but never filled in) could suggest that some patrons were more interested in the words than in the music. The 'blank' songs on the other hand could indicate that sometimes there was a shorter supply of music-scribes than of text-scribes, or that a musical source was not available at that particular moment, even though the scribe who ruled up the quire expected it would be.[74] But in any case it cannot seriously be argued that a generation of patrons/collectors/song-lovers who took the trouble to assemble the huge surviving repertoire of upwards of 1,500 separate melodies – some of them in six, eight, ten different copies – could conceivably have thought that the music was not an essential and admirable part of the tradition they were aiming to preserve.[75] The fact is incontrovertible. The existence, moreover, of a large number of *contrafacta* within the repertoire shows some people having a strong interest in the melodies as such, irrespective of their texts.[76]

However, the real answer to the charge that troubadour and trouvère musicians wanted art lies in the melodies themselves. I hope to have said something in my analyses to counteract this mistaken and depressing assessment. Unfortunately, the thorough analytical study which would be a

[72] There can, however, often be many discrepancies between texts also (see van der Werf (1972), 26); significantly, 'about the only elements in the text which rarely change from version to version are the number of lines per stanza, the number of syllables per line, and the sound of the rhyme syllables'.

[73] Van der Werf, ch. 2 *passim*; he rightly regards 'the theory of an exclusively written transmission' as 'very unsatisfactory'. In an impressive and detailed study of trouvère song (1977) Hans-Herbert Räkel has argued, on the basis of surviving *contrafacta*, that in the first half of the thirteenth century the art was essentially the province of the noble aristocratic amateur and the stylistic traits identify it as primarily oral, whilst in the second half of the century innumerable *contrafacta* reveal the stability of a written tradition now largely in the hands of a socially pretentious bourgeoisie (pp. 135–7 and 259–61 especially). On the terms 'parody' and *contrafactum*, see W. Lipphardt in *Jahrbuch für Liturgik und Hymnologie* 12 (1968) 104–11, and R. Falck in *MQ* 65 (1979) 1–21; *contrafactum* is not a medieval term.

[74] See Stäblein (1975), pl. 47, left-hand column (BN fr. 22543, Source 32, fol. 57v); also the Chansonnier St Germain (Source 31), *passim*. Many chansonniers have 'blank' songs; further information in *Raynauds Bibliographie*, pp. 1–11.

[75] Rosenberg and Tischler, p. xvii, estimate well over 2,000, but this is because they mis-leadingly classify as trouvère songs many which I should exclude. See chapter 14:1 below. *Raynauds Bibliographie* has over 2,130 entries; but this total includes many poems without melodies.

[76] The most detailed and up-to-date study is by Räkel.

necessary prelude to convincing generalization about their musical art has
scarcely been begun. Now, however, thanks to the publication of two impressive volumes of melodies in Musica Monodica Medii Aevi by van der
Werf himself, it begins to look like a practical possibility for the future.[77]
Meanwhile we must be content with selective and necessarily unsystematic
observations.

The concept of number realizing itself in the *armonia* of words and of music
is not confined to the high courtly art of the *canso* and chanson; it is apparent in
songs of a lighter type such as one finds, if not with great frequency, in the
output of most trouvères.[78] Thibaut's 'Pour conforter ma pesance / faz un son'
(R237)[79] is still a chanson, with five stanzas and an envoi, and in the form A A B;
but it is not in the grand manner.

Ex. 3

To relieve my heaviness, I am making a song; it will be good if it furthers my suit, for
Jason, who won the Fleece, never suffered such misery.

Lines of 7 syllables are interspersed with short lines of 3 and a non-verbal
refrain-line, 'e,e,e'. The syllable-count of 37 (40 if weak endings are included) is precisely maintained in the text and in the melodic setting. Light as it

[77] Van der Werf (1977) and (1979). Equally welcome is the complete collection of troubadour
melodies by de la Cuesta (1979). On the analytical side, the *New Grove* articles on individual
troubadours and trouvères (mostly by Theodore Karp) are the most solid contribution to
date.

[78] They are further considered in chapter 14:III and IV.

[79] Transcribed from all M S versions (six melodic lines represent eight M S S with music) in van
der Werf (1979), 11–17; the version in M S *T*, the Chansonnier de Noailles (Source 30), is
mensurally notated (see p. 685, under R237) but is not so transcribed by van der Werf. Text
ed. Wallensköld, p. 1 (no. 1); Ex. 3 is from M S *O*, the Chansonnier Cangé (no *b* flats)
(Source 29) fol. 35. See also chapter 14:III for discussion of the rhythm of this song.

is in tone ('I'd prefer to have her "acquaintance" than the kingdom of France!'), it is thoroughly craftsmanlike and establishes its verbal *armonia* out of two rhymes only (*-ance*, *-on* (*coblas unissonans*)). The music, similarly, is economical in its patterning. After the expected repetition of lines 1–2 as 3–4, we seem on first sight to have a *cauda* melodically designed C D E, but in fact all the melodic material has already been given in the *frons* (A B–A B). Phrase C approximates to A transposed down a fifth; phrase D incorporates B as 6.2–4, varied as 6.5–7; and phrase E, the refrain-line, consists (7.1–3) of an inversion of the end of A (1.6–7). So although 'Pour conforter' is a miniature, and has what is for a chanson disjunct, triadic movement and an uncharacteristic sort of refrain (the use of a refrain at all is rare in the grander styles),[80] it derives its 'aesthetic' from the same source as its bigger neighbours and confers a similar pleasure.

There will be more to say about these lighter chansons in the chapters on rhythmic interpretation. But I should like to conclude with an example of the art of one trouvère who stands outside the mainstream of tradition. Colin Muset was probably active throughout the second third of the thirteenth century, in the Champagne–Lorraine area.[81] Unlike other trouvères (and troubadours) he was a *jongleur*, a professional musician. According to Bédier, only seven chansons out of the total trouvère repertory mention the minstrel profession.[82] The trouvère is either an aristocrat by birth, like Thibaut, King of Navarre, or purposely adopts the aristocratic pose for the sake of writing courtly chansons, like Adam de la Halle. Colin Muset can do this too; but his characteristic tone is frankly that of a different kind of *serviteur*: 'Sire cuens, j'ai vielé / devant vous en vostre ostel / si ne m'avez riens doné' – he wants something in return for his professional skills.[83] If he can find a generous patron in the winter with plenty of 'porc et buef et mouton . . . et bons fromages en glaon [straw]', he'll leave it to others to ride out and get covered with mud ('de chevauchier toz boous').[84]

Doubtless the tone of these poems may be more subtle than it appears; but at least it is different. The nonchalance, real or affected, makes itself felt also – and this is our present concern – in metric and music. Colin Muset, for whatever reason, is often much less careful about syllable-counting, about consistent rhyme-schemes, and even about stanza-length. 'Number', and all

[80] The distinction between *refrains* (in a special sense) and refrains is discussed in chapter 5:11 and taken up again in chapter 14:11 and 111.

[81] The problem of Colin Muset's dates is complicated by the fact of doubtful attributions. 'It is . . . difficult to determine the actual extent of Muset's work; the confusion of sources may be related to his presumed humble origin' (Falck, 'Muset' in *New Grove*). The music of the songs is now available in van der Werf (1979), 435–67, which includes all the songs of Bédier's second edn (1938).

[82] The fact, in relation to Colin Muset especially, must encourage scepticism about the view that all courtly chansons were normally accompanied by instruments.

[83] R476. Van der Werf (1979) 439, 710.

[84] R893. Goldin, 438–41, text and translation. The attribution to Muset is on grounds of content and style.

that that implies, is far from being an imperious presence here. As an example I take his 'Il me covient renvoisier' (RI 300).[85]

Ex. 4

It is right that I should be gay in this summertime, and rejoice and take solace and pleasure. I have found my heart more in love than I am used to. But the evil-speakers think to cause me trouble and to separate [me from my lady].

The most striking thing about the text of this song is that, although in the unique source, the Chansonnier Cangé, the copyist clearly arranges it in three stanzas, the second is one line overlength, the third two lines short. There is also some uncertainty about the rhyme-scheme, as the different analyses of Spanke and van der Werf show.[86]

Musically, Colin Muset's song is some way away from the restrained and

---

[85] Van der Werf (1979), 444. Text of Ex. 4 from Bédier, 2nd edn, 22; music from Chansonnier Cangé, fol. 68v.

[86] Spanke, in entry RI 300 of *Raynauds Bibliographie*, following J. Jeanroy and A. Långfors, eds., *Chansons satiriques*, CFMA (Paris 1921), 76, 128; van der Werf (1979), 712.

ceremonious style illustrated by 'D'amourous cuer'; it has much more in common with Thibaut's 'Por conforter'. But whereas Thibaut keeps to the standard AAB form, Colin has adopted a quite un-trouvère-like bipartite scheme (1–4, 5–8). In tonality, again, there are strong similarities. But Colin makes more insistent use of a contrast between the triad on g (gbd) and one, less clearly stated, on f. This contrast, we shall see in the next chapter, is the tonal 'stuff' of dozens of melodies of the sequence/lai type and seems to show Colin Muset's affinities with a tradition of secular melody very different in style and import from that of the aristocratic chanson.

v   Words, notes and numbers

Detailed musical analysis of the kind attempted in the preceding pages, though laborious, is strictly necessary if generalizations about the inexhaustible inventiveness and sophistication of the 'noble style' in music are to have any substance. If the poems of these chansons are sophisticated creations in carefully designed forms, so indeed are the melodies. They are artefacts, delightful artefacts, every bit as rewarding to study and hear as the poems themselves. I do not claim in this respect to have made a novel discovery. But as van der Werf's comments show, there is still an inadequate appreciation both of the nature of our pleasure in their musical art and of its implications. By giving direct consideration now to that aspect of the chansons which has been most misunderstood – the relation between the poems and the melodies – I hope to increase our appreciation. The all-important concept of 'number' is as relevant here as elsewhere.

It was Dante's *De Vulgari Eloquentia* that first brought home to me the strangeness of some medieval attitudes to aesthetic problems, including the problem of words and music.[87] His technical description of, prescription for, a courtly *canzone* was discussed above. Dante never mentions, and I am sure did not have in mind, either a 'conceptual' relationship between the poem and the melody (the musician is not concerned with intellectual ideas as Renaissance composers so intensely were) or an emotional one (the musician is not concerned with real or imagined feelings). What is left? There is, obviously, the sound of individual words and the sound of words in phrases. The difficulty of doing justice to individual word-sounds in strophic songs at any time is notorious. But in any case where is the evidence in these songs that the composers cared at all? The evidence is almost solely in the rhyme-word. Brunetto Latini says 'the rhyme is not correct if the word-accent does not fit it' ('certe la risme n'ert ja droite se l'accent se descorde'). His advice about the rest

---

[87] See my paper '*La grande chanson courtoise*' (1974) p. 26. I have retained the term 'conceptual' for want of a better, even if with some misgivings; in the present context it is limited to relationships which concern *words* in all their denotations and connotations. (The term is not entirely satisfactory for the obvious reason that numerical relationships of the kind I have discussed can also properly be regarded as 'conceptual'.)

of the line has already been quoted; it amounts to this: 'If you wish to write good poetry, you must count all the syllables in your poems.'[88]

It is not possible to do justice to the sounds of individual words throughout a whole song unless every stanza has the same rhythmical pattern in its text. Such repeated patterns are often clearly recognizable in Latin songs of the period. They cannot be found in French and Provençal songs. There is room for disagreement about the details of accentuation in almost every chanson, but the main position can in my view hardly be challenged.[89] The chansons are evidently not in a regular and predictable metre; Jean Beck claimed to have examined more than ten thousand troubadour and trouvère chansons without finding a single one with perfect strophic construction. Moreover, it is rare to find *within a single stanza* the precisely repeated pattern of verbal accent which would enable the melodies of lines 1 and 2 to be used sensitively for lines 3 and 4, as in most chansons they are:[90]

	melody
Il ne *muet* pas de *sens* che*lui* ki *plaint*	A
paine et tra*vail*, ki a*quert* ava*nt*age;	B
pour *chou* ne *puis* ve*oir* ke *cil* bien *aint*	A
ki, pour goïr d'a*mors*, suffrance *gage*.	B

The point need not be laboured. It is a difficulty that all exponents of modal rhythm have had to contend with. On the other hand, it must be said that the music of these songs never goes so far as to do violence to the word-accent – unless it is edited into a rigid and unyieldingly measured metrical frame. A great deal of later medieval music seems positively hostile to the natural sounds of words. The trouvère style could be described as at least neutral and possibly even accommodating. The melody is a soft mould rather than a Procrustean bed.

To talk in these terms, however, perhaps implies a dominance of poem over melody which is not at all to be assumed. The normally accepted way of talking about these songs assumes that the words were written first and were then set to music. There are some reasons for thinking that the opposite may sometimes have been true. One reason is the testimony of the poets themselves. The troubadour Bernart de Ventadorn, for instance, says in one poem: 'tan sui entratz en cossire / com pogues bos motz assire / en cest son, c'ai apedit' ('I have been so worried as to how I might best 'seat' words [i.e. set them] in this melody which I have [?] constructed in *pedes*').[91] The other and

---

[88] See note 35 above.

[89] Dragonetti (1960) is perhaps the most influential of recent scholars to have propounded a different view.

[90] Stevens (1974–5), pp. 16–17 and Fig. I, presents an analysis of verbal accent in all five stanzas of Adam de la Halle's 'Au repairier en la douce contree' (R500). For Beck's comment see p. 495 and note 11 below. 'Il ne muet pas' (R152) is ed. Marshall, 43 (no. 4); the italicized syllables are those which seem to attract accent or stress.

[91] Ed. Nichols and Galm, no. 27, lines 4–6 (the reading *apedit* is doubtful).

main reason for believing that the melody often came first is the widespread practice of *contrafactum* composition. The facts have long been known and studied and speak for themselves.

This, however, is not the end of the enquiry. In the final chapter, on 'the balanced relationship of words and music', I shall pursue (see especially section IV) the implications of a theory of words and music which allows not simply for the possibility of the music preceding the words it sets but for the possibility that the two are not (in any sense familiar to us today) directly related to each other at all. Behind both words and notes lies 'number', a numerical Idea waiting to be incarnated; we may come to regard this as the only common term between the verse and the melody.

The present chapter has to end, however, by sounding one note of caution. The bulk of the musical evidence on which we have to draw is of the later thirteenth century; this is the period of the great chansonniers (the Chansonnier du Roi, the Chansonnier Cangé, the Chansonnier de Noailles, to mention only a few). They represent, as it were, the old age of the troubadour–trouvère tradition. Whether (to pursue the human analogy) they represent the rigidities of age and its dogmatism replacing the openness and flexibility of a more youthful style – which one might presume to be represented by twelfth-century melody – must remain to some extent an open question. However, I believe that the chapters which follow (2–4), describing the Latin song traditions, are informative on this point. The 'aesthetic of number' is dominant in the centuries which lead up to the codifying generations of chansonnier-makers; the code they were following was an ancient one.

2

LATIN SONGS: *CONDUCTUS* AND *CANTIO*

It may seem curious, indeed back-to-front chronologically, to have considered the 'numbers' of troubadour and trouvère song before those of the equally numerous (in a double sense) Latin songs of the early Middle Ages. I have done so because the French vernacular repertoire – at least in the form we have it, in the group of professionally written chansonniers of the late thirteenth and early fourteenth centuries – presents a single uniform and coherent picture; it is a tidy object for study.[1] The Latin repertoire, on the other hand, although fully international and in many respects coherent, is more variegated. It has, too, a much longer charted history, and documents survive from the ninth century onwards – written songs with musical notation. To take a comprehensive view of the whole is not easy, since there is, to date, neither a comprehensive study nor a substantial anthology.[2] In this chapter I shall only be able to treat in detail a few representative songs, but I

---

[1] The problematical degree to which this tidiness may have falsified the object is discussed at the end of chapter 1, above.

[2] There is no comprehensive substantial up-to-date account of the repertoire of Latin monophonic song. The older standard accounts by Ludwig (1930); Reese (1940) ch. 7, and Westrup (1955) are still useful though in some respects out-of-date. In *New Grove*, the articles 'Early Latin secular song' (Anderson), 'Conductus' (Knapp), 'St Martial' §11 (Planchart), and 'Versus' (Crocker) contain most of the required information and views but they are unco-ordinated and not related to one central account. The introductory pages, however, to §111 of the major article 'Sources' in *New Grove* ('Secular Monophony' by David Fallows) raise in a concise and lucid way basic questions about the nature of the monophonic repertoire as a whole; the relationship of Latin song to the vernacular (they have 'essential and fundamental common features'); their strikingly contrasted sources; the changing 'historical awareness' of copyists; the relation of learned song to folksong; and, in general, the problem of seeing what survives in the context of 'the great unwritten tradition'. Less specialist, but attractively specific in its presentation, is Hoppin, *Medieval Music* (1978a); the accompanying *anthology* (1978b) is unfortunately too restricted in size to present a balanced picture of monophonic song.

There is, surprisingly, no published anthology of Latin songs of any scope. Vecchi (1958) gives 34 examples (these include sequences and hymns). The editions by Anderson of Notre Dame *rondelli* (1978c) and *conductus/cantiones* (1978b) to some extent meet the need for scholars (but see note 66 below). Combined with Arlt's edition (1970) mentioned below they cover a good part of the later repertoire.

On the literary side the spacious histories by Raby (1953) of Christian Latin poetry and (1957) of secular Latin poetry, together with his Oxford anthology (1959) comprehensively describe the enormous repertoire of Latin texts (no translations are provided). Dronke's more up-to-date volumes, beginning with *Medieval Latin and the Rise of the European Love-Lyric* (1965), are particularly illuminating on secular Latin lyric in its total European

hope to establish some sense of the repertoire as a whole as well as certain obvious continuities in the handling of words-and-notes. The discussion will be confined largely to songs in strophic form; the remarkable, and remarkably complex, group of sequence, *planctus* and *lai* is reserved for the chapters following.

The oldest surviving collection (ninth- to tenth-century) of sacred and secular songs in various styles and forms comes from a southern French monastery dedicated to St Martin.[3] It constitutes fols. 98v–142 of the manuscript Paris BN lat. 1154, and contains pieces as diverse as a lament for Charlemagne (*planctus Karoli*), the Sibylline verses (*versus Sibille de die iudicii*, later incorporated into the Prophets play), a hymn for All Saints (*hymnus in festivitate . . .*), a *carmen* ('Spes mea, Christe / rex benedicte'), a *ritmus* on the Last Things, the well-known early sequence, 'Concelebremus sacram' (*prosa in natale Sc. Marcialis*), settings of poems from Boethius's *De Consolatione* (*versus, alius versus*) and 'Ut quid jubes, pusiole', an affectionate song addressed to a young friend (*versus Godiscalchi*).[4] The range of content and function is wide; the collection clearly raises some problems of general

---

[3] The provenance and the date of the MS are both disputed. See Chailley (1960), 75ff, in favour of St Martin (followed by Stäblein (1975), 146, 148 (notes) and pl. 32, 33). The basic studies of the so-called St Martial 'collection' as a whole are by Chailley (1960), and by Spanke, 'St Martial-Studien' (1932). For Spanke's study of Paris BN MS 1154 see note following. Crocker (1958), 161–2, discusses MS 1154 and lists some of its contents. See also Planchart and Fuller, 'St Martial' in *New Grove*, for an up-to-date survey and bibliographies; and L. Richter, 'Die beiden ältesten Liederbücher des lateinischen Mittelalters', *Philologus* 123 (1979) 63–8, for musical reconstruction of the *Song of the Sibyl*; Sesini (1949) ch. 9.
[4] The contents of these folios are most conveniently listed by Spanke (1931a: repr. 1977), 3–6.

(and wider) context as well as being more aware of musical issues and providing musical examples (1968, 1970). See also Szövérffy's weighty 'handbook' (1970).

The development of Latin song in the early Middle Ages can conveniently be seen in three stages: (i) the Carolingian, for which the sources are mainly the earlier MSS associated with St Martial; (ii) the Aquitanian repertoire of *versus* (verse-songs) and *conductus* in the later St Martial MSS, in MSS at Madrid and in many northern French sources; (iii) the Notre Dame (Parisian) repertoire of *conductus*, many of which I term *cantiones* (see section III below), the main source being the Florence MS (Source 10).

The principal sources of non-liturgical monophonic Latin song are listed, with the vernacular, in approximate chronological order by Jammers (1975) ch. 1 with detailed bibliographical notes; the index of MSS in Stäblein (1975) leads to further information and sometimes illustrative plates. See also Dronke (1965a), 11, for a bibliography of nearly 600 Latin love-poems according to their MS sources (musical settings not distinguished). The first-line indexes of Walther (1959), Anderson (1975) and Schaller-Könsgen (1977) are indispensable: Anderson is especially useful to the musician, because he charts for the first time with any thoroughness the repertoire of non-liturgical Latin songs (*conductus* and *cantiones*) from *c.* 1170 to 1300. The liturgical and paraliturgical *conductus* is described, analysed and illustrated in Arlt's massive study (1970) of the New Year liturgy (an extended festal occasion) from Beauvais. See, further, note 23 below on *conductus*. The List of Sources below includes brief descriptions of some important Latin manuscripts: BN lat. 1154 (Source 36); BN lat. 1139 (Source 35); The Cambridge Songs (Source 9); The Later Cambridge Songs (Source 8); The Carmina Burana (Source 21); The Florence MS (Source 10). See also the related non-musical MSS, Sources 13 and 23.

import. The first is the difficulty of defining the object: Latin song, with its tendency to run in and out of the liturgy, as it were, is a less clear-cut object than the courtly chanson; its variety is the result of widely differing functions (worship, public celebration, monastic entertainment, pedagogy, etc.). The second difficulty is one of terminology; the wide variety of terms is used in a way which is not always helpful. *Carmen* is, strangely enough, not much used in musical sources as a term of description; here perhaps it distinguishes this prayer to Christ written in a strophe of six short lines (6 × 5p) from the normal hymn quatrain (4 × 8).[5] *Planctus* is here used appropriately as to content, which is not always in fact the case. *Ritmus* is here used appropriately of a poem constructed on syllable-counting principles; the wonder is that it does not occur more often in this collection.[6] *Versus*, finally, is the compiler's favourite term and covers virtually every type of song. This is no idiosyncrasy of the particular scribe but the general usage of the early period. In its vernacular form *vers* it is frequently found referring to songs in the troubadour repertoire ('Faray un vers de dreyt nien': Guillaume IX) and even to early northern French songs ('. . . an chancons et an vers / chanter . . .': *Cligès*, 2804).[7] Two important terms used to describe Latin songs later in the period do not appear in this earliest song-anthology: one is *conductus*, the other *cantio*. *Conductus* came into general use in the mid twelfth century and was the principal term until *cantio* replaced it in the fourteenth.[8] Especially in the case of the popular designation *conductus*, it is often very difficult to tell whether a form (strophic as opposed to sequence-form) is being characterized, or a function (such as the escorting of a lesson-reader to the place appointed), or indeed neither.[9] Amongst other terms in regular use are *cantus*

---

[5] Evidently a *versus* could be referred to as a *carmen*; see, for example, the *versus de S. Mauritio* in this MS: 'Dulce carmen et melodum canimus ecce tibi' (Spanke (1977), 25ff), where *carmen* might refer to the text as opposed to the music. Norberg (1958), 92, cites a fourteenth-century author who seems to imply that *carmen* was the preferred term for a higher style of verse (i.e. hexameters) than *ritmus*; this seems to be confirmed by the dictionaries.

[6] *Ritmus*, a song constructed according to the principles of *musica ritmica* (see ch. 12:1). The lack of consistency in the use of terms is witnessed to by the fact that the author referred to in the previous note is willing for his hexameters to be called *ritmus*.

[7] Guillaume's eleven surviving poems are ed. A. Jeanroy, *Les chansons de Guillaume IX Duc d'Aquitaine* (Paris 1927); transl. of 'Farai un vers' in Goldin, 25–7. *Versus*: see Stäblein, 'Versus' in *MGG*, and Stäblein (1975), 60, 64, 73 etc. Crocker, 'Versus' in *New Grove*, gives its distinguishing features from the eleventh century onwards as rhyme, accentual scansion, 'frequent but varied and imaginative use of strophe, and "songlike" melody'. See also Chailley, 'Premiers troubadours' (1955b).

[8] *Cantio*: see Stäblein (1975), 74; the Latin equivalent etymologically, and often musically (see below), of Provençal *canso*, French *chanson*. Schlager (1972), 286ff, holds that from *c.* 1300, when it was most in use, *cantio* referred to a spiritual song which was not strictly part of the liturgy.

[9] *Conductus*: see especially Arlt (1970), I.207, and Reckow (1972). Roughly speaking, the historical shift is from functional definition, *c.* 1100, to broader generic uses during the twelfth century: first religious, or at least serious, secular song; eventually secular dance and love-song. I use the form *conductus, conductūs* (fourth declension) following classical usage (see also Arlt); the form *conductus, conducti* (second) is common in the Middle Ages.

and *cantilena*.[10] The medieval use of all these terms would be a study in itself – profitable but not necessarily conclusive. In the following pages I shall use them in the sense generally adopted by musical historians today, except that I shall limit the term *conductus* for the most part to songs associated with the liturgy and with its extended 'secular' festivities, especially at Christmas and New Year, whilst using *cantio* to refer generally to art-songs of a less obviously functional and, often, more ambitious nature. The *rondellus*, Latin dance-song, will be discussed separately in chapter 5: III below.

Only a limited amount of helpful information about the art of song can be gained from studying this early collection in detail, because not only are there no indications as to rhythm, but also the pitches of the notes are uncertain. The lines of text are well spaced, and this allows for a limited amount of heighting of the neumes. In Aquitanian notation of the eleventh century an embryonic stave consisting of one, or two, lines with clef forms a more precise guide to pitch. But in the present instance a rough idea of the relative pitches of adjacent notes is all that can be aspired to. The opening stanza of the *versus* by Gottschalk of Fulda (ninth-century) is neumed as shown on p. xviii:[11]

Ut quid iubes pusiole	What is it you command me, little one?
quare mandas filiole	Little son, why do you charge me to
carmen dulce me cantare	sing a sweet song, though far, far away I
cum sim longe exul valde	have been an exile, amidst the sea? O
intra mare	why do you command me to sing?
o cur iubes canere	

From this notation one may gather: that the melody was 'syllabic', in the sense that each syllable of the text was provided with a single note or short note-

[10] *Cantus*: song. Grocheo (see chapter 12:III below) in general distinguishes *cantus* (vocal music) from *cantilena* (non-vocal): there are three types of *cantus* – *gestualis* (*chanson de geste*), *coronatus* (?courtly chanson) and *versualis* or *versiculatus* (a lighter type of chanson, 'which some call *cantilena*'): Rohloff, 130–3. *Cantilena* is sometimes used by modern scholars as a generic term (e.g. by Reese, 322) to cover secular songs, monophonic and polyphonic. Grocheo restricts *cantilena* to the dance (or dance-related) forms – *rotunda*, *stantipes* and *ductia*. In *New Grove* (Sanders, 'Cantilena') 'the repertory of polyphonic songs produced by English musicians of the later 13th and the 14th centuries' is principally discussed, somewhat to the neglect of other meanings (which, however, he lists).

[11] 'Ut quid iubes' (fol. 131v); Schaller–Könsgen 16895: printed by Ludwig Traube in *Poetae Latini aevi carolini*, III (Berlin 1896), pp. 731–2, 'Godescalci carmina', no. vi, *Versus Godiscalchi*, ten stanzas; Traube's facsimile from BN lat 1154 is clearer than Stäblein's (1975, p. 146, pl. 32). See also Bernhard Bischoff, 'Gottschalks Lied für den Reichenauer Freund', in *Medium Aevum vivum: Festschrift für Walther Bulst* (Heidelberg 1960), 61–8, printing newly discovered verses from Angers MS 477. Bischoff gives details of the five surviving manuscripts. The only other one with musical notation is Montpellier, Fac.Med. 219, p. 1 (melody for lines 1–4 only). Dronke (1978) 34–6, gives a sensitive literary analysis of the poem. The melody in Coussemaker's transcription is not satisfactory ((1852), 231). A more recent transcription is by H. Sanden in *Mf* 26 (1973) 205–7.

group in ligature; that the flowing syllabic movement was not dislocated by any long melismas (there is one three-note neume, in the last line – *porrectus* on 'o');[12] that the melody was fairly but not entirely conjunct (the impression of five distinct *visual* levels is probably a simplification); that the melody of line 2 repeats that of line 1 (producing the musical form A A B C D E); that the style of singing was refined and subtle (see the use of the *quilisma*, an 'ornamental' note, on 1.2 *quid* and 2.2 qua*re*). These deductions, as far as they go, point to a style of song not essentially different except in its miniature scale from the trouvère chanson of the late twelfth and thirteenth centuries, or from many strophic Latin songs (yet to be described) of the intervening period. They point, too, to a relationship between poems and melody which can properly be described as numerical. On the evidence available it is hard to follow Stäblein in his characterization of the melody in simple outline as 'self-contained, rich in tensions and well managed', making a unity with the text which shows it was written 'for it and it alone'.[13]

Gottschalk's song, it seems reasonable to infer, is strophic. The first stanza only is neumed; but those that follow are in exactly the same form. To judge, however, from some other songs – the *planctus Karoli* (Lament on the death of Charlemagne), 'A solis ortu usque ad occidua', from the same collection, and 'Iam dulcis amica', found fully neumed in another southern French manuscript (BN lat. 1118; eleventh-century) – strophic song may in this early repertoire have allowed a good deal of (improvised?) variation from stanza to stanza. Some scholars even doubt whether 'A solis ortu' is truly strophic at all, the neume shapes and positions differ so much from stanza to stanza; the neumes of 'Iam dulcis', however, vary only slightly.[14]

I The medieval hymn

Recorded strophic song begins in the West with the hymn, which is of great antiquity.[15] It can be defined as a song with a non-Biblical text, metrically or rhythmically composed (i.e. quantitatively or numerically), put together out of stanzas structurally alike. It was sung in the Offices (the services of the Hours) and was characterized by a doxology (*Gloria patri* . . .) and by a

---

[12] There is probably also a *scandicus* (5.1 i*ntra*).

[13] Stäblein (1975), 146.

[14] 'Iam dulcis amica': see note 53 below. 'A solis ortu' (Schaller–Könsgen, no. 32). Facsimile: Coussemaker (1852), pl. 2, no. 1, and (first four lines only) in Sesini (1949), 168. The neumes (St Gall) are staffless and more or less unheighted. Attempts at transcription: Coussemaker, p. iv, no. 5; Sesini, 171. Text and German transl. in Kusch, 74–7. Szöverffy, 513–15, full discussion. See also Raby (1957), 1.211, printing the complete text.

[15] The earliest surviving Latin hymns in the form which was to become standard are those of St Ambrose and Prudentius (fourth-century). For texts, see Walpole (1922), and W. Bulst, *Hymni Latini Antiquissimi L X X V* (Heidelberg 1956).

concluding Amen.[16] Amongst the items of the early 'anthology' from which
Gottschalk's song came (and showing incidentally the unreality of any sharp
sacred/secular division) is the famous *hymnus in onore sancte crucis* by Venantius
Fortunatus, Bishop of Poitiers (d. after 600). It is not notated in the Paris
manuscript. The following version is from the earliest surviving English
hymnary (Worcester Cathedral, thirteenth-century).[17]

Ex. 5

My tongue, sing the battle of the glorious conflict, and of the trophy of the cross
proclaim the noble triumph – how the redeemer of the world was victorious in his
sacrifice.

This well-known melody from Worcester was not the only one sung in the
Middle Ages. On the right-hand side of the example I give one of two further

[16] Schlager (1972), 282. See Stäblein, 'Hymnus' in *MGG* (Section B, 'Der lateinische Hymnus'), the most comprehensive modern account; and his edition, *Hymnenmelodien* (1956). It is
easy for us to exaggerate the popular importance of the hymn because of its centrality in
Protestant worship since the Reformation. Latin hymns belonged to the Office, and the
Office belonged essentially to religious communities; it was monks not merchants who sang
Matins and Lauds, even on festival occasions. The hymn during the Middle Ages was not
congregational. It has its minor importance for vernacular literature and vernacular song
chiefly perhaps because clerks were familiar with it and had uses for it outside the liturgy.
[17] Worcester version: Stäblein (1956), 188 (no. 56/3); facsimile in *Paléographie Musicale* XII.216.
The Moissac version, Stäblein, 52 (no. 101).

melodies from the early Aquitanian hymnary (Moissac; eleventh-century).[18] Bruno Stäblein's massive *Die mittelalterlichen Hymnenmelodien des Abendlandes* (1956) contains yet others. The text is syllabically constructed (8 7 8 7 8 7); it has no rhymes or assonances. The predominantly trochaic movement of the lines is partly a matter of accent, partly a matter of quantity (i.e. of long and short syllables, agreeing with the traditional classical rules).[19] However it is achieved, a chief beauty of 'Pange, lingua' is in a verbal harmony, an *armonia* independent of rhyme.

The Worcester melody is, formally, more characteristic of the traditional hymn, in that it is completely through-composed. Untypical melodic symmetries, such as that established in the Moissac version by the repetition of the first two lines as lines 5–6, are avoided; and so, in general, is motivic play, though we can note the musical 'assonance' of 1.5–8 and 3.1–4. There is only one echo (rhythmic and pitch-shaped) which to my ear has an important balancing and rounding effect: line 5 is an aural 'shadow' of line 1. The only significant direct relations between the poem and melody are, it scarcely needs saying, structural (the matching of verse-lines and musical phrases) and numerical (every syllable has its single note or note-group).

There is one important respect in which 'Pange lingua' is untypical of the hymns known and sung in the early Middle Ages: it has six lines. The standard hymn-form follows the 'Ambrosian' pattern: a quatrain, unrhymed in the oldest examples, with a tendency also to iambic (rather than Fortunatus's trochaic) rhythm, as in the following:[20]

Ex. 6

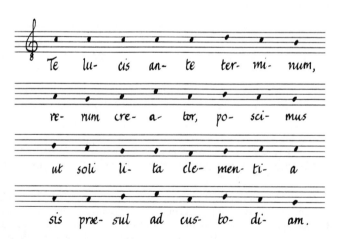

---

[18] Stäblein (1956), 188 (no. 563); 52 (no. 101).

[19] Norberg (1958), 23, gives instances of shift of accent in 'proclitic pronouns' including *super* as *supér* (*híc supér apóstolos*). See also his latest study (1984) of Latin verse accentuation. I thank Peter Dronke for this reference.

[20] Stäblein (1956), 176 (no. 136₂), thirteenth-century. See also Walpole, no. 83. 'Te lucis' had numerous seasonal melodies.

Before the ending of the day we beg you, O creator of all things, that with your wonted clemency you will be our leader to guard us.

This well-known Compline hymn, with (in this setting) an entirely single-noted melody (from Worcester), satisfies all the standard requirements, except that there are apparent concessions to modernity in the light assonance lines 1–2, 3–4, and that the musical form is A B C B' instead of A B C D. At the other extreme from this austerity are much more demonstrative, indeed jubilant, melodies such as this thirteenth-century French one, somewhat inappropriately, we might think, sung in Lent; the text is by Prudentius.[21]

Ex. 7

O_ Na- za- re- ne, dux Bethle- hem, ver- bum pa- tris,

quem par- tus al- vi vir- gi- na- lis pro- tu- lit,

ad- es- to cas- - tis, Christe, par- si- mo- ni- is;

fes- tum-que nos-trum, rex, se- re- nus a- spi- ce,

je- ju- ni- o- rum dum li- ta- mus vi- cti- mam.

O Nazarene, lord of Bethlehem, word of the Father, whom birth from a virgin womb brought forth, be present, O Christ, in our virtuous frugalities; look O King, propitiously on our festival, as we offer up the sacrifice of our fastings.

This is a rather more rhapsodic melody than one could easily find in the courtly repertory and it observes the verse-caesura (in this case after the fifth syllable) in a stronger style. Nevertheless, in its mingling of single notes with short melismas it is not unlike some *grands chants*; and close inspection reveals complex use of motifs and some melodic rhyme, or near-rhyme.[22] With all this it is still strictly a syllabic song; verse and music are constructed and held on parallel courses by the numbers $(5 + 7) \times 5$.

[21] Stäblein (1956), 117 (no. 178). See also Walpole, no. 25.
[22] Schlager (1972), 284, observes that the hymns which approach nearest to secular song-art in form and melodic style are those of Peter Damian (1007–72), often entitled *versus* (see note 7 above). See Stäblein (1956), 462–9 (nos. 788–98).

II The *conductus*

The medieval hymn was a traditional liturgical form and is not so frequently found outside the liturgy as its fashionable rival the sequence, to be dealt with later. Nor is it as interesting to us in the present enquiry as a third type of song, the *conductus*, which has less firm liturgical connections than either.[23] In twelfth-century liturgical use the *conductus*, as its name implies, is a song for 'leading' or escorting, especially for leading the lesson-reader in procession to his lectern. Wulf Arlt, to whose learned edition of the New Year ceremonies at Beauvais Cathedral I am much indebted, quotes this short conclusion to a song from the oldest source of a *conductus* collection (Madrid, BN MS 289; *c.* 1140):[24]

Ex. 8

Le- ctor, le-   ge   qui re- git om-ne; dic : Iu- be, dom- ne.
hoc de re-   ge

Reader, read about this King who governs everything. Say 'Jube, domne' [asking for a blessing].

Another, 'Resonet, intonet', ends with the words:

> Munda sit, pura sit, hec ergo concio,
> audiat, sentiat, quid dicat lectio.[25]

[23] Definition: see note 9 above. The present chapter is concerned with the monophonic *conductus*. The polyphonic *conductus* is the main concern of Janet Knapp's article 'Conductus' in *New Grove*. The early articles on *conductus* by Ellinwood (1941), Schrade (1953) and, especially, Handschin ('Conductus' in *MGG*; *NOHM*, II. 128–74; and 'Spicilegien' (1952)) should now be supplemented, for monophony, by: Arlt (1970), Falck (1981), Steiner (1964) and (1966), Stäblein (1975), *passim*, Anderson (1978) (an edition of all the eighty-three *conductus* from the Florence MS). Anderson's 'Catalogue raisonné' (1975) (cited below by letter and number, e.g. 'L45') is an indispensable guide to the repertoire of polyphonic and monophonic Latin song.

[24] Arlt (1970), I.208. The Madrid MS contains the earliest repertoire belonging to the pre-Notre Dame period; it is, like the later, international in character (see Arlt, I.207, for concordances). Three 'schools' of *conductus* have been distinguished: the Norman–Sicilian (largely monophonic), the Aquitanian (i.e. St Martial MSS), the Notre Dame (Florence MS etc.). Knapp ('Conductus' in *New Grove*) regards the existence of an independent Norman–Sicilian school as speculative and stresses the 'single artistic' movement, a single, all-encompassing repertory.

[25] Reckow (1972), 2, from Madrid MS 289, fol. 101. The *conductus* may or may not indicate at its close for what liturgical action or occasion it was intended; however, it is less closely bound up with the liturgy than the *Benedicamus*-trope (an insertion of words and music, characteristically in *conductus*-like verse and melody, into the *Benedicamus Domino*, which is a liturgical salutation (with response *Deo gracias*) occurring at the end of the Office and certain Masses).

So may this congregation be clean and pure to hear and understand what the lesson says.

'Resonet, intonet' was evidently popular: it figures at the beginning of a troped epistle for Christmas in a Naples manuscript of about the same date, where it is itself an additional trope (interpolation); it is connected again with the singing of the Epistle in a Vatican manuscript; and it appears in the Later Cambridge Songs without liturgical link (lacking indeed the final stanza quoted above).[26] The melody in the Madrid manuscript (the English one, alas, has only empty staves) is as follows:

Ex. 9

Re- so- net, in- to- net, fi- de- lis con- ci- o

men- ti- bus, vo- ci- bus, sol- lempni gau-di- o.

Let this faithful congregation sound forth and make a noise, with minds, voices and solemn joy.

This is a fairly typical simple *conductus* melody – mostly single-noted, with a few ornamental groups, stylistic rather than structural.[27] It is interesting to compare this with the slightly differently ornamented Naples version:[28]

Ex. 10

Re- so- net, in- to- net, fi- de- lis con- ci- o

men- ti- bus, vo- ci bus, so- lem- pni gau-di- o.

[26] Naples, B N vi.G.34, fol. 39v; Rome, Vat.Barb.lat. 603, fols. 3–3v; Later Cambridge Songs, fol. 2 (empty stave for strophe 1 and refrain). Stäblein (1975), pl. 30b (Naples), commentary p. 144 (not listing the Cambridge M S), amplifies Anderson L45 (with facsimile of Madrid version, opp. p. 208). Text: *A H* x x.58 (no. 30); music of Ex. 9 from Madrid M S.
[27] The polyphonic *conductus* in particular may have a *cauda* or *caude*, i.e. extended passage(s) of textless melisma. These are less common in the monophonic songs (see, however, section III below).
[28] Stäblein (1975), 144.

(The doubled notes (*pressus*-type) on 're-*so*-net' and 'men-*ti*-bus' suggest an (undefined) subtlety of rhythmic interpretation.) An even simpler *conductus* moving entirely in single notes is cited by Arlt from the Madrid manuscript:[29]

Ex. 11

The court of heaven rejoices in the birthday of the King of glory. The lord of treason is damned; his power dies.

These *conductus* are strophic songs and may have many verses. 'Natali regis glorie' is also, it happens, in the same metre (octosyllabic quatrain with iambic movement) as the 'Ambrosian' hymn. And yet it is unmistakably not a hymn. This is a matter chiefly of tonality, which has an obviousness avoided by hymn-composers. The movement of the finals *e f e d* epitomizes the pattern; and this is matched by the miniature reciting-notes in the first half of each line, *f g a f*. The balanced mono-tone three-fold figures add to the easy, attractive and (to repeat) obvious effect of the whole. Another way in which these simple *conductus* are distinguished from hymns is in the much firmer hold the verbal accent seems to take on the total song. This does not mean that they are necessarily *measured*, in longs and shorts;[30] it does appear to mean that 'number', with everything this implies, has taken on a new dimension, offers a new face, virtually unseen in the courtly chanson – repetitive pattern. In this new patterning, which we shall encounter again in the *lai*, words and music work together and not simply in parallel.

Only a small minority of *conductus* can be specifically attached to liturgical action in the way described, but some others are escort or processional songs in a wider sense. The Circumcision Offices (perhaps more revealingly described as liturgical festivities for New Year) of Sens, Laon and Beauvais contain various '*conductus ad*' designations: *ad tabulam* (? to the roster, for the reading out of the list of duties), *ad ludos* (to recreation, after the service), *ad bacularium* (apparently to the ceremony, connected with the Feast of Fools,

---

[29] Arlt (1970), 1.209.
[30] The problem of rhythmic interpretation is considered in chapters 11–15 below.

'ubi baculus accipitur'), *ad poculum* (to the drink).[31] Other songs called *conductus* occur in the liturgical drama. Contained in the same manuscript as the Beauvais Office for New Year is the *Play of Daniel*, in which we find *conductus Danielis venientis ad regem* (. . . for Daniel as he approaches the King) and *conductus referentium vasa* (. . . for those who carry the vessels).[32] And the Tegernsee *Antichristus* names a *conductus* 'Alto consilio divina ratio' which is sung whilst Ecclesia mounts her throne.[33] The manuscript of the play does not give the music, but it is thought to be the following *conductus*, which at Beauvais brings second Vespers, and thereby the whole Office, to a triumphant end. It is a piece of some magnitude and in other ways unlike the small, tuneful *conductus* so far described. It is in two parts, one highly melismatic in its style, in effect a florid, free sequence; I quote the first double versicle.[34]

Ex. 12

The divine purpose in its high wisdom renewing mankind will send from heaven the power of the Holy Spirit filling a virgin with it.

The second part, beginning with the fourth versicle (in AAB form) is in a *lai*-like style, mostly one note to a syllable, and full of the melodic (and melodious) clichés of that tradition, such as short telling phrases and clear tonality (see chapter 4):

31 E. Gröninger, *Repertoire-Untersuchungen zum mehrstimmigen Notre Dame Conductus* (Regensburg 1939), 12–13; for *bacularium*, see Arlt (1970), I.50 and n. 2. There was also sung at Beauvais and elsewhere a *conductus quando asinus adducitur* (Arlt, II.3 (no. 2), with commentary, 193–4).

32 For the *Play of Daniel*, see Beauvais MS (Source 15). Full details of the *conductus* references in Reckow (1972), p. 2, col. 2.

33 Anderson L35. See Stäblein (1966) on the music of the play, and his commentary on the *conductus*.

34 See Arlt (1970), II.157–9 (no. 25a) and 261. I read *immittet* for *immitet*.

Ex. 13

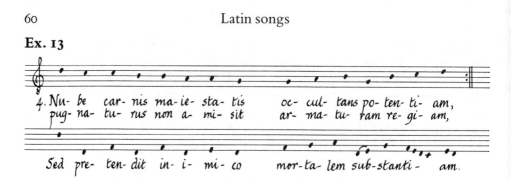

4. Nu- be car- nis ma- ie- sta- tis   oc- cul- tans po- ten- ti- am,
pug- na- tu- rus non a- mi- sit   ar- ma- tu- ram re- gi- am,

Sed pre- ten- dit in- i- mi- co   mor- ta- lem sub- stanti - am.

Hiding the power of his majesty in the cloud of [human] flesh, he did not put aside his royal armour as he went to battle but presented to the enemy his mortal substance.

'Alto consilio' is a magnificent song – 'magnificent' in a basic sense of the word, since its intention and effect is to magnify the divine purpose. It is a *conductus*, evidently, in the functional sense, and yet the term *conductus* seems less than adequate to describe it, because of its scope and its stylistic variety. However, in the rich repertory of the New Year Office in northern France *conductus* is in fact a word which may be used to designate songs in various styles and forms, some borrowed from elsewhere, some written especially for the occasion, to enlarge the festive liturgy. The great majority of these *conductus* are, it seems, essentially joyful songs filling out the Christmas liturgy and fulfilling its great purpose of celebration – *Natus est, natus est.*[35] Even when they are in strophic form, they are not necessarily simple by any means. The eight *conductus* of Matins include several with complex stanza-patterns; some also have refrains. Songs like 'Quanto decet honore' (with variable refrain marked *chorus*) and 'Eva virum' (with a 23-line strophe) could be described as short *lais*, the latter strophically repeated; their surface patterning, if not their inward design, is more complex than practically anything to be found in the *canso*/chanson repertoire.[36] A characteristic song of moderate complexity is 'Lux optata claruit'.[37]

Ex. 14

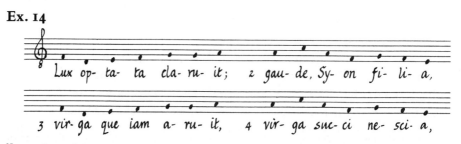

Lux op- ta- ta cla- ru- it;   2 gau- de, Sy- on fi- li- a,

3 vir- ga que iam a- ru- it,   4 vir- ga suc- ci ne- sci- a,

[35] For the well-known *conductus* beginning with these words (Anderson L132), see Arlt (1970), II.114 (no. 11), with comparative study of the five sources, *ibid.*, pp. ix–xvi.

[36] Anderson L128: with music, Arlt (1970), II.60–1 (no. 32). Anderson L30: with music, Arlt, II.71–2 (no. 47); concordance with Paris BN 1139 (Source 35).

[37] Anderson L29: musical text from Arlt (1970), II.68–9 (no. 43). The Sens version (Bibl. Mun.M. 46A, fol. 17v) is printed in Villetard, 110–11.

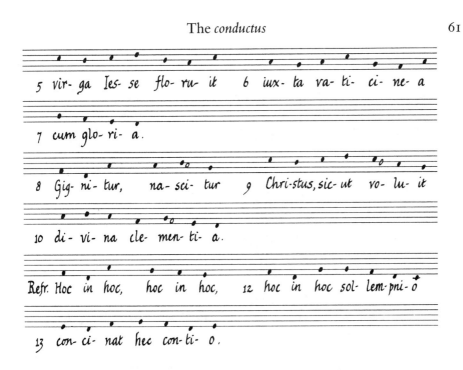

5 vir- ga Ies- se flo- ru- it 6 iux- ta va- ti- ci- ne- a

7 cum glo- ri- a.

8 Gig- ni- tur, na- sci- tur 9 Chri-stus, sic- ut vo- lu- it

10 di- vi- na cle- men- ti- a.

Refr. Hoc in hoc, hoc in hoc, 12 hoc in hoc sol- lem-pni- o

13 con- ci- nat hec con- ti- o.

The longed-for light has shone out. Rejoice, daughter of Sion, the rod which but now was dry, the rod which knew no sap, the rod of Jesse, has flourished according to the prophecies, with glory. He is brought forth, he is born, Christ, just as the divine mercy wished it. *Refrain*. Let this congregation sing this [song] on this festival.

'Lux optata' was sung both at Sens and at Beauvais. The short melodic figures are again reminiscent of the more extrovert sequences and of *lai* material. There is nothing here of the sustained dynamic of the courtly chanson, despite the superficial resemblance in form (*frons* AA + *cauda* B). At the same time, despite some triadic figures (phrases 2, 4, 8 (repeated as 12)) and a scarcely disguised sequential shift (5 and 6), the tonality remains, at least to my ear, subtle and elusive; it is hard to grasp the implications of the *e*-mode stated at beginning and end. The 'numbers' of the song, represented entirely by single notes and syllables, are easy to hear and pleasing in their variety, in the play of 3s and 7s.[38]

A different and less tractable problem is presented by the eighth and last *conductus* of Matins, 'Ex Ade vitio', the only one in the set to combine syllabic and melismatic style:[39]

[38] The total number of syllables is 86: (7×6) + 4; (3×2) + (7×2); *refrain* (3×2) + (7×2). This pattern could doubtless be made to carry a 'meaning', but there seems no reason to make it do so (see chapter 1:III above).

[39] Anderson L31: musical text from Arlt (1970), II.74 (no. 50). The more melismatic concording version in BN 1139 (Source 35) is transcribed by Handschin (*NOHM*, II.173) with variants from BN lat. 3549 (twelfth-century; ?Limoges).

Ex. 15

From the sin of Adam our damnation took its beginnings; [through the Lord Christ peace was made between God and men]. Eia, let the church of the faithful rejoice. A new mother has brought forth a son, redeemer of the lowly, remaining herself a virgin – a thing out of the course of nature.

This is a *conductus* from the St Martial repertoire and appears in the early collection BN lat. 1139 (before 1100).[40] The poem is by no means unusual in content or in manner:

> Ex Ade vitio
> nostra perditio
> traxit primordia.

The conventional syllabic movement of the verse itself is quite evident; and, apart from the characteristic little jubilation on *Eya*, the whole of the second half of the melody concords well with this movement – the syllabic pulse continues to be felt. But the sense of varied pattern, the overt play of

40 See note 36 above.

'number', which depends on syllabism, is completely obscured in the teeming melismas of the first four lines. There are vestiges of a different sort of pattern, a tonal one, in the musical 'rhyme' or 'half-rhyme' of lines 2, 3, 12 and 15; but the rhythmic–metric pattern is submerged.

III Latin art-song: the *cantio*

The Latin songs so far discussed have mostly had a use, and that use has been connected, even if sometimes marginally, with the liturgy. But such freedom of poetic and musical invention had never been, and never would be, confined to songs performed within even these generous limits. Writing of the twelfth-century state of the St Martial repertory – that is to say, about what can be deduced from the contents of southern French manuscripts (such as BN lat. 1139) assembled in the monastery of St Martial at or soon after that time – Bruno Stäblein says that the songs entitled *versus* (the free forms, as distinct from the tropes) were intended in a quite general way for festive occasions such as New Year, Christmas, St Stephen, the Holy Innocents and so on and at such a season would have been sung

extra-liturgically, in processions, at gatherings of clerks or monks; for example, during mealtimes and on social occasions. We have, then, to do with a kind of clerical entertainment [*klerikaler Unterhaltungskunst*] parallel to the secular courtly and aristocratic art of chivalric love-song, which similarly had already grown up in the region of southern France by the twelfth century, with Limoges as its centre.[41]

The existence of a huge corpus of Latin songs in the period *c.* 1050–1350 is attested by a whole series of collections large and small. Unfortunately, the two greatest anthologies of Latin lyric, the Cambridge Songs and the *Carmina Burana*,[42] while both containing some notated items, use a style of neuming which, again, is imprecise as to pitch. Such notation could be of use only to those who knew the melodies already; it served as a mnemonic, as in the case of earlier chant manuscripts. As moderns we can only interpret it securely when the song survives in another source with pitches clearly defined. In the case of the Cambridge Songs the neumes are few and far between. For one well-known song, 'O admirabile Veneris idolum', the pitches can be recovered with certainty from two notated versions of its pious contrafact, 'O Roma nobilis'; it has often been reprinted.[43]

---

[41] Transl. from Stäblein (1975), 64; and see note 7 above.

[42] See Sources 9 and 21.

[43] Vecchi (1958), fig. 2 (facsimile of Cambridge Songs, fol. 441v), with transcription of both songs as tav. ix (opp. p. 168). Westrup in *NOHM*, 11.221 (facsimile of 'O Roma nobilis' from Monte Cassino MS Q.38 fol. 291 and transcription of the Cambridge version using all three MSS). Facsimile of Vatican MS lat. 3327 in L. Traube 'O Roma nobilis' (*Abhandlungen der philosophisch-philologischen Klasse der Königlichen Bayerischen Akademie der Wissenschaften* 19 (1891) 299–309).

The anthology known as the *Carmina Burana* was compiled probably *c.* 1220–30 either at the monastery of Benediktbeuern in southern Bavaria or, as some now think, at Seckau.[44] Unusually for a manuscript of that date the neumes are unheighted and are therefore not transcribable with any certainty. About twenty melodies are apparently recoverable from other sources: half from the manuscripts associated with St Martial, mainly of the twelfth century and therefore older than the *Carmina Burana* M S itself; and half from more contemporary manuscripts recording the repertoire of Notre Dame in Paris.[45] I say 'apparently recoverable' because the list of surviving settings does not coincide with the list of neumed songs amongst the *Carmina Burana*, and some later melodies could be new ones. There is the further complication that some of the song-texts survive only in polyphonic settings, where they may of course have been altered in various ways, if not newly composed. However, the following extract shows how the staff notation of another source – in this case the Later Cambridge Songs – can to some degree be used to specify the pitchless neumes of the Benediktbeuern collection. Both versions are quite highly ornamented; and the differences between them are instructive. 'Vacillantis trutine' is a secular sequence with refrain, by an unknown author; it tells how *amor* pulls the scholar–poet in one direction whilst *ratio*, his desire to study, pulls him in another.[46]

Ex. 16

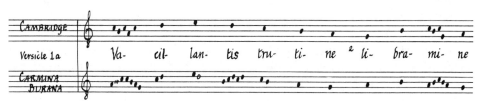

[44] See Source 21. The most thorough study of the music associated with the *Carmina Burana* is in two articles by Lipphardt (1955, 1961), who however made rigid assumptions about the rhythm of the songs, as well as about the relations of *CB* songs to other versions. He also misleadingly claimed novelty for his work. See also Spanke (1930–1). The practical anthology by Korth (1979) is not fully critical and the rhythmical solutions are disputable; but the notes give basic information about sources.

[45] All are listed, with their concordances, and transcribed in Lipphardt's articles (see preceding note).

[46] 'Vacillantis trutine' (Anderson L48): see note 48 below. The only other surviving version is in the large English anthology, the Arundel Latin Lyrics (Source 13) (fol. 234: no music). The *Carmina Burana* version is on fol. 80; see facsimile, ed. Bischoff. The Cambridge version (ed. Schumann (1943), no. 9, without its melody) is a shortened text. The full text is conveniently reprinted from Arundel in *The Oxford Book of Medieval Latin Verse*, no. 232. Ex. 16 is based on the reconstruction in Lipphardt (1961) no. 12, pp. 118–21; but I have de-mensuralized the transcription.

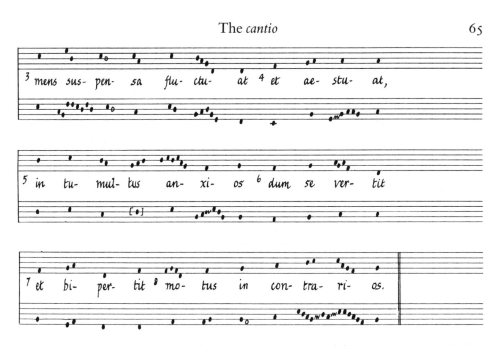

In the sway of the wavering scales my mind hovers to and fro in passionate agitation whilst it turns back to anxiety and commotion and splits between opposite impulses.

The Later Cambridge Songs (thirteenth-century) seems to be just such an anthology as might have been put together for the kinds of 'clerical entertainment' Stäblein describes – but in the region of Leicester, it seems, not Limoges:

the presence of numerous text scribes [in a collection of 16 pages only] argues a community at work, a community of clerics, perhaps the teachers or students of a cathedral or monastery school. The interlarding of a mainly sacred repertory with lively, though never gross, secular songs supports this opinion.[47]

Amongst the *conductus* are the widely popular 'Resonet, intonet', described earlier (here, unfortunately, with empty staves), and others of a similar kind – 'Magno gaudens gaudio', for example, for the Holy Innocents, and 'Virgo mater', a song for Candlemas. But scattered amongst these are 'international' songs of a different order, including three from the *Carmina Burana*.[48] It is songs of this more ambitious kind, the Latin counterpart to the vernacular *chanson* (and therefore, I have argued, more appropriately called *cantio* than *conductus*), which I wish now to consider. One of the three songs just men-

---

[47] Stevens, in Fenlon (1982), 43, based on Schumann (1943).
[48] 'Ecce torpet probitas' (Anderson L50): melody from Later Cambridge Songs, fols. 1v, 298; *Carmina Burana*, no. 3 (Hilka *et al.*, 3–5).
  'Licet eger' (Anderson L51): Later Cambridge Songs, fol. 297; *Carmina Burana*, no. 8 (Hilka *et al.*, 10–13).
  'Vacillantis trutine' (Anderson L48): Later Cambridge Songs, fols. 1–1v; *Carmina Burana*, no. 108 (Hilka *et al.*, 178–9).

tioned is 'Ecce torpet probitas' by Walter of Châtillon (d. *c.* 1190).[49] If it were
not for the Cambridge manuscript we should have no melody for it at all. As it
is, we have no absolute guarantee that the 'Cambridge' melody was the
continental one; nor, of course, that Walter composed it. The poem consists of
five stanzas of six lines with a refrain of three. The wording of the refrain
varies slightly from stanza to stanza; but it always starts with the same line –
Omnes iura ledunt (Everyone violates the laws). The refrain drives home the
message of the poem, which castigates vice, especially the vice of greed (*regnat
avaritia*). The wittiest refrain is the third:

> Omnes iura ledunt
> et in rerum numeris
> numeros excedunt

– 'in the numbers of their possessions [all] exceed proper measure' (?).[50] The
poet and composer of the song certainly observed 'number' in the way we
have come to expect.

Ex. 17

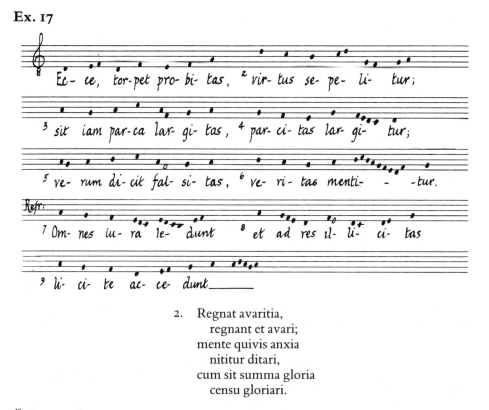

2.   Regnat avaritia,
         regnant et avari;
      mente quivis anxia
         nititur ditari,
      cum sit summa gloria
         censu gloriari.

[49] See preceding note.
[50] Hilka *et al.*, commentary, p. 5: 'beim Zählen ihrer Habe geraten sie über die Zählen hinaus';
      that is, they have so much that they cannot reckon it all up.

Refr Omnes iura ledunt
et ad prava quelibet
imple recedunt.

Look, integrity is asleep; virtue is in the grave. Let generosity now become niggardly; niggardliness is distributed. Falsehood speaks the truth; the truth lies. *Refr:* Everyone violates the laws and licitly broaches illicit deeds.
(2) Greed reigns, and greedy men reign also. Any and every person strives anxiously to get rich, for it is the highest glory to boast about your possessions. *Refr:* Everyone violates the laws and falls back wickedly to whatever crookedness he may devise.

It is not difficult to say the obvious things about this song. They characterize it as a *cantio* having behind it the numerical syllable-counting and phrase-balancing tradition which also produced the vernacular chanson: musical and poetical form are close, but not identical (the melodic material for the refrain marks it off from the verse, for instance); the melody corresponds precisely with the syllabic structure of the original in the usual way (except for the curious extended final melisma) and with the line-structure (each line is a complete melodic unit).[51] Procedurally, then, it is very similar to the troubadour/trouvère chanson – and to practically every other medieval song we have looked at. And yet there are important differences. The Latin stanza, in addition to its syllabism, has an unmistakable stress pattern created by the favourite 'goliardic' metre (the *Vagantenzeile*: 7pp + 6p).[52] This metre has an irresistible swing which Walter of Châtillon exploits to the full (see, for instance, his careful choice of verbs with an *i*-stem in lines 2, 4 and 6, to ensure the full weight on the penultimate – *sepelítur, largítur*). The text would seem to be a suitable candidate – or mate – for one of the tuneful, festive, equally 'obvious' *conductus* melodies looked at earlier. But the accompanying melody does not have the expected qualities. It does, admittedly, provide a fair number of single notes, and therefore has some phrases that move easily. But there are also melismas (phrases 6 and 7, especially) to impede the flow. However, the most puzzling feature is the structure of the melody itself. It is stable in a *d*-tonality and makes prominent use of the *a a* fifth above; it has its recurrent descending-thirds motif; and it appears to be working towards a developmental repetition (7, 8, 9, certainly; 2, 4, 6, perhaps). And yet, the total effect is, to my ear, inconclusive; it lacks the extroverted balance of simple *conductus* and *lai*, and it does not achieve the satisfying *armonia*, the melodic architecture, of the best chansons. Perhaps – though one hesitates to say it across the centuries – it is just not a very good melody.

The 'numbers' of the Latin *cantio* are not so very different from those of the

---

[51] The sense of line-structure is occasionally modified by light enjambement; it is most marked in strophe 5 lines 1–2: 'Si recte discernere / velis, non est vita'. However, it may be more appropriate, despite the rhymes, to regard each pair of lines as a single unit (Norberg (1958) 214, classifies the *vers goliardique* as a thirteen-syllable line). The final melisma has been designated, unconvincingly, as instrumental.

[52] See Norberg (1958), 151–2, 187–8.

twelfth- and thirteenth-century chanson, excepting only in the use of melisma and the role of verbal accent. Accent, it may be observed in passing, had not been a consistent or necessary feature of syllable-counting strophic verse in Latin, and many early songs (as well as sequences) depend on the more subtle *armonia* of the modulated line[53] –

> Iam, dúlcis amíca, veníto,   9
> quam sícut cor méum díligo!   9
> Íntra in cubículum méum   9
> órnaméntis cúnctis onústum!   9
>
> 2. Íbi sùnt sedília stráta   9
> àtque vélis dómus paráta,   9
> florèsque in dómo spargúntur   9
> herbèque flagrántes miscéntur.   9

> 'Come now, sweet friend,
> whom I love as my own heart!
> Come into my little room
> that's laden with all that is exquisite.
>
> There the couches are covered,
> the house is ready with curtains,
> flowers are scattered within,
> and fragrant grasses among them.'   (Dronke)

When accent predominates in verse of this period, as it does in so much of the *conductus–cantio* repertoire, the melody-maker (the poet?) has two choices: either to use it, or to minimize its effects. The latter is what seems to have been done in this song lamenting the exile of Thomas Becket:[54]

[53] 'Iam dulcis' (Schaller–Könsgen, 7489; Walther, 9697) survives in three MSS: the Cambridge Songs fol. 438v, heavily erased (facsimile Breul, p. 16); Paris BN lat.1118, fol. 247v (a St Martial MS), music in staffless and, only in part, heighted neumes (facsimiles Sesini (1949), 190–1, and Coussemaker (1852), pl. viii(2)); Vienna, Österr. Nationalbib, 116, fol. 157v, music in unheighted neumes (facsimiles E. Vuolo, 'Iam dulcis . . .', *Cultura Neolatina* 10 (1950) 6–7, and Coussemaker, pl. ix(1)). Dronke (1968), I.271–3, discusses the two versions of the text, sacred and profane; see also his article on the Song of Songs (1979). The metre of the poem has puzzling features, one of which is occasional slight variations in line-length; this occurs in all three versions. See Norberg (1958), 131; Bulst, 'Hymnologica partim Hibernica', in *Latin Script and Letters AD 400–900*, ed J. J. O'Meara and B. Naumann (Leiden 1976). Musical context and available transcriptions: see Stäblein (1975), 51, n. 493; Jammers (1975), 7, n.21; Chailley (1960), 336, with comments also on the rhythms of the text (especially line-endings).

[54] Anderson LI. The unique source is the Wolfenbüttel MS (Source 40), fol. 168v. For text, translation, commentary, facsimile (no transcription) see Denis Stevens (1970), 316–18. See also Reese, 242; and facsimile in Baxter, fol. 168v. Discussed Schrade (1953), 16–17.

Ex. 18

1. In Ra- ma so- nat ge- mi- tus,
2. plo- ran- te Ra- chel An- gli- e,
3. He- ro- dis nam- que ge- ni- tus
4. dat ip- sam ig- no- mi- ni- e.
5. en, e- ius pri- mo- ge- ni- tus
6. et Jo- seph Can- tu- a- ri- e
7. ex- u- lat, si sit ven- di- tus;
8. E- gip- tum co- lit Gal- li- e.

In Rama sounds the voice of weeping, as England's Rachel mourns, for Herod's offspring gives her over to ignominy. Behold her firstborn, her 'Joseph' of Canterbury, lives in exile as if sold [into slavery]; he inhabits the 'Egypt' of France.

In melodic structure (A A B; not imposed by the verse in this case), and in general style 'In Rama sonat' is much like a vernacular *grand chant*. The short note-groups (twos, threes and fours, mostly) are nicely balanced against the single notes; the movement is largely conjunct (broken only by the significant *en* of line 5, and by the climbing figure of line 6 which supplies energy for the climax, 6.4);[55] and the whole melody has the carefully designed arching shape that one so often finds in the high-style courtly art.

The repetition of motifs is perhaps a little more extended than in trouvère song, but it is very well and unobtrusively handled – especially in the way repeated phrases are differently disposed in the line-unit (compare 4.1–6 with 5.4–8; 7.3–7 with 8.1–6). With the possible deliberate exception of *en* (5.1),

[55] The treatment of *en* seems to fall into the small class of instances of a particular word-response. Cf. *O, eheu* etc. (see discussion chapter 8:VIII below).

the syllabic pulse is felt throughout, and accent does not oversimplify the
harmoniousness of the whole. The emphatic harnessing of verbal accent to the
melody would have produced a quite different balance of words and music, a
different manifestation of 'number', as in the simpler examples of *conductus*
quoted earlier (section 11).

The second respect in which the *cantio* may differ from the courtly chanson
is in the more liberal use of melisma – though on the evidence of the highly
florid *cansos* of the late troubadour Guiraut Riquier (*flor. c.* 1260–85) the
contrast is not an absolute one.[56] The melismas are applied in two quite
different ways – one, stylistic; the other formal. The stylistic use of melisma is
evident in an odd piece from the Later Cambridge Songs:[57]

> Argumenta faluntur fisice;
> ruunt leges Aristotilice;
> enervatur vis artis logice;
> sillogisme silent rethorice.
> *Refr.* Emicuit   deliciut   quod riguit
>   in litera;
>   apparuit   prevaluit   quem genuit
>   puerpera; . . .

The proofs of physics are found wanting; the laws of Aristotle collapse; the power of
the art of logic is weakened; the syllogisms of rhetoric are silent. What in the letter [of
the Old Testament] was harsh has become radiant and soft; the maiden's son has
appeared, has prevailed. And the power of the wicked which threatened rough blows
is restrained by the Son.

This poem celebrates Christmas in an ostentatiously academic manner; and
the melody seems to be its counterpart. The man who wrote it and perhaps
sang it had as much reason (or as little) to plume himself as the poet:

Ex. 19a

[56] The forty-eight surviving melodies of this late and prolific troubadour are given by de la
   Cuesta, pp. 592–700, in a neutral transcription.
[57] Music, Later Cambridge Songs, fol. 1 (no. 8); text, Schumann (1943), 63–4; Anderson L47
   (wrongly printed as 'Argument*ur* . . .'). This song is exceptionally difficult to transcribe.
   There are, for instance, no clef signs visible, as the left-hand margin is deeply discoloured by
   gum. Many details in Ex. 19a are conjectural.

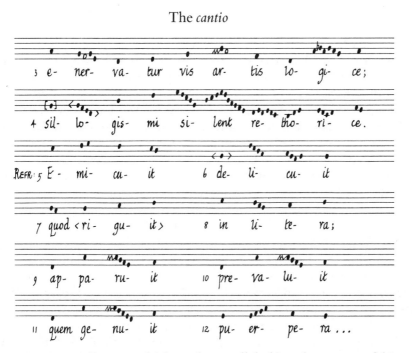

The extravagant melismas, which can be paralleled in other songs of this small collection, do not seem to have more than a decorative function. Most of the phrases could be rewritten in a simpler style without destroying the shape of the melody – Phrase 1, for example:

Ex. 19b

And this enables us to see that phrase 2 is another even more embellished version of the same, but with a 'closed' rather than an 'open' ending. Phrase 4, however, is more difficult to reduce to the conventional conjunct style. And phrases 9–11, with their un-chanson-like decorated repetitions, suggest that what lies behind the song is no single influence, but a complex. It might seem tempting to believe that the conspicuous roulades connected with Aristotle's laws and the arts of rhetoric are in some way illustrative, a sort of 'word-painting', but this would in my view be anachronistic. Rather, I believe, the song may be an unusually full, written-out version of a virtuoso performance – though why anyone should bother to write it out (and copy it so abominably) is a mystery. However this may be, the existence of such soloistic extravagances does not rule out, in the singer or in the listener, a sense of the syllabic pulse motivating the melody as a whole.[58]

---

[58] It might, however, cause us to wonder how the concepts of *armonia*, *consonantia* etc. were reconciled with such extravagances.

The other use of melisma, which I have called formal, is best illustrated from the Florence Manuscript (thirteenth-century). Besides being a major source of Notre Dame polyphony from early in the century, the manuscript contains in fascicles 10 and 11 the largest single collection of monophonic Latin songs.[59] Those in fascicle 11 are *rondelli*, the Latin equivalent of the French *rondeaux*, and will be considered in chapter 5 below (on dance-song). The others are usually referred to as 'monophonic *conductus*', but many of them belong rather with the Latin songs that I have been calling *cantiones* in order to stress their status as art-songs and their apparent complete independence of the liturgy and of devotional festivity. Of the eighty-three poems, thirty-six or thirty-seven 'are attributed in various sources to Philip, chancellor of the Cathedral of Notre Dame from 1218 to 1236';[60] most are religious, though non-liturgical, and some are satirical and moral, after the style of Walter of Châtillon's 'Ecce torpet' (Ex. 17, above). Amongst the other songs are many of topical interest: they eulogize or elegize (which is not so different) personages as diverse as Henry II (Count of Champagne), William Longchamps (Bishop of Ely and Regent of England during the third Crusade), St Bernard of Clairvaux, Francis of Assisi, Peter the Chanter (the Paris theologian).[61] Love is not at all as frequent a topic as the immoral greed of the clergy; and one of the few songs which deal with it, 'Olim sudor Herculis' (also in *Carmina Burana*), deals only to dispraise 'the love which takes the bloom from fame's deserts' (*Amor fame meritum / deflorat*).[62] 'Olim sudor' is in fact a sequence, not a strophic song, but it will serve to introduce the problem of melismas. I give the opening line from the Florence MS and also from the Later Cambridge Songs:[63]

Ex. 20

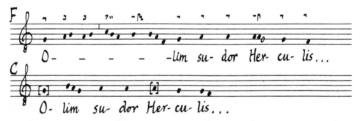

59 See Source 10.
60 Steiner (1966), 57–8; see also Raby (1957), II.227–35, for an account of Philip the Chancellor's poems, and Peter Dronke's forthcoming article in *Das Ereignis Notre Dame* ed. W. Arlt and F. Reckow (Wolfenbüttel 1986–7).
61 Steiner (1966), 56–7.
62 'Olim sudor' (Anderson K4): Florence MS, fol. 417.
63 There are five sources, of which only Florence and Cambridge (fol. 300) have music (both in non-mensural notation). Anderson (1978b), 5–9, gives both in full, in a measured transcription (for which he argues in his article on the monophonic conductus (1978d)). The melismas, or *caude*, could conceivably have been added to the songs of MS F after their original composition; some have independent existence elsewhere (see Bukofzer, in *AnnM* I (1953) 65ff), including the initial melisma of 'Olim sudor'.

Some songs in the Florence MS have even longer *preludia* – especially the sequences, but the more ambitious strophic songs may also be introduced and concluded with long melismas:[64]

Ex. 21

(In this case a shorter eight-note melisma decorates the second line of the verse also: 'O quorum studia . . .') These opening melismas are clearly not an integral part of the songs that they introduce, since they can be freely omitted, as in the Cambridge manuscript. Some scholars have related them to the *caude* of polyphonic *conductus*; but whereas the latter are normally copied according to the rules of a clearly defined mensural modal notation, the introductory melismas of the monophonic *conductus* are not. In this the different sources agree fairly consistently. The opening of 'Ve mundo a scandalis' in the important Wolfenbüttel MS (W^1), for example, is almost identical in notation to its opening in the Florence MS.[65] The *caude* in the latter are often broken up with short vertical strokes, such as are reserved elsewhere in this fascicle for important word-divisions and the ends of phrases; their meaning (see 'O curas hominum' above) in this context seems to be related to melodic structure – they are, as it were, phrase-marks. To sum up, these introductory melismas, as the Cambridge 'Olim sudor' demonstrates, are evidently not integral to the song. They lie outside the 'numbered' pattern and cannot possibly be incorporated into it. A melody with this type of opening may well proceed thereafter in a normal 'neumatic' style, with single notes and short note-groups; or it may introduce other melismas in introductory or final positions. Their intention and effect could be to heighten the style, to raise it perhaps above the level associated with courtly chanson on the one hand or festive *conductus* on the other.

iv Conclusion

A thorough stylistic analysis of the Latin songs in high style, the *cantiones*, in relation to other monody, is much needed and has not yet been undertaken.[66] I

---

[64] Steiner observes that '38 pieces begin with fairly long melismas, and 27 end with them. In 20 pieces there are melismas at the beginning of a new stanza within the work; in some there are further melismas within the stanza' ((1966), 70). 'O curas' (Ex. 21) is on fol. 424v.

[65] Wolfenbüttel MS (Source 40), fol. 185; Florence MS, fol. 426. Anderson k27. On this song, see the analysis of Steiner (1964), 95–102. The melismatic *cauda* in Las Huelgas MS (Source 4), fol. 157, is close melodically but not notationally.

[66] For studies of monophonic music in the Florence MS, see Source 10. Systematic wider study of the repertoire has not advanced far, partly because of the unavailability of usable transcriptions, partly because of the intractability of the rhythmic problem. The late Gordon Ander-

will conclude the discussion by presenting one further complete song from the Florence MS to show what an ambitious art this is, how little it deserves its present neglect, and how naturally it springs from the centuries–old tradition of numbered song. The song is 'Veritas veritatum / via vita veritas', attributed to Philip the Chancellor.[67]

Ex. 22

[67] 'Veritas veritatum' (Anderson K19): Florence MS, fols. 423v–424 (the only source with melody; but music was evidently intended for the *Carmina Burana* version, fol. 2 (edn no. 21, n. on p. 41)). Measured transcription, ed. Anderson (1978), no. K19.

son's welcome comprehensive edition (1978) does not altogether meet the former need, because his transcriptions, heavily metricalized and not set out to display the structures, somewhat obscure the object.

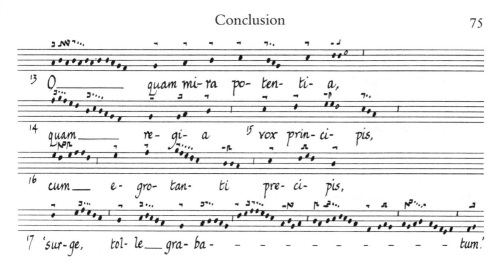

Truth of truths – the way, the life, the truth – casting out sin from throughout the paths of truth, to you, the Word Incarnate, cry faith, hope and charity. You are shaping again the primal peace after man's guilt, you give grace, after the pleasures of the flesh are past, that you may make men blessed. O marvellous power, O royal princely voice instructing the sick man, 'Arise and take up your bed!'

This by thirteenth-century standards – indeed, I think by any – is a massive melody. Some of the sequences and *lais* to be discussed later display an architectural power that is comparable but not the same. In their case the structure is more visible externally; one imagines that the building could be taken apart and reassembled quite easily. In this case the melody seems rather to grow than to have been built up. There is nothing comparable on this scale outside the corpus of Gregorian chant.

Taking the *grand chant* of the trouvères as a starting-point, we note the same basic principles of form. The composer is aware of the line- and syllable-structure of the verse. Even though he does not always keep strictly to the *grand chant* 'rule' (the 'rule' of practically all secular monophonic song) of one note or note-group to a syllable, this is still the norm from which, if he deviates, it is consciously, and to which he returns. In the first eight lines, well over half the syllables are 'set' with a single note, and only 6 syllables (out of 58) have a melisma of more than four notes. In this part of the song an expectation of syllabic movement, the pulse of the syllable, is set up. Nor, in my view, should this basic expectation be discarded in the more melismatic second half (lines 9–16). There is inevitably some dislocation – perhaps better thought of as suspension – of movement: as for instance, when the voice warbles the trill-like figures of '*Tu post carnis*' (9.1) and '*O quam mira*' (13.1). But these rhythmic 'suspensions' are mostly at the beginning or end of the phrase (14.1 '*quam*'; 17.6 '*grabatum*'), though not always; and the phrase, if not too short, has time to recover its momentum. To repeat, this is still 'syllabic melody', like the courtly chanson, however thickly ornamented.

Formally the song is most interesting. It does not use the AAB structure of the courtly chanson, though a good number of Latin *cantiones* do so. There are twenty-five such in this collection alone, according to Ruth Steiner's analysis, a fact which confirms links between the Latin and vernacular repertoires.[68] The melody of 'Veritas veritatum' is, by contrast, basically in an ABB' form where B' (13–17) is a greatly enlarged version of B (9–12). This tripartite division corresponds both to the formal division set up by the rhyme-scheme (there are only five rhymes in this sixteen-line strophe but they change after 1–8 and again after 9–12) and also to the division indicated in the manuscript by the scribe's careful capitalization of *Tu* and *O* (lines 9 and 13). Looked at a little more closely, the melody has the appearance of an *oda continuata*, to use Dante's term, in which each line of verse has a new musical phrase; this is only evidently untrue of the melismatic openings of 9 and 13. But the impression of continuous novelty (which can be represented as *ABCDEFGH*) is totally misleading: the song is developed from a small number of melodic ideas (even the term 'motif' may be too fixed and definite for them). The first arises as a series of afterthoughts to the opening, 'Veritas', *gaa*.

Ex. 23

(i)

Other melodic germs are:

(ii)  worked in phrases 4, 7, 8, 16 (twice).

(iii) worked in phrases 10–11, 12–13, ?15.

(iv) repeated in phrase 12 and suggested in the final cadence, 16.

One can in an allowable metaphor speak of organic growth in such a melody as this. It is a different principle to that of sequence and *lai*, which rely essentially on literal repetition, juxtaposition, contrast. But it is very much in keeping with the way the high courtly chanson comes into being and creates its unities.

---

[68] Steiner (1964), 136–7. The number is twenty-eight if three songs are included which have an introduction followed by AA or AA' form.

The melody of 'Veritas' seems from the page to have an active and energetic movement, but the impression may be misleading. The effective range is only a single octave plus the tone below. The movement is almost entirely conjunct, even between phrases. The conjunctness certainly contributes to the stateliness, the restrained opulence, of the melody, smoothing over the angles and corners implicit in the triadic harmony and, paradoxically, enforcing its stability. Tonally the melody is indeed very stable. If one follows the archings of the melody through the first eight phrases, for instance, one finds a recurrent insistence on the 'key-note' (the term seems fully justified) g, with subsidiary weight on the notes of the triad (b, d'). The upper g' is *the* climactic note. Counterpoised against the g triad and creating the lightest of tensions is an f–a tonal axis lightly touched at various points and becoming explicit in the final cadence. This tonality (not quite a 'harmony'), which seems positively to exploit the so-called forbidden interval, the tritone f–b, is one of the most common of all in the *lai* and sequence repertoire, is quite un-Gregorian, and does not appear often in the high courtly chanson.[69]

However, when all is said and done, it is still with the chanson that such a song as 'Veritas veritatum' has its closest affinities – which brings us back finally to the question of music, verse and number. In discussing troubadour and trouvère songs I wrote of 'the concept of number realizing itself in the *armonia* of words and of music'. It was possible to say everything that was necessary about the verbal artefact and about the musical artefact as separate entities without having to consider any direct relationship between them other than one based on 'number' in quite a narrow sense of the word. Poem and melody simply had the same number of lines/phrases and syllables/note-(groups), and they observed, normally, a common main (and very simple) structure – A A B. What we must now ask is whether the same general observations are valid in the case of this solemn and ambitious Latin *cantio*, 'Veritas', and other Latin songs which preceded it. Does the concept of number 'explain' the relation between words and notes? The answer is 'yes' – but not a completely unqualified one.

The truths about 'number' stand firm; I will not reiterate the arguments for believing that under the encrustations this is 'syllabic melody' still and belongs to the centuries-old tradition of song-making in which counting your syllables, balancing your lines, weaving an harmonious fabric of units, was the all-important thing. Nor is it necessary, I think, to argue expressly that both the poem and the melody are independent, self-sustaining and highly wrought. The question is whether there are any other points of contact between the words and the music. Generally speaking, the numerical theory of verse-making and melody-making implies a complete interchangeability between songs of the same pattern. (This is not quite as open a situation as it might seem when one remembers that over 1500 different strophic patterns

---

[69] The nature of the tritone and the reasons for assuming its validity in the *lai* and sequence repertoire are further discussed in chapter 4 below.

were invented for troubadour song alone.) There is only one aspect of 'Veritas' which perhaps does not fit in with this plan – the 'trilling' melismas on *Tu*
and *O*. These have the air of being specifically devised for these monosyllables
in this particular context. I am not sure, however, that a phrase like 'specifically devised' quite hits it off. Of all available sounds the 'O' is the one which
most readily invites a melisma – in plainchant, in this collection of songs, and
in general. It is, as it were, a primal sound, whether used as a vocative or (as
here) as an exclamation. Another song in the Florence M S, 'Anglia, planctus
itera' (fol. 422), for example, has a series of vocative *Os* – *O dies . . . O dies . . .*
etc. – and each *O* is melismatic. The melisma there, as here, stylizes *in sound* a
basic expressive cry, and conveys thereby the emotion already inherent in the
cry.[70] There are not many words of this kind in any language, for most words
are symbols not symptoms: they denote and refer. In 'Veritas veritatum' there
is only one other, the vocative *Tu*, which being at the beginning of a line and a
section (a favourite place on purely conventional grounds, we have seen, for a
melisma) rather unusually is accorded the same treatment that *O* will receive
three lines later. Formally, it is the necessary preparation for the coming *O*.
One cannot deny that these melismas do seem to constitute a point of particular contact, of a kind rare in medieval monody, between what the words mean
and what the melody does. However – and there is some sting in this tail –
these so expressive-seeming undulations of wonder are thought perfectly fit in
the subsequent verses to go with this series of syllables: *per, mor*(tis), *sed, non,
sed, et, nunc,* and *sic*!

One other possible 'particular contact' may strike the reader. The first
climax of the melody is in phrase 5; it has been carefully prepared in phrase 4,
which itself lies high, and starts on the highest note reached anywhere in the
melody, top *g*, used for the first and only time to begin the phrase. The words
are *te verbum incarnatum* (you, the Word made flesh). The force and appropriateness of this are so striking as to unsettle even an entrenched scepticism.
There is something at work here trying to break the bounds, though not the
bonds, of number. This something should perhaps be called rhetoric? The
effect is 'demonstrative', certainly, and meets one of the central injunctions of
the *ars rhetorica* – to persuade. If the composer of this melody thought he had
the duty of effective communication, then it is as a figure of rhetoric that he
might have explained this melodic emphasis. The highly educated Parisian
circle, such as must have been the birthplace of this 'anthology', would have
been a natural place for the arts of speech and number to mingle their ideas.[71]
But this remains conjecture. The true explanation of this striking and 'un-
numerical' effect may be simpler – and deeper – as a natural feature of human
song in all ages.

To conclude, the feature most characteristic of Latin strophic song in this
period – as it was characteristic of the high courtly chanson – is a consistent and

[70] See discussion of this issue in chapter 8:VIII (text to note 82) below.
[71] See Steiner (1966), 56–61.

unquestioning attention to 'number', in senses ranging from the purely arithmetical (syllable-counting) to loftier notions of number disposition – balance,
proportion, *armonia*. One result of this preoccupation is something which,
with seeming paradox, might be called a *non*-relationship between words and
music, except in the numerical sense described. To this 'non-relationship' I
shall return in Part III of this book, since it contains, I believe, an essential clue
to some of the outstanding problems of medieval song.

3

THE SEQUENCE

In chapter 8 below, 'Speech and melody', I give some account of the way words and melody work together in the liturgy. The subject is a forbidding one: the corpus of the chant is vast in itself and intricate beyond measure in its variations. I shall not attempt to describe it, even in the most general terms. However, there was in the early Middle Ages a new wave of creativity which produced new styles of liturgical and 'para-liturgical' song. Under 'para-liturgical' are included forms such as the sequence, the *Benedicamus*-trope and some dramatic ceremonies; their status in the liturgy was not official or obligatory, and they sometimes took on a life of their own outside the church and its services. The category is not easy to define with any precision. Some of the new 'songs' were deeply influential upon the non-liturgical songs which are the main subject of this study. Indeed, some of them – the sequence in particular – were more than merely influential; they provided models, often actual melodies, for so-called secular songs. They cannot therefore be omitted from this account of the art of melody.

Amongst the interesting songs squeezed into the musical pages of the Arundel Songs (London B L Arundel M S 248) is a *lai* which begins 'Flos pudicitie'; it is headed *Cantus de domina post cantum Aaliz* (Song of Our Lady, to the melody of 'Aaliz'). 'Aaliz', Alice, is presumably 'la bele Aelis' mentioned in many dance-songs of the period, and this song a religious contrafact, in two languages, of a song written in her honour.[1] It opens as follows:

Ex. 24

```
A  Flos pu-di- ci- ti-  e,        au- la mun-di- ti- e,
B  Flur 'de vir- gi- ni- te,      chambre d'o- nes- te - te,
```

---

[1] Concerning Bele Aaliz, see chapter 5:1 below. 'Flos pudicitie': Arundel Songs, fol. 153v (non-mensural notation), Anderson L144; facsimile in *EEH*, I, pl. 33. Diplomatic transcription: Maillard (1963), 235. The 'lyrical *lai*', a genre distinct from the narrative *lai*, is discussed below, chapter 4:IV. See also Source 12 (Arundel Songs). I am grateful to David Hiley, Susan Rankin and Janthia Yearley for their helpful comments on this chapter.

ma- ter mi- se- ri- cor- di- e,
de mer- ci mere e de pi- te,

2 sal- ve, vir- go se- re- na, vi- te ve- na, lux a- me- na, ro- re ple- na;
Deu vus saut vir- gne pu- re, ki na- tu- re d'en- gen- dru- re e por- te- u- re

sep- ti- for- mis spi- ri- tus
sur- mon- tez par vos bon- tez,

3 vir- tu- ti- bus or- nan- ti- bus ac mo- ri- bus ver- nan- ti- bus.
dont tanz a- vez ke bien po- ez ai- der as- sez as mes- ais- siez.

4a Ro- sa io- cun- da, cas- ti- ta- tis li- li- um,
Ro- se tres be- le, flur de lis en chas- te- te,

b pro- le fe- cun- da gig- nis de- i fi- li- um,
vir- ge pu- ce- le, en- fan- tas- tes le filz De;

c vir- go- que mun- da tu post pu- er- pe- ri- um ....
de ta ma- me- le dou- ce- ment fu 'a- lai- te....

Latin: Flower of chastity, palace of purity, mother of mercy. Hail, bright virgin, vein of life, pleasing light, full of dew – with the virtues of the seven-fold spirit embellishing you, and flowering in all your ways. Rose of delight, lily of chastity, you are the mother of God, fertile in offspring and still a pure virgin after childbirth.

French: Flower of virginity, chamber of modesty, mother of mercy and of pity, God save you, virgin pure, you who surpass nature's way of conception and birth through your virtues, in which you are so abundant that you are well able to give great help to those in distress. Most beautiful rose, lily-flower in chastity, virgin maiden, you gave birth to the son of God; from your breast sweetly he was given suck.

There are several features of 'Flos pudicitie' which clearly distinguish it from the kind of song we were considering in the last chapter, *la grande chanson courtoise* in particular. To begin with, it is a long, continuous and 'through-composed' song. The troubadour or trouvère chanson is strophic and repeats its complex stanza-pattern of metre and melody precisely, as many times as required; the *lai* 'Flos pudicitie', on the other hand, is full of repeated motifs, but its structure is non–strophic. A second feature is that it has two texts, one in Latin and one in French. The French text, presumably the second to be written, starts by being a close metaphrase of the Latin and occasionally returns to that ideal, but most of the way it is related only in its general pious sentiments. One reason for the thin, paraphrasing quality of the French is the necessity the author has imposed upon himself of keeping to the syllabic count of the original. This is obviously very important to him – more important than retaining the meaning; it is also exceedingly difficult in a language less highly inflected than Latin. Here we stumble at once, however, on the essential link between the songs to be discussed in the present chapter and those previously discussed. It is *the* distinguishing feature, indeed, of the whole monophonic repertoire in Latin and the romance vernaculars – syllabism. The counting and matching (in words and music) of syllables is just as important in sequence, *lai* and *planctus* as it is in *conductus, cantio* and chanson.

Sequence, *lai* and *planctus* are three genres which have frequently been discussed together in the musical scholarship of the last fifty years.[2] They make up a complex of extraordinary interest, one which is both unfamiliar to most modern students of song and also of fundamental importance for understanding the English song repertoire. Everyone is familiar in our day with the traditional strophic songs (such as ballad and hymn), with *aria*-form (ABA), with recitative as used in the seventeenth and eighteenth centuries. But the kind of song which the sequence is has no modern equivalent. Its structure will be more fully considered later; its essential structural principle is that of 'progressive repetition', which musically and metrically can be represented AABBCCDD... To put it another way, the sequence in its standard form is a through-composed song in which *each formal unit is stated twice.*

The prevalence of this form, or set of forms, in the English repertory has perhaps even now not received its full recognition. The Reading Abbey MS (BL Harley 978) has, of course, attracted much expert attention, because of 'Sumer is icumen in'; and Jacques Handschin many years ago fully recognized the dominant form.[3] The MS opens, musically, with a magnificent *lai* (a 'free' sequence, one might say) which is also a dramatic *planctus*, 'Samson dux fortissime', and follows it with two more *lai*-like pieces, 'Regina clementie' (a sequence addressed to the Virgin) and 'Dum Maria credidit' (another of the same but unique to the manuscript). Then comes the well-known sequence 'Ave gloriosa virginum regina' (the melody, which again has *lai*-like characteristics, appears elsewhere with French *lai*-texts). I need not detail the full contents here; but it is worth remarking that even the short motet 'Ave gloriosa mater salvatoris' was thought by Handschin to have connections

[2] The sequence, and to a lesser extent the *lai*, can essentially be defined by metrical–musical form. The *planctus*, or song of lament, is a more elusive entity but often has formal features which associate it strongly with the other two; in theory, at least, a *planctus* can take any musical form. See chapter 4:III below for fuller discussion.

[3] Handschin (1949), a detailed study of the Reading Abbey MS (Source 16). 'Sumer is icumen in' (*Index* 3223) is the only English song in the MS (Dobson and Harrison, no. 9).

with the sequence or *lai*.[4] Amongst these and other pieces occurs also the
well-known group of *estampies*, wordless instrumental pieces in sequence
form.[5] The Arundel Songs Manuscript, similarly, advertises its indebtedness
to the sequence–*lai* tradition in other songs besides 'Flos pudicitie' quoted
above.[6] The consideration of this tradition will take us back a long way before
the period which I have chosen for study. But such is the intrinsic interest of
the material and such its importance for understanding the relationship
between words and music that the excursion will be worthwhile. We may
begin with some early sequences.

I The early sequence: Notker

During the period stretching roughly from the ninth to the sixteenth century
thousands of sequences were produced. Some 4,500 texts were published in
Dreves's *Analecta Hymnica* (1886–1922). It is a major form of the art of song in
the Middle Ages.[7] The sequence in liturgical use, from which we may most
easily take our bearings, has its place 'in the first part of the Mass between the
lessons, more precisely between the Alleluia (with which it is connected in a
varying degree of closeness) and the Gospel'.[8] The standard order would be:

Alleluia with its *jubilus* – *Verse* – repeat of Alleluia – sequence replacing or
extending repeat of *jubilus*.

The *jubilus*, 'formerly called *neuma* . . . is the melismatic continuation of the
melody of the Alleluia on the final syllable of the word'.[9] Originally the

---

[4] The Latin pieces mentioned are indexed by Anderson, L42–44, K75, A13.
[5] Handschin (1929), and 'Estampie' in *MGG*. Facsimiles: *EEH*I, pls. 18, 19; Besseler–Gülke,
pl. 13 (with extensive commentary, p. 46). Wulf Arlt's article 'The "Reconstruction" of
Instrumental Music: The Interpretation of the Earliest Sources' in *Studies in the Performance of
Late Mediaeval Music*, ed. S. Boorman (Cambridge 1983), discusses the wordless *estampies* in
the Reading Abbey MS and Oxford, Bodleian Douce 139 (Source 24). The *estampie* is also
the name for a poetic form: see edn. by Streng–Renkonen. The most compendious account
of the *estampie*, musical and literary, is van der Werf, 'Estampie' in *New Grove*. All but two of
the nineteen *estampie* poems in the Lorraine Chansonnier (Source 25) are in sequence form
with double versicles.
[6] E.g. in the Mary Magdalene sequence 'Magdalene laudes plene', on the same page as 'Flos
pudicitie' *EEH* I, pl. 33), to the melody of 'Letabundus' (see Ex. 28 below).
[7] The recent research report by Nancy Van Deusen, 'The medieval Latin sequence' (1982),
makes an extensive bibliographical note unnecessary. Her report lists work on the sequence
'by region, by chronological period, by possible author or composer' etc. (Her short article is
not, of course, an 'edition'; it describes a projected plan for a manuscript catalogue.) I have
relied extensively on Stäblein, 'Sequenz' in *MGG* XII (1965). The works I have found most
stimulating on the particular subject of words and music are: the articles by Spanke reprinted
in *Studien* (1977); Crocker, *Early Medieval Sequence* (1977); von den Steinen, *Notker* (1948); de
Goede, *Utrecht Prosarium* (1965). The 'secular' sequence is discussed in chapter 4:1 below; see
especially notes 2 and 3 on types and terminology.
[8] Trans. from Stäblein (1965), col. 522. See also de Goede, p. ix: in the Roman Gradual the
sequence precedes the repeat of the Alleluia.
[9] De Goede, p. xiv. The relation between *sequentia* ('following things') and *jubilus* is often
obscure (*ibid.*, p. xxiii).

sequentia appears to have been a purely musical addition not distinguishable in essence from the *jubilus*. The *sequentia* becomes a *prosa* (or 'sequence' in modern scholarly usage) when words are added syllabically to the notes of the wordless melody.[10] Bruno Stäblein in his authoritative survey of the sequence gives the following example of the complete liturgical item outlined above. It consists of the Alleluia, with its verse *Letabitur justus in domino*, followed by the repeat of the Alleluia and its extension into the sequence. The latter is given in two forms by Stäblein, following the common practice of the early sources – the first is melismatic and has no words; the second has the text 'Fulget dies jucunda' from an English source (the Winchester Troper, *c.* 1000). In the example which follows, slurs indicate ligatures in the original wordless *sequentia* melody.[11]

Ex. 25

---

[10] De Goede, p. xxiii. A further term is also found – *prosula*, a text added to the Alleluia-*jubilus* itself. More generally a *prosula* is a text applied on the syllabic principle to any melismatic chant, such as a responsory (see Steiner, 'Prosula' in *New Grove*).

[11] Ex. 25 based on Stäblein (1965), following col. 528, who also prints the text of 'Concelebremus sacram': Schaller–Könsgen, 2503; Chevalier, 3692; text in *AH* VII.183 (no. 166), with references to nine MS versions amongst the St Martial MSS. See also Chailley (1960), 76, 135, 306, etc. 'Fulget dies jucunda': Schaller–Könsgen, 5415; Chevalier, 6620; text in *AH* XL.226 (no. 256) from Oxford, MS Bodley 775, and Cambridge, Corpus Christi 473, the Winchester Troper (Source 5) with heading *De s. Fusto Autissiodorensi*.

5a Ma- ter ad hec ver- ba to- to cor- de com- mo- ta in- quit Fe- li- ci- a:
5b 'Pro- les mi- hi ca- ra, fi- li mi, o Jus- te, quid lo- que- ris ta- li- a?

6a Si que ad- ver- sa ti- bi in vi- a con- tin- gant, e- go pro te
6b 'No- li, ma- ter mi,' in- quit, 'plo- ra- re; in- ter om- ni- a Christi

ma- gna fle- bo tris- ti- ti- a.'
me 'li- be- ra- bit gra- ti- a.'

7a Fre- ti vir- tu- te an- ge- li- ca per- gunt lon- gin- qua i- ti- ne- ra,
7b Jus- to pu- e- ro pre- ful- gi- da pre- pa- ra- ta an- te se- cu- la

fra- trem li- be- rant.
ad- est glo- ri- a.

8 Ter- re- a pas- sus membra, ce- lo dans a- ni- mam can- di- da,

ru- bi- cun- da ful- get in pur- pu- ra. Om- nes u- na

te vo- ce sup- pli- cant

9a Et in e- ter- na fac te- cum es- se le- ti- ti- a.
9b Tu- am com- men- da, pre- ca- mur, Christo fa- mi- li- am.

10 Laus de- o ma- gna per cun- cta se- cla.

Not all early sequences by any means can be accounted for in the way just
described, i.e. by the addition of words to a *sequentia* melody. But this way
seems to be one of the facts of their history.[12] Notker testifies to it in the
famous preface of which all historians of the sequence have taken account.
This monk of St Gall relates how as a young man he already found it difficult
to remember the *longissime melodie*, and how he therefore pondered on a better
means of fixing them in his memory. Inspired by an example in the Antiphonal of a monk who had fled from his monastery at Jumièges in Normandy,
which had been sacked by the Normans, he decided to provide these melodies
with texts.[13] Notker himself writes of their reception:

> When I took these lines to my teacher Iso, he, commending my industry while taking
> pity on my lack of experience, praised what was pleasing, and what was not he set
> about to improve, saying, 'The individual motions of the melody should receive
> separate syllables.'[14]

Some of the wordless melodies denoted *sequentie* are indeed very long, *longissime*, and in their surviving forms they have two features which distinguish
them from the traditional repertory of Gregorian melodies. The first is
parallelism, 'the systematic repetition of . . . melodic parts'; the second is
'melodic rhyme, the ending of a series of phrases with the same cadential
figure'.[15] Both these features are evident in 'Fulget dies': each melody is
repeated with one or two small exceptions; and the cadential figure consists of

Ex. 26

[12] See, e.g., Crocker (1977). On the origins of the sequence there are several views: C. Hohler,
reviewing Crocker (*JPMMS* 2 (1979) 65–7), re-asserts the theory of Italian (as against
Frankish) origins, which has some medieval authority; Crocker himself stresses the possibility that the early sequence was a new kind of sacred song consciously composed by Frankish
artists. Many of the sequences he discusses have no demonstrable relationship with an
Alleluia; and he finds it helpful to distinguish between 'large' and 'small' sequences in this
respect (ch. xxii, 'Sequence, Alleluia and Liturgy'). Another suggestion is that Notker's
sequences were for use in choir-practice rather than in the Mass. Further theories, chiefly of
secular origins: see below, chapter 4.

[13] De Goede, p. xx.

[14] Transl. Crocker (1977) 1. The Latin original of Notker's preface is printed by von den
Steinen, 8–10 (with German translation). The relevant passage runs:

> 'Cum adhuc iuvenulus essem et melodiae longissimae, saepius memoriae commendatae, instabile
> corculum aufugerent, coepi tacitus mecum volvere, quonam modo eas potuerim colligare. Interim vero
> contigit, ut presbyter quidam de Gimedia, nuper a Nordmannis vastata, veniret ad nos, antiphonarium
> suum deferens secum: in quo aliqui versus ad sequentias erant modulati, sed iam tunc nimium vitiati.
> Quorum ut visu delectatus, ita sum gustu amaricatus. Ad imitationem tamen eorundem coepi scribere:
> *Laudes deo concinat orbis universus, qui gratis est redemptus*, et infra: *Coluber Adae deceptor*. Quos cum
> magistro meo Isoni obtulissem, ille studio meo congratulatus imperitiaeque compassus, quae pla-
> cuerunt laudavit, quae autem minus, emendare curavit dicens: singulae motus cantilenae singulas
> syllabas debent habere . . .'

[15] De Goede, xxiii. The question of the origins, and therefore in some sense the authenticity,
of the repetitions in the (wordless) *sequentiae* is also disputed. In their earliest versions they

The approach to the final (*g*) from below does not occur in the Alleluia itself, nor in its verse *Letabitur* . . . These two features, it should be noted, are features of the wordless *sequentia* itself. They are purely musical and have nothing to do with the relation of words to the melody.

The application of the words to the *sequentia*, note by note, syllable by syllable, produced a characteristic verbal structure. It was called, as already mentioned, a 'prose' (*prosa*); and prose it is, but prose of a special kind, patterned and assonanced.[16] The syllabic pattern corresponds precisely with that of the melody, which being irregular in its 'numbers' produces a similar irregularity in the *prosa*; there seems to be no particular rationale in the succession 17, 13, 20, 19, 21, 25 . . . (syllables per strophe). In each strophe the *b* versicle follows the *a* with perfect regularity, until we come to strophe 8, which is a single (i.e. stands alone without repeat), and strophe 10 (the last). There are various ways in which the text might be set out. I have tried in the arrangement which follows to display the assonances and the occasional rhyme (1a.2 *Christi*; 1b.2 *Justi*). The prevalence of the *-a* rhyme, with its assonances *-am* and *-ant*, is a common feature of sequences which are connected with an Alleluia. But the author of the *prosa* is not concerned to produce absolute congruity between parallel versicles – and it could be that my editorial arrangement into short lines draws attention to supposed 'defects' (e.g. absence of correspondence in strophes 5 and 6) which are not really such at all. The author evidently had other types of patterning in mind, of a syntactical and grammatical kind and even occasionally of sense. These are more evident at the beginning of the piece than later: the second strophe, for example, contrasts the martyr's tender age with the vanities of the world in parallel noun-plus-adjective lines. In the central strophes the demands of a simple narrative style preclude this sort of tidy parallelism. There is nothing, however, to preclude a more basic phonetic parallelism based on number: the author often succeeds in matching a word in the strophe with a word of precisely the same syllabic count in the antistrophe. There are some twenty-five instances of this in 'Fulget dies'; that might not be sufficient in itself to establish a firm intention, but the example of many others (including Notker's) sequences leaves no doubt that this phenomenon is the result of conscious technique. In the text which follows, the words connected by number parallelism are italicized.[17]

---

[16] See alternative arrangement in *A H* XL.226 (no. 256).

[17] Text from Stäblein (1965), following col. 528 (first music example); *A H* XL.226 (no. 256). The sequence honours St Justus of Auxerre, whose head was brought to Winchester in Athelstan's reign (895–940).

---

may have had no repetitions. What is indisputable, however, is the essential structural function of the repetitions (double versicles) in the texted sequence as it survives early and late. The cadential rhyme figure *a-g-f-g* becomes a cliché of sequence and *lai* melodies (see below, chapter 4, Exx. 39 and 42).

Alleluia

1a   Fulget dies *jucunda*/in qua   1b   pro martyris *eterna*/sancti
     Christi/*gaudet* ecclesia,   *Justi*/*palma* et gloria.

2a   *Etas tenera,*/*virtus in* qua sed *valida,*   2b   *mundi prospera*/*temnit ac* vincit *fortia.*

3a   Gratia quem deus *mira*/facit *in*   3b   prophetie illi *dona*/mox et *ab*
     ipsa/pollere infantia,   *ipsa*/donans pueritia.

4a   *Patri* denique *prescia*/de   4b   '*Tecum*', inquit 'ad *propriam*/volo,
     captivo/pandit alumno/*monita.*   pater,/hunc revocare/*patriam.*'

5a   *Mater* ad hec *verba*/*toto* corde   5b   '*Proles* mihi *cara,*/*fili* mi, o Juste,
     commota/inquit Felicia: quid/loqueris talia?

6a   Si que adversa/*tibi* in   6b   'Noli, mater mi',/*inquit,*
     via/contingant, ego/pro te/magna   'plorare;/inter omnia/Christi/me
     flebo tristitia.'   liberabit gratia.'

7a   *Freti virtute angelica*/pergunt   7b   *Justo puero prefulgida*/preparata ante
     longinqua itinera,/*fratrem liberant.*   secula/*adest gloria.*

8   Terrea passus membra/celo dans
     animam/candida, rubicunda/fulget
     in purpura./Omnes una te/voce
     supplica[nt]

9a   Et in *eterna*/fac tecum *esse letitia.*   9b   Tuam *commenda,*/precamur, *Christo*
                                                     familiam.
10   Laus deo magna/per cuncta secla.

(1a) The joyous day shines, in which the church of Christ rejoices (1b) because of the immortal and glorious victory of St Justus [of Auxerre]. (2a) His tender age, in which however virtue is strong, (2b) disdains the good things of the world and conquers their strong appeal. (3a) God through the marvel of his grace gives him power even in his childhood, (3b) and straightway from merest boyhood gives him the gifts of prophecy. (4a) In due course he reveals to his father prescient warnings concerning his foster-brother in captivity. (4b) 'I wish, father,' he says, 'to go with you and recall my brother to his own country.' (5a) His mother, Felicia, is deeply disturbed within herself at these words and says: (5b) 'My dear child, my son, Justus, why do you say such things? (6a) If any harm befalls you on your journey, I shall weep for you with great sadness.' (6b) He replies 'Do not weep, mother mine! Whatever happens the grace of Christ will set me free.' (7a) Relying on the strength conferred by angels, Justus and his father set out on their long journey and set his brother free. (7b) For this just young man a supremely shining glory is prepared before all ages. (8) After suffering in his earthly body, he surrenders his soul to heaven and shines in the high dignity of the white and the red. All men with a single voice call upon you [*reading* 'supplicant']. (9a) Grant that they may be with you in eternal blessedness. (9b) Commend, we pray you, your family to Christ. (10) High praise be to God throughout all ages.

Notker's sequences also are written in patterned prose. I quote the opening of his 'Johannes, Jesu Christo' with the melody as reconstructed by Richard Crocker:[18]

Ex. 27

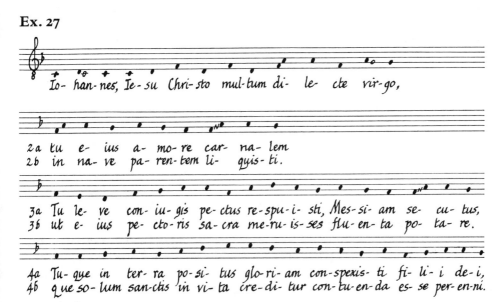

John, virgin most dear to Christ, you for love of him left your earthly father in his boat; you spurned the inconstant breast of your wife and followed the Messiah that you might be worthy to drink the sacred streams from his breast; and you, a man on earth, saw the glory of the Son of God, which it is granted only to the saints to gaze on in the life which is eternal.

The vertical alignment of the words in the text indicates the exactly parallel word-divisions where they occur; strophe 3 is particularly striking. The linear arrangement with the melody makes it easy to spot this particular type of verbal patterning, which (it must be emphasized) depends entirely on the 'numbering' of small units. An arrangement of the text in parallel columns would reveal other kinds more clearly. The strophes three, four and five, as de Goede observes, each form a complete sentence, in such a way that the *a*-versicle is the main clause and the *b*-versicle a sub-clause. This brings the

---

[18] Crocker (1977) attempts to establish the texts *and melodies* of the early-medieval sequences in their *ninth-century* form (i.e. their form at a time long before they were precisely noted). Notker's texts, he argues (p. 6), give 'precise reliable witness *from the ninth century* for the plans of the melodies he used' (this is because the sequence is syllabic song). The problem, then, is to reconcile the divergences between Notker's 'plans' and the plans of the sequences as they survive with their melodies (notated in heighted neumes) in later, especially Aquitanian, sources (c. 1000 onwards). The music example in the text is taken from Crocker, 148. Stäblein (1965), col. 69, records the existence (Karlsruhe Lichtenthal 60: Cistercian hymnary, thirteenth-century) of an irregularly measured version of this sequence, in breves and semibreves. De Goede, 11–12 (no. 6), prints the Utrecht Prosarium version (which is very close) and lists innumerable others.

symmetry of the parallelism strongly to the fore. This symmetry is further intensified by the parallelism of thought expressed, and by the multiple repetition of *Tu*, *Te* and *Tibi* at the beginning of the sentences. 'Johannes, Jesu Christo' is not an exception. It is a typical example of the relationship between text and melody in Notker's sequences.[19] De Goede also draws attention to another kind of numerical patterning – 'the words often have the same number of syllables as the corresponding neumes [i.e. the ligatured groups in the text-less *sequentia*] have notes'.[20]

This brief examination of some early ecclesiastical sequences has immediately brought out aspects of the central problem, the relation of words and music. In brief, there is a very close physical relationship between the two, but this relationship is one of pattern and parallel, not of *individualized* sound (that is to say, the particular sounds of particular words do not signify). Many sequences came into being as songs by the fitting of words syllable by syllable to the single notes of an often long and complex melody. The melodies (*sequentie*) were often systematically constructed with a succession of parallel units; this parallelism the authors observed and strengthened by verbal means. Precise syllabic counting was reinforced with rhyme, assonance, parallel syntax, etc. In some respects, one can see, the relationship between text and melody is not so very different from that which emerged two or three centuries later in the troubadour and trouvère chanson. It is syllabic (its basis is number in the most literal sense); and it is structural (words and music work together, line by line, strophe by strophe). However, some differences are obvious. The single-note progression of the melody is more dominant in sequence than in chanson, which relies much for variety on the mingling of single notes and simple neumes (of two to four notes). Moreover, the complicated verbal patterning within the strophe of a sequence, depending for its aural effectiveness on the shortness of the strophe and its immediate repetition, draws attention perhaps to the presence of similar configurations in the melody itself, melodic rhyme being one of them. We can, I think, usefully employ the concept of a 'double melody' of words and music (see p. 385 below), since the smaller patterns are not directly related to one another. But the effect at least of having the smaller verbal and musical units is of more continuous contact between the two, of a relationship somewhat less distant and rarefied. However, to avoid misunderstanding, I must stress the total absence (as it seems to me), in the sequences so far discussed, of any relationship which might in my definition be called either referential (that is, involving reference, intellectual, imaginative, emotional, to things outside the music itself) or phonetic (that is, mirroring the sounds of words as distinct from their syllabic, 'numbered', structure). The only possible exception is the matching of verbal and musical accent, a question which I defer till later.

[19] De Goede, p. xl; and see generally his section 7, 'Parallelism in the Texts'. The procedure is sometimes referred to by the technical term 'responsion'. See further Dronke (1965), 44ff, for a detailed analysis of structure and meaning in the early sequence 'Rex celi'; see also chapter 4, note 2, below.

[20] De Goede, p. xliii. See G. Reichert, 'Strukturprobleme der älteren Sequenzen', *Deutsche Vierteljahrschrift für Literaturwissenschaft und Geistesgeschichte* 23 (1949) 227.

II Later sequences: 'Letabundus'

Having established these bearings we can approach closer to the period in which the surviving vernacular song repertory was composed. The history of the sequence as a metrical form is often divided into three stages: the first, just sketched, in which the texts were in a sort of 'poetic prose', governed by symmetry and pattern but not by quantitative measure nor by qualitative accent;[21] the second, in which the texts became more regular in various ways and could without violence to the term be called 'verse'; and a third, having Adam of St Victor as its central figure, in which the strophes are so standardized in structure and rhyme that the poems resemble hymns – only the melodic progression (A A B B C C etc.) distinguishes them as sequences.[22]

As an example of the second, 'intermediate', type we may take the sequence 'Letabundus': it was evidently much loved from the eleventh century onwards and produced innumerable 'imitations', contrafacts in different languages and for different purposes.[23]

1a	Letabundus exsultet fidelis chorus, alleluia;	1b	regem regum intacte profudit thorus, res miranda.
2a	Angelus consilii natus est de virgine, sol de stella,	2b	sol occasum nesciens, stella semper rutilans, semper clara.
3a	Sicut sidus radium, profert virgo filium pari forma;	3b	neque sidus radio, neque mater filio fit corrupta.
4a	Cedrus alta Lybani conformatur ysopo valle nostra;	4b	verbum, ens altissimi, corporari passum est carne sumpta.
5a	Ysayas cecinit, synagoga meminit, numquam tamen desinit esse ceca;	5b	si non suis vatibus, credat vel gentilibus sibillinis versibus hec predicta.
6a	Infelix propera, crede vel vetera; cur damnaberis, gens misera?	6b	Quem docet litera, natum considera; ipsum genuit puerpera.

[21] A very few sequences survive using quantitative metre.

[22] These stages are conceived of only in a most general and abstract way. A thorough history of the sequence would have to take into account particular *repertoires*, a more elusive as well as a more particular concept (see N. van Deusen in *Forum musicologicum* 2 (1980) 44ff on Nevers Cathedral).

[23] Chevalier, 10012; Walther, 10087a; Kehrein, no. 13; Arlt (1970), 1.75–7; 11.11–12 (melody). Bartsch (1868), 224–5, lists twenty-six sequences in precisely the same form, presumed *contrafacta*; this list could easily be augmented, e.g. by the Mary Magdalene sequence mentioned in note 6 above, and by the 'Gemebundus/Marie decantet clerus/voce pia' (*AH* VIII, no. 55). According to Hesbert (1966), 20 n. 6, the 'Letabundus' sequence originated in

(1a) Let the faithful choir exult in gladness – Alleluia; (1b) the womb of a virgin has brought forth the king of kings – a marvellous event. (2a) The angel of counsel is born of a virgin – the sun from a star; (2b) a sun which knows no setting, a star that glows for ever, always bright. (3a) As the star produces its ray so the virgin her son, alike in nature. (3b) Neither is the star corrupted by its ray nor the mother by her son. (4a) The high cedar of Lebanon conforms itself to the hyssop in the valley of this world; (4b) the Word, the being of the Most High, has suffered itself to be embodied in the flesh it has taken. (5a) Isaiah sang, the synagogue remembers but never ceases to be blind; (5b) if the Jews will not believe their own prophets, let them at least believe the Gentiles', the predictions of these things in the Sibylline oracles. (6a) Unhappy people, make haste, believe the ancient [writings]; miserable nation, why should you be damned? (6b) Consider this child of whom scripture teaches us; a maiden gave him birth.

The poem is fresh and succinct. The exhortation to joy of strophe 1a is 'explained' by the triumphant statement of 1b: the reason for our 'Alleluia' is a 'marvellous thing' – *Letabundus* is answered by the 'king of kings'; the *chorus* rejoices in the (precisely matching) *thorus* (couch, bed). The second strophe plays with the traditional figure of Christ/sun coming from Mary/star; the sun knows no setting, the star shines for ever.[24] The image of light continues in the *sidus radium/sidus radio* parallel, before it gives way to the cedar (Christ's divinity) and the hyssop (His humanity), a humble herb in the vale of our world; 4b beautifully matches 4a – *cedrus/Verbum . . . altissimi; confor-matur/corporari; valle/carne*. In strophe 5 the Jewish blindness is set against the certain truth proclaimed by the Gentile verses of the Sibyl. And finally the Jews' resistance to truth is confronted by the fact of Christ's birth: the *puerpera* (maiden, 'child-bearer') matches the *gens misera*.

Although not fully regular in its use of rhyme (both 2a and 2b, for example, depend on assonance) this is verse not prose – a poem, in fact, and a most successful one. The account just given has revealed in passing some of its verbal 'music' as well as parallels of syntax and sense. It is also delightfully varied in its rhythms. The central strophes (2–5) are regular except for the extra line in 5; but strophe 1 is individual in syllable-count (4:8:4) and in the stress-pattern of line 2.

exúltet fidélis chórus / intácte profúdit thórus

The light dactylic effect returns at the end, strophe 6, phrase 2, *créde vel vétera*, in another strophe differing from all the rest (6:6:5:4). The general movement of the verse is trochaic. In particular, the refrain-lines (musical refrains, not verbal except in their monorhyme *-a*, which originates from the *Alleluia*)

[24] J. B. Pitra, *Spicilegium Solesmense* (Paris 1855), 11.68–9, gives the third of the eight properties of a star: *Stella ex se radium emittit: et virgo ex se radium illum emisit* (cited Arlt (1970), 1.76).

France in the late eleventh century (represented by about thirty MSS); the insular MSS (fewer in number) date from the late twelfth century. Arlt (1970), 11.201, quotes Laon MS 263: *prosa quando volueris* ('a sequence for any time').

insist on the trochees – except perhaps in the last lines (6.3): *gens miśera/ puérpera*.

The melody is worthy of the words. The transcription which follows is from a service book which belonged to the Benedictine Abbey of St Albans at the end of the twelfth century, a 'troper–proser' containing both tropes and sequences:[25]

Ex. 28

1a Le- ta- bun- dus   ex- ul- tet fi- de- lis cho- rus,   al- le- lui - a;

1b re- gem re- gum   in- tac- te pro- fu- dit tho- rus,   res mi- ran- da.

2a An- ge- lus con- si- li- i   na- tus est de vir- gi- ne,

sol de stel- la,

2b sol oc- ca - sum ne- sci- ens   stel- la sem- per ru- ti- lans,

val- de cla- ra.

3a Sic- ut sy- dus ra- di- um,   pro- fert vir- go fi- li- um

pa- ri for- ma;

3b Ne- que sy- dus ra- di- o,   ne- que vir- go fi- li- o

[25] Text and music from the St Albans Troper (Source 18), fol. 177. Norberg (1968) 178–80, gives text, translation, commentary and notes on the versification.

fit cor- rup- ta.

4a Ce- drus al- ta Ly- ba- ni   con- for- ma- tur y- so- po

val- le nos- tra;

4b Ver- bum, ens al- tis- si- mi,   cor- po- ra- ri pas- sum est

car- ne sum- pta.

5a Y- sa- i- as ce- ci- nit,   sy- na- go- ga me- mi- nit,

nunquam ta- men de- si- nit   es- se ce- ca;

5b Si non su- is va- ti- bus,   cre- dat vel gen- ti- li- bus

si- bil- li- nis ver- si- bus   hec pre- di- cta.

6a In- fe- lix pro- pe- ra,   cre- de vel ve- te- ra;

cur dam- na- be- ris, gens mi- se- ra?

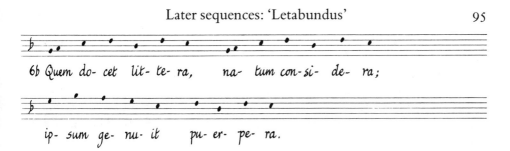

6b Quem do- cet lit- te- ra,   na- tum con- si- de- ra;

ip- sum ge- nu- it   pu- er- pe- ra.

There is precise parallelism between the strophe and the antistrophe through-out; and there are no 'irregular' (i.e. unmatched) stanzas, as there were in 'Fulget dies jucunda' (strophes 8 and 10). 'Letabundus' produces a very different effect from 'Fulget dies' even though they have some important features in common, such as clear syllabic movement and melodic rhyme. The most striking feature of the melody is its basis in the triad *c-e-g*: every phrase begins, or ends, or both, on one of those three notes. The leading motif which opens the sequence and constitutes its principal refrain firmly estab-lishes *c* and lightly touches *e*:

Ex. 29a

Other phrases circle round *e* and rest there; others centre upon their temporary final, *g*.

Ex. 29b

Ex. 29c

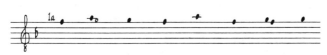

The climax of the melody, seen as a whole organism, is reached in strophe 5, whose first two phrases reach the higher *c* before falling back to cadence on *g* and *e*. This is balanced in the sixth and last strophe with the rare use of the lower octave, i.e. of the fourth below the centre *c*. (There is, incidentally, a small but not unimportant tonal ambiguity here. The St Albans Troper has *b* flats in strophe 6. The flattened seventh recalls the characteristic sequence/*lai* cadence of *g*-mode melodies such as 'Fulget dies' (Ex. 25 above), even though the final is not approached directly from below. Other versions, such as the one from Beauvais, do not flatten the seventh.) There is the occasional suggestion of a harmonic tension between f (associated with a above or d below) and the ever-returning resolution on c (strophe 1 phrase 2; strophe 4 phrases 1,3).

As usual, it is difficult to hear the melody with an innocent ear. Nevertheless, some such analysis as this in terms of the major triad seems right and inevitable. Similar fears of anachronism may haunt us when we come to consider the relationship between the text and the melody. But first, two more comments on the melody as such. Unlike 'Fulget dies' or the famous Easter sequence 'Victime paschali', which is often cited with 'Letabundus' as a masterly example of the 'intermediate' style,[26] this melody freely mingles note-groups of two or three with the single notes. Scarcely a phrase is without a ligature or *plica*'d note. The melodic style is, in the usual term, 'neumatic' (like the melodies of the troubadours and trouvères), neither fully melismatic nor strictly single-noted. The effect of this is to produce a labile and fluid melody in which the movement is fairly conjunct and many intervals are lightly bridged over. Its hallmark is sweetness rather than strength; it flows rather than marches along. The second necessary comment is on the structural devices of melodic 'rhyme' and internal repetition. The 'rhyme' is consistent and extended in the first three strophes. In the fourth and fifth it seems at first glance to be confined to the last two syllables; but perhaps it should be heard as extending back into the previous phrase:

Ex. 30

The whole of phrases 2–3 of strophe 4 is repeated in any case in strophe 5 – a clear instance of melodic repetition, an effect which is again contrived internally in strophe 6 (phrases 1 and 2 are identical). All in all, a closely knit and impressive melody, and one quite outside the Gregorian idiom.

The principal relationship between the words and the music in 'Letabundus' is a structural one, as in all medieval monophonic songs, so that a strong sense of the basic pattern underlies the double realization, verbal and musical. Moreover, since the basic patterns of this type of sequence are more complicated and interesting than those of the chanson (which has the fascinating complexity of a miniature), this is an important part of our experience of the song. In the sequence too – excluding the earlier 'prose' sequences – the members of the pattern tend to be short and succinct and telling; one can more easily spot, more readily respond to, the detail of the pattern – rhyme (verbal and melodic), motivic repetition, parallelism in sound and in syntax. Where I think the question is problematic and especially interesting in songs of the sequence/*lai* type is, as it was with *conductus*, in the relation between the verbal

[26] 'Victime paschali': the melody is given below, chapter 9, Ex. 142.

patterns and the musical. In the case of *la grande chanson courtoise* I argued that direct, close relationship was virtually non-existent; there seemed to be no evidence that musicians were responsive to any qualities in the words beyond their 'numbers' in the most literal sense – counted syllables.[27] In the case of the sequence something different appears to be happening in addition to the parallelisms already noted. It has to do with accent.

Common sense and common experience find that much Latin verse of the *ritmus* type, as distinct from the quantitative (*musica metrica*),[28] does indeed by the eleventh century have not only syllable-counting but accent as an organizing principle. *Ictus* (metrical stress) in this type of Latin verse usually coincides with the actual sounds of the words as established by spoken accent or stress.

> 1a Létabúndus
> éxsúltét fidélis chórus,
> Állelúia;

which is echoed in 1b by

> 1b Régém régúm
> intácté prófúdit thórus,
> rés miránda.

The degree of coincidence of accent throughout the sequence between the parallel versicles is very high indeed. This constitutes presumptive evidence that it is conscious and planned; especially convincing is the shift back from the regular trochaic rhythms of strophes 2–5 to the less predictable but still precise pattern of 6:

> 6a Ínfelix própera,
> créde vel vétera;
> cúr damnáberis,
> géns mísera?

> 6b Quém dócet lítera,
> natúm cónsídera;
> ípsum génuit
> púerpera.

---

[27] As previously remarked (chapter 1:1 text to note 35), one exception must be made: the accent of the rhyme-word has to be observed.

[28] 'Accentual' or 'stressed' or 'rhythmic' verse (as it is variously called) has a long history going back to classical times. See Norberg (1958), ch. 6, 'Les débuts de la versification rythmique', and the references there to his earlier book *La poésie latine rythmique du haut moyen âge* (1954). Norberg appears to conflate the concepts of 'rhythmical' verse and accentual, whereas *ritmus*, it seems to me, depends in the first instance on number (syllable-counting) and not necessarily on accent at all. Accent and (later) rhyme are the accidents rather than the essentials of the *musica ritmica* tradition.

If we look back to some of the earlier sequences, we shall find a far less perfect coincidence; as for instance in 'Fulget dies' (Ex. 25), strophe 6:

> 6a Sí que ádvérsa
> tíbi ín vía
> cóntíngant, égó
> pró té
> mágná flébó tristítiá.

> 6a 'Nóli, mátér mí',
> ínquit, 'plórárè;
> íntér ómnía
> Chrísti
> mè libérábit grátiá'.

It is clearly not an essential part of sequence style from its beginnings to have precisely matching verbal accents and phrasal stresses, whereas matching numbers of syllables and repeated melodies *are* essential. As a fairly brief example of the dilemma which arises we may refer to the strophe just quoted from 'Fulget dies', against which I have set the corresponding strophe of 'Concelebremus':[29]

Ex. 31

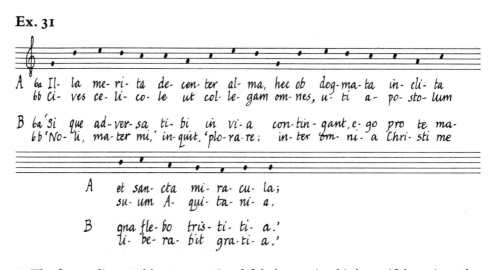

6a The former [i.e. earth's congregations] fitly honouring his bountiful services, the latter [i.e. hosts of heaven] honouring him for his glorious teachings and holy miracles; 6b All heaven's citizens honouring him as their fellow, Aquitania honouring him as its own Apostle.

---

[29] Concerning the French sequence 'Concelebremus', see note 11 above.

Even making allowances for our imperfect knowledge of Latin pronunciation (it may have varied from land to land and from century to century), it is obvious that there are different patterns of verbal accent which the melody has to accommodate. Between the two possible extreme readings of the song – one which preserves the full independence of the melody, in tension with a similar independence of the words, and one which subordinates the melody to the text in a neutral, submissive and flexible role – the choice is difficult. The answer depends, first, on one's sense of the importance and strength in the verbal text of clear metrical groups; on the evidence given, I should say that the verbal text of 'Letabundus' has clear metrical groupings but that 'Fulget dies' is more fluid, less emphatic (syllable-matching by numbers is not the same as accent-matching). The answer also depends on whether one believes the melody to have an innate and inalienable rhythmic shape which must not be violated.

What do we mean when we speak of the 'independence' or the 'innate' shape of the melody? An answer to this question is even harder to come by, especially as we do not know the rhythmic intentions. The rhythmic shape of a melody consisting of undifferentiated single notes can only be determined by such factors as modal idiom, change of melodic direction, range, energy of movement (by step or leap), and repetitions.[30]

Ex. 32

The markings over the notes of these two lines from 'Fulget dies' indicate one reading of the melody; there could be several others. Line 6 (which has the melodic shape A A^1) would, if sung without the words, clearly demand parallel, balanced phrasing. But to apply this when the words were present would be to beg the very question we are considering, since melodic repetition is of the essence of sequence style. How then are the demands of text and melody to be reconciled? I incline to the view that in the earlier sequences of the 'prose' type, with very variable accent and flexible melodies, the reconciliation should result from unforced recitation (as in the chanting of psalms) in which the words lightly mould the melody which carries them

---

[30] 'Undifferentiated', i.e. non-mensural (see Glossary). The melody of Ex. 32 is from 'Fulget dies' (Ex. 25) strophes 5–6.

along. In more regularly patterned sequences like 'Letabundus' the accentual pattern of each strophe, confirmed in every case by its repetition as a double versicle, is more emphatic and establishes, I believe, a *single* pattern of words-and-melody. To this pattern the other elements of melody are not strongly resistant and are sometimes quite inviting – in strophe 2, for instance where the alternation of single note and 'doubles' (on the light syllables) lightly reinforces the / . / . / . \ pattern. However, 'Letabundus' is a melody with more inherent rhythmic character than 'Concelebremus'/'Fulget', and there are places where it asserts its musical rights. The refrain itself is one of these. It varies in the sources between a simple form (a)[31] and a more florid one (b):

Ex. 33a

Le - ta - bun - dus

Ex. 33b

Le - ta - bun - dus

A further stage of elaboration is represented by:

Ex. 33c

Le - ta - bun - - dus

What these successively more elaborated versions demonstrate is the degree of purely musical weight attaching to the note before the final – not because of the word-accent, I suggest, but because of the shape $c \rightarrow d \rightarrow e \leftarrow c$.

III   The standard sequence: Adam of St Victor

Finally, some 'rhymed' sequences from the third stage. The form became highly standardized and, it must be admitted, less interesting. The tendency towards simplification and regularity (of accent and rhyme) set in during the

[31] The three versions of the refrain are from (a) the St Albans Troper (see Ex. 28 above); (b) the Arundel Songs, fol. 153v (contrafacted as 'Magdalene laudes plene'); (c) Aix-la-Chapelle, MS 13, fol. 122 (*Le prosaire d'Aix-la-Chapelle*, ed. R.-J. Hesbert (Rouen 1961), 55). Wagner (1911), III.484, gives a similarly contrasting set of melodic openings from Strasbourg and Trier.

eleventh century and at its strictest produced texts such as the following, *In conversione Sancti Pauli*, attributed to Adam of St Victor (d. 1192).[32]

1a	Iubilemus Salvatori qui spem dedit peccatori consequendi veniam,	1b	Quando Saulum increpavit et conversum revocavit ad matrem ecclesiam.
2a	Saulus, cedis et minarum spirans adhuc cruentarum in Christi discipulos,	2b	impetravit ut ligaret et ligatos cruciaret Crucifixi famulos. etc.

Let us rejoice in the Saviour who gave hope to the sinner of obtaining pardon, when he upbraided Saul and summoned him back, converted, to Mother Church. Saul, at this time still breathing slaughter and bloody threats against the disciples of Christ, procured that he might bind, and when bound crucify, the servants of the Crucified.

There are five double versicles in all, and the metre never changes. A slightly longer strophe, equally regular, is exemplified by 'Virgo, mater salvatoris' (rhyming aaab:cccb; same line-lengths as before).[33] And there are other patterns equally predictable. It would be wrong, however, to give the impression of tyrannical monotony. The nine-strophe sequence 'Gratulemur ad festivum', for instance, varies the three-line pattern of 'Iubilemus Salvatori' with one strophe of the four-line 'Virgo mater' variety and one extending to five lines (aaaab:ccccb).[34] Inventiveness is not dead, but its scope is more limited. Inventiveness expresses itself particularly in internal rhyme:[35]

1a	Prunis *datum* admiremur, *laureatum* veneremur *laudibus Laurentium;*	1b	Vener*emur* cum tremore, deprec*emur* cum amore martirum egregium.

Let us marvel at Laurentius thrust into the live coals; with our praises let us reverence him crowned with laurels. Let us reverence the good martyr with fear, let us pray to him with love.

We note also effects of verbal patterning (*cum tremore* /*cum amore*) and the vowel-play in 1a on *lau-*. Such 'harmonies' are common:[36]

> serva servos tue matris
> solve reos, salva gratis . . .

---

[32] Misset and Aubry, no. 10 (text, pp. 181–2): the double-versicle arrangement is mine; see also Stäblein (1965), col. 542. The still standard edition of the Victorine sequences by Misset and Aubry needs to be supplemented from Spanke (1941: repr. 1977), an essential article which analyses all the metrical–melodic forms and groups them. The attribution of any of the sequences to Adam of St Victor himself is highly disputable.

[33] Misset and Aubry, 180–1 (no. 9).

[34] *Ibid.*, 174–5 (no. 3).

[35] *Ibid.*, 205–7 (no. 31), strophe 1. Misset and Aubry set it out in short lines.

[36] *Ibid.*, p. 214 (no. 36), strophe 12. *Ibid.*, p. 215 (no. 38), strophe 2.

and

> Non discordet os a corde,
> sint concordes he tres chorde:
> lingua, mens et actio.

Preserve the servants of your mother, free the guilty, save them freely.

Let not the mouth be discordant with the heart; let all these three strings concord together: tongue, mind and deed.

The effects leap to the eye and should charm the ear, too. All this is in the tradition of the sequence, as we have seen, but tinged with new fashion.

One fine sequence in the Adam of St Victor collection is the famous 'Laudes crucis attollamus'. It will serve to illustrate points already made and to introduce discussion of the music of this later repertoire.[37] (I give the text and melody of the first four strophes only.)

Ex. 34

[37] *Ibid.*, no. 18 (text, pp. 189–90, but omitting strophe 1b, which however is given in the melody version (p. 260)). Misset and Aubry arrange strophes 3a and 3b as strophes 3 and 4. This is musically unsound despite the slight metrical irregularity. Analysis by Spanke (1941: repr. 1977), 224–5: he prints strophes 10–11 (Misset and Aubry, 11–12) as a single strophe. My transcription (Ex. 34: strophes 1–4) is from the Dublin Troper (Source 7), whilst Stäblein (1975), pl. 42, reproduces the first opening of the St Albans Troper (Source 18), fols. 173v–174, and in n. 15 (p. 162) lists a number of editions from other sequentiaries; Moberg, in his book on Swedish sequences (1927), II, no. 1, gives a conspectus of MSS. See Walther, 10162a; Chevalier, 10360. N. Weisbein, 'Le *Laudes crucis attollamus*', *Revue du moyen âge latin* 3 (1947) 5–26, discusses authorship (tentatively attributing the poem to Hugh of Orleans), manuscript tradition and formal structure, and edits the text.

dul-cis est sym-pho-ni-a.

3a Ser-vi cru-cis cru-cem laudent, qui per cru-cem si-bi gaudent

vi-te da-ri mu-ne-ra; di-cant om-nes et di-cant sin-gu-li:

A-ve, sa-lus to-ti-us po-pu-li, ar-bor sa-lu-ti-fe-ra.

3b O quam fe-lix, quam pre-cla-ra fu-it hec sa-lu-tis a-ra,

ru-bens a-gni san-gui-ne, a-gni si-ne ma-cu-la,

qui pur-ga-vit se-cu-la ab an-ti-quo cri-mi-ne.

4a Hec est sca-la pec-ca-to-rum per quam Christus rex ce-lo-rum

ad se tra-xit om-ni-a;

4b for-ma cu-ius hoc os-ten-dit, que ter-ra-rum compre-hen-dit

quattu-or con-fi-ni-a.

(1) Let us raise the praises of the cross, we who exult in the special glory of the cross. (2a) Let sweet music strike the skies; we believe the sweet cross to be worthy of sweet melody. (2b) Let life harmonize with the voice (of praise): when the voice does not reproach the life, the concord is sweet. (3a) Let the servants of the cross praise the cross – those who delight that through the cross the gifts of life are given to them. Let all say, let each man say: Hail, salvation for the whole people, hail, saving tree. (3b) O how happy, how illustrious, was this altar of salvation, red with the blood of the lamb, of the lamb without spot, who cleansed this earth of its ancient crime. (4a) This is the sinners' ladder, by which Christ, the king of heaven, drew all things to himself.

(4b) Its form shows this, the form which grasps in one the four corners [*lit.*: boundaries] of the earth.

'Laudes crucis' cannot be by Adam of St Victor himself. Friedrich Blume remarked on the earliness of some sources, and Hans Spanke on the use of the second versicle, 'Dulce melos', as a *Benedicamus*-trope in a manuscript of *c.* 1100.[38] In addition 'Laudes crucis' borrows the opening of its melody from an old sequence, 'Salve, crux sancta, arbor digna'.[39] However, the precise attribution of the sequence is not important; it is in any case part of the Victorine repertory. For present purposes it raises two major questions of compelling interest in the study of music and poetry. First, it belongs to a whole group of sequences all of which use the same metre and melody in one form or another; secondly, it points to the presence in this period of a treasury of melody available for common use.

The melody of 'Laudes crucis' was perhaps the most popular of all the Victorine sequences. Eight of Adam's texts are based upon it: 'Letabundi jubilemus' (Transfiguration) – not to be confused with the 'Letabundus exsultet'; 'Heri mundus exultavit' (Ascension); 'Lux jucunda lux insignis' (Whitsun); and so on.[40] The melody continued to be loved, and Thomas Aquinas took it for 'Lauda Sion salvatorem', in which form it survives into modern use.[41] The most immediately striking feature of the melody is its regularity; this is essentially a metrical–musical trait. As always, the same syllabic pattern is being worked out in the melody as in the verse, and there is no room for divergence (the only apparent exceptions are in 3b, 6b and 7b, and these are in fact slight divergences from the rule of *parallelism* not of syllabism). The effect of sturdy sameness is emphasized also by the continual use of the conventional cadence-figure on *g* (*agfgg*), modified, when necessary, to suit the context, but almost always incorporating these notes in this order. The repetitions are not confined to the closing phrases: the little phrase of 'melodic rhyme' just mentioned (repeated at cadences some twenty times) also figures in strophe 3, phrase 3; the second phrase of 5 is used again in 6; 10 and 11 are very similar; a half phrase from 9 and a full phrase from 10/11 appear in 12. The general effect is of a closely unified melodic style with many 'catchy' turns of phrase,[42] but one much more limited in scope and material than the earlier, or freer, sequences demonstrate.

From the beginning there were always more sequence texts than there were sequence melodies. This is partly because a good melody offered a challenge to a poet which could be met in different ways, provided the rules of structural division and syllabism were observed. Notker, who was perhaps primarily if not exclusively a poet, took a West Frankish prose 'Hec est sancta sollemnitas

---

[38] The earliest part of Paris B N 1139 (Source 35); see Spanke (1977), 225.
[39] *A H* LIII. 144 (no. 82); see Spanke (1977), 228.
[40] Stäblein (1965), Ex. 10, prints 'Letabundi jubilemus'.
[41] *L U*, 945.
[42] E.g. 10.2, repeated 11.2, 12.3 (see the complete melody in Misset and Aubry, pp. 260–62).

diei huius et veneranda . . .' and wrote his own 'Hec est sancta solemnitas solemnitatum insignita . . .' to the same melody.[43] Later he wrote a second contrafact, 'Quid tu, virgo', containing a lament of Rachel (the melody acquired the title *Virgo plorans*).[44] Notker's 'Hec est sancta' celebrates Christ the King and the triumph following the Harrowing of Hell.[45]

Against this difference of language and conception between the two proses must be set the fact that QUID TU VIRGO corresponds exactly – but exactly – in syllable count to HEC EST SANCTA SOLEMNITAS SOLEMNITATUM (word structure and accent patterns often coincide, too, but there are several important deviations). Having decided on a topic for the later prose, Notker proceeded to give the topic a verbal shape that corresponded exactly in numbers of lines and syllables to one already existing . . . a literary tour de force.

Deviations in accent patterns there certainly are, and it seems worthwhile to quote the opening line of the two songs:[46]

Ex. 35

(1) This is the holy solemnity of solemnities marked by the triumph of Christ . . . (2) Why do you weep, beautiful Rachel, maiden mother, you whose face gives delight to Jacob?

That Notker should permit such variation of verbal accent suggests strongly that he did not regard this melodic phrase as having a marked and inviolable rhythmic character of its own. This confirms the tentative conclusion reached above that in the prose sequences the words and the melody are reconciled to each other in an unforced recitatory or narrative manner. And it provides a clear contrast with the procedures of Adam of St Victor and/or his musician.

The whole problem of contrafacted melodies in the Adam of St Victor repertory is extremely complex. The 'Laudes crucis' group is the largest one, and it extends well beyond the bounds of the fifty or so sequences now associated with Adam of St Victor (Moberg has listed seventeen *contrafacta* of

[43] Crocker (1977), ch. 7, pp. 116ff.
[44] For 'Quid tu, virgo' see chapter 10, Ex. 156, below.
[45] Crocker (1977), 131.
[46] The music example conflates the texts of Crocker (1977), 119 and 132.

'Laudes').[47] But even within the corpus the *contrafacta* are not strictly conceived. 'Letabundi' has the whole of the melody plus an extra (13th) strophe; 'Heri mundus' omits five strophes but repeats two others; 'Corde voce' omits two, shortens one, and amalgamates two others into one; 'Laus erumpat' inserts some completely new material; and so on.[48] It is a method of creative imitation in which the poet has manipulated the musical material at the same time as he manipulated the patterns of his verse. Or, according to a slightly different theory, the poet, perhaps Adam, having created a poem in a mould related to 'Laudes crucis', then handed his verses over to a helpful musician, a 'melody-maker' in the monastery, with instructions to make the necessary musical dispositions for it. It is correct to refer to this group of sequences as contrafacts based originally on a single model, the 'Laudes crucis', since, despite the variations to which I have referred, the later versions preserve the original *order* of the melodies – which is essential, of course, to the notion of an individual musical structure.[49]

Such free contrafacting as the groups of Victorine sequences illustrate is itself interesting evidence of the working relationships between music and poetry, especially of the interchangeability of standard units, as it were, of notes and of words. It is important to realize that such procedures were not confined within the limits of a single repertoire or a single language; and my last example in this chapter will be of a sequence (not one of Adam of St Victor's) which became extremely popular in various guises; some dozen Latin monophonic versions are known. 'Ave gloriosa virginum regina', by Philip the Chancellor, appears in the Dublin Troper with other Marian sequences; it also appears non-liturgically in the Reading Abbey MS, amongst the *conductus/cantiones* of the Florence MS, and elsewhere.[50] The interesting thing about 'Ave gloriosa' is that three *lais* with French texts use the same melody: a religious *lai* 'Virge glorieuse' (R1020) and two secular ones, the *Lai de la Pastourelle* (R1695) and the *Lai des Hermins* (R2060).[51] The Latin song opens, in the Reading version:

Ex. 36

la A- ve glo- ri- o- sa   vir- gi- num re- gi- na,

[47] Moberg, 1.151.
[48] Stäblein (1965), Ex. 10, gives a useful table of this group. The melodies can be found in full in Misset and Aubry, nos. 30, 18, 2, 20, 23, 37, 27 and 19, respectively. Analysis in Spanke (1941: repr. 1977), 224–5.
[49] See Spanke (1941: repr. 1977), 228–9.
[50] Ex. 36 is from the Reading MS (Source 16) fols. 7–8v. See Anderson K75 for a substantial list of versions. Also Ludwig (1910), 251–62.
[51] The group is discussed by Spanke (1938: repr. 1977), 175–8. A fragment of another French *lai* to the same melody also survives (R362a).

vi- tis ge- ne- ro- sa,   vi- te   me- di- ci- na,

cle- men-ci- e   re- si- na.

1b A- ve co- pi- o- sa   gra- ci- e pis- ci- na,

car-nis ma- cu- lo- sa   mun-da nos sen- ti- na

mun-di- ci- e   cor-ti- na.

2a Cla- ri- ta- te ra- di- o- sa,   stel-la ma- tu- ti- na,

bre-vi- ta- te le- gis glo-sa,   per te lex di- vi- na

ir- ra- di- at do- ctri- na.

2b Ve- nus-ta- te ver-nans ro- sa,   si- ne cul- pe spi-na,

ca- ri- ta- te vi- sce- ro- sa   au- rem huc in- cli- na,

nos ser- ves a ru- i- na.

(1a) Hail, glorious queen of virgins, noble vine, elixir of life, resin of mercy. (1b) Hail, abundant pool of grace, cleanse us of the filthy dregs of the flesh in the basin of purification.

(2a) Morning star, radiant in brightness, yourself a gloss on the brevity of the law, through you the Divine Law illuminates with its teaching. (2b) O rose blooming with loveliness, having no thorn of sin, with inward love incline your ear hither and save us from destruction.

Obvious reasons for the popularity of the melody are: the extreme simplicity of the melodic materials; its 'tunefulness' (within the favourite *g*-mode, but with an excursion into the *c-e-g* triad above, in strophes 7 to 10); its repetitive-ness (ten phrases serve 81 lines of verse); and the incantatory nature of the quasi-refrain (strophes 1–6, 11–12). 'Ave gloriosa virginum regina' does not display the ambitiously varied structure of some of the big Latin *lais* (see chapter 4, below) or of the early sequences. But it is more freely conceived than the sequences of Adam of St Victor. Did Philip the Chancellor write the text intending to divert a known melody to liturgical use? This is thought unlikely. Yet it found its way into the liturgy sometimes – though in the Dublin Troper it is placed equivocally between the Marian sequences and a Latin *lai*, 'Omnis caro', which is evidently not liturgical (see Ex. 55, below). There is, it appears, no connection between its music and the music of the Victorine sequences. One remains in doubt as to whether it is best called a sequence or a small *lai*.

There is reasonably close agreement between the sequence- and the *lai*-versions of the song. The question is, what kind of a song is it? Ludwig, who was the first to point out the existence of the vernacular *lais*, believed that the Latin sequence came first, and that the French texts were written as contra-facts. Spanke, on the other hand, argued that the *Lai des Hermins* was the earliest surviving text; its anonymous author makes, moreover, the interest-ing revelation, 'El lai des Hermins / ai mis reson roumance / por toz amanz fins' (I have set a vernacular text to the *lai des Hermins* for the benefit of all courtly lovers).[52] This certainly means there was a pre-existent melody, with or without words. In view of the known association of *lai*–sequence melodies with instruments, Spanke states dogmatically, but without specific evidence, that the original melody was instrumental.[53] This dubious premise does not, however, diminish the force of his observation that the original melody 'was interpreted in completely different ways by the poets who wrote words for it; the conclusion could be drawn from this that . . . the melody had no marked rhythm [*ausgeprägte Rythmik*]'.[54] The pertinence of this for an enquiry into words and music is that the melody, whether instrumental or not, was to some extent malleable. This is true of the main structure; the number of repetitions within a strophe can be varied at will. It is also true of the detail. The fourth phrase of strophe 1 takes an extra note and becomes phrase 5; another phrase, first appearing in strophe 3, is modified in strophe 4 and again in strophe 5.

Ex. 37

[52] Spanke (1977), 175; Ludwig (1910), 258.
[53] Spanke (1977), 176. A recent full discussion of the instrumental problem is by Harrison (1979), 79ff.
[54] Spanke (1977), 176.

It is as if it were not so much *a* melody as a series of melodic ideas. (One finds a similar kind of freedom in the performance of the traditional folk-ballad.)

In this case do we have to modify concepts of the relation between words and music? Certainly in this complex of melodies there is, as compared with the courtly chanson, a much less sacrosanct notion of 'number' as ideal pattern. This is not to say that an author like Philip the Chancellor did not work out in his *poem* a carefully conceived scheme of syllables numerically disposed. But it is evident from the analysis of the music above, and from the free way in which the French *lai*-writers handled the same melody, that the music was to some degree subordinate. The inordinate amount of repetition suggests some affinity perhaps with 'narrative melody'. And this is an aspect of sequence–*lai* music which we shall have to consider in the following chapter.

4

LAI AND *PLANCTUS*

The sequence 'Ave gloriosa', quoted at the end of the previous chapter, reminds us that we cannot proceed as if the sequence were purely and simply an ecclesiastical form. This was never the case. From the earliest times there is evidence of a secular tradition – though one hesitates to use a word which implies a sharp division. The beginnings of the sequence have traditionally been placed in the first half of the ninth century, some thirty years before the enterprise which Notker recounted. But Peter Dronke in an important article has argued that 'both the "classical" and the "archaic" sequence existed already in the eighth century; and that the beginnings of the sequence lie in the domain of secular as well as of sacred song, in the vernaculars as well as in Latin'.[1] Much of the evidence is formal; examples of the 'double-cursus' and of alternating and other parallel structures are drawn from various early European sources as far apart as Ireland and Byzantium.[2]

1 The secular sequence

The secular connection, if not the early date, has long been evident from the existence of a group of textless melodies in sequence form with titles such as *planctus cigni*; *planctus sterilis*; *planctus pueri captivati*; *planctus Bertane*. The titles are all suggestive. Dronke writes: '*planctus sterilis* (the lament of the barren woman) possibly belonged to a profane sequence before it was "sanctified", once by Notker (Benedicto gratias deo) and once by an anonymous contemporary of his (Iste dies celebris). The title *planctus sterilis* may well take us back to the world of women's songs, passionate and often tragic *winileodas*.'[3] The *planctus cigni* melody has been studied in detail by Bruno

[1] Dronke, 'The beginnings of the sequence' (1965b), 69. For some observations on these new 'explorations', see Szöverffy (1970), 1.525.

[2] The 'double-cursus' sequence, exemplified by 'Rex celi' (Dronke (1965b), 46), is one in which 'not only is each half in its own right a perfectly constructed "classical sequence" . . . but the entire second half . . . is also a precise rhythmic–syllabic counterpart to the first'. The melody of 'Rex celi' was first discovered by Handschin, who prints it entire ((1929), 19–20) from the *Musica Enchiriadis* (ninth-century) indicating the 'double-cursus'. The most recent study of the genre is by Nancy Phillips and M. Huglo, 'The versus *Rex caeli* – another look at the so-called archaic sequence', *JPMMS* 5 (1982) 36; they provide a most useful table of the eight generally accepted examples and argue that they are not liturgical but 'sacred/secular art-song'.

[3] Dronke (1965b), 58–9. The textless melodies are frequently referred to as *sequele* (see the edition by Dom Anselm Hughes, *Anglo-French Sequelae*, PMMS (London 1934)); but

Stäblein. In its textless versions it is variously entitled *planctus cigni filii plangant*, *sequentia candidi planctus cigni*, *plangam*, and *sequentia planctus cigni*. The transcription which follows is taken from a Paris manuscript (BN lat. 887), a troper–sequentiary from St Martin, Limoges.[4]

Ex. 38

Clan-gam, fi- li- i,   plo- ra- ti- o- ne u- na

2a A- li- tis cy-gni,   qui transfre-ta- vit e- quo- ra.
2b O quam a- ma- ra   la- men- ta- ba- tur, a- ri- da

3a Se de- re- li- quis-se flo- ri- ge- ra
3b Ai- ens, 'In-fe- lix sum a- vi- cu- la,

et pe- tis- se al- ta ma- ri- a,
heu mi- hi, quid a- gam mi- se- ra?

4a Pen-nis so- lu- ta in- ni- ti   lu- ci- da non po- te- ro
4b Un-dis qua-ti- or, pro- cel- lis   hic in- ten-se a- li- dor

hic in stil- la.
ex- u- la- ta.

5a An-   gor in- ter ar- ta gur-gi- tum ca- cu- mi- na,
5b Cer-   nens co- pi- o- sa pis- ci- um le- gu-mi- na,

ge-   mens a- la- ti- zo in- tu- ens mor-ti- fe- ra,
non   que- o in den-sos gur- gi- tes as- su- me- re

[4] BN lat. 887 (early-eleventh-century): see Planchart, 'St Martial' in *New Grove*; Chailley (1960), 98–100. The transcription is from Stäblein, 'Schwanenklage' (1962), 494. His article lists twenty sources of the melody under various titles and with various texts.

sometimes the Latin *sequentia* is used (as by de Goede), contrasting with the English term 'sequence' (melody and words together). See further, Apel (1958), 444ff. For a list of titles, some obviously secular, see Spanke (1934: repr. 1977), 110, and Frere (1894), 239–46, index 4: a summary list of proses and their corresponding *sequentiae*.

non con-scen-dens su- pe- ra.
a- li- men- ta op- ti- ma.

6a Or- tus, oc- ca- sus, pla-ge po- li, ad- mi- nis- tra- te
6b Suf- fla-gi- ta- te O- ri- o- na, ef- fla- gi- tan- tes

lu- ci- da si- de- ra.
nu-bes oc- ci- du- as.'

7a Dum hec co- gi- ta- ret ta- ci- ta, ve- nit ru- ti- la
7b Op- pi- tu- la- ta af- fla-mi- ne ce- pit vi- ri- um

ad- mi- ni- cu- la au- ro- ra.
re- cu- pe- ra- re for- ti- a.

8a O- va- ti- zans iam a- ge- ba- tur in- ter al- ta
8b Hi- la- ra- ta et iu- cun-da- ta ni- mis fa- cta,

et con- su -e- ta nu-bi- um si- de- ra.
pe- ne- tra- ba- tur ma-ri- um flu- mi- na.

9a Dul-ci- mo- de can-ti- tans vo- li- ta- vit ad a- me- na a- ri- da.
9b Con-cur-ri- te om- ni- a a- li- tum et con-cla-ma- te a- gmi-na:

10 'Re- gi ma-gno sit glo- ri- a.' A- men.

We know about the *Lament of the Swan* not, as one might in later centuries, through a collection of 'secular' songs but because its melody was so widely current in ecclesiastical use. It is found, as Stäblein shows, in Western manuscripts from *c.* 850 to *c.* 1100. During the eleventh century the melody was provided with texts for the celebration of the Holy Innocents (28 December); and in the twelfth it was especially popular in the south of France and the north of Spain as a Whitsun sequence.[5] The earliest MSS transmit the text given in Ex. 38, but variously beginning 'Clangant . . .' or 'Plangam . . .'; it is not without its puzzles.

[5] Stäblein (1962), table of sources. See also *ibid.*, 114–15, with pl. 6, 7a–c, from the Winchester Troper.

A swan has left the firm land, with its flowers, and flown out over the sea. It begins a lament for its unhappy state, shaken by winds and storms. Full of anxiety, it attempts to rise above the mountainous waves [*gurgitum cacumina*] but cannot; it sees fish in abundance for food but is unable to get hold of them. Then as dawn breaks its strength returns and, singing sweetly [*dulcimode cantitans*], it flies again to the delights of firm earth [*ad amena arida*]. 'Gather together, all creatures, and praise the high king. Amen.'[6]

It has been conjectured that this is allegorically intended, perhaps having the same meaning as the parable of the Prodigal Son; and one manuscript does indeed have the rubric *allegoria ac de cigno ad lapsum hominis* – 'allegory of the swan concerning the fall of man'.[7] The matter cannot be finally decided; but it looks on the whole likely that the rubric is an example of that most common medieval practice, allegory-after-the event. May the *Lament of the Swan*, then, be in origin non-Christian? This does not necessarily follow: 'the song', Dronke writes, 'is in effect a single, complex image, with a deliberately unexplicated, and therefore highly evocative, figural meaning, of a type and technique that has parallels in early Christian Latin poetry'.[8] It is not some simple pagan popular song. The text is one of the early 'prose' type, in which syllable-count is the chief prosodic feature (see chapter 3:1); the syllabism is, however, supplemented with a consistent proparoxytone rhythm at the end of each line (*équorá, áridá; súperá, óptimá*), very occasionally rhymed (*cacúmina, legúmina*) or half-rhymed, and always with a final sonority on -a – a feature which may, as already said, indicate some connection with the liturgical Alleluia (though the assonance could of course be purely literary). The verbal patterns are sufficiently marked to be evidently intentional, as in the Notker sequences (see 'Johannes, Jesu Christo', Ex. 27 above), even though they are not thoroughly consistent. These prosodic parallels are particularly striking in the eighth strophe:

8a: Ovatizans	jam	agebatur	inter	alta	et consueta	nubium	sidera
8b: Hilarata	et	jucundata	nimis	facta	penetrabatur	marium	flumina

The melody of 'Clangam, filii' is, like many of the sequence melodies, almost strictly one note to a syllable. Like them, too, it mirrors the 'progressive repetition' of the metrical form with precise melodic parallelism; only the first and last strophes of the song are singles. But what is remarkable and unlike most sequences in this melody is its complex use of small segments, repeated over and again.[9] The clearest example on a small scale is strophe 8 with its triple repetition of the motif *e-d-e-c* followed by its extension

[6] The summary is mine. Norberg (1968), 174–6, gives text, translation and commentary.

[7] Stäblein (1962), 493, mentions as a possible but wholly unsupported source the ancient legend of the swans coming from the north; they are the holy creatures of Apollo the god of light.

[8] Dronke (1965b), 57–8, n. 36.

[9] But see, however, the comments above (chapter 3:III and Ex. 34) on 'Laudes crucis' and pattern in the Victorine sequences.

e[*f-g*]*e-d-e*[*d-d*]*c*[*e-e*]. But this motif is not isolated. Indeed, strophe 8 is a longer variant of strophe 6; and strophe 7 not only rhymes melodically with both but contains more or less the same material differently arranged. All three include a rising figure *e-f-g*. This figure enlarged to *d-e-f-g* is the basis of strophe 9 (stated twice) and occurs also in the final versicle, 10. This 'net' of motifs extends further and is by no means easy to disentangle, since one motif is merged with another. Strophe 5, for instance, makes much use of the rising *c-d-e-e* figure (five times in the strict form plus two initial variants) but incorporates the descending form as well. The earlier strophes, 1–4, which might seem at first to be outside this particular 'net', in fact are not. They centre on *g* and *a* rather than on *c* and *d*, but much of their matter is the same, at a lower pitch, as I have already analysed (cf. the close of 3 with the close of 6, 7, 8). Strophe 3, moreover, has the same trick of internal repetition as occurs later in the melody. As Stäblein observes, these melodic idioms – short points, tonally stable, easily memorable – are outside the usual bounds of the ecclesiastical sequence;[10] rather, they link the *planctus cigni* with the music of the *lai* and suggest, like the enigmatic image of the swan, that traditions other than Gregorian chant are alive and working in the imagination of the poet–musician.[11] The relationship between words and music in the *lai* will be our principal concern in the final part of this chapter. But some prior attention must be given to indisputably secular uses of sequence-form, and to the *planctus* itself as a neighbouring genre.

II   The Cambridge Songs

Sometime in the middle of the eleventh century an interesting educational manuscript was compiled at St Augustine's, Canterbury. Its fame and a major part of its interest arise from the fact that the scribes had to hand a collection of songs imported, apparently, from the district of the lower Rhine, and copied them into the book – love-songs, *planctus*, *fabliaux*, celebratory and political songs.[12] They were perhaps all intended to be sung, but only two of them have musical notation. One of them, 'Quisquis dolosis', is in sequence form. It tells a story from the Life of St Basil.[13]

---

[10] Stäblein (1962), 494–5: '. . . in einer besonders auffallenden Weise aus den üblichen Rahmen der Kirchlichen Sequenz'. He also stresses the un-ecclesiastical nature of the *e*-modality (see especially the cadences in strophes 5–8).

[11] David Hiley has kindly drawn my attention to a sequence with remarkably similar melodic patterning, 'Arce summa', with the title *Berta vetula* (text in the Winchester Troper, Source 5 elsewhere, often 'Alme sanctorum'). It makes much play with the figure *g-a-f-a-g*, especially at cadences. There is no apparent connection with *planctus Bertane*.

[12] The Cambridge Songs manuscript (Source 9).

[13] Strecker's edn (1926), pp. 79–82 (no. 30a). The poet has made up the narrative from the Latin *vita* of St Basil. The same source was used by Hrotsvita (see P. von Winterfeld, ed., *Hrosvithae opera* (Berlin 1902), 76–84).

The servant of a young woman marked out for the religious life falls in love with her. In despair he enters into a compact with the devil; he agrees to repudiate the Christian faith, and in return the devil imbues the maiden with a violent passion for him. Nothing the maiden's father can do or say will deter her. The couple get married. And then, soon after, the wife discovers her husband's treachery. She persuades him to accept the sacrament from the blessed St Basil. As Basil leads him out to be reconciled to the Church, they are confronted by the devil waving a legal document and claiming his rights. But such is the power of the saint's prayers, supported by the congregation of the faithful, that the document slips out of the devil's hands and is caught by the saint and torn up into small pieces.

The story is told in quite a lively style. The following double versicle gives the dialogue between the young woman and her anxious father:

3a Continuo
    tacta a diabolo
    clamat virgo: 'Miserere,
    miserere, pater, filie!
    Moriar, mi pater, modo,
    si non iungar tali puero.
    Noli, pater kare,
    noli tardare,
    dum potes me salvare.
    Si moraris,
    natam tuam non habebis,
    sed in die iudicii
    quasi pro peremta
    poenas et tormenta
    tu subibis
        supplicii.'

3b Ast flebilis
    contra pater inquit:
    'Nata, heu quis te cecavit?
    Nata, quis te fascinavit?
    Ego te Christo dicavi,
    non te mecho destinavi.
    Patere, mi filia;
    sine me modo
    perficere, quod volo.
    Si consentis
    mihi, tempus adveniet,
    quando multum letaberis
    pravam quod non
    voluntatem perfeceris,
    male sana
        quam nunc geris.'

Forthwith, touched by the devil, the maiden cries out: 'Have pity, father, have pity on your daughter! I shall die now, father, unless I am married to that young man. Dear father, please, please do not delay, while you are still able to save me. If you hold back, you will no longer have your daughter, but in the Day of Judgement you will undergo the pains and torments of punishment as if you were a murderer.' But, with tears in his eyes, her father replies: 'Daughter, who has blinded you, alas? Who has bewitched you? I dedicated you to Christ; I did not intend you to marry a fornicator. Be patient, my daughter, give in to my wishes. If you give me your consent, the time will come when you will greatly rejoice that you did not execute the evil intention which now, ill in mind, you entertain.'

'Quisquis dolosis' is a big song – over 150 lines long, each versicle of thirteen to fifteen lines. There is almost total syllabic correspondence between the pairs of versicles. Where 'imperfections' occur, it is impossible to be sure whether they are the result of the poet's indifference (it could hardly be incompetence), scribal error, or editorial misunderstanding. The use of rhyme is well developed but not entirely regular; the poet is obviously working for some 'harmonies' but disregarding others. As compared with the *planctus cigni*, this secular sequence (non-liturgical, at least) is in many ways less of a 'prose', more obviously verse. Yet one is more conscious of local verbal patterning in the earlier song and – what is more – of accentual patterning as well. The rhythms of 'Quisquis dolosis' seem to depend very little, as versicle 3 shows, on regularly recurring accent. They are in the sharpest contrast to those of, for example, the 'Letabundus' sequence discussed earlier. If *tácta á diábolo* is predominantly iambic, the corresponding *cóntra páter ínquit* seems even more consistently trochaic.[14] Syllable-counting is the underlying, consistently sustaining principle.

Musically, it is not possible to say much about 'Quisquis dolosis', since only stanzas 1a and 2a have notation and this notation consists of unheighted neumes squeezed in between the lines of words:[15] the pitches of the notes are thus irrecoverable. What one can see, however, from the simplicity of the notation is that the melody was in the familiar note-to-syllable style without melisma. 'The simple vertical stroke for the *virga* . . . alternates with a *punctum* consisting of a dot which is, rarely, squared.'[16] The simple syllabic relation does not, of course, imply that there was anything simple about the melody itself, which may have been every bit as complicated and interlocking as that of *planctus cigni*. One would wish to know more about the music. We might again have here an example of one of the central paradoxes of words-and-music in the repertory of secular sequence and *lai* – that a fairly straightforward, not at all unusual, narrative is cast into a mould of high artifice, melodic as well as prosodic.

The sequence form is used for numerous pieces in the Cambridge Songs, with widely differing subjects and tones of voice. 'Voces laudis' (Strecker no. 3) celebrates the coronation of the Emperor Conrad II; 'Grates usie' (no. 4)[17] sings the praises of Christ; 'Advertite, omnes populi' (no. 14) tells the folk-tale of the Snow-Child; 'Mendosam quam cantilenam' (no. 15) on the other hand is a jest, a *gab*. The following double versicle from the Snow-Child song shows how lightly the formal patterns of the sequence could be adapted to a swift-moving *fabliau*-like narrative. During her husband's absence, a wife has been unfaithful. In this encounter with him on his return she explains how the unwanted birth had occurred.

---

[14] *Tacta a diabolo* (3a.2) could perhaps be dactylic. The argument is not affected. The accent *páter* is confirmed at 3a.7 and elsewhere, assuming that adjacent strong accents are ruled out.

[15] Facsimiles of 'Quisquis dolosis': Fenlon (1982), p. 22; Breul's edn (1915), opp. p. 17; Bernt, 'Carmina Cantabrigiensia' in *MGG*, II, col. 1327.

[16] Stevens in Fenlon (1982), p. 21.

[17] Certainly a sequence, as Strecker observes (p. 7, n.), but an 'imperfect' one, at least in the text as we have it (see, for instance, the variable syllable count in strophes 1a and 1b). Spanke (1942: repr. 1977) is rightly critical of Strecker's attempts to regularize these sequence texts of the Cambridge Songs. In another article, on the liturgical sequence, Spanke dubs them as *Spielmannslieder* ((1932: repr. 1977), 96).

3a   Duobus   3b   At illa
     volutis annis   maritum timens
     exul dictus   dolos versat
     revertitur.   in omnia.
     Occurrit   'Mi', tandem,
     infida coniux   'mi coniux', inquit,
     secum trahens   'una vice
     puerulum.   in Alpibus
     Datis osculis   nive sitiens
     maritus illi   extinxi sitim.
     'De quo', inquit, 'puerum   Inde ergo gravida
     istum habeas,   istum puerum
     dic, aut extrema   damnoso foetu
     patieris.'   heu gignebam.'[18]

(3a) When two years had passed, the aforesaid exile returned. His unfaithful wife ran to meet him, pulling a little boy after her. They greeted one another with kisses, and then her husband said, 'Who may be the father of that boy you have there? Tell me, or it will be the worse for you.' (3b) But she was frightened of her husband and thought of every way she could trick him. At last she replied, 'Husband dear, one day in the Alps I was thirsty and I quenched my thirst with snow. As a result I became pregnant and, alas, I bore that boy – an injurious birth.'

This is a poem without rhyme – in some sense, therefore, a *prosa*. But as the above double versicle shows there is a fair correspondence of accentual pattern, so far as the modern ear can judge it, and some suggestion of the phonetic parallelism based on word-division which we have already encountered (e.g. lines 2–3, 9–10). Of the two features the accentual patterning is the more striking and significant. It seems to indicate, even in this swift-moving style, a consciousness of the artefact, an awareness of 'number' in one of its newer manifestations.

This verse-*fabliau* has no music surviving in this or any other MS. What can we deduce about it? Very little from the text itself. The division into short lines which could suggest short *lai*-like melodic motifs is, of course, purely editorial. It seems appropriate because it brings out the phonetic and accentual parallelism mentioned above; but it has no manuscript authority. The only clue to the formal nature of the song is in the title, *Modus Liebinc*, which does not appear in the Cambridge Songs manuscript but is found in one of the other two sources.[19] It means evidently 'the Liebinc tune' and may refer to one Liuppo, *egregius miles*, who saved the life of Otto II in battle.[20] The supposition is that a Latin *lai* celebrating this exploit formed the pattern, musical and metrical, for the present very different poem. However this may

---

[18] Strecker, no. 14, *Modus Liebinc* (pp. 41–4). The poem survives in two other MSS; it was edited from all three by W. Meyer, *Fragmenta Burana* (Berlin 1901), 175–6. Meyer argues that it and *Modus Ottinc* must be by the same author.

[19] Wolfenbüttel, MS Cod. Aug. 56 16/18, fol. 16v.

[20] Strecker, p. 44, n.

be, the Snow-Child poem is one of four Cambridge songs to which a *modus* is attributed. The others are *Modus florum* for 'Mendosam quam cantilenam' (no. 15), *Modus qui et Carelmanninc* for 'Inclito celorum' (no. 5), and *Modus Ottinc* for 'Magnus cesar Otto' (no. 11).[21] About the *Modus florum* nothing is known. The 'Charlemagne melody' is only a little less shadowy. The *Cambridge Songs* text is an unmemorable poem recounting the life of Christ; though not connected with Charlemagne, it is presumably based on a song which was. The lost original was also imitated by Ekkehard of St Gall in a sequence honouring St Paul.[22] Concerning *Modus Ottinc* we are better informed. The opening lines of the song mention the name of the melody and indicate how it came into being:

1a. Magnus cesar Otto,
      quem hic modus refert
      in nomine,
      Ottinc dictus,
      quadam nocte
      somno membra
      dum collocat,
      palatium
      casu subito
      inflammatur.

1b. Stant ministri, tremunt,
      timent dormientem
      attingere,
      et cordarum
      pulsu facto
      excitatum
      salvificant
      et domini
      nomen carmini
      inponebant.[23]

(1a) Whilst Great Emperor Otto to whom this *lai* (?) refers in its title, 'Ottinc', is asleep one night, his palace by sudden accident catches fire. (1b) His servants stand by, they tremble, they fear to touch the sleeper. Only when he is wakened by the strumming of strings do they bring him to safety; they then gave their master's name to the song.

This Otto (936–73), who was so formidable a character, it seems, that his servants were afraid to waken him except by music, even when his palace was on fire, was the grandfather of the Otto, yet uncrowned, who is celebrated towards the end of the poem. Having effected this musical rescue they gave Otto's name to the song. The way the title is thus explained at the beginning of the poem is reminiscent of the style which later writers, such as Marie de France, will adopt in the prologues to their *lais*.[24] But there is a further point of interest. This opening anecdote speaks of stringed instruments; the emperor is awakened by a harp or similar plucked instrument (*cordarum pulsu facto*). The original *Modus Ottinc* may, then, have been a textless melody, possibly instrumental.[25] However, in its surviving musical version (it is the only one of

---

[21] Spanke (1932: repr. 1977), 97–8, discusses the '*Modus*' songs.

[22] Spanke (1942), 121–2.

[23] Strecker, no. 11 (pp. 33–6).

[24] E.g. *Marie de France: Lais* no. x, 'Chaitivel', lines 6–8: 'Le Chaitivel l'apelet hum, / E si [i] ad plusurs de ceus / Ki l'apelent les Quatre Deuls' (ed. A. Ewert, Oxford 1960, p. 116).

[25] *Lai* and 'secular' sequence form one group of medieval monophonic songs of which it can safely be said that they habitually received instrumental accompaniment. A good deal of evidence has been assembled by: Handschin (1929); Spanke (1934); Maillard (1963) and

the four named *modi* for which we have music) it has the text given above. The neumes of the Wolfenbüttel manuscript are only vaguely heighted and cannot be satisfactorily transcribed.[26] They indicate, however, a syllabic, principally single-noted melody, with no melismas and no clearly identifiable repetitions. It is a melody which in this respect obeyed the rules of number, even if it is related to a more popular tradition in which syllable-counting and precise patterning were of little account.

III   *Planctus*

The reader will already have become aware of the problem of terminology in this chapter: what is the best term to use to refer to non-liturgical songs in sequence form, in Latin or the vernacular? The early manuscripts have no single term corresponding to the twelfth-century term *lai* (and German *Leich*) to describe songs related to the ecclesiastical sequence. Terms there are, however. *Modus* is evidently one of them; and *planctus* is, as we have seen, another. The term *planctus* is in fact widely and loosely used over this whole long period and at least in one source denotes nothing more than 'song'.[27] However, in the huge majority of instances *planctus* means what we should expect it to mean – a lament. The term clearly does not denote any one particular metrical–musical shape; the *planctus* may or may not be in sequence or *lai* form. I shall concentrate chiefly on those that are.[28]

There are *planctus* amongst the Cambridge Songs and in other early manuscripts, and they are generally of a highly formal kind, informed not by personal sorrow but by a sense of public loss.[29] 'Iudex summe medie' (no. 9)

[26] The opening of 'Magnus cesar Otto' (*Modus Ottinc*) is reproduced by Coussemaker (1852), pl. 1. The lines of the Wolfenbüttel version (see note 19 above) are reasonably well spaced – i.e. as if neuming was envisaged by the text-scribe. There is some slight heightening.

[27] In the fourteenth-century Provençal play *Le Jeu de Sainte Agnès* (ed. Jeanroy, CFMA, 1931) the Latin term *planctus* is used in a quite general sense to introduce a variety of songs (see *ibid.*, pp. xi–xiv, and appendix, 'Les Mélodies', 58–9, by Gérold).

[28] There is as yet no full study published of the *planctus* as a musical phenomenon, the meeting-place as it seems of several genres of song. I have, however, benefited greatly from the researches of Janthia Yearley, who has generously allowed me to make use of her unpublished dissertation, 'The medieval Latin planctus' (1983); it lays the groundwork for a fuller understanding. Her published bibliography of European *planctus* (1981) is an essential scholarly tool. See also Corbin, 'Teatro Religioso': v, 'Il "Planctus" ' in *La Musica* (IV.623ff).

[29] There is evidence of the following types of *planctus* from the ninth century (the classification is based on Dronke (1970), 27–9): (a) vernacular *planctus* to be sung by women; (b) 'Germanic complaints of exile and voyaging'; (d) fictional, as distinct from real-life, *planctus* on classical or Biblical themes. From the twelfth century onwards, (e) dramatic or semi-dramatic laments of the Virgin and (f) *complaintes d'amour* in a courtly style are common. The *Marienklage* was especially important as a dramatic nucleus in Germany (see Stevens, 'Planctus' in *New Grove*).

(1959); and Harrison (1979). In the case of the sequence it is chiefly of two kinds – the evidence of melody titles and the evidence of internal literary references. There is no reason to believe that any instruments other than the organ were permitted in normal liturgical use.

laments the death of the Emperor Henry II (1024) and the shortness of his reign. He is praised for his legal skill, the clemency he showed to clergy and people, his support of the church, his subdual of barbarian peoples, and so forth. The sequence is punctuated by, and ends with, a refrain asking Christ to bless his soul:[30]

> Imperatoris Heinrici
> catholici
> magni ac pacifici
> beatifica animam,
>   Christe.

The public style of this *planctus* is characteristic. As so often in the European tradition, elegy and eulogy are merged together to assert the values of a society. Paradoxically, many of the most moving *planctus*, and the ones which seem most personal, are not 'real' but fictional – or, at least, historical (based on biblical stories, for example). Of these the six *planctus* of Peter Abelard are outstanding.

Music survives for all Abelard's *planctus* in a single manuscript in the Vatican Library (Reg. lat. 288).[31] Unfortunately the melodies are written in unheighted neumes and cannot be transcribed with any certainty as to pitch. However, one which may have been especially popular – David's lament over Saul and Jonathan, 'Dolorum solatium' – survives in three versions; the latest of these, recently discovered in an English manuscript, is clearly written in square notation.[32]

'Dolorum solatium' is based on the biblical lament, but its emphasis differs

---

[30] Strecker (1926), pp. 27–8.

[31] The standard text of Abelard's *planctus* is W. Meyer's edition in his *Gesammelte Abhandlungen* (1905), I.340. A new edition of *Planctus Dine Filie Iacob* is published by Dronke (1970), 146, at the end of his chapter 'Peter Abelard: *Planctus* and Satire' (which see, also, for references to earlier literary studies). For the music of Abelard, see Weinrich's two articles (1969) and (1968), making a substantial addition to previous knowledge. Also Vecchi's edition (1951); A. Machabey, 'Les planctus d'Abélard: remarques sur le rhythme musical du XIIe siècle', *Romania* 82 (1961) 71. The most recent general study is by M. Huglo, 'Abélard, poète et musicien', *CCM* 22 (1979) 349–61.

[32] Oxford, MS Bodley 79, fols. 53v–56 (the conventional dating is late-thirteenth-century, but Pächt and Alexander give early-thirteenth-century), an anthology of Latin poems written in England. Abelard's *planctus*, which Weinrich (1968) was the first to identify in this source, is followed by Walter of Châtillon's 'Frigescente karitatis' with melody, in the same hand (Walther, 6909; Anderson L23a). Facsimile of Abelard's *planctus* in E. M. Bannister, *Monumenta Vaticani di Paleografia Latina*, 2 vols. (Leipzig 1913), pl. 48. The transcription here is my own, from Bodley 79, with text checked from Dronke (1970). Weinrich (1969), 468ff, gives parallel transcriptions from Bodley 79, from the Vatican MS, Cod.Reg.lat. 288, fols. 63v–64v, and from Paris BN n.a.lat. 3126, fols. 88v–90v. Weinrich reconstructs the melody (unheighted) of the Vatican MS with the help of the other two MSS. The Paris MS is a twelfth-century troper from Nevers, first described by M. Huglo, 'Un nouveau prosaire Nivernais', *Ephemerides liturgicae*, 71 (1957) 3–30; the neumes are heighted around two stave lines, c^1 and f. Text edition (of Vatican MS), Meyer (1905), I.372–4. For a measured transcription, see Ian Bent in Dronke (1970), appendix, pp. 203–9.

from the biblical in ways which have been succinctly described by Peter Dronke:

> It begins, like the biblical dirge of David, with a lament over the humiliation of Israel in battle. But where the biblical song goes on to give almost equal emphasis to Saul and to Jonathan, here Saul as a person is given only three lines, Jonathan more than thirty.[33]

Saul is the king, and no more. But Jonathan is addressed, 'Plus fratre mihi, Jonathe' – 'more than a brother to me'.

David recalls not only the oneness of the love they shared, but a shared agony of guilt . . . of which the Bible knows nothing, and which is never explained within the *planctus* itself . . . In the longest and most moving stanzas of the *planctus* David sings to his dead friend of his wish to have died at the same moment as he, his bitter regret not to have been at his side in battle then, 'that even death would join us more than sunder us'. For to live without Jonathan 'is to die constantly'.[34]

Ex. 39

---

[33] Dronke (1970), 116.
[34] *Ibid.*, 116.

2a A- ma- lech in- va- lu- it,   Is- ra- hel dum cor- ru- it;

in- fi- de- lis iu- bi- lat   Phi- lis- te- a,

dum la- men- tis ma- ce- rat   se Iu- de- a.

2b In- sul- tat fi- de- li- bus   in- fi- de- lis po- pu- lus;

in ho- no- rem ma- xi- mum   plebs ad- ver- sa,

in de- ri- sum om- ni- um   fit di- vi- na,

2c In- sul- tan- tes in- qui- unt: Ec- ce   de   quo gar-ri- unt?

qua-li- ter hos pro- di- it   de- us ser- vus,

dum a mul- tis oc- ci- dit   di- is pro- stra-tus.

2d Quem pri- mum hiis pre- bu- it   vic- tus rex oc- cu- bu- it;

ta- lis est e- lec- ti- o   de- i   su- i,

ta- lis con- se- cra- ti- o   va- tis   ma- gni.

3a Sa- ul, re- gum for- tis- si- me,   vir- tus in- vic- ta Io- na- the,

qui vos ne- qui- vit vin-ce- re   per- mis-sus est oc- ci- de- re.

3b Qua-si non es- set o- le- o con- se- cra- tus do- mi- ni- co

sce- les- te ma- nus gla-di-o iu- gu- la-tur in pre- li- o.

3c Plus fra-tre mi-chi Io-na-tha, in u- na me-cum a- ni- ma,

que pec-ca- ta que sce- le- ra nos- tra sci- de- runt vis-ce- ra.

3d Ex-per- tes, mon-tes Gel-bo- e, ro- ris si- tis et plu- vi- e,

nec a- gro- rum pri-mi- ci- e ves-tro suc-cur-rant in-co- le.

4a Ve, ve ti- bi, ma-di- da tel- lus ce- de re-gi- a,

qua et te, mi Io- na-tha, ma- nus stra-vit im- pi- a!

4b U- bi Christus do-mi- ni Is- ra-hel-que in- cli- ti

mor-te mi- se- ra- bi- li cum su- is sunt per-di- ti!

4c Planctus, Sy- on fi- li- e, su- per Sa- ul su- mi- te,

lar- go cu- ius mu-ne- re vos or- na-bant pur-pu- re.

4d Tu mi-chi, mi Io- na- tha, flen-dus su-per om- ni- a,

in- ter cun-cti gau-di- a per- pes e- ris la- cri- ma.

5a He- u, cur con-si- li- o ad- qui- e- vi pes- si- mo,

ut ti- bi pre- si- di- o non es- sem in pre- li- o?

vel con- fos-sus pa- ri- ter mo- re- rer fe- li- ci- ter,

cum quid a- mor fa- ci- at ma- ius hoc non ha- be- at,

et me post te vi- ve- re mo- ri sit as- si- du- e,

nec ad vi- tam a- ni- ma sa- tis sit di- mi- di- a.

5b Vi- cem a- mi- ci- ci- e vel u- nam me red-de- re

o- por- te- bat tem-po- re sum-me tunc an- gus- ti- e,

tri- um-phi par- ti- ci- pem vel ru- i- ne co- mi- tem,

ut te vel e- ri- pe- rem vel te- cum oc-cum- be- rem,

vi- tam pro te fi- ni- ens quam sal-vas-ti to- ci- ens,

ut et mors nos iun-ge- ret ma- gis quam dis-iunge- ret.

5c In- fau-sta vic-to- ri- a po- ci- us in- te- re- a;

tam va-na quam bre-vi- a hic per- ce- pi gau-di- a!

quam ci-to du-ris-si-mus est se-cu-tus nunti-us,

quem, in su-am a-ni-mam lo-cu-tum su-per-bi-am,

mor-tu-is quos nun-ci-at il-la-ta mors ag-gre-gat,

ut do-lo-ris nun-ti-us do-lo-ris sit so-ci-us.

6a Do qui-e-tem fi-di-bus; vel-lem ut et plancti-bus

sic pos-sem et fle-ti-bus!

6b Le-sis pul-su ma-ni-bus, rau-cis plan-ctu vo-ci-bus,

de-fi-cit et spi-ri-tus.

(1a) My harp, my consolation in sorrow and cure for pain, (1b) is now the more needful to me, as my sorrow is greater and my grief more fitting. (1c) The great slaughter of the nation, the king's death and his son's, the triumph of the enemy, (1d) the desolation of the leaders, the commons in despair – these fill all things with mourning.

(2a) Amalek has grown powerful while Israel has fallen in ruins; infidel Philistia exults while Judah torments itself with lamentations. (2b) The faithful are mocked by an infidel nation. The people of the enemy have come to the highest honour, God's people meet the derision of all. (2c) The mockers say: see in what manner their god, of whom they babble, has betrayed them, seeing that he has perished, laid low by many gods. (2d) The first king he granted them has fallen in defeat. So much for election by their god, so much for consecration by the great prophet!

(3a) O Saul, most valiant of kings, O invincible courage of Jonathan, one who could not defeat you was permitted to slay you. (3b) As if he [Saul] had not been consecrated with the oil of the Lord, he is slaughtered in battle by the sword of a wicked hand. (3c) O Jonathan, more than a brother to me, sharing a single soul with me, what sins, what wicked deeds have sundered our living flesh. (3d) Mountains of Gilboa, may you be without dew or rain, and may no first fruits of the fields grow up for those who dwell in you.

(4a) Woe, woe to you, earth drenched with royal blood, where a hand of wickedness felled you too, O my Jonathan! (4b) Where the Lord's Anointed and Israel's men of renown with their followers were piteously slain. (4c) O daughters of Sion, take up the lament over Saul, by whose bounteous gift you were adorned with purple robes. (4d) O my Jonathan, it is for you I have to weep above all else; amidst all that gives delight, my tears shall be unending.

(5a) Alas, why did I assent to the worse counsel, so that I could not protect you in the battle? Or else, struck down at your side I could have died happy, since love has no greater thing than this that it can do, and since for me to live on after you is a perpetual death. For life half a soul is not enough. (5b) Then at the time of utmost distress I should have paid friendship's debt, either in one way as a sharer in your victory or else as your companion in death; then I should either have rescued you or have fallen with you. In your defence I would thus have ended this life which you saved so often; thus would death have united rather than parted us. (5c) Meanwhile I had won an ill-starred victory; as empty as they were brief were the joys I gained from it! How speedily there followed the grimmest of messengers whose speech of pride was fatal to his own life: death, thus summoned, adds him to the dead whom he announces, so that the messenger of grief shall be grief's companion.

(6a) I give rest to my harp-strings; would that I could do so to my lamentations and tears. (6b) My hands are sore with striking, my voice is hoarse with lamenting and my breath fails me.

The form of David's lament is quite elaborate. It divides into six sections, each containing metrical/musical repeats. Schematically it can be represented:

1:	3-line strophe	4	versicles
2:	6-line strophe	4	versicles
3:	4-line strophe	4	versicles
4:	4-line strophe	4	versicles
5:	12-line strophe	3	versicles
6:	3-line strophe	2	versicles

The musico-poetical structure of this *planctus* is by no means unusually complex, as we shall later see.[35] For instance, the variation of line-lengths (measured, as is proper, by the number of syllables) is not great. But it shows, metrically, the clearly distinctive features of the Latin *lai* – as the term may helpfully be used to distinguish it from the much more regular ecclesiastical sequences of the same period (Adam of St Victor was only one generation junior to Abelard).[36] Abelard's *lai* is recognizable as a sequence-type because it is neither fully strophic (i.e. stanza-repeating) nor through-composed; it is made up of a series of repeated versicles, not consistently of 'doubles' as in the standard sequence, but of threes and fours (as the second column above shows) with a 'double' at the end. No strophe has precisely the same metre as another. The distinction may be a fine one – only line-length distinguishes

[35] For the more varied forms of Abelard's other *planctus*, see Spanke (1931: repr. 1977), 48–52.
[36] Abelard was born in 1079; Adam of St Victor, whose date of birth is not known, flourished *c.* 1130 onwards.

strophes 3 and 4, for instance – but it is indisputably there. The *lai* calls for the exercise of metrical invention on a large scale.

Consistent and skilful use of rhyme supplements and varies the poetic pattern of Abelard's *lai–planctus*. In this 'Dolorum solatium' differs from the *planctus cigni* (see Ex. 38 above). The interest in sound-pattern is present in both; but the signs of it have changed. Abelard in this *planctus* shows less concern, it seems, with cunning abstract patterns based on parallel word-divisions – the little numerical mirror-effects where the 'counters' are syllables – but rather more with sonorities, especially the end-sonorities of rhyme.[37] At least the rhymes are identifiable even if 'imperfect' by later and stricter standards (3d: *Gelboe/pluvie/primitie/incole* – where most of the work is done by the comparatively light final syllable). Perhaps the relics of older usage, of an older fashion of assonance, are present? At the very end of the poem Abelard does not trouble to complete his set of six -*ibus* rhymes but admits *spiritus*, chiming but not fully rhyming with *manibus*, *vocibus*, and others. Other sound-patterns which make witty play with the stanza he obviously enjoys, as a rhetorician should:

> 5c (end) . . . mórtuis, quòs núntiat,
>
> illátà mòrs ággrègat,
>
> ut dóloris núntius
>
> dolóris sit sócius

As the quoted strophe shows, there is some ambivalence about accent in this *planctus*. In the reading of the fourth line one might wish to preserve the trochaic movement of the third, but this would disturb the echo on *doloris*. The departures from strict alternation of stressed and unstressed which I have tentatively indicated underlie, it seems to me, the rhythms of the whole poem. The fact that many lines fall naturally into patterns of alternation is no argument for forcing the rest into the same mould. The slightly teasing fluidity is a positive gain.

> 3a Saül régum fortíssime . . .
>
> 3b Quási non ésset óleo . . .
>
> 3c Plus frátre míchi Iónatha . . .
>
> 3d Expértes móntes Gélboe

This fluidity is a factor also in the relationship between the words and the music, and to this I now turn. There are 110 lines in the poem, and each of them (as is usual in songs of the period) is set to a single melodic unit. There are, however, fewer than twenty distinct melodic units. The precise number depends on how you categorize what are clearly variants of the same tune: the first phrase, for instance, in strophe 5, has four slightly differing endings of

---

[37] On the other hand his *Planctus virginum Israel* displays great interest and skill in verbal patterning, as the opening in particular shows.

which the first and third are more 'open' than the second and fourth. The *g*-tonality is extremely stable throughout; the proportion of tunes which end on the note *g* is very high, and of those that do not end on *g* practically all end on a note of the *g*-triad. The melodies of strophe 4 provide an excellent example:

Ex. 40

The emphasis on a *g*-tonality goes even further in this example: not only the finals but the initial notes are members of the *g*-triad. Moreover the seven-note melody seems to fall naturally into a / ˇ / ˇ / ˇ / pattern, the fifth note taking a subsidiary accent *and* reinforcing the triadic feeling.[38] Every single versicle throughout the *planctus* closes on *g*. We might on the basis of the Oxford version, from which these examples are taken, naively think we were dealing with a much later melody, so clearly does it seem to fall into the idioms of *g*-major (though with flattened seventh). However, variants in the Paris MS suggest a somewhat more modal, more 'medieval', view. Strophe 4 there reads:

Ex. 41

The notes *a* and *c* play a more important part here. Though the melody remains basically as I have described it, the *g*-tonality is counterbalanced by an *f*-triad which emerges clearly in the fourth phrase. This particular modal

[38] I am aware that the argument could become circular: we, as moderns, feel the power of the major triad, hear the melody according to its patterns, and then invoke the presumed medieval response to the triad to confirm our reading. However, the continual recurrence of these patterns in this repertoire, but not in Gregorian chant, the objective nature of the acoustical–mathematical relations within the triad, and the indisputable evidence (in the history of polyphony) of the fundamental aural appeal of octave, fifth, fourth and third lead one to have confidence in the reading.

juxtaposition of *g/f* natural is one of the hallmarks of *lai*-like melody;[39] it is especially the characteristic of its cadences which approach the final from the tone below (see phrase 4 of strophe 2):

Ex. 42

A song of this length – it might take some eight minutes to perform – with such an unvarying and insistently limited tonality is quite removed from the Gregorian tradition. It has common links with some sequences (see the discussion of the tonality of 'Letabundus' above and of 'Laudes crucis'), but the exceptionally high incidence of repetition of small, rather 'catchy' phrases sets it apart even from them. One concluding observation on the melodic idiom: unlike some of the other *lais* and *lai*-like pieces to be discussed, 'Dolorum solatium' does not regularly pick up melodies used earlier in the song and repeat them later. In this respect it is more through-composed than other *lais*.

David's lament over Jonathan is a most moving event in Abelard's re-creation:

> 5a Heu, cur consilio
> adquievi pessimo,
> ut tibi presidio
> non essem in prelio?
> > Vel confossus pariter
> > morerer feliciter,
> > cum quid amor faciat
> > maius hoc non habeat,
> et me post te vivere
> mori sit assidue,
> nec ad vitam anima
> satis sit dimidia.

The human truth of this feeling vibrates in the words of the poem. What, then, is the function of the music in the totality of 'Dolorum solatium'? One could say, I suppose, that the swift-moving, unimpassioned melody (strophes 3 to 5 are almost entirely syllable-to-note) is in some way a solace for griefs. But this would hardly be convincing. In fact, the relation between the words and the music is once again purely formal. Structures and patterns are what matter. The form of the melody is the form of the poem; the shape of the musical strophe coincides with the metrical; the musical phrase is the poetic line; each note or short note-group has its corresponding syllable. The governing

[39] See, for example, 'Flos pudicitie' (Ex. 24 above), 'Omnis caro' (Ex. 55 below), 'Samson dux' (*EEH*, II.16, an out-of-date transcription).

principles are pattern, balance and proportion – in a word, 'number'. The absence of emotional, intellectual, 'imagistic' connections between the text and the melody is too obvious to need comment. We need not imagine the composer searching for the *mélodie juste* to fit the moving stanza quoted above, and cannot imagine, indeed, what principles he might invoke to help him. Conversely (as may well have been the case), faced with this *lai*-melody as a structure on which to devise a lament, would Abelard have seen any especial fitness in making this particular conjunction (versicle 3c)? –

Ex. 43

He had already used the same melody to set lines celebrating the power of Saul: 'Saul, regum fortissime, virtus invicta Jonathe'. The music is clearly not a commentary of any sort; it is a vehicle. (It would be possible, of course, for a skilled singer to give such a song a highly emotional *performance*. But this is a different matter. I return to it in chapter 10:III below, in relation to the drama.) There are two sorts of vehicle that a melody can be. One is the vehicle which has full and substantial meaning of its own as a piece of music; this, I have argued, is the case with *la grande chanson courtoise*. The other is the vehicle of 'narrative music' in which the purely musical interest is subdued and subordinate; this is the case with epic, ballad and romance (see chapter 6 below). The music of this *lai–planctus*, like most *lai* melodies, falls between the two. The aesthetic involved may be further considered in relation to another song.

'Dolorum solatium' was sufficiently well known to find its way into an English manuscript. Another Latin *lai*, or *lai*-like sequence, with a strong English connection is a twelfth-century lament of the Virgin 'Planctus ante nescia'.[40] The text is a dramatic monologue.

After announcing her grief in the opening stanza, Mary addresses two stanzas [i.e. two double versicles] to Christ, describing their mutual suffering. Then follow three stanzas of sheer lament (4, 5 and 6), in the course of which she recalls Simeon's

---

[40] 'Planctus ante nescia' by Godefroy of St Victor: Anderson L79 (many surviving texts with musical notation; my transcription is from Evreux, Bibl.Mun., MS 2, fols. 3v–4v). The text is printed by Young (1933), I.496–8; *AH* xx.156–8 (no. 199); and, most recently, collating eight MSS, Dobson in Dobson and Harrison (1979), 116–17 (Dobson argues strongly in favour of the attribution to Godefroy). See also Yearley (1981), L123, and (1983) III, nos. 58a–g (pp. 176–95). Harrison (1979), 238–40, prints parallel melodies of the *planctus* from three main sources, and in his Introduction (p. 84) transcribes the melody from the unheight-

prophecy that a sword should pierce her spirit. In the next three stanzas she appeals to death to spare her Son's life, and to take her in his place. Finally, after denouncing the Jews (10, 11 and 12), she closes with an appeal for sympathy addressed to the women of Jerusalem. The poem, then, is assumed to be spoken at the foot of the cross, during the last moments of Christ's agony.[41]

Ex. 44

1a Planctus an-te ne-sci- a,   planc-tu las-sor an-xi- - a,
1b Or-bat or-bem ra-di- o   me Iu-de-a fi-li- - o,

cru-ci-or do- - lo- re.
gau-di-o, dul- - co- re.

2a Fi-li, dul-cor u-ni-ce,   sin-gu-la-re gau-di-um,
2b Pec-tus, men-tem, lu-mi-na   tor-quent tu-a vul-ne-ra.

ma-trem flen-tem re-spi-ce,   por-ri-ge so-la- -ci-um.
que ma-ter, que fe-mi-na,   tam fe-lix, tam mi-se-ra?

3a Flos flo-rum, dux mo-rum, ve-ni-e ve-na,
3b Proh do-lor, hinc co-lor ef-fu-git o-ris,

quam gra-vis in cla-vis est ti-bi pe-na!
hinc ru-it, hinc flu-it un-da cru-o-ris.

4a O quam se-ro de-di-tus,   quam ci-to me de-se-ris,
4b O quis a-mor cor-po-ris   ti-bi fe-cit spo-li-a,

o quam di-gne ge-ni-tus,   quam ab-ie-cte mo-re-ris!
o quam dul-cis pi-gno-ris   quam a-ma-ra pre-mi-a!

---

[41] Young (1933), I.498. I am grateful to Jill Mann and Michael Lapidge for advice on the translation following Ex. 44.

5a O pi- a gra- ci- a   sic mo- ri- en- tis,
5b O fe- ra dex-te- ra   cru- ci- fi- gen-tis,

o sce- lus, o ze- lus   in- - vi- de gen- tis.
o le- nis in pe- nis   mens pa- ti- en- tis.

6a O ve- rum e- lo- qui- um   ius- ti Sy- me- o- nis;
6b Ge- mi- tus, sus-pi- ri- a   la- cri- me- que fo- ris,

quem pro-mi- sit, gla- di- um   sen- ci- o do- lo- ris.
vul- ne- ris in- di- ci- a   sunt in-te- ri- o- ris.

7a Par- ci- to pro- li,   mors, mi-chi no- li!
7b Mor-te, be- a- te,   se- pa- rer a te,

tunc mi-chi so- li   so- la me- de- ris.
dum- mo- do, na- te,   non cru-ci- e- ris.

8a Quod cri- men, que sce- le- ra   gens com-mi-sit ef- fe- ra!
8b Na- to, que- so, par- ci- te;   ma-trem in- ter- fi- ci- te,

vin- cla, vir- gas, vul- ne- ra,
aut in cru- cis sti- pi- te

spu- ta, spi- nas, ce- te- ra   si- ne cul- pa pa- ti- tur.
nos si- mul af- fi- gi- te;   ma- le so- lus mo- ri- tur.

9a Red-di- te mes-tis- si- me   cor-pus vel ex- a- ni- me,
9b U- ti- nam sic do- le- am,   ut do- lo- re pe- re- am,

ut sic mi- no- ra- tus   cres-cat cru-ci- a- tus
nam plus est do- lo- ri   si- ne mor- te mo- ri,

o-[s]cu- lis, am- ple- xi- bus,
quam pe-ri- re ti- ti- us.

10a Quid stu-pes, gens mi- se- ra,   ter- ram se- mo-ve- re,
10b So- lem pri-vas lu- mi-ne,   quo-mo-do lu- ce- ret?

ob- scu- ra- ri si- de- ra,   lan-qui-dos lu- ge- re?
e- grum me-di- ca-mi- ne   un- de con-va- le- ret?

11a Ho- mi- ci- dam li- be- ras,   Ihe- sum dans sup-pli-ci- o;
11b Fa- mis, ce- dis, pes-ti- um   sci- es do-cta pon-de- re

ma- le pa- cem to- le- ras,   ve- ni- et se- di- ti- o.
Ihe-sum ti- bi mor-tu- um   Bar-ra bam-que vi- ve- re.

12a Gens ce- ca, gens fle- bi- lis,   a- ge pe- ni- ten- ti- am,
12b Quos fe- cis- ti fon-ti- um   pro-sint ti- bi flu- mi- na,

dum ti- bi fle- xi- bi- lis   est Je- sus ad ve- ni- am.
si- tim se-dant om-ni- um,   cun-cta la- vant cri-mi- na.

13a Fle-te, Sy- on fi- li- e,   tan-te gra-te gra-ci- e –
13b In am-ple-xus ru- i- te,   dum pen-det in sti- pi- te,

iu- ve- nis an- gus- ti- e   si- bi sunt de- li- ci- e –
mu-tu- is am-ple- xi- bus;   se- pa- rat a- man-ti-bus

pro ves- tris of- fen- sis.
bra-chi- is ex- ten-sis.

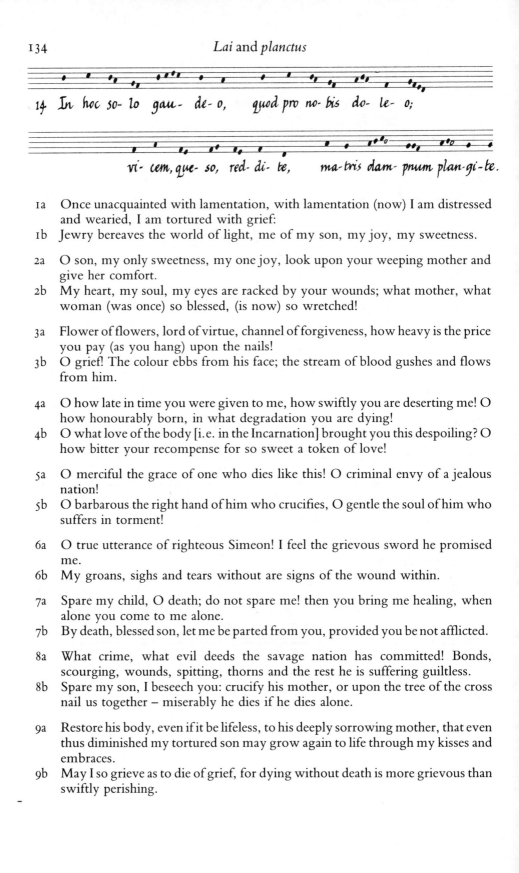

14 In hoc so-lo gau-de-o, quod pro no-bis do-le-o;

vi-cem, que-so, red-di-te, ma-tris dam-pnum plan-gi-te.

1a Once unacquainted with lamentation, with lamentation (now) I am distressed and wearied, I am tortured with grief:
1b Jewry bereaves the world of light, me of my son, my joy, my sweetness.

2a O son, my only sweetness, my one joy, look upon your weeping mother and give her comfort.
2b My heart, my soul, my eyes are racked by your wounds; what mother, what woman (was once) so blessed, (is now) so wretched!

3a Flower of flowers, lord of virtue, channel of forgiveness, how heavy is the price you pay (as you hang) upon the nails!
3b O grief! The colour ebbs from his face; the stream of blood gushes and flows from him.

4a O how late in time you were given to me, how swiftly you are deserting me! O how honourably born, in what degradation you are dying!
4b O what love of the body [i.e. in the Incarnation] brought you this despoiling? O how bitter your recompense for so sweet a token of love!

5a O merciful the grace of one who dies like this! O criminal envy of a jealous nation!
5b O barbarous the right hand of him who crucifies, O gentle the soul of him who suffers in torment!

6a O true utterance of righteous Simeon! I feel the grievous sword he promised me.
6b My groans, sighs and tears without are signs of the wound within.

7a Spare my child, O death; do not spare me! then you bring me healing, when alone you come to me alone.
7b By death, blessed son, let me be parted from you, provided you be not afflicted.

8a What crime, what evil deeds the savage nation has committed! Bonds, scourging, wounds, spitting, thorns and the rest he is suffering guiltless.
8b Spare my son, I beseech you: crucify his mother, or upon the tree of the cross nail us together – miserably he dies if he dies alone.

9a Restore his body, even if it be lifeless, to his deeply sorrowing mother, that even thus diminished my tortured son may grow again to life through my kisses and embraces.
9b May I so grieve as to die of grief, for dying without death is more grievous than swiftly perishing.

10a Why are you astonished, O wretched nation, that the earth shakes, that the stars are darkened, that the sick are lamenting?

10b If you deprive the sun of light, how should it shine? If you deprive a sick man of medicine, from what source may he regain his health?

11a You set free a murderer; you hand over Jesus to execution; peace you reject – insurrection will follow.

11b Taught by the oppressive weight of famine, slaughter, pestilence you shall know that for you Jesus is dead and Barrabas is alive.

12a O blind nation, lamentable nation, do penance, while you may still move Jesus to forgiveness.

12b May the streams from the fountains (of blood) you have caused bring you benefit: they quench all men's thirst, they wash away all sins.

13a Weep for your transgressions, O daughters of Sion, in gratitude for such grace: his distress is a delight to him.

13b Rush into his embrace, while he hangs upon the tree, with embraces in return; he makes himself ready for those who love him, with his arms outstretched.

14 In this alone I rejoice, that I suffer grief on your behalf. Do me a service in return, I pray: bewail a mother's loss.

The *planctus* is in double versicles throughout, except only versicle 14 (the last), which is a single. In this respect it is like the standard sequence. One slightly unusual feature – unusual at least at this late date – is the short 'double-cursus': the metrical form and the music of strophes 2 and 3 are repeated for 4 and 5. This reminiscence of the earliest (the so-called 'archaic') sequences fits in with the fact that 'Planctus ante nescia' has, as I said, *lai*-like characteristics: these are chiefly observable in the contours of the melody, which falls into short segments as did 'Dolorum solatium'. Thus each half of stanza 3 falls into two repeated sections of three members with an 'open' and a 'closed' cadence:

Ex. 45

(repeated as 3b, 5a, and 5b, with different words). The short descending figure (a 'sequence' in the modern musical sense) adds to the predominant sense of patterned repetition. The repetition takes place, once again, within a very stable tonal scheme which, though somewhat more varied and flexible, is extraordinarily similar to that of 'Dolorum solatium'. The mode is the same.

And again every single versicle has *g* for final.[42] Many cadence on *g* at
the half-versicle also (2, 3 and 4, for example); but a characteristic tonal
effect is that of a half-close at the half-versicle on a different degree of the scale.
Thus in strophe 6 the *d* is maintained in phrase 2, before the relaxation of
phrase 3 (to *a*? – or is this just a passing note?) and the finality of phrase 4,
on *g*.

Ex. 46

It is, incidentally, worth comparing this melody with one of the favourite
tunes of the *planctus cigni* (Ex. 38 above) for its play with the third-on-*c*:

Ex. 47

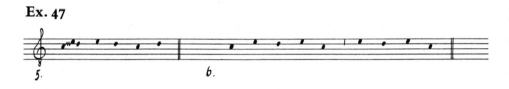

Generally speaking, however, the closer links of 'Planctus ante nescia' are
with 'Dolorum solatium', through the use of the *g*-triad (*g-b-d*) and its contrast
with quasi-harmonic formation on *f* (either *f-a-c* or *d-f-a*). Such a melody as
this (strophe 2) sums it up:

Ex. 48a

Compare with this the tonality of these phrases from Abelard's *planctus*:

[42] The characteristics of *g*-mode melody are discussed with many examples from chant,
chanson, *refrain* and popular song by U. Aarburg in *Festschrift Helmut Osthoff*, ed. W. Stauber
et al. (Tutzing 1969) 33–50, but without reference to *lai* and sequence modality.

Ex. 48b

The tritonal effect set up by the juxtaposition of *b* natural and *f* natural is, as I said earlier, characteristic of the numerous *lai*-melodies in the *g*-mode.

The melodic similarities between the two *planctus* led Lorenz Weinrich, who first drew attention to the existence of the Oxford version of 'Dolorum solatium', to posit a direct link between them. He argued that Godefroy of St Victor 'probably knew and utilized Abelard's . . . "Dolorum solatium" when he created his Marian lament'.[43] A wider acquaintance with the repertory of *lai* and *planctus* might have given him second thoughts. The similarities are real; but they arise from a larger situation. It is evident that there was a 'treasury' of melodic material – motifs and 'tunes' on which anyone might draw. Much work needs to be done on the musical vocabulary of sequence, *lai* and *planctus* before it will be safe to generalize further. But this much may be posited. The music of the Latin *lai* is formulaic; some of the formulas are shared with sequences (cf. 'Laudes crucis') and extensively used also in some *planctus* (whose borrowing does not, of course, stop there).[44] This richly various shared idiom has an unmistakable flavour of its own which is quite different on the one hand from the idioms of Gregorian chant in its various traditional forms, and on the other from the idioms of troubadour and trouvère song.[45] It is characterized by short motifs, often many times repeated with slight variations; by tonal stability, the *g*-mode being a favourite; by a syllabic and non-melismatic treatment of the text; and, consequently, by a fairly strong sense of the words as a significant presence.

One aspect of this presence which I have so far not mentioned is epitomized by the short quotation from 'Planctus ante nescia' in Ex. 45 above. The balance of the closely juxtaposed rhymes *florum/morum* and the parallel *gravis/clavis* gives a strong feeling of verbal harmony, composed of matching sonorities and matching accents, and reinforced by the terse sequential figure in the melody. It is natural to invoke again the term *armonia*, which I used

[43] Weinrich (1969), 485.
[44] There are perceptive analyses and comments by Harrison (1979), 83–7, in his discussion of 'Planctus ante nescia'. See also Stäblein (1975), 96, on the essential characteristics of *lai*-style (quoted p. 142 below).
[45] I return in chapter 14:1v below to the question of genre-styles within the trouvère repertoire. The position is far from clear-cut. The *pastourelle* in particular will not fall neatly into any of these stylistic categories.

extensively to describe the aural, not merely numerical, realization of 'number' in *la grande chanson courtoise* (chapter 1 above). But this is *armonia* with a difference: it is a *linked* 'harmony' in which words and music contribute together. Verbal accent plays a significant part in creating this 'harmony', and we feel that most of these succinct verbal/musical phrases have a rhythm, a definable rhythm (which is, of course, not at all the same as saying that the melodies must be measured into longs and shorts). At the same time there is a residual fluidity, a relic of a purely syllabic, non-accentual relationship. These two phrases from 'Planctus ante nescia', for instance, cannot be made perfectly parallel without some violence being done:

Ex. 49

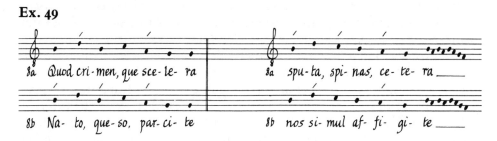

We find ourselves back with the paradox that the *lai*, like some sequences (especially the earlier, non-liturgical ones), and like the *planctus* when it adopts this style, hovers between the requirements of 'narrative music' – speed, self-effacement, flexibility, open-endedness – and the requirements of a closed artefact – pattern, 'character', fixity, balance, structure.[46]

Not all *lai*-type songs draw exclusively on the same melodic treasury as those just discussed. The 'free sequence' 'De profundis ad te', for instance, is a *d*-mode, not a *g*-mode, melody; it opens with the eight statements of the following double phrase – the passage is, in effect, sixteen statements of a decasyllabic line in alternately 'open' and 'closed' forms with a refrain after every fourth line:[47]

Ex. 50

---

[46] See also Harrison (1979), 83: 'If there is an element of truth in the hypothesis that the sequence had a secular prototype, this was probably a kind of verse-with-formulaic-music on a scale somewhere between a relatively short song and a relatively lengthy piece of hieratic chanting. On this and other grounds, the most likely prototype was the lay . . . a median between song and formally delivered prose . . .'

[47] *AH* x.54–5 (no. 66); Chevalier, 4238; Yearley (1981), 124. Transcription: Yearley (1983) III, 29–32, from B N n.a.lat. 3126, fols. 87–88. For this Troper from Nevers, see note 32 above. The melody of the *planctus* was not previously known: it derives, as Huglo observes, from the responsory 'Libera me' (from the Office for the Dead) and associated verses.

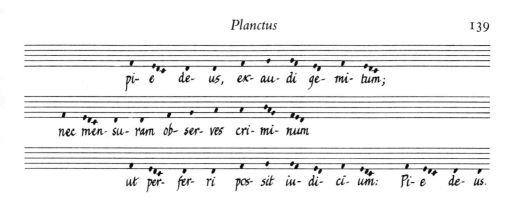

pi- e de- us, ex- au- di ge- mi- tum;

nec men- su- ram ob- ser- ves cri- mi- num

ut per- fer- ri pos- sit iu- di- ci- um: Pi- e de- us.

Merciful God, hear the groaning of those who call to you from the depths. Do not regard the measure of our offences lest we be unable to bear your judgement. Merciful God.

This is followed by other melodies predominantly in the *d*-mode, but not all so conjunct in their movement:[48]

Ex. 51

4a Ad me- den- dum con- tri- tis a- ni- mo

de- scen- dis- tis pa- tris im- pe- ri- o.

To heal those who are bruised in soul, you descended from the Father's kingdom.

Then, with curious abruptness, the style changes to a typical *g*-mode *lai*-melody.

Ex. 52

6a Ve, ve no- bis mi- se- ris se- ro pe- ni- ten- ti- bus

et de ne- gli- gen- ci - is tar- de iam ge- men- ti- bus.

Woe, woe, to us wretched beings who are too late repentant and for our negligences at this late hour are groaning.

---

[48] Lipphardt, *Die Weisen der lateinischen Osterspiele des 12. und 13. Jahrhunderts* (Kassel 1948), distinguishes an older tradition of *d-a* type melodies in the Latin *planctus* repertoire from later *f-c* and *g-d* types.

Melodies of this kind, already sufficiently described, continue for the remainder of the song. There are the usual *lai* repetitions – the two lines just
quoted, themselves repetitive, occur a further three times. There is however one curious feature. The melody to the climactic words *Miserere, miserere,
miserere nostri* is a single; it is also singular, starting as it does on *e*, rising to
d and ending on *f*, all of which melodic happenings are unique in this
section:

Ex. 53

Mi- se- re - re,   mi- se- re- re,   mi- se- re- re   nos- tri

The neumes are quite clearly heighted. There could, of course, be scribal
error; but the likelihood is that this melodic segment, which is not out of
keeping stylistically, does represent a direct, though rare, response to the
rhetoric of the text with its climax of repetition. Otherwise the relationship
of words and music is of the formal, patterned kind that we have come to
expect.

IV *Lai*

In the course of describing *planctus* written in forms which can in a broad sense
be called sequence-forms, to distinguish them from the strophic forms of
chanson and *cantio*, I have inevitably found myself frequently referring to
characteristics of the *lai*. In this final section of the chapter I wish to consider
the relation between words and music in the *lai* and especially in one
substantial Latin *lai*. But before this can be done something needs to be said
about this ubiquitous and confusing term.[49]

The first distinction that has to be made is between the narrative *lai* and the
lyrical *lai*. It is the narrative type to which Chaucer refers in the Prologue to
the *Franklin's Tale*:[50]

[49] Bec, *La lyrique française . . . une typologie* (1977–8), I.189ff, summarizes the types of French *lai*
and gives a bibliography, chiefly literary. The most comprehensive study is by Maillard
(1963), but this has to be supplemented by Fallows' lengthy article 'Lai' in *New Grove*, which
provides a complete check-list of the French *lai* and of the German *Leich*. The music of the
French *lais* was published in full by Jeanroy, Brandin and Aubry (1901); the edition is now
not wholly satisfactory. The numerous studies by Spanke (collected 1977) are, however, still
basic for the formal study of the genre. The Latin *lai* is not substantially covered by any of the
above. The category is indeed difficult to establish and to distinguish from the early
sequence. See, however, the list in Spanke (1936), section v, 'Sequenzenformen', 88–9; also
Stäblein (1975), 98 (n. 1012–15).
[50] Ed. Robinson, 135, lines 709–12.

> Thise olde gentil Britouns in hir dayes
> Of diverse aventures maden layes,
> Rymeyed in hir firste Briton tonge;
> Whiche layes with hir instrumentz they songe . . .

Such are the *lais* that Marie de France wrote in the late twelfth century, almost entirely in rhymed octosyllabic couplets like the courtly romance. (The question of whether they were ever sung belongs to the discussion of 'narrative melody' in chapter 6 below.) There may originally have been some connection between these narrative *lais* and the lyrical ones which are our concern here. The 'Breton *lai*' to which Marie and Chaucer refer was perhaps half-spoken, half-sung, a *chante–fable* like *Aucassin et Nicolette*, or perhaps a form in which a *note* (an improvised(?) instrumental composition) was directly related to an *aventure* (an interesting happening or event). None survive, and speculation is rife.[51]

The term 'lyrical *lai*' itself leaves room for further clarification since it is used both by medieval and by modern writers to refer to two different sorts of lyric. The first are usually labelled 'independent *lais*'; the second, 'Arthurian *lais*'.[52] The latter are mostly found fictionally embedded in the voluminous French prose-romances such as *Tristan*, where they are sung and/or played (since instrumental accompaniment of some sort is constantly mentioned) by the characters. They are formally as different as could be from the independent *lais*, being written in short strophes (much shorter than the chanson's), mostly quatrains.[53] It is only the first kind, the independent *lais*, which resemble the sequence. They are 'independent' in the sense that they are not given a literary context; the vernacular *lais* survive as individual items in major trouvère chansonniers,[54] where they are aptly placed because their thematic affinities are, with few exceptions, all with *la grande chanson courtoise* –

> Un descort vaurai retraire,
> s'il porroit ma dame plaire,
> mais tot li vient a contraire,
> kanques sai dire ne faire.   (Thomas Herier)

I should like to recount a *descort*, if it could please my lady; but whatever I can say or do is tedious to her.

They are also 'independent' in the sense suggested by the word *descort* – that is,

---

[51] See *Marie de France: Lais*, ed. A. Ewert (Oxford 1960), introd., p. xiii; Maillard (1963), 1–11, sets out the various theories of origin; see also Bec, 1.194. For *Aucassin et Nicolette*, see chapter 6:IV, Ex. 86, below. See also R. Bromwich, 'A Note on the Breton Lays' *MÆ* 26 (1957) 36–8; and Bullock-Davies, 'Breton Lay' – a detailed and stimulating discussion.

[52] Maillard (1963) 84; Bec, 1.191.

[53] They are thought to be older than the prose-romances in which they occur (Maillard (1963), 85). The oldest source of the prose *Tristan* is *c.* 1230 (Maillard (1959), 341), and sixty MSS attest its popularity right up to the Renaissance. See chapter 6:IV, Ex. 89 below for a musical example.

[54] The largest number of independent *lais* is in the Chansonnier de Noailles (Source 30).

formally independent. A number of French *lai*-writers refer to their poems by
this term, which is borrowed from the troubadours. The *discordia* may be the
effect produced by the perpetual change of the form of the strophe; it is a
defining feature of the *lai* as it is of the sequence, and this is possibly why the
word was chosen to denote certain *lais*.[55]

There will be opportunity in chapter 14 to return to the independent
vernacular *lai*. At this point I will simply quote from Bruno Stäblein's succinct
characterization of the *lai* as a distinct musical genre.[56] The *lai*, he says, has
essentially more freedom of movement than even the 'archaic' sequence,
which compared with the *lai* looks already like a simplification. The features
of the *lai* are: that it is not a narrative; that it is often larger than the sequence;
that it is not strophic but is composed of double (or treble, or quadruple)
versicles; that the progressive 'run' of the versicles is often interrupted by the
repetition of material used earlier; that, moreover, the *lai* may repeat single
phrases of melody *within* the versicle up to four or five times; that it has a
distinctive melodic idiom consisting of short, telling (*schlagkräftig*) phrases,
catchy and often repeated, constructed out of single notes mostly, and rarely
using more than two to a syllable – in short, a skimming, dance-like (*tänzerisch
beschwingt*) style that carries the audience along with it, is essentially
independent of the words, and may also be instrumental.

Stäblein offers this excellent epitome as a characterization of the earliest *lais*
in the French vernacular, such as the *Lai des Amants*, the *Lai de la Rose*, and the
Note Martinet.[57] It serves equally well as a summary of the Latin *lais*. In fact,
the two (vernacular and Latin) are not to be regarded as distinct and separate
forms. The general similarities are unmistakable; and the survival of
contrafacts puts the issue beyond doubt. To take an example, one of the only
two Provençal *lais*, the *Lai Markiol*, provided the metrical–musical pattern for
the French 'Flour ne glais' (R192), which in one manuscript has the rubric *Un
lai de Nostre Dame contre le Lai Markiol*.[58] The same pattern was also provided

[55] Another possible meaning of *descort* is a poem with different stanzas in different languages.
On the term see especially R. Baum, 'Le descort ou l'anti-chanson', *Mélanges . . . Jean
Boutière* (Liège 1971), 75–98, who summarizes all previous scholarship. His positive conclusion emerges as an 'anti-chanson' hypothesis: 'A côté de la chanson régulière et qui suit le
principe de la régularité, ils conçoivent la chanson irrégulière, qui suit celui de l'irrégularité.'
The irregularity may be of structure, of music, or of meaning, or a combination of these
elements.
[56] Stäblein (1975), 96.
[57] For the music of these *lais*, see Jeanroy *et al.* (1901), nos. xx (p. 123) and xxi (p. 127), in
modern square notation.
[58] On the contrafacts, see Stäblein (1975), 96, footnote 993. The *Lai Markiol (Marquiol)* is
printed from two MSS in de la Cuesta, 765ff, with English translation following. Discussion in Maillard (1963), 241ff; F. Gennrich, 'Zwei altfranzösische Lais', *Studi medievali* n.s. 15
(1942), 1–68, with modal transcription of 'Flors ne glais' (pp. 4ff). Spanke (1938: repr.
1977), 163, discusses Abelard's *Planctus* III and *Lai des pucelles* (no music). Vecchi (1951)
gives the *lai* with its melody (from Chansonnier de Noailles) and reconstructs the melody for
the *planctus* (Vat.Reg. 288) by combining the imprecisely pitched neumes with the pitches of
Noailles.

with a Latin text by Philip the Chancellor; it is a moral satire, 'Veritas, equitas'.[59] I give the opening of the Provençal *lai* and of the Latin *lai* to show the closeness of the contrafact to the original (it does not matter which is which, since the numerical–metrical–musical pattern is the essential thing):

Ex. 54

Gent m'e-nais quand del cais

Ve- ri- tas e- qui- tas

en eis lais Mar-qui- òl.

lar- gi- tas cor- ru- it;

Non cuid mais jorns m'en-grais

fal- si- tas pra- vi- tas

ni m'a- pais si com sòl;

par- ci- tas vi- gu- it;

per que n'ai dòl et ai còr mòl.

ur- ba- ni- tas e- va- nu- it.

Provençal: I am pleased that from my mouth comes forth Marquiol's lay. I do not think that any day can ever feed me and sate me as this; and yet I am full of sorrow and my heart is full of pity.

Latin: Truth, equity, generosity are destroyed; falseness, wickedness, miserliness have flourished; true civility has vanished away.

It would, incidentally, be hard to find a neater demonstration than these three *lais* provide of the truth – by now, I hope, a truism – that the relation between the poems and the melody is a purely formal one, a matter of numbered notes and syllables. The Provençal poet is longing for a secret kiss (*un bais, sol a sol*); the northern French poet fears that we will all be damned if the Blessed Virgin's prayers do not rescue us; and Philip the Chancellor lashes out at corrupt clergy, patrons of Caiaphas (*Cayphe fautores*). The same melody serves for each purpose.

---

[59] The Florence M S version of 'Veritas, equitas' is in Anderson (1978b) no. κ62, with English translation (pp. lxxxiv ff). Ex. 54 is taken from the Egerton Chansonnier, fol. 28v. 'Gent menais' (Pillet–Carstens, 428), see de la Cuesta, 765, from two M S S. The version in the text is from the Chansonnier du Roi (Source 28), fol. 212, which is also a principal source of trouvère music. Transl.: de la Cuesta, 783.

v Conclusion: the Song of the Flood

The Latin *lai* which I wish to analyse by way of summarizing the chapter is
'Omnis caro peccaverat'. It is a song of the Flood, describing God's dealings
with Noah. Despite the fact that it appears in four insular sources, three of
them with music, it remains virtually unknown. Apart from 'Samson, dux
fortissime', it is the most ambitious of the Latin *lais* surviving from thirteenth-
century Britain.[60] The *Song of the Flood* is a long piece and has a large design. In
order to give a sense of this, it will be necessary to quote the text in full and to
give a substantial part of the melody.

Ex. 55a

```
1a  Om-nis ca- ro  pec- ca- ve- rat,       vi- am su- am  cor-ru- pe- rat;
 b  Hinc con-di- tor  i-  ra- sci- tur,    in-tus do- lo-  re  tan-gi- tur;
 c  'Me  co-ram ca-ro  cor- ru- it,        ho- mo  tur- pe  de-si- pu- it;

 a  ho- mo de- um  re- li- que- rat,       lex na- tu- re  pe- ri-  e- rat.
 b  qua-si  de se  con-que-ri- tur         et  ad No- e  sic lo- qui- tur:
 c  le- gem na-tu- re  pol- lu- it,        nil ni- si  mor-tem me-ru- it.

2a  Ut  sci- at  hu- ma- ni- bus           lo- cu- tum fu- is- se,
 b  Stu-por et  pro- di- gi- um,           quod su- per- bit  ci- nis;
 c  Ho- mi- nes  dis- per-de- re           cum ter- ra  pro- vi-di;

 a  pe- ni- tet me  pe- ni- tus            ho- mi- nem fe-cis- se.
 b  co- ram me mor- ta- li- um             im- mi- net  iam fi- nis.
 c  ti- bi  vo- lo  par- ce- re            nam te  ius-tum vi-di.
```

[60] 'Omnis caro': Anderson L160. The sources are: the Dublin Troper, fols. 126–7 (not listed
by Anderson); Paris BN fr. 25408 fols. 116–17; Gonville & Caius MS 240, pp. 12–13 (not
known to Hesbert (1966)); BL Cotton Titus A. xx, fol. 70v (no music). The song has not
been edited entire, though Hesbert (1966) prints the melody and the text separately (pp.
97–105). He observes that the melody resembles many ancient sequences in Mode 7 (*g*
authentic) such as 'Epiphaniam', which survives in the Dublin Troper, and dozens of other
MS sources, and 'Sancti spiritus adsit' (some eighty MSS including Dublin). My
transcription is from the Dublin Troper (Source 7) fols. 126–7. The notation is in the same
style as that of the preceding sequences; the copying is professional but was evidently done at
speed; the staves are hand- (not rastrum-) ruled. The distinction between breve and
semibreve-shaped rhomb is neither consistent nor clear.

3 a Tu- que tu- i fi- li- i   ves- tris cum ux- or- i- bus,
   b Vos in- dem-nes e- ri- tis   cum con-demp-nem no- xi- os;
   c Per-dam vo- la- ti- li- a,   per- dam om-nem bes- ti- am;

   a ni-chil es- tis no-xi- i   tan- tis in ex- ces- si- bus,
   b oc- to re-ma- ne- bi- tis,   om-nes per-dam a- li- os.
   c pau-ca se- mi- na- ri- a   vo- bis- cum cus-to- di- am.

4 a Er- go, No- e, con- ci- to,   ar- cham ti- bi fa- ci- to;
   b Le- vi- ga sa- ga- ci ter   et con- iun-ge pa- ri- ter;
   c fac-que man-si- un- cu-las,   plu- res et non pau- cu-las,

   a de li- gnis e- li- gi- to   que sunt a- pti- o- ra.
   b o- pus fac vi- ri- li- ter,   to- ta vi la- bo- ra;
   c ar- che per par-ti-cu- las –   non te tar-det mo- ra!

5 a Li- ni- es in- trin-se- cus   ar- cham et ex- trin-se- cus
   b ut in a- qua flu- vi- da   sit for- tis et so- li- da
   c Ci- bos a- ni- man- ti- um   in- fe- res in- tran-ti- um,

   a te- na- ci bi- tu- mi- ne,
   b pi- cis ne- xa glu- ti- ne.
   c pe- co- ris cum ho- mi- ne.

1a   All flesh had sinned, had perverted its way;
    Man had forsaken God; the law of nature had perished.
 b   At this the Creator was angry; his heart was touched with sadness.
    He lamented as it were for himself and spoke thus to Noah:
 c   'In my presence flesh has gone to destruction; man has acted with base folly;
    He has polluted the law of nature and deserved nothing but death.

2a   (I wish) him to know that I have spoken to him as a man;
    I repent deeply of having made man.
 b   Astounding marvel! Dust is taking on proud airs.
    The end of all things mortal is at hand, and in my presence.
 c   I have planned the destruction of men, and of the earth with them;
    You I wish to spare, for I have seen that you are righteous.

3a   You and your sons and your wives,
     You have no sin in you amongst these great evils.
 b   You will be saved when I sentence the wicked.
     You eight will survive; all the rest I shall destroy.
 c   I shall destroy all things that fly, I shall destroy every animal;
     A few only, to breed for the future, shall I keep safe with you.

4a   Therefore Noah, speedily make yourself an ark!
     From your store of timber choose the best for the job!
 b   Plane the wood skilfully and joint it evenly!
     Perform your task with energy and work with all your strength.
 c   And make little cabins – plenty, not just a few –
     In every corner of the ark! Don't allow any delay!

5a   Daub both the inside and the outside of the ark with strong pitch,
 b   So that, bound together with this tarry glue, it will ride firm and stable in the
     moving waters.
 c   Load on food for the living creatures who are embarking, beasts and men.

6a   Bestias inferius   Put the animals down below and the
     et aves superius   birds up top with you.
     tecum collocabis.
 b   Ostium in latere   If you are wise you will arrange to have a
     deorsum componere   door in the side of the ark, low down.
     prudens procurabis.
 b¹ Fenestram in culmine   And on the top deck you will construct a
     ut fruaris lumine   window so that you may enjoy the light.
     sursum preparabis.⁶¹
 c   Culmen sursum ducito,   Put a roof on the top, and at last you will
     et tandem in cubito   complete the ark within one cubit.
     archam consummabis.

7a   Trecentorum cubitorum   The ark will be 300 cubits long,
     arche [longitudo],
 b   Quinquaginta cubitorum   fifty cubits wide,
     erit [latitudo],
 c   et triginta cubitorum   and thirty high.
     erit altitudo.⁶²

8a   Hanc intrabis,   By entering the ark and living there you
     habitabis,   will avoid the danger that threatens –
     et vitabis
     imminens periculum.
 b   Tu et nati   You and the sons that have been given
     tibi dati   you, born to keep the world going.
     procreati
     ut sustentent seculum.

⁶¹ Strophe 6, versicle *b*¹ is unique to the Dublin Troper.
⁶² Strophe 7, versicles *a* and *b*: M S reads *latitudo* and *longitudo* respectively, inverting the proper
   order.

c Intret sexus
   cuius nexus
   per amplexus
   dilatabit populum.

Let male and female embark; their intertwining embrace will multiply the people.

9a De mundis animantibus
    in singulis generibus
    tolles septena paria.

From pure living creatures in their several kinds you will take out seven couples.

b De immundisque macula
   feda sit simplex copula,
   serves ut seminaria.

From the impure who are loathsomely tainted, let a single couple [be chosen], so that you may be sure of breeders for the future.

c Tu cum ista compleveris –
   vide moram ne feceris –
   descendit a me pluvia.

When you have done all this – see you make no delay! – I shall send down rain.

10a Archam cum ingressus eris –
     vide moram ne feceris –
     de supernis ego pluam
     et omne nefas diluam.

When you have entered the ark – see you make no delay! – I shall rain down from the heavens and wash away all wickedness.

b Quater denos simul dies
   nulla tenebit requies;
   incessanter ymbres ruent
   omnem humum superfluent.

For forty days together there shall be no respite whatsoever; violent rains will tumble down without cease and overflow the whole earth.

c Vita, salus et pax erit
   illis quos archa clauserit;
   et qui foris eam erunt
   omnes discrimen perferunt.'

Life, salvation and peace will be the lot of those whom the ark encloses; those who are outside are all exposed to danger.'

11a Archa parata
     Noe mandata
     domini peregit.

Noah got the ark ready and fulfilled the Lord's commands;

b Et bene nota
   quod unum iota
   justus non infregit.

note this well – that righteous man did not break one iota of them;

c Omnia dicta
   fide non ficta
   complere sategit.

with true faith he was busy in carrying out all his orders.

Ex. 55b

12 a Im-bres ru- unt, nu- bes plu- unt, un- de flu- unt
    b Cre-scunt a- que cir- cum-qua-que flu- mi- na- que
    c Sic im- mun-dum car-ne mun-dum in pro- fun-dum

a   la- ben- tes cum im- pe- tu.
b   cum im- men-so stre- pi- tu.
c   per- is- se cum so- ni- tu.

13   In- vol- vun-tur flu- cti- bus   iu- ve- nes cum se- ni- bus,

fi- li- e   cum ma- tri- bus.

14a   Sic mer- gun- tur im- pi- i,   ma- le si- bi con- sci- i,

pa- ren- tes et fi- li- i.

b   So- los sal- vat ar- cha ius- tos   cu- ius fi- des est et cus- tos

de- i mi- se- ri- cor- di- a.

12a   The rainstorms hurtle down, the clouds pour down water, the waves overflow, running strongly.
  b   The waters increase on every side; the rivers also with a huge roaring.
  c   Thus perishes the carnal world with a resounding fall into the depths.

13   Young men and old, girls and their mothers, are swallowed up in the waves.

14a   Thus the sinful are drowned, parents and children, knowing their own evil.
  b   The righteous alone are saved in the ark; its security and guard is the mercy of God.

Although it is generally true, as Stäblein says, that the *French* songs classed as *lais* are not narrative, this does not hold for the Latin (cf. 'Samson, dux fortissime'). The *Song of the Flood* tells a dramatic story, and one which in the Middle Ages would have had a significance beyond the merely historical. In Genesis the story is part of Hebrew myth and legend; but in medieval biblical interpretation it was essentially Christian. Typologically, every person and event in the Old Testament pre-figures something in the New. In the story of Noah there are two important prefigurations. The Flood is a type of the Last Judgement, when once more God will separate the just from the unjust and the world will come to an end. And the Ark is a type of the Church: *ecclesia est navis* (the 'nave' of the Church preserves this typology in its very name). In the Ark of the Church all the just, like Noah, will be saved, whilst the unjust will perish in the primal flood. This prefiguration (*figura*) certainly explains why the song ends not with the subsiding of the waters, the flight of the dove, the new earth and the disembarkation of Noah and his family but at the very height of the flood, with the drowning of the impious and the assured salvation of those in the Ark – *Solos salvat archa iustos*. The *Song of the Flood* may be compared with 'Samson, dux' in this respect too. Samson is a traditional type of Christ, and his triumph is Christ's triumph.

This episode from the drama of salvation is embodied in an elaborately constructed musical and poetic edifice. Like all *lais* and 'free' sequences, it is built out of a number of varied stanzas each of which may be repeated. 'Omnis caro' differs from others in that each of the stanzas, with one exception (see note 61), is repeated three times – which could have an obvious, probably a too obvious, symbolic meaning. This makes for formal unity. On the other hand, the strophe (the stanza-form) itself is subtly varied: each one has a different combination of syllable-count and rhyme-scheme (except that strophe 8 is repeated as 12 and 9 as 14). Another 'artificial' feature is that scarcely a single rhyme or rhyme-sound is repeated throughout the whole poem of 128 lines. The author is so strikingly consistent in this it must be deliberate. 'Samson dux' seems to have taken up a similar challenge; but some *lais* work on an entirely opposite principle. 'Regina clementie' deliberately eschews variety: not only is it written throughout in the so-called 'goliardic measure' of 13 syllables (7pp + 6p), but it manages its 86 lines with only two rhymes (*-ata* and *-isti*), the change of rhyme having no apparent relation to the *lai*-like structure (metrical–musical) of the piece.[63]

The musical form of 'Omnis caro' is, as is usual in the *lai* and unusual in the courtly chanson of the troubadours and trouvères, closely and continuously linked with the metrical form. I speak for the moment chiefly of the larger aspects of form, stanza-building and strophic repetition (the internal structure of the line will come later). The melodic unit is the line; a strophe of four lines has four melodic phrases contributing to a whole. Since in this song each strophe form is repeated three times, each melody is also precisely repeated. Conversely, as each strophe has a pattern different from all the rest, with the exceptions mentioned, each strophe has a different melody.

The melody is analogous to the metre in another way also. Just as metrical diversity is achieved by small but significant variations in line-length and

[63] 'Regina clemencie' (Anderson L43); to the texts listed in Anderson should be added BL Harley 524, fol. 65. The Reading Abbey version (Harley 978) is the only one with notated melody. Text printed Mone, II.411. See also Handschin (1949), 59.

rhyme-scheme, so melodic diversity arises from variation within a distinctly restricted ambit – the by now familiar *g*-triad, set off occasionally by the conspicuous use of *f* natural. (It is, I must repeat, not easy to say how thirteenth- and fourteenth-century ears would have reacted to this tonality and this contrast; but one thing we can say with confidence is 'How un-Gregorian!')

Ex. 56

The extreme tonal stability appears in analysis of the cadences: the forty-two cadences of the first thirteen strophes (all, that is, except the last) are with two exceptions on *g*, *b* or *d*. In the two instances when *f* is used, it is with an evidently open 'first-time-bar' effect, or transitionally (strophes 4 to 5). The melodies themselves tend to be triadic, and it is amazing how the composer manages to go on devising motifs within the close limits he has set himself; twenty-five distinct motifs can be identified in the fourteen strophes. Part of the art of composing *lais* (and this remains pre-eminently true of Machaut's also) is to show inventiveness. In strophe 1, for instance, the melodic form is AA^{1}BC; in strophe 2, using new material, ABAB^1; in strophe 3, new again, ABB^{1}C. Given the evidently deliberate search for continuous novelty, renovation, a copiousness of invention such as any rhetorician would have approved, one is entitled to ask why certain motifs *are* brought back. There seems no reason in narrative logic why, for instance, strophe 3 should chime with strophe 5 or either with strophe 13; even less, why the melody which in the first strophe carried the striking statements of man's corruption and God's judgements on it should be used again, somewhat prominently, for the tedious business of carpenter's measurements – 'The ark will be 300 cubits long, fifty cubits wide', etc. (strophe 7).

The melodic structure of this *lai* seems, in fact, to obey laws of musical logic which have little if anything to do with the 'drama' of the story of the Flood. In musical logic the first five strophes obviously form a whole, a total melodic shape. A symptom of this is the sense of rise and climax given by the triadic pattern of initial notes: *g-b-d-g'-g'*. The role of strophe 4 as the climax of these five strophes is emphasized by the unusual ascending scale ending on high *f* and leading (after the necessary repeats) to the 'concluding' strophe (5) which neatly resolves the tensions as it works down the triad to the 'final', *g*.

Ex. 57

In the context of this analysis the melodic repetition of B and C from strophe 3 creates the effect of musical rhyme and makes musical sense.

The generalization that the musical logic and the dramatic logic of 'Omnis caro' are quite unconnected[64] calls for one qualification. One cannot fail to recognize a sense of mutual climax at the end of the piece, strophe 14, when the composer, having denied himself the use of the top *g* since its use in the first climax (strophes 4 and 5), lifts the melody up an octave for (a), with its even more emphatic repetition (b).

Ex. 58

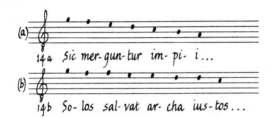

The *armonia* of the *lai* (to repeat Dante's term for a set of beautiful proportions) must also take into account the internal structure of the line. The question of the proper accentuation of Latin in the period is, as previously said, an extremely difficult one; and the question whether Latin accent affects, or should affect, melody is no easier.[65]

The opening of 'Omnis caro' will provide a good example or two of the problem:

> (1a) Ómnis cáro péccavérat
> víam súam córrupérat
> hómo déum réliquérat
> léx natúre périerat.

---

[64] The same generalization applies to the even more dramatic story of Samson in the Latin *lai* 'Samson, dux fortissime', Reading Abbey MS, fols. 2–4v (Anderson L42).

[65] Many writers assume without demur that rhythm is determined by word-accent (see below, ch. 15:1).

(1b)   Hínc cónditór iráscitúr
       Íntus dolóre tángitùr
       qüasi de sé conquéritùr
       ét ad Nóe sic lóquitùr.

There appears to be a genuine ambivalence in this strophe between iambic and trochaic metre. Of course the ambivalence may arise, in part, from our ignorance of how thirteenth-century Latin was pronounced. But there is an instance here that fortunately removes the doubt from a purely subjective or ignorant position and puts it on solid ground. The fourth line of 1a and the third line of 1c both use the word *nature*:

    4   léx natúre périerat . . .
   11   légem natúré pollúit

Whether an iambic or a trochaic accentual scansion is chosen for strophe 1, *nature* will have its 'correct' stress violated in one line or the other. This opens various possibilities – either the predominance of the metre following a regular scheme; or predominance of some 'absolute' musical scheme (i.e. a rhythmic pattern inherent in the melody); or a more varied and flexible manner of interpretation in which there is a slightly unpredictable interplay between words and music.

The Dantean notion of an *armonia* goes some way to explain what *lai*-writers as well as trouvères were trying to do, I think. But, unlike the courtly *chanson*, the *lai* embodied other traditions which may explain its essential individuality. 'Narrative melody' is one of them. The *lai* is a narrative music. Some of the longer French ones very obviously betray (or for special reasons deliberately parade) their origins, jogging along in the unstoppable way that probably characterized many a clerk's or jongleur's performances. I take as an example that portion of the *Lai de l'Ancien et du Nouveau Testament* by Ernoul le vielle which briefly tells of Noah and the Flood: in it a single snatch of melody is repeated eighteen times, with one break in the middle.[66]

Ex. 59

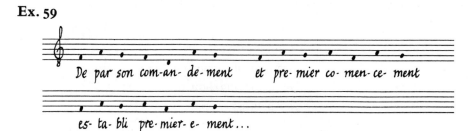

De par son com-an- de- ment   et pre- mier co- men- ce- ment

es- ta- bli pre- mier- e- ment . . .

By means of his commandment, at the first beginning,
he established first of all . . .

[66] Jeanroy *et al.* (1901), 114; I have given the readings of the MS, the Chansonnier de Noailles. See also chapter 6:IV, Ex. 88, and chapter 14:V, Ex. 189.

A more interesting example is the Latin *lai* 'Flos pudicitie' with French text also underlaid (from the Arundel Songs: see Ex. 24 above). Strophe 4 consists of the six-fold repetition of the following phrase:

Ex. 60

Mo-do mi- ro si- ne vi- ro pro- le fe- cun- da- ris

In a marvellous way, without a man, you are pregnant with a child

There seems to be a compromise here perhaps between the purely functional – one might say 'vehicular' – style of the French *Lai de l'Ancien* melody and a more truly musical melody.

What may seem to us the obvious characteristics of melody designed for the purpose of telling a story may not coincide with the medieval reality. Indeed, in chapters 6 and 7 we shall see that they often do not. But there are three things that may safely be said about 'narrative' melody: (i) that it will consist largely of single notes or short note-groups, since melismatic melody makes it impossible to follow the story; (ii) that it is likely to have 'open' and 'closed' forms (i.e. differentiated cadences) because language itself has such forms (e.g. 'commas' and full-stops); (iii) that it will be formulaic (that is, will involve the repetition of stock motifs), since the continuous invention of new melody in a long narrative, one lasting some hours perhaps, would be humanly impossible. Other questions, relating to rhythm and melodic contour, are best left open. The various *lais*, and *lai*-like *planctus* and sequences, that we have been considering in this chapter conform to the three narrative criteria I have named. The third, the use of formulas, phrases belonging to common stock, needs systematic investigation; but even without that one becomes increasingly aware of remembered phrases. A comparison of the opening phrases of 'Samson, dux fortissime' and the *Song of the Flood* is instructive:[67]

Ex. 61

Sam-son dux for- tis- si- me,   Om- nis ca- ro pec- ca- ve- rat,

vi- ctor po- ten- tis- si- me,   vi- am su- am cor- ru- pe- rat;

[67] For the sources of 'Samson', see chapter 13, note 60, below. Compare also kindred phrases in the sequence 'Laudes crucis' (extract in Ex. 34 above), such as strophe 10 phrase 2; 11, 2; 12, 3. For Ex. 61, see note 64 above (*Samson*) and Ex. 55 above (*Flood*).

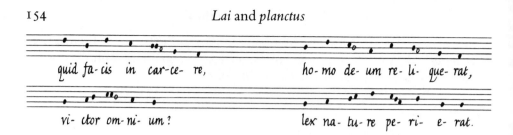

quid fa-cis in car-ce- re,   ho- mo de- um re- li- que- rat,

vi- ctor om- ni- um?   lex na- tu- re pe- ri- e- rat.

There is no reason to suppose direct borrowing from one by the other. The assumption of a common stock is much more likely. The same is doubtless true of a precise melodic parallel between the second, *lai*-like, section of the *conductus* 'Alto consilio' (strophe 4: *occultans potentiam* – see Ex. 13 in chapter 2, above) and the *Song of the Flood* (strophe 8: *imminens periculum*); both use the phrase *g-a-b-g-b-c-d*.

The 'narrative' melody is what keeps a *lai* moving, fluent, dynamic. By comparison the movement of a high courtly chanson – with its alternance (though not regular alternation) of single notes and small melismas, its conjunct melody and its more elusive tonality – is leisurely, even clogged. This narrative movement (often combined, as in *Samson* and the *Song of the Flood*, with actual story-telling) enables us to experience the patterns quickly, easily, repetitively.

How, then, in conclusion, may we define the 'aesthetic' (if this is not too grand a term) of the *lai*, i.e. the composer–poet's attitude to his art and our proper response to it? The *lai* is, first, a sort of aural geometry, an *armonia*. The strong sense of pattern derives in part from verbal factors: (i) a continuously displayed rhythmic contrast between strophes, between iambic and trochaic metres, between lines of from four to eight syllables, with weak or strong endings, disposed in units of varying length; (ii) a *discontinuous* but not infrequent ambivalence in the stresses of the individual line; (iii) the play of rhyme. Parallel to these verbal patterns, and coinciding with them in their larger structures, are musical patterns: they have their own relations, echoes, contrasts, building up into a 'net' of sounds that fits perfectly over the 'net' of words but has a different mesh. But 'net' and 'mesh' are static images, whereas the *lai* is nothing if not dynamic. It owes its dynamic energy to the narrative element, especially the 'narrative melody' which I have described. So, perhaps, an analogy with another of the medieval arts of number, fanciful as it might seem, may help to convey the combination of pattern and flow. I have constantly invoked the art of Arithmetic in this chapter, and just now the image of Geometry. But it is Astronomy which is nearest to music in its patterned measuring of time. The stars – 'fixt they are nam'd, but with a name untrue,/For they all move, and in a Daunce . . .'

To return to earth, sequence, *planctus* and *lai* are harder to define and analyse than the high courtly chanson. But 'number' in its various senses is the key to all. In none is the musician governed by words *as words* – that is, as entities having individual meanings, individual sounds. In the *grand chant*, as I see it, an elaborate and particular melody is devised to a numerical Idea, the *musica* of which is also realized in the verbal 'music' of the poem. In the *lai*, short, telling, tuneful melodies, evidently derived from a common treasury, are cleverly diversified; they become the flexible vehicle for elaborate verbal patterns. The words and the music in this baffling genre are not mutually responsive in any obvious modern way; but theirs is not the cool 'non-relationship' of the chanson. The new 'rhythmical' Latin verse and the new (or newly recorded) melodic idioms of the *lai* make contact in a dazzling interplay.

PART II
RELATIONS OF SPEECH, ACTION, EMOTION AND MEANING

FOREWORD

In the preceding chapters I have attempted to uncover the 'world of mathematics' in the principal forms of Latin and vernacular song from *la grande chanson courtoise* to the stately and yet vivacious *lai*. There has, I think, been no distortion in presenting these songs as mainly compositions of Number. Only the *planctus*, or lament, might seem to raise issues which need discussion in other terms, and to this we shall return in chapter 10. However, it would be strange indeed if every aspect of words and music in the period could be embraced within this single concept. The following chapters display a multiplicity and variety of relations briefly indicated by the heading above – 'speech, action, emotion and meaning'. Words and music combine differently in the courtly *caroles*, the *vitae sanctorum*, the elaborate chants of the Palm Sunday ritual, and Christmas 'plays' of Rouen Cathedral, to mention only a few typical examples. The 'aesthetic of Number' will not be found altogether superseded. Far from it: in some instances it provides the unquestioned basis of composition. But it comes under pressures and into circumstances which hitherto we have not had to consider.

5

THE DANCE-SONG

We shall not go seriously wrong if we think of the art of dancing as having as wide a range of interest, skill, social use and aesthetic appeal in the early Middle Ages as it has today.[1] Between the courtly *carole* –

> A lady karolede hem that hyghte
> Gladnesse, [the] blisfull and the lighte[2]

– and the trained antics of a visiting jongleur's bear there was a whole world of saltation and delight. There was, indeed, as might be expected, one kind of dance, or dance-idea, which is not dreamt of in our present-day philosophy: the dance of the heavens. The 'sweet symphony' (*la dolce sinfonia di Paradiso*) is often expressed in medieval writers, and supremely in Dante, under the form of a dance. In the *Paradiso*,

those who take part in the dance do so to symbolize their joyful participation in the Divine Order. The saints in the Heaven of the Fixed Stars are dancing *caroles* . . . Dancing is not confined to Paradise itself. The image is used often elsewhere to signify unity and joy. For instance, near the end of the *Purgatorio*, when Dante, now in the Earthly Paradise, sees the Divine Pageant. With it come three ladies dancing – *tre donne in giro*. They are the three theological virtues (Faith, Hope and Love) dressed in white, green and red (xxix.121).[3]

Dancing is simply another manifestation of the all-embracing, all-pervading concept of *musica*. Generally speaking, the descriptions of the dance as a spiritual activity tell us as little about actual dancing in this sublunary world as descriptions of angelic music tell us about the practice of polyphony, or

---

[1] I am indebted to recent essays on aspects of European dance-song: in Dronke, *Medieval Lyric* (1968), ch. 6, concentrating on its importance for medieval lyric; in Axton, *European Drama* (1974), ch. 3, 'Dancing-game', i.e. the dramatic activity; and in Greene, *Early English Carols* (1977), Introduction, ch. 11 'Carol as Dance-song', with numerous quotations. References to the earlier literature are available in these studies; but of particular interest are: Bédier, 'Les plus anciennes danses' (1906); Chambers, *Medieval Stage* (1903); Sahlin, *La carole médiévale* (1940). See also *New Grove* articles 'Carol' and 'Carole' (Stevens) and 'Dance', III.1 (Brainard), with bibliographies. The latter does not perhaps sufficiently distinguish the genre of dance-*song* (my sole concern in this chapter) from that of the instrumental dance. The question whether dance-songs were accompanied by instruments has not been systematically investigated. But see C. Page's forthcoming book, *Harmonia: Voices and Instruments in Medieval France*.
[2] Chaucer, *The Romaunt of the Rose*, lines 745–6 (all references are to Robinson's second edn).
[3] Stevens (1968), 3.

monophony, in thirteenth-century courts and cathedrals. More to our present purpose are accounts like the following, which, purporting to instruct us in the nature of the celestial motions by allegorizing dances on earth, in fact do precisely the reverse:

Per choreae autem circuitionem voluerunt intelligi firmamenti revolutionem: per manuum complexionem, elementorum connexionem: per sonum cantantium, harmoniam planetarum resonantium: per corporis gesticulationem, signorum motionem: per plausum manuum, vel pedum strepitum, tonitruorum crepitum.[4]

By the circling of the dance moreover they wished the revolution of the heavens to be understood; by the joining of hands the linking of the elements; by the sound of singers the harmony of the resounding planets; by bodily gestures, the movements of the constellations; by hand-clapping or the stamping of feet, the crashing of thunder.

From which may be inferred the existence in the first half of the twelfth century of a round-dance in which the participants held hands; it was a dance-*song*, punctuated evidently by the clapping of hands and the stamping of feet, and may have had some mime in it (*corporis gesticulationem*).

Dance-song, in fact, not the whole range of dance, is what we are concerned with in this chapter. I should like to consider how the relationship between words and notes is conditioned by the presence of an element of which elsewhere there is less need to take account – the element of movement. In the first part of the chapter I shall describe the main types of dance-song which we know existed, their poetic texts and the social function they performed. After that, I shall turn to the music of the dance-song, its notation and known characteristics; and, finally, to the words and melodies in their inter-relationship.

Any social history of the dance must distinguish, for the period 1100–1400 as for other periods, between professional dances and social dances. The first are danced as an exhibition before spectators; they are performances. The second are danced for the amusement and delight of the dancers themselves. The historian of twentieth-century dance might find that he is much better informed about professional than about ordinary social, sociable, dancing. The reverse is true of the Middle Ages.[5] The information often comes from account-books and tells us, for example, merely that a Venetian dancer named John Katerine was paid the huge sum of six pounds, thirteen shillings and fourpence for dancing before King Richard II.[6] The excessive size of some of

---

[4] Honorius of Autun, *Gemma Animae*, lib. I, cap. 139 (*PL* 172. 587), cited by Gougaud (1914), 16–17. Honorius lived in the mid twelfth century, apparently near Regensburg.

[5] Information about professional dancing can be gleaned from many sources; see Faral, *Jongleurs* (1910), especially 90–2; Salmen, *Fahrende Musiker* (1960); Bullock-Davies, *Menestrallorum* (1978); Sachs, *History of Dance* (1963), 250 (*joculatores*) and *passim*; Jusserand, *Wayfaring Life* (1950), 116–18; Chambers, *Medieval Stage* (1903), 1.70–1; etc.

[6] Cited by Jusserand, 117, from Frederick Devon, *Issues of the Exchequer* (London 1837), 212. John Katerine is not among the household musicians of Richard II (see R. Rastall in *RMA Research Chronicle* 4 (1964) 23–5) and was presumably on a visit.

these payments makes one wonder whether they do not sometimes cloak rewards for other activities. Another difficulty arises from the fact that dancing as such is not always distinguishable from general acrobatics:[7]

There were the *tombeors*, *tombesteres* or *tumbleres*, acrobats and contortionists, who twisted themselves into incredible attitudes, leapt through hoops, turned somersaults, walked on their heads, balanced themselves in perilous positions. Female tumblers took part in these feats, and several districts had their own characteristic modes of tumbling, *le tour français*, *le tour romain*, *le tour de Champagne*.

The daughter of Herodias, 'dancing' before Herod, is often depicted in manuscript illuminations upside-down, dancing on her hands, and sometimes she holds knives as well.[8] Such performances could be accompanied by instruments but not, presumably, by dance-song.

About the other kind of dancing, dancing in company, we are better – though still imperfectly – informed. Often, as we shall see, we are in the curious position of knowing, or thinking we know, the meaning of what was happening without having too clear a grasp of the physical details. There are three main categories of company dance – the popular, the courtly and the clerical. Of these, the first, it must be conceded, is not easy to describe. Our knowledge of it is derived partly from the denunciations of moralists through the ages and partly from its adaptation into courtly modes. The official Church took its cue from St Augustine's remark that it is better to dig and plough on festival days than to dance.[9] The often-told legend of the cursed carollers of Kölbigk depicts a ring-dance. Cursed by the priest for not obeying his command to leave the *carole* and come to the Christmas Eve service,[10]

we found that we could not break the circle or stop dancing for a whole year . . . Meanwhile we danced and leapt and clapped, mocking our own pain with the refrain [*regressus*] of our song, *Quid stamus? Cur non imus?* [Why are we standing still? Why don't we move?]

The chorus circles to the left around a soloist who seems often to have been a woman: 'a *ring-dance* is a circle at whose centre is the devil, and everyone is turning perversely' (*vergunt ad sinistrum*, to the left), as a French preacher says.[11] Another clerical condemnation (Council of

---

[7] Chambers, 1.70. For a further example of the term *tour*, see below, Ex. 62, from *Robin et Marion*. On the category 'acrobat', see Bullock-Davies, 55–60, who also analyses the *tours* performed by the jongleur in *Del Tumbeor Nostre Dame* (ed. E. Lommatsch (Berlin 1920)).

[8] Jusserand, 117, refers *inter alia* to stained-glass representations at Clermont-Ferrand and at Lincoln. Some manuscript references are given by Bullock-Davies, 57.

[9] Gougaud (1914), 9; Chambers, 1.162, from Council of Bayeux (1300).

[10] For the Latin text, see Andre Wilmart, 'La légende de Ste Edith en prose et vers par le moine Goscelin', *Analecta Bollandia* 56 (1938) 287–8.

[11] Cited by Axton, 49, from Lecoy de la Marche, *La chaire française au moyen âge* (Paris 1886), 447: *chorea: enim circulus est diabolus et omnes vergunt ad sinistrum*. See also Gougaud (1914), 14, on the place of women in such dances.

Avignon, 1209) puts popular song and dancing in an equally unfavourable light:[12]

Statuimus, ut in sanctorum vigiliis in ecclesiis historice saltationes, obsceni motus, seu choree non fiant, nec dicantur amatoria carmina, vel cantilene ibidem . . .

It is our edict that in churches on saints' eves there shall be no dance-mimes, no obscene movements and no round-dances; nor shall love-songs be sung there, nor dance-songs . . .

This does admittedly only prohibit such dances and other entertainment *in ecclesiis* (? church premises, not necessarily the church itself) and on festival eves; but those were perhaps particularly the times, and places even, where a thinly disguised paganism was most likely to break out.

It may be that we shall never know more than we do at the present time about the dances which were 'popular by origin'. That there must have been many such – genuine 'folk', as distinct from 'popular', dances and dance-songs – goes without saying. Peter Dronke has argued that

the two best-known types of medieval dance-song, the carol [which I shall call the *carole*, to distinguish it from the later insular development] and the rondeau, are essentially popular forms . . . their melodic and poetic simplicity made them intrinsically suitable for dancing and festivities irrespective of class . . . It is highly probable that carols and rondeaux flourished long before any were written down, and there is no evidence whatever that they were originally restricted to an exclusive milieu.[13]

Dronke emphasizes that we do not have to believe they must have been 'composed in the first instance by uncultivated men and women'. And this is surely true. But it would be quite in keeping with the evidence to allow that in some form or other many dance-songs (one thinks of 'Bele Aaliz' for instance)[14] may have originated 'below', to be later taken up by courtly writers and musicians and given the shapes we know today. Certainly in later periods courtly–popular songs were all the vogue. The poetic and musical characteristics of some early Tudor court songs ('A robyn, gentyl robyn', 'And I war a maydyn', 'My love sche morneth for me') scarcely allow a doubt that they are popular art transformed by courtly needs, tastes and technique.[15] *Carole* and *rondeau* as we know them are courtly–popular, and sometimes fully courtly, forms, but behind them we can sense, touch and hear dances and

[12] Chambers, I.162, from *Sacrorum Conciliorum Nova et Amplissima Collectio*, ed. J. D. Mansi, 30 vols. (Florence 1769–92).
[13] Dronke (1968), 188–9. The insertion in brackets is mine.
[14] 'Bele Aaliz': see note 54 below. Langton's moralized allegory confirms that it could be a dance-song, but the metrical form is unusual.
[15] Stevens (1961), chs. 3 and 6, with texts on pp. 405, 418, 393.

dance-songs with deeper roots, wider appeal, and greater popularity (in more than one sense of that word).[16]

1 Courtly dance-song: *carole* and *rondeau*

One of the fascinations of attempting to describe the courtly dance-songs of the thirteenth century, even if we confine ourselves mostly to the French-speaking parts of Europe, is that there is no such thing as a purely 'literary' form or genre. The *carole* is no exception. In fact, the *carole* is perhaps the most elusive form as it was also the most popular, apparently, of all. Considering that it merits literally hundreds of mentions in poetry and prose, it is odd, to say the least, that there is no collection of poems or songs headed *caroles*. Even the Oxford manuscript known as the Lorraine Chansonnier, containing *grans chans, estampies, jeus partis, pastorelles, balletes* and *sottes chansons*, all without music, has no section for *caroles*.[17] (The date – 1300–25 – might seem late, but it is only slightly later than that of many of the other chansonniers and well within the *carole* period.) However difficult precise definition may be (and we shall return to the various aspects of it), the *carole* is well provided with a social context – it was 'un élément essentiel des divertissements populaires et courtois du moyen âge, et l'on s'y adonnait avec frénésie'.[18]

The best introduction to the high courtly, social meaning of the *carole* is through the first part of the *Roman de la Rose* (c. 1235) by Guillaume de Lorris. In this first masterpiece of medieval love-allegory, the poet dreams that he comes upon a garden surrounded by a wall, the mysterious Garden of Love; outside on 'the highe walles enbatailled' are depicted hateful qualities – Felonye, Vilainye, Coveitise, Envye, Elde, and so forth. 'A mayden curteys' opens the wicket gate for him. Her name is Ydelnesse (i.e. Leisure). The lord of the garden is Sir Myrthe (in the French, *Deduiz*), and with him is Lady Gladnesse (*Leesce*). Lady Curtesie (*Cortoisie*) invites the Dreamer to join the *carole* in which the God of Love and his Squire, Swete-Lokyng (*Dolz Regart*), are taking part together with *Biautez, Richece, Largesce* and *Franchise*.[19] The dance is both a figure in the allegory and a self-contained symbol. In the allegory it

[16] The difference in emphasis between Dronke and myself arises in part from our different selections of dance-song; his ranges widely over the whole of Europe, whilst mine is centred on the north and on the twelfth and thirteenth centuries.

[17] Lorraine Chansonnier (Source 25). The *carole* is not mentioned, either, in *Las Leys d'Amors* (Toulouse, fourteenth-century), which lists and specifies the requirements for many courtly genres, *dansa, bal, estampita*, etc., and observes that the *rondeau* (which the author will not discuss) is spreading from the north of France to the south. The term for *carole* – *corola* – is admittedly very rare (Sahlin, 59–60).

[18] Sahlin, 1.

[19] The account is slightly expanded from my *Medieval Romance: Themes and Approaches* (London 1973), 53.

unites into one movement, as it were, all the desirable qualities which the lover must have if he is to grow and succeed in love. As symbol it 'betokeneth concorde', the social joy of the courtly élite, the delights and rewards of the good life, the desirable life, on this earth. But, furthermore, it is contemporary *reality* – idealized, of course, but not to the point of pure fancy. This, we feel, is how the privileged few wished and were able to enjoy their pastime.

About the courtly meaning of the *carole* as it is described there can be no doubt. The extraordinarily sophisticated aristocratic and courtly circles of the late twelfth and thirteenth centuries rejoiced in the ideal world they had created. The romances of Chrétien, the narrative *lais* of Marie de France, the first part of the *Roman de la Rose* all testify to the imaginative hold of *fine amour* and to its all-embracing significance in the noble life. In the social realization of this ideal world, its acting out in the forms of social life – ceremony, entertainment, game – the *carole* held a central position. Nor was it confined to France or French society. There are many references in medieval English literature to the *carole*/carol as a courtly as well as a popular dance-song. By the nature of the case it is the courtly activity which is best documented. To take some fourteenth-century instances, which reflect, if in an idealized form, the festivities and amusements of English courts: thus, 'damisels carols ledeth' (*Arthur and Merlin*, 1714); 'the hovedance and the Carole/ . . . A softe pas thei daunce and trede' (*Confessio Amantis*, viii.2679); 'Where as dawnsyng many maidenis were with many karoles & ryht merye song' (*Merlin*, 2.9275).[20] These works, if not direct translations, are deeply indebted to the romance tradition, of which the principal language was French. But this does not mean that the references are 'merely literary'. The English courtly tradition up to Chaucer's time was essentially French and French-speaking; and a *carole* was a *carole* on either side of the Channel. Gower makes it clear that an 'English' author, like a 'French', would relate the *carole* to the refrain-forms of French medieval song: 'he can carolles make / Rondeal, balade, and virelai' (*Confessio*, i.2708).[21] A large proportion of references specifically mention dancing-with-singing.

So much for the meaning of the *carole* as a courtly form. What, next, can be said about its actual performance? About this we are not too badly in-formed. Even in the dream-world of the Rose there is a welcome and convincing particularity, as in the portrait of *Leesce* (Gladness). Some of the detail is properly effective as allegory, and there is a general appropriate-ness in the link between music and the happiness of love. But some other of the detail is there, surely, because it *was* there, in the world not of dream but of fact.

[20] For these citations and many others, see Carter, *Dictionary of ME Musical Terms*, s.v. 'Carol' (sb.). The most extended account of the *carole*/carol phenomenon is in Greene (1977), Introduction ch. 11, 'The Carole as Dance-song'.
[21] The terms 'French' and 'English' are here used linguistically, not geographically.

[725]　This folk, of which I telle you
　　　　　soo,
　　　Upon a karole wenten thoo.
　　　A lady karolede hem that hyghte
　　　Gladnesse, [the] blissful and the
　　　　　lighte;
　　　Wel coude she synge and
　　　　　lustyly, –
　　　Noon half so wel and semely, –
　　　And make in song sich
　　　　　refreynynge,
　　　It sat hir wondir wel to synge,
　　　Hir vois ful clere was and ful
　　　　　swete.

[733]　She was nought rude ne unmete
　　　But couthe ynow of sich doyng
　　　As longeth unto karolyng;

[737]　For she was wont in every place
　　　To syngen first, folk to solace.
　　　For syngyng moost she gaf hir
　　　　　to;
　　　No craft had she so leef to do.

[741]　　Tho myghtist thou karoles
　　　　　sen,
　　　And folk daunce and mery ben,
　　　And made many a fair tournyng
　　　Upon the grene gras springyng.
　　　There myghtist thou see these
　　　　　flowtours,
　　　Mynstrales, and eke jogelours,
　　　That wel to synge dide her
　　　　　peyne.
　　　Somme songe songes of
　　　　　Loreyne;
　　　For in Loreyn her notes bee
　　　Full swetter than in this contre.
　　　There was many a tymbestere,

And saillouris, that I dar wel
　　swere
Couthe her craft ful parfitly.
The tymbres up ful sotilly
They caste and hente full ofte
Upon a fynger fair and softe,
That they failide never mo.
Ful fetys damyseles two,
Ryght yonge, and full of
　　semelyhede,
In kirtles, and noon other wede,
And faire tressed every tresse,
Hadde Myrthe doon, for his
　　noblesse,

[761]　Amydde the karole for to
　　　daunce;
But herof lieth no
　　remembraunce,
Hou that they daunced
　　queyntely.
That oon wolde come all
　　pryvyly
Agayn that other, and whan they
　　were
Togidre almost, they threwe
　　yfere
Her mouthis so, that thorough
　　her play
It seemed as they kiste alway.
To dauncen well koude they the
　　gise . . .[22]

[741]　. . . *quarole aler*
　et gent mignotement baler
　et faire mainte bele tresche
　et meint biau tor

The poet concludes the description by saying that he could have stayed there for ever just watching them (*cestes genz*) *queroler* and *danser*.

　　The first thing to note about this is that it is not a description of one *carole*,

---

[22] Chaucer's translation (lines 743–89) of Guillaume de Lorris (lines 725–69). The French and English texts are conveniently available in parallel in Ronald Sutherland, '*The Romaunt of the Rose*' and '*Le Roman de la Rose*' (Oxford 1967). The most recent edition of the whole *Roman* is by Félix Lecoy, CFMA, 3 vols. (Paris 1965–70).
　　The bracketed line numbers refer to the French text in Lecoy's edition, not to Chaucer's translation.

but of a variety of dances. The lines 725–40 are about the main *carole* in which Gladnesse (*Leesce*) is the leader and solo singer, a role to which she is accustomed (737) and which she performs with skill – including skill as a dancer (735). In lines 741 ff there appears to be a contrast between *quarole aler* and *baler*, which the poet now turns to. *Tresche* indicates perhaps a line of dancers, not a ring; the *meint biau tor* may refer to various sets of steps, or solo 'turns'.[23] The general scene is further enlivened by the efforts of various professionals, minstrels and jongleurs etc. Some are playing instruments, some singing in various styles, others (female entertainers) toss their tambourines in the air and catch them cunningly on their fingers. At line 761 we are directed back again to the *carole*. Deduiz graciously gives the centre of the ring – the centre of the stage, as it were – to two young women of special charm ('ful fetys damyseles', says Chaucer) where they perform a 'routine' of a delicately erotic nature.

The choreography of the *carole* is extremely difficult to establish. A lot of important references, such as the one just quoted, clearly refer to a round-dance: the dancers form a ring, men and women alternately (though this is not essential), and move to the music of their singing leader. In the centre of the ring some action may be taking place. But, as Margit Sahlin conclusively showed in *Étude sur la carole médiévale* (1940), a number of references weigh against the round-dance hypothesis, such as for instance the long procession described in *La Manekine* by Philippe de Remi:

> Tel carole ne fu veüe,
> Pres du quart dure d'une liue.
> Par les caroles s'en aloient
> Chevaliers, dames qui cantoient . . .

Such a *carole* was never seen – it was nearly a quarter of a league in length. Through the *caroles* knights were moving, ladies singing . . .

In the performance of a courtly dance there could evidently be an element of 'game', perhaps even of drama. It was of varying prominence. One of the most circumstantial accounts of the 'action' of an aristocratic dance-game is in a courtly narrative by Jacques Bretel, *Le Tournoi de Chauvency* (after 1285). It resembles the account just quoted in so far as an element of game or 'play' (the word, like *jeu* and *ludus*, is helpfully ambiguous) was present in the *deux demoiselles mout mignotes* who were invited to dance *en mi la querole*; but Bretel's account is much more detailed.[24] It tells, in Richard Axton's words,

---

[23] Chaucer's translation evades the problem of *tresche*; and Lecoy's gloss, *danse*, is unhelpful. Sachs, 250–1, suggests 'stamping dance'. The context of *Robin et Marion* line 211 is not explicit: Varty in his edition says that it is a dance in which the dancers hold hands and are in a long line; Gennrich (1962), 36 (n. on line 226), says it is a walking dance in a chain. The passages cited by Godefroy, s.v. 'Tresce', and Tobler–Lommatzsch, s.v. 'Tresche', are mostly ambiguous or contradictory. On *tor*, see note 7 above.

[24] The element of 'game' was first propounded in two fundamental articles by Bédier, 'Les fêtes du mai' (1896) and 'Les plus anciennes danses' (1906). I supply line-references to *Le Tournoi*

How the Countess of Luxembourg led a dance called the *chapelet* [4192, 4202] for the solace of the wounded knights. The structure is simple: the girl provokes the advances of a young man, 'leading him a dance' before granting him a kiss. Delicacy of performance was all, and required, it seems, some improvisation on a known pattern. The heroine plays with a garland of flowers (her *chapelet*), putting it on and off her head, as she dances alone, singing softly as if to herself: *Si n'a plus joliete de me* (There's no one more joyful here than I). The minstrel [*menestreus de viele*] asks why she stands all alone, without a lover; she replies in song

> Sire qu'en afiert il a vos? Ne vos voi pas bien sage.
> j'ai fait mon chapelet jolif, la jus en cel boschage.   [4235–6]

> (What business is it of yours? I see you are not wise. I have made my pretty garland down there in the wood.)

He asks, *Douce dame, volez baron?* Does she wish for a husband? She replies that she would rather a maiden's garland than a bad marriage:

> J'aim mieux mon chapelet de flors que mauvais mariage.   [4250]

The minstrel promises to find her a good one; she dances provocatively towards an imaginary wood, possibly a ring of dancers, a 'grove of love' to await the man. A knight is chosen by the minstrel, at first denying his own worthiness, but then allowing himself to be led to the girl as she sings:

> Dieus! Trop demeure; quant vendra? Sa demouree m'ocira.   [4282]

> (Lord! He delays too long; when will he come? His delay will kill me.)

She takes him by the hand and gives thanks to God for her great delight.

As Axton observes, 'This light-hearted *ballerie* expresses the aspiration of a leisured, courtly society to aesthetic and erotic refinement through "game".'[25]

Apart from some representations in art, it is from the fictional presentation of dance occasions in courtly, and in a few other, texts that we get our understanding of the significance, spirit and style of performance as well as the literary content of the dance. It was early in the thirteenth century that the practice became popular in the north of France of interlarding romances and other poems with the texts of songs, or excerpts from them, or even shorter pieces called *refrains*. This practice continued to be part of the musical–poetical tradition; Machaut's *Remede de Fortune* (before 1342), for instance, develops it

---

[25] Axton, 48–9. See also Dronke (1968), 198ff, who translates the whole scene from the edition by M. Delbouille, *Le Tournoi de Chauvency*, Bibliothèque de la Faculté de Philosophie et Lettres de l'Université de Liége, 49 (Liége–Paris 1932), lines 4215ff. The romance contains a huge number of *refrains*; they are listed by Boogaard, p. 315. 'Si n'a plus joliete de me' is *refrain* no. 1730. I discuss the nature and significance of the French *refrain* as a genre in section 11 below.

---

de Chauvency, ed. Delbouille (see note 25 below), where the spellings differ slightly from Axton's.

to the point where, in his work, we are faced with what is virtually a *summa* of the art of song-writing in his time presented in the course of a love-allegory.[26] Jean Renart's romance *Guillaume de Dole* (*c*. 1228) is not one of the major works in the courtly tradition, but it may have set the fashion for such insertions,[27] followed by *Le Roman de la Violette* (1230 or soon after) and in about 1310–14 by the most famous example of the genre, the *Roman de Fauvel* (1310–14).[28] Renart refers to his enterprise in the opening lines:

> Cil qui mist cest conte en romans,
> ou il a fet noter biaus chans
> por ramembrance des chançons,
> 4 veut que ses pris et ses renons
> voist en Raincïen en Champaigne . . .
> 8 car aussi com l'en met la graine
> es dras por avoir los et pris,
> einsi a il chans et sons mis
> en cestui *Romans de la Rose,*
> 12 qui est une novele chose
> et s'est des autres si divers
> et brodez, par lieus, de biaus vers
> que vilains nel porroit savoir.
> 16 Ce sachiez de fi et de voir,
> bien a cist les autres passez.
> Ja nuls n'iert de l'oïr lassez,
> car, s'en vieult, l'en i chante et lit,
> 20 et s'est fez par si grant delit
> que tuit cil s'en esjoïront
> qui chanter et lire l'orront . . .

He who translated this story into French and then had fine songs 'noted' in it lest they should be forgotten wishes his reputation and renown to reach the district of Reims in Champagne . . . For just as red dye is put into garments for the increase of fame and reputation, in the same way the author has puts songs and melodies into this *Romance*

[26] See Stevens, 'The "music" of the lyric: Machaut, Deschamps, Chaucer' in *Medieval and Pseudo-Medieval Literature: the J. A. W. Bennett Memorial Lectures Perugia, 1982–1983*, ed. P. Boitani and A. Torti (Tübingen and Cambridge, 1984), pp. 109–29.

[27] Jean Renart, *Le Roman de la Rose ou de Guillaume de Dole* (*c*. 1228) has no direct connection with the famous *Roman de la Rose* by Guillaume de Lorris and Jean de Meun. Renart's poem is ed. F. Lecoy, CFMA (Paris 1962), who observes that it is 'a veritable anthology of French lyric, corresponding to the taste of the cultivated public at the beginning of the thirteenth century'. Interpolations are not confined to *refrains* and refrain-forms, though these predominate in the long narrative poems. Two unpublished dissertations are helpful to understanding the whole phenomenon of lyric insertions: M. B. M. Boulton, 'Lyric Insertions in French Narrative Fiction in the thirteenth and fourteenth centuries' (University of Oxford, 1981); M. V. Fowler 'Musical interpolations in thirteenth and fourteenth century French narratives' (Yale University, 1979).

[28] Gerbert de Montreuil, *Le Roman de la Violette ou de Gerart de Nevers*, ed. D. L. Buffum, SATF (Paris 1928). Boogaard, *Rondeaux et Refrains* (1969), p. 338, lists over thirty *refrains*. *Roman de Fauvel* (Source 27): this satirical and anticlerical *roman* by Gervais de Bus is an important source of polyphonic as well as of monophonic music.

of the Rose. This romance is a novelty and quite different from others, and is decorated in various places with fine verses, such as an uncourtly person could not comprehend. And you can be absolutely sure that it is far superior to other romances. No one will ever be tired of hearing it, for there's both song and speech in it at pleasure. There was so much delight in the making (of this poem) that all those who hear it sung and read will rejoice in it.[29]

The author goes on to claim that he has introduced the *chans et sons* so naturally, so skilfully, that his readers/listeners will think they are his own. They are not, of course – at least not the majority. So what does this claim amount to? Is it an assertion of the author's skill in observing rhetorical decorum? Or is it – could it be – intended to validate the social scene and action? I suspect only the former. Nevertheless, Jean Renart does give us a vivid sense of scene, even if rose-tinted (it never pours with rain on a courtly *carole*). And, what is more, he gives us texts. No music, unfortunately; but this can often be supplied from elsewhere, as we shall see. The following scene is part of a long description of a courtly festivity. The guests have all been feasted (and not with mere rustic fare – 'slices of toast dunked in red wine') and now settle down to entertain and be entertained.[30]

> Les dames et les conpegnons
> l'empereor s'en issent hors.
> Main a main, em pur lor biau cors,
> 508   devant le tref, en un pré vert,
> les puceles et li vallet
> ront la carole commenciee.
> Une dame s'est avanciee
> 512   vestue d'une cote en graine,
> si chante ceste premeraine:
>   C'est tot la gieus, enmi les prez.
>   *Vos ne sentez mie les maus d'amer!*
> 516   Dames i vont por caroler.
>   Remirez voz braz!
>   *Vos ne sentez mie les maus d'amer*
>   *si com ge faz!*
> 520   Uns vallez au prevost d'Espire
> redit ceste, qui n'est pas pire:
>   C'est la jus desoz l'olive.
>   *Robins enmaine s'amie.*
> 524   La fontaine i sort serie
>   desouz l'olivete
>   *E non Deu! Robins enmaine*
>   *bele Mariete.*

---

[29] Renart's claim that he had the songs 'noted' in the text of the poem may well be true, even though the surviving MS (Rome, Vat.Reg. 1725) does not contain music. The thirty *refrains* are listed by Boogaard, p. 324.
[30] Ed. Lecoy (see note 27 above), lines 492–4 (the feast), 505–37 (the dancing).

528 Ceste n'ot pas duré .III. tours,
     quant li filz au conte d'Aubours
     qui mout amoit chevalerie
     reconmencë a voiz serie:
532   Main se levoit Aaliz,
         – J'ai non Emmelot –
         Biau se para et vesti
             soz la roche Guion.
536   *Cui lairai ge mes amors*
             amie, s'a vos non?

The ladies and knights of the emperor came out. Hand in hand, without their cloaks, in front of the tent, in a green meadow, the maidens and squires began their *carole* again. One lady came to the fore, dressed in a scarlet coat, and sang this first [*carole?*]:

          Down there amongst the meadows –
     You do not feel the woes of love at all –
          Ladies go dancing the *carole.*
              Look at your arms!
     You do not feel the woes of love at all
              As I feel them.

A squire of the Provost of Espire sang this next [dance-song], which is certainly not inferior to it.

          Down there, beneath the olive-tree
     Robin leads his sweetheart away.
          The fountain swells up gaily
              beneath the olive.
     In the name of God! Robin leads his
              beautiful Mariete away.

This [dance] had not gone three times round when the son of the Count of Aubours, a great lover of 'chivalry', began [another] in a pleasing voice:

          Alice rose in the morning,
          – My name is Emmelot –
          dressed and made herself pretty
              beneath the Rock Guion.
     To whom shall I give my love,
          my dear one, if not to you?

The form of the first two *caroles* quoted in this passage is that of the *rondeau*; here it appears at its simplest: aAabA B (the capital letter indicates repetition of words and music in a refrain-line). The *rondeau* is capable of, and later underwent, great elaboration; but it never loses the defining characteristic of a 'half-refrain' occurring in mid-verse. On the basis of this passage it might seem as if the *carole* and *rondeau*, so far from being two genres of dance-song, were one and the same. This, however, would be an over-simplification. As will emerge, the *carole* is not in the formal sense a genre – or, at least, it is not a lost *forme fixe.* And in this respect it differs from its descendant, the Middle

English carol. The *carole* is, rather, a set of constituents which may be fitted
together in a number of ways to make a dance-song – of which the *rondeau* is
perhaps the only one that can be certainly identified as a regularly recurrent
form. The words of the dance-songs to which *caroles* were performed are
variously described in the literary sources as *chançons, chançonetes, cançons de
carolle, rondets, rondelets, motez, conduiz*. Such a mélange of forms and genres
suggests no simple answer to the question: Did the medieval *carole* have a
specific form?

II The French *refrain*

The constituent of the *carole* that is most important from the poetico-musical
point of view is the *refrain*, and it is to this that we must now turn.[31] I have
italicized the word *refrain* not for emphasis but to indicate that the French
word has in the study of the period *c.* 1150–1350 a special meaning: a *refrain*
was a sort of courtly aphorism, a love-tag, usually with a melody attached to
it. To take an example – in a scene of hilarious rejoicing in Renart's *Guillaume
de Dole* (lines 2360ff) the handsome Galerans de Lamborc, 'who hadn't
enjoyed himself so much for a long time' (*qui ne s'envoisa mes pieça*), sang this
song (the context makes it reasonably clear that it was the dance-song for a
carole, and this is confirmed by the fourth line):

> La jus desouz l'olive,
> *– ne vos repentez mie, –*
> fontaine i sourt serie:
> Puceles, carolez!
> *Ne vos repentez mie*
> *de loiaument amer.*   (2369–74)

---

[31] The essential guide to the large, and generally somewhat neglected, corpus of *refrains* is van
den Boogaard's *Rondeaux et Refrains du xiie siècle au début du xive* (1969), which prints 198
rondeaux and 1,933 *refrains* and relates them to distinct and separate repertoires of chansons,
motets and romances. In his indispensable introduction Boogaard comments on the comparatively few previous studies, including Gennrich's *Bibliographisches Verzeichnis der französischen Refrains* (1963), the third volume of his study *Rondeaux, Virelais und Balladen* (1921ff).
Gennrich's studies are, on Boogaard's showing, full of error and cannot be used with any
confidence; they are, however, still necessary to the musician, as no one else has yet covered
the ground. The texts as printed are, as Apel says ((1954), 128), 'reconstructed with rather
more boldness and license than is admissible in scholarly studies'. Furthermore it is impossible to tell from the transcriptions whether the original melodies are in mensural or non-
mensural notation; Gennrich's studies were commented on in detail by Spanke (1929). 'In
type and tone [the *refrains*] are "popular" rather than aristocratic or learned – brief, rhyming
verses . . . singable or danceable, emotionally direct, swift in thought and simple – even if
they are at times hard to grasp analytically, it is never difficult to get the feel of them'
(Dronke (1965a), 1.22–3). The *refrains*, it should be added, do not always rhyme in themselves (see the *refrains* quoted above in the extract from *Guillaume de Dole*, lines 518, 526,
536).

> Down there beneath the olive tree
> *– Do not repent ever –*
> the fountain rises there gaily:
> Maidens, do your *carole!*
> *Do not repent ever*
> *of loving loyally.*

The italicized lines are the *refrain* of this dance-song in basic *rondeau*-form –
first, a single line (which breaks the syntax of the stanza, lines 1 and 3); and, at
the end, both lines. The interesting thing is that these same two lines, which
incidentally do not have any very obvious connection with the rest of the little
poem, occur in six other contexts. Four of them are *chansons-avec-des-refrains* –
a peculiarly medieval genre – a chanson with a different *refrain* in each stanza
(different in words and often in metre and in melody: see p. 466). One is
quoted in a religious *dit* called *La Court de Paradis*; another, in Gautier de
Coinci's long religious narrative, *Les Miracles de Nostre Dame*.[32]

One thing is quite evident. This *refrain*, 'Ne vos repentez mie / de loiaument
amer', was well known and enjoyed an independent existence. The question
is, how independent? What, more precisely, was a *refrain*? First, it could be and
very commonly was a refrain in the ordinary, accepted sense – i.e. that part of
a stanza in a strophic song which is common to all the stanzas (in this ordinary
sense I give the word 'refrain' in roman, not in italics). Such an internal refrain
may or may not have an obvious connection with its poetic context, as this
famous lyric shows

> When that I was and a little tine boy
> *with hey ho, the winde and the raine:*
> A foolish thing was but a toy,
> *for the raine it raineth every day.*   (*Twelfth Night*, v.i.389)

The medieval *refrain* in the special (italicized) sense has marked characteristics
of its own. More often than not it is a courtly aphorism or amorous proverb, a
tag of the kind that courtly poets (and presumably courtiers, too) like to play
with. Such a saying as Chaucer's favourite 'For pitee renneth soone in gentil
herte' would qualify as an English *refrain*.[33] Typical of the repertory are such
refrains as these – the first which we have already met: 'Vos ne sentez mie les maus
d'amer, si com ge faz' (You do not feel the woes of love at all as I feel them);
'Au vert bois deporter m'irai: / m'amie i dort, si l'esveillerai' (I'm going to the

---

[32] Boogaard, refr. 1375, lists the six occurrences: the *chansons-avec-des-refrains* are by Pierre de
Corbie (R2041), Colart le Boutellier (R839), Baude de la Kakerie (R1509), and an anonymous
writer of religious chansons (R1963). *La Court de Paradis* (late-thirteenth-century, anony-
mous) describes a fête given by God to the saints in heaven; it is ed. E. Vilamo-Pentti
(Helsinki, 1953) the *refrain* is at line 271. Gautier de Coinci (d. 1236), *Les Miracles de Notre
Dame*, is a prime source for religious *contrafacta* of all kinds; the *refrain* is at III.502 (ed. F.
Koenig, TLF (Geneva and Paris, 1955–6)). The musical aspect of Gautier's work is studied
by Chailley (1959), with transcriptions and commentary.

[33] Chaucer, *Knight's Tale*, I.1761; *Merchant's Tale* IV.1986; *Squire's Tale* v.479; *Legend of Good
Women*, Prol. F 503 (see Robinson's note, pp. 675–6).

wood to enjoy myself: my sweetheart is asleep there and I'll wake her); 'Se la bele n'a de moi merci, / je ne vivrai mie longuement einsi' (If that beauty doesn't take pity on me, I shan't live a moment longer); 'Biaus doz amis, por quoi demores tant?' (Good sweet friend, why do you delay so long?).[34] If all these *refrains* are, as I have said, typical, then there is more variety in them than my definition may have suggested. Perhaps the range in tone between the two terms 'aphorism' and 'proverb' gives us the necessary room to move in. Some *refrains* are of the court, courtly; others belong to the courtly–popular realm described earlier. The *refrain* 'Au vert bois . . .' is an example. It reminds one of the burden of a much later medieval song, from a song-book of Henry VII's time,

> Smale pathys to the grenewode,
> Will I love and shall I love,
> Will I love and shall I love
>   No mo maydyns but one.[35]

This is contrasted with a stanza which begins in would-be high courtly style, 'Love is naturall to every wyght / Indyfferent to every creature'. The playful juxtaposition of courtly and popular (or near-popular) could not be clearer. The same juxtaposition is possible within the huge repertory of *refrains* and the texts to which they attach themselves.

Refrains, it should be emphasized, were current in early medieval England as well as in the north of France, their favourite habitat. Since the court circles of England (as well as many other circles) were French-speaking, and French-thinking, this is hardly surprising. A few *refrains*, not many, are found in two collections of proverbs. Such a collection survives in Hereford Cathedral Library: it includes, for instance,

> Je sent les max d'amer por vos;
>   sentez les vos por moi?

(I feel the pangs of love for you; do you feel them for me?)[36]

This *refrain* reappears in two chansons, two motets, a romance, and another proverb collection. 'Vos ne sentez mie les maus d'amer', quoted above, is also in the Hereford proverbs as well as in a *pastourelle*, a romance (*Guillaume de Dole*), and a chanson to the Virgin.[37] Another well-known *refrain*, 'E, dame jolie', serves as a refrain to a *ballete* in the Lorraine Chansonnier. But it has also been found 'written in a fourteenth-century English hand on a flyleaf of an

---

[34] Boogaard, refrs. 1865, 198, 1692, 220.
[35] Text in Stevens (1961), 382–3 (Fayrfax MS no. 46); music edn *Early Tudor Songs and Carols*, Musica Britannica XXXVI (London 1975), no. 66.
[36] Boogaard, p. 331: *Proverbia vurgalia cum cuncordanciis sacre scripture* (J. Morawski, *Romania* 48 (1922) 513). The MS is Hereford Cathedral, Close P.3.3 (described Morawski, 511ff); in this MS not only the proverbs but the *refrains* are provided with commentary, mainly in the form of Biblical allusion. 'Je sent les max': see Boogaard, refr. 1127.
[37] See Boogaard, refr. 1865.

Italian manuscript of the Code of Justinian';[38] it occurs, additionally, as a tenor in the famous Montpellier Codex, and as a *refrain*, simply, in the *Renart le Nouvel* (line 6286). What clinches the English connection is the appearance of the *refrain*, yet again, at the end of an Anglo-Norman love-letter written in verse.[39]

> Ey, Mergrete jolie,
> Mon quer sans fauser
> [met an vostre baillie,
> Ke ne sai vo peir].

Hey, merry Margaret, I put my heart into your keeping without falseness, for I know no equal to you.

N. J. van den Boogaard's careful and systematic catalogue has done more to set the study of the *refrain* genre on a secure scholarly footing than any other published work. His approach is primarily bibliographical, but he has a succinct paragraph on the generic nature of the *refrain*:

c'est vraiment comme un genre ayant ses propres 'lois' que se présente le refrain. Ce en quoi il se distingue des autres genres, c'est qu'il pourrait s'appeler 'parasite' dans le sens biologique du terme: le refrain semble toujours (à part quelques *probationes penne* sur des feuillets de garde) vivre en symbiose avec un autre genre littéraire, que celui-ci soit chanté comme le refrain, ou qu'il ne le soit pas.[40]

It is in truth as a genre with its own 'laws' that the *refrain* brings itself to our notice. The thing which distinguishes it from other genres is that it could be called a 'parasite' in the biological sense: the *refrain* always appears (setting aside a few *probationes penne* on guard-leaves) to live in symbiosis with another literary genre – whether the latter is sung, as the *refrain* is, or not.

The concept of the *refrain* as 'parasite' seems to me just what is required; it is not only a literary but also in some sense a social parasite and, finally, as we shall see, a musical one, too. The older view was rather different. Alfred Jeanroy argued that all the *refrains* were excerpts from, i.e. originated in, the dance-songs, such as the *rondeau*.[41] This would imply that they were all fragments of some larger whole. But this seems too narrow. However, it is evident that the *refrain* was an important, and the most memorable, constituent of the dance-song.

The ordering of the *refrain* (in its use as song-refrain) in relation to the rest of the stanza – or, to put it in other terms, the ordering of the chorus and solo sections – was one of the features which distinguished one dance-song from

---

[38] Legge, *Anglo-Norman Literature* (1963), 343; Boogaard, refr. 806, and R1168 (Gonville and Caius MS 11, flyleaf).

[39] P. Meyer (1909), 435; the letter begins, 'M., ma especiele / Vus estes bone et bele' (Gonville and Caius MS 54). The bracketed lines are not in Meyer's sources but are in all others.

[40] Boogaard, p. 17.

[41] A. Jeanroy, *Les Origines* (3rd edn, 1925), ch. 5, 'Les refrains' (p. 114).

another. I would go further and say that this distinguished one *carole* from another. The *carole* must surely have been not *a* single form but a potential for form, a dance-*idea* waiting to be realized in various forms. Since the fourteenth-century *formes fixes*, as they are called (*rondeau* in its complexly developed shapes, *virelai*, *ballade*), developed from earlier dance-songs embodying *refrain* material, it is reasonable to suppose that they are themselves ossified versions of the *carole* showing at least three forms the *carole* could take.[42]

Before we leave popular and courtly dance, some account of the *refrain* as used by Adam de la Halle in his pastoral play (dramatic-*pastourelle-cum-bergerie*) *Robin et Marion* may be of interest.[43] It was probably written in about 1283 – not in Arras, his home-town, but in Naples, where Adam's patron, Robert II, Count of Artois, had gone with his army that year. However, there is nothing Italian about it; it is written in Adam's native dialect for a French courtly audience and consists of two parts, a dramatized *pastourelle* followed by a dramatized *bergerie* (shepherds' games). To decide what kind of experience the exiled aristocrats (and common soldiers?) were to get from this play is exceedingly difficult. It is not close enough to the common earth of the Arras district to satisfy an ordinary homely nostalgia, though at the same time there is an undeniable freshness about it, as about many medieval *pastourelles* – the atmosphere is different from and less artificial than that of its Elizabethan counterpart. Perhaps the term I have used before, 'courtly–popular', will serve again. What we have in *Robin et Marion* is a stylized version of life and love amongst country folk to please a courtly taste. Part of the stylization is in the songs. They occur chiefly in the first half of the play and, as Jacques Chailley first pointed out, they all belong to the repertory of *refrains*.[44] Adam inserted *refrains* into his dramatized *pastourelle* just as they were inserted into the *pastourelles* from which he drew his inspiration: there are nine in all, of which four are found elsewhere.

The play opens with Marion singing one of the most popular of the *refrains*: 'Robins m'aime, / Robin m'a; / Robin m'a demandée, / si m'avra'. It occurs in two *chansons-avec-des-refrains* (both are *pastourelles*) and in a motet.[45] Another well-known ditty is sung by *li compaignie* after the intruding Knight's final departure: 'Aveuc tele compaignie / Doit-on bien joie mener'. This, unusually, is found elsewhere only in three literary sources – *Renart le nouvel*, *Le Tournoi de Chauvency*, and *Salut d'Amours*.[46] There is no evidence that either

---

[42] The variety of *carole* forms (and, by implication, the impropriety of reconstructing earlier texts to match the rigidities of the later *formes fixes*) is one of the points which emerges strongly from Bédier's articles (see note 24 above).

[43] I have principally used the edition by Varty (1960), supplementing it on the musical side with Gennrich's edition (1962). The translation by Axton and Stevens (1971) also contains transcriptions of the music.

[44] Chailley (1950b), the basic study of *refrains* in drama.

[45] Line 1: Boogaard, refr. 1633.

[46] Line 421: Boogaard, refr. 200; and see his pt 3, index IV, 'Les Romans'.

of these *refrains* was danced to in the context of the play: the first is sung solo by
Marion; the second could be the cue for a dance-song, but as it stands it is a
simple couplet (with music). So a particular interest attaches to the most
extended musical item in the play, the dance-song dialogue of Robin and
Marion 'Robin, par l'ame ten pere'.[47]

It is not easy to classify this 'bit of merriment' (*poi de feste*), as Marion calls it.
In response to her demands Robin demonstrates his skill in four separate
dance-figures: *aler du piet* (which goes forwards and backwards); *le tour dou
chief*; *le tour des bras*; and *baler au seriaus* (for which the editors suggest no
convincing gloss). The texts for these patterned exchanges are not *refrains*, yet
the music which accompanies them is very *refrain*-like.[48] Whether the repeated
melody for the dialogue (in A A B form) has any connection with the dance-
figures named it is impossible to say. It certainly looks as if Robin dances to
them as he sings – but they are extremely short.[49]

Ex. 62

MARION
Ro- bin, par l'a- me ten pe- re, Ses tu bien a- ler du piet?

ROBIN
O- il, par l'a- me me me- re, Re- gar- de comme il me siet!

A- vant et ar- rie- re, be- le, a- vant et ar- rie- re.

MARION
Ro- bin, par l'a- me ten pe- re, Car nous fai le tour dou chief.

ROBIN
Ma- rot, par l'a- me me me- re, J'en ven- rai mout bien a chief!

I fait on tel chie- re, be- le, i fait on tel chie- re?

MARION
Ro- bin, par l'a- me ten pe- re, Car nous fai le tour des bras!

[47] Line 187: not in Boogaard.
[48] In the absence of a musical index to the French *refrains* it is impossible to say whether they are
known *refrains* or not.
[49] The melody is transcribed from the clear but not totally unambiguous mensural notation of
the Adam de la Halle M S (Source 34), fol. 41v. There is music also in Aix-en-Provence,
Bibliothèque de Méjanes M S 572, fols 1–11.

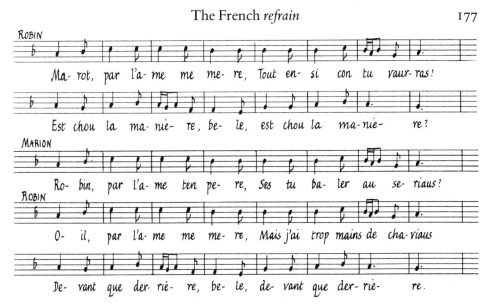

ROBIN: Ma- rot, par l'a- me me me- re, Tout en- si con tu vaur- ras!

Est chou la ma- nie- re, be- le, est chou la ma- nie- re?

MARION: Ro- bin, par l'a- me ten pe- re, Ses tu ba- ler au se- riaus?

ROBIN: O- il, par l'a- me me me- re, Mais j'ai trop mains de cha- viaus

De- vant que der- rie- re, be- le, de- vant que der- rie- re.

M: Robin, by your father's soul, do you know how to dance The Foot (?).
R: Yes, by the soul of my mother, look how it suits me – forwards and backwards, my sweet, forwards and backwards.
M: Robin, . . . Now please do the figure of The Head for us.
R: Marot, . . . I will come to a head very easily. Is this how one does it, darling? Is this how one does it?
M: Robin, . . . Now please do the figure of The Arms for us.
R: Marot, . . . Absolutely as you would wish.
   Is this the style of it, darling? Is this the style?
M: Robin, . . . Do you know how to dance *au seriaus*
   [? at evening parties?].[50]
R: Yes, . . . but my hair is very much shorter in front than behind . . .

The courtly dances of the period did not always win the approval of the moralists. I have more than once had occasion to mention 'Bele Aaliz', who seems to have occupied a singular place in the affections of both popular and courtly dance-singers. There are no fewer than six *rondeaux* in the text of *Guillaume de Dole* alone which mention her name and seem to quote from a popular song about her.[51] Another strong testimony to her popularity is, paradoxically, a sermon attributed to Stephen Langton (d. 1228), Archbishop of Canterbury, turning 'vanity to truth' and showing his listeners what in truth Bele Aaliz is – she is 'the mother of mercy and the queen of justice who bore the king and Lord of the heavens', the Virgin Mary.[52] What is of more interest to us is that the sermon, which survives in three English manuscripts, gives the whole text of one stanza; I quote the text from the Trinity Miscellany (see Source 6):

[50] For *au seriaus* I have followed Langlois's conjectural translation (edn CFMA, 1924), adopted by Varty: *assemblée du soir*.
[51] Printed Boogaard, rond. 2, 3, 7–9, 15, from Lecoy's edition (note 27 above).
[52] Reichl, *Religiöse Dichtung* (1973), pp. 379ff, quotes the sermon at length, editing it from five MSS. In line 7 another MS (Arundel 292) reads *trahez vos en la*.

Bele Alis matyn se leva,
sun cors vesti e appara.
En un verger s'en entra,
cync florettes i trova.
Une chapelette feit en ha,
    de rose flurie.
Pur Deu, trevus en la,
vos qui ne amet mie.[53]

Beautiful Alice got up in the morning, dressed and got herself ready. She went into an orchard; there she found five flowers. She made a hat of them, of the rose in bloom. For God's sake, get away, you who do not love.

We learn from the preacher's moralization of this that it was a dance-song, requiring 'a resounding voice, intertwining of the arms and steps with the feet keeping time to the song'.[54]

III Clerical dance-song: *rondellus*

It is to the efforts of determined and pious clerics such as Langton that we owe at least some of our knowledge of the other, non-courtly, realm of early-medieval dance – the ecclesiastical. It is striking that the only substantial corpus of Latin dance-song to survive from the period *c.* 1150–1350 consists of monophonic *rondelli*, Latin *rondeaux* paralleling in metrical form, and perhaps also borrowing melodies from, secular (courtly or popular) dances in the same form.[55] Dancing was a problem for the Christian Church from the

---

[53] Reichl, 379. In the Trinity Miscellany (Source 6), of which Reichl's book is a complete and authoritative edition, the last line reads: *vos qui me ne amet mie*. Other MSS, more characteristically, omit *me*.

[54] *Vox sonora, nexus brachiorum, strepitus pedum (concordans voci)* (Reichl, 381). The phenomenon of 'Bele Aaliz' is studied by R. Meyer, Bédier and Aubry in *Bele Aalis* (1904), an edition of the *chanson-avec-des-refrains*, 'Main se leva la bien faite Aelis' (R1509) by Baude de la Quarière (de la Kakerie). On the genre, see chapter 14: II below. It is unclear what the original *Aaliz* song was – if indeed one can meaningfully speak of an 'original'. A narrative stanza can be reconstructed from Baude de la Quarière's chanson similar to the stanza allegorized by Stephen Langton. 'Bele Aaliz' is not a *refrain* but seems rather to have provided the narrative material for a group of dance-songs with *refrains* (which were also refrains in the metrical–musical sense). One of the more puzzling references is the heading *Cantus de domina post cantum Aaliz* to the *lai*-type song 'Flos pudicitie' in the Arundel Songs; see Ex. 24 above.

[55] For information on the Latin monophonic *rondeau* (*rondellus*), see especially H. Spanke, 'Das lateinische Rondeau' (1930a), basic on sources and the history of the form. The most important source is the Florence MS, the eleventh fascicle of which contains sixty items. These were transcribed by Y. Rokseth, 'Danses Cléricales' (1947); the most recent edition is by Gordon Anderson (1978c), who also edits the *rondelli* of other sources. Further on the Florence MS, see List of Sources (no. 10). See also Stäblein (1975), pp. 160–1, pl. 44 and n. 16–18, on Latin and French dance-song. The term *rondellus* is also used by musicologists (following W. Odington, *c.* 1300) to denote a technique of three-voice composition or a polyphonic piece so composed (see Sanders, 'Rondellus', in *New Grove*). The whole complex of terms (*rondellus/rondeau, rota* and others) is expounded in detail by Reckow, 'Rondellus' in *HMT*.

earliest centuries.[56] This was not at first for the reason that it was considered sinful in itself but, as Margit Sahlin has pointed out, because dancing was a ritual act, cultic, and therefore to be feared as a rival. A well-known passage from the apocryphal *Acts of St John* (before A.D. 150) describes Christ meeting his disciples; he says

Before I am delivered up unto them let us sing an hymn to the Father, and so go forth to that which lieth before us. He bade us therefore make as it were a ring, holding one another's hands, and himself standing in the midst he said: Answer Amen unto me. He began, then, to sing a hymn and to say:
    Glory be to thee, Father.
And we, going about in a ring, answered him: Amen . . .[57]

This account of a mystic ring-dance, taking the place of the Last Supper, suggests there may have been dance within the Christian Church itself – on the margins, at least, if not in the centre. Liturgical dancing in the early Church seems, however, not to have been confined to heretical or deviant sects; it could be a proper and acceptable act of adoration.[58]

The expanding Church feared especially the dances of paganism with their tenacious imaginative hold on the people and their often disreputable associations, and a long series of pronouncements by the Councils of the Church, denouncing dance and song, stretches from the year 589 into the seventeenth century.[59] They provide evidence for the fact of ecclesiastical dances but not much more, except in the latest period. For the twelfth and thirteenth centuries, fortunately, other witnesses are available. The liturgical commentator Durandus (1230–96) states that on the eve of St Stephen's Day the deacons, to honour their patron saint, 'joining together in dance sing an antiphon of St Stephen' (*in tripudio convenientes cantant antiphonam de Sancto Stephano*).[60] And in Limoges on the feast of St Martial there was dancing to psalms in the church; the singers and dancers concluded their psalm with the refrain[61]

[56] See Gougaud, 'La danse dans les églises', (1914); Spanke, 'Tanzmusik in der Kirche' (1930c); Sahlin, ch. 7, 'Etude sur la danse rituelle chrétienne au moyen âge'.
[57] Transl. James, *Apocryphal New Testament* (1953), 253.
[58] Sahlin, 137ff, citing numerous authorities.
[59] Sahlin, 139; and Gougaud, listing the Councils' denouncements from 589 onwards (pp. 10–14).
[60] Gougaud, 233, from Durandus, *Rationale*, VII.42; Spanke (1930c), 150. There may have been a special connection between antiphons and dance (Spanke); but the word *antiphona* is often very loosely used in the period.
[61] Gougaud, 236; Spanke (1930c), 150. *Bous* is a dialectal form for *vous*; *epingarem* is glossed by Gougaud as cognate with O Fr. *espringuier* ('sauter', 'danser'). A more famous ecclesiastical dance-song from Limoges is the macaronic 'Mei amic e mei fiel' for the Annunciation: see Axton, 56–7; Roncaglia in *Cultura neolatina* 9 (1949) 67; Gennrich, *Nachlass der Troubadours* (1958–65), no. 1 (with music). Bischoff (1967, introduction) suggests that in the *Carmina Burana* 'the long, rarely interrupted series of love, dance and spring songs to each of which a German strophe has been added (nos. 135–48, 150–3, 155, 161–75, 179–83) . . . were sung to the round dances of the *clerici*'.

Sen Marsau, pregat per nous
Et nous epingarem per bous.

St Martial, pray for us and we will dance (?) for you.

This context would seem to support the translation of *tripudia* in the following as 'dances', the normal but not invariable meaning: *Fiunt autem quatuor tripudia post nativitatem Domini in ecclesia* – 'There are four dances in church after Christmas'.[62] The four are on St Stephen's Day (deacons), St John the Evangelist's Day (priests), Holy Innocents' Day (choirboys), Circumcision or Epiphany (sub-deacons). These were the well-known occasions for some licence (and occasionally worse) in medieval church establishments. Festivities were evidently not confined to secular cathedrals nor to men clergy; a visitation to a nunnery near Rouen in 1261 found occasion to lament:

Item in festo S. Johannis, Stephani et Innocentium nimia jocositate et scurrilibus cantibus utebantur, utpote farsis, conductis, notulis; precepimus, quod honestius et cum majori devotione alias se haberent.[63]

on the feast(s) of St John, of St Stephen and of the Innocents they engaged in immoderate foolery and scurrilous songs, namely 'farsing', *conductus*, *lais* (?); we have instructed them to behave more decently and with greater devotion in future.

However, the authorities evidently allowed dances when they were decorous and disapproved of them only when they got out of hand. A perhaps characteristic instruction comes from the cathedral at Sens: the clergy are permitted to dance at great festivals – *non tamen saliendo*, 'provided they do not leap off the ground'.[64]

There survive in manuscripts of the period a good number of Latin songs, many with music, which may have been the dance-songs of the Church. Again, the direct evidence for the connection is a little later than one would wish. 'In Besançon the clergy danced, according to a manuscript of the early fifteenth century, a dance at Easter called *bergerette*, to the melody of "Fidelium sonet vox sobria". We recognize at once the rondeau [*rondellus*] beginning thus . . . with the form: a[10] *a* aa *aa'* – [musically] A A A B A B.'[65] The surviving songs

---

[62] Gougaud, 233, n. 1, from Jean Beleth, *Rationale*, 72 (*PL* 202, col. 79). Spanke (1930c), 151, observes that *tripudium*, besides its special meaning of 'dance', can mean simply 'jubilation' in general.

[63] Spanke (1930c), 168–9; he argues that *notula*, diminutive of *nota*, is a type of song, derived from the earliest Latin sequences, originally instrumental in character. It is discussed by Grocheo (see chapter 12:III below) together with *ductia* and *stantipes*, and is distinguished from them by the number of its sections, *puncta* (Rohloff, 136: '. . . notae vocatae quattuor punctorum').

[64] At Moosburg a procession from the church to a round-dance outside in the forecourt was the occasion for dance-songs surviving in the 'Moosburg Gradual' (Munich, Universitätsbibliothek M S 156); see F. A. Stein in *Festschrift Erich Valentin*, ed. G. Weiss (Regensburg 1976), 231–4.

[65] Spanke (1930c), 154–5. The text is in *A H* xx.44 (no. 57), the music in the Florence M S, fasc. xi, fol. 465. See Anderson, M17. The small letters denote the rhyme-scheme (see note 82 below); the superscript figure 10 indicates that the lines have 10 syllables in them.

are mostly in *rondeau*-form like the one just quoted, and this in itself is *prima facie* evidence that they were dance-songs. This is not simply a matter of analogy with the French *rondeau*, for it can be shown that some Latin *rondelli* (as I prefer to call them) were actually written as *contrafacta* to French songs. A manuscript in the Bibliothèque Nationale, Paris, of the late thirteenth century, contains twenty-seven songs written by a clerk, perhaps a schoolmaster of St Victor.[66] Several are in *virelai*-form (i.e. similar to the English carol with initial burden repeated between stanzas), and many have snatches of French (i.e. *refrains*) attached to them; for example, this for St Nicholas:

> Joi le rossignol
> chanter de sus un rain
> u jardinet m'amie
> desus l'ante florie

> *Contra in Latino: Sancti Nicolai.*
> Sancti Nicolai
> vacemus titulis
> cum summa letitia
> pangentes Alleluja.[67]

I heard the nightingale sing on a branch in the little garden of my friend, under the blossoming engrafted tree.

Alternative Latin text for St Nicholas:
Let us give our attention to honouring Holy Nicholas, sounding Alleluia with great gladness.

Another piece of evidence incontrovertibly associating Latin songs with dance comes, admittedly, from well outside the northern European area with which we are primarily concerned, but it should be mentioned here. The most interesting section of the *Llibre Vermell* of Montserrat (fourteenth century) is 'a carefully made and handsomely written collection of ten songs, in the Catalan vernacular and in Latin, with considerable variety of musical and literary style'.[68] The Latin preface to the songs states

---

[66] BN lat. 15131, fol. 178v: see *AH* xx.24 (description of collection); *AH* xx–xxi (Latin texts); Hauréau, *Notices et extraits de quelques manuscrits latins de la Bibliothèque Nationale* (Paris 1890), IV.278; Greene (1974), introd., p. xxv. Boogaard, p. 316, lists seventeen *refrains* from the MS. Gennrich (1921ff), II.291, prints their French texts; the MS gives no music. The relation of the Latin texts to the French refrains can be seen clearly only in Spanke (1929).

[67] The text as printed by Greene (1974), p. xxv, appears to be corrupt. Boogaard, refr. 1159, gives it as follows: *J'oi le rousignol chanter / dessus le raim / u bois qui reverdie / souz une ente flourie*, referring also to its use by Jehannot de l'Escurel (?–1304). I thank Janthia Yearley for checking this text with the manuscript.

[68] Greene (1974), introd., pp. xxvii–xxviii.

quia interdum, diu, peregrini quando vigilant in ecclesia beate marie de monte serrato volunt cantare et trepudiare, et etiam in platea de die. Et ibi non debeant nisi honestas ac devotas cantilenas cantare.[69]

that from time to time over a long period pilgrims keeping vigil in the church of the Blessed Virgin of Montserrat have been eager to sing and dance, even in the square by broad daylight. And in that place they should not do any singing unless the songs are decent and devout.

The second song, 'Stella splendens in monte' (2 voc.), is headed[70]

Sequitur alia cantilena omni dulcedine plena ei[u]sdem domine nostre ad trepudium rotundum.

There follows another song for a round-dance full of all the sweetness of that same Lady of ours.

The burden which precedes the first verse puns on the name 'Montserrat':[71]

> Stella splendens in *monte*
> ut solis radium
> miraculis *serrato*
> exaudi populum.

Star resplendent with miracles, like a ray of the sun, on Monte Serrato (saw-shaped mountain), hearken to your people.

The last song of all takes death as its theme: 'Ad mortem festinamus / peccare desistamus'. It is especially interesting since it appears to make a *virelai* (perhaps, therefore, a dance-song) out of a version of a Latin song, 'Scribere proposui', which survives in several other manuscripts, three of them British.[72]

A final example of a probable Latin dance-song is connected with a well-known and often-discussed yet still mysterious English lyric, 'Maiden in the mor lay'.[73] This haunting piece has always attracted attention because of its elusive and baffling quality. Latter-day Stephen Langtons have brought their patristic learning and moral fervour to bear on it and produced results of which no medieval homilist need have been ashamed. Others have pointed out the fact that the (or an) original lyric, 'Maiden in the moor', must have had

---

[69] G. Suñol, 'Els cants dels Romeus' (1918), 106. Suñol prints texts and melodies and provides plates of the *Llibre Vermell* (Source 20). The music is in mensural notation. Spanke (1936), 127–30, analyses the metrical and melodic forms and comments on the inadequacies of the texts printed in *AH* xx.160ff. The most recent study is by H. Anglès, 'El Llibre Vermell' (1955), who also prints the melodies.

[70] Suñol, pl. 2 and p. 122. No music in MS, space provided.

[71] Suñol, *ibid*.

[72] Suñol, pl. 11; 187 faulty text; 191 musical transcription. Anderson, L161. The English sources are: the Dublin Troper, p. 187; BL Add. 16559, fol. 220 (no music); Paris, BN fr. 25408, fol. 120 (Source 33).

[73] Oxford, Bodl. Rawl. MS D.913: single leaf. *Index MEV: Supplement* 2037.5 lists numerous studies; Dobson and Harrison, no. 16b (with Latin text 'Peperit virgo'), commentary, 189–93.

a secular meaning, since in the earlier fourteenth century the Bishop of Ossory apparently classed it with *cantilenis teatralibus*. The evidence is in the moralizing anthology of Latin songs, The Red Book of Ossory;[74] the preface runs

Attende, lector, quod Episcopus Ossoriensis fecit istas cantilenas pro vicariis Ecclesie Cathedralis sacerdotibus et clericis suis ad cantandum in magnis festis et solaciis, ne guttura eorum et ora Deo sanctificata polluantur cantilenis teatralibus, turpibus et secularibus, et cum sint cantatores provideant sibi de notis convenientibus secundum quod dictamina requirunt.[75]

Be advised, reader, that the Bishop of Ossory has made these songs for the vicars of the cathedral church, for the priests and for his [the bishop's] clerks, to be sung on the important holidays and at times of recreation in order that their throats and mouths, consecrated to God, may not be polluted by songs which are associated with revelry, lewd and worldly; and, since they are trained singers, let them provide themselves with suitable tunes according to what these sets of words require.

Along with the sixty poems, none of which have music in the manuscript, are a number of marginalia in English and French, such as 'Have mercie on me, frere / Barfote that y go' (three times) and 'Harrow! ieo su trahy / Par fol amour de mal amy'. The barely legible heading to no. 11, 'Peperit virgo', first deciphered by Richard Greene, is 'mayde yn the moore lay'.[76] This must, all agree, indicate an English song, to the tune of which the Latin poem could be sung. In strict logic, of course, it does not follow that this is a song the Bishop thought 'lewd', but simply that his scribe or his *cantatores* knew that tune would fit; it might refer indeed to a religious song in the vernacular. Be this as it may, the stanza-forms with a minimum of adjustment run closely parallel.

Maiden in the mor lay –	Peperit virgo,
in the mor lay –	Virgo regia,
sevenyst fulle,	Mater orphanorum,
sevenyst fulle.	Mater orphanorum;
Maiden in the mor lay –	Peperit virgo,
in the mor lay –	Virgo regia,
seuenistes fulle,	Mater orphanorum,
[seuenistes fulle]	Mater orphanorum,
ant a day.	Plena gracia.[77]

A maiden, a royal virgin, has borne a child;
[she is] the mother of orphans, full of grace.

---

[74] There are editions of The Red Book of Ossory (Source 11) by E. Colledge, *The Latin Poems of Richard Ledrede* (Toronto 1974), Greene (1974), and T. Stemmler, *The Latin Hymns of Richard Ledrede* (Mannheim 1975); comparative review, *Anglia* 98 (1980) 487. See also Greene (1977), introd., pp. cxv–cxvi. The MS is described in detail by Stemmler, pp. xiii–xvii: 'the contents range from *Magna Carta* to a treatise on *aqua vitae*'.

[75] Text and translation (slightly emended) from Greene (1977), pp. iii–iv.

[76] R. L. Greene, '"The Maid of the Moor" in *The Red Book of Ossory*', *Speculum* 27 (1952) 504–6.

[77] English text from Robbins (1952), no. 18 (pp. 12–13), with slight rearrangement.

It has always seemed possible that 'Maiden in the mor lay' was a dance-song if only because of the refrain-like repetition of lines within the stanza. I say 'refrain-*like*' because, surprisingly, no material is repeated from one stanza to the next, though the incantatory pattern of apparently incomplete lines continues and is intensified:

> Welle was hire mete.
> Wat was hire mete?
>> the primerole ant the –
>> the primerole ant the –
> Welle was hire mete.
> Wat was hire mete?
>> the primerole ant the violet.

In 1968 Peter Dronke published an imaginative interpretation of the lyric as a dance-song with mime, based on a Germanic legend of a water-sprite: 'she tends to appear at village dances in the guise of a beautiful human girl, and to fascinate young men there, but she must always return into the moor at a fixed hour, or else she dies'.[78] In view of the dance-song possibility, Siegfried Wenzel's discovery a few years later of a specific reference to the moor-maiden song as a *carole* is most satisfactory. The preacher of an anti-Wycliffite sermon in 1381 writes:[79]

In the first age, that of gold, men lived in mutual love, innocence, moderation and peace. Their food was fruit that grows of its own: figs and dates, apples, nuts and acorns. And what was their drink? The answer appears in a certain song [*cantico*], viz. a *karole* that is called 'The mayde be wode lay' . . . [they drank] 'the colde water of the welle spryng'.

This, with the mention of the well-water, clinches the matter; the Middle English poem must be a dance-song, and indeed a *carole*. If this is right 'Peperit virgo' and other Latin poems in the Red Book may possibly have been not only sung but danced to.

The Latin ecclesiastical dance-songs centre upon the festivals of Christmas and Easter, with Christmas predominant:[80]

Festa dies agitur –	a
Mundo salus redditur –	a
in qua sol exoritur	a
qui mundum replet lumine.	b
Mundo salus redditur	a
Christo nato de virgine.	b

---

[78] Dronke (1968), 195–6.
[79] S. Wenzel, 'The moor maiden: a contemporary view', *Speculum* 49 (1974) 69–74.
[80] The Egerton Chansonnier (Source 14), fol. 47. See *A H* xx.89 (no. 91); xx.248, music; Anderson (1978c), pp. lii, 35. Anderson N16 gives further references. See especially Spanke (1930a), 123.

The festal day is here – *salvation is given back to the world* – the day on which the sun rises filling the world with his light. *Salvation . . . as Christ is born of a virgin.*

Characteristically, in many texts the Blessed Virgin is the centre of attention and adoration rather than the new-born Christ:[81]

Sol est in meridie –	a
Laudes demus Marie –	*a*
Fulget dies gratie	a
et gaudii.	*b*
A laude Marie	a^1
non debent conscie	a^2
lingue demi.	b^2

The sun is in the south – let us give praises to Mary – the day of grace shines out, the day of joy. The perceptive tongues of sinners should not be torn from Mary's praise.

(These two songs, which follow each other in the Egerton Chansonnier (BL Egerton 274), show incidentally that the form of the Latin *rondellus* is as flexible as that of the French *rondeau*. The first song is in the regular form; the second, in a freer.)[82] The largest single collection of *rondelli* is in the Florence MS. The fascicle opens with a group of Easter songs, including:[83]

In hac die Dei –	a
Dicant nunc Hebrei –	*a*
sepulcrum Iudei	a
male servaverunt –	b
quomodo Iudei	a^1
regem perdiderunt.	b^1

In this day of the Lord – let the Hebrews now declare – the Jews have failed to guard the sepulchre – how the Jews have destroyed their King.

Later in the same fascicle the tone seems to change. On the surface it is not Easter which is being celebrated but simply the return of spring, as in this delightful *reverdie*:[84]

---

[81] The Egerton Chansonnier, fol. 47v. See *A H* xx.212 (no. 298); Anderson (1978c), pp. lii, 35. Anderson N17 gives further references.

[82] The small letters denote rhyme-schemes; an italic letter indicates a refrain-line with that rhyme; a superscript figure indicates a verbally different refrain-line with the same rhyme again.

[83] Florence MS, fol. 463. *A H* xx.38 (no. 44). Anderson (1978c), pp. iv, 2. Anderson M4 gives further references.

[84] Florence MS, fol. 468. *A H* xx.93 (no. 101). Anderson (1978c), pp. xxix, 18. Anderson M40 gives further references. Spanke (1930a), 119, states that this is a Christmas song, but the phrase *novi candor lilii* (the brightness of a new lily) in strophe 3 hardly seems specific enough to support it. However, the following *rondellus* says that *Floralis gaudia / Dat Epiphania* (flowery Epiphany brings joy). See also the texts of 'Illuxit lux' (fol. 468) and 'Christo sit laus' (fol. 468); texts printed Anderson (1978c), pp. xxviii–xxix.

Ecce tempus gaudii –	a
Gaudeamus, socii! –	a
Cesset labor studii.	a
In hoc florali gaudio	b
Floris renovatio	b^1
Lusus est incitatio.	b^2

Behold the season of joy – *Comrades, let us rejoice!* – let the studious grind come to a stop. *In this time of flowery joy, the flowers' renewal incites us to play.*

The second stanza refers to *vox tripudii* (the 'voice/sound of dance'?).

These two *rondelli* from the Florence M S (which, it will be recalled, is huge in its totality and is one of the principal sources for the liturgical polyphony of Notre Dame of Paris) are different in form from the Egerton *rondelli*. But form in these songs is not to be described in purely literary terms. It will be most illuminatingly dealt with as part of a general discussion of the music of dance-song, to which we must now turn.

iv   The music of dance-song

The music of medieval dance-song comes from many sources, few of which contain whole musical texts on which we can fully rely. The Latin *rondellus* collections just referred to are in fact examples of apparently whole musical texts; no more music is required to perform the poems given. And for the French *rondeau* we have, for instance, whole musical texts for the ten *rondeaux* of Guillaume d'Amiens, *li paignour* (second half of thirteenth century). Otherwise our knowledge of dance-song music must be derived largely from the corpus of French *refrains*. These occur notated in three main types of source, in addition to the *rondeau* collections:[85]

(i) as isolated *refrains* in literary contexts, principally romances (in these sources they are more often without their music);
(ii) as integral parts of *trouvère* chansons of the genre *chanson-avec-des-refrains* (and particularly in *pastourelles* written in this form);
(iii) as integral parts of the polyphonic motets contained in such sources as the Montpellier and Bamberg collections of the thirteenth century.

There is, it should be made clear, no repertoire of Latin *refrains* quite in the sense defined for the French. Of course many Latin songs and all the *rondelli* (by definition) have refrains in the purely formal sense, but these are not of the individualized, aphoristic kind with their own tunes. They may be found to have taken their origin from favourite hymns or antiphons or sequences; they are even more likely to repeat the thousand clichés of medieval devotional verse.[86]

---

[85] References to all these sources can be found in Boogaard's indexes.
[86] Stäblein (1975), 160, argues that the *refrain*/refrain, Latin as well as French, was *always* a 'given' (*vorgegeben*) but does not substantiate.

The little collection of *rondeaux* by Guillaume d'Amiens occurs in a trouvère chansonnier of quite varied scope and content: the Chansonnier du Vatican dates from the turn of the thirteenth century and contains *chansons, pastourelles, jeux-partis, motets, rondeaux,* a group of Adam de la Halle's works, and *chansons pieuses* addressed to the Virgin.[87] The last *rondeau* but one is entitled 'C'est la fins'.[88]

Ex. 63

It is certain:
whatever any one says I'm going to be in love.
It's down there in the middle of the meadow –
It is certain: I wish to be in love –
down there a dance has begun;
I have a beautiful sweetheart.
It is certain:
whatever any one says I'm going to be in love.

The transcription of this widely known melody poses a rhythmic problem which must be mentioned as a preliminary. The notation of this whole group

[87] The Chansonnier du Vatican (Source 38).
[88] Melody, fol. 119v (non-mensural notation). See Boogaard, rond. 92 (refr. 338). See also Gennrich (1921ff), I.37–8 (no. 49) in measured transcription; II.32–5 commentary and further musical texts. As Ludwig first pointed out ((1910), I.201), a version of the *refrain* melody occurs at the end of the *duplum* of a Notre Dame *clausula* and in three Latin motets with different Latin texts, as well as in French motets. Gennrich gives all the melodies but does not distinguish their notations.

is non-mensural: as the conventionalized original symbols added over phrase
I show, the single notes appear as *virgae* (undifferentiated 'longs', to use the
terms of mensural notation); the note-groups or melismas appear as simple
ligatures. I shall not enter on a discussion of the rhythmic problem here; it is
deferred to Part III.[89] The problem is not, to my way of thinking, crucial in
the present context. I assume it as axiomatic that all choral dance-songs,
dances sung and performed in company, must have a metrical base, an
underlying regular rhythm – and one not so very *under*-lying, since it must
be immediately recognizable by the dancers. Subsequent discussion will
show, I think, that Gennrich's triple-time transcription is more likely to be
right than a transcription based on the isosyllabic principle. However, the
essential point is the difference between an 'irregular' rhythm and a regular
metre; an isosyllabic transcription could in fact here be measured in duple
metre.

The next and last *rondeau* by Guillaume d'Amiens is worth quoting in full
because it raises this and other points of analysis:[90]

Ex. 64

---

[89] Its complexity can be gathered from the mass of material referred to in note 88 above. One
thing is certain: this sequence of musical notes may have had different rhythmical and
metrical shapes in different contexts.

[90] Melody, fol. 119v (non-mensural notation). Boogaard, rond. 93 (refr. 1531). See also
Gennrich (1921ff), 1.38 (no. 50), for a slightly different transcription; 11.35–6 for commentary and other melodic versions. The *refrain* also occurs in the *Renart le Nouvel*; two MSS
give this melody, the third a totally different one.

7 Pren-dés i gar- de, s'on mi re- gar- de;

8 s'on mi re- gar- de, di- tes le moi.

Take care, lest someone sees me!
If someone sees me, tell me.
It's right down there in that wood –
Take care, lest someone sees me! –
the shepherdess was looking after her cows there.
Sweet brown-haired one, I offer myself to you.
Take care! . . .
If someone . . .

It is interesting and I think significant that it is the initial (and final) refrain of this dance-song that is virtually *un*ambiguous as to metre. It would, I think, be perverse to frame it in duple measure. It is unambiguous because of the number of syllables – five – in each phrase member. The most natural way to measure and balance the phrase is to lengthen the rhyme syllable.[91] The relationship between the words and the melody seems totally unsophisticated – naive to a degree that we shall rarely encounter in other types of medieval songs. This naiveté comes about not only because the words of the refrain are what they are but because the music has special characteristics which distinguish it from other types.

The characteristics of 'Prendés i garde' as a melody are: short, concise phrases more or less of even length; the answering of one 'open' phrase by a 'closed' (e.g. phrases 1 and 2), or of several by a 'closed' (phrases 3–6); rhythmic balance of a rather obvious kind; a clearly defined tonality; a small melodic range; simple note-to-syllable relationship with virtually no melismas. All these features are found in other *refrains* and *rondeaux*; to describe one is virtually to describe them all. It is perhaps the clear modern-sounding tonality and phrasal balance, that most clearly mark off the music of dance-song from that of most courtly chansons (questions of rhythm apart). The 'd minor' tonality of 'Prendés i garde', for instance, is strongly, even monotonously, emphasized throughout: the insistent *a* (the 'dominant' of the scale) is repeated three or four times at the beginning of each phrase. The phrase then hinges on a stressed *g* before either turning back up in its 'open' form or descending firmly down to *d*, the tonic or key-note (the apparently anachronistic terms of classical harmonic analysis seem fully justified). It has all the simplicity and irresistibility of a favourite nursery rhyme.

[91] Duple measure could, of course, be achieved by halving notes 1.2–4, compressing 1.7–8, halving 1.9, and so on.

An equally obvious balanced effect, this time in 'C major', is apparent in another rondeau by Guillaume d'Amiens: 'Ses très dous regars'.[92]

Ex. 65

1. Ses tres dous re- gars 2. m'a mon cuer em- blé;
3. Ce n'est mie a gas~ 4. ses tres dous re- wars ~
5. el- le m'o- cir- ra 6. se li viegne a gre.
7. Ses tres dous re- gars 8. m'a mon cuer em- blé.

Her sweet look / has stolen my heart away;
It's not a joke – Her sweet look –
She will kill me / if it pleases her.
Her sweet look
has stolen my heart away.

Here there is a simple oscillation between tonic (*c*) and dominant (*g*). All the characteristics of the *rondeau* 'Prendés i garde' are also found here without exception. They are both, in consequence, 'catchy', easily memorable – which is what a dance-song needs to be.

On an earlier page I noted the poetic form of the *rondeau*: at its simplest it is *aaabab*. The musical form is equally, or even more, repetitive and may consist of two phrases only, one normally with an 'open' end, the other moving to a full close. So in 'Prendés i garde' we have

	words	music
Prendés i garde, s'on mi regarde;	a	A
S'on mi regarde, dites le moi.	b	B
C'est tout la jus en cel boschaige,	?a	A¹
– *prendés i garde, s'on mi regarde* –	a	A
la pastourele u gardoit vaches;	?a	A¹
plaisant brunete a vous m'otroi.	b	B
Prendés i garde, s'on mi regarde;	a	A
s'on mi regarde, dites le moi.	b	B

(The symbol ?*a* indicates imperfect rhyme, or assonance)

[92] Melody, fol. 118 (non-mensural notation). Boogaard, rond. 87 (refr. 1717). See also Gennrich (1921ff), I.33 (no. 44); II.31. The *refrain* occurs in a *chanson-avec-des-refrains* (R816), without music, and in the *Roman de Fauvel* (Source 27), notated fol. 24v.

This happens to be a 'regular' *rondeau* by later, fixed, standards. But we are not entitled on the evidence to think that such a conception existed in the late twelfth and most of the thirteenth centuries; and it is mistaken scholarship to try to force all the surviving material into such a mould. To perform a dance-song of this type the chorus only had to learn a simple two-phrase melody with its words, while the soloist (*qui chante avant et fiert dou piê*) needed more words but virtually the same segments of melody. Since the *refrain* would often contain all or nearly all the musical material needed to perform the piece, it was obviously cardinal. Hence its status as an independent unit, if it was not one before (the question of pre-existence does not seem here to be of essential importance), and its availability as a basis for other dances or for other compositions of a different kind.

Before considering other aspects of the French *refrain*, it will be useful to look at some Latin *rondelli* to see how they compare with their French counterparts. We may start with one from an English source, 'Qui passus est pridie resurrexit hodie'.[93]

Ex. 66

He who lately suffered,
has risen today.
A new giant, of twin substance,
has risen today, the king of glory.

From the literary point of view this looks like a 'regular' rondeau, except that there is no contrasted rhyme (a/b). Musically it is somewhat different, as shown: AABCBC. It differs from the 'regular' form in that the melody for the internal refrain (line 2) is not the same as the melody for the end-refrain with the same words (line 5). But the practicality of the form is evident: the chorus have only to repeat the music the cantor has just sung. There is no chance of their forgetting it.

[93] Melody, Bodleian, MS Bodley 937 fol. 446v (non-mensural notation); *AH* xxi.31 (no. 31). Anderson (1978c), pp. xlv, 30 (from Tours MS 927). See further Anderson N4.

From the Egerton Chansonnier comes a Whitsuntide *rondellus* based on the sequence 'Veni sancte spiritus'.[94]

Ex. 67

Come, holy Spirit, hope of all,
and send [your light] from heaven. – *Come, holy Spirit –*
You are the glorious searcher of hearts.
Come, holy Spirit, hope of all.
. . . Bestow your light on the hearts,
your purity on the the minds, of faithful people.

'Veni sancte', like most Latin *rondelli* including the others I have quoted, is strophic. In this instance, I have underlaid to the melody the words of verse 2 to show how they fit; the scribe wrote them, and verses 3 and 4, as prose following the melody. In this respect the Latin dance-songs differ from the French. Out of 198 *rondeaux* edited by Boogaard only one is strophic; it comes from *La Panthère d'Amours*, a romance by Nicole de Margival.[95]

In other ways the *rondelli* and the *rondeaux* are very similar. Both enjoy a good deal of formal freedom in this earlier period. The Latin dance-songs, we can see from the two examples, have the same balanced rhythms, lucid tonality, 'open' and 'closed' phrases, syllabic movement, and so on. There is only one additional comment that should be made about the two particular pieces: it is that they both use the major triad (*g–b–d*) and touch the *f* below (presumed *f* natural) in a way which, especially in 'Veni sancte', is reminiscent of one of the favourite melodic clichés of the *lai*.

[94] Melody: Egerton Chansonnier, fol. 49 (non-mensural notation). *AH* xxi.56 (no. 80) wrongly arranged. Anderson (1978c), pp. liii, 46. See further Anderson n19.
[95] Ed. H. Todd, *SATF* (Paris 1883); it contains several pieces by Adam de la Halle.

The *rondellus* 'Veni sancte spiritus' is interesting, too, in another way: the melodic similarities to *rondeau* melody are not simply a matter of stylistic conjecture. There occurs in various motets a French *refrain* to this identical tune; its form seems to be remarkably constant.[96]

Ex. 68

A ma dame ai mis mon cuer et mon pen-sé.

I have set my heart and my thought on my lady.

There is also a complete French *rondeau* with this refrain in BN fr. 12786, amongst a group of thirty-five ruled for three-voice setting, like the *rondeaux* of Adam de la Halle, but never completed with music.[97] The question of priority (French *v*. Latin) is, for us, unimportant – though it is worth remarking that *contrafacta* and borrowings are by no means always *from* Latin *to* the vernacular. The simple fact of shared tunes is to be remarked; the two repertoires, French and Latin, are related in more than a formal way.[98]

Another link between Latin and French dance-song seems rather more artificial, but supports the case. Adam de la Bassée's *Ludus super Anticlaudianum* is a re-writing, paraphrase and, in some respects, simplified version of the famous and influential Latin allegorical poem *Anticlaudianus* by Alanus de Insulis (Alain of Lille). Adam de la Bassée, canon and priest, was also of Lille, and in *c*. 1280, a hundred years after his fellow townsman had written the original, he re-worked it.[99]

The original allegory is . . . rendered more accessible, much less severe. Adam seems also to have tried in another way to make the work entertaining: he emphasises the underlying musical framework by adding to the poem 38 pieces of music, some of which may well have been song-hits of the late thirteenth century.[100]

Some of the pieces may be original compositions by Adam; others are *contrafacta* and are advertised as such. Amongst the latter is a dance-song headed

[96] Montpellier M S (Source 19), fol. 231v; Boogaard, refr. 662; Gennrich (1921ff), 1.85 (no. 108); 11.96–7, giving the melody from three motet M S S. The *refrain* also occurs in two *chansons-avec-des-refrains* (R1957, R1099) without music.

[97] Boogaard, rond. 186, from B N fr. 12786 (Gennrich (1921ff), 11.90); only the *refrains* would have been notated.

[98] See note 66 above (and text) and note 88 above.

[99] A. Hughes, '*Ludus super Anticlaudianum*' (1970). The M S is Lille, Bibl. Mun. M S 316; see RISM, B.IV[1], 269–70 (late-thirteenth-century).

[100] Hughes (1970), 3.

Cantilena de chorea super illam que incipit 'Qui grieve ma cointise se iou l'ai ce me sont amouretes, c'au cuer ai'.[101]

Dance-song to [the tune of] that one which begins 'Qui grieve . . .'

This *refrain* is not otherwise known; but fortunately Adam de la Bassée, as usual, provides the melody, which has all the expected characteristics.[102]

Ex. 69

Nobility, finely decked in virtuous manners has no equal in this world below. She despises sins – *Nobility, finely decked* – She is not haughty, not puffed up by her polished manners; she governs her people by the mirror of [her own] behaviour.

The discussion of the music of dance-song has so far covered only *rondeaux* and *rondelli* with complete surviving texts, even if only single-stanza texts as in the case of the French. I turn now to the scraps of melody associated with *refrains* in the text of *Renart le nouvel*. It is not the only romance to contain musical notation (the *Roman de Fauvel* is another, infinitely richer, more celebrated); but in *Renart* the music is traditional and old-fashioned.[103]

[101] Boogaard, refr. 1599 (*unicum*). Gennrich (1921ff), II.219–20, fits the French words to Adam's melody.
[102] fol 36: diplomatic transcription, Hughes (1970), 8 (Ex. 2). The notation is mensural.
[103] Boogaard, refr. 1862, rond. 195; the melody is from the Adam de la Halle MS, which contains a text of *Renart le nouvel*. The *refrain* occurs at line 2544 (ed. Roussel). See also Gennrich (1921ff), II.96.

Ex. 70

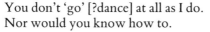

You don't 'go' [?dance] at all as I do.
Nor would you know how to.

(This *refrain* forms the refrain for a complete *rondeau* found elsewhere without music.) The *Roman de Renart le nouvel* (completed 1289) is a continuation of the famous *Roman de Renart* (*c.* 1170–*c.* 1205). To be 'continued' was a fate wont to befall all successful medieval narratives. *Renart le nouvel* survives in four sources, three of them supplied with, and the fourth ruled for, music. The versions of the poem do not agree about the *refrains*. Sometimes one manuscript will have a different *refrain* from the others; sometimes they will differ as to the melody which goes with the text in question. Thus for the *refrain* following the one just quoted there are three separate tunes.[104]

Ex. 71

I will never be without love in all my life.

The melodies are clearly distinct, but they all follow the 'rules': they are the same length because of the syllabic 'rule', for example; each in its different tonality establishes the 'open'/'closed' effect we have noted before; they are balanced; and have the accustomed 'obvious' tunefulness.

The fact of the interchangeability of *refrains* within the same poetic narrative

[104] Gennrich, II.157: (a) the Adam de la Halle MS, fol. 129; (b) BN MS fr. 372, fol. 18v; (c) BN MS fr. 1593, fol. 18 (I have emended the last measure of (c)).

is most interesting: it suggests that even though there was evidently a stable corpus of well-known *refrain*-melodies, a singer could nevertheless invent a new tune, if he wished to, to the same old tag. The fictional context of this *refrain* in all three texts is moreover the dancing of a *carole*:[105]

> 'Or carolon et si cantons
> haut et cler, je cuit nos arons
> anquenit le pris de le feste.'
> A che jor n'i ot onques beste
> qui ne carolast et cantast
> et qui son cors n'i esprouvast.
> N'i ot chelui ne fache joie,
> Et Rois Nobles pour che c'on l'oie,
> en haut commença a canter:

'Now let us dance and sing as well, loud and clear; I think tonight we shall get the prize of the festival.' This day there was never an animal that didn't dance and sing and show his paces. There was no one who didn't make merry. And the *Rois Nobles* began to sing out loudly so that everyone could hear him.

This *carole* seems to have been a sequence of four dance-songs.[106] Some degree of flexibility, even spontaneity, may evidently have governed the choice of melody for a *carole*.

Other *refrains* in the text of *Renart le nouvel* are referred to variously as *ce motet, cest cant, une cançon, rondet, rondet à carole, cançon de carole*. We can be sure that, as in many later periods (one has only to think of Elizabethan England or of England and America in the 1930s), dance-song provided many of the popular songs that the age required, whether or not they were always *used* with dancing. People, of whatever class, surely did not go around singing the high courtly chansons? They sang *refrains, rondeaux*, and *rondelli*.

In chapter 14 I shall consider some of the wider uses of this huge, and often strangely neglected, repertoire of *refrains*, in order to see if they throw any light on the central enquiry – the relationship of words and music, and what this means for an understanding of medieval song. In conclusion to the present chapter I shall briefly review what can be deduced about that relationship from the straightforward examples of *rondeau* and isolated *refrain* which have been given above.

v   Words and music

The relationship is different from that we have seen in *la grande chanson courtoise* and shall see in narrative poetry, in Gregorian chant and elsewhere. It is a physical thing, basic and close to ordinary human experience. Granted the rightness of my initial assumption, that 'all choral dance-songs, all dances sung and performed in company, must have a metrical base' – a strictly

[105] Ed. Roussel.
[106] Different MSS of the poem insert different refrains at will (see Boogaard, p. 332), making a total of eight surviving.

measured regular rhythm – words as well as music are likely to contribute to this effect. And they do: either by being themselves accentually measured, or by allowing themselves to be used *as if they were*. The Latin *rondelli* provide the most accessible examples, for the tradition of versifying to which they belong is well understood and was understood at the time. They are *rhythmi, ritmi*; syllable-counting verse clearly distinguished by nearly all medieval theorists as *musica rhythmica*, as distinct from *musica metrica* which is 'measured' in feet (i.e. quantitative verse, with longs and shorts: see p. 416). Whatever may be the case in some other types of Latin song, especially earlier ones, the thirteenth-century *rondelli* generally have alternating strong and weak beats; they are usually accentual trochaics (/./.), but the pattern need not remain constant even in a short song. Thus, if we look back to Ex. 67, we see that the refrain-lines (1–2) are respectively trochaic and iambic:

Veni sancte spiritus / spes om-ni-um.

The preceding example, 'Qui passus est' (Ex. 66), introduces a light complication. The first line, taken on its own, sounds like two dactyls with an upbeat

Qui passus est pridie

but the rest of the song contradicts this; the metre must be

Qui passus est pridie resurrexit hodie *etc*

The melodies of both these *rondelli* fit naturally into the patterns set up by the words; and any transcription, whether in duple or triple time, has to acknowledge this. I have said 'set up' by the words, and this is one way of putting it. But it could be misleading. It might be better to think of the pattern being set up by movement – the movement of the dance. The words themselves do not *require* this particular kind of pulsed, metrical response and can easily have their natural subtleties over-ridden – as indeed the first line of 'Qui passus est' shows. Perhaps the argument can be made clear by an analogy – the marching-song. If a platoon is trudging along on a route-march and starts singing (let us say) 'It's a long way to Tipperary; it's a long way to go', it is their feet, swinging left–right left–right, that set up the pulse. The words and the tune fit into the pulse, and emphasize and stimulate it. Something similar happens in dance-song: movement is primary; words and melody are subordinate to it.

Our difficulty is that we do not know the movement, and certainly not the movements, the choreography, of early medieval dances. We are dependent therefore on the words or the music to give us the necessary clue. In the case of mensurally notated dance-songs and *refrains*, such as those in *Robin et Marion* or *Renart le nouvel* or *Ludus super Anticlaudianum* etc., the music tells us all we need to know. In other cases – the non-mensural (which is not to say unmeasured) *rondeaux* of Guillaume d'Amiens, for instance – the words may give a hint as to the 'movement'. It is seldom that a French text makes such unambiguous rhythmic gestures as does Ex. 64 above:

Prendés i garde, s'on mi regarde;
S'on mi regarde, dites le moi

The verse part of this *rondeau*, be it noted, is less assertive. A line like

C'est tout la jus en cel boschaige

seems to have a typically smooth, though more or less iambic, movement. But once the 'movement' of the song, of the dance, has been set up, all the lines must conform. So what happens is that the words lend their 'roughage', their consonantal edge and physical substance, to the music and give it drive, irrespective of their own natural accents and durations. The words give extra impetus to the melodic line – much needed if it was unaccompanied by instruments – making it not flow but bound. The phenomenon is familiar in the work-songs, game-songs and nursery rhymes of all periods. It is also a feature of the medieval English carol in the first half of the fifteenth century.[107]

The wider uses of the *refrain* – to speak only of musical uses – include its appearance, often as a refrain in the formal sense, in the *pastourelle* and similar songs of a lighter kind, in that curious courtly medley the *chanson-avec-des-refrains*, and in the sophisticated polyphonic motet. These uses, informative as they are in other ways, tell us nothing new about dance-song as such, and therefore nothing about the relationship of words and music in dance.

---

[107] See Stevens (1952; rev. edn 1958), especially the earlier carols there edited (e.g. nos. 5, 6 and 7 from Cambridge, Trinity College MS 0.3.58).

6

NARRATIVE MELODY I: EPIC AND *CHANSON DE GESTE*

In ordinary thinking – or 'not-thinking' – about music and literature, the notions of song and of story seem naturally opposed. We think of the 'song' as a completed object in which formal sound–pattern has achieved roundness and gives satisfaction; we think of 'story' – narrative – as, if not infinitely extensible, at least flexible, elastic, and malleable. In the early Middle Ages such a view would not have seemed a natural one: the amount of narrative music in people's ears may well have exceeded the amount of song in the narrower sense. In this chapter I shall sketch the north European scene in some of its teeming variety and try to give the reader an idea of the many ways in which song and story might be combined.[1] It is fruitless to attempt questions about the singing of narrative poetry in Britain, where the direct evidence is sparse indeed, without first having an idea of the different ways in which early-medieval story was sung in France and in Germany – in French, one should rather say, since England is a node in the international French-speaking complex, and in German, the interest of German being that it gives us the opportunity to see music at work in a stressed language sharing many phonetic and structural qualities with our own.

We may begin by formulating distinctions – by establishing the meaning, that is, of some key terms – before proceeding to consider the principal musical types from an analytical point of view. Between 'singing' on the one hand and 'speaking' on the other there is not so much a gulf as a sort of no man's land, in which move shadowy creatures of indeterminate allegiance. 'Song' in the strictest sense has clearly defined pitches and rhythms and a melodic shape which can be essentially, even if not entirely, accounted for in musical terms. 'Speech' has the same elements in its composition as music – pitch, rhythm, timbre, intensity – but the pitches and rhythms are not precisely defined. Terms which might be needed in a full discussion of the performance of medieval narrative poetry are the intermediate ones – 'intone', 'chant', 'recite', 'declaim', with the different shades of meaning they imply.[2] However, the present discussion will be confined almost entirely to the musical end of the spectrum; that is, to narrative singing capable of at least

---

[1] I am particularly indebted in this chapter to Karl Reichl for stimulation and advice.
[2] Historical evidence on this point is extremely hard to come by. Some of the possibilities are apparent from twentieth-century performances of narrative poems. See chapter 7: VI below, text to note 62.

skeletal representation in musical notation, even if the subtleties are elusive.

The problem of terminology is also one of understanding and extends back into the sources. Can one be sure, for instance, that the distinction between *canter* and *conter* in French is as straightforward as it seems? It seems that in medieval German, at least, the terms *singen* and *sagen* may point to the difference between song and what might better be called chanting or intoning.[3] This is the same distinction as can sometimes be made in Latin between *modulatio* (song-like melody) and *pronuntiatio* (the formal utterance of 'chant'), between *concentus* and *accentus*.[4] And when Chaucer prays for his 'litel bok' of *Troilus*, 'And red whereso thow be, or elles songe, / That thow be understonde, god I biseche' (v. 1797), the alternatives may not be so clear as they seem.[5]

A further set of distinctions is necessary to clarify the relations between an oral and a written literature. Setting aside for the moment the vexing problem of oral *composition*, whatever that may entail, there is a whole large area (which includes folk-ballad, for instance) which can properly be called 'oral literature' (if the contradiction in terms may be allowed). That we know about it at all, have records of it, is an accident not a consequence of its nature. At the other end of the scale is 'reading literature' intended for private and individual delectation. But between the two is the important medieval hybrid – literature written indeed, but *written for oral performance*. A fair number of the works we shall be considering in this chapter come under this heading.[6]

1 Melodic types

Narrative melody in the Middle Ages is of several distinct formal types:

(i) The *recitation*-tone.[7] This type is best illustrated from the plainchant

---

[3] The alliterative formula *singen und sagen* (originating from the liturgical *cantare et dicere*?) when adopted by secular musicians was made to express a distinction between a lyrical and an epic style of performance (see F. Kluge's *Etymologisches Wörterbuch der deutschen Sprache*, 19th edn (Berlin 1943) by W. Mitzka, pp. 709–10).

[4] See Jammers, 'Mittelalterliche Epos' (1957), 33–4: *pronuntiatio*, liturgically, is not speech but *accentus* ('musikalisch geordnete Rezitativ', i.e. recitation-melody); also van der Veen, 'Chansons de geste' (1957), 95.

[5] An even more startling prospect is opened up by Lydgate's reference in his *Pilgrimage of the Life of Man* (ed. F. J. Furnivall, EETS e.s. 77 (1899)), lines 114ff, to his original (Deguileville's *Pelerinage de la vie humaine*), 'maad and compylyd in the French tonge / ffull notable to be rad *and songe*'. (I thank Helen Houghton for this reference.)

[6] See, on these general problems, Ruth Finnegan, *Oral Poetry: its nature, significance and social context* (Cambridge 1977), especially Introduction, section 3, 'What is "oral" in oral poetry?'

[7] This 'recitation' melody (Ger. *Rezitativ*) has to be distinguished from 'recitative' (*stilo recitativo*), the seventeenth-century declamatory style in which music is subordinated to speech in a totally different way. Other examples of 'recitation' melody are the chants used for the Passions in Holy Week (see chapter 9:I), for the Genealogy of Christ (see chapter 9:III), for the psalms, for litanies, and for prayers. See Wagner (1911), III, part I, for an extended discussion (pp. 19–278) of liturgical recitation and psalmody; and Apel (1958), part 3, ch. I.

repertory. From the earliest days of the Church prayers and lessons have been intoned to very simple formulas; psalms to formulas only slightly more complicated. As an example we can take the reading-tone for the prophetic readings (*lectiones*) at Mass on Ember Days.[8]

Ex. 72

The lesson of Isaiah the prophet; the Lord God speaks these things: Say ye to the daughter of Sion, Behold thy salvation cometh, behold his reward is with him. Who is this that cometh from Edom, with dyed garments from Bosra? . . . the praise of the Lord according to all that the Lord our God hath bestowed upon us. (Isaiah 6:11; 63:1,7)

In addition to the simpler melodic flexions – the *flexa*, equivalent to a comma; the *punctum*, a full-stop; the *interrogatio*, question – some recitations require a stop heavier than a comma but less heavy than a full-stop, the *metrum*.[9]

The principal characteristics of this kind of narrative melody are its closeness to speech and its infinite extensibility. The melody, such as it is, stylizes the speech-tunes, the common intonations, of European speech – the slight lowering of the voice for a comma, the deeper fall at the end of a sentence, and so on. 'And so on', indeed, for there is no musical reason why such melody should not continue for ever.

(ii) The *laisse*-type melody. This is the type associated with the singing of the Old French epic, the *chanson de geste*, and perhaps with the singing of saints' lives. The very few surviving melodies will be discussed below. They appear

---

[8] The musical example is from *L U*, 102–3. See also Wagner (1911), III.44, from B L M S Add. 17001. The *Sarum Antiphonal*, II, pp. 1–9, gives many further examples (in facsimile).
[9] Apel (1958), 204.

to be more 'musical' than the recitation-tones of (i) above: they have a certain melodic life of their own which cannot be accounted for by the texts. They are, admittedly, highly repetitive but have certain turns of phrase for use at different parts of the *laisse*, which is a stanza of indeterminate length held together by assonance or a single rhyme. This first *laisse* from the *Chanson de Roland*, assonancing on the sound *e/ai/ei* would have, it is thought, one melody with perhaps alternative endings (*ouvert* and *clos*, 'open' and 'closed'); the mystifying letters 'A O I' may indicate a refrain.[10]

> Carles li reis, nostre emperere magnes,
> Set anz tuz pleins ad estet en Espaigne,
> Tresqu'en la mer cunquist la tere altaigne.
> N'i ad castel ki devant lui remaigne,
> Mur ne citet n'i est remés a fraindre,
> Fors Sarraguce, ki est en une muntaigne;
> Li reis Marsilie la tient ki Deu nen aimet,
> Mahumet sert e Apollin recleimet;
> Ne.s poet guarder que mals ne l'i ateignet.   A O I

Charles, the king, our great emperor, has been in Spain for seven full years. He has conquered that mountainous land right down to the sea. Not a castle remains standing before him; not a wall or a citadel is left for him to break down, except for Saragossa which is on a mountain. King Marsilie holds it, who loves not God; he serves Mahomet and calls upon Apollo. He cannot prevent woe coming upon him.

The clearest and best-authenticated example of a *laisse*-type melody comes from *Aucassin et Nicolette*, a prose-tale with verse interpolations (see Ex. 86 below).

(iii) The *lai*-type melody. This is more 'musical' again. It is not possible to say in general terms whether the music or the words came first. The musical characteristics of the 'lyrical' *lai* have already been described (ch. 4: IV): the form is closely related to that of the sequence (A A B B C C etc.) but is freer. This 'lyrical' *lai* could be and was used for straight narrative, as in the *Song of the Flood* (see Ex. 55, above).

(iv) Lastly, the *strophic* type of narrative melody. Most of the surviving melodies for the medieval German epic as well as for the English and Scottish folk-ballad are strophic: that is to say, the melody devised for the first stanza,

---

[10] The puzzle is still unsolved. Brault, in his two-volume edition of the Oxford MS (1978) gives a bibliography (II.253) of scholarly attempts. He prefers the solution of A. B. de Mandach (*Symposium* 11 (1957) 303–15), *Aoi<Am<Amen*. Some kind of sung refrain, at least, seems indicated (cf. *La Chançun de Willame*, ed. N.V. Iseley (Chapel Hill 1961), pp. xiv and lines 10, 87 etc.). Grace Frank (*PMLA* 48 (1933) 629–35) proposes that A O I abbreviates *pAx vObIs* by analogy with the *sEcUlOrUm AmEn* frequent in liturgical sources. Other possibilities are considered by Chailley, 'Chanson de Geste' (1955a), 8–10, who derives it from *Alleluia*.

or chosen for it, is repeated throughout the tale. The stanza, or strophe, is an unchanging metrical–musical unit. The structure of the unit may vary considerably. In British folk-ballads a four-line stanza is by far the most common, as in this Argyll melody for *Tam Lin*; here the poetic form is the usual – four-stress lines alternate with three-, the second and fourth lines rhyming – and the musical form is simply ABCD.[11]

Ex. 73

Mar-gret stood in her high cham-ber,

She'd sewn a sil-ken seam.

She loo- ked east an she loo- ked west

An she saw those woods grow green.

In this type of narrative melody we have come a long way from recitation chants; we have arrived at song proper, the self-sufficient musical structure which 'contains within itself the reasons why it is so and not otherwise'. This is the moment, then, to emphasize the obvious – that there is no separate domain of narrative melody. *Lai*-form, like strophic song, has an independent life of its own, as we shall see. The range of melody available runs from the simplest formula to the developed art-form; and even the simplest formula may serve other purposes as well as story.

In the discussion which follows I shall describe as best I can from the fragmentary evidence the way that medieval narrative poetry was or may have been sung in the German, French and English vernaculars. The second part of the discussion (chapter 7) will deal primarily with musical narrative in Latin, mostly hagiography, since it is here that the greatest number of clues are to be found.

---

[11] The melody is from Bronson, ed., *The Singing Tradition of Child's Popular Ballads* (Princeton 1976), p. 101 (no. 39: 2.1).

II The Old English period

Each 'literature' presents a different kind of problem in interpretation. Whereas with German we are faced with a dearth of texts but have some musical facts, however scarce, to work on, with English we have a considerable body of texts but no direct musical evidence at all.

There is a special appropriateness in the fact that *Widsith*, perhaps the oldest poem in the English language (seventh-century, though with later additions), is a poem about a singer of heroic songs. [12] Widsith, 'far traveller', who speaks the monologue (lines 10–134), is an idealized *scop*, poet, 'maker'. We learn from the poem how he travelled the world (no real historical bard could ever have gone so far in space or time) telling tales of heroic deeds among the Huns, the Goths, the Swedes, the Geats, the South Danes, the Saxons, the Burgundians, the Assyrians, Hebrews, Egyptians, Medes, Persians and many other tribes. He tells not only of *gesta* but of his own success as a public entertainer and of the fine gifts he received:[13]

> Forthon ic mæg singan   and secgan spell,
> mænan fore mengo   in meodohalle
> hu me cynegode   cystum dohten

Wherefore I may sing and utter a measure [?], recite before the company in the mead hall how the noble ones were liberal to me in their generosity.

In another passage he refers to the manner of his performances in the court of Eadgils, his *hleodryhten*, lord protector; he 'said in song' (*be songe secgan*) the praises of Queen Ealhhild. [14]

> Thonne wit Scilling   sciran reorde
> for uncrum sigedryhtne   song ahofan,
> hlude bi hearpan   hleothor swinsade;

When Scilling and I with clear voice raised the song before our victorious lord – loud to the harp the song made music.

From even these brief quotations we can gather that the office of a *scop* was one of standing and honour, that music (especially harp music) came within his province, that he was valued because he sang of heroic deeds, and probably that the performance of heroic narrative could be the joint work of two

---

[12] See, for a broader context, Dronke (1968), 'Introduction: performers and performance', especially pp. 17ff. The derivation of *scop* is uncertain; the word has often been derived from O E *scieppan*, 'create' (see Opland, *Anglo-Saxon Oral Poetry* (1980), 232); but it seems that it should rather be related to Icelandic *skop*, 'railing, mocking' (I thank Karl Reichl for advice on this point). Opland discusses the four words for poet (*scop, gleoman, wothbora* and *leothwythta*) at length, 232ff. His conclusions, scrupulously balanced, are on p. 253 (see further note 15 below).

[13] *Widsith* (ed. Malone) lines 54–6 (the mid-line spacing is mine); trans. Gordon, 68.

[14] *Widsith*, lines 103–5; trans. Gordon, 69, who gives 'the words sounded in harmony' for *hleothor swinsade*.

performers. (It could be that 'Scilling' was simply a *gleoman*, a lower class of entertainer standing in the same relation to a *scop* as a *jongleur* to a trouvère.)[15] Not all performers, of course, were professionals. A well-known story from Bede makes it clear that rustic workers also could sing to the harp: the poet Caedmon, when a young cattle-herd, would get so alarmed, when the harp passed round his companions and his turn came to sing, that he would leave the house and go outside.[16] At the other end of the social scale, a king himself might perform. In *Beowulf* we read of the old Hrothgar[17]

> Þær wæs gidd ond glēo;   gomela Scilding,
> felafricgende   feorran rehte;
> hwilum hildedēor   hearpan wynne,
> gomenwudu grētte,   hwilum gyd āwræc
> sōth ond särlic,   hwilum syllic spell
> rehte æfter rihte   rūmheort cyning;

There was singing and merriment. An aged Scylding of great experience [i.e. Hrothgar] told tales of long ago. At times one bold in battle drew sweetness from the harp, the joy-wood; at times [one] wrought a measure true and sad; at times the large-hearted king told a wondrous story in fitting fashion.

Firmer evidence, because historical not literary, refers to the high reputation of St Dunstan (*c.* 908–88), of the royal line of Wessex, as a harper. The 'most vain songs of ancestral heathenism' (*avite gentilitatis vanissima carmina*) which he is alleged to have learnt must surely have been epic narratives.[18]

A few basic facts, then, are clear. But as soon as we begin to ask what precisely is meant by *gidd (gied, gyd) glēo, singan and secgan, drēam, spell, lēod, hlēodor, galdor, fit* and other words used to describe music, song, and epic recitation, we realize how little we actually know. It is not always clear, for instance, whether in a particular context the *hearpa* is envisaged simply as an

---

[15] There has been disagreement about 'Scilling' in this passage. Some have held that Scilling is the name of Widsith's harp (see Werlich, *Der westgermanische Skop* (1964), 256); but most scholars believe that a fellow-*scop* is referred to (Malone edn, pp. 50–1, 194). On the office and standing of a *scop*, see Opland, 243: 'a serious and respected member of the community whose role was more significant than that of entertainment'; the *scop* is to be distinguished from the harpers and gleomen, professional entertainers, perhaps itinerant (259).

[16] Bede, *Ecclesiastical History of the English People*, ed. B. Colgrave and R. A. B. Mynors (Oxford 1969, 414–21 (parallel text edn).

[17] *Beowulf* (ed. Klaeber), 2105–10; and see p. 205 (n. to line 2105): 'What relation there is between this *gyd*, the *syllic spell* and the harp playing, we are unable to determine.'

[18] This is certainly what is insinuated by those who attacked him for cultivating not only the vain songs of their pagan ancestors but also 'the frivolous incantations of charms from histories' (*historiarum frivolas . . . incantationem naenias*). The account is from the earliest extant life of St Dunstan, written *c.* 1000 by a continental Saxon priest (Author B). For this passage and for other information about St Dunstan, see the full account in Opland, especially 178–80.

accompaniment to song, or whether it makes music independently.[19] The
passage about Hrothgar is a case in point. The following, from a minor poem,
The Fortunes of Men, similarly leaves the connection between singing and
playing quite open.[20]

> Sum sceal mid hearpan   æt his hlafordes
> fotum sittan,   feoh thicgan,
> ond a snellice   snere wræstan,
> lætan scralletan   sceacol, se the hleapeth
> nægl neomegende

One shall sit at his lord's feet with his harp, receive treasure and ever swiftly sweep
the strings, let the leaping shackle [?plectrum] sound aloud, the nail making sweet
melody . . .

Some lines, however, from the prose *Apollonius Tyrii* are quite explicit about
the use of the harp as an accompanying instrument:[21]

Tha eode heo ut and het feccan hire hearpan, and sona swa heo hearpian ongan, héo
mid winsumum sange gemægnde thare hearpan sweg.

Then she went out and ordered her harp to be fetched; and as soon as she began to harp
she mingled the harp's sound and her pleasing voice together.

Jeff Opland, in the most detailed study yet published, comes to the conclusion that the tradition of song for ceremonial and work occasions was probably distinct from the tradition of poetry.[22] There are, of course, two questions to be answered: one is, 'Was Old English narrative poetry sung?'; the
other, 'If it was sung, was it accompanied?' To the latter question he would
return a sceptical answer: 'the onus would seem to rest on those who assume
lyre accompaniment for apparently all the extant Old English poetic texts to
prove their case'.[23]

It would be foolish to maintain that all types of Old English verse were

[19] On the interpretation of *hearpa* in literary, pictorial and other contexts, see the unpublished
dissertation of Christopher Page, especially ch. 2, 'Terminology': 'In the poems of wisdom
and learning the *hearpe* stands for all musical pursuits. The presentation of indoor music in
Old English verse is emblematic: the *hearpe* stands for all' (p. 133). The dissertation is full of
fascinating information, and I thank the author for permission to refer to it.

[20] Lines 80–4, ed. G. P. Krapp and E. Van K. Dobbie, The Anglo-Saxon Poetic Records III:
The Exeter Book (London 1936), 154–6. Trans. Gordon, 319 (emended). See Bosworth and
Toller, s.v. 'SEACEL', shackle ('the word also glosses *plectrum*'). Page (see note 19), 179ff,
emending the text, produces a different interpretation, namely that the fingers were used
rather than a plectrum. R. G. Lawson in his unpublished Ph.D. dissertation 'Stringed
Musical Instruments: artefacts in the archaeology of Western Europe', 2 vols. (Cambridge
1981) also discusses the matter in detail and, while not ruling out the plectrum theory
entirely, regards it as dubious – '*naegl* could refer to the harper's own nail' (153ff). I thank the
author for permission to refer to his work.

[21] P. Goolden, ed., *The Old English Apollonius of Tyre*, Oxford English Monographs (Oxford
1958), 24 (lines 26–8). The MS is mid-eleventh-century.

[22] Opland, 259.

[23] Opland, 256.

invariably sung on all occasions. But the arguments in favour of concluding that the normal public performance of *narrative* poems was in some sense 'musical' still seem to me strong albeit circumstantial. Two points seem worth emphasizing: first, we should distinguish the different genres of verse – some may always have been sung, some not; and, secondly, the discussion of terms opens a logical trap – the use of a non-musical terminology by the poet does not necessarily mean that the passage in question was not sung, but only that a non-musical aspect of it was being singled out.

Any discussion of narrative singing in Old English must start from the text itself, since (as I have said) there is no music of any kind to start from. All Old English poetry is written in the balanced alliterative line which characterizes older poems in the Germanic languages. The passage just quoted from *Beowulf* (2105–10) will serve for analysis. Each line is in two halves – an 'on-line' and an 'off-line', an *a* and a *b*. In each half-line two, sometimes more, syllables have a stress (which usually coincides with the natural verbal accent). Grouped around the 'strong' syllables are 'weak', unaccented ones. The alliteration normally links two strong syllables in the 'on-line' with the first of the 'off-line': *a a / a x*. The standard classification of metrical types – i.e. recurrent patterns – is that of Eduard Sievers. As a basis for *description* Sievers's five types are still useful, and still used.[24] But the 'rules' are not prescriptive. Marjorie Daunt has taken this notion to a logical conclusion. In an often-quoted article she contested the fundamental assumption of 'all previous commentators',

namely, that in Old English poetry we are dealing with a 'poetic metre', a definite artistic medium which needed to be acquired, of the same nature as later verse forms, though quite different in shape.[25]

Her conclusion, based on the analogies between the rhythms of Old, Middle and Modern English, was that the Anglo-Saxon poet simply 'tidied up' the spoken language; his rhythms are valid because they are the rhythms of that language. '*Old English verse is really conditioned prose*, i.e. the spoken language specially arranged with alliteration, but arranged in such a way that does no violence to the spoken words.'[26]

The thesis is a stimulating one – it has indeed stimulated much disagreement. The cardinal objection to it, in my view, has been well put by Thomas Cable in *The Meter and Melody of 'Beowulf'* (1974):

If the patterns of meter are simply a set of selected linguistic patterns, by what principle can one explain the basis of selection? Why should just those patterns occur

---

[24] They are conveniently set out by T. A. Shippey, *Old English Verse* (London 1972), 101, who rightly replaces the concept of 'rules' or 'types' with that of 'verbal patterns of an almost abstract order, never perhaps reaching conceptual awareness but still exercising rigorous constraint on generations of poets' (102).

[25] M. Daunt, 'Old English Verse and English Speech Rhythm', *Transactions of the Philological Society* (1946) 56.

[26] *Ibid.*, 57.

that do occur, and why should other patterns, which there is every reason syntactically to expect, fail to occur?[27]

Cable lists numerous rhythmic patterns which prose syntax seems to have
allowed over the centuries and which are not used, at least by the *Beowulf*-
poet.

It is time now to ask whether these century-old controversies about the
essential nature of the balanced alliterative line have any bearing on the
question 'Was Old English poetry spoken, recited, chanted, intoned or sung?'
The earlier commentators, Sievers himself and Andreas Heusler, took the
view that the poems could not have been sung in the strictest sense; but they
did so chiefly, it seems, because their own musical experience did not contain
musical models compatible with their view of the metre. For Sievers, the
verse lacked a regular beat and could not sustain a 3/4 or 4/4 melody.[28]
However, Sievers, Heusler and numerous other scholars recognized that the
verse might be intended for heightened speech-recitation (*zum gehobenen
Sprechvortrag bestimmt*), and some particularly envisaged the heightened recitation of liturgical chant, such as the psalm, as a model, with the harp admitted
as an accompaniment.[29]

The next serious attempt to make sense of the narrative music problem was
that of J. C. Pope, who in *The Rhythm of Beowulf* (1942) 'mensuralized', so to
speak, the verse of the poem. His basic assumptions, openly held and stated,
were that the normal half-line or verse contains two bars of quadruple time;
that in consequence the rhythmic basis of every normal line is what in music
would be a four-bar phrase divided into two twos; that in order to preserve the
sense of quadruple measure without violating the normal rhythms of speech,
'rests' must be introduced, as in music, even on strong beats of the measure.
Pope believed that *Beowulf* not only was in a regular, indeed a four-square,
rhythm but was intended to be *sung* so:[30]

In an effort to find a degree of order in Beowulf that would allow it to pass as
reasonably metrical spoken verse, we have been led to the establishment of a rhythm
so strictly governed that it approaches the realm of music and to the introduction of
rests of a sort that musical accompaniment alone can justify.

Pope envisages the harp accompaniment, then, as essentially rhythmical – or,
more precisely, in a regular metre, since the harpist will (for example) have to
provide the missing first beat of a measure if the words have not supplied it.
Melodically, the music will be stichic, not strophic: each line 'has a simple but

[27] Cable, 11. He is, however, no more successful than anyone else, as it seems to me, in
explaining positively why the 'metrical selections' are as they are.
[28] E. Sievers, *Altgermanische Metrik* (Halle 1893). See Werlich, 187ff, for further references.
[29] M. Kaluza, *A Short History of English Versification*, transl. A. C. Dunstan (New York 1911),
sect. 90, drew attention to the comparison between the expanded, balanced lines of Old
English poetry and the structure of psalm-verses (see further Clemoes, 'Liturgical influence
on punctuation' (1952), p. 15, n. 2).
[30] Pope, 93–4.

complete melodic pattern, which is repeated *ad infinitum*, or exchanged for another at will'.[31] Pope's whole rhythmic conception now seems anachronistic; it savours of the 'double-double beat' school of Riemann and others – it is pure *Vierhebigkeit*.

More recently Thomas Cable has proposed a melodic scheme for the singing of Old English verse, the key to which is a relation between verbal stress and musical pitch. Five 'contours', using up to four distinct pitches, form the basis of Cable's 'musical score' for the opening lines of *Beowulf*.[32]

Ex. 74

Hwæt, wē gār- de- na   in gēar- da- gum,

þēod- cy- nin- ga   þrym ge- frū- non,

hū ðā æþel- in- gas   el- len freme- don!

Oft Scyld Scē- fing   sceaþe- na þrēa- tum,

mone- gum mæg- þum   meodo- set- la of- tēah,

eg- so- de eor- [lās],   syð- ðan æ- rest weard

fēa- sceaft fun- den;   hē þæs frō- fre ge- bād,

wēox un- der wolc- num   weorð- myn- dum þah

---

[31] Pope, 93, n. 70. The quotation refers to the performance of Serbian epic; but he takes it as a model for Old English.

[32] Cable, 96; it has to be emphasised that the 'score' is entirely conjectural in general and in detail. Transl. Gordon, 3.

oð þæt him ǣg- hwylc   ymb- sit- ten- dra

o- fer hron- rā- de   hy- ran scol- de,

gom- ban gyl- dan;   þǣt wæs god cy- ning!

Lo! we have heard the glory of the kings of the Spear-Danes in days gone by, how the chieftains wrought mighty deeds. Often Scyld Scefing wrested the mead benches from troops of foes, from many tribes; he made fear fall upon the earls. After he was first found in misety (he received solace for that), he grew up under the heavens, lived in high honour, until each of his neighbours over the whale road must needs obey him and render tribute. That was a good king!

Cable's suggestion that pitch and ictus were linked may have some historical support by analogy with the conjectured 'accents' in Otfrid's *Evangelienbuch* (see below, p. 212). But he oversimplifies the general situation when he says 'there is good reason to believe that much medieval music, religious and secular, was composed in accordance with rules similar to these'.[33] On the contrary, it is a striking feature of hundreds of medieval songs that there is no coincidence of 'beat' or accent between words and notes. And certainly other modes of narrative singing do not require it, or even in some cases allow it.

Another approach to the problem is palaeographical. Whether the conclusions reached by Egon Werlich are right or wrong, they rest on amongst other things a close examination of the manuscript text of *Beowulf*. The manuscript evidence which Werlich takes into account includes the division of the poem into 'fitts', the use of *puncta* (dots, points), small capital letters, and accent-marks. Thus all the 'points' (stops) of this manuscript are to be interpreted as meaningful performance signals, rather like the 'expression marks' in a (modern) musical score; and they indicate the temporary abandonment of the placid narrative mode (*ruhiger Erzähltlon*) for a heightened and emphatic one (*emphatische Sprechlage*). Werlich does not expound further what this might mean in specific melodic or other musical terms.[34]

Werlich's views are highly speculative and have not been generally

---

[33] Cable, 102. He accepts without question from Ferretti (1938) and others that there was 'a clear relationship of grammatical accent and musical pitch' in Gregorian chant. For a different view, see chapter 8:III below.

[34] Werlich (1964) also sets out a view of the *scop* as 'Germanic poet–priest'; he dispensed heroic praise but was also an entertainer, a singer, and originally a dancer. Werlich's views on manuscript 'notation' are summarized on his pp. 323–5.

accepted. But the problem of accents, at least, remains. The accents in the *Beowulf* and other Old English manuscripts present fascinating matter for speculation. They have been interpreted variously as scribal ornaments, as signs of lengthening over vowels, and as pronunciation aids which indicate the 'quality' of the sound; others have argued for a pitch-heightening significance, for verbal accent (intensification of syllable or word), or for rhetorical emphasis.[35] One scholar, G. C. Thornley, commenting in detail on the Junius Manuscript, which contains four religious poems, has suggested that the accents are in fact notational signs designed to help monks familiar with liturgical intonation to sing/intone the poems.[36] In view of the likely connection between neumatic notation in liturgical books and medieval scribal punctuation (see chapter 8:11), the position could be a sound one – that the accents, as well as the other visual signs in the text, relate to the practical performance of the poem.[37] But here a distinction should perhaps be drawn between ecclesiastical tradition and the native Germanic tradition of heroic epic. A particularly interesting text of the eighth century, taken from the twelfth canon of the Council of Clovesho in 747, forbids priests to mutilate the style of singing appropriate to liturgical chant by the introduction of secular styles:[38]

Ut presbyteri saecularium poetarum modo in ecclesia non garriant, ne tragico sono sacrorum verborum compositionem at distinctionem corrumpant vel confundant, sed simplicem sanctamque melodiam secundum morem Ecclesiae sectentur: quo vero id non est idoneus adsequi, pronunciantis modo simpliciter legendo, dicat atque recitet quicquid instantis temporis ratio poscit, et quae episcopi sunt non præsumant.

The priests are not to prate in church in the manner of worldly poets, lest they should break up and confuse the ordered structure of the sacred text with the utterance of a tragic actor [?]. On the contrary, they are to strive after a simple and devout style of singing in accordance with the usage of the Church. However, let him who is not capable of this utter his speech and recite, reading straightforwardly in the manner of a public speaker whatever the necessity of the moment requires. They should not take on themselves what belongs to the bishop.

This passage is specific and is almost contemporary with the composition of some of the earliest surviving Old English poetry. It has weight, therefore, even though it seems to be a unique testimony. However, it does not necessarily imply so great a difference between two types of narrative song as some

[35] Werlich, 292, (3) 'Die Funktion des Akzents in der Beowulfhandschrift', gives references to the text and to the scholarly literature.
[36] G. C. Thornley, 'The Accents and Points of MS Junius II' *Transactions of the Philological Society* (1954) 178–205. The question is further discussed by Page, 244–55, who is sympathetic to Thornley's theory but points out difficulties.
[37] See chapter 8:11 below for the question of the relation of neumes to speech-marks (whether accents or punctuation signs).
[38] Cited Werlich, 297, from A. W. Haddan and W. Stubbs, *Councils and Ecclesiastical Documents*, 3 vols. (Oxford 1869–71), III.366.

have argued.[39] A difference in *style* is indeed stated: secular poets evidently sang in a more elaborate and perhaps a more histrionic style than was appropriate in church (is this the connotation of *tragico sono?*). But the actual melodic material and musical principles could have been similar. This would help to explain why confusion and malpractice had arisen.

To sum up, there is a mountain of conjecture about the performance of Anglo-Saxon narrative but only a very small mound of ascertainable fact.[40] It seems likely, from the accumulation of circumstantial evidence, from the analogy of other European 'literatures' and from ethnic parallels in other cultures, that some Old English poems were sung. Of the manner of their performance, the music to which they were performed and the function (if any) of the *hearpa* in all this we are at present sadly ignorant.

III German narrative song

There is no lack of evidence to establish that throughout its later-medieval history not only lyrical but narrative German poetry was sung – 'sung', again, in a variety of senses which may have included intoning and chanting. There is evidence, first of all, of a literary kind, such as there is for the *chanson de geste*: references in the texts of poems to their being sung; references to other singing occasions. Literary evidence must not be naively interpreted; equally, it must not be naively disregarded. I shall not, however, go over that ground again here, since the musical evidence as such will sufficiently occupy us.[41]

The musical evidence for the singing of German story may be best considered chronologically. In the Old High German period texts are scarce and musical hints almost non-existent. Between the *Hildebrandslied* (copied *c*. 810) and the *Nibelungenlied* (*c*. 1200–10) four centuries passed leaving virtually no trace of epic music from what must have been a richly endowed period.[42] All the more important, then, is a right assessment of one unusual text supplied in the manuscript with neumes indicating, it is argued, some kind of musical performance. The text is Otfrid's Gospel-book (*Evangelienbuch*); it was completed by Otfrid, a Benedictine monk, in his monastery at Weissenburg in Lower Alsace around the years

---

[39] E.g. Werlich, 97. However, it could be that *sono* as distinct from *modo* refers to a different melody.

[40] See the sensible, sceptical conclusions reached from a literary historian's point of view by D. Pearsall, *Old English and Middle English Poetry* (London 1977), 16–17.

[41] See Bertau and Stephan, 'Zum sanglichen Vortrag' (1957), 253–4, on the general problem. My account of the musical side of German epic is much indebted to the work of Karl Bertau, especially his article 'Epenrezitation im deutschen Mittelalter' (1965), which gives the most lucid exposition of the relevant material. The articles of Ewald Jammers on medieval (1957) and Old German narrative (1959) are basic; see also his *Melodien des Minnesangs* (1963), introd. p. 74, 'Die epischen Melodien'.

[42] The *Hildebrandslied* is a textually corrupt fragment of sixty-eight lines, *c*. 800, written on the spare pages of a devotional MS. (The so-called *Jüngeres Hildebrandslied* is a sixteenth-century ballad).

865–70.[43] It is the earliest example of end-rhyming verse in the German language. Taking as his subject the passages of the Gospels set for daily reading, the author interprets them in the manifold senses which characterized the whole medieval period.

There has been much controversy about the performance of Otfrid's verses, but decades of argument are judiciously summed up by Karl Bertau, whose account I follow.[44] A typical 'Otfrid-stanza' is given in Ex. 76 below, where its structure may be clearly seen. Scholars used to hold that this verse was not sung, though it might have been spoken as in a liturgical recitation. A crucial phrase is that of Otfrid himself in a preface to the work; he says his aim was

ut aliquantulum huius cantus lectionis ludum secularium vocum deleret

that to some extent the chant of this lesson should do away with the frivolity of worldly tunes.[45]

The monastery of Weissenburg, where Otfrid lived, was in the diocese of Mainz, where instead of the 'Roman' tone a special tone known as the *Accentus Moguntinus* was used. In contrast to the tones of the Sarum Use, the Mainz tone has a special peculiarity: it usually gives accented syllables higher notes. Thus, to borrow Jammers's example, a formula for the consecration of oil runs (the pitches are conjectured).[46]

Ex. 75

[43] Bertau (1965), 1–6, with reference especially to Jammers (1959).
[44] Bertau, 2.
[45] *Ibid.*
[46] Jammers (1957), 50; in 'Zum Rezitativ in Volkslied und Choral', *Jahrbuch für Volkslied-forschung* 8 (1951) 86–115, he gives a reconstruction of the neumes (from the Mainz sacramentary, ninth- and tenth-century) which differs in some details.

For David also, by the spirit of prophecy foreknowing the sacraments of thy grace, sang that our faces should be made to shine with oil.

In order to represent this in a notation which has no stave to indicate pitches, each accented note is given a *virga* sign (/), and in one of the manuscripts of the Gospel-book Otfrid has written the signs in his own hand, producing a result as follows (the pitches are based on the 'oil' formula, though with a conjectured major not a minor third):[47]

Ex. 76

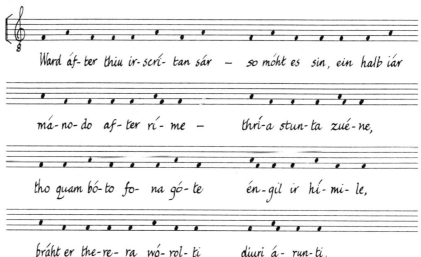

Soon after that – it might be half a year, by common reckoning thrice two months – there came a messenger from God, an angel from heaven, who brought to the world a precious message.

The conclusions drawn are: that Otfrid intended his verses to be sung; that the 'accents' which had previously been thought to have a textual significance are neumes; and that the chants indicated for the singing of his Gospel texts are, as might be expected, the lesson-tones of the locality, *cantus lectionis*.

It is tempting to seize on this scrap of evidence and to suppose that if the Old High German epic, typified by the *Hildebrandslied*, was sung, this is the type of melody which was used. The lesson-tones have, indeed, two features which make them suitable for the rendering of the balanced line of alliterative verse (alliterating *a a · a x*): they are infinitely extensible – i.e. can accommodate any number of syllables – and they have a system for marking accents. But the possibility remains extremely nebulous. There is for one thing a fundamental metrical difference between the two: the *Hildebrandslied* is in an alliterative metre, whilst Otfrid's *Evangelienbuch* is in rhymed verse. In these lines from

[47] Bertau (1965), 4.

the German epic we can hear, even without understanding them, the *Beowulf* sound:[48]

> Hiltibraht gimahalta Heribrantes sunu.   her was heroro man
> ferahes frotoro.   her fragen gistuont
> fohem wortum.   hwer sin fater wari
> fireo in folche   . . .

Hiltibraht spoke, Heribrant's son – he was the older man, the more experienced in life; he began to ask with few words who his father was of the men among the people . . .

Moreover, it is a far cry from heroic epic to the confinements of Otfrid's devout didacticism. It is like the distance in English between *Beowulf* and the plodding *Orrmulum*.[49]

The next period is that of Middle High German, the counterpart roughly of the Middle English period. Amongst the narrative masterpieces of the age are the *Nibelungenlied*, the *Parzival* of Wolfram von Eschenbach and the *Tristan* of Gottfried von Strassburg, all composed in the early years of the thirteenth century. From the point of view of narrative music, it would be neat and convenient if one could make a firm distinction between romance (*das höfische Epos, der höfische Versroman*) and epic (*das Epos*, without qualifying adjective). There is in fact one essential distinction: it is between short-line poems written in imitation of the French octosyllabic couplet (often a rather curious imitation) and long-line poems written not in alliterative paragraphs nor in the assonancing *laisse* of the French *chanson de geste* but in a variety of short strophic forms. The matter of the octosyllabic poems is usually taken from French romance; the matter of the long-line strophic poems is usually from Teutonic epic stock. These distinctions of form and content are not absolute, but they are firm enough to raise a question. Are we to assume that poems in the romance style were spoken or recited, whilst epics, in long lines, were sung? Immediately we come up against difficulties. The choice between spoken and sung performance was sometimes left open: thus, in the strophic verse-chronicle of Michel Beheim (1416–?1474) we have the author's specific comment 'das man es lesen mag als ainen spruch, oder singen als ain liet' – it can be spoken as speech or sung as song. He meant the second suggestion seriously, too, since he provides a tune in his own hand – but the evidence is of late date.[50]

Further blurring of the epic/romance distinction arises from the fact that it is of a romance text, *Der jüngere Titurel* (early-fourteenth-century) that the

---

[48] Ed. W. Krogmann, *Das Hildebrandslied* (Berlin 1959), p. 46 (lines 6–9).

[49] *Orrmulum* (*c*. 1200+), a collection of metrical English sermons, phonetically written; ed. R. M. White and R. Holt (1878).

[50] Ed. Th. G. von Karajan, *Michael Beheims Buch von den Wienern* (2nd edn, Vienna 1867). A facsimile of the first page of this rhymed chronicle is in *Geschichte der Stadt Wien*, III.1 (1907), pl. viiia; see Bertau and Stephan, 254. Further on Beheim, and this final stage of epic recitation, see C. Petzsch, 'Zum Gesangsvortrag', in *Mitteilungen des Kommission für Musikforschung im Anzeiger der Österreichischen Akademie der Wissenschaften* 109 (1972) 266–315.

author, Albrecht von Scharfenberg, says 'daz iz ir aller herzen tugnde bringe, diez lesen oder hoeren, der iz sage oder in dem done singe' (6031).[51]

. . . that I may instil into all their hearts the ability [power] to read or hear what I am saying, or singing to the melody.

The singing performance is again confirmed by the fact that the corrector of the M S (Vienna, Nationalbib. M S 2675) has written out the 'Titurelstrophe' with its musical notes; it may be that the original *Titurel* of Wolfram von Eschenbach was sung to the same *Ton*.[52]

Ex. 77

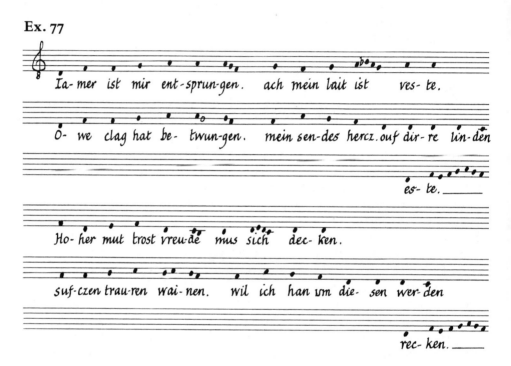

There is, of course, no particular reason why melodies should ever have been written down for the singing of long poems. It has been pertinently asked, 'For whom needed they to be written?'[53] Professional *Spielleute* could hardly have needed them even if they were able to read notation, which seems

[51] *Der jüngere Titurel*, ed. W. Wolf (Berlin 1955), is a later expanded version of Wolfram's fragmentary and perhaps abandoned *Titurel* (early-thirteenth-century), ed. Karl Lachmann, *Wolfram von Eschenbach*, 6th edn (Berlin and Leipzig, 1926), 389ff. (The *don* or *Ton* is a fixed metrical–musical structure. I thank Peter Johnson for help with this text.)

[52] The music example is from Bertau (1965), 9, checked against the facsimile of the Vienna M S in Bertau and Stephan, opp. p. 258. The latter discuss other versions of the *Ton* and argue a convincing case for its having been used by Wolfram. The melody is well copied in non-mensural Gothic neumes with *c*- and *f*-clefs.

[53] Bertau, 6.

very unlikely. Interested amateurs, perhaps: it may be through their coopera-
tion that some medieval German plays include the stanza-forms used in
narrative poems (*Epenstrophen*) and occasionally notated melodies as well. A
particularly interesting example is found in the Trier–Alsfelder play (Ex.
78).[54]

Ex. 78

1. Ez wuohs in Bur-gon-den ein vil e-del ma-ge-din,
2. daz in al-len lan-den niht schoe-ners moh-te sin, ___
3. Kriemhilt ge-hei-zen : sie wart ein e-del wip.
4. dar um-be muo-sen de-ge-ne vil ver-lie-sen den lip. ___

There dwelt in Burgundy a most noble maiden; there could not be a more beautiful
one anywhere in the world. Her name was Kriemhild; she became a noble woman.
For her sake many knights are due to lose their lives.

As Bertau and others have pointed out, this strophe is very similar to that of
the *Nibelungenlied*.[55] Too much should not be built on the formal likeness
between the Trier–Alsfelder and the *Nibelungen* strophe; there is simply a
tendency for the somewhat variable *Nibelungen* strophe to fall into the form
presented in the Passion play.

It used to be thought that *Der jüngere Titurel* was one of only four strophic
narratives for which specific notated melodies were available. However, the
recent researches of Horst Brunner have established a small corpus of recoverable melodies. He concludes,

the existence of these melodies establishes in principle beyond question the possibility
that the medieval German *Epos* constructed in strophic form was sung in
performance.[56]

[54] Facsimile, Bertau, opp. p. 6; with transcription, 7. In Ex. 78 I have underlaid a *Nibelungenlied*
stanza; the fit is approximate. The notation is non-mensural. Four-line strophe (in eight
half-line phrases) rhyming *a a b b*; melodically the strophe falls into two equal parts,
producing the musical structure A B C D A B C D.

[55] Ed. James Boyd (Oxford 1948); and see Bertau, 7–8.

[56] Brunner, 'Epenmelodien' (1970), 160. The supplementary melodies come from the Meistersinger MSS of the fifteenth to the seventeenth centuries. He calculates that in all seven

One important feature of the singing scene revealed now more fully than before is that there were in circulation for centuries not merely a number of melodies attached to particular epics but a set of *Töne*, accepted and established musical–metrical shapes, available to poets and 'story-singers' as required. To Wolfram's *Hönweise* Hans Sachs wrote *Das Christliche Schliffein*, in the sixteenth century, versifying a Gospel story.

Ex. 79

Matthew writes in his eighth chapter – Christ entered into a ship, and his disciples kept watch. Christ lay there and slept. The sea was stormy; it covers the boat with waves around and about and frightens the disciples.

---

melodies have been handed down for six out of the thirteen strophic forms used in narrative or lengthy didactic poems of the German Middle Ages (p. 159). Stäblein (1975), 100, gives a table of the melodies and summarizes the research. His plates 84, 85a, 85b illustrate the *Flammweise* melody. My Ex. 79 is from Brunner, 169; he gives four versions of Wolfram's *Hönweise* (*Heunenweise*) of which this is the second. The words were written to the *Ton* by Hans Sachs.

It remains to consider the problem of short-line narrative verse (see also p. 245, Ex. 97). A passage from Gottfried's *Tristan* will show how much less regular the metre of the German *Kurzzeilenepen* is than that of their models, the French courtly romances (those of Chrétien, for instance – a particularly relevant example, since they were known in Germany and translated):[57]

> si stiezen an und fuoren dan
> mit hôher stimme huobens an
> und sungen eines unde zwir:
> 'in gotes namen varen wir',
> 5 und strichen allez hinewart.
>   Nu was den frouwen zuo zir vart
> mit Tristandes râte
> ein kielkemenâte
> nâch heinlîcher sache
> 10 gegeben ze ir gemache.

Then they put to sea, and, as they got under way, began to sing the anthem 'We sail in God's name' with high, clear voices, and they sang it once again as they sped onward on their course.

Now Tristan had arranged for a private cabin to be given to the ladies for their comfort during the voyage.[58]

The number of syllables varies between 5˘ and 8, and adjacent strong stresses (lines 7 and 8) are admissible.

Ewald Jammers supposes that rhymed-couplet romance (*Reimpaar-Epos*) may have been intoned after the style of recitation melodies in the Roman Use and gives an illustration of how *Parzival* might have been sung.[59]

Ex. 80

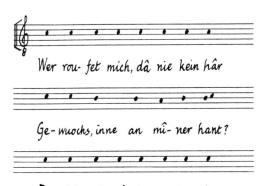

Wer rou-fet mich, dâ nie kein hâr

Ge-wuochs, inne an mî-ner hant?

Der hât vil nâ-he griffe er-kant.

---

[57] Ed. K. Marold, *Gottfried von Strassburg: Tristan*, 3 edn, rev. by Werner Schröder (Berlin 1969), lines 11535–44. The variable line length is reminiscent of Middle English *King Horn* (thirteenth-century).

[58] Transl. A. T. Hatto, *Gottfried von Strassburg: Tristan* (Harmondsworth 1960), 193.

[59] Jammers (1963), 75, and 144, Ex. 6; the example is entirely conjectural.

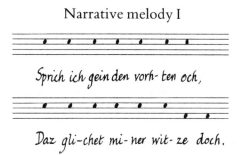

Sprich ich gein den vorh- ten och,

Daz gli-chet mi- ner wit- ze doch.

Who tweaks my palm where never a hair did grow? He would have learnt close grips indeed! Were I to cry 'Oh!' in fear of that, it would mark me as a fool.

The idea of singing a poem as intellectually and imaginatively demanding – and as long – as *Parzival* is one that arouses the strongest resistance in a modern mind. In general this resistance has to be overcome; it is quite anachronistic. The particular case is supported with no direct evidence; but it cannot be dismissed out of hand. A *Leich* by the late-thirteenth-century poet known as Der Wilde Alexander provides us with an example of short-line verse repeated to a single melody. The *Leich* is the German equivalent of the French *lai*; it follows, therefore, that this is only one of the patterns which occurs in the song:[60]

Ex. 81

Truly here comes Amor flying. He brings torches and bows, his arrow pierces right through walls. After that he throws the flames. Thus a fire and a yearning arise soon in the breast of those longing for love.

---

[60] Bertau (1965), 15, who however omits to observe that it is an excerpt from a *lai*. See chapter 4:IV above for further comments on the relationship between *lai*-melody and narrative music. The *lai* is printed from *Carl von Kraus Deutschen Liederdichtern* in the selection by H. Kuhn, *Minnesang des 13. Jahrhunderts* (Tübingen 1962), 1–6 (the quotation is strophe 10b). For more on Oswald von Wolkenstein's couplet settings, and on the tension between strophic and stichic form, see Petsch in *Werk-Typ-Situation* (Stuttgart 1969), 281–304.

A more convincing example of short-line recitation can be seen in the *Reimreden* of Oswald von Wolkenstein. The date is comparatively late (the poet lived from 1377 to 1445); but we can see here a twenty-line stanza involving repetition and near-repetition of very simple formulas.[61]

Ex. 82

1. Sich man-ger freut das lan-ge jar 2. gen des lieh-ten mai-en schein,
5. Ains al-ten wei-bes nam ich war, 6. von der ich kom in swä-ren pein,

3. und al-so hab ichs auch ge-tan; 4. hört wie es mir er-gie.
7. und het sie halb, wes ich ir gan, 8. si hunk an ai-nem knie.

9. Un-rüe-win ist ir nam, 10. des ward mein rugg wol in-nen,
15. Fürs grien und für den kram 16. ward mir die haut er-pe-ret

11. da si mich zue der lie-ben prächt, 12. und ich nicht mocht en-trin-nen.
17. von vie-ren, die des nicht ver-dross; 18. got waiss, was mich er-ne-ret.

13. un-ruew ge-wan mein ar-mer leib, 14. ich west nicht sel-ber wie.
19. Erst rau mich ser, das mich ain weib 20. gar alt so dick em-pfie.

Many a man looks forward all the year to the light of shining May, and so did I. Hear what befell me. I took notice of an old woman, and through her I got into sore straits. And if she got only half of what I wish her, she would limp on one leg. Unrüewin [Great Painer] is her name; of that my back became well aware, when she brought me to my beloved and I couldn't get away. With great pain my poor body was afflicted, I don't know how. Instead of a chat and trinkets, my skin was bared [? I was stripped] by four fellows who were not put off; God knows what saved me. It makes me very angry that such an old woman has led me on so often.

To sum up what is known about the singing of German narrative poetry in the Teutonic early Middle Ages, direct evidence is very sparse indeed for the early period, and much turns on the correct interpretation of the unheighted neumes, formerly thought to be speech-marks, in the *Otfrid* manuscripts. The likelihood is that some religious poems were sung to melodies similar in

---

[61] Music example based on Bertau (1965), from the diplomatic text of J. Schatz and O. Koller, ed., *Oswald von Wolkenstein: geistliche und weltliche Lieder* (Vienna 1902), Denkmäler der Tonkunst in Österreich XVIII, no. 61 (p. 165). Bertau, 14, speculates whether these quasi-recitation melodies may be especially connected with *Spruchdichtung* (proverbial, aphoristic verse).

character to the liturgical tones, melodic formulas used for the intoning of the lessons; but whether these would have been used for *heroic* poems is, to say the least, dubious. The interesting feature about the later period is the prevalence of strophic melody for the singing of narrative. Metrical–musical shapes (*Töne*), mostly small, are repeated over and over again. In this respect Germany seems to differ from France, where the predominant mode is (as we shall see) that of the *laisse*, which combines predominantly stichic (line-by-line) form with variable closes and half-closes. In neither language area is there any reason to doubt that heroic, or otherwise lofty, subjects called for a sung or intoned performance.[62] On the other hand no convincing case has yet been made out for the general singing of German short-line poems modelled on the French octosyllabic couplet.

There is much more one would like to, and may never, know about the way heroic verse was performed in the last centuries of the first millennium. If the performance was a musical one, did (an) instrument(s) accompany the singer? And if they did, was the instrument used rhythmically to mark the alliterated or stressed syllables? Would this also mean metrically, at precisely measured intervals? Or would an instrument have a primarily melodic, perhaps a heterophonic, role?

IV   The French tradition: *chanson de geste*

The Norman writer Wace, author of an English history, the *Roman de Brut*, wrote another long poem, the *Roman de Rou* (*c.* 1170–5), in which the following famous account of the Battle of Hastings occurs:[63]

> Taillefer, qui mult bien chantout,
> Sor un cheual qui tost alout,
> Deuant le duc alout chantant
> De Karlemaigne e de Rollant
> E d'Oliuer e des uassals,
> Qui morurent en Ronceuals.

Taillefer, who was an excellent singer, went before the duke on a swift horse, singing of Charlemagne and Roland and Oliver and the warriors who died at Roncevalles.

[62] There is one other source of evidence about the way German epic may have been sung: melodies associated with other Germanic languages may provide models and analogies. Old English, as we have seen, has nothing to offer; but something is known about Icelandic, i.e. Old Norse, melodies or melodic formulas. This 'something' does not amount to very much and is, unfortunately, mediated through a very late source, J. B. Laborde's *Essai sur la musique ancienne et moderne* (Paris 1780). He got his melodies from a Danish court musician, his contemporary J. Hartmann. These can be supplemented by a few others collected in the second half of the nineteenth century and published by B. Porsteinsson in 1909. See further W. Danckert, *Das europäische Volkslied* (Berlin 1939), 191–3; Jammers (1964), *passim*, with music examples; and D. Hofmann, 'Die Frage des musikalischen Vortrags der altgermanischen Stabreimdichtung in philologischer Sicht', *Zeitschrift für deutsches Altertum und deutsche Literatur* 92 (1963) 83–121.

[63] *Le Roman de Rou*, ed. H. Andresen (2 vols., Heilbronn 1877–9), lines 8035–40.

This passage may not tell us anything we can absolutely believe about the conduct of the battle, but it does assure us for certain that a twelfth-century author regarded the *chanson de geste* (the *Chanson de Roland* must be referred to) as a sung form. This mention is supported by others. In the *Moniage Guillaume* (twelfth-century),[64]

> Dist l'uns a l'autre: 'J'ai öi un jougleur.
> Oïés con cante de Guillaume au court nés.'

> One said to the other: 'I've heard a jongleur.
> Hear how he sings of Guillaume the Short-nosed.'

And the fame of Guillaume is to the fore again in the *Roman de la Violette* (1225), where the hero is made to sing twenty-four lines from the *chanson de geste* entitled *Aliscans*:[65]

> Lors commencha si com moi samble
> con chil qui molt estoit senés,
> un ver de Guillaume au court nes
> a clere vois et a douch son:
> 'Grans fu la cours en la sale a Loon;
> mult ot as tables oisiaux et venison.'

Then like (as it seems to me) one who was most skilful, he began a *laisse* [?] of Guillaume the Short-nosed, in a clear voice and to a sweet melody:
'The court in the hall at Laon was a huge gathering; there were many tables of fowl and venison.'

Examples could be multiplied. The Arras poet Jean Bodel (late-twelfth-century) boasts of the skill required for the *chant* as well as for the *vers*.[66] This hint of two separate entities is borne out by a troubadour, Guiraut del Luc (fl. 1190), who remarks that his *sirventes* 'Ges sitot m'ai ma voluntat fellona' was written *el son Beves d'Antona*.[67] The tune to which *Beves* was sung in Provence may or may not be the same as that used for the Anglo-Norman *Boeve*. But the reference does seem to imply that there could be some individuality in a narrative chant, enough at least to make it adequate to the needs of a *sirventés*. (A *sirventès* is normally in strophic chanson-form, and the reference could

---

[64] *Le Moniage Guillaume*, ed. W. Cloetta, S A T F (2 vols., Paris 1906, 1911) lines 471–2. On the performance of the *chansons de geste* see Gennrich (1923), 6.

[65] *Le Roman de la Violette ou de Gerart de Nevers*, by Gerbert de Montreuil, ed. D. L. Buffum, S A T F (Paris 1928), lines 1403–8. *Aliscans*, a *chanson de geste* of the Charlemagne cycle, is ed. F. Guessard and A. de Montaiglon (Paris 1870); the passage is lines 3036–59.

[66] Bodel was a trouvère, a playwright, and the author of a *chanson de geste* dealing with Charlemagne, the *Chanson de Saisnes*. See F. Menzel and E. Stengel, eds., *Jean Bodel's Saxonlied* (Marburg 1906), p. 29 (lines 4–5: *Jamais vilains jougleres de cesti ne se vant! Car il n'en saroit dire ne les vers ne le chant*).

[67] Gennrich (1923), 9: 'Gessi tot m'ai ma voluntat fellona / No.m lais mon chant el son Boves d'Antona'. See de Riquer, no. xxiii; he prints the poem, pp. 550–2, and points out that it was composed to the melody of *Daurel et Beton*, a Provençal *chanson de geste* whose hero was Boves d'Antona.

mean that the Provençal *Beves* was a strophic narrative, not a *laisse*-built one.)

Not much music survives from the abundance that must have existed once for the singing of the *chansons de geste*. The best-known melody is one quoted in the course of Adam de Halle's dramatic entertainment *Robin et Marion* of *c.* 1282 (see ch. 5: 11 and Ex. 62). Towards the end of the play (it verges towards 'musical comedy') the traditional *pastourelle* has developed into a *bergerie*, shepherds' games; one of the rougher characters, Gautiers, is flirting boisterously with the heroine, Marion, and sings a bawdy snatch after boasting 'Je sai trop bien canter de geste' (726).[68]

Ex. 83

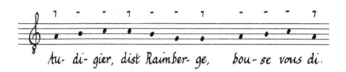

Au- di- gier, dist Raimber- ge,   bou- se vous di.

'Audigier,' said Raimberge, 'I say shit to you.'

Here we evidently have a ten-syllable line with an additional weak syllable *-ge* after the caesura at the sixth. (The principal metre of *Robin et Marion* is octosyllabic.) This line is quoted from a poem about Audigier which is an obscene parody of a *chanson de geste*; the particular passage parodies a scene in *Girart de Rousillon* which is also written in the 'major decasyllable' (6+4).[69]

A second melody is found in a British Library manuscript which preserves a short epic poem on the subject of the battle of Annezin. It is written in a single *laisse* assonancing on the sound *in*. At the end occurs the following melody.[70]

Ex. 84

in   in   in   in   in   in   in

[68] Ed. Varty, line 729. The music example is from the Adam de la Halle MS (Source 34): the notation is black full with a mixture of tailed and untailed notes, but not mensural. The Aix-en-Provence MS (Bibl. Méjanes 572) is similar, but different notes are tailed. Gennrich (1962), p. 11, reproduces both in diplomatic facsimile and suggests numerous transcriptions all based on the assumption that the melody should be measured. Differing rhythmic transcriptions will be found by Eric Hill in Varty's edn (p. 37); in Axton and Stevens, 299; in Gérold, 82; in Reese, 204; etc.

[69] Van der Veen, 87–8; the question, unresolved, is whether the *Audigier* melody was also used for the singing of other *chansons de geste*. See also Gennrich, *Formenlehre* (1932), 40–5, for a reconstruction of a complete *laisse*.

[70] On musical aspects of the *chansons de geste*, see van der Veen, 88–9, with references to the earlier literature. The music example is transcribed from BL Roy. MS 20.A.xvii, fol. 177; diplomatic facsimile in Gennrich (1923),15.

The poem is written in lines of twelve syllables, which is quite common. But the wordless melody only has seven note-groups and seven *in*-sounds to go with them. What is the solution? One suggestion is that the jongleur performed an instrumental postlude based upon it; another, that it is the music for a rounding-off or refrain line such as we meet elsewhere; a third, that somehow this melody should be adapted for the twelve-syllable line of the poem as it stands. In considering this third suggestion we have to bear in mind that notes bound together in ligature are not, as a rule, broken up to provide for more than one syllable, but in this case they must be. Here are two possible adaptations of the tune to the line of the *geste* in which the author, 'Thomas', names himself: the first is in a modal rhythm, the second in an isosyllabic transcription (but one made possible only by the breaking of ligatures).[71]

Ex. 85

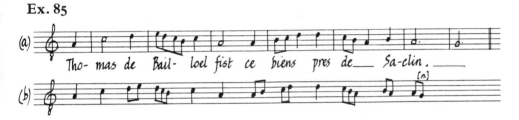

Thomas de Bailloel did this good deed near Saclin . . .

A third narrative melody is frequently named in connection with those just discussed: it has already been mentioned from the manuscript of *Aucassin et Nicolette*, a *chante-fable* of the thirteenth century.[72] *Aucassin* is a delightful romantic tale about the love between the son of a *seigneur* and a Saracen slave-girl, who is revealed in the end to be of royal birth. It is essentially a narrative, though some have thought it might have been put on as a play, and it is unique in its combination of *chant* and *fable*, song and story. Sections in verse headed *or se cante* alternate with prose passages headed *or dient et content et fablent*. The verse passages have a special interest: they are *laisses*, as in the *chansons de geste*, with assonance not rhyme though in short lines. The music, once again in non-mensural notation, falls into three phrases; the third phrase is clearly intended for the short line at the end of the *laisse*, the first two for the rest. The question is whether phrases A and B simply alternate (a simplicity which lets us down when we come to the end of an *odd* number of lines), whether one phrase or the other predominates (Riemann suggested that phrase B was the recitation melody, phrase A an 'intonation' only), or whether

[71] Music example (a) is from Gérold, 83; (b) is my own transcription. Gennrich (1923) 15, supplies others.
[72] Ed. Roques (1962); facsimile Bourdillon (1896); transl. Matarasso (1971). The tonality of the melody is considered at length by U. Aarburg, in *Die Musikforschung* 11 (1958) 138–43, because of its unusual end (phrase C cadencing on *c*) which she thinks may be the result of an error.

the performer followed his improvisatory whim. The whole of section ix
with one possible arrangement of melodies would run as follows.[73]

Ex. 86

Au- cas- sins oï du bai- sier
por cent mi- lë mars d'or mier

qu'il a- ra au re- pai- rier:
ne le fe- sist on si lïe.

Gar-ne-mens de-man-da ciers,
il vest un au-berc du- blier

on li a a- pa- rel- liés;
et la- ça l'iaume en son cief,

çainst l'es-pee au poin d'or mier,
si mon-ta sor son des- trier

et prent l'es- cu et l'es-piel.

Re- gar-da an-dex ses piés –
bien li sis- sent es es- triers;

a mer-vel- le se tint ciers.

De s'a-mi- e li so- vient,
il li cort molt vo- len- tiers:

s'es-pe-ro- na le des- trier.
tot droit a le porte en vient –

C   a la ba- tail- le!

Aucassin hears of the kiss he is going to have at his return. With a hundred thousand
marks of pure gold one couldn't have made him so happy. He asked for expensive
garments; they were got ready for him. He put on a padded hauberk and strapped the
helmet on his head, girded on his sword with its pommel of pure gold, mounted his
steed, and took the sword and the spear. He looked at both his feet – they fitted well
into the stirrups – and held himself marvellously brave. He thought of his beloved and
spurred on his steed. It galloped for him fully of its own accord: straight to the gate he
goes – into battle!

About these *laisse*-type melodies and their presumed connection with the
chansons de geste I will say no more at the moment, except that the surviving
melodies are very different from the recitation tones of Gregorian chant; they
seem for one thing to have no clear reciting-note. On the other hand there

[73] BN fr. 2168, fol. 70. The melody is written, *passim*, a number of times in the course of the
piece, which extends over fols. 70–80v. The notation is black full and consists of undifferentiated square notes lightly tailed on a red four- or five-line stave.

seems no reason why they should be interpreted as *measured* melodies (that is
with longs and shorts). At least two other rhythmic possibilities should be
considered, both requiring roughly equal notes. Either the rhythm is neutral,
and subservient to verbal accent, or it is metrical, with regular groups of twos
or of threes.[74]

An interesting feature of the *Aucassin* melodies which leads one to think that
they may not have been especially composed for this *chante-fable* is that the
second phrase is identical, almost, with a phrase in the anonymous *Lai des
Amants*. As Théodore Gérold commented, the concordance could be purely a
matter of chance or the phrase could be one 'très repandue', one that belonged,
so to speak, 'au domaine public'.[75] The *lais* are, in fact, full of phrases which
seem to qualify as narrative tags. They deserve some examination.

The *Lai de Notre Dame* by Ernoul le vielle (late-thirteenth-century) is one
of several in which narrative tags are used extensively; these three phrases
serve for the first twenty-six lines of the *lai* and recur again later in the
piece. The whole melody is notated in the only source, the Chansonnier de
Noailles, so one is able to see how the three phrases are used. The parallel
with *Aucassin* is instructive: phrase A is always followed by phrase
B; phrase B can, however, stand on its own (e.g. lines 9–13); phrase C rounds
off a section.[76]

Ex. 87

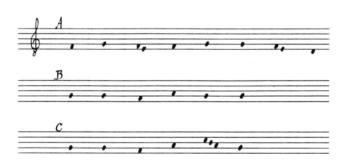

Another *lai*, the longest of its type from this period, is the *Lai de l'Ancien et du
Nouveau Testament*, attributed to Ernoul (see ch. 14: Ex. 189 below). It uses
from time to time even shorter segments of melody.[77]

---

[74] On the use of the terms 'measured', 'metrical' and 'mensural' see Glossary.

[75] Maillard (1963), 272, gives both melodies; see Gérold in Roques edn (see note 72 above), p. xxv.

[76] 'En entente curieuse' (R1017) from the Chansonnier de Noailles, fol. 62 (black full notation, undifferentiated as to rhythm). Ed. Jeanroy et al., no. XVII. See also Maillard, *Ernoul de Gastinois* (1964), pp. 24–32.

[77] 'S'onques hom en liu s'asist' (R1642) from the same MS, fol. 63 (attributed to Ernoul on grounds of MS location and style). Jeanroy et al., no. XVIII; Maillard (1964), 13–24.

Ex. 88

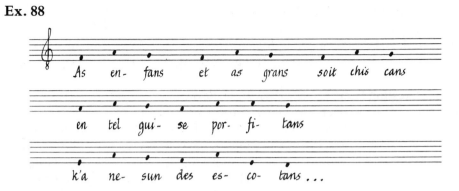

To young people and to their elders may this song be profitable in such a way that to
none of the hearers . . .

A type of narrative song of some length to which the title *lai* is frequently
but misleadingly attached in the French prose-romances of the Arthurian
cycle ought just to be mentioned here. Formally it has nothing in common
with the *lai* proper; it is strophic narrative. The so-called *Lai mortel* from the
French prose-romance *Tristan*, for example, uses strophic melody with
recitation-type features.[78]

Ex. 89

I have made chansonettes and *lais*,
but now I am forsaking all of them.
I'm composing my last *lai*;
'Love is killing me' – is this not a fine *lai*?

[78] On this special type of 'Arthurian' *lai*, see chapter 4:IV above. Music example: Vienna,
Österr. Nationalbib. MS 2542, fol. 63; transcr. Steiner (1974), 144, with full list of variants.
'Ja fis canchonnetes' has 31 stanzas.

Jean Maillard sets the opening phrases of the *Lai mortel* alongside a chanson by the trouvère Conon de Bethune (? *c.* 1150–1220) on which two German songs are also modelled.[79] The chanson could have given the melody to the *lai*; but the two are not in the same metrical form, and it seems more likely that they are both drawing on common stock. Conon de Bethune's chanson is a Crusade-song in which the poet laments at having to part from his love but protests, with doubtful orthodoxy, that although his body goes to serve God his heart will always stay at home with her. Another Crusade-song (R401) shows the tendency of some chansons on the margin of the standard repertoire to adopt a repetitive structure: 'Parti de mal' has the musical form A A¹ A A¹ A² B B¹ (B is a part-'rhyme' with A, B¹ a 'rhyme' with A). In the second line the poet says he wants all people to hear his song about God's need for the service of Christian men (*voil ma chancun a la gent fere oïr*), and the 'narrative' structure of the melody may be modelled on simpler songs which do just that.[80]

Ex. 90

[79] 'Ahi, amours, con dure departie' (R1125); see Maillard (1963), 196ff.
[80] On recitation-type melodies in trouvère *chansons* generally (i.e. other than *chansons de croisade*), see van der Werf (1972), 47–8, and his article 'Recitative Melodies' (1967). 'Parti de mal' (R401) is from an English source (?*c.* 1300), BL MS Harl. 1717, fol. 251. Crusade-songs are assembled in Bédier and Aubry, *Chansons de Croisade* (1909).

Escaped from evil and prepared for good deeds, I wish my song to be heard widely,
for God has called us at his need, and no honourable man ought to fail him, since he
deigned to die on the cross for us. He should be properly rewarded, since by his death
all of us were saved.

One category of trouvère song which has a special interest in this connection is that of the *chansons de toile*.[81] As the name which has been given to them
('weaving-songs') lightly implies, they pretend, at least, to be the songs which
women sang at their looms whilst their husbands or lovers were away. They
are genuine 'story-songs' (*chansons d'histoire*) in so far as they are sung by a
narrator *about* the lovelorn ladies and not by the ladies themselves. Not only
are they 'narrative' songs musically, with their repeated melodies, but metrically also, since their monorhymes and half-rhymes recall the *laisse*-style
already described ('Bele Doette' assonances *siet/tient/-vient*/tornoier).[82] The
musical form of 'En un vergier' is A A A A¹B C, which again suggests that a
standard way of singing a *laisse* was by the subtle variation (possibly improvised) of a recurrent melodic figure, rounded off at the end by a different or
modified melody.[83]

Ex. 91

1 En   un   ver- gier   lez   u-   ne   fon- te-   ne-   le
2 dont clere est   l'on- de et   blan- che   la   gra- ve-   le
3 siet fille a   roi,   sa   main a   sa   ma-   xe-   le;
4 en   sos- pi-   rant   son   douz a-   mi   ra-   pe-   le :
REFR: Ae,   cuens Guis a-   mis!

---

[81] Bec (1977), I.107–19, gives a detailed 'typology' of the genre. Gérold, 125: 'pièces lyrico-
épiques de style ancien'; he gives a measured transcription of Ex. 91, 'En un vergier' (R594).
The *unicum* in the Chansonnier St Germain, fol. 65v, is in non-mensural notation (Messine
neumes).

[82] 'Bele Doette' (R1352), monorhymed with refrain-line (aaaaB).

[83] Cf. in Latin song, e.g. the Latin *alba* 'Phebi claro' (Walther 14086), transcr. Jammers (1963),
146, from Rome, Vat.Reg. M S 1462, fol. 50v. Musical scheme A A A B A¹. 'En un vergier'
(R594) is from the Chansonnier St Germain (Source 31) fol. 65v (notated in Messine
neumes). Line 2 has a superfluous note after syllable 5.

b   la   vos-tre a-   mors   me   tout   so-   laz   et   ris.

In an orchard, by the side of a spring with clear water and shining pebbles, sits the daughter of a king, her chin in her hand. Sighing she calls on her sweetheart – *'Ah, Count Guy, my dear! Your love is all solace and gladness for me.'*

Related to the *chanson de toile* in several respects is the *pastourelle*.[84] Once again it is a genre which pretends to be popular, 'belonging to the people', rather than actually being so. There is a disingenuousness, a mock-simplicity, at the heart of pastoral in every age. The medieval 'pastoral lyric', the *pastourelle*, is also a narrative song; it tells a story which always begins something like this:

> Au tems pascor
> L'autrier un jor
> Par un ries chevauchoie –

The other day, at Eastertide, I was riding through a clearing . . .

and goes on to describe an encounter between a knight and a maid. The *pastourelle* shows its relation to the *chanson de toile* not only in its assumed naiveté but also musically, in its tendency to use 'narrative melody'. One of four *pastourelles* beginning with the words 'L'autrier par un matinet' is an extremely repetitive one by the trouvère, Moniot de Paris (fl. *c.* 1250); the melodic range is limited to a fifth, and several phrases are contained within a third.[85]

Ex. 92

L'au-trier par un   ma-ti-net –   2   un jor   de   l'au-tre se-mai-ne –

3   che-vau-chai les   un   bos-chet,   4   come a-   ven-tu-re   gent mai-ne,

5   par de-joste un   jar-di-net,   6   sos le   ru   d'u-ne fon-tai-ne

---

[84] On the *pastourelle* as a genre, see Bec (1977), I.119ff.

[85] R965; ed. in measured style by Gérold, 126–7; in neutral style, van der Werf (1979), 407. My transcription is from Chansonnier de l'Arsenal (Source 26) fol. 193. For the *refrain*, see Boogaard no. 1629. Falck, 'Moniot de Paris' in *New Grove*, comments on 'the prevalence of relatively simple forms with refrain' in Moniot's small *oeuvre*. Van der Werf prints all the songs. Rosenberg and Tischler, in their anthology of trouvère songs (1981), print three in measured rhythm (nos. 202–4); no. 202 is particularly *lai*-like in tonality.

7 *choi-si en un pra-e- let* 8 *pa- sto- re qui mult ert sai- ne,*

9 *et d'au-tre part Ro- bi- net* 10 *qui grant po- ne- e de-mai- ne;*

11 *pipe a- voit et fla- io- let,* 12 *et fla- iole a douce a- lai- ne,*

13 *car por Mar-gue- rot se pai- ne* 14 *qui plus ert blan- che que lai- ne.*

REFR :15 *Ro- bi- net chante et fres-te- le,* 16 *et trepe et cri-e et sau-te- le.*

17 *Mar-got en chan-tant a- pe- le.*

The other day in the morning – it was during last week – I was riding beside a copse, as chance leads one to do, in the neighbourhood of a garden, when I saw by the water of a fountain in an open space a shepherdess who was very pretty, and opposite her, Robinet in high spirits. He had a pipe and a flageolet and he fluted with sweet breath because he was suffering for [love of] Marguerot, whose complexion was whiter than wool. [*Refrain:*] *Robinet sings and pipes and shouts and leaps. And as he sings he calls out to Margot.*

With the *pastourelle* we make contact with another tradition of medieval melody, a tradition which has been described more fully in the chapter on dance-song – the *refrain* (ch. 5:11). To summarize, the *refrain* (which may or may not be used as a refrain in the modern sense) is a short aphoristic saying of usually two or of three lines, a sort of courtly proverb, as for instance[86]

> Onques més ne les senti
> les maus d'amer,
> més or les sent.

I never felt them before – the pangs of love; but now I feel them.

These *refrains* are frequently met with in the *pastourelle*, where they raise a new question about narrative song.

The problem is this. The *refrain* is metrical melody; it belongs to the tradition of medieval dance-song. More than 'metrical', it is also 'measured' – i.e. durationally proportioned. This we know from the fact that a great many

[86] Boogaard, no. 1424 (three occurrences).

of them are found written out in a clear mensural notation. Should we assume from this that the association of narrative with *refrain* in the *pastourelle* means that some narratives at least were sung in a metrical, even in a 'measured', style? At this stage it would be foolish to close our minds to this possibility, even though it is diametrically opposed to what a modern might regard as a 'natural' way of singing narrative – that is, with the flexibility experienced in the recitation tones of Gregorian chant, such as psalmody. Our conceptions of what is 'natural' may, as often, not provide a safe guide.[87]

There is nothing in Johannes de Grocheo's well-known remarks about singing narrative poems (see ch. 7: 1) to suggest a connection with dance-song. All he says about the performance of *gesta* is that the number of lines is not fixed but variable and that each line should be sung to the same melody (*idem etiam cantus debet in omnibus versibus reiterari*) – the evidence suggests that this latter prescription can only be true in a general sense. However, there is an early southern French saint's life which makes a specific connection between dance-song and narrative: it is the *Chanson de Sainte Foi d'Agen*, of the first half of the eleventh century.[88]

> [L]egir audi sotz eiss un pin
> del vell temps un libre Latin;
> tot l'escoltei tro a la fin.
>
> . . .
>
> Canczon audi q'es bella'n tresca,
> que fo de razo Espanesca;
> non fo de paraulla Grezesca
> ne de lengua Serrazinesca.
> Dolz'e suaus es plus que bresca,
> e plus qe nulz pimentz q'om mesca;
> qui ben la diz a lei Francesca
> cuig me qe sos granz pros l'en cresca
> e q'en est segle l'en paresca.
> Tota Basconn' et Aragons
> e l'encontrada delz Gascons
> sabon quals es aqist canczons
> e ss'es ben vera 'sta razons.
> Eu l'audi legir a clerczons
> et a gramadis, a molt bons,
> si qon o monstral passions
> en que om lig estas leiczons.
> E si vos plaz est nostre sons,
> aisi conl guidal primers tons,
> eu la vos cantarei en dons.

---

[87] The problem of rhythmic interpretation created by mixed styles and conflicting traditions in the *pastourelle* is discussed in more detail below, chapter 14:1 v.

[88] Van der Veen, 85–6, from the edn by A. Thomas, CFMA (Paris 1925), lines 1–33, giving Thomas's modern French translation. The *Chanson* is in monorhymed octosyllabic *laisses* of unequal length.

I heard read under a pine-tree a Latin book of antiquity; I heard it all right through to the end . . . I heard a song which is good to dance to, and its content was Spanish; it was not in Greek words nor in the Saracen tongue. It is sweet and succulent, more than a honeycomb, and more than a spiced drink poured out ready. He who utters it well in the French manner, I think that he will get great profit from it, and that the profit will be evident in this world. All the Basque country and Aragon and the land of Gascony know what a song it is and if what it has to say is true. And I heard it read by clerks and scholars of note exactly as the 'passion' shows it – the 'passion' [i.e. Office of the saint] in which those 'lessons' are read. And if our melody pleases you, then I will freely sing it to you in the style set by the first melody.

In this interesting passage, which itself is in *laisse* form, the Provençal poet tells us he has used three sources for his poem – a Latin book, a dance-song (*canczon . . . q'es bella'n tresca*) and 'the passion in which one reads those lessons' (*estas leiczons*). One of the poem's editors has identified the Latin book as Lactantius's *De mortibus persecutorum*;[89] and the 'lessons' will call for comment later. Meanwhile the reference to the dance-song is far from being crystal clear. We know that it had Spanish subject-matter and that it could be uttered, performed (?), in the French style (*Qui ben la diz a lei francesca*). It was widely known, and everyone in those parts to the southwest knew 'if what it said was true'. And the narrator had heard it read/sung by educated people.

  The question is whether the matter of the dance-song was sung to the melody of the *lectio* (that is, a recitation tone) or, on the other hand, whether the matter of the *lectio* was sung to the melody of the dance-song.[90] What in any case might the author have had in mind when he referred to the *leiczons*? In order to answer this question we must now turn to the saint's life as a genre of narrative melody – to its association with the *chanson de geste*, on the one hand, and its association with the liturgy, on the other.

[89] See Hoeppffner and Alfaric, ed. (Paris 1926), II.27.

[90] Karl Reichl has drawn my attention to the use of dance-song melodies by the folk-singers of Uzbekistan up to the present day for the singing of epic narratives. See his informative article 'Oral tradition and performance of the Uzbek and Karakalpak Epic Singers' in *Fragen der mongolischen Heldendichtung*, ed. W. Heissig (Bonn 1983). His further researches and field-work (in 1985) among the neighbouring Kirghiz have brought to light *epos* melodies of an indisputably metrical and measured type, predominantly in triple time and sung unaccompanied.

7

NARRATIVE MELODY II: SAINT'S LIFE AND LITURGICAL NARRATIVE

I Saint's Life and *chanson de geste*

Towards the end of the thirteenth century an Englishman, Thomas de Cobham (d. 1327), Sub-Dean of Salisbury and Archbishop of Canterbury, wrote a passage in a Penitential in which he distinguished three kinds of *histrio* (the term covers actors, minstrels, entertainers). The first two kinds are utterly damnable in the strictest sense. One kind consists of those who disfigure their own bodies with disgusting dances (acrobatics?), nude displays, and the wearing of shocking masks. The second are idle, criminal and footloose; they frequent courts, curry favour and spread evil slanders. But there is a third kind:

Est etiam tertium genus histrionum qui habent instrumenta musica ad delectandum homines, et talium duo sunt genera. Quidam enim frequentant publicas potationes et lascivas congregationes, ut cantent ibi diversas cantilenas ut moveant homines ad lasciviam, et tales sunt damnabiles sicut et alii. Sunt autem alii, qui dicuntur joculatores qui cantant gesta principum et vitas sanctorum et faciunt solatia hominibus vel in egritudinibus suis vel in angustiis suis et non faciunt nimias turpitudines sicut faciunt saltatores et saltatrices et alii qui ludunt in imaginibus inhonestis et faciunt videri quasi quedam phantasmata per incantationes vel alio modo.[1]

But there is a third kind of entertainer: they have musical instruments to delight men with. And this kind can itself be subdivided. For some of them frequent public drinking places and licentious gatherings: there they sing various sorts of songs to incite people to licentious pleasures. And these entertainers, like the first two kinds, are in peril of damnation. But there are others, called jongleurs, who sing the deeds of princes and the lives of the saints and give people comfort both in sickness and in distress; these jongleurs do not perform the extremely disgusting acts that dancers do, male and female, and also those others who disport themselves in unseemly shapes and make themselves appear virtual apparitions by means of enchantments or in some other way.

So far as the Archbishop is concerned, there is only one kind of good minstrel – one who sings the deeds of noble persons and the lives of the saints. The

[1] F. Broomfield, ed., *Thomae de Chobham Summa Confessorum*, Analecta Mediaevalia Namurcensia, 25 (Louvain 1968), 291–2. In the second sentence he reads *ut cantent*; other editors emend. There is dispute about Cobham's identity and date: Broomfield argues for a date of *c.* 1216 for the *Summa*.

interest of this passage has more than once been commented on: there were minstrels whose efforts had the approval of some churchmen; no important distinction is made between *gesta principum* and *vitam sanctorum* for the purposes of edification and solace, and minstrels perform both.

Another well-known passage, written by the Parisian Johannes de Grocheo in his *Theoria* (*c.* 1300), confirms the connection between the performance of *chansons de geste* and the performance of saints' lives:[2]

Cantum vero gestualem dicimus, in quo gesta heroum et antiquorum patrum opera recitantur, sicuti vita et martyria sanctorum et proelia et adversitates, quas antiqui viri pro fide et veritate passi sunt, sicuti vita beati Stephani protomartyris et historia regis Karoli.

We call a song a *chanson de geste* in which the deeds of heroes and the achievements of our forefathers are recounted, like the life and sufferings of the saints and the conflicts and adversities which men of old endured for the faith and for the truth – the life of St Stephen the first martyr, for example, and the story of Charlemagne . . .

The weight of these two passages taken together leads us to expect a close connection between the two types of heroic narrative, the 'secular' epic and the 'sacred' life, and allows us to suppose that evidence about the singing of the one may be evidence about the singing of the other. We should not, of course, fall into the easy, anachronistic error of imagining that we are linking disparates together. The 'sacred' and the 'secular' are not so easily distinguished in an age which saw Christianity through an heroic lens – and heroes through a Christian lens. Is not Roland designated in old Passionals as *Sanctus Rolandus comes et martyr in Roncevalla* and commemorated, wearing the saintly nimbus, in the window of Chartres Cathedral?[3] And it is not simply that epic heroes are canonized. The reverse is also true: saints are seen as heroes. A thoroughly convincing example from the Anglo-Norman domain is that of *La Vie de St Alexis* (mid-eleventh-century).

Alexis of Rome probably never existed, but his Legend was extremely popular in the Middle Ages. Alexis 'left his wife on his wedding night and went on a long pilgrimage, returning afterwards to Rome and living there unknown as a beggar [under the stairs] in his father's house for seventeen years. He was identified after death by documents in his handwriting, by voices from heaven and by miracles.'[4] The following passage is taken from his father's lament:[5]

---

[2] Ed. Rohloff, 130.

[3] Emile Mâle, *The Gothic Image* (London 1961), 351, from C. Cahier, *Caractéristiques des saints dans l'art populaire* (Paris 1867–8), II.778 (n.).

[4] Farmer, *Dictionary of Saints*, s.v. 'Alexis'. For the history of the legend in more than a dozen languages see Odenkirchen's edn (note following) pp. 11–13.

[5] Ed. C. Storey (1946), lines 406–15, p. 14. The edn by C. J. Odenkirchen (1978) reads *l'aveie* in the second line (407), repunctuates and translates 408 'And yet for yourself you never had any concern for it.' The MS (now at Hildesheim, taken there by English monks in the seventeenth century) is part of the St Albans Psalter.

Blanc ai le chef e le barbe ai canuthe;
Ma grant honur t'aveie retenude
Ed anpur tei, mais n'en aveies cure.
Si grant dolur or m'est apar[e]üde!
Filz, la tue aname el ciel seit absoluthe!

Tei cuvenist helme e brunie a porter,
Espede ceindra cume tui altre per;
E grant maisnede doüses guverner,
Le gunfanun l'emperedur porter,
Cum fist tis pedre e li tons parentez.

My head has white hairs and my beard is hoary with age; my honourable estate I had reserved for you and because of you. But you cared nothing about it. What heavy sorrow is now my lot! Son, may your soul be absolved in heaven!

For you it would have been fitting to wear helmet and coat of mail, to gird on sword like your companions in age; you should have been lord of a great retinue and should have carried the emperor's standard, as your father did and all your kin.

Admittedly, this is a lament for the kind of hero Alexis decided *not* to be. But the poem has it both ways: Alexis could have been a hero in the mould of the feudal *barun*, and the poem, couched in epic idiom, does nothing to repudiate this ideal.

The closeness of the two modes, heroic and hagiographical, also extends to romance and amounts in some instances to interchangeability, as in the case of the story of Amis and Amiloun.[6] The two types of narrative – or perhaps we should rather think of three, saints' lives, heroic epic, and romance – were not sharply distinguished one from another. The same stories availed for all, and the high idealism of each mode could borrow or be borrowed. The same performers could, we have seen, manage sacred and secular narratives. It remains to be investigated whether there were sufficiently close formal (i.e. physical, metrical) links between the various types of narrative to allow evidence about the singing of one to hold as evidence for the singing of others.

The earliest vernacular saints' lives are in Old English.[7] In so far as they have excellences, these are the excellences of Anglo-Saxon heroic epic, whose characteristics they share. The problems of their performance have by implication already been considered. Apart from them, the earliest lives are in French: they are a short poem in sequence-form about St Eulalie,[8] a Life of St

---

[6] The editor of the ME text (EETS 1937, repr. 1960), MacE. Leach, writes (p. ix), 'The hagiographic group uses the same story skeleton (as the romantic), but adds new incidents; it changes the story theme from the testing of romantic friendship to an exposition of the virtues of two friends, so beloved of God and the Blessed Virgin that miracles are worked on their behalf . . .' See further K. Hume in *JEGP* 69 (1970) 89–107, on hagiographical features of romance.

[7] Pearsall, 40–4, judiciously surveys the surviving examples, distinguishing between a 'lavishly inappropriate use of heroic diction' and 'a blending of values'.

[8] Ed. with facsimile in R. M. Ruggieri, *Testi antichi romanzi*, 2 vols. (Modena 1949), no. 21; transl. by L. S. Porter in *SinP* 57 (1960) 590. See also P. von Winterfeld, 'Rhythmen und

Leger, and a Passion (it seems logical and apt to include certain narratives about Christ under the general heading; the sufferings and martyrdom of a saint, it is worth noting, were often termed his *passio*). Of these *St Leger* and the Passion are of immediate interest because they have some musical notation.[9] The notation is in Aquitanian neumes, 'heighted' to some extent but not on a stave. In each case the neumes are squeezed in above and between the lines. The melodies, therefore, cannot be transcribed satisfactorily: but something may be learnt from them nevertheless.

The *St Leger* manuscript cannot, it is thought, be later than the early eleventh century. Leodegar, Bishop of Autun, was remembered most actively in Poitou and Burgundy. The feast of St Leodegar/Leger was perhaps first celebrated at Autun; and it was there in all probability that some clerk composed this not too inspired Life – 'son récit strophique en roman, destiné a être chanté au peuple'.[10] The conjecture as to use may be true; but Gaston Paris adduces no evidence except the presence of the notation – a dubious argument in any case. The notation is unfortunately minimal in extent, being confined to the first five syllables; the neumes are simple *puncta*. What the notation, combined with the manuscript presentation, does suggest is that the narrative was written in six-line stanzas and was sung strophically (i.e. each stanza had the same melody) – though of this we cannot be sure. The line-structure of each stanza is a a b b c c; the lines are octosyllabic; the couplets are linked by assonance, and only occasionally by full rhyme:

> Domine deu devemps lauder
> et a sus sancz honor porter
> in suamor cantomps del sanz
> quae por lui augrent granz aanz.
> et or es temps et si est biens
> quae nos cantumps de sant lethgier

We are bound to praise the Lord God and to honour his saints. For love of him we sing of the saints who for him suffered great torments. And now it is time, and an excellent thing too, that we should sing of St Leger.

The St Leger Life is 240 lines long. The stanza-melody was, then, repeated 40 times, if it was strophic. The Passion presents a very similar picture and

---

[9] In Clermont-Ferrand MS 240. Text: G. Paris, 'La vie de St Léger', *Romania* I (1872) 303ff; facsimile in G. Paris, *Les plus anciens monuments de la langue française; Album*, SATF (Paris 1875), pl. 7–9.

[10] Paris, 'La vie de St Léger', 302; the poem was composed in the mid tenth century. On the life of St Leodegar, see E. Auerbach in *Syntaktika und Stylistika, Festschrift für E. Gamillscheg* (Tübingen 1957), 35–42.

Sequenzenstudien I: Die lateinische Eulaliensequenz und ihre Sippe', *ZfdA* 45 (1901) 133–49; Dronke (1970), 2–3. Both the Clermont Passion and the *Vie de St Léger* 'were originally composed in French but subsequently copied by a Provençal scribe' (P. Rickard, *A history of the French language* (London 1974), 37); J. Linskill, *Saint Léger: Etude* (Paris 1937), 142, argues that two different scribes copied the poems.

comes from the same manuscript.[11] It is much longer and consists of 129 quatrains, again assonanced a a b b. This, of course, is not long as medieval narratives go; but a great deal of melodic repetition must have been involved, if it was sung strophically – and the evidence is that it was. Each quatrain forms a syntactic unit and is introduced in the manuscript with a capital letter. Furthermore, the whole of stanza 1 is notated and no other. This is not conclusive evidence, but it is suggestive. We know from other evidence that long narratives were often sung strophically (p. 228). The notation, untranscribable though it is, clearly shows that the melody was syllabically conceived (no neume contains more than two notes) and contained no large leaps. So far as can be deduced from the heighting and grouping of the neumes, there is no melodic repetition, or very little – but this is to venture on unsure ground. The example shows the opening of the poem with its neumes:

Ex. 93

Now I tell you the true story of the Passion of Jesus Christ. I wish to call to mind his sufferings, for he has redeemed this world of ours.

II Epistles of the saints

In the centuries which followed, the twelfth and thirteenth, it is still the saints' lives around which the largest amount of circumstantial evidence accrues. In an important article of 1948 Jacques Chailley proposed a connection between the singing of saints' lives and the singing of certain lessons in the Mass and in the Offices of the church (the services of the Hours from Matins to Compline). He printed, from a Chartres MS, a troped epistle (that is, an

---

[11] G. Paris, 'La Passion de Jésus-Christ', *Romania* 2 (1873) 299ff, prints the text. Facsimile in Paris, *Monuments* (note 9 above), pl. 3–6.

epistle with interpolations) from the Mass of St Stephen's Day (26 December).[12]

Ex. 94

Masters, listen all of you and you will be able to hear briefly the 'passion' and the sufferings of St Stephen openly [declared]. *The lesson from the Acts of the Apostles.* The apostles wrote this lesson with true intent about St Stephen the good knight. *In those days* – Around the day when Christ was born and placed on earth for us St Stephen was stoned. *Stephen full of grace . . .*

[12] Chartres MS 520 (destroyed 1944), fol. 311. See Chailley (1948) 12, for the music example. Texts: *AH* XLIX, nos. 383–414. See Stäblein (1975), 61, for the relation of epistle tropes to others; M. Huglo, 'Epistle' and 'Farse' in *New Grove*, gives details.

When the interpolations are in the vernacular, as here, the procedure is often called 'farsing' (ME *farsen*, OF *farcir*: 'to stuff'). The purpose of 'farsing' an epistle is celebratory rather than didactic; it magnifies the importance of the reading.[13] Indeed, the new matter is sometimes referred to as *ornatura sive farsitura*, and farsed epistles are most commonly met with at seasons of joyous ceremonial, especially Christmas when the following feasts are celebrated, besides St Stephen – St John the Evangelist (27 December), the Holy Innocents (28 December), St Thomas of Canterbury (29 December), the Circumcision (1 January), the Epiphany (6 January). This was also a season of jollity (to give it no grosser name) as well as joy, the season of the Feast of Fools; and the potentially 'jolly' character of an epistle sung in dialogue between two deacons, one singing in Latin and the other in French, can be gauged from directives such as the one quoted earlier (p. 180) from the Archbishop of Reims who in 1261 equated 'farses' with scurrilous songs.[14] The surviving texts of farsed epistles do not seem in the least 'scurrilous'. Perhaps the scurrility was improvised for the occasion.

The prominence of St Stephen is especially noteworthy in view of the fact that Grocheo singles him out and links his name with that of Charlemagne (p. 236 above). The following epistle of St Stephen survives in two versions of which one is in Provençal (in a manuscript of the early thirteenth century) and one is in Northern French (from a manuscript of the early fourteenth). I give the opening of the text in parallel columns as edited and arranged by Gaston Paris:[15]

i. *Incipit vita sancti Stephani*
    Oués trestout conmunaument:
    Moustrer vous veuil regnablement
    La passion et le tourment
    De saint Estienne apertement,
    Que il souffrit mout doucement
    Pour l'amour Dieu omnipotent.
    Juis le trairent laidement
    Dehors les murs de chasement
    Ou Dieu fu mort corporelment,
    Dont il prendra son vengement
    Quant il vendra au jugement.

    Epistola beati Stephani prothomartiris
    Entendes tug cominalmen:
    Mostrar vos vuiel apertamen
    De sanc Esteva lo turmen,

    Ques el sofri mout dousamen
    Per amor Dieu omnipoten.
    Jusieu lon traisson laiamen
    Defors los murs Jherusalem
    On Dieus fo mortz corporalmen
    Don el penra so vengamen
    Quant il venran al juggamen.

---

[13] Huglo, however ('Farse' in *New Grove*), observes that in medieval sources the word 'trope' is more frequently used of the longer interpolations, 'farse' of interpolations into lessons.

[14] See ch. 5 above, note 63 and text; also L. Gaudin, 'Epîtres farcies inédites de la Saint-Etienne', *Revue des langues romanes* 2 (1871) 133, who prints *motulis* (? motets) instead of *notulis*.

[15] G. Paris, 'Une épître française de Saint Etienne', *Romania* 10 (1881) 218–23, prints both texts (BN fr. 1555 and Montpellier, Bibl.Mun. MS 120); he argues that the northern French version is the earlier. Facsimile of the Provençal version with its music are in Gaudin (note 14 above). Yet other versions survive (Paris, 223, gives details).

Lectio actuum apostolorum

ii. Uns livres est que nous avon:	Us libres est que nos avem:
Faiz des apostres l'appellon . . .	*Fags dels apostols* l'apelam . . .

Listen all of you together: I wish to give you a rational account of the 'passion' and the
sufferings of St Stephen openly [declared], for he suffered most mildly for the love of
Almighty God. The Jews dragged him cruelly outside the walls of the town, where
God died in his bodily form and because of which he will take his vengeance when he
comes to the Judgement. *Reading from the Acts of the Apostles.* There is a book which we
have here: we call it 'The Deeds done by the Apostles' . . .

The text, we see, is arranged in rhymed *laisses* of the *chanson de geste* type (see
above, p. 201), except that the lines are short – octosyllabic – and rhymed. In
each case the vernacular text follows the Latin, which it greatly expands and
glosses. The northern French text proceeds as follows:

> *Lectio actuum* (see above) = *laisse* ii (7 lines)
> *In diebus illis* = *laisse* iii (9 lines)
> *Stephanus plenus gratia, etc.* = *laisse* iv (13 lines)
> *Surrexerunt autem quidem, etc.* = *laisse* v (6 lines)
> *Et non poterant resistere, etc.* = *laisse* vi (6 lines)

and so forth. No *laisse* has more than 13 or fewer than 5 lines. The whole piece
is 126 lines long.

Some historians have seen connections between the 'farsed' epistle and the
beginnings of drama. It is, however, its interest as a narrative form which
concerns us. The expansions of the vernacular text contain several of the
formulas familiar to us in saint's life and romance, such as the assurance to the
audience

> Et vous mesmes pas n'en doubtez,
> Fu saint Estienne lapidés:
> Ja l'orreis bien se vous voulez . . . (lines 25–7)

And you yourselves can be quite assured of this, St Stephen was stoned. You can
indeed hear all about it, if you're willing to listen . . .

or the final prayer for intercession

> Or lui prion tuit a un cry
> Qu'il prie Dieu qui ne menty
> Que de nos ames ait mercy . . .   (122–4)

Now let us all pray to him [Stephen] with one voice, that he will pray to God who is
truth itself, to have mercy on our souls . . .

But what is most important is, first, that it, the vernacular text, is indeed a *vita*
of the saint, a narrative of his acts not a hymn of praise; and, secondly, that the
vernacular text is in verse and in a significant metre. The metre may, in fact, be
a little more complicated than I suggested just now. The Provençal text is in a

form which combines *laisse* technique with strophic repetition. This is where the manuscript presentation of narrative may be significant.[16] Line 6 of the text is distinguished by a capital letter 'I', dividing an apparent *laisse* of ten lines into two stanzas of five monorhymed lines each. However, the text is by no means precisely strophic throughout, and the length of the stanzas varies from three to seven lines.

What information do these various texts give us about the singing of narrative? The troped epistle of St Stephen from Chartres (quoted at the beginning of this section) shows the simplest form of potential narrative melody. Phrase A has an 'open' and a 'closed' form (A'). According as to whether there are three or four lines of vernacular interpolation, so the strophe is expanded or contracted. Without the rest of the text it is impossible to say for how many lines these phrases could serve. The other epistle of Stephen gives us a better idea. The northern French manuscript unfortunately contains no music; but the earlier Provençal one does, in a clear and elegant square notation which shows an evident derivation from the neumes of the Aquitaine 'family'. The whole *vita*, as one heading calls it, is sung to three melodies; here they are as used in the final *laisse*.[17]

Ex. 95

When the martyr's blood had spoken, it was the time that he should die. The angels came at his death to request his soul. He neither sobbed nor sighed. Rather, God let him pass away so peacefully that it was as if it was time to fall asleep.

---

[16] See facsimile in Gaudin.

[17] Transcr. from facsimile in Gaudin, p. 8. The MS has only one capital letter (line 1, *Cant*), except for the last letter of *adormiR*. The phrase-divisions are mine; the scribe has written in some fourteen vertical strokes indicating the carefully syllabic word-division.

Once again we find a narrative musical structure composed of three melodies (cf. *Aucassin et Nicolette* above, Ex. 86). But on this occasion they are differently combined. The rules appear to be: the *laisse*, or stanza, always begins with phrase A and always ends with it;[18] the standard five- and six-line stanzas always end B C A; that a four-line or a three-line stanza omits C (which to a modern ear seems the necessary answer to B) and runs A A B A or A B A. However, despite these principles of combination, which are slightly different from ones we have met before, we are still dealing with a narrative style in which a fairly simple basic melody is freely repeated as required (it allows incidentally of slight melodic variants) but is occasionally set into relief by other melodies of still simple but contrasting contour. Although it is not directly relevant, it is interesting to note that the melodies in this MS for the recitation of the Latin text of the epistle contrast, on the whole, with those for the vernacular 'stuffing'; they contain some unusually florid writing (e.g. for *Lectio actuum apostolorum* itself) and the longer passages use *d* as a reciting-note with a recurrent flexion quite unlike anything in the trope.

Ex. 96

Et tes- tes de- po- su- e- runt ves-ti- men-ta su- a se- cus

pe- des a- do- le- scen-tis qui vo- ca- ba- tur Sau- lus.

And the witnesses laid down their clothes by the feet of a young man whose name was Saul.

Another farsed epistle of the Christmas season shows a more complex musical structure. It comes from Amiens and is dated mid-thirteenth-century: *In die sanctorum innocentium epistola.*[19] It opens:

> Or escoutés, grant et petit,
> traiés vous cha vers chest escrit,
> Si attendés tant que j'aie lit
> cheste lechon et chest chant dit . . .

> Now listen, old and young,
> draw near to the book here
> and give your attention until I have read
> this 'lesson' and performed this melody [*lit.*: said this song] . . .

[18] The only exception is a single couplet, B A.

[19] Previously printed P. Aubry, *La Musique et les musiciens d'église en Normandie au xiiie siècle* (Paris 1906), 34–40.

Once again we find an opening, quite non–liturgical in tone, addressed to an audience of old and young with rhymed *laisses* of varying length. The *laisse* here quoted has, in fact, three rhymes: *-er* ×10; *-ant* ×11; and *-ie* ×7.[20]

Ex. 97

Et au-di-vi vo-cem in ce-lo, tan-quam ro-cem a-qua-rum mul-ta-rum,

et tan-quam vo-cem to-ni-tru-i ma-gni; et vo-cem quam au-di-vi si-cut

ci-tha-re-do-rum ci-tha-ri-zan-ti-um in ci-tha-ris su-is.

laisse 1 De loins au-y ia-ves ver-ser,   tout au-tre-si com-me de mer;

et puis au-y for-ment ton-ner   et ton-noir-res en-tre-con-ter.

A-pres au-y har-pes son-ner,   les har-pe-ours a-vec chan-ter.

Or, de-vons bien chi en-sei-gner   nos fais, nos dis, nos-tre pen-ser,

que nous nous puissons as-sam-bler   a Dame-dieu et a-cor-der.

laisse 2 Les ya-ves sont li peu-ple grant,   et mal et bon et mes-cre-ant,

que Dieux fait naistre en ter-re tant,   com il a fait d'ya-ve cou-rant.

Tous doib-vent los en leur vi-vant   a Da-me-dieu le tout puis-sant;

---

[20] My transcription of the epistle is from Amiens, Bibl. de la Ville 573 (Source 1), fol. 206v. The notation is square, well written in a professional service-book hand.

et che que j'o- y Dieu ton-nant, ch'est che qu'il nous va ma-ne- chant,

et par be- son- gnes de- ba- tant, par faim, par guer-re cha-ste- iant,

comme li pe- res son en- fant.

laissez Les har-pes don-nent me-lo- di- e, quant li homs dit sa psal-mo-di- e

et par je- ü- ne se cru- ci- e, qu'il n'y ait point d'y-po-cri- si- e,

et sans or-geuil et sans en- vi- e chan-te a Dieu par sympho-ni- e

et si li rent doulche ar-mo-ni-e.

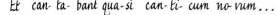

Et can- ta- bant qua-si can-ti- cum no-vum . . .

Latin: And I heard a voice in heaven, as it were the voice of many waters, and the voice of great thunder; and the voice that I heard was as of harpers harping on their harps. *French:* I heard the flowing of waters afar off, just as if it was the sea. And then I heard loud thundering and thunderclaps meeting. After that I heard harps sounding, the harpers with singing also. Now we must make quite clear here our deeds, our words, our thoughts, so that we gather ourselves before the Lord God and reconcile ourselves to him. The waters signify the multitude of peoples, bad, good and unbelievers, whom God made to be born on earth, just as he made the running waters. They all owe praise to God the all-powerful, for as long as they live. And that I hear God thundering means that he comes to threaten us, subduing us through our needs, through hunger and war chastising us, as a father does his child. The harps give melody, when man sings his psalms and disciplines himself with fasting, provided that there is no hypocrisy in it, and that without pride or spite he sings to God with his music and offers sweet harmony to him. *Latin:* And they sang as it were a new song . . .

As the rest of this long epistle confirms, there is an underlying basic melodic quatrain A B C D. But it is continuously varied: D (or one of its variants) always ends a *laisse* or marks the end of a monorhyme section; A normally begins a melodic cluster but can occasionally be preceded or replaced; phrases B or C can be omitted; and indeed if the 'closing' quality of D is not required, then D itself can be omitted. There is also a sixth melodic member, F (and its variant), which can be used to fill out, but never in a beginning or ending position. This is an extraordinarily interesting piece of narrative melody (the same six 'tunes' are used throughout the whole epistle) and may show *in extenso* how melodic units might be combined in kaleidoscopic variety by other singers of narrative.

The 'farsed' epistles just discussed provide melodies that are suitable for – and, indeed, are actually used for – the singing of narrative verse in octosyllabic lines. Another piece of music, from the well-known manuscript associated with St Martial (Paris BN lat. 1139), seems to provide for decasyllabics.[21] It is not itself a farsed epistle but may be connected with lesson-singing.

> Ben deu hoi mais finir nostra razos –
> un panc soi las que trop fu aut lo sos.
> Leven doi clerc que dijen lo respos:
> '*Tu autem, Deus*, qui es paire glorios,
> nos te preiam que t'remembre de nos
> quant triaras los mals d'entre los bos.'

Now it time to finish our 'story' for today – I'm rather tired because the melody lay very high. Two clerks get up who make the response: '*Tu autem, Domine*, who art our glorious father, We pray Thee to have remembrance of us when Thou shalt pick out the evil from the good.'

Chailley comments that this appears at first sight to be a trope to the familiar formula which concluded the chanting of the lesson(s) during the night office of Matins:

Versicle: Tu autem, Domine, miserere nobis. *Response:* Deo gratias.

But, he argues, the tone of line 2 is too colloquial for a liturgical occasion – 'I'm rather tired because the melody lay very high'. Rather, it might be the terminal stanza (*laisse?*) 'of one of the sung Lives based on the Latin Lives which were sung in psalm-style like the lessons in the Office of these same saints' – possibly, he suggests, a stanza for general use in a conclusion.[22] The *Tu autem* formula was used at the end of mealtime readings in religious houses; and a very likely occasion for the recitation or chanting of a saint's life would be when the monks were gathered in the refectory – in silence, be it remembered – for meals. One traditional formula for the *Tu autem* is[23]

---

[21] Chailley (1948), 16, with conjectural transcription of the staff-less neumes.
[22] Chailley (1948), 18.
[23] See *Sarum Antiphonal*, vol. II, p. 11, col. 1 (Advent I).

Ex. 98

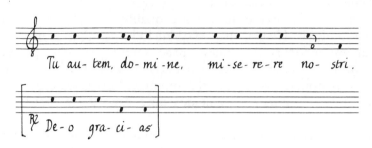

Musically speaking, the melody of 'Ben deu hoi mais' (which I do not give here because the precise pitches are uncertain) is interesting because it shows a different principle at work. Instead of the repeated single-line formula, we seem to be dealing with half-line formulas.[24] One would like to know more about chants constructed in this way. However that may be, this vernacular adornment of the *Tu autem* appears to provide one kind of model to which six monorhymed lines of decasyllabic verse might be sung. What is not clear, on the evidence, is whether the musical material permits extension and contraction or whether it is of fixed length. To put the question another way – is this a six-line strophe to be repeated only in its entirety, or does it provide, like the previous example, the material for a *laisse* of variable length?

Whatever the answer, one of the links between liturgical and non-liturgical narrative chanting could have been the use of such common, endlessly repeated and repeatable formulas as the *Tu autem*. It is especially interesting, therefore, to find the words of the formula quoted again in the final lines of the Anglo-Norman *Horn*, a romance which owes much to the *chanson-de-geste* tradition and which is written in *laisses* (the alexandrines are monorhymed not merely assonanced):[25]

> Or en die avant ki l'estorie saverat:
> Tomas n'en dirrat plus, 'Tu autem' chanterat:
> 'Tu autem domine miserere nostri'.

Now let him who knows it carry on with the story. Thomas will tell no more of it. He will sing 'Tu autem': ['And thou, O Lord, have mercy upon us']

This reference may, of course, be purely metaphorical, and Thomas's 'chanterat' may be in genuine contrast to his 'dirrat' earlier in the line. There could, on the other hand, be a link of a melodic kind, if the romance was sung – that is, the *Tu autem* melody might form a suitable cadential phrase for the *laisse*. If this were so, amongst the melodies used for the performance of the

---

[24] As I analyse it, there are two 'beginning' phrases, 'intonations' as it were, and three 'ending' phrases ('terminations'). The 'beginnings' (A and C) cannot be used in the second half of the line; the 'endings' (B, D, E) cannot be used in the first half.

[25] M. K. Pope, ed., *The Romance of Horn*, Anglo-Norman Text Soc. vols. IX–X (1955, 1964), lines 5238–40. Legge, 97 n. 1, gives some further *Tu autem* references.

chanson de geste, or at least of the saints' lives, we might include the epistle tone itself. However, against this it must be said that there appears as yet to be a total absence of positive evidence that liturgical recitation tones were so used. And in some of the farsed epistles there is indeed, as we have seen, an implied *contrast* between the chant for the Latin *lectio* and the more tuneful syllabic melodies used for the vernacular farse or gloss.

III The rhymed Office

The material so far considered does not exhaust all the sources of melodies associated with the *vitae* of saints. The 'rhymed office' of the twelfth and thirteenth centuries provides yet another.[26] It was one of many outlets for the stream of creative musical and poetic activity which was flowing continually into the composition of tropes and sequences. In a way it was an extension of the same activity, since it consisted in adding yet further to the amount of 'measured' and 'rhythmical' poetry in the liturgy. The 'rhymed Office' was one in which all the musical items except for certain fixed ones were turned into verse. All the services of the Hours from Matins and Lauds through to Vespers and Compline could be so treated:[27]

A rhymed office begins, as a rule, with the six antiphons which on the vigil of the Feast itself were sung to the five psalms and the Magnificat. Then follows the antiphon to the invitatory psalm of Matins and the nine antiphons and nine responsories which alternate with psalms and lessons in the three 'nocturns'. The six antiphons for the psalms and [the canticle] of Lauds are added. At the end normally comes another antiphon for the Magnificat at Second Vespers.

Some idea of the poetic output can be gauged from the fact that this standard rhymed Office requires some thirty or more texts, though each antiphon would normally only crystallize as a single stanza to be grouped with others. This number may be multiplied by nine hundred or more (865 Offices are printed in *Analecta Hymnica* alone).[28] What gave the impulse to this wave of creativity was essentially the desire to honour the saints. Some five hundred separate saints were thus celebrated, most of them in a single surviving Office

[26] There is no satisfactory comprehensive study of the rhymed office. The best available is by Wagner (1911), 1.260 (ch. 15, 'Offices in metrical form'). A large number of texts are collected in *AH*, vols. v, xiii, xviii, xxiv–xxviii, xlv. Andrew Hughes reports progress (*ML* 65 (1984) 136) on a two-volume summary; his article in *New Grove*, however, is slight and does not supersede the article 'Reimoffizien' by W. Irtenkauf in *MGG*. Stäblein (1975), 162–5 (colour pl. 45a and b), reproduces part of the popular rhymed Office of St Thomas Becket from a southeast German antiphoner and discusses it.

[27] Schlager (1972), 293 (transl.); he gives the canticle of Lauds as the Nunc Dimittis, but the proper New Testament canticle is the Benedictus Dominus (see Steiner, 'Lauds' in *New Grove*, with comments on its especial appropriateness).

[28] W. H. Frere (*ML* 15 (1934) 353), reviewing E. Jammers, *Das Karlsoffizium 'Regali natus'* (Strassburg 1934), calculates the number at 1000; his review includes a lucid short history of the rhymed Office. Most of the Offices are singular, individual and local (Schlager (1972), 293).

designed for local use only. One of the earliest rhymed Offices is, however, for the Trinity (c. 920, by Stephen of Liège).[29] The ordinary festivals of the Church are little affected. The exercise was in inspiration a hagiographical one: the rhymed Office was frequently entitled *historia* and told and celebrated the story of a saint.

A rhymed Office is, in effect, a double *historia*. The lessons, which are left in prose, tell the Legend of the saint who is being honoured. At the same time, interspersed with the lessons and with the required psalms are the versified antiphons and responsories which sometimes themselves narrate, sometimes celebrate, the very same deeds. Thus, in an Office in honour of St Eustace (formerly called Placidus), the fourth and fifth antiphons for First Vespers run:[30]

> 4. Venando cervum capitur
>   hic Domino venante,
>   hunc dum vox alloquitur
>   cruce coruscante:
>
> 5. Cur me fugas, Placide?
>   Ego, quem ignoras,
>   sum Christus, cui splendide
>   res tuas dividebas.

As he is hunting the stag, God the hunter captures him. A voice addresses him, and the cross shines: 'Why do you pursue me, Placidus? I, whom you do not recognize, am Christ, for whom you nobly distributed your worldly goods.'[31]

In between these two verses would, of course, have come the singing of a psalm. Then in the responsory which follows we curiously jump backwards in the story to a more detailed account of Eustace's meeting with the stag (the metre here changes to quantitative hexameters):

> ℟ Ivit venatum
>   Placidus sibi prendere gratum.
>   Conspicit elatum
>   cervum cruce significatum,
>   cornibus innixum
>   simul aspexit crucifixum.
> ℣ Insequitur cervum,
>   nullum socians sibi servum.

[29] Sometimes attributed to Hucbald (d. 930); see Schlager, 293.

[30] *A H* xxvi.20 (no. 4: *De sancto Eustachio*).

[31] 'The historically worthless legend tells of a Roman general called Placidus under Trajan, who was converted by seeing a stag with a crucifix between his antlers, changed his name and that of his wife and children, lost his fortune and his family, was recalled to command the army at a critical time, was reunited with his family, and with them suffered martyrdom through being roasted to death in a brazen bull after refusing to sacrifice' (Farmer, s.v. 'EUSTACE').

Placidus went hunting to give himself pleasure. He sees a stag in a high place signed with the sign of a cross. At the same time he saw the crucified one supported upon its horns. He follows the stag, keeping no servant in attendance.

Obviously, if you did not know the story of St Eustace and wished to make its acquaintance, you would not attend his rhymed Office for this purpose.

In the absence of a properly grounded musical study of this odd and now little-known liturgical genre, it is not possible to generalize confidently about the melodies. However, one or two things are clear from the available material. I shall take as principal example the Office of St Thomas of Canterbury, since he was also, as we have seen, a favourite saint for celebration in the vernacular and his office is given in Sarum sources. The Office for St Thomas, one of the most elaborate of its kind, begins with a procession on the eve of the feast, during which this rhymed responsory is sung with its *versus*:[32]

> Jacet granum   oppressum palea,
> justus cesus   pravorum framea
> celum domo   commutans lutea.
> ℣ Cadit custos   vitis in vinea,
> dux in castris   cultor in area.

The grain lies overwhelmed by the chaff, the just man killed by the sword of the wicked, exchanging a home of clay for heaven. The guardian falls, the vine in the vineyard, the general in the camp, the husbandman in his plantation.

Ex. 99

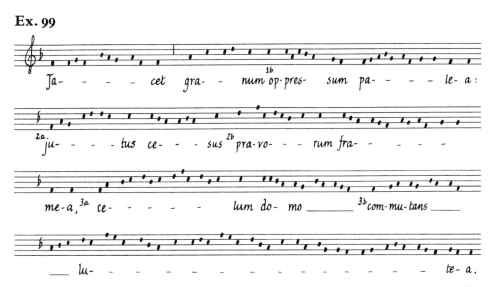

[32] See *Antiphonale ad vsum ecclesie Sa(rum)* . . . (Paris 1519), fol. lxxxiii v. (There is no music for this responsory in the *Sarum Antiphonal*, p. 72, as published in facsimile (Frere 1901); the whole office is much defaced.) Text in *Sarum Breviary*, I, cols. ccxlv ff. The first rhymed office for St Thomas (text in *AH* XIII.238–40, no. 92) corresponds only in a few items.

The *versus* is in similar style.

The melody of this responsory (traditionally one of the elaborate chants of the liturgy) is much more complicated than the text. It is fully melismatic, which is stylistically appropriate to its liturgical genre but not in any obvious way to the lightly patterned text (the change in accentual pattern in the *versus* may be deliberate). But what is most striking about it is its un-Gregorian tonality.[33] It is firmly based throughout on the 'major triad' of F, and has a consistent unvarying 'sweetness' more in keeping with the new sequence melodies than with traditional chant. Each phrase – indeed, looking more closely, each word – closes on *f* or on *c*; and many begin in the same way, or on the third, *a* (*granum*), or with a little phrase, *d-(c-)f* (*pravorum*; *lutea*), lifting to the octave above the 'key-note' – as in this context the final may properly be called. There is a great deal of melodic repetition or near-repetition: the opening phrase *jacet*, for instance, provides material and shape for several cadences and much else besides. This is interesting, of course, as an aspect of the 'new melody' associated especially with the sequence (the resemblance of this opening to that of 'Letabundus exultet fidelis chorus' (see Ex. 28) is noteworthy). But it does not help us at all with the problem of narrative melody; the style is too continuously and heavily melismatic.

The other main liturgical genre in the music of the rhymed Office – apart from the psalms and canticles, which were never metricalized – is the antiphon. The following antiphons are from the beginning of the service of Matins, which on solemn occasions was divided into three Nocturns.[34]

Ex. 100

[33] Cf. Stäblein's analysis ((1975), 162–3) of the 1st responsory of Matins, 'Studens livor'.
[34] *Antiphonale* (see note 32 above); *Sarum Breviary* I.ccxlix (text only).

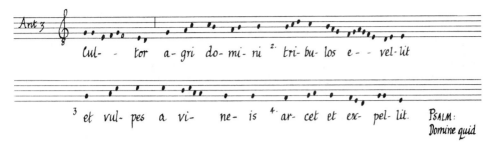

Ant 3

Cul- - tor a- gri do- mi- ni ² tri- bu- los e- - vel- lit

³ et vul- pes a vi- ne- is ⁴ ar- cet et ex- pel- lit. PSALM:
Domine quid

(1) Elevated to the highest priestly office, Thomas was suddenly changed into another man. *Ps. 1*: Blessed is the man . . . (2) The monk, secretly hairshirted under [the garb of] a cleric, stronger than his flesh, subdues the stirrings of his flesh. *Ps. 2*: Why do the heathen . . . (3) The husbandman of the Lord's field roots out the thistles; he wards off the foxes and drives them out from amongst the vines. *Ps. 3*: Lord, how are they increased . . .

These little pieces, written and composed on the same scale as the traditional antiphons which they imitate, do look at first sight like a potential narrative music; that is, the melodies are for the most part susceptible of an equal-syllable (isosyllabic) movement which would not much distort natural speech-flow (they are 'neumatic' rather than 'melismatic'). However, their interest seems to me – judgement must be partly subjective – too purely musical: they are conceived as flowing wholes not as patterned, schematic piece-work. Nothing could be more different from the narrative music of *laisse* or *lai* (to refer to two of our principal formal categories). The only narrative type remaining – apart from 'recitation' melody which is out of the question – is the strophic type. That medieval narrative could make use of strophic forms we have already seen in the early French Passion, in Middle High German epic, and elsewhere. However, one of the most striking facts about the strophes of the rhymed office antiphons is the totally *unrepetitive* manner of their use. The three antiphons quoted above do not, admittedly, teem with dramatic event, but they are connected and form part of the story of St Thomas's martyrdom which is to be unfolded in the Office as a whole. Moreover, they are in the same metrical form – a rather 'catchy' metre which the music tends to disguise, unless it is sung in an isosyllabic rhythm. If these melodies were thought of at all as having narrative implications or narrative suitability, they would surely have been more obviously devised to show it in the quasi-narrative setting of the rhymed Office. But, of course, it is essentially still a liturgical setting, and there can be no doubt that what the composers were aiming to do was to write new *liturgical* melody, contrasting, incidentally, with the sacred recitation of the lessons themselves.

The new fashions in tonal construction so evident in the responsory 'Jacet granum' (Ex. 99) can also be detected here, if less markedly. Each of the antiphons quoted makes some use of the triad formed on the final, stressing either the fifth (antiphon 1) or the third (antiphon 3). It is unlikely that this is a

matter of conscious theorizing. However, one aspect of the musical
construction of this Office, as of many others, is fully conscious and seems to
represent a new intellectual fashion: each antiphon is written in a different
mode, starting with Mode 1 ('authentic' on *d*) and proceeding through to
Mode 8 ('plagal' on *g*) – and the ninth antiphon, 'Felix locus' (the last of the
third Nocturn), returns to Mode 1. As Bruno Stäblein comments, 'Thus, in the
construction [of the Office] a regularity and clarity dominate, which remind
one of "scholastic" ordering'; and he quotes St Anselm's *fides querens
intellectum*. As symptoms of this 'ordering' mentality Stäblein mentions also,
in his analysis of a responsory, two features of special interest in a study of
words and music, both 'un-Gregorian' – the use of melismas on accented
syllables and the tendency to shape a melodic phrase, in the melismatic style,
so as to confine it to a single word.[35] Both these features can be seen in the
responsory 'Jacet granum'.[36]

   The procession on the eve of the feast of St Thomas, martyr, also contained
a sequence, incorporated into the structure of the responsory 'Jacet granum'; it
is a strong, rather unsubtle, piece which can be identified as a sequence only by
the fact that the melody changes after each double versicle. In fact, the strophe
throughout is a single decasyllabic line; it is the sequence reduced to its
ultimate simplicity. According to the rubric anyone may sing the sequence
who wishes to, the choir (*chorus*) taking up the melody after each versicle and
repeating it without its words (*sine littera*).[37]

Ex. 101

[35] Stäblein (1975), 162.
[36] The clearest instances of the single-word melisma, in which the melisma is also on the
accented syllable, are *jacet, palea*; but *granum, oppressum, justus, cesus* etc. all show the same
tendency (their prominent use of triadic resting-points accentuates the point).
[37] *Antiphonale* (see note 32 above), fol. lxxxiiij; *Sarum Breviary* 1.ccxlv (text only). The latter
directs: *Chorus respondeat cantum Prosae post unumquemque Versum super litteram A* (the chorus
shall answer with the melody of the sequence singing it to the vowel *A* after each line).

(1a) Let the shepherd sound a blast on his trumpet of horn, (1b) that the vineyard of Christ be fruitful – (2a) the vineyard which, beneath the stately cloak of the flesh he had assumed, (2b) he has set free by his shining cross.

(There are five double versicles and a single.) This simple song should not certainly have taxed the memories of those who had to walk in the procession. It also sketches the story of Thomas's martyrdom. We should not lose sight of the fact that more complex sequences than this could often be, and had often been, narrative poems and that there was nothing inherently unlikely in the combination of an intricate musical and metrical form with telling a story (see ch. 4: 1).

To sum up, then, the rhymed Office, for all its popularity, does not on the face of it look like a source of melodies to which vernacular saints' lives, or by adoption other narrative poems, might have been sung. Their 'aesthetic', the way they handle words and music, whether in the rhymed responsories or the rhymed antiphons, seems to betray quite other interests, of a kind I hope to have shown. Only the simple sequence melody just quoted seems to have the qualities of memorability, flexibility and a certain self-effacingness required in a melody that is going to be borrowed for general purposes (as distinct from a specific *contrafactum*). And if sequence melodies were required, it was not necessary to seek them in the rhymed Office; there are many elsewhere.[38]

iv Narrative singing in drama

A further possible source of narrative melody has been more or less entirely neglected, perhaps because it has been labelled 'drama' and tucked away in a different corner. The so-called Fleury Playbook of the late twelfth or early thirteenth century is remarkable in several ways – not least because it is the earliest manuscript of its kind: four quires are devoted entirely to a collection of sung Latin 'plays'.[39] Some are the familiar dramatic ceremonies which embellished the liturgy (like the *Visitatio Sepulchri*); others, more unusual, are plays on sacred topics, including four legends of St Nicholas.[40] *Tres Filie* tells

[38] Interesting in this narrative context is the sequence, unique to the Mass of St Thomas, 'Solemne canticum hodie'; see Denis Stevens, 'St Thomas' (1970), 321–2, who analyses its musical form and its narrative content. He comments, rightly, that 'the rapidly changing moods of the sequence do not always coincide with the musico-poetical form, as when the brutal knights burst into the middle of verse 3 and usurp the melody which has just been used for jubilant Canterbury'. The present chapter shows, I hope, how extremely rare and unusual such coincidence would be in medieval narrative music. On narrative in sequences honouring St Nicholas, see Young (1933), II.309–10.

[39] The title is usually given to Orleans Bibl. de la Ville MS 201 (Source 22), or more particularly to pp. 176–243 of it.

[40] The Fleury St Nicholas plays are printed and discussed by Young, *The Drama of the Medieval Church* (1933), II, ch. 36, together with other plays of the saint, 'the only saint, in fact, whose legends are treated in Church plays that are extant and complete' (Young, II.308). See also: Albrecht, *Four Latin Plays* (1935), ch. 6, for a careful and objective discussion of the music; Jones, *St Nicholas Liturgy* (1963), for the liturgical context (especially the rhymed Office); and C. Hohler's review-article of Jones, 'The Proper Office of St Nicholas', *MÆ* 36 (1967) 40–8, and Source 22 below.

the story of the well-known miracle. It is not lacking in dramatic possibilities: the saint, by hurling gifts of money through the window, dowers three daughters, and so saves them from prostitution and sees them safely into marriage. Yet it is sung throughout to two melodies. The first serves for the opening statements of father and daughters, in which they lament their poverty (*O rerum inopia!*).[41]

Ex. 102

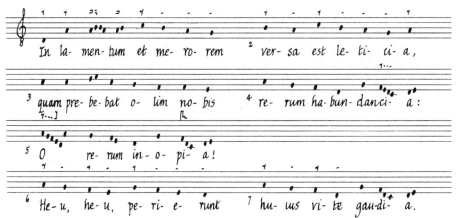

Gladness is turned into mourning and sorrow – the gladness which formerly an abundance of possessions conferred on us. O poverty! Alas, alas, the joys of this life have passed away.

Apart from the onomatopoeic melisma on O (phrase 5), the melody is syllabic or lightly 'neumatic'. Despite the common *d*-mode opening the melody is, technically at least, 'in' *e*: three important cadences have an *e* final. (I say 'technically' because the characteristic falling semitone *f–e* is totally avoided.) It follows that it has none of the, to our ears, catchy tuneful effects of the lai-type melodies on *g* (see ch. 4:1v). However, it is with *lai* and sequence, rather than with Gregorian chant on the one hand or courtly chanson on the other, that it belongs. There is something rather 'obvious' about its melodic procedures: the descending fourths in series (lines 6–7); the musical rhyme (4, 5 and 7); and the general tendency to repeat, with slight variations, limited material (see the *a–c–a* oscillation in 1, 2 and 3). The fact of its repetition as a complete unit means that it belongs formally in the class of strophic melodies for narrative singing.[42]

---

[41] Fleury Playbook, p. 176. The notation is non-mensural. All the melodies of the MS are written in cursive neumes on a four-line red stave; the presentation is informal but professional and clear – well below the standard, however, required for a liturgical service-book. A measured transcription is in Smoldon, *Medieval Church Dramas* (1980), 261.

[42] I adopt the slight rearrangement of these stanzas proposed by Young (1933), II.316, n. 3.

The tune that is used for the whole of the rest of the play (lines 15–168) is tonally compatible but structurally simpler.[43]

Ex. 103

My daughters, dear pledges of love, only treasures of a treasureless father and solace of my misery, pray have regard for me in my sadness. Oh, wretched me!

This melody hovers between being a short *laisse*-type (i.e. stichic, based on the line–phrase) and being a consistent strophe. The important thing about it is that it can be shortened as required by the omission of a line, or two, provided that the music of the short final line is preceded by the music of phrase 4 (=2). Like more extended *laisse* music (see above p. 225), it has three phases of melody – the staple melody in its 'open' (A) and 'closed' (A') forms and a short melody to round things off. The formal parallel with *Aucassin et Nicolette* is noteworthy.

Similar in its musical mechanism to *Tres Filie*, and indeed even simpler, is *Tres Clerici*. Three students lodging at an inn are murdered by their host and his wife for money; Nicholas arrives, confronts the inn-keepers with their crime and brings the students back to life. There are no detailed rubrics; the murder was presumably mimed. The whole of this dramatic *miraculum*, except a closing prayer, is sung to one melody.[44]

---

[43] MS p. 177; there are occasional very slight modifications to the melody on repetition. Measured transcription in Smoldon (1980), 262, who points out (as had Albrecht, 105) that it is used in another of the Fleury St Nicholas plays, *Filius Getronis*. It is, as he rightly observes, 'common property'.

[44] MS p. 183. See Coussemaker (1860), 100; Smoldon (1980), 264 (measured); Young (1933), II.330ff (text only).

Ex. 104

Let us, whom the zeal of humane learning has sent among foreign peoples, seek a lodging for ourselves whilst yet the sun lights us with his rays.

This narrative strophe could be precisely repeated eighteen times to produce the necessary 72 lines of music, but it does not work like that. When a speech occupies two lines instead of four, phrases B and C are omitted, producing in effect a short *laisse*:[45]

Senex:	Acquiescam tuo consilio,	A
	et dignabor istos hospicio.	A
Senex ad Clericos:	Accedatis, scolares, igitur;	A
	quod rogastis uobis conceditur	A
Senex, Clericis dormientibus:	Nonne vides quanta marsupia?	A
	Est in illis argenti copia;	A
	hec a nobis absque infamia	B
	possideri posset pecunia.	C

Old Man [to his wife]: I will agree with what you advise and will reckon them worthy of hospitality. *To the clerks:* Come forward, then, students! What you're asking is granted you. [To his wife] *when the clerks are asleep*: Do you not see how big their purses are? There is much money there. We could seize hold of this wealth without getting a bad name.

This melody (A A B C) does not, then, constitute a closed form, in the sense that a courtly chanson is 'closed'. It is extensible, versatile. In this connection it is interesting that the only other contemporary dramatic version of this 'miracle', from Hildesheim (no music survives), is in monorhymed quatrains with unrhymed short fifth line, suggesting another kind of connection with *laisse* structure.[46] Perhaps these quatrain forms, found also in the strophic *lai* (see Ex. 89), are as it were epitomes of *laisse* melodies?

45 Young, II.331.
46 Young, II.325–7.

The previous play, *Tres Filie*, ended with a liturgical antiphon. *Tres Clerici*, however, ends (apart from the choir's Te Deum) with a prayer of St Nicholas. The melody is only sung once; but it has a shape similar to that of the main narrative melody.[47]

Ex. 105

Gracious God, whose all things are, the heaven, the earth, air and sea, command these [murdered clerks] to rise again, and hear them as they cry to you!

Is this also a narrative strophe – that is, an inconspicuous vehicle repeated almost endlessly, as opposed to a chanson strophe which is of a complexity to demand attention? It is impossible to be sure. On the one hand, the sweeping range of the melody in each single phrase (phrase 4 goes up and down the octave twice) is in striking contrast to the restrained movement of most of the narrative melodies we have met. On the other hand, it is exceedingly economical in its use of melodic material; the composer seems only to have had the melody of phrase 1 in his head throughout. The general structure (AABC) could just be represented as stichic: A; A; A^1 with 'open' cadence; A^2 with 'closed' cadence. The melisma at the end presents no insuperable obstacle to narrative singing.

The other two plays about St Nicholas in the Fleury manuscript are quite different musically. They are the *Iconia Sancti Nicholai* and *Filius Getronis*. Each of them employs a large number of melodies – over forty and over thirty respectively – and each of them could well be described as a dramatized *lai*. They have sections of purely narrative melody: the *Iconia* opens with eleven statements of the following:[48]

---

[47] MS p. 187. See Coussemaker (1860), 105; Smoldon (1980), 264 (unmeasured 'because of the melismas', in 'free rhythm').

[48] MS p. 188. See Coussemaker, 109; Smoldon, 267 (measured); Young, II.344–8 (text only).

Ex. 106

If any sayings are ascribed to you, servant of God . . .

But the overall scheme is *lai*-like, not strophic. These more ambitious pieces require further investigation, since their proper interpretation raises general questions about the relationship of music and dramatic action. I confine my attention here to the straightforward narrative forms, the present purpose being simply to uncover material that might have been used as 'narrative melody'.

The play of the Raising of Lazarus (*Versus de resuscitatione Lazari*) is another dramatized narrative from the Fleury manuscript, and it is entirely strophic. The melody is as follows.[49]

Ex. 107

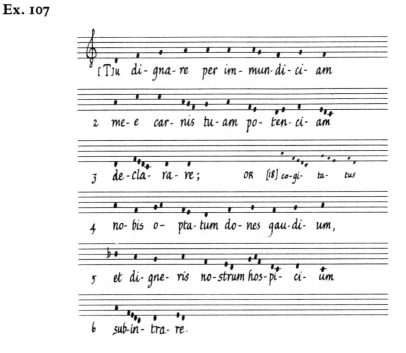

---

[49] MS p. 233. See Coussemaker, 220; Smoldon, 280 (transposed, measured); Young, II.199–208 (text only).

Deign through the impurity of my flesh to declare your power; give us the wished-for joy and condescend to enter into our dwelling.

(There are a number of small melodic variants; whether these are purely scribal or represent genuine improvisational practice it is not possible to be sure.) The melody is repeated some fifty times – to the alarm and dismay of an earlier generation of scholars, but to the interest and pleasure of those who believe that narrative melody has its own peculiar power and rewards those who subject themselves to its experience.[50] This is genuine strophic melody for story-singing and would, presumably, be suitable for any stanzaic narrative in this metre – sacred or secular.[51] Unlike some of the other melodies we have looked at, its detailed structure is not taut. The hint in phrase 1 of a recitation-type melody with intonation rising to a 'tenor' on *a* is not entirely lost sight of later (lines 4 and 5), but there is nothing very firm about its handling. The tonality is the familiar *d*-mode; and several phrases recall other narrative melodies from the Fleury manuscript.

These Latin plays, despite their liturgical connections, are peripheral to the main corpus of liturgical drama which will be discussed in chapters 9 and 10, and their procedures are very different. It is only in the most ambitious and extended of the Easter plays that room can be found for episodes of 'narrative music'. Such is, for instance, the *Ludus paschalis* from Origny-Sainte-Benoîte, with its long vernacular encounter between the three Marys and the spice-merchant.[52] The basic strophe for this scene (lines 16–75) is:[53]

Ex. 108

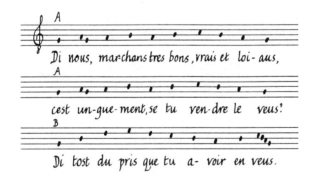

Di nous, marchans tres bons, vrais et loi- aus,

cest un-que-ment, se tu ven-dre le veus?

Di tost du pris que tu a-voir en veus.

---

[50] Cf. Smoldon's comments, 280–2: 'intolerable monotony, verbal and musical'.

[51] When one character has a three-line speech only the first (and always the first) half of the melody is used.

[52] St Quentin, Bibl. de la Ville, M S 86, pp. 609–25 (*Le Livre de la Trésorerie d'Origny-Sainte-Benoîte*). See Young (1933), II.412–19 (text only); Coussemaker (1860), 256–79; and, with full discussion of the manuscript and its music, Rankin, 'Music of Medieval Liturgical Drama' (1981), II.85–9, followed by complete musical text, 90–7 (modern neutral transcription syllabically displayed). The extended vernacular scenes are highly unusual; a possible explanation is the fact that this Benedictine house was for women.

[53] Lines 32–5 (Young, I.414); Coussemaker, 258–9; Rankin (1981) II.91.

REFR. He- - las, ver-rons le nous ja-mais.

Tell us, O best, true and faithful merchant,
that ointment – are you willing to sell it?
Say now what price you want to get for it.
Refrain. Alas, shall we ever see him [Christ] again?

Like the *Tres Clerici* melody, this one also is not a closed form; it has some of
the flexibility of a *laisse*.[54] The preceding quatrain (the merchant's speech), for
example, uses two melodies only – A A A B – making in all an eight-line *laisse*
(28–35) A A A B A A B C.

There is a second vernacular melody in the Origny *Ludus* which serves for
the dialogue between Mary Magdalene and the two angels. In this episode the
angelic statement uses two members of the melody; Mary's reply uses these
and adds two more (3 syllables + 8˘ syllables). The whole once again forms a
laisse-like structure, but in this case an unvaried one.[55]

Ex. 109

Angels
Dou- ce da- me, qui si plou- res,

2 di- tes nous ou vo- les a- ler.

3 Je crois mout bien, se diex nous gart,

4 de vraie a- mour li cuers vous art.
Mary
5 Las- se do- lan- te, que fe- rai

de mon si- gnour que per- du ai?

---

[54] The stanzas, also, are often assonanced rather than strictly rhymed.
[55] Lines 100–8 (Young (1933), 1.417); Coussemaker (1860), 265; Rankin (1981), 11.90ff (transcription T2:04).

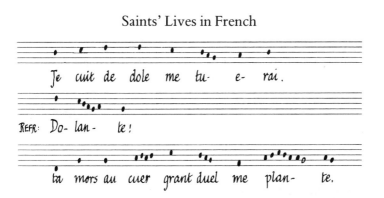

Angels: Sweet lady, you that weep so, tell us where you want to go. I believe surely (God keep us!) that your heart is afire with true love. *Mary*: Weary and sad, what shall I do about my lord whom I have lost for ever? I think I shall kill myself with sorrow. *Refrain*. Sad I am! Your death makes great sorrow grow in my heart.

Both these Origny melodies are in the *g*-mode and tonally very stable; they have a good deal in common, as eye and ear can tell. But the second in particular has the telling cadence-figure *f–g*, which we have noted in *lai*-type melody from Abelard's 'Dolorum solatium' (Ex. 39) onwards.

v Saints' Lives in French

In the several sections of this chapter I have tried to describe the principal materials available for the singing of vernacular narrative; I should like to look in conclusion at the repertoire of surviving Anglo-Norman texts in order to see how the assembled musical materials might have been used in the performances of other poems.[56] What I hope is now confirmed is that narratives in French, especially the *chansons de geste* and the lives of saints, were sung, at least if they were in the form of assonanced monorhymed *laisses* or in simple strophic forms. Music is available either separately notated or in the form of notated interpolations within the chanting of the Latin epistle – the so-called 'farsed' epistle. An Anglo-Norman text such as *St Alexis*, mentioned earlier, is clearly one which is catered for by these provisions. The five-line assonanced strophe seems to have been a favourite compromise between the fully variable epic *laisse* and the short rhymed strophe. *St Alexis* is in this metre, which occurs in its precise decasyllabic form in a troped epistle from Tours (once again for St Stephen) where the text begins.[57]

> Por amor de vos pri Saignos Barun
> Se et vostuit escotet la lecun
> de Saint Estevre le glorieux Barrun –
> Escotet la par bonne entention –
> qui a ce jor recu la passion.
> *In diebus illis Stephanus*

[56] I hope to consider texts in Middle English in a future volume.
[57] *Laisses* of variable length are quoted in section 11 above, including a five-line 'strophic *laisse*' in an Epistle of St Stephen.

By your love I pray you, noble seigneurs, that you one and all listen to the 'lesson' of
St Stephen, the noble knight – listen to it with a good understanding – Stephen who on
this day 'received his passion'. *In these days Stephen* . . .

One of the manuscripts of *St Alexis* has an interesting prologue which begins[58]

Ici comencet amiable cancun e spiritel raisun d'iceol noble barun, Eufemien par num,
e de la vie de sum filz boneüret del quel nos avum oit lire e canter . . .

Here begins a pleasant song and edifying account of that noble knight called
Eufemien, and of the life of his blessed son, concerning whom we have heard reading
and singing.

This short advertisement is not without its puzzles. One of the poem's editors
says it establishes that *St Alexis* 'was intended to be sung in church'.[59] I cannot
understand why. The fact that the writer of the prologue refers to having
heard 'reading and singing' about St Stephen in the past tense might rather
indicate that after 'we' had heard the Latin *vita* chanted (is this the force of *lire e
canter*?) in a liturgical service we were going to hear this 'pleasant song'
(*amiable cancun*) in the vernacular – possibly in the refectory?

Another favourite saint, with a well-documented set of Lives, was Thomas
Becket. Hagiographers set to work almost immediately after his murder in
1170, even before his official canonization three years later. The most
interesting *vita* for our purposes was written by a French clerk (perhaps a sort
of 'ecclesiastical minstrel'), Guernes de Pont-Sainte-Maxence.[60] Six
manuscripts of this survive, all of them Anglo-Norman. Not that Thomas's
fame and cult were at all confined to England; but Canterbury was the
principal shrine. And Canterbury played an important role in the composition
of Guernes' poem, about which he is quite informative. We gather from his
prologue that Guernes wrote a first version of his poem from hearsay (it is in
fact based on the earliest Latin *vita* by Edward Grim) but, not being content
with it, went to Canterbury and rewrote it on better authority, that of
Thomas's friends. At the end he gives us some more facts:[61]

> Guernes li Clers del Punt fine ici sun sermun
> del martir saint Thomas e de sa passiun.
> E mainte feiz le list a la tumbe al barun.
> Ci n'a mis un sul mot se la verité nun.
> De ses mesfaiz li face li pius Deus veir pardun!

[58] Ed. Storey, p. 23. This prose prologue is found only in the Hildesheim M S (twelfth-
century). Described by Storey as 'the earliest, the most complete and the least contaminated
by scribal errors' (pp. ix–x). The most recent edn, by Odenkirchen, gives comparative
versions in Greek and Latin.

[59] Ed. Storey, p. ix.

[60] Guernes de Pont-Sainte-Maxence, *La vie de saint Thomas Becket*, ed. E. Walberg, C F M A
(Paris 1936).

[61] Ed. Walberg, stanza 123. He may of course have gone to Canterbury 'in search of a more
generous audience' (Legge, 249).

Guernes, the clerk of the Pont[-Sainte-Maxence], ends his discourse at this point about the suffering of St Thomas and about his 'passion'. And many times he read it at the great man's tomb. Here he has not put in a single word that is not the truth. May the good God give him true pardon for anything he has done wrong.

At Canterbury he performed his *romanz* (i.e. vernacular history) or *sermun* (discourse) many times at St Thomas's shrine. The word Guernes uses for his performance is *lire*, which in an undefining context may mean anything from singing to saying. The opening stanza seems in fact to set *lire* and *chanter* in a light contrast – 'Tuit clerc ne sevent pas bien chanter ne bien lire' – but this is done in such a way as to imply that both activities, 'singing' and 'reading', are part of a *clerc*'s proper attainments. Once again we are driven back to the metrical form; the stanza above exemplifies it – a five-line monorhymed stanza repeated 1,236 times.

   The Life of St Thomas, like that of St Alexis, occupies the formal middle ground between *laisse* and strophic structure. The only difference between them is that *Alexis* is in decasyllabics, *Thomas* in alexandrines (12-syllable lines). The likelihood is, I think, that both were sung to melodies of the kind already discussed – the farsed epistle melodies. Is the length of Guernes' poem an objection? I do not think so. We are so totally unaccustomed to narrative singing in our culture that we are scarcely in a position to judge the issue. The peoples of other cultures have not found it strange, and in some cases still do not. A poem nearly twice as long as the *Chanson de Roland* would, needless to say, not have been performed in a single sitting – nor necessarily to a single melody. It may not have been sung throughout; might some portions have been recited? Finally, the possibility of instrumental accompaniment or interludes cannot be ruled out, even though the material we have been considering (much of it liturgical or para-liturgical) does not provide any positive warrant for this.

VI   Conclusion

The reflections in the last paragraph bring home what an extremely limited view we get of narrative music from the fragmentary musical evidence which I have been trying to piece together in these two chapters. It seems to me worthwhile, nevertheless, to have assembled the bits, as it were, and by establishing musical types – recitation, *laisse*, *lai* and strophe – to have given a notion how words and music may have gone together in the singing of epic, *chanson de geste* and saint's life. But the total reality must have been infinitely variable and far more colourful than my almost purely musical speculations suggest. A recent parallel may make this more vivid.

   While this chapter was being written, Karl Reichl was visiting one of the few regions where there is still a live tradition of epic singing – Uzbekistan, in the south-east of the U S S R. Reporting informally on his researches, he wrote:

In northern Uzbekistan, among the Karakalpaks, there are two types of epic singers and hence epic songs: Singer 1 (called a *dzhiraw*) specializes in heroic epics and accompanies himself on a horse-string fiddle; singer 2 (called a *bakshi*) specializes in romantic epics and accompanies himself on a lute-like plucked instrument. They are genuine oral singers, i.e. they have learned their epics from other singers and perform them without the help of printed or written texts. The *dzhiraw* performed a heroic epic, formally a mixture of prose and verse (chante-fable) with the prose portions spoken and the verse portions sung. The verse portions could be monologues, dialogues, or complaints, but also simple narrative (the hero mounting his horse etc.). 'Speaking' meant reciting in an expressive voice, a somewhat heightened speech intonation, just like an old-fashioned poetry recital. The singer would now and then tune his instrument, play a few notes (chords), sip hot water. The verse portions were sung to a melody (it was a melody, more 'melodious' than say the gospel 'tone'), which was repeated in *laisse*-like fashion. Being repeated did not mean that there weren't slight modifications according to the text; the melody changed also: it started off lower down, with a pressed voice, and got gradually higher and 'clearer'. The Kirghiz sing their epics in a similar fashion (all verse), epics several times the length of the 'Iliad'!

Singer 2 recited the prose-portions of his text also. The verse-portions in the so-called romantic epics (comparable to the medieval love-romance) are also sung, but this time to tunes close to folk-song. There are several tunes to be found in an epic (depending on the skill of the singer), and the tunes are 'strophic' rather than '*laisse*-like'. In Chorezm, another region of Uzbekistan, these portions are normally performed by the singer plus a group of musicians. In southern Uzbekistan one and the same singer performs in both styles (heroic and romantic), with a preponderance of romantic epics.[62]

The communication speaks for itself.

Amongst modern attitudes, a prejudice against (or at least a complete indifference to) the singing performance of narrative is deep-seated and almost unquestioned. We allow some exceptions, of course – the *recitativo secco* of the Bach Passions, the narratives in the *Ring*, not to mention folk-ballad. Perhaps, then, the objection is rather to the presentation in this style of poems having a serious content and claims on our continuous imaginative attention? In the case of the lyric we do not in fact object; we are prepared to accept even the abstruseness of a Donne sonnet in a musical setting. So where precisely is the prejudice located? It may be that, with more recent music in mind, we cannot accept the idea of a totally inconspicuous music, one that is so transparent that we are conscious only of the object behind. Much medieval narrative melody has this 'see-through' – 'hear-through' – quality. But the experience of hearing narrative melody (it is, indeed, *heard*, not listened to) shows that the reluctance is ill founded.

The evidence in the foregoing pages is mostly for an inconspicuous music. This is achieved in various styles which, however, seem to have one thing in common – they do not correspond, or indeed respond, to the story except in

---

[62] Karl Reichl, in a private letter. See also his article cited chapter 6, note 90, above.

its structural features (*laisse*-type, strophic, stichic, or other). This leads to a certain impersonality in the relation between the words and the music, an impersonality which is confirmed by the dry, neutral performance style of British folk-singers as we can hear them on record. But – a final word – such an impersonality is a positive effect and makes a positive contribution towards the way we take in the narrative. Such music is, in its own terms, a part of the story.

8

SPEECH AND MELODY: GREGORIAN CHANT

Of the various ways in which man may have become conscious of music – by blowing, banging or scraping – the use of his own voice is the most basic. We all have some music in ourselves – pitched sounds, at least, and rhythm. Common sense and common experience suggest that the earliest urges towards music, organized sound, may accompany regular movement (dance, marching, rocking a cradle) or may arise from speech. Not from all speech, however, but from certain kinds – the heightened speech of ritual and cult, the impersonal speech of heroic narrative, perhaps the anguish of pain and the release of joy (the dirge and the *Alleluia*).

In this chapter we shall be considering the implications for medieval song of the many-faceted relations of music and speech in ritual. The topic must be made manageable, and to make it so I shall concentrate on liturgical chant in its traditional forms.[1] If we are hoping to discover how medieval musicians felt about words, plainchant provides one obvious starting point. Except for the hymns, which have in any case a less central place in medieval Catholic than in Protestant worship, the texts of the liturgy are in prose.[2] 'Prose' may seem an

---

[1] The 'new' liturgical and para-liturgical chants of the period *c.* 1000–1200 are here omitted; they are discussed in other chapters (3, 4 and 9). I am much indebted to Susan Rankin for her comments (especially on notational problems) and for several important references; and to Mary Berry for observations on the chant analyses.

[2] The secondary literature on plainchant is huge (see the 24-column bibliography to 'Plainchant' in *New Grove*). I shall do no more here than mention some standard works that I have found especially useful; they relate to that part of the plainchant repertoire known as Gregorian (in effect the music of the official liturgy of the Church of Rome). The best account of the liturgy, its ritual and its music in medieval England (the 'Uses' of Sarum, York etc) is by Harrison, *Music in Medieval Britain* (1958 ch. 2). For an extensive non-musical exposition of the liturgy in its Roman form (which is in all essentials the same as the medieval), see Young, *Drama of the Medieval Church* (1933), i, ch. 1, who prints all the texts of his norm – 'a solemn Mass . . . sung on Easter Day in a well-appointed Church' – commenting on their significance and on the liturgical actions; ch. 2, 'The Canonical Office', deals in the same lucid manner with the services of the Hours of Christmas Day. The *Oxford Anthology* (Marrocco and Sandon 1977), items 10–11, gives *in extenso* the music for the Sarum Mass of Easter Day and the solemn procession which preceded it. The multifarious service-books of the earlier centuries, each containing a specialized part of the repertoire, became to some extent standardized in the course of time. By the thirteenth and fourteenth centuries the principal books of chant (i.e. music-books) were the Antiphonal, containing the music of the Office, and the Gradual, containing the music of the Mass. (I generally refer to and quote from those of the Sarum rite.) The *Liber Usualis* is an extremely useful compendium of the two in their traditional Roman form (N B the majority but not all of the

inappropriate term, to say the least, with which to characterize some of the greatest poetry in the Western inheritance – the Psalms, the Lamentations, the Canticles, for instance. In the present context I mean, simply, writing which does not conform to any of the main traditions of medieval verse – syllable-counting, accentual or quantitative. The texts are non-poetic according to the purely formal canons of the age. (I speak only of the traditional 'Gregorian' repertoire; many tropes, sequences and rhymed offices are, of course, verse by medieval definition.) The importance of considering the traditional chant repertoire, even if only selectively, is self-evident; it is simply the most magnificent monument of Western monophonic art, pervasive, enduring, inescapable. Its particular usefulness to us in the present study is that it enables us to examine the relations of words and notes without the distracting complications of metre.

1 Words and action in the liturgy

One of the ways in which the Middle Ages expressed their 'blessed rage for order' was in the structure of the liturgical day:[3]

On any of the days of the liturgical calendar the service of divine worship is organized according to a definite and nearly invariable plan . . . Eight times during the day a service for the offering of prayer and worship is held. This is called the Divine Office (*Officium divinum*), Canonic Hours (*horae canonicae*, from *canon*, i.e. rule, law), or Office Hours. These are:

> 1. Matins (*matutinum*): before sunrise
> 2. Lauds (*laudes*): at sunrise
> 3. Prime (*ad primam horam*)
> 4. Terce (*ad tertiam horam*)
> 5. Sext (*ad sextam horam*)
> 6. None (*ad nonam horam*)
> 7. Vespers (*ad vesperam*): at sunset
> 8. Compline (*completorium*): before retiring.

[3] Apel (1958) 13.

chants go back at least to the early Middle Ages). For other service-books (Processional, Ordinal, etc.), see Glossary.

The authoritative survey by Peter Wagner, *Einführung in die gregorianischen Melodien* (1911–21) deals with all aspects of the chant, historical, palaeographical and stylistic, and has formed the basis of later studies such as Apel, *Gregorian Chant* (1958), which is concerned in detail chiefly with stylistic matters. For specialized studies on notation (e.g. Cardine (1968) Corbin (1977)); for new approaches to written/oral transmission (e.g. by Treitler (1974, 1981, etc)); and for questions of aesthetic and words-and-music (Johner (1953) and others), see the notes below. For facsimiles illustrating the enormous wealth and variety of plain-chant, see *Paléographie Musicale* in 21 volumes from 1884 onwards. Recent general histories of medieval music have paid much more attention than formerly to Western Christian chant: see, especially, the spacious account by Richard Hoppin (1978), ch. 2–7; the more com-pressed and technical opening chapters of John Caldwell (1978); and Cattin's contribution (1984 transln) to a new Italian history of music.

The Hours formed the frame of daily ritual of which the centre-point was the Mass.[4] In the table which follows, the left-hand column gives the generalized structure of the Mass, the right-hand its manifestation on one particular day of the year, 28 December, the day on which the Holy Innocents were celebrated.

THE MASS: Ordinary and Proper   *In die sanctorum innocentium*[5]

Introit (introitus or *officium)*	Ex ore infancium deus et lactencium . . .
KYRIE ELEISON	
GLORIA	
Epistle (subdeacon) or Lesson	Apoc. xiv. 1–5: In diebus illis vidi supra montem Syon agnum stantem . . .
Gradual (gradale)	Anima nostra [sicut passer erepta est . . . .℣] . Laqueus cont[ritus est]
{ *Alleluia* or *Tract*	Alleluia.℣. Te martyrum cand[idatus]
{ *Sequence*	Celsa p[ueri]
Gospel (deacon)	Matt. ii. 13–18: In illo tempore Angelus domini apparuit in sompnis . . .
CREDO	
Offertory (offertorium)	Anima nostra [sicut passer erepta est . . .]
Preface (celebrant)	
SANCTUS and BENEDICTUS	
The Canon (the consecration)	
Pater noster	
AGNUS DEI	
Pax (kiss of peace)	
Communion	Vox in rama audita est ploratus et ululatus, Rachel plorans . . .
Postcommunio (prayer)	
ITE, MISSA EST (dismissal)	

The liturgies of the greater festivals in the Church's year all have their individual elaborations, their individual beauties. The festival I take as the main text, as it were, for the present enquiry is that of Palm Sunday, encompassing as it does a wide range of Christian responses, ecclesiastical chants and liturgical actions. Palm Sunday (*Dominica in Palmis*) is the Sunday before Easter and introduces Holy Week. The ceremonies which mark the day as a special one are the blessing of palms and the procession, both representing Jesus's triumphal entry into Jerusalem a week before the Resurrection. At Salisbury, when Terce was finished, a procession, somewhat different

---

[4] Further on the Hours, see M. Berry 'Liturgy of the Hours' in *New Grove*.

[5] My tabulation of the liturgy for the Holy Innocents is based on the *Sarum Missal*, 32–3. In the left-hand column, the italicized items belong to the Proper; that is to say, their words and music vary according to the liturgical season or occasion. The items in capitals belong to the Ordinary; their verbal texts are invariant (unless expanded by troping), their melodies less so. The other items are spoken or intoned to the simplest formulas.

from the usual Sunday one, formed for the sprinkling of the altars with holy water.[6] After the *aspersio aque* followed the blessing of flowers and branches (*florum vel frondium*): they too were sprinkled and censed. Whilst they, the 'palms' of the Jerusalem entry, were being distributed, two antiphons were sung; and as the procession moved from the west door of the choir around the cloisters to the first station near the south-east corner of the church, yet more antiphons.

Meanwhile two clerks of the second form had carried the relics and the Blessed Sacrament to the first station. There a lesson from the Gospel was read, and the antiphon *En rex venit* was sung for the adoration of the Sacrament . . . Two antiphons and, if needed, two responds accompanied the procession to the next station at the door of the north transept where seven boys in a high place (*in eminentiori loco*) sang . . . *Gloria laus et honor* . . . Then with the antiphon *Collegerunt* the procession continued along the north side of the church to the third station before the north-west door . . . From there a respond brought the procession through the west door to the fourth station at the rood. The cross, which had been covered since the first Monday in Lent, was uncovered, and the officiant began the antiphon *Ave*, the choir singing *rex noster*, with a genuflection to the rood. These three words were sung twice more at a higher pitch each time, and at the third time the antiphon was continued and completed by the choir. Then the crucifix on the high altar was uncovered, and the procession entered the choir to the singing of a respond.[7]

All this formed a stately prelude to the central act of worship – the Mass of the Day, which differed from the standard form already described in only two particulars. Since Palm Sunday is in Lent, instead of the Alleluia is sung a Tract, *Deus, deus meus, respice*; and after this comes not the usual fairly short passage from one of the Gospels but a complete sung narration of the Passion as recounted by St Matthew (ch. xxvi–xxvii), lasting some twenty to twenty-five minutes.

If I have set the liturgical scene at a generous length, it is to emphasize an aspect of words and music in this period which can all too easily be lost sight of. They are not to be seen as concerned with each other in a mutual self-regard but as combining together for other, external purposes: here, the purpose of worship, the worship of a community. Furthermore, this worship does not consist simply of offering song to God. As the first part of the liturgy for Palm Sunday shows, the chants are bound up with action; they are part of a total ritual of movement, colour and gesture. Nor should this observation be confined to the processional rite; the Mass itself centres upon an action – or, rather, is a series of actions. Three of the chants of the Proper (those portions

---

[6] The Palm Sunday liturgy is printed in the *Sarum Missal*, 92–8; the music is in the *Sarum Gradual*, 78ff. The liturgical actions are described and indexed in Frere, *Use of Sarum* (1898), vol. I, an edition of the Sarum Consuetudinary (?c. 1210) and the Customary derived from it (early-fourteenth-century).

[7] Harrison (1958), 91–2; his footnotes draw attention to the detailed ways in which the ceremonies of other places differed from those of Sarum (e.g. at York, Hereford and Lincoln).

of the service which change perpetually according to season and occasion) – the Introit, the Offertory and the Communion – are chants accompanying liturgical actions. We are extremely fortunate to have such a wealth of documents, stretching over all the medieval centuries. There is surely no other domain of medieval life about which we are so well informed: we can follow the people concerned from minute to minute, sometimes in the very places they knew and used.

ii Notation and speech

In the traditional chant of the Church there is one basic relation between words and music of a particular sort which, for scarcity of written documents, can only be glimpsed elsewhere: it is the closeness of early musical notation to speech signs. In recent years it has become much easier for the ordinary musician to gain access to the notations on which interpretation of plainchant must rest.[8] The earliest manuscripts containing musical notation are of the ninth century. From the next six centuries hundreds of liturgical manuscripts survive with notated music. It is incomparably the best-documented area of medieval music.

There are two kinds of early notation: one kind is used mainly in theoretical sources and indicates pitches by means of the letters of the alphabet or through the so-called Daseian symbols;[9] the other occurs in most of the practical sources (chant-books) and consists of staffless neumes. In the latter case the pitches of the notes are generally uncertain, at best roughly relative (they will indicate some melodic shapes in outline).[10] Such melodies can be reconstructed only with the help of later manuscripts which contain the music written (as in later centuries) on staves. This does not mean that the earlier sources are worthless, or redundant: far from it. Amongst them are liturgical books, such as the St Gall *Cantatorium* (i.e. soloist's book) of the late ninth century, containing subtle indications of the style of performance which are quite lacking from the later manuscripts.[11] These subtleties take two main

[8] See *Graduel Neumé* (1972) and *Graduale Triplex* (1979).

[9] Daseian notation: a ninth- and tenth-century system of precise pitch notation 'in which the tones of the scale are represented by signs derived from the *prosodia daseia*, i.e. the aspirate sign in ancient Greek' (*HDM*; see also *New Grove*, s.v.). Plates in Smits van Waesberghe, *Musikerziehung* (1969), no. 70; and Stäblein (1975), 220–5.

[10] The various systems of early medieval non-neumatic notation are lucidly set out by Reese, 134–7. Treitler, 'Reading and Singing' (see note 16 below), discusses their significance for an understanding of the relationship of text and melody, with special reference to the treatises *Musica Enchiriadis* and *Musica disciplina*: the notation 'is a depiction of the voice moving through the sound space as it declaims the syllables of a text'.

[11] St Gall 359, 'le plus ancien, le plus parfait, et le plus précis des manuscrits de l'école sangallienne' (Cardine, *Sémiologie* (1970), 3). A selection of readings from the 'best' St Gall MSS is now handily available (see note 8 above). Facsimiles of nearly all these MSS are in *Paléographie Musicale*. The neumes of the earliest MSS are enormously varied and constitute various 'families' or 'dialects'. The complexities of the subject are best approached *via* Corbin, *Die Neumen* (1977) or the same author's article 'Neumatic Notations' in *New Grove*. The plates and commentary in Stäblein (1975) are invaluable; see also Jammers, *Tafeln*.

forms: the graphic modification of the neumes (e.g. by the addition of a short serif, the *episema*, showing a lengthening – ⌐ instead of ╱) and *littere significative* (such as *t* = tenete) telling the singer what to do with a particular note or neume.[12] With the help of recent editions, it is now easily possible to see (though not necessarily to interpret) the music for the Mass in a more authentic version than before.[13] The neumes of earlier manuscripts are shown above and/or below the edited melody, and it is at least possible to check whether the suggestions for performance (the lengthening or accenting of particular notes) might correspond to early practice or not. We cannot assume, of course, that there was ever a single, correct style. The manuscripts do not always agree amongst themselves; it is not to be expected that they should. Apel, however, may be going too far when he says not only that 'rhythm . . . was an accessory element which was greatly variable in time and in locale', but that 'each of the early manuscripts has its own rhythm'.[14] The notations differ in their styles of communication; but the rhythmic meanings may be close or identical.

In what way do these early notations bear on the problem of words and notes? In the first instance they keep us in mind of the pristine closeness of the two arts in sound – speech and music. To look at a neumed text is more like looking at two sign systems in intimate relationship than at song as we today notate it. And this is how, traditionally, the origin of the neumes has been explained. The theory most generally accepted in this century 'interprets them as being derived from the grammatical accents of Greek and Latin literature, the same accents as survive to the present day in the French language as *accent aigu*, *accent grave*, and *accent circonflexe*. In fact, the very term *accentus* suggests such a semi-musical connotation, being derived from *ad cantum* (perhaps *signum ad cantum*, sign for the song).'[15]

Recent research, notably that of Leo Treitler, has shrewdly questioned this account. Treitler has shifted the direction of the enquiry away from 'origins', as conceived in a somewhat restricted palaeographical sense, towards function and context – 'the study of notations in the light of their use in particular conditions', especially the condition of a long-established oral tradition.[16] In

---

[12] The bearing of the *littere* on rhythmic interpretation is much disputed: some scholars hold that they indicate strictly proportional lengthening (a mensuralist view); others, that subtler effects, nuances of rhythm and style, are being registered. See further note 27 below.

[13] The concept of 'authenticity', here as elsewhere, is difficult to apply. In this context I mean 'in accordance with the earliest written records'. But there are numerous 'authenticities' varying with time and place. For recent helpful editions see note 8 above.

[14] Apel (1958), 132, n. 7.

[15] *Ibid.*, 108–9. It has sometimes been argued that there was a third dimension, that of gesture – 'le neume est un geste écrit'. The neumes are nothing other, wrote Peter Wagner, than 'the written representation of gestures, movements of the hand, by means of which the *rector chori* was accustomed to direct his singers' (II.16). The whole concept is sharply questioned by H. Hucke, 'Die Cheironomie und die Entstehung der Neumenschrift', *Mf* 32 (1979) 1–16.

[16] Treitler, 'Reading and Singing' (1984). 'Music Writing, (1982b), 238: the 'shift of focus' is from palaeography as traditionally practised to semiotics, concerned with 'the functional

practical, pedagogic sources the function of the notation was principally to guide the singers 'in adapting language to melody, and in giving the right sounds to the melodic turns'. The earliest notation, then, has nothing to do with a classical tradition of *verbal accent* but it is directly related to *sentence punctuation*, the function of which was to help the reader 'bring out the sense of a text as he read it aloud'.[17] (The concept is one that is still familiar, or should be, to students of the original texts of Shakespeare and Donne.) To regard the earliest musical notations as groping 'evolutionary' attempts to indicate pitch relationships for their own sake is mistaken. Their function was less intellectually ambitious, more pragmatic. Notation was similar to punctuation: 'it did its work by marking off the sense units of the text, conceived as the hierarchy, *comma, colon* and *periodus*'.[18] I shall take up again, in a later section, the larger relations between text-structure and melody. For the moment we turn to some details of the connection between minutiae of neumes and word-sounds.

Amongst the neumes in all their richly inventive variety there were a great many to be sure, by the end of the first millennium, whose meaning was purely musical; they belonged (if the distinction can be maintained) to the singing rather than to the speaking realm. But a few survive in contexts which show a sensitive relation between melody and syllable-sound. The best example is the liquescent neumes. Strictly speaking they are not a separate class of neume but modified versions of standard neumes. Thus, in the notation of St Gall a *virga* is written as a single stroke / , but in its liquescent form it is written ℐ; the *punctum* is • or –, but as a liquescent it is ʋ or ꜱ. In each of these cases the addition of an apparently lighter note to the main note is signalized, although the precise manner of its performance and its pitch remain matters of dispute.[19] This leads us to the point at issue. A liquescent is a sound in the music corresponding directly and physically to a sound in the words. The verbal sounds which may provoke a liquescent include groups of two consonants of which the first is a 'liquid' (*l, m, n, r*), the consonant group *gn* (A*gn*us), or certain diphthongs (ga*u*dete, ele*i*son) etc. The following antiphon 'Hosanna, filio David', contains four liquescents.[20]

[17] Treitler (1982b), 269.

[18] For recent studies of medieval punctuation, see T. J. Brown, 'Punctuation' in *New Encyclopedia Britannica*, xv (London 1974), and Parkes, 'Punctuation' (1978).

[19] See Cardine, p. 4, Tableau des Signes; he writes (p. 133) that liquescence is 'a vocal phenomenon brought about by a complex syllabic articulation which causes . . . a certain lessening or choking [*étouffement*] of the sound'. Apel (1958), 104: 'the liquescent neumes are also called *semivocales*, and both terms suggest that a special kind of voice production is involved, with the last note sung in a "fluid or half-voiced" manner . . .'

[20] *Graduale Triplex*, 137, with diplomatic transcription of the neumes of the M S S of the St Gall

relationships of sign systems and what they signify' in the social and historical situation of those who use them. See further the Afterword, at the end of this chapter.

Ex. 110

Liquescents do not properly occur except in the right phonological situations. On the other hand, there is no consistency in the manuscripts as to their introduction: sometimes one would expect a liquescent for ease of singing and it is not there, sometimes the opposite. This makes one wonder whether there were other conditions for their employment.

In addition to the liquescents there are a number of special neumes which are not it seems directly related to word-sound: they include the *pressus* , the *oriscus* , the *quilisma* , and various others (I give the neumes in their St Gall forms from Cardine's table).[21] Their meanings and the manner of their performance are a matter of dispute. The *quilisma*, which always occurs in an ascending progression, may simply have been a lightly treated note; on the other hand, it was defined in the ninth century as a *tremula adclivaque vox*, and its written form suggests something more than a single light note. Wagner said it was 'without doubt a portamento-like tremolo figure'; Apel, 'a short ornamenting group involving several pitches'.[22] Most authorities agree at least that the *quilisma* had the effect of lengthening the note preceding it. Modern chant books, written in the square notation that became standard by the thirteenth century, usually record the *quilisma* while neglecting other special neumes.[23] The *quilisma* does not have the particular phonological interest for us of the liquescent neumes. But, together with the other special neumes, it reminds us not only that there is much we do not know about the performance of the chant in the tenth and eleventh centuries, but even more

---

[21] Cardine, p. 4, presents a convenient 'Tableau de Signes Neumatiques de Saint-Gall' (reproduced in Cattin (English edn), p. 67).
[22] Wagner (1911), II.149, basing his arguments on Aurelian of Réôme (from whom the Latin definition in the text is taken) and Aribo.
[23] In Germany, however, the standardized square (quadratic) notation was not adopted; hooked neumes remained in use up to the sixteenth century.

'family'. For a full classification of the phonetic situations in which liquescents occur, see Mocquereau in *Paléographie Musicale*, II (1891) ch. 2 (pp. 37–57, with Table, 54–5). See also Apel (1958), 104–6, with references to other studies. For the antiphon, see *Sarum Antiphonal*, 206 (*Sarum Breviary*, col. dcclx), antiphon for Prime, Palm Sunday.

importantly that chant, the greatest manifestation of medieval monody, was closer to speech in its flexibility, fluidity, nuance of sound (and 'unnotatability') than the singing styles to which we are more accustomed.

I spoke above of 'the chant in the tenth and eleventh centuries'. It might reasonably be objected that this is somewhat too early to be relevant to the present enquiry. The question is whether the flexible, nuanced style so evidently (if in details so puzzlingly) represented by the earliest musical manuscripts survived in the following centuries, when the chant was notated in the much simpler square notation. Of course, the chant like every other human activity is subject to change – growth and decay and renewal; and the chant as surely reflects the musical taste of an age as does any other musical activity. Thus, in the early sixteenth century we find the humanists 'mensuralizing' the chant and editing it in accordance with good principles of *musique mesurée*; and in the nineteenth century we find it romanticized.[24] It could well be that by the thirteenth century something of the aesthetic of the new polyphony with its clearly defined metrical patterns (the rhythmic modes) began to influence the chant, at least to the point of clarifying its melodic movement and cleaning up its rhythmical ambiguities. Such at least is the impression given by the liturgical sources of the period, from which many of the notational subtleties have been banished. Changes in the performance of the chant are lamented two hundred years earlier by Aribo in his *De Musica* (second half of the eleventh century):[25]

Antiquitus fuit magna circumspectio non solum cantus inventoribus sed etiam ipsis cantoribus, ut quidlibet proportionaliter et invenirent et canerent. Quae consideratio iam dudum obiit, immo sepulta est.

Of old a great deal of care was taken, not only by those who composed the chant but also by the singers themselves, that everything should be composed and sung proportionally (?). This concern expired some time ago – more than that, it is buried.

This is usually taken to mean that 'the rhythmic performance of chant was an early practice which was lost after *c.* 1000' (Apel); but much turns on the meanings of *antiquitus* and of *proportionaliter*.[26] What did Aribo actually know of the performance of the chant even a century before his own time? How could he have known it? As for *proportionaliter*, does it mean music measured in strict proportions (2:1, 3:2 etc.)? Or is Aribo invoking a wider ideal of harmony and proportion? Or, as his mention of the rhythmic letters *c*, *t* and *m*

[24] See Sister Thomas More (Dr Mary Berry), 'The Performance of Plainsong in the Later Middle Ages and Sixteenth Century', unpublished Ph.D. diss. (Cambridge 1968), for mensuralized chant. Romanticized chant is still with us in the tradition of organ accompaniment.

[25] Aribo, *De Musica*, ch. 21, ed. Smits van Waesberghe, p. 49.

[26] Much turns also on the word 'rhythm', which Apel (1958), 132, here uses loosely. In the context Apel is preferring Wagner's measured, but not metricalized, interpretation of the chant to other 'rhythmic' interpretations. The concept of chant 'rhythm', however, must embrace a host of more subtle possibilities than he here envisages.

might suggest, is he talking of 'lengthenings' and 'shortenings' rather than longs and shorts? Whatever Aribo had in mind, a change had taken place.[27] The general point at issue is whether the somewhat simpler style of *notation*, which dates in its beginnings from the introduction of the stave in the eleventh century, necessarily indicates a simpler style of *singing*. There is at least one practical fact that is worth mentioning: the very existence of stave lines, however finely drawn, is an obstacle in the way of the finer nuances of penmanship. This applies to the *episema*, for instance, in its St Gall forms. However, it does not apply over the full range of neumatic signs, and certainly not to the 'rhythmic letters'.

This brief excursus into chant notation, if it has not brought many absolutely firm and specific results, does at least open our minds to an unfamiliar style of melody, in which there existed refinements, nuances, sophistications. In some cases these were directly related to the sounds of speech; in others, they had a purely musical impulse, an impulse of delight in song. I shall now turn back to the Palm Sunday liturgy and attempt to analyse the relationship between words and music in the chant from various other points of view.

III The chant and the text: accent and duration

The notational relations between words and music which we have just considered point back to a time when, it is clear, the two arts were not clearly distinguished. As in the music of the Greeks, ceremonially heightened speech in liturgy or in drama *was* chant, and one system of sound-inflexions only was required. The relations we now turn to are more deliberately conceived, or – if this makes the process of creation and transmission seem too conscious – the two sets of sounds may at least be deliberately and properly separated in analysis. I start by considering the musical treatment of the syllable.

It is, indeed, by their treatment of the syllable that three main stylistic categories of the chant can be distinguished. They are the 'syllabic', the neumatic and the melismatic. The liturgy for Palm Sunday contains, as indeed does almost every single service except the lesser Hours, examples of each kind of chant. Into the 'syllabic' group come the psalms, the Passion, the lesson-chants etc., together with the psalm-antiphons, the hymns, and the Gloria and Credo of the Mass. The first of the antiphons in the Palm Sunday procession will serve as an illustration.[28]

---

[27] The so-called 'Romanus' letters or *littere significative* include both melodic direction for staffless neumes (e.g. 'A' *monet alta peti* – 'A' tells you to ascend in pitch) and 'rhythmic' indications (*c* = *celeriter*, quickly; *t* = *tenere* or *trahere*, drag; *m* = *mediocriter*, at a moderate speed (?)). See Wagner (1911), II.234ff; more briefly, Apel (1958), 117; and the detailed account by J. Froger, 'L'épître de Notker sur les "lettres significatives": édition critique', *Etudes grégoriennes* 5 (1962) 23–71.

[28] *Sarum Antiphonal*, 207; *Sarum Breviary*, col. dcclxi (at Sext).

Ex. III

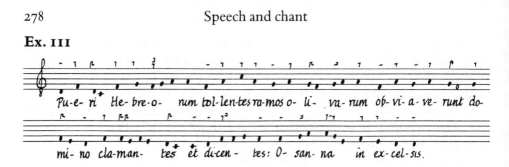

The children of the Hebrews, carrying branches of olive, came to meet the Lord, shouting and saying: 'Hosanna in the highest'.

Each syllable takes one, or two, notes – exceptionally three (e.g. the *climacus* of 'Hosan*na*'). The so-called 'neumatic' style is slightly more elaborate: the defining feature is that the notes for each syllable are mostly represented by a single neume or note-group; single notes and short melismas occur but are rarer. The 'neumatic' chants include Introits, Communions, the Sanctus and Agnus Dei from the Mass, and some special antiphons, such as those in honour of the Virgin. The processional antiphon (for Palm Sunday) 'Cum appropinquaret Dominus' is also of this type, as the opening will show.[29]

Ex. 112

When the Lord came near to Jerusalem, he sent two of his disciples, saying . . .

The third category of musical speech, the 'melismatic', defines itself by name. Single notes and small note-groups are not excluded from this style; but it gains its character from extended melismas such as we find for the opening of the verse of the Palm Sunday Gradual, 'Tenuisti manum dexteram meam'.[30]

Ex. 113

[29] *Sarum Gradual*, 79; *Sarum Missal*, 94.
[30] *Sarum Gradual*, 86; *Sarum Missal*, 97.

. . . How good is the God of Israel . . .

These examples may not seem at first to tell us much, except that there were three main styles of chant – or, to put it more precisely, that it is possible to impose three stylistic categories on the chant without too much falsification. But, actually, one important fact begins to emerge. The choice of style is not a matter of inner meaning or rational appropriateness of melody to words. It depends on genre and is related to function. Thus, all Introits tend to belong to the middle group, the neumatic, and all Graduals to the melismatic, along with Great Responsories, Offertories and Tracts. It is a common event in the chant for the very same words to be set in more than one style, depending on what the text is being used for. For instance, in the liturgy which we are examining the psalm-verse for the Introit is 'Deus, Deus meus, respice in me' (Ps. 21, verse 1); it is sung in a 'syllabic' style which is almost as unadorned as the psalm-tone to which the whole psalm will be recited on Good Friday (at the service of *Tenebrae*) and is in fact a version of that tone.[31] However, a few minutes later in the Palm Sunday Mass the same psalm, or verses from it, form the Tract. Whereas in the Introit sixteen notes suffice for the words quoted, in the Tract over sixty are required. The classic example of this procedure has been tabulated by Peter Wagner in his magisterial *Ein-führung in die gregorianischen Melodien* (1895–1921). He took the text (Ps. 91, verse 13)

> Justus ut palma florebit:
> sicut cedrus Libani multiplicabitur
>
> The just man shall flourish as a palm-tree;
> like the cedar of Lebanon he shall be multiplied

and traced its setting from a simple monotone recitation through psalmodic uses to the variously elaborate chants of the Prophet – Introit, Offertory and Alleluia.[32]

The relationship between words and music is not a matter of individual creative attention so much as of convention. This idea endures throughout the Middle Ages and, indeed, in some shape, beyond. For the present enquiry it provides a valuable insight, but one that can only serve as a point of departure. Despite the wide stylistic divergence between, say, a psalm-tone and an Alleluia, there may still be fundamental principles in common governing the treatment of words in a melody. One 'law' common to many Gregorian melodies, for instance, is set out by Wagner: 'as a rule the melodic line begins

---

[31] For the psalm see *Sarum Antiphonal*, 223; *Sarum Breviary*, col. dcclxxxvi: psalm incipit following the antiphon 'Astiterunt reges' (Matins of Good Friday, first Nocturn). This is from the second of the ancient services of *Tenebrae*, sung, by anticipation of Matins, late on the evenings that precede Holy Thursday (*In cena Domini*), Good Friday (*In Parasceve*) and Holy Saturday (*In sabbato sancto*). The Introit and Tract (Palm Sunday Mass) are in *Sarum Missal*, 97; *Sarum Gradual*, 86–7.

[32] Wagner (1911), III.7–13.

at a low pitch, rises to a point of climax and gradually descends to its final'.[33]
This feature cannot be without relevance to the way words and music are
related, as we shall see later.

   The next aspect of speech-music that I should like to examine is the way
melody corresponds, or not, to the sounds of words, phrases and sentences,
starting with individual words. Each word in a language, even a word of one
syllable, has its own 'tune' or intonation. Thus, one could plot possible
speech-tunes of 'individual', 'sentences', and 'corresponds' as follows.[34]

Ex. 114

These 'tunes' are not unalterably fixed even within the speech of a single
person; they are affected, for instance, by the degree of emphasis attached to
a word in a particular sentence or a particular situation, since emphasis
will determine the pitch, length and intensity of the constituent syllables.
With this in mind we may turn to some liturgical texts in their liturgical
settings.

   Each Latin word of more than one syllable had in classical times a single
main accent. This accent occurs either on the next-to-last syllable
(paroxytone) – *pálma, florébit* – or on the syllable before that (proparoxytone) –
multiplicábitur.[35] In accentual Latin of the Middle Ages, the main accent, now
defined by stress not quantity, may be counterbalanced by secondary, lighter,
ones: thus, *òrnaméntum, vèrecúnda, sánguinìs*. The question is whether these
accents are represented in the melody of the chant and, if so, how. Since we
know nothing, and can know nothing, about accents of intensity in the chant,
we are left with two possibilities – shortening or lengthening (accents of
duration) and heightening (accents of pitch, usually called 'tonic' accents).[36]
Three versions of 'Justus ut palma' will illustrate the problem and show how
difficult it is to assess the evidence.[37]

---

[33] *Ibid.*, III.9.

[34] Intonation is, of course, not simply a function of the word, or of its placing (in the sentence)
or of its emphasis. It may be a function of the speaker's individual manner or nationality (e.g.
a high-pitched voice, a Welsh intonation, etc.).

[35] Dom A. Mocquereau, *Le nombre musical grégorien*, 2 vols. (Rome and Tournai, 1908, 1927)
II.125ff, citing classical and later authorities. Mocquereau's fluctuating views are the subject
of critical discussion by Apel (1958), 280–1.

[36] A caveat: it does not necessarily follow, and should not be assumed, that when a high note or
a melisma (accent of duration) does coincide with a verbal accent, the reason for it must be
something to do with the text–melody relationship.

[37] Wagner (1911), III.10–11: (i) Introit (Mode 8); (ii) responsorial 'office'-psalmody; (iii)
Introit (Mode 2). There are various other 'Justus ut palma' settings in the *Sarum Gradual* and
one responsory in *Sarum Antiphonal*.

Ex. 115

(i) Ju- stus ut pal- ma flo- re- bit ...

(ii) Ju- stus _____ ut pal- ma flo- re - bit ...

(iii) Ju- - - stus ut pal- ma flo- re- - bit _____ ...

In the first example only the word *florébit* seems to be set 'naturally' (assuming for the moment that it is 'natural' to lengthen or heighten the accented syllable); *jústus* has a lower and shorter note on the accent. In the second example, *florébit* again has justice done to it by lengthening, though not by pitch; *jústus*, quite the opposite – the light syllable has ten notes. In the third example, the first syllable of *jústus* is markedly lengthened, the second is short. Throughout these examples *pálma* receives a somewhat neutral and ambiguous treatment, though in yet another setting of the words there is a melodic flowering (having, admittedly, nothing to do with the proper accentuation of the word).[38]

Ex. 116

...pal- - ma _____

The objection could be made that all the examples given are 'intonations', i.e. the opening phrases of chants, and as such are governed by particular 'rules'. But every chant is governed, in its whole and in its parts, by conventions which meet other needs than those of a conscious relation between words and music. The observation still, I think, stands that there is great freedom in the treatment of accented syllables. Even from these few examples – an absolutely infinitesimal proportion of the available evidence (how many thousands of words, one wonders, make up the sung portion of the liturgy in the year?) – it is certain that valid general principles will not be easy to find and to formulate.[39] No wonder the foremost scholars in the field

---

[38] Cited Wagner, III.12 (Offertory). See also *Sarum Gradual*, 17, for a slightly different text of this chant. The Sarum scribe has taken much care over the underlay: the music was written over an insufficiently spaced text and the syllable divisions are indicated by short vertical strokes.

[39] Apel (1958), 282, calculates there may be forty to fifty thousand words with an accent – i.e. words which are not monosyllabic.

have not been able to agree. For the school of Solesmes, 'the word accent of medieval Church Latin is high and short and . . . these qualities are reflected in the music'. For Ferretti, 'the tonic [i.e. pitch] accent receives the status of a universal law of Gregorian chant while, on the other hand, the melodies are said to be indifferent as to the sustaining [i.e. lengthening] accent.' Apel prefers to say that 'both the tonic and the sustaining accent are formative principles of the chant, the former more fully than the latter, neither of them, however, attaining the status of a law'.[40] In the extremely interesting and characteristically thorough section of his *Gregorian Chant*, on 'Melody and Text', Apel declares himself forced against his personal inclination to adopt a statistical approach as a check to the subjective and selective procedures of previous scholars. He analysed the chants of the Proper (Introit, Alleluia, Gradual, Offertory and Communion) in twelve successive Masses of the Christmas season; he also analysed a group of Responsories of Matins. He found that word–accent and melisma (lengthening of syllable) tended to coincide in the antiphonal chants far more often than not, whereas in the Graduals and Responsories this was not the case.[41] Apel's similar investigation of the tonic, or pitch, accent was based on a completely different and simpler group of chants – the antiphons of the Advent season: here he found a 57 per cent 'positive' result, though only two or three antiphons could be singled out as entirely conforming to the 'rule'. Here is one of them.[42]

Ex. 117

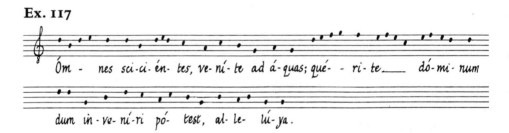

Om - nes sci-ci-én-tes, ve-ní-te ad á-quas; qué- - ri-te.___ dó-mi-num

dum in-ve-ní-ri pó-test, al-le-lú-ya.

All ye that thirst, come to the waters; seek the Lord whilst he may be found. Alleluia.

One is bound to be grateful to Apel for his determined attempt to put the study of this question on to a more scientific basis, but even his 'entirely

[40] The quotations are taken from Apel's summary (p. 279) of the position he adopts, which is a moderate and moderately sceptical one. In addition to Mocquereau, *Le nombre* (see note 35 above), the influential study of Ferretti, *Esthétique grégorienne* (1938), receives close attention. Apel concludes (p. 286) 'that Mocquereau's thesis of the *brièveté de l'accent* as a governing principle of chant is entirely without foundation, and that the more recent theory of "indifference", proposed by Gastoué [*Les origines du chant Romain* (Paris 1907)] and Ferretti, is correct for the responsorial chants (probably also the Tracts), while the other chants, considered as a whole, show a decided preference for the melismatic accent'.

[41] Apel, 282ff.

[42] For the investigation of the antiphons, see Apel, 294ff. He cites 'Omnes sitientes' as fig. 79 (his example is apparently based on *LU*, 324, but stripped of redundant Solesmes editorial markings). I have used the *Sarum Antiphonal* version (p. 13), which differs in a few details.

conforming' examples, such as this, raise doubts about the method of analysis and about what may be expected from it. To start with an obvious point, the tonic accent 'exists only if the accented syllable is higher in pitch than the subsequent weak syllables or, at least, than the first of these'; but it is only on a literal, a *visual*, reading of *ómnes, Dóminum* and *pótest* that the tonic accent seems to exist, since the higher note in a musical, 'singing' rendering may be the lightest note, ornamental, unweighted – the first syllable of *omnes*, for instance, is no more than a decorated note *d*, and there is no felt fall to the second syllable.

Similar doubts come to mind about the accent of duration, irrespective of 'pitch' – i.e. the so-called 'sustaining' accent. The word 'accent' is indeed singularly inappropriate in this connection; first, because the effect of a melisma, a long note-group, is more or less to destroy our sense of the word-sound itself (for example, *gen . . . . . tem* in phrase 4c of 'Collegerunt pontifices' below (Ex. 122, p. 289)) and, secondly, because a melisma does not necessarily have an accenting effect in any case and may, if short, be rhythmically light (see the neume for *gens* in phrase 7c – the whole phrase is fairly light). However, one may say that the effect of an extended melisma must in some degree be to draw attention; it underlines, as it were, a word or syllable whilst paradoxically exercising the utmost musical freedom. This is where the melody lifts off and flies on its own.

The inadequacy, in so many instances, of these two long-standing theories about the treatment of verbal accent ('tonic' and 'durational') make one wish to ask a further question. Could there not be broad musical considerations governing the structure of a chant which make the identification of verbal accent by lengthy note-group (melisma) or by pitch (higher-to-lower) of subsidiary importance if not in fact irrelevant? Such musical considerations certainly exist. Perhaps the most important relation between word-accent and melody depends on the use of structural notes – notes, that is, such as the main reciting-note in a particular mode. Examples of this will be seen in analysis of the Responsory 'Ingrediente Domino' in the next section, and discussion of them will be postponed until that point, since the argument is dependent upon the musical sense of whole units of chant, which we must now consider.

iv   Chant and text-structure

The study of words-and-music in the chant starts from the most minute and detailed identities of sound as represented in the notation and proceeds to a consideration of the syllable as a unit of sound. In the present section larger units are in question – the phrase, syntactical and musical, and the larger structures it builds. We may return to Palm Sunday for our main example.

The Responsory 'Ingrediente Domino' is sung as the procession re-enters the church:[43]

Ingrediente Domino in sanctam civitatem, Hebreorum pueri resurrectionem vite pronuntiantes *Cum ramis palmarum: 'Hosanna, clamabant, in excelsis'. ℣ *Cumque audisset populus, quod Iesus veniret Ierosolymam, exierunt obviam ei.* *Cum ramis [palmarum: 'Hosanna, clamabant, in excelsis']

As the Lord entered the holy city, the children of the Hebrews, announcing the resurrection of the life with palm branches [in their hands], cried out, 'Hosanna, in the highest'. *Verse*: When the people heard that Jesus was coming to Jerusalem, they went out to meet him. With palm branches . . . [*as before*]

Ex. 118

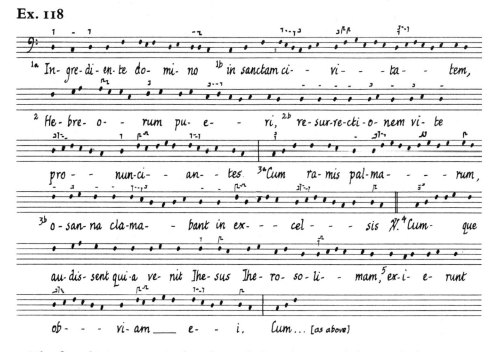

The first thing to note is that the verbal structure and the musical structure are very close; there is no conflict between them.[44] The intonation covers the

---

[43] *Sarum Antiphonal*, 205; *Sarum Missal*, 96 (*in introitu ecclesie*).

[44] See Guido of Arezzo (early-eleventh-century) in *Micrologus*, ch. xv: *ut in unum terminentur partes et distinctiones neumarum atque verborum* . . . (ed. Smits van Waesberghe, pp. 173–4; trans. Babb, p. 70). Wagner (1911), III.285 n., quotes the theorist Anonymus I (Coussemaker, *Scriptores* II.474) who put the matter in more practical terms: *Ibi quoque in vocibus fiat respiratio, ubi in sensu literarum congrua est repausatio, ut verborum et cantus una possit esse distinctio.* See also Gallo, *Il Medioevo II* (1977), 4–5 (English edn, 2–3). M. Bielitz, *Musik und Grammatik* (Munich 1976), works out in detail the hierarchically structured system of musical and parallel verbal entities. Jonsson and Treitler, 'Medieval Music and Language' (1983) appeared too late for me to make full use of it, but I am glad to find some of my main arguments confirmed.

noun and verb of the 'ablative absolute' clause (*Ingrediente Domino*), the next phrase completes that clause, the next double phrase presents the subject of the main clause (*pueri*) with its dependent present participle (*pronuntiantes*); and so on. It is all clear and logical. The barlines, half-bars and quarter-bars of the Solesmes texts, it should be observed, are mostly editorial; nevertheless, they conform to the obvious musical and verbal structure. Although I have given a syntactical analysis, the same result would emerge from straightforward reading aloud: the units are also the natural phrases of speech.

The total musical structure is a slightly different thing from the structure just described, because of the repeat required by the responsorial form. After the *cantor*, the soloist, has sung his verse, the choir takes up the response again, singing from *Cum ramis* to the end. As, in addition, there is 'musical rhyme' between the phrase that precedes *Cum ramis* (i.e. *pronuntiantes*) and the phrase that ends the solo section (i.e. *obviam ei*), the total structure is quite complex. Once again, this larger formal structure arises from function and conventions of performance not from the verbal text as such.

The musical form – the melodic shape which may be distinguished from structure rather as a man's bodily form may be distinguished from his skeleton – is a harder thing to describe in words. It depends on factors such as tonality, melodic range, rhythmic grouping and so on. 'Ingrediente Domino' is in the second mode – that is, it has *d* as its last note, or 'final' (phrase 3b, *excelsis*), but it ranges both above and below the 'final' – in theory from *A* to *a*; in practice here from *c* to *a*. The important cadences are on *d c d, d c d*. This pattern of cadences, combined with the unusually limited range, makes the piece tonally stable. But, though stable, it is not dull; it is, in fact, most subtly modulated. To make some of the obvious points in terms necessarily oversimplified –

Phrase 1a starts modestly, *d c d d*, within the central range, touching lightly on the other most important note of the whole melody, *f*, the reciting-note (see Verse).

Phrase 1b, emerging from the *c*-cadence of phrase 1, moves quickly up to *f* and insists on it (contrast neume-forms with 1a), having enough energy to get to *g*, to fall away and then go back to *f*.

Phrase 2a develops its power from the newly established height of *f*, moves lightly up to *a* (the highest point yet) and, with a gradual release of energy, declines to *d* (note that the slightly weighted neumes on -*rum*, *pu*- and -*e*(ri) prevent this happening too slackly).

Phrase 2b runs along on *d*, in neutral, as it were – even the little excursus of (pro)*nunti*(antes) is lightly conceived, with a slight dwelling on -*an*(tes).

Phrase 3a, beginning the third section, takes flight anew and returns the melodic weight to the *f-g* area (extended neumes on (pal)*ma-rum*).

Phrase 3b is thus enabled to cruise along lightly on reciting-note *f* before falling away to the final cadence on *ex-cel-sis* – this latter is finely balanced, the weightier neumes and repeated *f* of *ex*(celsis) seeming to resist the descent, the lighter neumes and single *f* of (ex)*cel*(sis) assenting to it.

Phrases 4 and 5 make up the Verse, which is in decorated recitation style, first on *f*;
    then on *d*, moving to *f* and back to cadence on *d-c* ('rhyming' with phrase 2b).

The more closely one examines this melody, the more one admires the skill
with which tensions are built up and resolved, and all with such economy of
means. A further point which analysis brings out is the way in which the detail
of the early neumatic notation supports and confirms the musical sense of each
phrase. (This detail is suppressed in the Sarum square notation.) There is, I am
aware, a danger of circularity in this argument; but I believe an analysis carried
out on purely melodic grounds – and mine is primarily that – is indeed
confirmed *after the event* by observation of the way the notation works. That
is, the importance of the structural notes to which I have referred is confirmed
by the notational devices of the *episema* (indicating a slight lengthening) and
the *coupure* (the 'cutting', i.e. division, of a component neume into two or
more constituent parts).[45]

We may now turn back to the question of verbal accent which I left
somewhat in the air at the end of the preceding section. The most striking
feature of the melody just analysed, from the formal point of view, is its use of
the structural notes *d* and *f*.[46] These are in fact the final and the *tenor* (the
reciting-note) of mode 2. The emphasis on these notes, and the characteristic
formulae associated with them, are essentially what allow us to speak of a
mode 2 (plagal *d*-mode) melody. The emphasis also deeply affects the
word-setting and explains, I hope, what was meant by saying above that in
such a chant as this the attempt to identify verbal accent by duration (melisma)
or by pitch (higher-to-lower) might be irrelevant. It is in fact psalmody which
gives the clue to an understanding of the way the words (as sounds) relate to
the notes. In the respond alone, a dozen verbal accents come on one of the two
'structural notes' (cf. Ingred*ie*nte, D*o*mino, s*a*nctam, civi*ta*tem, etc.). The
most important relationship turns out to be basic and simple; it is essentially
that of recitation, at least in those chants – and they are legion – which have
developed from the psalms.[47]

v Formulaic, adapted and 'free' melodies

The analysis so far has not, I hope, been entirely fruitless. But the problem has
another whole dimension which will enable us to see our way much more
clearly towards answers to the questions raised. The Responsory 'Ingrediente

[45] For examples of the *episema* as found in the St Gall M S S, and suggestions as to its meaning,
    see Cardine, 6, 11–13. The term *coupure* (Ger. *Neumentrennung*, neume-division) is much
    used by Cardine (see especially, ch. ix, 'La coupure neumatique'). The rhythmic importance
    of the *episema* and *coupure* in Cardine's revisions of the traditional Solesmes non-mensuralist
    interpretation of the rhythm of plainchant is discussed by Corbin, *Neumen* (1977), 195ff, 'Die
    Rhythmik der Neumen'.
[46] I am grateful to Mary Berry for her observations on this feature of chant analysis.
[47] See below, section VII and Ex. 131a–c in section VIII.

Domino' is not an individual melody in the ordinary sense of the word 'individual'; that is to say, it was not written as a setting for the particular text attached to it in the Palm Sunday procession. This Responsory is one of a group in mode 2 all of which use the same basic material. Peter Wagner transcribed the following Responsory as representative of the type.[48]

Ex. 119

Do-mi-na-tor Do- - mi- ne ²ce-lo- - - rum et___ ter- - - re, ³cre-a- - - tor a- qua- - - rum, ⁴rex u-ni-ver-se cre - - - tu-re___ tu- - e: ⁵Ex- au-di o- ra- ti- o- - nem ⁶ser-vo- rum tu- - o- - - rum.

O Lord, governor of heaven and earth, creator of the waters, universal king of your creation, hear the prayer of your servants.

Comparison between this melody and that of 'Ingrediénte Domino' will reveal the fundamental similarity. There are some minimal differences – for example, in the way phrase 1 opens. Phrase 3 of 'Dominator' attains a *b* flat, but this does not alter the 'sense' of the phrase. The only rather substantial difference is at *orationem* (phrase 5), where the melody does not closely follow the contour of *palmarum*; the last phrase, too, is somewhat foreshortened since it is necessary to accommodate only six syllables instead of ten. The use of the words 'follow the contour' gives perhaps a false impression, since they suggest that 'Dominator Domine' was the first Responsory to be written and that the others took up its melody and copied it. This would be quite false. These Responsories are not *contrafacta* as the term is properly used (denoting a precise syllabic fit); and to my knowledge it is not possible to date them in any chronological sequence. The process by which they came into being has to be explained in some other way. The terms traditionally used to describe the process are 'adaptation' and 'centonization'.

Centonization might seem to be a process analogous to what in literary

---

[48] Wagner (1911), III.336, from Lucca, MS Bibl. Cap. 601 (monastic antiphoner); facsimile, *Paléographie Musicale* IX, pl. 292. The neumes are heighted around a continuous *f*-line and an intermittent *c*-line.

studies is usually referred to as 'oral–formulaic composition'; but the process
of centonization is by definition more conscious than that of traditional
formulaic composition.[49] The term hints at skilful patchwork rather than at
the way memory works with shared melodic ideas, traditional musical
'images', the idiom of a particular repertoire. Even the term 'adaptation'
smacks rather too much of conscious building and contrivance –
'composition' in the modern sense. This group of Responsories seems, in fact,
to show the art of the traditional improviser, with emphasis on 'traditional'
and on the constraints that the word implies but also on the freedom for
'invention', re-creation within those constraints.

This group not only uses the same material but uses it in the same order.[50]
Phrases 1–2 are almost standard, phrases 3–4 only slightly less so; phrases 5–6
(the third section of the response) vary rather more. The re-creations evince
the degree and kind of limited melodic individuality which we have already
seen in 'Ingrediente Domino' and 'Dominator Domine'. So far as the words
and their underlay are concerned, the problems seem fairly easily dealt with.
In the Responsory 'Judas mercator pessimus', the second phrase has nine
syllables instead of the six of 'Dominator', so the adaptor adds a two-note
intonation (c, d), as in 'Ingrediente', and one extra note before the penultimate
group.[51]

Ex. 120

... os- cu-lo pe- - - ci- it_____ do- mi- - - num

(Judas, most wicked of traders,) sought the Lord with a kiss . . .

It is characteristic of the inventor's method that the melismas are always the
most stable part of the melody. It is not uncommon to find some re-

[49] The question of chant transmission up to c. 900 and how we should use terms such as
     memorization, improvisation, oral–formulaic, 'centonization' etc. is the subject of Treitler's
     stimulating article 'Homer and Gregory' (1974). Building on concepts borrowed from the
     Parry–Lord theories of oral transmission, Treitler argues that formulaic system and formula
     'stand for a kind of knowledge which a singer had when he knew a melodic type' (p. 353). 'A
     formulaic system can be transmitted only *through* melodies, but that is not to say that the
     singer can assimilate it only *as* a melody . . . At some point his inventions do not refer back to
     the models of concrete melodies but are based on his internalized sense of pattern' (p. 360).
[50] Apel (1958), 332ff, developing the observations of Wagner (1911), III.336. The most
     extended discussion, with numerous comparative melodies, is in Frere's introduction to the
     Sarum Antiphonal. He writes (p. 8): 'It may seem, if merely these lists and the formulas
     attached to them are considered, that the composition of responds of this type was a very
     mechanical affair, being simply the combination of certain clichés. But this is not the case;
     and in order to see the skill of composition it is necessary to examine the different component
     phrases, and see how each is skilfully handled being delicately and skilfully adjusted to the
     words . . .' The 'adjustment', it should be emphasized, is a matter of sound and structure.
[51] *Sarum Antiphonal*, 217.

arrangement of the melismas;[52] but it was by the addition or removal of single 'syllabic' notes that the adaptor/scribe/singer preferred to work. One last example should clinch the point. The Responsory 'Obtulerunt pro eo Domino' (Candlemas procession) has only four syllables for this same phrase 2 (*par turturum*); all that survives of the melodic phrase is the last two melismas, but these characterize it (Ex. 121).[53]

Ex. 121

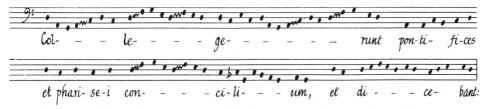

The very existence, in the heart of the Gregorian repertoire, of a body of chants which are mostly the same chant is itself a comment on the relationship between words and music. The Responsories, it must be added, are not a unique instance of this. Two other chants of the Proper, the Gradual and the Tract, have similar internal connections. Of the Tracts, Apel writes that they show 'the extensive use of standard phrases which not only recur within the various verses of one and the same Tract, but are also transferred from one Tract to others, so that, in each mode, the entire group is closely bound together by the use of identical thematic material'.[54] In view of this, there seems to be little point in attempting a detailed analysis of, say, the Palm Sunday Tract 'Deus Deus meus', since it would lead us to the same generalizations about words and music as we have already reached.[55] It may be more interesting and more fruitful to take a so-called 'freely composed' chant. The responsory 'Collegerunt pontifices' was sung in the Sarum rite at the return of the Palm Sunday procession as it approached the doors of the church; it followed the processional hymn *Gloria, laus et honor*.[56]

Ex. 122

---

[52] As Frere's tabulations show, the cadential melismas seem to be particularly stable.

[53] 'Obtulerunt' is not in the earliest MSS; the melody in the *Sarum Antiphonal*, 398, differs from the one given here (a 2nd-mode melody which I take from the *Graduale Triplex*, 542) but is itself formulaic (see Frere, introd., 34, on 4th-mode responsories). See also Apel (1958), 332, table.

[54] Apel, 315.

[55] See analysis by Treitler (1974).

[56] *Sarum Gradual*, 84; *Sarum Missal*, 96. The melody as given in *Graduale Triplex*, 135–6, differs in numerous details.

The chief priests and Pharisees brought together a council and said: 'What shall we do, for this man makes many signs? If we thus let him be, all men will believe in him. The Romans might come perhaps and take our place away from us, and our nation too.' *Verse*: One of them, Caiaphas by name, being the chief priest for that year, prophesied saying: 'It is expedient for you that one man should die for the people rather than that the whole nation should perish.' Therefore from that day onward they thought how they might destroy him, saying, 'The Romans might come . . .' [*as before*]

Of this piece (called *antiphona* in the Sarum Missal without any particular reason, except perhaps to distinguish it in style from other responsories) Apel writes:

The ample melisma on 'Collegerunt', with its repeated scale formation rising through a full octave, from G to g; the ascending and descending leaps of a fifth on 'Quid facimus'; the descent from a to A on 'veniant', with its quasi-sequential pattern: these are traits never encountered in any of the typical Responsories of the second mode. Equally exceptional is the verse [Unus autem], which is not sung to the responsorial tone but to a free melody that incorporates, on 'Ab', the melisma on 'veniant' from the respond.[57]

What can we say about the relation of text and music in this apparently more freely invented Responsory? Regarding structure, we find once again a total and natural agreement between the spoken, phrasal structure and the musical structure. To write out the text phrase by phrase without reference to the melody, following only the sound and sense of the words, is to discover that one has defined the melodic structure as well. The general parallel holds, as always. Within the structure, the external melodic shape, the true organic form of the melody is much more subtle. Space forbids a full analysis. I will simply draw attention to one or two features which make the shape unusual: the unusually weighted opening phrase, low and heavy with repetition, counterbalanced at the end of the respond by the long melisma on gentem; between the two comes what one feels to be the main musical climax, on omnes (phrase 3), after which the unusual quasi-sequential melisma on ve-niant comes as a gradual and restrained relaxation of tension; in this long melody (phrases 1–4) the animation of Quid facimus (phrase 2) is another musically necessary moment – it creates energy to carry the chant through the following phrase.

Next we must ask once more whether agreement extends from the general structure to the detail of word- and phrase-formation. So far as the so-called 'tonic' or pitch accent is concerned, the answer must assuredly be 'no'. There are comparatively few words which conform to the strict definition of this accent (see above): autem ex illis provides an instance in the first phrase of the verse; and illius another, two staves later. So far as the durational, or melismatic, accent is concerned, are the melismas in 'Collegerunt pontifices' concentrated on the accents? That is, do they have at any rate notionally a relation to the sounds of the words? This kind of connection is more marked towards the end of the respond section than elsewhere, with véniant, románi and géntem. The phrase immediately before this also conforms: ómnes crédent in éum. However, a completely opposite practice can be found, too: the first two phrases of the respond contain scarcely a word which is 'naturally' lengthened (and proportionately), but have several (concílium being the most striking) in which melisma is totally unrelated to word-accent. In any case, as I have

---

[57] Apel (1958), 336. Johannes Afflighemensis, De Musica, ch. 21, discusses this 'antiphon' as an example of a chant that is often corrupted by ignorant singers performing from staffless neumes. 'Rarely do three men agree about a chant, far less a thousand' (trans. Babb, 147). This seems to be borne out by the different versions given by Johannes (ed. Smits van Waesberghe, p. 136); by Sarum Gradual, 84; and in Gradual Neumé (St Gall MSS), 155–6.

already argued, neither of these types of accent has any necessary relation to the melodic accent or 'weighting' in which the life of the chant resides. The relation between melody and verbal accent seems once again to be based largely on the 'structural note' principle. The way the chant responds to sound of words is not by 'tonic' or lengthening accent but by bringing together the accentual syllable with the final or with the *tenor* of the mode. In this case it is the final, *d* (cf. in phrase 7 alone the setting of the words *moriátur, hómo, pópulo, péreat*).

VI   Sound and sense

If relationships of sound and sound in the two media of music and words are hard to describe adequately, relationships of sound and sense are no easier. I touched upon them in my discussion of the Responsory 'Ingrediente', but broke off because it was evident that speculations about the treatment of textually important words were rendered null by knowledge of the Responsory's formulaic character. If the same melody is apt both to the text 'Dominator Deus' and to the sharply contrasted text 'Judas mercator pessimus', to take an extreme case, then aptness cannot be a matter of verbal meaning.

Rather too much has been made over the years, by scholars and other commentators, of the way the chant reflects (such is the general view) the words which it carries – and rather too few distinctions have been introduced in their analysis of their observations. Paolo Ferretti, for example, in a work that is still much quoted (*Esthétique Grégorienne*, 1938), writing of Gregorian melodies freely composed, says

The composer in creating them is inspired by his individual genius; but his imagination, warmed by the sentiments expressed in the sacred text – the *ideal* source of his inspiration – was guided also by the grammatical principle of tonic accent (*l'accentuation tonique grammaticale*) – his *technical* source.[58]

This statement is, in its general form, acceptable: at least, no one would wish to deny that the source of ideas/ideals for the Gregorian musician, or musician*s* (if one does not believe in the single act of creation), was the same as for those who shaped the ceremonial – the sacred text. The notion of 'guidance' by the accentuation of the text is more dubious, as we have seen, but enshrines a partial truth – an original, if outgrown, truth. What is alarming, however, is the ease with which Ferretti moves from this modest position to one, not two pages later, where he can quote with approval Dom Gajard on the Offertory 'Jubilate Deo universa':[59]

Another fine piece . . . Here again, we have repetition of the first phrase, but this time with a splendid development of the opening double theme; the phrase climbs by a

[58] Ferretti, 93.
[59] *Ibid.*, 94–5.

succession of leaps, in the manner of a mighty wave hurling itself into an attack on some cliff – a formidable acclamation to God. Then the solemn summons *Venite et audite*, which proclaims before the face of the whole world the goodness of God towards his creature; and then the melody climbs down again and becomes altogether humble and devout.

This quotation is a prime example of 'one thing leading to another'. We can hardly enter here on a discussion of the 'proper language' of musical analysis – musical criticism, as it must be called if it ventures beyond the purely objective. But a moment's reflection on this passage by Gajard will suffice to show how the ground of his description shifts as he writes. The melody is the following:[60]

Ex. 123

---

[60] Transcription of Roman version (see *Graduale Triplex* 227) with variant readings from *Sarum Gradual*, 20; *Sarum Missal*, 42. Offertory for the first Sunday after the octave of Epiphany. It is quoted *in extenso* with its verses by Wagner (1911), III.422–3, from a German MS (Graz 807) of the twelfth century. I have neumed the longer melismas from Sarum to give some indication of phrasing.

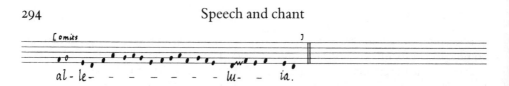

al - le - - - - - - - - lu- - ia.

Rejoice in God, all you lands: recite a psalm to his name! Come and hear, and I will tell you, all you who fear God, what great things the Lord has done for my soul. Alleluia.

Dom Gajard's first comment is factual: there is repetition of the first phrase (1–2 is expanded as 3–8). He refers both to the text and to the music. (It is a unique characteristic of the Offertories, alone amongst Gregorian chants, to allow extensive text-repetitions.) His description of the amplified phrase is at first unexceptionable: the melody does ascend by a succession of leaps (4 → 6). This then suggests to him mighty waves hurling themselves at a cliff, indeed attacking it, a process which is described as a mighty acclamation. Here there is a shift from what I should regard as legitimate simile of waves – 'legitimate' because waves have an existence *in time*, like melody, and height and depth, like melody[61] – to an 'illegitimate' attribution to the waves, and by transfer to the melody, of determination and courage, as if the waves were warriors attacking a fortress. The underlying meaning is rather unhappy, as it turns out, because it involves a central contradiction: God may well be *ein' feste Burg*, 'a safe stronghold', but in that case the acclaiming believers are inside, not attacking it from without. However, it is not just the faulty logic that we must object to; it is also the unspoken 'expressive' assumption behind the description (the melody is assumed to carry quite complex emotions, to 'express' them).

It might be thought that I am cavilling unnecessarily, since Dom Gajard has taken shelter behind a simile (*à la manière*); but the remainder of the passage does not allow any doubt of his insidious emotionalism. The notion that the believer must proclaim God's goodness *à la face de l'univers* seems perhaps to continue gratuitously the battling imagery; if not gratuitous, it smacks rather of romantic than of medieval Christianity.[62] But it is the last observation that really gives the position away, where the melody is seen 'humbling itself' and behaving in a thoughtful and contemplative way. To attribute human feelings of this kind to music – an attribution seriously meant, even if expressed in fanciful anthropomorphic terms – is very misleading. And in this case the non-sense is multiplied by the fact that ninety-nine out of a hundred Gregorian melodies 'humble themselves' at the end; that is to say that they never *rise* to final cadence (unless 'locally', as it were – a small ascent in the very last notes counterbalancing a deeper descent in the final phrase as a whole).

---

[61] One must regard the universally accepted and totally 'dead' spatial metaphor for pitch – high/low – as being in effect objective, literal, *non*-metaphorical.

[62] The 'battling' imagery which is abundant in medieval spirituality characteristically pictures Christ (or the Christian) fighting the Devil.

However, it is one thing to dismiss the old-fashioned romanticized accounts of the relations between words and music with which twentieth-century literature on the chant used to abound; it is quite another to formulate a theory which will fit the facts and help us to understand our experience of the chant. On the negative side Apel has written with his usual trenchancy. He quotes examples of 'expressive' interpretation from the works not of popular devotional writers but of outstanding scholars of the chant – Gevaert, Frere, Johner, Ferretti. He then observes that if

descriptive explanations such as these occur in scholarly writings . . . they adopt the connotation, not of a modern exegesis, but of a historical statement

and he registers his opposition to

attempts to explain Gregorian chant as the result of mental processes [in medieval and pre-medieval 'composers'] so obviously indicative of nineteenth-century emotionalism . . .[63]

Apel carries the matter no further; he does not supply the basis for a positive view of the relations between words and music in the chant, apart from the all-important structural parallelisms and the disputed accentual links. This is no criticism, since his massively detailed study is concerned with other matters of prime importance. To the best of my knowledge there is only one extended study of the subject, Dominicus Johner's *Wort und Ton im Choral* (1940). Johner was a Benedictine, and it is the natural, and in a sense reassuring, result of his deep practical, worshipping knowledge of the chant, as well as of his wide learning, that no more than forty-odd of his 460 pages are directed to the problem of expressiveness. He rightly stresses the 'will to form' above all ('Der Choral hat einen klar bestimmten Willen zur Form') and the continual use of the 'type' (*die Typik*).[64] And yet as a child of his time (the book was evidently conceived in the 1930s) he cannot find, and clearly does not wish to find, any other way of talking about the detailed relations between the words and the notes than that supplied by outmoded romantic presuppositions. Thus, 'the Gradual "Dirigatur" makes the prayer climb up like clouds of incense before the countenance of God' (*zum Antlitz Gottes*); and, in the second part of the chant, the man who prays 'spreads out his arms and lifts them in yearning request for divine grace and help'.[65] An up-to-date account of words and music in the chant is much to be desired. In the remaining pages of this chapter I do not presume to do more than provide a hypothesis which may serve to distinguish traditional Gregorian chant from the repertoire of mainly non-liturgical song. The hypothesis may also perhaps help to explain why our experience of the chant is always one in which the presence of the words is pervasively felt, and felt to be peculiarly important.

[63] Apel (1958), 303.
[64] Johner, 429; and see part C, 'Der Choral als Ausdrucksmusik', *passim*.
[65] Johner, 435.

VII Detailed relations: 'important' words, rhetoric

The music of the chant, except in simple recitation, has its own *raison-d'être*; it does not need words. Of course, the same could be said of many good songs, though it could not be said, for instance, of a seventeenth-century declamatory lament, or of the Evangelist's part in one of the Bach Passions. Nevertheless, there are in most chants some words which appear to get more attention than others. Emphasis can be placed on a word by pitch, by extension in time, or perhaps (but we can never know much about this) by a peculiarity in the manner of performance. We may take as an example the Palm Sunday responsory discussed earlier, 'Ingrediente Domino' (Ex. 118):

As the *Lord* entered the holy city, the children of the Hebrews, announcing THE RESURRECTION OF THE LIFE with palm branches [in their hands], *cried* out, 'HOSANNA, IN THE HIGHEST'. When the people heard that *Jesus* was coming to Jerusalem, they *went out to meet* him.

Musically speaking, the words in this responsory which seem most prominent to eye and ear are *civitatem* (city), *pronuntiantes* (announcing) and *palmarum* (palms); in the second rank come *clamabant* (cried out) and *obviam* (to meet). These words are singled out by lengthening, emphasis by duration. Why? Are they the important words of the text? From the literary–liturgical point of view, clearly not. 'Importance' is a nebulous concept; but one cannot entirely do without it. In this short responsory, it might be argued, the words printed in small capitals are the most important in the sense that they carry the most solemn weight of meaning – though that meaning, with all its ironies, cannot be fully grasped except in the knowledge of the Gospel story as a whole. The italicized words are also important, since this is a matter of degree; and none of the rest could in fact be dispensed with without loss, not even the single adjective 'holy'. The melody does not, in my opinion, decisively favour the significance of the text. Or, to put it more strongly, the melody carries the text firmly but rather neutrally, burgeoning out only occasionally and then in the *musically* expected place towards the end of a phrase. It is these musically placed melismas and the scarcely concealed recitatory nature of several phrases which result in the revealing casualness, if that is the word, of the treatment of *resurrectionem vitae*.

Neither 'Ingrediente Domino' nor any other melismatic chant quoted in this chapter lends much colour to the view that the detailed significance of words in the text is of moment to the musician. Nevertheless, it is proper to ask whether chant-'composers' (to use a handy if anachronistic term which covers all those who may have moulded the melodies over the centuries) were in any way influenced by an artistic discipline of even greater antiquity than their own – the discipline of rhetoric. The ancient *ars rhetorica* was inherited by the Middle Ages from the Greco-Roman world and in particular from the

Latin writers Cicero and Quintilian. Rhetoric – one, with grammar and dialectic, of the three arts of the word – was essentially an art of persuasion; it concentrated the speaker's or writer's attention on communication, on 'getting things over' to his audience. Hence, the emphasis on style in poetry and in prose, on figures of speech – figures of sense and sound. The concepts of rhetoric 'penetrated into all literary genres. Its elaborately developed system became the common denominator of literature in general.'[66] Ernst Curtius, in a book fundamental to the understanding of rhetoric in Western culture, did not exaggerate its importance when he wrote:

Rhetoric signifies 'the craft of speech'; hence, according to its basic meaning, it teaches how to construct a discourse artistically. In the course of time this seminal idea became a science, an art, an ideal of life, and indeed a pillar of antique culture.[67]

The influence of rhetoric on music is more evident in some periods than in others; in the sixteenth century numerous parallels can be worked out, some of them certainly indicating a conscious possession by composers of the ideals and procedures of this all-pervading art of communication. But what of Gregorian chant? There is no doubt whatsoever that musical theorists, being educated men, knew their rhetoric. The oft-quoted fifteenth chapter in Guido of Arezzo's *Micrologus* (eleventh-century), 'De commoda vel componenda modulatione' (Concerning proper melody and how it is composed), contains a series of instructions which are identifiable as rhetorical techniques applied to music. Quintilian appears to be laid most under tribute.[68]

If there was a live and practical rhetorical connection between words and music in the chant, one would expect it to work towards making the chant more communicative, more persuasive to the listener. Is there not the possibility that at least on occasion melismas have the function of drawing out meaning by 'amplifying' (*amplificatio* is a rhetorical device) the words that are most important and meaningful in a text?

There are two main objections in principle to this 'important word' theory. The first objection is that the concept of 'important' words is essentially foreign to the chant.[69] It is, paradoxically, not in the nature of *liturgical*

---

[66] Curtius, *European Literature and the Latin Middle Ages*, 70.

[67] *Ibid.*, 64. For more recent work on rhetoric, especially in the Middle Ages, see Murphy's history of rhetorical theory (1974) and the same author's bibliography (1971).

[68] The connection with the ancient rhetoricians is remarked upon and annotated by Crocker (1958a), 12ff, in his comments to his translation of Guido's ch. xv. For the further influence of Quintilian on musical theory, see chapter 11:iv below.

[69] There could be, however, another side to this. In possible modification of my argument one has to consider Cardine's view that in the earliest neumed manuscripts one use of the *episema*, the serif-like lengthening sign (see section 11 above), is to mark 'important monosyllables'. I can only say that the eight notated examples given by Cardine (pp. 11–13) do not seem conclusive to me, though the 'underlining' of the words *rex* and *cor* in psalmodic examples is striking (p. 13). The significance here, however, could be purely musical, having to do with the *sound* of the phrase not its particular meaning. A careful reading of the earliest practical

reading, reciting, intoning, or chanting to bring out meaning; the meaning is simply there. Amongst the psalms, for instance, are some of the most dramatic and moving texts in the whole Bible ('Out of the depths have I cried unto thee, O Lord'; 'The heavens declare the glory of God'; 'Lift up your heads, O ye gates, and be ye lift up, ye everlasting doors'). But liturgical performance is not designed to heighten their drama; it is, properly, impersonal and inexpressive. The music, in the first place, simply carries the text, and then by its positive indifference and neutrality discourages individual engagement, or at least the manifestations of individual engagement; it holds the emotions in check, encourages no display, indulges no personal emphasis. The psalms, however, are not just *an* example of the way the chant works: in an important sense they are *the* example and type of its working in relation to words. The number of chant genres related to psalmody (apart from the antiphons themselves, they include Introit, Gradual, Tract, Offertory and Communion) is sufficient to show the central importance of psalmody to the growth of the Gregorian repertoire. Peter Wagner opened his introduction to the study of the 'free forms' of Gregorian chant with the words

In regard to the commanding position of psalmody in liturgical song, it is significant that even the melodically freer chant (*die melodisch freiere Lyrik*) has for the most part grown out of psalm models (*psalmodischen Gebilden*); and, what is more, in so far as it may find its way into the realm of artistic expression, it but seldom to this very day disowns its relationship to psalmody.[70]

Is it too bold to deduce from this that the aesthetic of the words/music relationship in the chant remains essentially that of psalmody? This is not to say that the music does not develop characteristics very different indeed in its effects from those of psalmody, but that in its relation to the meaning of the text the music remains in general emotionally uncommitted.

The second objection to seeing the relations between text and melody in rhetorical terms, with the expectation that 'important' words will be singled out by musical 'figures' in order to make them more emotive and persuasive,

---

[70] Wagner (1911), III.281.

---

instructions in psalm-singing seems to bear this out; the treatise (?*c.* 1000) is the St Gall *Instituta patrum de modo psallendi sive cantandi* (Gerbert, I.5–8). The writer stresses the necessity for precision and unanimity, for structural phrasing, for observing the accent of individual words and phrases, for matching liquescent sounds in the words and the music, for breathing musically, for feeling the 'roundness' of each melody, for careful listening to other singers – qualities of good performance, in fact, familiar to choirmasters throughout the ages, all expressed in purely *musical* terms. The only hint of another consideration is when the author explains that the words will not be understood if *accentus vel concentus verborum* are neglected. Wagner (1911), III.270–2, prints the text with German translation. Apel (1958), 239, refers. *Accentus* and *concentus* are common terms for types of chant, simple and ornate respectively (Apel, 288), but here must mean something other (Wagner: *Akzent* and *Verbindungen*).

is that it seems to put liturgical chant into a wrong perspective. The chant is not addressed to a human audience but offered in reverence to God. There is, then, no one to be persuaded. The aesthetic of post-Reformation chant is rather different. A group of conservative bishops wrote, around 1540–3,

The sober, discrete and devout singing, music and playing with organs used in the church for the service of God are *ordained to move, and to stir the people* to the sweetness of God's word the which is there sung, and by that sweet armony . . . *to excite them to prayers and devotion.*[71]

This emphasis on the congregation's taking a feeling part in what is going on is not entirely new, but the explicit belief that liturgical music was originally 'ordained' to this end surely is.[72] Gregorian chant is not directed at the feelings of the congregation; and, although certain aspects of the chant may properly be, and were, talked about in rhetorical terms, this central function of rhetoric (human persuasion), is, I believe, irrelevant to its understanding.

VIII   Detailed relations: the sound of meaning

Gregorian chant is the music of stylized speech. As a simple statement this is obvious enough and would, I think, be widely accepted. Perhaps a slightly more precise way of putting it would be to say that the chant stylizes the 'music' of speech.[73] We have, in fact, already seen this at work – quite clearly and unambiguously in some aspects of the chant (its structure, corresponding as it always does to the structure of the words as spoken, phrase by phrase), and rather less clearly in others (the relation of musical to verbal accent) since few examples show the delicate mutuality of the antiphon 'Lapidabant Stephanum'.[74]

[71] C. S. Cobb, ed., *The Rationale of Ceremonial: 1540–3* (London 1910), 14 (my italics); the book was never published.
[72] There are naturally a few medieval exceptions, or modifications, to this. The Abbess of Barking devised *c.* 1370 a ceremony for the Elevation of the Host which would dispel the *torpor humanus* of the faithful and excite their devotion (see ch. 9:I and note 25 below). More appropriate in date to the present enquiry and less radical in their implication are the comments of Johannes de Grocheo (see ch. 11:III and note 55 below), who specifically directs style of performance to emotive effect.
[73] Jammers, 'Die Wahrheit der Sprache und die Musik in der mittelalterlichen Dichtung', in *Festschrift für Bert Nagel*, ed. W. Pelters *et al.* (Göppingen 1972), 15–23, puts forward the stimulating idea that the (metaphysical) truth of music also authenticated the truth of the words it set.
[74] Cit. Wagner (1911), III.289, from the Lucca Antiphoner (*Paléographie Musicale*, IX, facs. p. 47, from which Ex. 124 is taken. The antiphon was apparently not in Sarum Use; it survives almost unchanged into modern Roman Use (see *L U*, 414, and *Antiphonale Monasticum*, 250) as *Lapidaverunt Stephanum*. Wagner comments: 'Das melodische Kleid lässt immer die sprachliche Verfassung [grammatical disposition] des Textes durchschimmern.'

Ex. 124

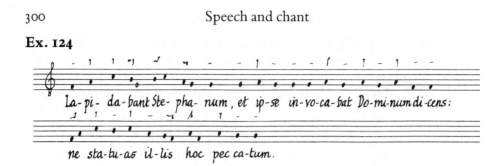

They stoned Stephen, and he called upon the Lord, saying, 'Lay not this sin to their charge.'

What I wish to suggest – and this is the crux of the argument – is the extension of this idea into the mimetic realm. I use the terms 'mimesis' and 'mimetic' to describe the relations between the music and the object or event, if any, which has stimulated it.[75] The stimulus may be a sound in the natural world, or the sound of a word, a movement, a sight, or an idea. If the stimulus is an internal state (mood, feeling, emotion), then I shall use the term 'express/-ive' (e.g. 'This melody *expresses* anger'), carefully distinguishing it from 'emotive', which I reserve strictly to describe the effects which the music has on the listener (e.g. 'This melody arouses anger'). This is not the place, nor have I the philosophical skills, to pursue the general aesthetic question as to whether music is a mimetic art. My more limited aim is to define the nature and to estimate the importance of the mimetic element as it appears in the chant.

To put it briefly, mimesis in the music of the chant follows the same laws as it does in speech, and is subject to the same limitations. The sound of words is not normally mimetic in a direct way; if I say 'horse' or 'table' or 'parliament' or 'love', I have not made a noise which directly represents a horse or a table (or whatever) or any aspect of them. The sign is a purely conventional one. On the other hand, if I say 'cuckoo' or 'whinny' or 'purr' I am making a sound which, although normally taken as purely conventional, did originally have, and can be made to have again, a mimetic relation to the thing signified. (In each of these cases the mimesis is of an associated sound – i.e., the words are onomatopoeic.) The question of the relationship between sound and sense *in words themselves* is a traditionally thorny one, and fortunately we need not enter upon it.[76] What concerns us is the analogous question in regard to the music of the chant.

'The chant stylizes the "music" of speech.' The makers of the chant over the centuries responded, one might say, not so much to the meaning of the words which accompany the chant as to the *sound* of that meaning. To take an

[75] See chapter 11:v below.

[76] I have discussed the matter in a preliminary way in relation to medieval and Renaissance English poetry (Stevens (1982)).

obvious example (it happens also to be a *locus classicus* of the 'word-painting' controversy),[77]

Ex. 125

Pas-ser in-ve-nit si-bi do-mum, et tur-tur ni-dum

The sparrow has found her an house and the turtle-dove a nest . . .

The usual account of this Communion is that it contains a 'charming imitation, through the use of liquescent neumes, of the cooing of the turtle-dove': Apel counters this by saying that actually 'the liquescent neumes are the result not primarily of the imagery of the words but of their spelling, there being always two consonants after each vowel' (see p. 274 above).[78] However, there is I believe a neater way of resolving the difficulty in accordance with the general rule I have just formulated. The Latin word *turtur* (like English 'cuckoo', and unlike, say, English 'starling') is onomatopoeic. The Gregorian composer responds not to his memory of the sound a dove makes but simply and directly to the sound of the word *turtur*. Apel is correct in what he says, but we need to add to his explanation: there is in fact 'word-painting' but of a secondary, indirect kind. By responding to the onomatopoeic *turtur* with the notation demanded by the complete word-*sound* (not simply the spelling), the 'composer' in fact produces at one remove a stylized imitation of the cooing turtle-dove.

This onomatopoeic category is the simplest to deal with. Far more questionable is the category of metaphoric music. This is a domain of musical expression, musical mimesis, of the highest importance in sixteenth-century music, especially in the madrigal. It is where a genius like Marenzio or Weelkes most clearly shows his wit, his *ingenium*; it is where lesser composers most certainly show their banality and lack of resource. A spiritual madrigal like Marenzio's 'Qual mormorio soave' or a witty conceit like Weelkes's 'Thule, the period of cosmography' provides a wealth of illustration. In 'Thule', for example, the phrase 'how strangely Fogo burns' is represented by 'strange' harmonies. This may be termed 'metaphor' in a broad sense because a point of comparison is implied, though not directly stated: the music is 'strange' – a burning volcano is 'strange'. There is no direct imitation as in musical onomatopoeia. In musical metaphor sound is related to non-sound. The most extended uses of musical metaphor are, of course, to be found in

[77] Roman version from *Graduale Triplex*, 306, with the neumes of the Laon M S (Bibl. Mun. 239). In the earlier M S S the upper note of the *pes* on *et tur-tur* is usually a liquescent as here; contrast the *Sarum Gradual* notation (pp. 55–6).
[78] Reese, 168; Apel (1958), 303.

Romantic music, the *Lied*, the programme overture, the descriptive orchestral
prelude, and other nineteenth-century forms.

   If I am right in my suggestion that the chant-makers were working with the
sounds of words and not directly as musicians with their meaning, the concept
of musical metaphor would be foreign to them and its procedures not part of
their craft. The only instances of metaphor would occur indirectly as the
stylization of word-sounds *which were themselves metaphoric.* Such words seem
to be very rare. The use of verbal sound as a metaphorical device is common in
English, and other poetry, from the mid sixteenth century onwards. But it
usually depends on whole phrases or lines and is often contrived through
rhythm, metre and syntax. Such metaphorical usages, in music and in poetry,
may be altogether the creation of a later age.

   It is often said that one particular concept – that of movement, ascending
and descending – is often represented by musical simile in the chant, and that
words associated with such movements (*celi, inferi, resurrexit,* etc.) are set
accordingly. This is an extremely difficult question to resolve conclusively. A
typical ambiguity is posed by the Alleluia 'Angelus domini descendit': the
word *descendit* occurs in mid-phrase, so it both rises and falls (falls perhaps
more strikingly) to end on the same note that it started on.[79]

Ex. 126a

The Offertory with the same opening words reverses the motion and is
ambiguous in a different way.[80]

Ex. 126b

(It also rises to great heights for *de caelo* ('*down* from heaven'), which could be
in itself contradictory.) A reading through the Mass chants for the week after
Easter discloses many cases of height/depth words, some 'positive', some
'negative', some ambiguous like these. The very Introit for the Easter Mass
itself is enough to establish doubt. On the great word of assertion that all
believers have been waiting for through the long darkness of Lent – *Resurrexi,*
'I have arisen' – its restrained neutrality is striking.[81]

[79] *Sarum Gradual,* 125: (*Versus alleluiaticus:* Eastertide).
[80] *Sarum Gradual,* 118.
[81] *Sarum Gradual,* pl. K (supplying missing leaf of BL Add. 12194 from Add. 17001).

Ex. 127

Re- sur-   re- xi _____   et   ad-huc te-cum sum. __

The fact of the matter is that the characteristic movement of plainchant, as has
already been said, is in the shape of an arch. Except in cases of plain recitation,
the chant is rising or falling. Words like *ascendit* and *descendit* seem, on the
whole, to take their chance with the rest.

I am aware that in the course of the argument I have omitted one whole
category of musical speech-sounds which bears directly on the problem.
There are many words in Latin, as in other languages, which are directly
expressive of feeling or emotion.[82] The monosyllable O, for example, may be
either a vocative or an exclamation: even as a vocative it may carry a heavy
weight of emotion, and not always the same emotion. Slightly more 'verbal'
than such simple expressions of pain and pleasure, is a large class of expressive
words with vocative or exclamatory or exhortatory meaning – *Ave* (hail),
Alleluia (praise ye the Lord), *Hosanna* (literally, 'save now'; a shout of praise),
Ecce (behold). There are also the semi-onomatopoeic words which represent
in stylized form human expressive cries – *ululatio, planctus, ploratio* (expressing
misery); *jubilatio, clamare* (expressing the opposite). All these words are in
themselves 'expressive'; they imitate the sound of human feeling. Even this
third class – of semi-onomatopoeic words, which can only be used indirectly,
to denote rather than to utter woe, joy, etc. – contain in their sound-imitating,
or onomatopoeic, elements relics of basic human cries. When expressive
words occur in Gregorian chant one's sense of the actuality of human emotion
is at its strongest and most vivid. Because the word-sounds are not mere signs
but actual *symptoms* of feeling, the musical sounds have the same effect, as in
the following example:[83]

Ex. 128

Al- le-   lu- - - - - ia

In the process, however, of stylizing the 'music' of speech, the chant-
makers are not bound by any law that 'self-expressive' words will necessarily
receive melodic treatment which clearly marks them off from others. The
word *Alleluia*, which is set hundreds if not thousands of times during the
liturgical year, can be sung quite simply – for instance, when it comes at the
end of an Eastertide antiphon such as 'Angelus autem Domini':[84]

[82] Expressive sounds need to be distinguished from mimetic (literal or metaphorical).
[83] *Sarum Gradual*, 137 (*Versus alleluiaticus*: Pentecost).
[84] *Sarum Antiphonal*, 237.

Ex. 129

... al- le- lu - ia,   al- le- lu- ia

This is stylistically in keeping with the syllabic style of the antiphons. We have
continually to bear in mind the point made earlier that the choice of melodic
style is not primarily a matter of 'aesthetic appropriateness', even in the
limited sense in which we are at present discussing it – as music for the 'music'
of speech. To repeat an earlier phrase, it 'depends on genre and is related to
function'. In this at least the chant-makers are following precepts which
rhetoricians could approve: *decorum* is crucial.

However, questions of style apart, there are always two contrary principles
at work in chant, which pull in opposite directions and affect our sense of the
relation of melody to text. On the one hand there is the principle of psalmody,
and on the other a principle which rather loosely one may call *jubilus*. The first
is extremely restrained and, whilst allowing itself to be diverted from pure
syllabic monotone by the needs of phrases and sentences, gives little or
nothing away to individual words. The second is free, creative, and in its final
forms ecstatically liberated from all the demands of a text – its characteristic
genre is the Alleluia of the Mass, but all melismatic chants seem to aspire to
this state. The first is dominated by the sound of words; the second, by the
sound of music. Even the simplest of small chant forms, the Versicle with
Response, shows the two principles in balance.[85]

Ex. 130

Versicle: Send forth your spirit and they will be created; *Response*: And you will renew
the face of the earth.

If we return to a text mentioned earlier, from the Holy Week liturgy, 'Deus,
deus meus, respice in me', we shall be able to see the two principles and their
effects. The text (Ps. 21.1) is sung three times:[86] as a psalm (*Tenebrae* of Good
Friday),

---

[85] Wagner (1911), III.33, with full discussion (pp. 31–6) of versicle and response forms.
[86] *LU*, 666 (with the tone written out); *Sarum Antiphonal*, 223 (incipit only).

Ex. 131a

De-us, de-us me-us, re-spi-ce in me : quare me de-re-li-qui-sti?

lon-ge a sa-lu-te me-a ver-ba de-li-cto-rum me-o-rum.

O God, my God, look upon me, why hast thou forsaken me? Far from my salvation are the words of my transgressions.

as a psalm-verse to the Introit 'Domine, ne longe facias' (Palm Sunday),[87]

Ex. 131b

De-us, de- us me-us, re- spi- ce in me: qua-re me de-re-li-qui-sti?

lon-ge a sa-lu-te me-a ver-ba de-li-cto- rum me-o- rum _____

as the Tract (Palm Sunday), another psalm-based chant.[88]

Ex. 131c

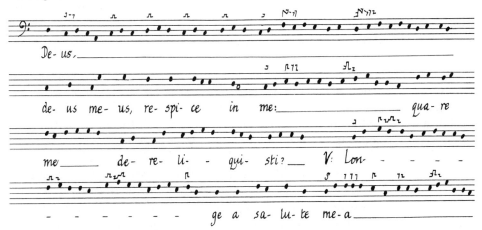

De- us, _____

de- us me- us, re- spi- ce in me: _____ qua- re

me _____ de- re- li- - qui- sti? ___ V: Lon- - - - -

- - - - - - - ge a sa- lu- te me- a _____

---

[87] *LU*, 590–1 (complete); *Sarum Gradual*, 86 (incipit only, with Amen).
[88] *Sarum Gradual*, 86–7.

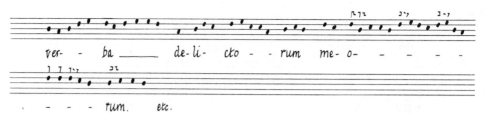

I have deliberately chosen a highly emotional text: it is emotional in the expressive sense, inasmuch as the words express not only the grief of the psalmist but, as spoken from the cross, Christ's grief and agony also. In the first two versions the recitation-style depersonalizes the emotion. The effect is not easy to describe: the formal monotony of the chant (almost in a literal sense) and its indifference to individual words diminishes our sense of pain, releases us from the intolerable realization, whilst at the same time enhancing through its generalizing power the importance and the significance. There is a higher level of experience than the merely personal, and the chant helps us to reach it.

I have deliberately chosen a highly emotional text: it is emotional in the expressive sense, inasmuch as the words express not only the grief of the psalmist but, as spoken from the cross, Christ's grief and agony also. In the first two versions the recitation-style depersonalizes the emotion. The effect is not easy to describe: the formal monotony of the chant (almost in a literal sense) and its indifference to individual words diminishes our sense of pain, releases us from the intolerable realization, whilst at the same time enhancing through its generalizing power the importance and the significance. There is a higher level of experience than the merely personal, and the chant helps us to reach it.

The Tract (Ex. 131c) is also a psalm – not simply a psalm-text (all the verses come from the same psalm) but psalmodic melody. On a first glance, and with only an extract from this very long piece before us, this may not be immediately apparent. But the chant is in fact highly decorated psalmody. Whereas in Ex. 131b the decorations were extremely modest, here they are flowingly complex and unrestrained. After a long embellished intonation on the first *Deus*, which has to be briefly recapitulated for the second *Deus*, there is a short recitation on *f* with a long *flexa* settling to *c*; the second phrase of this first half of the verse circles around *f* again before the mediant cadence on *d*. The answering second phrase (*Longe a salute . . .*) is recited round *f*, 'flexes' to *d*, 'recites' again on *f* (though often touching *d*), with a temporary resolution on *c*, and so on even more floridly, but oscillating always in the same range, to cadence finally again on *d*.

The placing of the melisma – or, to put it in other terms, the breaking out of jubilant melody – does not, however, follow any simple, consistent rule in this or any other Tract. If we take the whole chant into consideration we see that sometimes the melisma falls on an accented syllable, sometimes on an unaccented (*Deus*; *mea*; *exaudies*; etc). Sometimes the word so distinguished will be a seemingly important one – *longe* (*far* are my sinful words from you, God, my salvation) laus *Israel* (. . . the holy place; *Israel*'s ancient boast) etc. Sometimes it will not; *autem* is twice picked out in places where it has (it is true) logical force but none other; a 'natural' (i.e. post-medieval) setting would probably stress *ego* and *vermis* (*Ego* autem sum *vermis*) to make the really important contrast clear between 'our forefathers' who trusted in God and 'I' who am 'a worm and no man'. In so far as there is a principle of relationship between the words and the melody in this Tract it is, as the tonal analysis showed, the psalmodic, structural-note principle which the *jubilus* decorates.

To conclude – working from the position that the music of the chant is based on speech-music, on the sound not on the sense of the words, we have come, I hope, to reject relations between text and melody which seemed to rest on a direct apprehension, a direct representation or expression, of *ideas* in musical terms. The music of the chant is essentially non-referential; it does not express the meaning of words directly. On the rare occasions when it responds at all to the detailed meaning, it responds to the *sound* of that meaning as realized in the sound of the words, whether the words are onomatopoeic or expressive of human emotion.

9

DRAMA I: LITURGY, CEREMONY AND PLAY[1]

In thirteenth-century Padua, on the day of the Annunciation of the Blessed Virgin, clerics representing Mary, Elizabeth, Joseph and Joachim went in procession from the sacristy round the cathedral carrying silver books (*libros argenteos*).[2] These persons took their appointed places in the church. Then the rest of the procession went to the Baptistery,

where there shall be a boy-chorister dressed to represent Gabriel [sitting on] a chair [*cathedra*]; he shall be carried from the baptistery and taken into the church on the side of the piazza [*a latere platee*] and carried up the steps to the choir; the clerics shall halt in the middle of the church to represent a choir [*in modum cori*]. Meanwhile the subdeacon shall begin the prophecy [i.e. the Epistle for the day] *Locutus est Dominus ad Achac dicens*. When this is finished the deacon shall begin the Gospel, that is *Missus est angelus Gabriel*, until he gets to the words *Et egressus angelus ad eam dixit*.

At this point Gabriel shall come forward, and kneeling down, with two fingers of his right hand lifted up, he shall begin this antiphon in a loud voice [*alta voce*: ? at a high pitch]:

Ex. 132

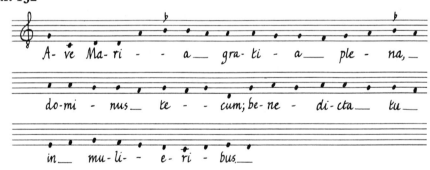

A- ve Ma- ri - - a — gra- ti - a — ple - na, —

do-mi - nus — te - - cum; be- ne - di-cta — tu —

in — mu- li- - e- ri - bus —

---

[1] I am indebted in this chapter to Richard Axton, with whom I have discussed medieval drama over many years, and to Susan Rankin, whose specialized knowledge of the melodies and their transmission has been a great boon.

[2] The Latin text of this dramatic procession is printed in Young (1933), II.248–50; the music is ed. by Vecchi, *Uffici drammatichi* (1954), 66–75 (facsimile, 219–21) with Italian translation of the text. The present account is based on my article 'Music in some early medieval plays' (1968b). My transcriptions are from the facsimiles in Vecchi's edition; the music is clearly and professionally written in square notation with many vertical strokes to indicate word-division.

When this antiphon is finished the deacon continues with the singing of the gospel, up to *Et ait angelus ei*. At this point the angel [comes forward] again and, standing with his right hand in the air, fully extended, shall begin the antiphon *Ne timeas, Maria* . . .

And so the ceremony continues. The deacon's singing of the Gospel narrative is regularly interspersed with the sung speeches of the persons in the story.

When the angel reaches the words *Spiritus sanctus superveniet in* [*te*] a dove shall be displayed for a moment. At the end of the verse [*versus*] the deacon shall continue down to *Dixit autem Maria ad angelum*. At this point Mary shall get up and, standing with her arms wide, shall begin in a loud [? high] voice [*alta voce*] the antiphon *Ecce ancilla*; before the end of it the dove shall be released, and Mary shall receive it under her cloak.

The ceremony ends with the narrative of Mary's visit to Elizabeth:

Meanwhile let Mary descend from her own station [*locus*] and go to that of Elizabeth and Joachim. And let them both receive her, as it is written in the Gospel [which has just been sung]. Then Elizabeth, on bended knees, touching Mary's body with both hands, shall begin the following antiphon:

Ex. 133

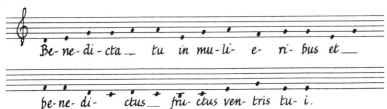

Blessed art thou among women, and blessed is the fruit of thy womb.

Finally, the boy representing Mary turns towards the congregation and (*alta voce*, again) begins the Magnificat. He sings the first three verses; the rest of the canticle is 'sung' in alternation between the organ and the choir before everyone returns, presumably in procession, to the sacristy.

I have chosen to start with this dramatic ceremony from Padua partly because it is attractive and little known, but more because it raises in a clear and simple form many of the issues with which we shall be concerned in this chapter. Padua is a long way from England and the north of France; but the phenomenon known as 'liturgical drama' is an international one and, despite regional and local differences, presents everywhere the same lineaments and the same problems.[3] The Padua Annunciation 'happening' is delicately poised

---

[3] An extensive bibliography of medieval drama and music will be found at the end of the article 'Medieval Drama' in *New Grove* (Stevens (1980)); the first section of the article gives some guidance as to the basic studies. See also the descriptive bibliographical articles on liturgical drama by C. Clifford Flanigan in *Research Opportunities in Renaissance Drama*, vols. 18 (1975) and 19 (1976). The journal (from the University of New Orleans) regularly

between liturgy and drama; one does not know whether to to call it a
'ceremony' or a 'play'. It is evidently not in the most literal sense a 'liturgical
drama', since it does not take place (as many do) as part of the service itself.
The rubric directs: 'After dinner, at the usual time, the great bell shall be
rung . . .' (this is the signal for the clerics to assemble in the sacristy). Otherwise,
it is liturgical: the two manuscripts which contain it are processionals of the
cathedral church;[4] the characters are those mentioned in the Gospel of the day
(Luke i. 26–38); the words they utter are the speeches of the Gospel narrative;
the melodies they sing them to are mainly the traditional chants of the
Church;[5] and the clothes they wear are liturgical vestments. Does this mean
that in the Annunciation ceremony we are dealing simply with liturgy (or
para-liturgy) and not with drama at all in the true sense? Not in the least, for
the implied contrast is wholly misleading. I shall return later to the 'drama' of
the liturgy, and the 'liturgy' of the drama. For the moment it is sufficient to
observe that what was performed in Padua had many of the elements of a
'play', even if its setting was a liturgical procession. One of the phrases most
often used by the rubricator is in modum, 'in the manner of . . .' (e.g. in modum
angelorum). It is probably going too far to say that the choirmen and choristers
'pretend to be' the Biblical characters whose speeches they borrow; no one
was deceived, or was intended to be. But there is dramatization here, if not a

[4] Padua, Bibl. Capit., MSS c55, c56. See Vecchi (1954), p. (3); Young (1933), II.248, n. 5.
[5] The antiphons 'Ave Maria' and 'Ecce ancilla' are still sung at Second Vespers of the
   Annunciation in Roman use (LU, 1416) to the same melodies, slightly simplified. For
   further information about the early use of these antiphons, see Hesbert, Corpus antiphonalium
   officii, nos. 1539 and 2491. 'Ne timeas' and 'Benedicta tu' (Hesbert, 3863 and 1709) were also
   widely known in monastic and secular use.

---

publishes medieval supplements. For the liturgical drama, the fundamental work is Karl
Young's The Drama of the Medieval Church (1933), assembling virtually all the texts then
known, without their music. On the literary side this has now been supplemented from
Donovan (1958), examining texts from Spanish sources, and especially from Lipphardt's
six-volume collection (1975–81) of Easter ceremonies and plays (no music). On the musical
side, Lipphardt's major article in MGG 'Liturgische Dramen' (1960) provides the best
starting-point though its sheer compression is a disadvantage. Smoldon's posthumous Music
of the Church Dramas (1980), is the only book-length study in English. It is fresh, idiosyncratic
and deeply personal and sums up valuable work published in NOHM II (1954) and in the
fifth edition of Grove's Dictionary (1954); but the interpretations are often anachronistic and
the scholarship was already out-of-date on publication. The collection of Medieval Church
Music-Dramas, ed. Fletcher Collins, Jr. (University Press of Virginia, Charlottesville 1976) is
of use to amateur dramatic companies, though it may in some respects mislead them. The
projected study of the music of the liturgical drama by Susan Rankin incorporating the
material and insights of her dissertation (1981) will provide a surer basis for understanding
the music of the drama and the complex processes of its 'composition'. At present Coussemaker's Drames liturgiques of 1860 is the best available edition. I have not referred often to
performing editions in this and the following chapter. Most of the better ones are by
Smoldon and are listed on p. 442 of his book. Over two dozen Latin texts with English
translations (no music) are conveniently provided by D. Bevington, ed., Medieval Drama
(Boston 1975). For more detailed bibliographies see the notes below: note 19 (Marienklagen); notes 53, 72 ('Quem queritis' dialogues); note 57 (Rouen ceremonies and plays); note
68 and Source 22 (Fleury Playbook).

full attempt at illusion. The Gospel story has undergone a process which might be called dramatic *realization* (it is far removed from realism) and to which the key is symbolic. Spiritual events like the moment of conception are put into images that every eye can see – the dove, immemorial symbol of the Holy Spirit, plunges from the roof of the church and is hidden by Mary under her cloak. Parallel to this symbolic (to us, at first, startlingly naive) use of 'properties', there is a symbolic employment of space (Gabriel comes from the choir, the heavenly part of the church, to visit Mary in the nave, the mundane or earthly region) and of time (Mary's journey to Elizabeth's house takes only a few seconds), symbolic costume (how else could a choirboy represent an angel?) and symbolic action (Elizabeth lays her hands on Mary's body whilst singing 'Blessed art thou among women').

This dramatic ceremony – the double term is the most precise – suggests also how drama and narrative can in a medieval, as in a modern, representation constitute a mixed mode. The gospeller tells the story at the same time as the other clerics act it. There is a sort of analogy to this in the liturgical singing of the Passion during Holy Week (see Ex. 136 below): in the singing of the Passion, however, there was never any dramatic action.

Finally, the Padua Annunciation raises the issue which will be my main concern in this chapter: the relationship between music and the other elements of drama. The nature of the musical experience which the 'play' offers is inseparably bound up with the nature of the dramatic realization – here mainly figural, typological, symbolic. There are complications here which we shall address later; I will for the moment only suggest that, as moderns, we have inherited two expectations of musical drama (whether it comes to us under the name of opera or of a film-score, or in a production of a Shakespeare play). The first is that the music shall convey, or reinforce, atmosphere; the second, that it shall, if sung, represent and deepen our sense of 'character' – that is to say, that the song of an actor shall be, even if stylized, an utterance of his feelings. The first of these requirements is totally anachronistic; no medieval drama, liturgical or vernacular, knows anything of 'atmospheric' music – that is, music unrelated to specific actions or speeches.[6] The second may raise complex questions, as the preceding chapter has shown; but not perhaps in the present instance. In the Annunciation ceremony the angel Gabriel, the Virgin Mary and Elizabeth all sing the same kind of music in the same style. Their musical utterances are no more personal than their stylized gestures; perhaps even less so.[7] When Mary stands with her arms wide stretched (*bracchiis*

[6] 'There is, of course, a legitimate sense in which the music of the Padua play "creates an atmosphere" – one of restraint and dignity, a liturgical atmosphere, helping to give the play a significance beyond the mere temporal and occasional. What is certain, however, is that . . . the atmosphere is not peculiar to the play – it is an intensification of the liturgical experience proper to the feast' (Stevens, 'Medieval Drama' in *New Grove*, XII.35; in subsequent notes in the present chapter, '*New Grove*, art. cit.' refers to this article).

[7] We have to recall that the two principal women's parts would have been sung by grown men. On some occasions, at least in the later Middle Ages, female roles were assigned to the *younger* men, *juvenes* (e.g. in the Bordesholm *Marienklage* (*New Grove*, art. cit., 40–1)).

apertis), she seems to be expressing in a stylized form her humble welcome to the Holy Spirit. But her song surely, as music, expresses nothing of her humility or of her exaltation.

The Padua Annunciation ceremony falls into the broad category generally known as liturgical drama. My main concern in this chapter is with this drama; its full range would be better indicated by the term 'ecclesiastical' drama, since amongst the items referred to are several having only a tenuous connection, if any, with the liturgy, whilst remaining within the ambience of the Church. Such a one is the *Ludus Danielis* (*c.* 1230) written, it is thought, by the students of the cathedral school at Beauvais. It is in a manuscript the other principal matter of which is the Office for the Feast of the Circumcision (in effect, liturgical festivities for New Year); and it ends with the singing of the Te Deum. It calls itself a *ludus*, and properly so, for it is an independent and self-contained entity.[8]

I shall not attempt to describe all dramatic manifestations that involve music. My principal aim, once again, will be to distil from particular examples the experience of music and the ways this might be defined by its relationship with words, in this case words-in-action as drama. The experience of dramatic song is certainly as complex as any we have so far considered; perhaps more. And it is bound to be of crucial interest in this enquiry, since drama, however stylized and formal it may be, is to do with human beings in action, with their fears and desires, conflicts and amities. The argument does not, I think, demand a precise definition of drama. Karl Young's requirements, of impersonation and action and dialogue, seem for present purposes unduly limiting;[9] I shall use the word 'dramatic' to refer to experiences as diverse as those provided by *The Song of the Sibyl* (a short prophetic monologue), *The Play of Daniel*, 'Samson, dux fortissime' (a *lai* with several singers), the 'Reproaches' or *Improperia* (sung liturgically on Good Friday), the 'Quem queritis' dialogue, and the *ballerie* from *Le Tournoi de Chauvency*. All of them involve at least some element of mimesis; and this element is presented, not simply narrated. Although a precise definition of drama may not be necessary (or possible), a brief word about medieval terms can hardly be avoided. Amongst the many Latin terms used by medieval writers to refer to dramatic

---

[8] The text of *Ludus Danielis* (from the Beauvais MS) is in Young (1933), II. 290–301, where it is preceded by the only other liturgical play on this theme, by Hilarius *Historia de Daniel representanda* (BN lat. 11331, twelfth-century; no music). The musical edn by Smoldon (1960) is helpfully presented in a neutral unmeasured transcription, with Latin text and English translation underlaid. In his *Church Dramas* (1980), ch. 11, he sets out his views on its performance and gives numerous transcriptions in modal rhythm (i.e. metricalized). The Circumcision Office is ed. in exemplary fashion by Arlt (1970). The attribution of the Daniel play to the cathedral school seems a natural interpretation of the opening lines: *Ad honorem tui, Christe, / Danielis ludus iste / in Beluaco est inventus, / et inuenit hunc iuuentus* (the young people composed it).

[9] See Young (1933), 1.80; for him impersonation is 'the essential element', not speech or movement. 'A play, that is to say, is, above all else, a story presented in action, in which the speakers or actors impersonate the characters concerned'.

representations are *ordo, officium, ludus, festum, representatio, miraculum* (rare), *misterium*. Each vernacular has a comparable variety. None of these terms is used consistently, nor is any used exclusively to denote a drama. *Ordo* and *officium*, for instance, are commonly used to describe liturgical ceremonies as well as plays; this draws attention to a fundamentally important but elusive distinction between ritual and drama.[10] Most of the texts with music which are to be discussed in this chapter occupy a sort of middle ground between these two. For this reason I shall rarely use the word 'play' with all its anachronistic associations, preferring to speak of 'dramatic ceremonies', for this is what most of them are.

A full assessment of the evidence would have to take into account the fact that the liturgical drama, though by no means universal, is found in centres all over Europe, and that there would have been local and regional diversities of style.[11] Whether these could have amounted to outright *incompatibilities* of attitude is a different matter. I find it hard to believe that singers in places even as far apart as the north of England and the north-east of Spain would have felt in fundamentally different ways about the nature of the music they were performing and its relationship to dramatic ceremony. The liturgical drama, to sum up, is attendant, and dependent, upon the liturgy itself: the 'plays' are found for the most part in liturgical books; their material is often the matter of the liturgy itself (antiphons, responsories etc.); and they are animated by the spirit of the liturgy and not by the spirit of theatre (a totally anachronistic word and concept). Western Christendom did not, of course, have a single liturgy even in the Middle Ages; but an impressive unity, an impressive imaginative unity, is evident beneath the diversity of use. Karl Young writes:[12]

The liturgy, or plan of public worship, in the midst of which the Christian drama of the Middle Ages arose is that of the Church of Rome . . . The plays, to be sure, seem never to have been sanctioned or performed at Rome itself; but wherever they appeared, in France, England, Germany, Spain or Northern Italy, they were associated with a liturgical design over which the Roman See formally presided.

The liturgical drama is far and away the most substantial and important dramatic object for study in this period; but no one now believes either that

---

[10] This distinction has been increasingly insisted upon in recent scholarship, notably by de Boor, *Textgeschichte* (1967). In the first chapter of this fundamental textual study of the Easter trope 'Quem queritis', he establishes a basic distinction between 'Feier' and 'Spiel': 'I designate as 'ceremony' everything that was created for the purpose of presentation within the bounds of ecclesiastical ceremony and was so used; or, put in external terms, everything that was copied in liturgical books . . . 'Play', for me, means everything that has no place in the liturgical realm, irrespective of whether it is written in Latin or in the vernacular, and irrespective of whether it is presented by clerics on church premises or with lay participation . . . in public places' (p. 5).

[11] The riches of eastern European traditions are still largely unexplored (*New Grove*, art. cit., 53, and bibliography). On regional diversity within W. Europe see Lipphardt, 'Dramen' in *MGG*; de Boor; Rankin (1981).

[12] Young (1933), I.15.

European drama perished utterly with the destruction of the Roman theatres in the sixth century, or that it had to be re-invented in the tenth. All the evidence, fragmentary as it is, testifies to a wealth of dramatic activity of various kinds in the early Middle Ages, much of it involving music.[13] Travelling minstrels – variously called *mimi, histriones, joculatores, menestrelli, lusatores, scurre*, and so on – combined music and acting with other sorts of entertainment: tumbling, bear-leading, juggling, puppetry. They were professionals, playing (in many senses) for hire; and their repertoire must have been diverse. It could have included simple pieces of the *fabliau* type, i.e. comic tales, such as the *Interludium de clerico et puella* or *Le garçon et l'aveugle*, both of the thirteenth century; mimed monologues, such as Rutebeuf's *Dit de l'herberie* (which recalls the 'sales-talk' of the spice-merchant in some Resurrection plays); scolding matches, 'flytings', *estrifs*, or demonstrations of clever repartee, such as *Le roi d'Angleterre et le jougleur d'Ely*; courtly narratives with interpolated song, such as the *chante-fable Aucassin et Nicolette*; semi-dramatic lyrics, such as 'Mei amic', a late-eleventh-century dance-song dialogue for the Annunciation.[14] Some awareness of this professional activity and of other quasi-dramatic traditions is essential if the musical elements of the liturgical drama are to be seen in their proper and diverse nature.

One important tradition, that of the dance-song, has already been described at some length (chapter 5 above). Another basic human activity, combat, produced not only folk-drama (sword-plays and the like) but also courtly performances from the Dark Ages on.[15] The existence of the Teutonic warrior-play and the presence of musical effects in it are mentioned by the German chronicler Gerhoh of Reichersberg (*c.* 1160), and its influence can be traced in the sung 'liturgical–political' play *Antichristus* (*c.* 1160) from Tegernsee in Bavaria.[16] A later courtly milieu was enlived by the dramatic spectacle of the heroic tournament, a 'species of mimed heroic drama' at which ladies were present and in which music and dancing were added to the social delights.

Other types of sung lyric besides dance-song may sometimes have sprouted into drama. These include the *aube* or *alba* (the lovers' dawn-song in which the

---

[13] To the short bibliography (on professional dancing) given in chapter 5, note 5 above should be added for present purposes Nicoll, *Masks, Mimes and Miracles* (1931); J. D. A. Ogilvy, in *Speculum* 38 (1963) 603; and Axton, *European Drama* (1974).

[14] *Interludium*: see J. A. W. Bennett and G. V. Smithers, *Early Middle English Verse and Prose* (2nd edn, Oxford 1968), no. xv. *Le garçon*: ed. M. Roques, CFMA (2nd edn, Paris 1921); trans. Axton and Stevens, 197ff. Rutebeuf: *Le dit de l'Erberie* (quack-doctor's monologue), ed. E. Faral et J. Bastin, *Oeuvres complètes de Rutebeuf* (Paris 1960), 272. *Le roi*: ed. A. de Montaiglon et G. Raynaud, *Recueil général et complet des Fabliaux* (Paris 1877), II.242 no. 52). (See also Chambers, I.85, n. 1). *Aucassin*: see chapter 6, Ex. 86, above; 'Mei amic': see chapter 5 note 61 above.

[15] See Axton, ch. 2.

[16] Axton, 45. The Latin text of the Tegernsee *Ludus de Antichristo* is in Young (1933), II.371–87; see also ed. G. Günther (Hamburg 1970). The music for the play, which does not survive in the unique MS (Munich, Staatsbibl., MS lat. 19411), is studied by Stäblein (1966) (see also chapter 2, Ex. 12, above for the one traceable song, 'Alto consilio').

watchman has a part), the *chanson de toile* (the lady in her chamber laments her lover's absence), the *bergerie* (shepherds' games) and the *pastourelle* (an encounter between a knight and a maiden). The two last-named, for instance, with their associated music, form the basis of Adam de la Halle's *Robin et Marion* (see ch. 5: 11). Another poetic type, the debate, is self-evidently a dramatic form and has a long musical as well as literary history. Sung dramatic debates range from the ridiculous (the *jeux-partis*, some of which are truly absurd, e.g. of Adam de la Halle and his contemporaries in thirteenth-century Arras) to the sublime (Hildegard of Bingen's *Ordo Virtutum*, *c.* 1155, the earliest known morality play).[17]

It might be objected that all lyrics spoken in the first person could be admitted as 'dramatic' in a loose and wide sense of the term. Such a characteristic poem as 'With longyng Y am lad, / on molde Y waxe mad, / a maid marreth me' certainly dramatizes the lover's situation ('Leuedi, thou rewe me!') even if only sketchily.[18] But there are at least differences of degree: the *chanson de toile*, for instance, much more than most other types seems to imply a 'scene' and sometimes an 'action' (e.g. the lover's return during the course of the song). And there is one distinct difference in kind: the poem 'With longyng' is uttered as if it were the poet's autobiography; the *chanson de toile*, on the other hand, is a little dramatic monologue invented by the poet and put into the mouth of 'bele Aaliz', 'bele Doette', or whoever she may be.

One genre of Latin and vernacular song of particular importance for this and the following chapter is the religious *planctus* or lament. It is sometimes, like the *chanson de toile*, dramatic by implication rather than explicitly. But as the implied context is often that of known plays (particularly the lament of the Blessed Virgin at the foot of the cross) some historians have seen the whole of medieval drama growing from this embryo. In German medieval drama, certainly, the *Marienklage* is of central importance.[19] The *planctus* naturally develops as sung dialogue between the lamenter and the bystanders – between Mary and the beloved apostle, St John; between Rachel and her comforters.

1 The 'drama of the liturgy'

When all is said and done, the most imaginative and impressive form of drama in the Middle Ages remains the liturgy itself.[20] Honorius of Autun, in his

[17] *Jeux-partis*: see A. Långfors *et al.*, *Recueil général* (1926). *Ordo Virtutum*: ed. Barth, *Hildegard, Lieder* (1969), 165ff (musical text), 300ff (Latin text and German transl.); and, independently, Dronke (1970), 180ff.

[18] *Harley Lyrics*, no. 5 (p. 34).

[19] There is to my knowledge no comprehensive modern study of the *Marienklagen*; they are briefly characterized in Stevens, 'Medieval Drama', *New Grove* XI.40–1 with bibliography. The three articles by Lipphardt there listed (1932–4) are of basic musical importance.

[20] On the 'drama of the liturgy', see Young (1933), I, ch. 3; and Hardison, *Christian Rite and Christian Drama* (1965).

Gemma Anime of *c.* 1100, describes the Mass as a drama analogous to ancient tragedy:[21]

Sic tragicus noster pugnam Christi populo Christiano in theatro Ecclesiae gestibus suis repraesentat, eique victoriam redemptionis sue inculcat. Itaque cum presbyter *Orate* dicit, Christum pro nobis in agonia positum exprimit, cum apostolos orare monuit. Per secretum silentium, significat Christum velut agnum sine voce ad victimam ductum. Per manuum expansionem, designat Christi in cruce extensionem. Per cantum praefationis, exprimit clamorem Christi in cruce pendentis.

Thus our tragic actor [i.e. the celebrant] represents by his gestures in the theater of the Church before the Christian people the struggle of Christ and teaches to them the victory of His redemption. Thus when the celebrant [*presbyter*] says the *Orate* [*fratres*] he expresses Christ placed for us in agony, when he commanded his disciples to pray. By the silence of the *Secreta* he expresses Christ as a lamb without voice being led to the sacrifice. By the spreading out of his hands he represents the extension of Christ on the Cross. By the chant of the Preface he expresses the cry of Christ hanging on the Cross.

This passage is striking not for its general approach (since the practice of allegorization-after-the-event was ubiquitous in medieval thinking) but for its quite specific use of theatrical terms – *tragicus, theatrum*. More immediately dramatic in their imaginative impact are, in particular, the ceremonies of Holy Week. In the preceding chapter (section 1) I briefly described the Palm Sunday procession and commented on the way the words-and-music of the chant were bound up with action, were part of a total ritual of movement, colour and gesture. Dramatically speaking, the procession of palms re-enacts the procession of those who welcomed Christ with Hosannas as he entered into Jerusalem. With significant doubleness those who take part are both the fickle crowd, applauding the popular hero for whose death they will call in a few days' time, and also the congregation of the faithful, honouring Christ the King – 'Gloria laus et honor tibi sit, Rex Christe redemptor'. Sometimes, especially in Germany, a figure representing Christ riding upon an ass, the *Palmesel*, was brought in procession into the church.[22] A procession is part of the action of, or forms the setting for, a number of liturgical ceremonies.

Two Easter ceremonies in particular may be singled out as dramatic: the *Depositio Crucis*, commemorating the Burial of Christ, and the *Elevatio Crucis*, celebrating the Resurrection. 'The *Depositio* occurs on Good Friday, between Mass and Vespers, and consists essentially in the burial in the sepulchre of a consecrated Host (*Viaticum, Corpus Domini*), . . . the essence of the *Elevatio* is the taking up of the Host from the sepulchre, before Matins on Easter

---

[21] Transl. after Hardison, 39, from Migne, *PL*, vol. 172, p. 570 (but with my own translations of *tragicus* and *expansionem* where Hardison uses 'author' and 'extension'). The Latin is as printed by Young (1933), 1.83, from the same source. Honorius of Autun is indebted to Amalarius of Metz, *De ecclesiasticis officiis*, but this passage is his insertion (see Young, 1.81–2, setting both authors in their medieval context).

[22] Young, 1.94–8.

morning.'[23] The ceremonies, as Young observes, could be called extra-liturgical since they are neither universal, necessary, nor obligatory. But the speech and music that accompany them are traditional Responsories taken from the Easter, or pre-Easter, services. The 'drama' here is entirely in the symbolic action.

Combined sometimes with the return of the Palm Sunday procession to the church, sometimes with the two ceremonies just named, is a striking liturgical action which had a long history in drama, literature and the visual arts – the Harrowing of Hell.[24] In this ancient, non-Scriptural legend Christ descends to Hell, calls on Satan to open the gates ('Attollite portas'; cf. Psalm 24 (Vulgate 23), verses 7–10), defeats him and releases the imprisoned souls of the prophets and patriarchs. Of especial interest for us, even though the music for it does not survive, is an elaborate Harrowing devised between 1363 and 1376 by the venerable Lady Abbess Catherine of Sutton for her convent at Barking, Essex. The elaborate rubrics describe, or rather prescribe, how the ceremony shall be conducted:[25]

First the Lady Abbess shall proceed with the whole convent and certain priests and clerks dressed in copes, one priest and clerk carrying a palm and an unlit candle. They shall enter the chapel of Saint Mary Magdalene, representing [figurantes] the souls of the holy Fathers going down to hell before the coming of Christ. Then the duty-priest approaches the said chapel, clad in alb and cope, with two deacons, one carrying the cross with the banner of the Lord hanging from it, the other swinging a censer in his hand, and other priests and clerks with two boys carrying candles. At the door of the said chapel he three times begins this antiphon:

Tollite portas

And this priest shall indeed represent the person [representabit personam] of Christ about to descend into hell and break down its doors; and the aforesaid antiphon is to be begun each time at a higher pitch [in altiori voce], and the clerks shall repeat it each time. And every time the priest intones the antiphon he shall strike with the cross on the door of the chapel, symbolizing [figurans] the assault on the doors [of hell]. And at the third stroke the gate shall open. Then he shall enter in with his attendants. Meanwhile one of the priests, being inside the chapel, shall begin this antiphon:

A porta inferi

which the cantor [cantrix] shall take up with the whole community

Erue, Domine

[23] Young, I.113. See also S. Corbin, *La déposition liturgique du Christ au Vendredi Saint: sa place dans l'histoire des rites et du théâtre religieux* (Lisbon and Paris 1960).

[24] The principal source for the theme is the *Descensus Christi ad Inferos* legend recounted in the apocryphal Gospel of Nicodemus (transl. James, *Apocrypha*, 132–3: the Ps. 24 quotation is in all three texts). The liturgical ceremonies are assembled by Young (1933), I, ch. 5, 'The Harrowing of Hell'. For English versions, see W. H. Hulme, ed., *The Middle-English Harrowing of Hell and Gospel of Nicodemus*, E E T S e.s. 100 (1907).

[25] Transl. from the complete Latin text in Young (1933), I.165–6 (from Oxford, Univ. Coll. M S 169, a fifteenth-century Ordinal).

and so on. Then the priest-in-charge shall lead all who are in the chapel outside, whilst intoning this antiphon:

Domine, abstraxisti,

and the cantor follows him with

Ab inferis.

Then all shall leave the chapel, that is, the limbo of the Fathers [who died before Christ], and the priests and clerks shall sing this antiphon processionally through the middle of the choir up to the sepulchre,

Cum rex gloriae,

each one of them carrying a palm and a candle, denoting [*designantes*] victory regained from hell, followed by the Lady Abbess, the prioress and the whole convent as before.[26]

Once more the 'drama' is in the symbolic action. In this case, however, human persons are part of the action. The precise interpretation of, and distinction between, the terms *representare*, *figurare*, and *designare* is not easy. But it seems that none of them belongs to a drama of illusion. The priest who strikes on the doors of the chapel is not pretending to be Christ, any more than he does when he celebrates the Mass, though he in some sense *stands for* him. The same applies to the nuns who are shut inside and wait to be liberated. As symbolic actors in this ceremonial drama their status is as ambiguous as that of those taking part in the Palm Sunday procession.[27]

The richly dramatic nature of some parts of the liturgy, especially at the time of major feasts – Christmas and Easter and others – is an impressive and unforgettable experience. So in considering music and drama in the widest context it is appropriate to begin, as we are doing, with music in the 'drama of the liturgy'.

One of the most striking moments in the Good Friday liturgy is the Adoration of the Cross, which occurs during the Mass of the Presanctified.[28] After the singing of the Passion narrative (from St John's Gospel), solemn prayers follow. Then, according to the tenth-century *Regularis Concordia* (the code of monastic observance in England), the cross is made ready before the altar and held in position by two deacons who sing:[29]

---

[26] For the full text of 'Cum rex gloriae' (the so-called *Canticum triumphale*), see Young, 1.151: it was 'frequently used in the processions of Easter', i.e. it was a pre-existent liturgical composition.

[27] It may be a symptom of the comparatively late date (?*c.* 1370) of this ceremony that the Abbess in her preface explicitly stresses its emotive power.

[28] 'A shortened form of the Eucharistic Liturgy without consecration . . . In the Latin Church it is restricted to Good Friday' (*Oxford Dictionary of the Christian Church*, p. 1100).

[29] So also in Sarum Use (*Missal*, 112–13). Young gives the full Latin text of the Adoration of the Cross from the *Regularis Concordia* (B L M S Cott. Tib. A.III) drawn up and approved by the Synod of Winchester, *c.* 970). See edn by T. Symons (London 1953). Hardison, 130–4,

Populus meus, [quid feci tibi? Aut in quo contristavi te? Responde mihi. ℣. Quia eduxi te de terra Egypti: parasti crucem Salvatori tuo.]

My people, what have I done to you? In what have I grieved you? Answer me. *Christ*: Because I led you out of the land of Egypt, you have prepared a cross for your Saviour.

The answer to this 'reproach' comes from two other deacons standing in front of the cross. They sing the praises of God in Greek, which are repeated by the rest of the choir (*scola*) in Latin:

Agios o Theos, Agyos yschiros, Agios athanatos, eleison ymas. Sanctus Deus [sanctus fortis, sanctus immortalis, miserere nobis].

Holy God, holy and mighty, holy and immortal, have mercy on us.

An acolyte brings a cushion and the cross is laid on it. Two more reproaches follow, in which Christ (i.e. the first two deacons) recalls how he led his people through the desert and fed them with manna, planted them as a vineyard; in return they have given him vinegar to drink and pierced his side with a spear. After each reproach, the Greek and Latin praises are again sung. Meanwhile the cross has been raised again; three antiphons are sung, and the hymn of triumph:[30]

> Pange, lingua, gloriosi
> prelium certaminis;
> et super crucis tropheo
> dic triumphum nobilem . . .

My tongue, sing the battle of the glorious conflict, and of the trophy of the cross proclaim the noble triumph . . .

The dialogue between Christ and his people in the *Improperia* or 'Reproaches', as they are called, is intensely emotive. Hardison speaks of the 'bitter refrain' *Populus meus* – and the impact may indeed have been so.[31] In some versions of the rite, the abbot and half the choir prostrate themselves and sing the seven penitential psalms before everyone 'adores' the cross by kissing it. The implied extremes of emotion – puzzlement, reproach, awe, self-abasement, exaltation, grateful love – are there, and there to be felt. The question for us is what part the music has in all this.[32]

[30] *Sarum Missal*, 113; ed., with detailed glosses, Walpole, no. 33; see chapter 2:1, Ex. 5 above for other versions.
[31] Hardison, 131. For important distinctions between 'expressive' and 'emotive' musical experience, see discussion chapter 11:v below.
[32] Music, *Sarum Gradual*, 101.

gives the historical background to the Adoration ceremony, but his comment that priest and choir reply 'in the manner of a tragic chorus' hardly seems appropriate. In these versions (*Regularis Concordia* and *Sarum*) of the Improperia Christ utters only three 'reproaches'.

Ex. 134

The *Improperia* are certainly very ancient. Duchesne refers to them as part of the preliminaries to 'the ceremony of Indulgence' prescribed by the fourth Council of Toledo (633). The melody is also presumably ancient; much more so than even the earliest notated version (Laon, Bibl. Mun. 239), of the tenth century (after 930).[33] It is a restrained melody of limited range: many of the phrases span only a sixth; the high point is where one would expect it to occur

[33] L. Duchesne, *Christian Worship: its Origin and Evolution*, 2nd Eng. edn, transl. M. L.

for ritual significance rather than verbal emphasis – in the third choral response with its reduplicated top *c* on *eleison/miserere*. There is much repetition, both structural (a necessary feature of the antiphonal singing of the Trisagion) and motivic (the short melisma on *quo* in stave 1 is repeated for *-ra* (*de terra*), stave 3, and *-ra* (*parasti*), stave 3; another turn of melody, *quid feci*, recurs for *eduxi*). The cumulative effect – and we have to remember that there are two further reproaches to be sung for which I have not given the music – is ritualistic, almost incantatory. Music less calculated in itself to mirror the variety of emotions implied can hardly be conceived. What the music does is to heighten the solemnity.

The 'drama of the liturgy' during Holy Week included the singing of the four Gospel narratives of the Passion, beginning on Palm Sunday with St Matthew. The Passions were sung to the Gospel tone for simple feasts with special formulas added; in Sarum use, *est notandum quod triplici voce debet cantari aut pronuntiari, scilicet voce alta, bassa, et media.*[34] The division of the narrative into three 'singing parts', as it were – at a high pitch for the Synagoga, medium for the narrator-Evangelist and low for Christ – would seem a dramatic device, in the sense of distinguishing the speakers' roles. And so it may be. But, curiously, until comparatively late in the Middle Ages all three parts continued to be sung by a single deacon.[35] 'Curiously' perhaps only to us, since the Gospel was normally and as a matter of course intoned by a single cantor on every day of the year. Nevertheless, the letters *c*, *s* and *t* which in the earliest manuscripts are used to denote recitation at three different pitch levels and speeds could indicate a degree of dramatization. A truer way of looking at it might be to see the three *voces* as clarifying features rather than anything more subtle. In a long narrative – and the Holy Week Passions are very long – something has to be done to elucidate the structure of the story. On a smaller scale this clarification is achieved by melodic inflexions articulating the syntactical structure.[36] Certainly, there is only an intermittent propriety, for

---

[34] Hardison, 71, from *Missale Sarum*, ed. F. H. Dickinson (Burntisland 1861–83), col. 264.

[35] Young, 'Observations on the Origins of the Medieval Passion-Play', *PMLA* 25 (1910) 309–33; see also Young (1933), I.550. He explains how the 'significative letters' *c*, *s*, and *t* (see chapter 8 note 27 above) were mistakenly interpreted as meaning *cantor* or *chronista*, *synagoga*, and (*t* = ✠) *Christus*. Kurt von Fischer, 'Die Passion' (in *Gattungen*, 574) and 'Passion' (in *New Grove*), corrects Young's view that the Passions were sung by a single deacon until the fifteenth century. Fischer emphasizes that the choice of pitch is to be understood not as dramatic in intent but as didactic.

[36] Concerning recitation tones in general, see chapter 6:1 and note 7. The fifteenth-century use (Cambridge, Trinity Coll. MS B.11.13) of 'melodical accents' in the recitation of the Passions as well as other Gospels is set out in detail by Rankin in Fenlon (1982), 90–4.

McClure (London 1904), 442. According to Steiner, 'Reproaches' in *New Grove*, 'it is rare to find two MSS of the 10th or 11th century in agreement on the number and order of Reproaches or their precise liturgical use'.

example, in having Synagoga sing at a high pitch, since he (or that range of his voice) has to utter the disciples' chagrin at the waste of precious ointment, Judas' greeting to Christ, the High Priest's interrogation, the maid-servant's challenge to Peter and Peter's denial, the mocking homage of the soldiers, and so on. However, there is propriety – *liturgical* propriety at any rate, even if not dramatic – in having Christ sing in a bass register and, perhaps, more slowly. The more solemn the feast, the slower the singing of the chant, was an accepted principle.[37] In this Sarum version of the Passion Christ commonly recites on *e* or *f*, the narrator on middle *c*, and Synagoga on the *f* above.[38]

Ex. 135

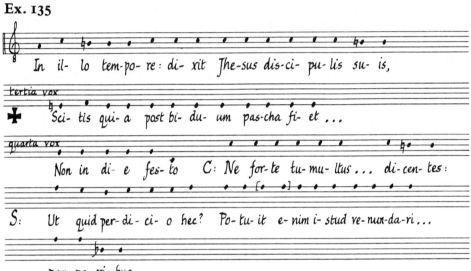

At that time Jesus said to his disciples, Ye know that after two days is the feast of the passover . . . [the Jews said] Not on the feast day, lest there be an uproar . . . [When his disciples saw it they had indignation] saying, To what purpose is this waste? For this ointment might have been sold [for much and given] to the poor.

The most striking feature of the Sarum Passion as it is transmitted in this version from a fourteenth-century Missal is the way in which at the climactic

---

[37] 'It should . . . be remembered that, traditionally, three different *tempi* were recognized by the Church. The fastest was that of ordinary weekdays and vigils. A slower *tempo* was adopted for Sundays and minor festivals, and the slowest of all was used on solemn feast-days' (Sister Thomas More [Mary Berry], 'The Performance of Plainsong in the Later Middle Ages and the Sixteenth Century', unpublished Ph.D. diss. (Cambridge 1968), p. 261; see also her ch. 10, '*Tempo* and expression').

[38] Transcription of the Passion (according to St Matthew) for the Sarum rite (CUL MS Dd.1.15; fourteenth-century). Fischer, in *Gattungen*, 581ff, and 'Passion' in *New Grove*, XIV.277, gives details of the tones to which Passions were variously sung; 'the English Sarum Gradual . . . has its own Passion tones'.

moment, when Christ calls upon God in despair from the cross, the lower register assigned to Christ is abandoned. The reciting-note for Christ is now the high *d* and, more remarkable still, the inflexion is upwards by one semitone to the strikingly rare note *e* flat.[39]

Ex. 136

Et cir-ca ho-ram no-nam: cla-ma-vit Jhe-sus vo-ce ma-gna di-cens,

He-lý : He-lý: la-ma zi-ba-ta-ni. Hoc est ✠ De-us me-us:

de-us me-us: ut quid de-re-li-qui-sti me? C: Qui-dam il-lic stan-tes etc.

And about the ninth hour Jesus cried out with a loud voice saying, Eli, Eli, lama sabachthani? That is to say, My God, my God, why hast thou forsaken me? Certain of those that stood by . . .

The departure from the norms of recitation for the cry of dereliction and for the Evangelist's translation of it was clearly a deliberate inventive choice at some particular moment in time. The interesting problem is what this choice implies. Was the chromatic alteration conceived as directly expressive of Christ's agony? Or is this another instance of the general aesthetic principle which I tried to establish in the preceding chapter – 'the chant stylizes the "music" of speech'; 'the makers of the chant responded not so much to the meaning of words as to the *sound* of that meaning'. Or, a third possibility, is the oscillation of *d* and *e* flat, which is so unusual and so unexpected, more a sign to the listening congregation than a symptom of imagined, dramatized feeling? Has it, that is to say, a quasi-rhetorical, effective function? By simply drawing musical attention to itself, it makes us attend to a crucial utterance. It is not easy for us to provide certain answers to these questions, and in this particular instance I think they should be left open.

Historians of drama have naturally given considerable attention to the recitation of the Passions but, for reasons some of which must now be obvious, have not been able to conclude that it contributed anything of

---

[39] The special *d* / *e* flat tone for Christ's words from the cross appears to be confined to the Sarum Passions. The same reciting note and inflexion are found in the Sarum Gradual (Parma, Bibl. Pal. 98: thirteenth century) and in the fifteenth-century Sarum Gospel book described by Rankin (see note 36 above). I refer, of course, to notated not absolute pitches; the concept of standard pitch for the performance of chant would not have been relevant or necessary.

significance to the development of the liturgical drama. The salient fact is that liturgical drama has to do with celebration; it is for the most part an ornament, and a splendid ornament, to triumphant ritual. It was mostly left to vernacular dramatists to present the 'human interest' of the great Christian festivals of Easter and Christmas. There is nothing in liturgical drama resembling Joseph's anxieties about his wife's unexplained pregnancy, the shepherds' comic puzzlement when they hear music in the heavens, or the painful screaming of the mothers at the slaughter of their innocent babes.[40] If one wished to add a musical buttress to the impregnable case made by Young and others, one could observe that the recitation-tones which are the invariable vehicle for the Passion narratives are never found in the liturgical drama, even though it has a place for 'narrative music' (see below, Ex. 145).

ii   The liturgical drama

Instances of the 'drama of the liturgy' (taking 'drama' in the widest sense) could be multiplied; I do not believe that other examples would, however, display music in a vastly different light from the examples chosen. We come now to a second category of texts: their shared characteristics are a traditional association with the liturgy and the fact that they are sung throughout. 'Association' is an imprecise word, and it needs to be so because the dramatic ceremonies to be considered can occur either fully integrated into the liturgy, or in a form which makes an explicit connection, or quite independently (at least so far as we can tell). The 'Ceremony of the Prophets' (Ordo Prophetarum) is one of these ambiguous cases; it has a non–liturgical origin but becomes liturgical in certain places at certain times.

The Ordo Prophetarum, Young writes, 'differs from all the other dramatic compositions of Christmas in its origin, for it arises not from tropes, antiphons, responsories, or lyric poems, but from a sermon'.[41] The prophecies originated in the pseudo-Augustinian sermon Contra Judeos, in which the preacher summons witnesses – Isaiah, Jeremiah, Daniel, Moses, David, et al. – who will refute the errors of the Jews from within their own tradition. Here are some excerpts from the Ordo, taken from the only surviving musical manuscript.[42]

[40] See, for instance, plays X, X II and X V I in the Towneley (Wakefield) Cycle, ed. G. England and A. W. Pollard, E E T S (1897, repr. 1952).
[41] Young (1933), II.125. Young prints that substantial part of the sermon which was in frequent use 'as a separate liturgical lectio . . . in Matins of Christmas or of some other day of the Christmas season' (II.125–31). Axton, 72, discusses the dramatic nature of the Ordo Prophetarum, a 'pageant of animated icons'.
[42] Transcr. from B N M S lat. 1139 (Source 35) fols. 55v–58, where it follows the Sponsus (see Stevens, 'Medieval Drama', New Grove, section III, 2(ii)). See Smoldon (1980) 150–2, for some discussion of the music of the Prophets, and excerpts transcribed one tone lower. (On the pitch problem in this M S see note 49 below.) The only complete musical transcription is by Coussemaker, Drames, 11–15 (in modern square notation at the lower pitch).

Ex. 137

Om-nes gen-tes con-gau-den- tes dent can-tum le-ti- ci- e:

De- us ho- mo fit, de do- mo Da- vid na-tus ho-di- e...

Is- ra- el, vir le- nis, in-que de Chri-sto <que> no- sti fir- me.

Dux de Ju- da non tol- le- tur do- nec ad-sit qui mit-te- tur;

sa-lu- ta- re De- i ver- bum ex-pe- cta-bunt gen-tes me- cum.

Le-gis- la- tor, huc pro- pin- qua, et de Chri-sto pro-me di- gna...

Est ne- ces- se vir-gam Jes- se de ra-di- ce pro-ve- - hi...

Sic__ est, hic____ est De- us nos- ter,

si- ne quo non e- rit al- ter.

Da- ni- el, in- di- ca vo- ce pro-phe- ti- ca

fa- cta do-mi- ni- ca.

San-ctus san-cto-rum ve- ni- et, et un-cti- o de- fi- ci- et.

Let all the peoples rejoicing together offer a song of gladness: God is made man, born today of the house of David . . . [CANTOR]: Israel, you man of mildness, speak of what you know for certain concerning Christ. [ISRAEL]: A leader will not be raised up out of Judah until he is here who shall be sent; the nations will await with me the Word

of God bringing salvation. [CANTOR]: Draw near, lawgiver [Moses], and utter
notable things concerning Christ . . . [ISAIAH]: It is necessary that a rod should spring
from the root of Jesse . . . [JEREMIAH]: So it is, here is our God, failing whom there
will be no other. [CANTOR]: Daniel, proclaim with prophetic voice the works of the
Lord. [DANIEL]: The holy of holies will come, and he will lack anointing [i.e. as a
crowned king].

The Limoges 'Prophets' is fairly closely modelled on the *sermo*, though it
slightly rearranges the order of events – and it is in verse. The favoured
metrical form is the opening one, with a trochaic movement:

> Omnes gentes
> congaudentes
> dent cantum leticie;
> Deus homo
> fit de domo
> David, natus hodie.

But Virgil, introduced in an iambic couplet, himself utters a hexameter
(though with internal rhyme).[43] So also does the Sibyl, one of the prophetic
women of the ancient world, in three famous lines which, originating in a
clandestine Greek pamphlet, are considerably older than the *sermo* itself. The
Cantus Sibille became the best-known of all the prophecies of Christ and
survives separately in numerous liturgical books, usually to the same melody
as it has in the Limoges MS. I give it here in a different form, from an
eleventh-century lectionary.[44]

Ex. 138

Au- di- te ___ quid di- xe- rit :

℞ Iu- di- ci- i si- gnum : tel- lus su- do- re ma- de- scet;

E ce- lo rex ad- ve- ni- et   per se- cla fu- tu- rus:

sci- li- cet in car- ne pre-sens ut iu- di- cet or- bem.

---

[43] *Ecce polo demissa solo noua progenies est* (Young (1933), II.142).
[44] BN lat. 5304, fol. 12v. See Anglès (1935), Table I opp. p. 294 (Ex. 138 is the fourth of
twenty-three versions of the melody there reproduced and differs considerably from that in
BN lat. 1139). The song of the Erythrean Sibyl, one of the many prophetic women of
ancient times, was incorporated into the Christmas office in the eighth century, and has been
found sung in present-day Majorca. See, further, S. Corbin, 'Le Cantus Sibyllae: origines et
premiers textes', *RdM* 31 (1952) 1.

Hear what she said. *Response*: The sign of judgement: the earth shall become wet with sweat. A king shall come from the sky, a king for all ages, that he may, whilst manifestly present in the flesh, judge the world.

Solange Corbin has distinguished three types of source for this ancient prophecy: liturgical books (the largest number by far); a few 'processions of the Prophets'; pious *florilegia* of the ninth and tenth centuries.[45] The second category (which is what we are concerned with) can itself appear as a liturgical item. The whole, or an abbreviated version, of the *sermo* itself had its place, usually as the sixth *lectio* of Matins of Christmas. Dramatized versions of the *Ordo Prophetarum*, like the Limoges one, were also performed liturgically. And to judge from a thirteenth-century version from Laon Cathedral the presentation may have been quite colourful.[46] The rubric prescribes a slightly odd mixture of ecclesiastical vestments (for the Old Testament prophets) and more 'impersonating' details. Thus, Isaiah is bearded with a dalmatic and red stole; Elizabeth is in woman's clothing, pregnant (with a cushion?); John the Baptist has a hairy garment, and carries a palm; Virgil, writing materials and a garland of ivy; and the Sibyl, woman's dress, cropped hair and a mad look. Finally comes Balaam – an addition to the list – riding on his ass, which he urges on with spurs.[47] The ceremony is similar to that of Limoges, with its highly formalized structure of summons and answer. Neither the Limoges nor the Laon text has any clear indication of where the *Ordo Prophetarum* was placed liturgically; but an evidently similar ceremony at Tours was presented at Matins of the Circumcision (1 January) between the ninth lesson and the ninth Responsory.[48]

It is a great pity that music survives only for the Limoges ceremony, since what we have there raises questions which other musical texts might have solved. The melodies of the Limoges text are written in Aquitanian neumes, heightened around a dry-point line; this means that the relative pitches are reasonably precise – except for the fact that there is no indication of clef. The exception is important since it affects the relation of tones and semitones. If the dry-point is on *f*, for instance, the note below is *e* (at the interval of a semitone); if, however, it represents *g*, the note below is *f* (a full tone). In the transcription in Ex. 138 I have taken the line to be *g*.[49]

The music for the *Ordo Prophetarum* is very different from that of the Passion

[45] Corbin (see preceding note), p. 1, says that about fifty liturgical MSS are known. Her brief chronology of sources (pp. 5–7) categorizes them.

[46] Young (1933), II.145, gives Latin text; I have abbreviated the descriptions considerably from the detail in the original. The Sibyl with her mad look is *insanienti simillima*.

[47] Young, II.153, warns us against modern assumptions that Balaam's ass must be comic and reminds us of 'the medieval attribution of noble virtues to this patient and sober beast'.

[48] Young, II.153.

[49] I have assumed that the clef-line is *g* chiefly because that assumption, if carried over to the *Song of the Sibyl*, is consistent with a transcription of the latter in agreement with numerous other surviving sources. Taking the line as *f* would produce an anomalous reading of the song. The problem is one that affects many pieces in the Limoges MS (Source 35), from which musical Exx. 139–40 are transcribed.

and also from that of most dramatic ceremonies. Whereas the Passion melodies are essentially those used for the chanting of the lessons (*lectiones*) – that is, they are recitation melodies – the *Prophetarum* melodies are infinitely more varied. Yet despite this diversity they are even less fitted to the speakers involved than the three chants of the Passion – low for Christ, middle pitch for Evangelist, high for Synagoga. The rationale behind the composition of the *Prophetarum* melodies appears to be purely musical, but it is not arbitrary nor without parallel elsewhere. In using the word 'composition' I do not intend to suggest a purely modern meaning. The piece has been 'put together' (composed), and much of the thematic material may have been drawn from tradition, from stock. The stock was not, it seems, that of Gregorian chant but rather that of the *lai* (and the related genres *planctus* and sequence). There are some two dozen or so distinguishable melodies corresponding to units of the verse. Some of them have three 'members', others have two.

Ex. 139a

Ex. 139b

These two melodies not only demonstrate the normal, exact correspondence between music and verbal form that we find in 'rhythmical' song throughout the period but also other important features of the *Ordo*. They are the firmness of the tonal centre on *g* (I assume this is the pitch for the purpose of analysis) and the balancing of melodies each side of it within a small range – up to the *d* above, and down to the *d* below. The tonal centre is continuously affirmed by *g* finals; about twenty melodies close on *g* and nearly as many of their 'members'. None of the melodies rises above the upper *d*, and only one makes use of lower *c*.[50] However, the most interesting feature of the music is the extensive, though apparently unschematic, use of repeated motifs – seven or eight are readily identifiable, and several are derived from the first member of Ex. 139b (*Sanctus sanctorum*) which presents an important melodic structure in its basic, simplest form. Variations on the rising or falling fifth are too frequent to list exhaustively, but, for example, the piece opens with one. The usual procedure is for each melody to begin on the tonal centre, *g*, and to work upwards and then downwards again. But there are some striking reversals of this, some unusually melismatic.

---

[50] The *Sibilla* has a single non–structural *e'*; *Isaias* has a median cadence on *c* (and incidentally a unique final cadence on *e*).

Ex. 140a

A- ba- cuc,...   Dic, Ba- pti- - sta...

Ex. 140b

Sic___ est. Hic_____ est.

Finally there are some cadence motifs (Ex. 140c) which do much to unify the *Ordo* from the musical point of view.

Ex. 140c

The general style of the word-setting is syllabic; and, since very few of the syllables carry more than three or four notes, an isosyllabic manner of performance would be as feasible here as for the Latin *lai*.[51]

In short, the musical affinities of the *Ordo Prophetarum* from Limoges are more, it seems, with the *lai* than with any other tradition. The repetition of stanza-forms two or three times, with their melodies; the interspersal of other stanzas which are sung once only; the extensive but unsystematic use of small melodic motifs; the limited ranges of the melodic phrases; their tonal stability and essentially triadic construction; the syllabic or 'neumatic' word-setting – these are all featured in *lais* such as 'Samson, dux fortissime' and 'Omnis caro' (Exx. 55 and 61). It is tempting to add the fact of the *g*-mode, but this must remain less than certain, for the reasons given earlier. Certainly, the general affinities with *lai*-type songs and sequences give encouragement to the conjecture that *g* is the tonal centre; but this falls short of proof. In any case the main observations of this analysis are not dependent upon its truth.

Smoldon found the music of the *Ordo Prophetarum* 'bewildering' – 'As regards the music itself, there is a manifest state of disorder that nevertheless sometimes hints at intentions misplaced and schemes gone astray.'[52] The Paris manuscript may indeed not present a perfect and uncorrupted text. But the reason for Smoldon's bafflement in the face of this object is quite evidently its wayward refusal, as he saw it, to present any *dramatic* scheme, to attach recognizable melodies to recognizable 'characters'. Such can never have been the intention. Instead we have an endlessly varied stream of melody in which what is memorable is the combination of pattern with spontaneous creative inventiveness.

[51] See chapter 4:IV above, and chapter 11:V below.
[52] Smoldon (1980), 152.

By starting my account of music in liturgical drama with the Procession of the Prophets, I have skipped round the usual starting-place, the dramatic dialogue 'Quem queritis'.[53] Amongst the simplest forms of dramatized ceremony are dialogue tropes, many of them for the Introit of the Mass. By far the most important and common are the 'Quem queritis' dialogues of Easter and Christmas. At Easter the dialogue is between *Christicole* (worshippers of Christ) and *celicole* (dwellers in heaven); in many texts the former are precisely identified with the three Marys visiting the tomb (*sepulchrum*) of Christ and the latter with an angel or angels in the tomb. At Christmas the dialogue is between the shepherds seeking the crib and the midwives (who are non-Scriptural). Other tropes on the 'Quem queritis' model are found for the Feasts of the Ascension, St John the Baptist, the Assumption of the Blessed Virgin.[54] Over seven hundred written versions of the Easter dialogue survive, not all with music, spanning six centuries and the whole of Europe.

Particularly in its enlarged forms the Easter dialogue is frequently found from the tenth to the sixteenth centuries at the end of Matins, following the last responsory, 'Dum transisset sabbatum' (When the Sabbath was past), and

---

[53] The origin, nature and development of the 'Quem queritis' have been warmly disputed over recent years. Various sources have been suggested from time to time for the words of the dialogue (Gospel narratives, antiphons and responsories of Easter) and to account for the fact of dialogue; but no single source accounts for all its features. The same may be said of the music. It is a free traditional composition – that is to say, newly composed in the traditional 'neumatic' (middle) style of Gregorian chant using familiar tonalities and melodic formulas. The collection of 'Quem queritis' texts in Young (1933), I. 201ff, has now been effectively replaced by W. Lipphardt's massive edition of texts alone (without melodies), *Lateinische Osterfeiern und Osterspiele* (1975–81), in six volumes; and the relationships of the texts more objectively described by de Boor (1967). Smoldon (1980), full of the author's enthusiasm and detailed observation, does not answer fundamental questions about the music. Here I have been much helped by Susan Rankin's unpublished dissertation (1981), the first sustained systematic attempt to discover 'how the melodies in any ceremony or group of ceremonies were composed' (p. 2). The dissertation is not a study of the 'Quem queritis' as such, but half of it is devoted to the *Visitatio Sepulchri*, in which the 'Quem queritis' is consistently the centre-piece. Traditional and recent scholarship is conveniently summarized in David A. Bjork's article 'On the dissemination of *Quem quaeritis* and the *Visitatio sepulchri*', *Comparative Drama* 14 (1980) 46. The traditional view of the 'Quem queritis' as a trope has been challenged by Hardison (1965) and by T. J. McGee, 'The liturgical placements of the *Quem quaeritis* dialogue', *JAMS* 29 (1976) 23–6. Hardison's argument that the dialogue was an Easter Vigil ceremony is quite unacceptable on musical and liturgical grounds (see Smoldon (1980), 98 and *passim*; Bjork, 62). McGee's contention that it formed part of an elaborate procession outside the church before Mass adds a further perspective. There were clearly three positions for 'Quem queritis' already widespread by the tenth century: (i) as an Introit trope to the Easter Mass; (ii) following the third responsory of Matins; and (iii) in procession. Bjork's own contribution is, on the basis of Lipphardt's edition of the texts and de Boor's regional allocations, to stress the importance of the geographical as against the chronological distribution of texts: 'the versions associated with Mass were limited geographically to the South of Europe' (p. 63); 'the dialogue was sung at Matins across the North of Europe – in England, the North of France, the Rhineland, and in most of East Frankish territory' (p. 60).

[54] See *MMMA* III and IV (Introit tropes). Donovan, 96: the Assumption trope (Santa Maria del Estany, fourteenth-century) was genuinely 'dramatic', acted dialogue (text in Donovan). In reply to the traditional question, the seekers reply *matrem Natzareni*.

leading into the Te Deum. The enlargement consists of prefatory and concluding sentences, mostly well-known antiphons. These amplified dialogues
are known generically as the *Visitatio Sepulchri* and account for over four
hundred of the surviving texts. This huge corpus of texts can be categorized in
various ways according to the interests of the categorizer. Historians of drama
normally distinguish three types: 'one in which the dialogue is conducted by
the Marys and the angel, a second in which are added the apostles, Peter and
John, and a third which provides a role for the risen Christ'.[55] The *Visitatio
Sepulchri*, it is essential to realize, is never extended backwards in time to
include scenes from the Passion and Crucifixion; it exists solely to celebrate
the joy of the Resurrection.

Musically these amplifications call for additions of various kinds. First,
there are the liturgical antiphons – 'Surrexit dominus de sepulchro', 'Venite et
videte locum', 'Currebant duo simul', for example, all three of which are
found in Hartker's Antiphonary (980–1011).[56] They are simple 'neumatic'
chants (i.e. neither strictly one note to a syllable, nor properly melismatic).
The following *Visitatio* from the Benedictine monastery of Fécamp (midway
between Dieppe and Le Havre) shows the basic dialogue enlarged by antiphons; the manuscript is a processional.[57]

After the third Responsory three of the brothers [shall come forward] in the semblance of women [*in specie mulierum*]. One of them in a red cope, between the two
others, shall carry a thurible; the others on each side, wearing white dalmatics, shall
carry vessels resembling pyxes. They shall stand by the candleholder and sing in a low
voice [*humiliter*] making this complaint:

Ex. 141a

From there they shall go forward slowly to the door [*ostium*] by the altar, and a
single brother standing by the 'sepulchre' in the semblance of an angel [*in specie angeli*]
shall reply:

[55] Young (1933), I.239. The classification originates with C. Lange, *Die lateinischen Osterfeiern*
(Munich 1887), and is still widely used for its convenience. A word such as 'types' is
preferable to Young's 'stages' to avoid evolutionary, or simple chronological, connotations.
[56] They are listed as nos. 5079, 5352, 2081, in Hesbert (1963). The third is found principally in
German sources of the *Visitatio*, which includes 'the Race to the Sepulchre' of Peter and John.
[57] Transcribed from Rouen, Bibl. Mun. MS 253 (A538), a processional from the Benedictine
Abbey of Fécamp, fourteenth-century (Lipphardt (1975), VI.410). Facsimile in Dolan,
Drame liturgique (1975), 55ff. Latin text: Young (1933), I.264; Lipphardt, II, no. 404. See also
Rankin (1981), II.61–2 (analysis: I.50); she gives the sources of the chants, which are all
Office antiphons apart from the basic dialogue (in its traditional form with slight variants).

Ex. 141b

Quem que- ri- tis in se- pul- chro, o chri-sti- co- le?

The women to the angel

Jhe- sum na- za- re- num cru- ci- fi- xum,

o— ce- li- co- le.

The angel

Non est hic, sur- re- xit si- cut pre- di- xe- rat;

i- te, nun-ci- a- te qui- a sur- re- xit di- cen- tes:

The women

Al- le- lu- ia re- sur- re- xit do- mi- nus.

The angel

Al- le- lu- ia re- sur- re- xit do- mi- nus.

The women to the people

Al- le- lu- ia re- sur- re- xit do- mi- nus.

The angel to the women

Ve- ni- te et vi- de- te lo- cum u- bi po- si- tus

er- at do- mi- nus: al- le- lu- ia, al- le- lu- ia.

The women to the people

Sur- re- - xit do- - mi- nus de se- pul- chro,

qui pro no- bis pe- pen- dit in li- gno:

al- le- lu- ia, al- le- lu- ia, al- le- lu- ia.

O God, who shall roll back the stone for us from the entrance to the tomb? / Whom are you seeking in the sepulchre, O worshippers of Christ? / Jesus of Nazareth the crucified, O dwellers in heaven. / He is not here; he has risen, as he had foretold. Go, announce that he has risen, saying, / Alleluia, the Lord has risen. / Come and see the place where the Lord was laid. / The Lord has risen from the sepulchre, he who for us hung upon the cross.

The ceremony ends, as usual, with the singing of the Te Deum.

Another frequent addition to the basic dialogue is the Easter sequence 'Victime paschali', an eleventh-century composition attributed to Wipo, an Imperial chaplain.[58] It is usually sung in a dramatic arrangement, but always to its traditional melody. The following ceremony from a Parisian breviary of the fourteenth century, shows the usual way in which it was arranged.[59]

Ex. 142

[58] Young (1933), I.273, gives the complete medieval version from *A H* LIV. 12–13 (no. 7). This famous sequence survived the Reformation and is sung, somewhat abbreviated, in modern Roman use (*L U,* 780). Its use as a text in the liturgical drama is analysed by de Boor, 101ff, with reference to the ceremonies printed by Young.

[59] Paris BN lat. 10482 fols 176v–177. Lipphardt (1975), no. 129 (St Victor, Paris; Augustinian; first half of fourteenth century), described VI.382. Rankin (1981), II.41, notes that of the thirty or so Parisian sources listed by Lipphardt 'only six have music'; also (I.37) that 'all the Parisian *Visitatio* ceremonies, with few exceptions . . . consist of the first three phrases of the ['Quem queritis'] dialogue, followed by . . . *Victime paschali laudes*'. See also de Boor, 102–4.

To the victim Christians offer praises in song. The lamb has saved the sheep, Christ the innocent has reconciled sinners to the Father. Death and life have fought an astounding duel. The lord of life, once dead, reigns alive. 'Tell us, Mary, what did you see on the road?' 'I saw the tomb of the living Christ and the glory of the Riser, / the angel-witnesses, the napkin and the grave-clothes. / Christ our hope has risen and goes before his own into Galilee.' It is better to trust simply in Mary, the truthful one, than in the deceitful multitude of Jews. We know Christ has truly risen from the dead. Victorious king, have mercy on us.

It is time to ask once more the central question: what kind of music-drama do we experience in these ceremonies from Fécamp and Paris? The first and fundamental observation must be that we experience something that is scarcely distinguishable from the liturgy itself, and for the very obvious reason that the ceremonies are 'composed' – perhaps 'compiled' would be a better word – out of already existent chants. The only exceptions are the melodies of the 'Quem queritis' dialogue itself, to which I will return in a moment. It is possible that the dramatization of 'Victime paschali' lent its performance a livelier and more human note than when it was sung in its normal style and liturgical position, after the Gradual and Alleluia on Easter Sunday; but this is pure hypothesis. No amount of dramatization of this kind is likely to have altered the cool balance between words and notes described in the previous chapter. The liturgical occasion is one of great joy, but the melodic restraint of (for instance) the antiphon 'Venite et videte locum . . . Alleluia, alleluia' does not seem to encourage a particularly demonstrative joy. But, then, this is the function and effect of the chant at large. Neither our joys nor our sorrows must seem too overwhelming. The musical material is liturgical and keeps, surely, its liturgical values even when used in a new context.

It is in the central dialogue itself, the 'Quem queritis', that one might expect to find evidence, if anywhere, of musical individuality and dramatic consciousness. The melodies were, after all, expressly written for the exchange of question and answer. But the evidence is wanting. The music of the dialogue is a free composition in a traditional chant-style.[60] It is not difficult to point out analogies between the melodies of the 'Quem queritis' and other chants of greater antiquity, such as the Whitsuntide antiphon 'Paraclitus autem'.[61]

Ex. 143

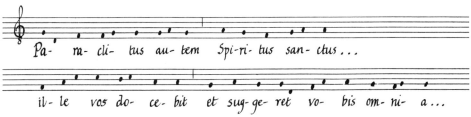

But the Comforter . . . he will teach you and will supply all your needs.

The fact that liturgically the two are quite unrelated makes it all the more likely that we have to do not with conscious borrowing but with unconscious recall of formulas, the 'marks', the manner of musical speech, as it were, in particular modes. This was surely the way that new melodies came into being for most of the liturgical dramas. In a thorough study of the Tours *Ludus Paschalis* (the most extensive form of Easter play) Krieg has shown the nature and extent of the melodic 'borrowing' in unidentified drama-melodies by approaching the problem from the opposite angle.[62] The parts of the liturgy most familiar to the medieval singer were the Ordinary of the Mass and the Requiem Mass. Musical thoughts were naturally taken from these as well as from the chants of the most important season of the Christian year – Passiontide and Easter. One of the most haunting phrases of the famous Easter sequence given above, 'Victime paschali', sets the words 'quid vidisti in via'; it recurs at least fifteen times in the Tours play.[63] From the Lent and Easter liturgies phrases are taken out of the Lamentations of Jeremiah, out of the

---

[60] We are principally concerned with French and English repertoire; it has, however, to be recorded that there was a second 'Quem queritis' melody common in Germany with an altered text. See Young (1933), I.253; Smoldon (1980), 121 (with melody and facsimile (pl. 6) from Einsiedeln, Stiftsbibl. MS 366; twelfth-century); Lipphardt (1975), no. 563.

[61] *LU*, 900; cited by R. Brandel, 'Some unifying devices in the religious music drama of the Middle Ages', in *Aspects of Medieval and Renaissance Music: a birthday offering to Gustave Reese*, eds. J. LaRue and others (New York 1966), 40. 'Paraclitus autem' is antiphon to the Magnificat at Vespers on the Friday of Whitsun week.

[62] Krieg (1956); see especially ch. 6, 'Über den Ursprung der Melodien'.

[63] Krieg, 33–8. Even if some of the parallels seem strained, the general thesis is totally convincing.

Gloria, Sanctus and Benedictus of Mass I (*in tempore paschali*) and out of the
'Popule meus'. The list could be greatly extended. The arranger–composer of
such a play as this from Tours must have been a cleric who lived this music
year in and year out in a singing community. He put it together, with
intellectual control certainly, but out of a teeming hoard of deeply known and
only half-consciously transmuted material.

The serious analytical study of the music of the liturgical drama is only just
beginning and has a long way to go. When it is completed, it should be
possible to distinguish the different layers and styles of melody more precisely
and to say which plays are related to which others. But what, perhaps, is
*un*likely to emerge is any completely new view of the plays as music-drama – a
view in which music will suddenly appear relevant to character, 'scene' and
action in ways which at the present state of our knowledge seem wholly
inappropriate. So much at least may be said about the huge majority of the
dramatic ceremonies which come under the title of liturgical drama. However, there are a number of more ambitious and lengthier pieces, in which
other musical elements enter: these elements may be passages of 'narrative
melody' in a markedly non-liturgical style, or laments (*planctus*), or – though
exceedingly rare – songs (*conductus, cantiones*).

iii   The Rouen Ceremony of the Shepherds

By way of rounding off this section of the argument and summarizing its
themes, I should like to consider in some detail one more dramatic ceremony –
the Rouen *Officium Pastorum* (the Ceremony of the Shepherds). I choose it
because it is an interesting and well-documented example of a Christmas
ceremony, and because it comes from Rouen, one of the great centres of
liturgical drama. There was almost certainly an *Officium Pastorum* being
performed in Rouen in the late eleventh century.[64] But by the next century in
the new cathedral (the original Romanesque building was burnt down in the
year 1200) a more elaborate ceremony had been devised; it survives in a
thirteenth-century Gradual, which gives the music in full, and in a fourteenth-
century Ordinal without music but with extensive rubrics describing the
liturgical action.[65] In the account which follows I shall conflate the two. But
first we must get a sense of context.

[64] See Young (1908), 2ff, describing *inter alia* Montpellier, Fac. Med. MS H304 (late-eleventh-
or early-twelfth-century), which contains the earliest known *Officium Pastorum* (no music).
In the same MS is the treatise of Jean d'Avranches, *De Officiis Ecclesiasticis*; Jean became
Archbishop of Rouen in 1067 but the treatise may belong to his time at Avranches. It
includes a description and explication of the Christmas liturgy in which seven young men
(*iuvenes*) represent shepherds. The text of the treatise is further discussed by Rankin I.168 ff;
the *Officium* is pr. Young, II.12–13.

[65] The Rouen Gradual (with music): Paris BN lat. 904. Latin text, Young, II.16–19, with facs.
of fol. 12 (pl. xiv); facs. of the whole MS in Loriquet, *Graduel* (1907). The music was first
publ. by Coussemaker, 235–8. The transcriptions in the text of the *Officium* and the

The experience of a liturgical drama such as this is, or should be, conditioned by our experience of the liturgy around it. We have not come to the theatre to watch a play; we are taking part in a sequence of worship lasting at least a couple of hours on one of the most solemn and joyfully ceremonious occasions of the Christian year, the vigil of Christmas.[66] The sequence begins with the celebration of Matins, which on this great festival is divided into three Nocturns. Each Nocturn is a service on its own and contains three psalms with their antiphons and three lessons with their responsories. (A Responsory, it will be recalled, is a big chant, and the singing of a *single* Responsory occupies more time than the singing of the standard 'Quem queritis' dialogue and several short antiphons as well.) We can get an idea of the richness of this liturgical event even if we only imagine ourselves joining in it near the end of the third Nocturn. The cantors begin the hymn 'Jesu redemptor omnium', which is taken up antiphonally by the choir. Psalm 97 follows – 'Cantate domino canticum novum' (Sing unto the Lord a new song). Then there is a versicle, 'Tamquam sponsus', and its response, 'Dominus procedens de thalamo suo'. The intonation of the Pater Noster is followed by its silent recitation. The last of the nine lessons of Matins is chanted by one of the canons – the passage from St Luke's Gospel '. . . the shepherds said one to another, Let us now go even unto Bethlehem, and see this thing which is come to pass', to which is added a brief homily on it by St Ambrose. The last of the Responsories follows, 'Beata viscera', an elaborate chant which opens

Ex. 144

Blest is the womb of Mary the Virgin . . .

At this juncture occurs one of the unique features of Christmas Matins as celebrated in medieval rites – the recitation of the Genealogy of Christ

[66] For a further sense of context, see Young, I.47–64, who prints and comments on the whole of the Matins of Christmas (Roman rite).

Genealogy are my own; for the liturgical items I am indebted to Mary Berry, who transcribed them from Rouen, Bibl. Mun. M S A486 (St–Ouen Antiphoner; fourteenth century), supplemented by other Rouen M S S (mainly M S A 233, Jumièges Gradual).

according to St Matthew, chanted by a deacon;[67] the chant at Rouen was as follows.

Ex. 145

The book of the generation of Jesus Christ, the son of David the son of Abraham. 2. Abraham begat Isaac; and Isaac begat Jacob . . . 3. And Judas begat Phares and Zara of Thamar . . .

The contrast between this recitation and the 'Beata viscera' is striking. The Genealogy may not, on paper, look very interesting, but is in fact extraordinarily moving in its context, and never more so than when from the ground, as it were, of recitation there flowers momentarily, as at 'Judas aut*em*', a little melisma at higher pitch. At the end of the Genealogy a sudden variation of the chant formula, which by that time feels as if it has indeed been flowing on from generation to generation, gives a sense of freedom and release wholly appropriate to the announcement of Christ's own birth. And without pause the cantor intones the Te Deum which forms the triumphant conclusion to Matins. Immediately after this the *Ordo Pastorum* begins.

This may seem a long preamble, but what I have described is only a small fraction of the Office, and in describing it I have omitted the ceremonial that attended every significant action. (To mention only one example, the deacon who sang the Genealogy would have been blessed, then censed, then escorted to the lectern.) The drama is placed, it is true, at an important, indeed an

[67] The singing of the Genealogy was introduced with double versicle and response. Arlt (1970), II.77ff, prints the Beauvais Genealogy; the two versions are recognizably related and contain some phrases in common (cf. Rouen 'Ysaac autem . . .' with Beauvais 'David filii', a characteristic *e*-mode phrase which is repeated in both versions), but they are not the same. See Joseph Pothier, 'Chant de la Généalogie a la nuit de noël', *Revue du chant grégorien*, 6 (1897–8) 65; Stäblein, 'Evangelium' in *MGG*; also, Arlt's commentary (II.234).

intensely expectant, moment, when the long preparations of Matins are over and the Mass (*Missa in Galli Cantu* – 'at cock-crow') is about to begin. But in some obvious senses it is dwarfed by its magnificent surroundings. The Ceremony of the Shepherds is a preludial ornament to the Mass itself.

A crib has been set up behind the main altar, and in it has been placed an *imago* of the Virgin Mary – presumably some three-dimensional representation, a statue perhaps. (It was St Francis of Assisi who first got Papal permission to set up a Christmas crib, at Grecchio, with a live ox and ass. We need not imagine anything so elaborate.) The crib will be the focal point of the drama; it is where the dialogue takes place. It does not, of course, constitute a 'scene' in the sense in which later plays have scenes. There is little sense of place – only an area where the action happens.

The first event is the angelic announcement 'Fear not: for behold I bring you tidings of great joy . . .' The verses from St Luke (ii. 10–12) are sung by a boy (it could possibly have been a young man, since the word *puer* is slightly ambiguous); he is positioned up in the roof to the west of the choir, 'announcing the birth of the Lord in the likeness of an angel' (*in similitudinem angeli*).[68]

Ex. 146

Fear not: for, behold, I bring you tidings of great joy, which shall be to all people. For unto you is born this day in the city of David the saviour of the world. And this shall

[68] Does *in similitudinem angeli* mean the same as *quasi angeli* in the next rubric? It is unclear whether these phrases refer to garments worn, to physical position (in 'heaven'), or to style of announcement. The melody of Rouen is almost identical with that from the *Officium Pastorum* of the Fleury Playbook (Source 22) for the same text (Smoldon (1980), 204). The music of Fleury was first published by Coussemaker (1860), 143–5 (the first part of the *Ordo ad representandum Herodem*); a more scholarly transcription is in Rankin (1981), II.124–6.

be a sign unto you: ye shall find the babe wrapped in swaddling clothes, lying in a manger.

Then a number of boys 'up in the vaults like angels' (*in voltis ecclesie quasi angeli*) sing 'Glory to God in the highest'.[69]

Ex. 147

The shepherds, who are canons of the cathedral or their deputies, enter meanwhile through the great west door of the choir and proceed, when they hear the angels' song, to the place where the crib has been prepared singing 'Pax in terris nunciatur' (Peace is announced on earth). I give verse 1 only.

Ex. 148

[69] The material for this melody is taken more or less entirely from the 'Nolite timere'. In the Fleury ceremony the Gloria text is set to the melody of the Office antiphon (Rankin (1981), I.176).

Peace is announced on earth, glory on high; earth and heaven are joined through the agency of grace. The Man–God mediator descends to his own, so that guilty man may ascend to the joys which are sanctioned. *Refr*: Eya, eya, let us go and see this Word which has been born; let us go, that we may know what has been proclaimed.

This metrical refrain-song has a very *un*-chantlike melody, as will be shown. It occurs also in the Later Cambridge Songs manuscript slightly more elaborated; and it appears to have been borrowed 'from outside', as it were, for the liturgical drama.[70] The refrain echoes the shepherds' words in the ninth lesson, 'Let us now go . . . and see this thing which has come to pass.' As the shepherds approach the crib they sing these words yet again, to a chant-type melody.[71]

Ex. 149

Let us go to Bethlehem and see this Word which has been created, the Lord's doing which he shows to us.

At the crib the shepherds meet the two priests who represent the midwives, and the usual Christmas dialogue takes place, the midwives pulling back a curtain to reveal first the Christ-child and then his Mother, to whom they point as they sing their second *versus*, 'Behold a Virgin shall conceive and bear a Son . . .'.[72]

[70] This refrain-song (facsimile in Young (1933), opp. II.16, pl. xiv; Anderson L55; Walther 13899) is unusual in so far as it has two concordances outside the corpus of liturgical drama: (i) Paris BN MS lat. 4880 (early-thirteenth-century; no music): contains a small anthology of poems with some attributions to Walter of Châtillon (see A. Wilmart, 'Poèmes de Gautier de Châtillon dans un manuscrit de Charleville', *Revue Bénédictine* 49 (1937) 121; 322); (ii) the Later Cambridge Songs (Source 8), where it is untidily notated in cursive square notation.

[71] This is virtually the same melody as in the Fleury ceremony (Smoldon (1980), 205, gives a parallel transcription). Rankin reports that she has not found it outside the *Officium Pastorum* but notes its similarity in style to that of the Office antiphons ((1981), I.174).

[72] On the Christmas dialogue (a trope to the Introit of the third Mass of Christmas), which is generally thought to have been modelled on the Easter one, see: Young (1933), II.3–8; Smoldon (1980), 102–5 (with transcription of the earliest surviving version from Paris, BN MS lat. 1118 (? Toulouse, *c*. 1100: see Lipphardt (1975), VI.371)); Rankin (1981), I.162–6, with special attention to the geographical disposition of the trope (cf. R. Jonsson, ed. *Cycle de Noël*, Corpus troporum I (Stockholm 1975)). There is essentially no musical connection between the Easter and Christmas dialogues.

Ex. 150

Whom are you seeking in the crib, shepherds? Tell. / The Saviour who is Christ the Lord, a babe wrapped in swaddling clothes, according to, the words of the angels. / The little one is here with Mary his mother; it is he of whom formerly Isaiah the prophet had prophesied, saying: /Behold, a virgin shall conceive and bear a son. As you journey, declare that he is born.

The shepherds reverence the Child Jesus with bent heads and sing a hymn to the Virgin.[73]

Ex. 151

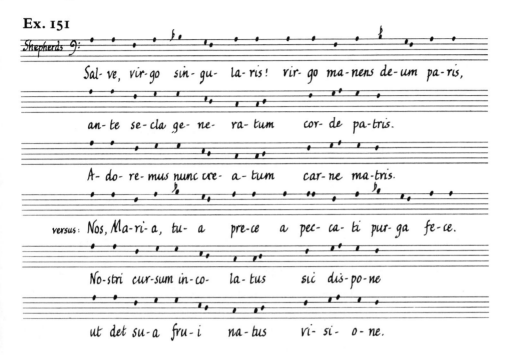

Hail, matchless Virgin; remaining a virgin you give birth to God, conceived in the heart of the Father before all time. Now let us worship him created from the flesh of his mother. Mary, by your prayers cleanse us from the dregs of sin. So dispose the course of our dwelling [in this world] that your Son may grant us to enjoy the vision of himself [in the hereafter].

And finally, as they make their way to their 'rulers' ' bench in the middle of the choir they sing, 'Alleluia . . . now we know truly that Christ is born on earth: of him sing you all, saying with the prophet'.[74]

Ex. 152

[73] This strophic song in the style of the simpler *conductus* has not been found elsewhere. It may well, like 'Pax in terris', have had an independent existence. For pieces in a similar syllabic style with much simple repetition, see Arlt (1970), I.120–38, 206–17; and chapter 2:11 above.

[74] This is the last melody of the standard dialogue, with some variants especially in the concluding phrase to the words *omnes . . . dicentes* (cf. Smoldon (1980), 105).

na- tum in ter- ris, de quo ca-ni-te om-nes cum

pro- phe- ta di- cen-tes:

In the Mass that follows, as if to minimize the difference (which assuredly they did not feel as we, *reading* the text, think we should feel it) between the Ceremony of the Shepherds (*Officium pastorum*) and the ceremony of the Mass (*ordo misse*), the shepherds have a prominent role – they 'rule the choir', which means amongst other things that they sing the splendid trope to the Gloria:[75]

Gloria in excelsis deo (quem cives celestes sanctum clamantes laude frequentant.) *Et in terra pax hominibus bone voluntatis* (ut ministri domini verbo incarnatum terrenis promiserant) . . .

Glory be to God on high (whom the citizens of heaven call the Holy One and celebrate with praise) *and in earth peace to men of good will* (as the ministers of the Lord had promised the Incarnate-by-the-Word to dwellers on earth) . . .

and other portions of the liturgy. Nor is their work finished with the Mass. In the office of Lauds, which follows immediately, the shepherds take part in a dramatized singing of the first antiphon. The archbishop, or celebrant, sings 'Quem vidistis, pastores? dicite: annuntiate nobis, in terris quis apparuit?' And the shepherds reply 'Natum vidimus et chorus Angelorum collaudantes Dominum, alleluia, alleluia.'[76] At the end of the service they sing a trope to the Benedicamus, 'Verbum patris hodie'.

This account has been long – necessarily so, if we were to understand the nature of the object. The Rouen *Pastorum* is the most extended of the dramatic ceremonies on this theme; but its extent is as nothing compared with the whole magnificent liturgy in which it is embedded. It can, of course, be taken out and regarded as a 'play'; but in reality it is a very small part of a much larger 'drama'. If representation (one thing standing for another) is part of the essence of drama, then the idea of the world as a stage (*theatrum mundi*) must have had a particularly deep meaning for the Middle Ages. In a sacramental universe we are all actors. But the metaphysical considerations apart, 'all the liturgy's a stage'. The 'drama' of Christmas was enacted, a symbolic enactment in time and space not just of a historical event but of an eternal verity – *Verbum caro factum est*. The *Ordo Pastorum* points this event in a specific, moving and jubilant ceremony; but, as I said before, we must not exaggerate its imaginative impact as a thing in itself. Such force as it has is not

[75] This trope for the Gloria is in Rouen MS A233, with its music.
[76] 'Shepherds, whom do you see? Speak. Announce to us – who has appeared on earth?' – 'We saw the newborn [child] and the choirs of angels praising the Lord together, alleluia, alleluia'. A responsory with almost identical text was sung at Matins (Beauvais), sometimes with an extensive trope (Arlt (1975), I.106–7).

self-generated, since it has little to offer of what we normally look for in a play; its force is derived from the larger 'drama' of which it is a small episode. The senses in which it is bound to appear inadequate, if we are looking for the signs of a naturalistic drama, are obvious. There is little impersonation and no illusion. The earliest text of the ceremony speaks of the young men as 'supporting themselves on their staffs *in the likeness of* shepherds' (*in similitudine pastorum*). This might be called an act of *denotation*. They are not pretending to be shepherds; nor are we expected to suspend our knowledge that they are canons of the cathedral. For one thing, none of the versions of the *Ordo* suggests that the 'actors' were dressed up. On the contrary the shepherds wore tunics and amices (*amictus*) and the midwives dalmatics, which were worn only on festive occasions. The fact that the shepherds had prominent duties prescribed for them in the Mass and at Lauds does not indicate a sustained attempt at 'let's pretend'; it is no dramatic essay. The apparent, only apparent, blurring of a 'play' world and a 'real' world (to use the crudest categories) is in fact the clearest refutation of the existence of those categories. Moreover, the principal personages of the little scene – the Blessed Virgin and the Child Jesus – are not even live but artificial figures, hidden for most of the time behind a curtain and (though this is not quite certain) in a part of the church where the congregation, if there was a congregation, could not possibly have seen them.[77]

Finally, what is to be said about the music and its contribution to the dramatic ceremony? With the exception of two metrical pieces, 'Pax in terris' and 'Salve virgo singularis', the melodies are all chant-like. Thanks to the researches of Susan Rankin, it is now possible to state with some certainty that they are not, like many of the *Visitatio Sepulchri* additions, taken from the known repertoire of liturgical chant; they are apparently new-composed in traditional styles.[78] However, there is no question of a unique composition for the Rouen ceremony. As Rankin shows, it has many outside links. The Christmas dialogue-trope 'Quem queritis in presepe' appears with its traditional music except for slight variants which Rouen shares with Fleury (the so-called Fleury Playbook). Moreover, the opening 'Nolite timere' uses the same melody as Fleury. However, whereas Fleury has the melody of the Office antiphon for 'Gloria in excelsis', Rouen puts together a 'new' melody, almost entirely out of the music of 'Nolite timere'. 'Transeamus', finally, is held in common with Fleury. The Rouen text is once called *antiphona* and once *versus*.[79]

---

[77] The fourteenth-century Rouen Ordinal (MS 384) directs that the crib be set up *retro altare* (Young (1933), II.14). At Fleury, however, it was placed 'at one of the doors of the church' (*ad januas monasterii*) (Young, II.89).

[78] Rankin (1981), I.179ff. See also Smoldon (1980), 204–5, who notes the Rouen–Fleury connection and gives parallel melodies from the two ceremonies.

[79] Young (1933), II.13 (*antiphona*); II.17 (*versum*). The text also occurs in the MS fragment Shrewsbury School MS VI, a single 'actor's' partbook. See F. Ll. Harrison in *Non-Cycle Plays and Fragments*, ed. N. Davis, EETS (Oxford 1970), 128; and S. K. Rankin in *PRMA* 102 (1975–6) 129.

The interesting question next arises as to how the new melodies, whether composed for Rouen or for a common tradition centring in the province of Rouen, came into being. It is not easy to frame the question rightly, since the sources of a creative act are necessarily mysterious. However, in the case of the 'Nolite timere' the melodic germs, the mode, certain turns of melody and cadence, seem to be there for the picking up in the Genealogy sung at the end of Matins. 'Nolite timere' does not have the stable recitatory formality of the Genealogy but the falling cadences *g-f-e*, in variously ornamented forms, the tendency to centre the melody in an oscillation between *g* and *a*, and the rising figure *g-a-c'* all seem possible signs of a creative indebtedness.[80]

The two metrical songs stand in marked contrast to the rest of the music for the ceremony. Given the almost invariably syllabic setting of metrical texts and an only lightly melismatic style (never so much as to disturb the basic syllabic movement, unless at the final cadence – 'nun*ciatum* est'), such a song falls naturally into balanced phrases which tend to have tonal implications, at least to a modern ear, out of keeping with chant-melody. The melody of 'Pax in terris', for instance, makes striking use of the 'major triad' on *g*, though its handling of cadences on *d, f, a, c* is often baffling and unexpected. 'Salve, virgo singularis' is equally un-chant-like. The final on *f*, it has been noted, is very rare in the liturgical drama.[81] As with 'Pax in terris', there may be an outside source for this song which waits to be discovered. It could not be argued that these two songs were in themselves dramatic, even in the wide senses that I have allowed to the word; but they are dramatically effective, at least. As in the liturgy itself, so here there is a propriety of music and action. 'Pax in terris' has the function of a *conductus*, a song designed especially to accompany liturgical movement (see ch. 2: 11), and the shepherds sing it processionally. 'Salve, virgo' partakes more of the function of a processional antiphon (though its style is more *conductus*-like) – that is, a piece sung during procession, usually at the altar of a particular saint. Indeed, unlikely as it might at first sight appear, the liturgical drama was often connected with processional rites. One way of viewing, and of understanding, the Rouen *Pastorum* as a whole is, in fact, as a dramatic procession.

Perhaps then, finally, the key to the significance of music in this Ceremony of the Shepherds is liturgical propriety. A procession was an occasion for greater liturgical freedom, and therefore inventiveness, than Mass or Office. But processions were conducted also with high ceremoniousness and decorum. The music is above all decorous – not in the enfeebled drawing-room sense of the word but in the rhetorical. What the music does, in its restraint and impersonality, is to deepen a conception of the shepherds' visit to Christ the child in the manger as an eternal, a timeless, act of homage. There are two other ways of looking at their visit. One is as the historical event which the

---

[80] This does not imply that there was a simple, direct and exclusive connection in this particular
       case. On the prevalence of *e*-mode melodies for the Genealogies, see note 67 above.
[81] Rankin (1981), 1.184.

Bible presents. Needless to say, only a few exceptional men in the Middle Ages were capable of, or interested in, taking a historical view of the past; the realities of a shepherd's life or of tavern conditions in Palestine were not the concern of the clerks of Rouen.[82] The other is the way of the vernacular Mystery cycles. There the shepherds' plays epitomize the contemporaneous, everyday view of Christian truth; their visit and present-giving is an occasion for sentimental fun, and the midwives' curiosity about parthenogenesis is sometimes distinctly prurient. The temptation to humanize the shepherds cannot have been at all strong in the Rouen festival; the nature of the music itself could only confirm the hieratic quality of the event.

[82] The unusual representation of the shepherds in the *Carmina Burana* (Benediktbeuern) Christ-mas play does not turn quite on this historical issue. The dilemma of the shepherds, tellingly presented as rivalry between *angelus* and *diabolus*, is of purely psychological interest.

10

DRAMA II: MUSIC, ACTION AND EMOTION

It would be convenient for my general argument if the whole of the liturgical drama presented a smooth hieratic consistency – formality, restraint, decorum. But it does not. There are several aspects of the tradition which disturb this comfortable notion of impersonality. We may consider three of them: the presentation of angry Herod; the presence of lamenting women, Rachel in particular; and the puzzling, ambiguous nature of certain rubrics which direct the singer how to perform his 'speeches'.

1 Dramatic emotion: 'angry Herod'

Herodes iratus is a feature, to a greater or lesser degree, in all the surviving 'plays' of the Magi. The usual name for the episode, which in the Fleury Playbook follows directly on from the shepherds' ceremony, is *Officium Stelle*, ceremony of the star. Fleury, however, gives to the two ceremonies (Shepherds and Magi) the single significant title *Ordo ad representandum Herodem*. Although the terms *ordo* and *officium* are still used, we encounter in this Fleury *ordo* something that might have been called *ludus* and which without unease can be referred to as a play.[1] Even setting Herod's anger aside, dramatic interest as contrasted with ceremonial necessity is evident, as the following summary will show:[2]

At the end of the shepherds' scene they invite 'the people standing round' (*populum circumstantem*) to adore the child Jesus. Meanwhile the Magi advance, announce the prophetic nature of the star and greet each other. The star goes before them. At the entrance to the choir, they sing 'Dicite nobis, O Ierosolimitani' (O citizens of Jerusalem, tell us where the world's expectation is . . .). Herod sends his *armiger* (knight), who asks them who they are and reports back to the king. The Wise Men are next interrogated by the king's *oratores vel interpretes*, and finally by the king himself. They describe their purpose in following the star – 'rex est causa vie' (a king is the cause of our journey) – and display their gifts. Herod consults his scribes – 'Tell me, is there anything written in the books of the prophets about this boy?' They cite the prophecy of Matthew, ii. 6 (part of the Gospel for Epiphany): 'Bethleem, non es minima in

---

[1] The prominence of 'dramatic interest' is evident in the Freising *Officium Stellae* (eleventh-century; text in Young (1933), II.92–7; music discussed briefly by Smoldon in relation to other versions). It is evident, too, in other texts earlier in date than the Fleury Playbook (Source 22).

[2] Text in Young, II.84–9; exemplary modern performing edn by T. Bailey (Toronto 1965).

principibus Juda . . .' which occurs in all these ceremonies and plays. Herod in a fury (*furore accensus*)[3] hurls the book away; his son Archelaus hears the noise and comes to placate him. Archelaus offers to revenge the affront, and as the Magi go off, following the star, he and his royal father make threatening gestures with their swords (*minentur cum gladiis*).

In the remainder of the play the shepherds appear rejoicing, and the Magi sing a sequence, 'Quem non prevalent', and have a completely decorous encounter with the midwives.[4] They then adore the Child and offer their gold, myrrh and incense. Departing they sing a liturgical antiphon, 'O admirabile commercium . . .', and greet their brothers in choir ('Gaudete fratres . . .'). Then the cantor intones the Te Deum.

There is, unfortunately, no thorough analysis available of the music of the various *Officia Stelle*.[5] But it is clear that as usual there is a mixture of sources and of styles. The opening utterances of the Magi (*Stella fulgore / Que regem regum / Quem venturum*) are set to a common, i.e. shared, melody.[6] I quote the first phrase.

Ex. 153

Stel- - - la ful-go- re ni- mi- o ru-ti-lat

The star glows with exceeding brightness.

It is probably not a liturgical chant; but the opening phrase is the same as that of the first antiphon, 'Rex pacificus', of First Vespers of the Nativity (cf. also First Vespers of the Circumcision, antiphon to the Magnificat).[7] The chant at the end of the play, however, is liturgical, Hartker's antiphon 'O admirabile commercium', still in use today in Second Vespers of the Circumcision.[8]

Young surmises that the Fleury performance occurred at the end of Matins of the Epiphany and sums up his impression of the whole as maintaining 'the

---

[3] Young, II.87, follows MS reading (p. 211) *accessus*; Tintori and Monterosso, 39, emend to *accensus*.
[4] Young, II.446, gives the text from *AH* LIV.9 (no. 4).
[5] See, however, Lipphardt's analysis of the Herod play from Le Mans in *Organicae voces: Festschrift Joseph Smits van Waesberghe* (Amsterdam 1963), 107–22. The music of the Fleury version here transcribed was printed by Coussemaker (1860), 143–56 (unmeasured modern square notation). The edition by Tintori and Monterosso of the whole MS (1958) does not greatly further understanding; the rigidly metrical transcription of the neumes for every style of 'play' and chant is not generally accepted and gives a misleading impression of homogeneity.
[6] Smoldon (1980), 127–8, sets out what he calls the 'core' of the 'Magi-Herod Music-Dramas', printing the melodies of the Rouen Gradual (see chapter 9 note 65 above). My examples (Exx. 153–5) are from the Fleury Playbook, pp. 205–14.
[7] See *LU*, 364, 440.
[8] Hesbert (1963) III.362 (no. 3985); *LU*, 442.

dignified tone which may be considered characteristic of a Church play'.[9] I
believe this may be right, though in such a problematic case much must have
depended on the style of performance and manner of singing, to which we
shall turn later. The presentation of Herod in medieval churches could vary
between the perfectly sedate (his anger was, after all, Biblical not invented)
and the wildly riotous: in thirteenth-century Padua he had licence to hurl his
spear at the choir, read the lesson *cum tanto furore* and dash around 'belabouring
bishop, canon and choristers with an inflated bladder'.[10] There is no
suggestion whatsoever that this kind of topsy-turvydom, similar to that
which prevailed in other allowed revels at Christmastide, was practised by
Herod in the Fleury or Rouen plays. Nevertheless, this leaves questions still
open. What place was there in this and other dramatic ceremonies and plays
for the display of dramatic emotion? And what light can a study of the music
shed on this?

At the angry moment of the play the following exchange takes place
between Herod and his son:[11]

Ex. 154

Son: Hail, noble father. Hail king most excellent, ruling everywhere and holding
royal power. *Herod*: Dearest son, deserving the tribute of praise, manifesting in your

[9] Young (1933), II.92.
[10] Young, II.99–100, quotes the Ordinal in full; see also Chambers, II.56, on this puzzling
two-faced aspect of Christmas celebrations.
[11] Young, II.87; Smoldon (1980), 208, with melody transcribed in triple metre.

very name [Arche-laus] the pomp of royal praise, a king is born, stronger and more powerful than we are; I fear lest he may oust us from our kingly throne.

The first thing to note is that they both sing the same tune even though Herod is in a fury and Archelaus in a pacifying mood; the second, that the simple *conductus*-type melody is very conjunct and in musical terms restrained; and the third, that it is related to other melodies in the play. For example:[12]

Ex. 155

Behold the Wise Men come . . . / By the king's command, we come, o kings, to discover . . .

The dialogue has a regularly metred text (seven syllables to a line). This does not affect the argument that the 'angry Herod' melody has musically no iconographic value. It can be regarded as one of the musical motifs of the play, but it does not constitute a moment of especial 'drama'. Its use in this exchange is more after the 'narrative' music style – A A A¹B. Tonally A is *ouvert*, B *clos*.

II Dramatic emotion: 'mourning Rachel'

I mentioned three features of the drama which seemed to work against any facile generalizations about its musical impersonality. In the case of 'angry Herod' the emotional neutrality of the melodic material has seemed to be confirmed. We turn now to the second feature, the dramatic *planctus* or lament.

An important lamenter in medieval liturgical plays was Rachel. Indeed, in dramatic ceremonies to do with the slaughter of the Holy Innocents her *planctus* was so central that at least in one instance the Innocents' 'play' is called *Ordo Rachelis*.[13] But – and this is of particular interest – the figure of the lamenting Rachel in itself is clearly other than, and perhaps older than, her appearance in drama. The earliest musical occurrence is in the *Liber hymnorum*

---

[12] MS p. 209 ('En Magi'), pp. 208–9 ('Principis').

[13] The Freising 'play' is in Munich, Staatsbibl. MS lat. 6264 (text in Young (1933), II.119); for the *planctus* itself, see Yearley (1981) 194. On *planctus* in general, see chapter 4:III above.

(880) of Notker 'Balbulus', monk of St Gall. There it appears, or rather can be reconstructed, as follows.[14]

Ex. 156

1 Quid tu, vir- go ma- ter, plo- ras, Ra-chel for-mo-sa,

cu- ius vul- tus Ia- cob de- le- ctat?

2a Ceu so- ro- ris an- i- cu- le
2b lip- pi- tu- do e- um iu- vet!

3a Ter- ge, ma- ter, flu-en- tes o- cu- los!
3b Quam te de- cent ge- na- rum ri- mu- le ?

4a 'He-u, he- u, he- u, quid me in- cu- sa- tis fle-tus in- cas-sum
4b Cum sim or- ba- - ta na- to, pau-per- ta- tem me-am qui so- lus

fu- dis- se,
cu- ra- ret ?

5a Qui non ho-sti- bus ce- de- ret an-gu- stos ter- mi- nos quos mi- hi
5b qui-que sto- li- dis fra-tri-bus, quos mul-tos proh do- lor ex- tu- li,

Ia-cob ad- qui -si- vit
es- set pro- fu- tu- rus.'

6 Numquid flen-dus est is- te, qui re-gnum pos-se- dit ce- le- ste;

[14] For Notker and the early sequence, see chapter 3:1 above. Mus. ex., see Crocker (1977), 132; and the discussion in his ch. 7. Yearley (L134) lists some thirty-five MS sources, most of them with unheighted neumes, for 'Quid tu virgo mater ploras' and comments that 'the full number of liturgical sources . . . is not yet determined'. In strophe 5a I follow Norberg (1968), 176–8.

7 qui-que pre-ce fre-quen-ti mi- se- ris fra-tri-bus a- pud de-um

au-xi- li- a- tur?

(1) Why are you weeping, virgin mother, comely Rachel, you whose countenance gives joy to Jacob? (2) As if the red eyes of your older sister could please him! (3) Mother, wipe your flowing eyes. Do streams of tears down your cheeks become you? (4) [RACHEL]: 'Alas, alas, why do you find fault with me for pouring vain tears, when I am deprived of my son, who alone would care for me in my poverty? (5) He would not yield to the enemy the narrow bounds which Jacob acquired for me; he would have been a help to his foolish brothers, whom being many, alas, I have brought to birth.' (6) Is he, then, to be lamented who has gained the heavenly kingdom, (7) and who helps his poor brothers with continuous prayer before God?

It should not surprise us that the *planctus* is in the form of a free sequence, since there are well-established relations (already sketched in chapter 4) between sequence, *planctus* and *lai*. More interestingly, this melody and these words were not originally conceived for each other. The melody, as observed earlier, is that of an earlier sequence by Notker, 'Hec est sancta solemnitas' (ch. 3, Ex. 35). Notker gives his new topic, the sorrows of Rachel, 'a verbal shape that corresponded exactly in numbers of lines and syllables to [the sequence] already existing'; he is writing a precise *contrafactum*.

The writing of *contrafacta* – a very popular procedure indeed throughout Middle Ages – itself weighs against the likelihood that men normally looked for a 'conceptual' or 'referential' connection between words and music. Richard Crocker, however, thinks or assumes otherwise and describes with a persuasive amount of detail the way Notker's mind may have worked as he devised his new 'prose' to the melody he had originally used to celebrate Easter and Christ's Harrowing of Hell (*qui devicit imperium malipotens diaboli*). Notker shows, it is argued, a 'heightened response . . . to the expressive shape latent in the melody'. For instance,[15]

It seems easy to relate the clear emotional inflections of these lines [2 and 3] to the melody – the gently scolding tone of 2a, b, to the brief, pert musical quality; the gesture of comfort expressed in 3a, b, in which the interlocutor can be seen bending over the weeping Rachel, then goes perfectly with the gracious downward curve in the melody.

The truth or falsity of this account cannot, of course, be established by particular comment on this song. I can only say that Crocker is here begging

---

[15] Crocker (1977), 131, 133. What Notker seems most interested in aesthetically is fitting *words* to *words* (i.e. two syllables to two syllables, four to four, etc.); cf. chapter 3:1 above, where patterning is discussed in more detail.

the question which it is a central purpose of the present book to examine. To me, the survival of the same melody with three different sets of words (the West-Frankish 'Hec est sancta sollemnitas' celebrates the martyr St Stephen) is strong presumptive evidence that the virtues of the melody are purely musical. The 'gracious downward curve' of the third section, for example, seems on the 'expressive' argument strangely ill-sorted to Christ's 'snatching' us (*eruens*) out of the Devil's power in the earlier prose.

The next lament of Rachel to be considered is found in the well-known Limoges manuscript (Source 35) which contains the *Ordo Prophetarum*, discussed earlier, and the play of the *Sponsus*.[16] The ceremony is very short: it consists of a liturgical responsory (Matins of Holy Innocents) 'Sub altare Dei audivi voces' (Beneath God's altar I heard the voices of the slain saying: Why do you not defend our blood? . . .); the *Lamentatio Rachelis*, so headed; and the angel's reply, 'Noli, Rachel, deflere pignora' (he tells her not to grieve but rather to rejoice at the happier life the slain children now have). The lament, in nine lines of twelve syllables, is sung throughout to the same melody.[17]

Ex. 157

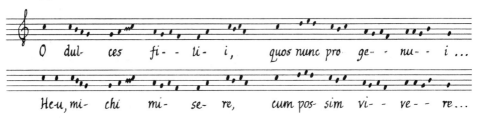

O sweet sons whom but now I brought forth . . . Alas, miserable as I am, that I can go on living . . .

Musically, the conception is totally different from that of the *planctus* as Notker conceived it. The continuous repetition of the same melody belongs to the *laisse* type of narrative music. On the other hand, the comparatively melismatic treatment seems somewhat untypical (only two syllables have a single note each); moreover, there is no sign of a variant melody (*ouvert* instead of *clos*), nor of the expected end-of-*laisse* cadential phrase.[18] It is a totally static invention (or borrowing) to which it would be hard to point a parallel.

The *Ordo Rachelis* from the Fleury Playbook is a very different affair. Here

---

[16] Yearley (1981), L95 (*unicum*); Latin text, Young (1933), II.109. For the complete musical text including 'Sub altare Dei', see Yearley (1983), III, transcription 48 (p. 131). In Sarum Use the responsory (Hesbert (1963), 7713) is sung at Vespers, Matins of Holy Innocents (*Sarum Antiphonal*, p. 68). For the MS (Source 35) and its problems, see chapter 9 notes 42 and 49.

[17] Fol. 32v. Smoldon (1980), 136–7, has 'no doubt . . . that the melodies were performed rhythmically' (i.e. in my terms 'metrically'), and he transcribes various excerpts to demonstrate agreement of musical and verbal accents.

[18] The third item of the ceremony, the Angel's consolation to Rachel, is almost equally static, consisting of a 'narrative' melody in syllabic style, sung seven times with an intermediate and final refrain, 'Ergo gaude' (Therefore, rejoice), which is more florid.

the *planctus* in an extended threefold form is embedded in a dramatic ceremony of scope and power.[19] It must be briefly summarized. It opens with the Innocents (the choristers of the choir) processing through the church singing 'O quam gloriosum est regnum' (liturgical antiphon). Then 'a Lamb, suddenly appearing, bearing a cross, shall go before them . . . and they following shall sing "Emitte agnum, Domine" ' (liturgical antiphon). This process continues during the Angel's warning to Joseph, Herod's attempted suicide and his command for the slaying of the children. As the slayers approach, the Innocents salute the Lamb once more, 'Salve, Agnus Dei'. The distraught mothers are allowed a prayer of five words for mercy. Immediately an angel appears and exhorts the murdered children to rise and cry out. Dead on the ground, they sing a sentence from the Matins responsory of the Limoges manuscript quoted earlier, 'Quare non defendis sanguinem nostrum, Deus noster?' They continue to lie prostrate during Rachel's long lament but rise to their feet when the Angel sings the antiphon 'Sinite parvulos' (Christ's words 'Suffer the little children . . .'). They then process to the choir, praising Christ in the words of the sequence 'Festa Christi'. Archelaus succeeds Herod as king (in dumbshow); the angel summons the Holy Family back to Galilee; Joseph sings 'Gaude, gaude' (liturgical antiphon), and the play ends with the Te Deum.[20]

This brief summary cannot do justice to the skill with which the deviser has blended three planes of reality: a traditional story (almost entirely Scriptural), a liturgical celebration (for the Feast of the Holy Innocents), and a *planctus* of typological significance (Rachel is the Old Testament type of the mourning mother, from Jeremiah xxxi. 15). But it demonstrates the essentially non-realistic character of the play. The slaughtered children are not only little Jewish two-year-olds but also the Innocents of Revelation xiv. 1ff, the 144,000 virgins who follow the Lamb singing 'a new song' in the Heavenly City. When they are swiftly and decorously slaughtered, they are not so dead that they cannot continue to sing.

The Fleury *Ordo Rachelis* is evidently unusual for a play of its length in having so many items taken direct out of the liturgy. Like the main text (i.e. what remains when Rachel's *planctus* is removed) its music also is 'a mosaic of passages from service-books':[21] at least seven separate liturgical chants are

<hr/>

[19] This account of the *Ordo Rachelis* is based on my article 'Medieval Drama' in *New Grove*, section 11.7(iv). The Latin text is in Young (1933), II.110–13; musical transcription, Coussemaker (1860), 166–72; long extract in *New Grove* article, with facsimile. Smoldon (1980), 214ff, discusses the play at some length in his theatrical terms and gives musical excerpts in a modern metrical transcription.

[20] The following liturgical items can be traced (Hesbert (1963) nos. in brackets):

'O quam gloriosum' (4063)	Antiphon of Vespers for Vigil of All Saints; or Holy Innocents
'Emitte agnum' (2642)	Antiphon of Lauds in Advent
'Super solium' (5064)	Antiphon of Lauds, second Sunday before Christmas
'Egipte, nole flere'	Responsory of Matins, third Sunday before Christmas (Young)
'Sinite parvulos' (4966)	Antiphon of Lauds for Innocents Day
'Anxiatus est' (1442)	Antiphon of Lauds for Good Friday
'Gaude, gaude' (?2924/5)	? Antiphon for Assumption

[21] Young (1933), II.116, referring to text alone.

borrowed, from half a dozen different Offices. Set in the midst of this and occupying a very substantial part of dramatic time is the *planctus*. It is threefold; and like the *planctus* from Limoges it is a dialogue.[22]

Ex. 158

1. RACHEL

He-u, te- ne- ri par- tus la- ce- ros quos cer- ni- mus ar- tus!

he-u, dul- ces na- ti so- la ra- bi- e ju- gu- la- ti!

he-u, quem nec pi- e- tas nec ves- tra co- er- cu- it e- tas!

he-u, ma- tres mi-se- re que co- gi- mur is- ta vi- de- re!

he-u, quid nunc a- gi- mus, cur non hec fa- cta sub- i- mus?

he-u, qui- a me-ro- res nos- tros-que le- va- re do- lo- res

gau-di- a non pos-sunt, nam dul- ci- a pi- gno- ra de-sunt.

2. CONSOLATRICES

No- li, vir- go Ra- chel, no- li, dul- cis- si- ma ma- ter,

pro ne- ce par-vo- rum fle- tus re- ti- ne- re do- lo- rum.

Si que tris- ta- ris, ex- ul- ta que la- cri- ma- ris,

---

[22] In 'Medieval Drama' (*New Grove*) I refer to Rachel's *planctus* as fourfold; but on reflection I think it better not to include the liturgical antiphon 'Anxiatus' within the lament structure.

nam-que tu- i na- ti   vi- vunt su- per as- tra be- a- ti.

3. RACHEL

He- u, he- u, he- u!

quo- mo- do gau- de- bo   dum mor-tu- a mem-bra vi- de- bo;

dum sic com-mo- ta   fu- e- ro per vis-ce- ra to- ta?

Me fa- ci- ent ve- re   pu- e- ri si- ne fi- ne do- le- re.

O_____ do- lor, O_____ pa- trum

mu- ta- ta- que gau- di- a ma- trum

ad lu- gu- bres lu- ctus;   la- cri- ma- rum fun-di- te fle- tus,

Iu- de- e flo- rem,   pa- tri- e la- cri- man-do do- lo- rem.

4. CONSOLATRICES

Quid tu, vir- go ma- ter Ra- chel, plo- ras for-mo-sa,

cu- ius vul- tus Ia- cob de- le- ctat? Ce- u so- ro- ris an- i- cu- le

lip- pi- tu- do e- um___ iu- vet.

Ter- ge, ma- ter, flen- tes o- cu- los.

Quam te de- cent ge- na- rum ri- vu- li?

5. RACHEL

He- u, he- u, he- u!

quid me in- cu- sas- tis fle- tus in- cas- sum fu- dis- se,

cum sim or- ba- ta na- to, pau-per- ta- tem me- am [qui solus] cu- ra- ret

qui non hos- ti- bus ce- de- ret an- gus- tos ter- mi- nos

quos mi-chi Ia- cob ad- qui- si- vit,

qui-que sto-li- dis fra-tri-bus, quos mul-tos pro do- lor

ex-tu- li, es- set pro-fu- tu- rus.

6. CONSOLATRICES

Num-quid flen-dus est is- te, qui re- gnum pos-si- det ce- les- te,

qui-que pre-ce fre- quen-ti mi- se- ris fra- tri- bus

a- pud de- um au- xi- li- e- tur?

Rachel: Alas, for the tender young whose limbs we see torn! Alas, for the sweet children, their throats cut in a single act of fury! Alas, for him (the murderer) whom neither mercy nor your age could restrain! Alas, pitiable mothers – we who are forced to witness such deeds! Alas, what are we now to do when we cannot submit to these things! Alas, joys cannot alleviate our griefs and sorrows, for our sweet children are no more.

Consolers: Maiden Rachel, sweetest mother, do not hold back your tears of grief for the slaughter of your little ones. If you are sad, rejoice that you weep, for your children live blessed above the stars.

Rachel: Alas, how shall I rejoice, when I see their dead limbs, for I shall be so convulsed throughout my whole being? Indeed, my children will cause me to mourn without end. O grief! O joys of fathers and mothers turned now into mourning laments; pour down floods of tears, weeping for the flower of the Jewish nation, for the grief of our land.[23]

[The remainder of this passage is translated following Ex. 156]

Rachel then sings her concluding antiphon, and her consolers, who are never identified, lead her away.

Although it is in dialogue, there is no musical connection between this Fleury item and the Limoges ceremony, which it will be recalled uses only one melody for Rachel's lament. This scene is altogether more interesting. I use the anachronistic word 'scene' deliberately – even though 'episode' might be safer – because it looks as if the *planctus*-dialogue could well have been a separate tableau round which a more extended ceremony has been constructed. There appear to be virtually no musical links between it and the 'liturgical' part.[24] The liturgical scene is complete in itself. The most striking and curious thing about it is the fact of its incorporating the Notker prose 'Quid tu, virgo', discussed above. This divides it in point of literary style (the earlier part is in quantitative hexameters) and to some extent musically as well. Before pursuing this, however, I should emphasize one feature which is crucial to the present argument: the musical unity of the whole, and the closer musical unity of the separate parts (items 1–3 and 4–6), over-rides and disregards the 'dramatic' distinction between Rachel and her comforters. To put it another way, the composer–compiler has not taken a *planctus*, with music appropriate to lamenting, and set against it a different sort of music appropriate to consolation. So whatever the reason for the slight stylistic break at the halfway point, it has nothing to do with dramatic propriety.

The musical unity of part one, containing two laments and one consolation, is established and maintained by the constant repetition of short motifs. The first lament is a sort of miniature sequence with three pairs of lines and a single. They are firmly held together (and bound in with the second lament and with the consolation between them) in particular by two cadence figures.

Ex. 159

cer- ni- mus   ar- tus   fa- cta sub- i- mus

---

[23] M S pp. 217–19; previously printed, Coussemaker (1860), 166–77; 'Medieval Drama' (*New Grove*), Ex. 13 (p. 34).

[24] An exception is the mothers' brief prayer to the slaughterers 'Oremus, tenere . . .' which uses material from the *planctus* to come (e.g. 'parcite vite' rhymes musically with 'cernimus artus').

Only one line out of seventeen deviates more than minimally: it is line 4 of the second lament. The highly melismatic 'O's are rounded off with what can be judged to be an ornamental version of motif *x*. Other motivic correspondences are clearly evident in analysis. But it is especially to be noted how much of the consolers' music (in fact, virtually all) is related to that of the laments. The patterned style of melody is familiar from sequence and *lai*; it is both formal (the double versicles of 'Heu, teneri partus' are still visible in 'Noli, virgo', though disguised in ornament) and informal (the favourite motif *x* is not restricted to the cadence position, for example).

After Rachel's second lament the music changes. The second consolation (section 4, 'Quid tu virgo') has a new pair of motifs.

Ex. 160

The first is an initial motif; the second, a cadence-figure (slightly varied each time). The form of the section is again sequence-like but very free as to number of syllables. There is no apparent musical recall of the Notker sequence melody (Ex. 156), and evident ignorance or neglect of its verbal–musical structure. The Fleury arranger has imposed his own musical shape on the 'prose', and it is quite unambiguous. Another interesting change at this point is in tonality. The first three sections stick determinedly to a *g*-tonality (even the first-half lines cadence regularly on *g*). 'Quid tu, virgo' is just as firmly centred on *e*, though interestingly it avoids characteristic Phrygian effects.

The third lament re-establishes contact with the first part of the episode: it opens with a reminiscence of the falling thirds at the beginning of the second (*d'-b-c'-a*) and is back in the *g*-tonality. New features are the use of the *g*-triad (lines 1–3) and a cadence figure falling in varied figures from *c'* to *g*. The third consolation returns to the *e*-tonality of consolation 2 but is less obviously patterned (each of the four *e*-closes is different). Although, like every other item, it has phrases recalling the opening of the very first lament (*g→c'→g*) –

Ex. 161

its main function, for which it could conceivably have been especially
composed, seems to be to lead into the moving little *e*-mode antiphon 'Anxiatus est'. The underlying structure of the third consolation may be AA¹A²B,
i.e. a short narrative form.

   The purpose of embarking on a discussion of these three *planctus* of Rachel
was to test again the principal thesis of this chapter, that there is 'no overt and
obvious connection' between the musical material of the ceremonies and plays
and the human actions or emotions implied in their 'drama'. In my view the
thesis still stands, in so much as the melodies of the Fleury lament-*and*-
consolation dialogue are clearly all of a piece. I have tried to show that the
dialogue displays clearly defined musical characteristics which are neither
determined nor developed according to the needs of Rachel's situation or the
anguished sentiments she utters. The underlying musical procedures are those
of narrative music, free sequence and *lai* which I summarized in concluding
the brief analysis of the *Ordo Prophetarum* (p. 329 above). There is, however,
one obvious feature of the lament which requires comment before we leave it
– the settings of the words 'Heu' and 'O'. Those in the first lament are purely
neutral, but the descending thirds at the opening of 'Heu, heu, heu, quomodo
gaudebo' are clearly not. More striking still are the repeated melismas of 'O
dolor, o patrum' in line 5.

Ex. 162

Such effects must be calculated (the three 'Heu's, incidentally, are extra-
metrical). Musically they are ornamental rather than structural; but they are, it
must be conceded, expressive ornaments. In chapter 8: vIII (and note 82)
when considering Gregorian chant I discussed a category of words 'directly
expressive of human feeling or emotion', such as 'Alleluia'. Here as there it is
true to say that in their musical treatment 'one's sense of the actuality of
human emotion is at its strongest and most vivid'. Because the word-sounds
themselves are 'not mere signs but symptoms of feeling', the musical sounds
which amplify and stylize the verbal ones have the same effect. The provision
of expressive ornaments is not so lavish, I believe, even in a highly emotional
scene such as this, as to require us to modify the basic argument, which in sum
is that the music of medieval drama, when not wholly subject to laws of
liturgical ceremony, is a sort of extended song, a lyrical narrative shared
between different voices.

III Dramatic singing: the evidence of the rubrics

On the evidence of the dramatic ceremonies and plays so far considered, there is in general no overt and obvious connection between their musical material and the human actions or emotions implied in their 'drama'. If dramatic emotion was displayed it must, therefore, have come direct from the singers' real or pretended feelings; it must have been imported, as it were, into the medium. The process is perfectly familiar in everyday speech; the words 'Yes' or 'I don't know' can be said in countless different ways with countless different meanings. The meanings are in tone, timbre and intonation, and other factors. The next task is to consider the evidence provided by the texts of ceremonies and plays – the evidence of *rubrics* – on this point. Not all the texts include rubrics, by any means. It depends on the purpose for which they were compiled; an Ordinal will be better provided with them than a Gradual, for example. And naturally the absence of an 'emotional' rubric can never on its own be taken to mean that a neutral, formal, impersonal style of singing was positively required. I have taken my examples almost entirely from Karl Young's great corpus, with the more confidence because his primary interest was in this problem of dramatic presentation, in effects of illusion and in realistic techniques. When he had a choice of texts, he printed precisely those which were richest in indications of mise-en-scène, of costuming, 'propertics', gestures, movement and style.

Some caution is necessary, particularly because of the huge spans of space and time involved: Young's texts are taken from sources ranging widely over Europe from the tenth to the sixteenth centuries, a period longer than that which separates us from Shakespeare. During the course of that time profound changes came over Western spirituality. To set the epic, heroic Christianity of Anglo-Saxon religious poems or of such fine early hymns as 'Pange, lingua, gloriosi' against the emotional warmth of St Bernard's sermons on the Song of Songs is to see the strength of one crucial change. Another, the excessive emotionalism of much late medieval devotion, may further have coloured the presentation of liturgical plays in the century before the Reformation. And geographically the number of 'emotional' rubrics from the German area is bound to strike the reader. The question is enormously complex and deserves full investigation.[25]

Perhaps the principal difficulty is in the semantic interpretation of the texts themselves. In practically every case the rubrics are in Latin, and many of the crucial terms are ambiguous. To take the simplest case – the word *humilis*. A thirteenth-century *Visitatio Sepulchri* from Rheinau contains the direction: '. . . three women, representing [*figurantes*] those who first went to the

---

[25] Anke Roeder's study of gesture, *Die Gebärde im Drama des Mittelalters: Osterfeiern, Osterspiele* (Munich 1974) includes an interesting discussion of 'music as a means of representing sorrow and joy', with rubrics taken, as mine are, from Young (1933). A wealth of secondary literature is referred to but fewer analytical distinctions are made than my argument requires.

Sepulchre, sing in turn their respective verses *humili voce*.[26] In a *low* voice? In a *quiet* voice? In a *humble* voice? It is hard to say. A direction as to pitch or loudness makes no emotional statement; a direction to sing in a *humble* voice is an emotional requirement and suggests that in some way the melody will reflect, or its performance could reflect, the necessary emotional pretence of the singer. In this particular instance, the three verses are those of a well-known *planctus* which frequently occurs in the plays – 'Heu! nobis internas mentes quanti pulsant gemitus' (Alas, the weight of the sighs which make our minds throb within us). It is a characteristically emotional text. However, the fact that all the other directions in this Resurrection play are neutral and non-committal (*cantare, affari, respondere, repetere, interrogare, dicere* etc.), inclines me to believe that *humilis* here has the basic physical meaning of *low*. Between *low* and *soft* the Middle Ages did not always clearly distinguish, as the history of the French terms *haut* and *bas* shows.

It is possible to distinguish among the directions for performance certain broad categories. The physical categories comprise directions as to speed (tempo), loudness, pitch, and texture (or timbre) of voice. The 'emotional' categories comprise directions appropriate to the general liturgical season, to the particular significance of the text about to be sung, and to the supposed feelings of the singer taking that particular role. Let us begin with the physical categories.

Speed. Few directions are found. Practically all specifically refer to the liturgical context of a play or dramatic ceremony. Thus after the dramatic presentation of a *planctus* in dialogue at Regensburg (fifteenth-century) during the Adoration of the Cross on Good Friday the priest, with or without his assistants, is twice required to sing *lenta voce* (in a slow voice).[27] And before a Pentecostal ceremony at Halle (sixteenth-century), in which the figure of a dove, 'surrounded by a circle of lighted candles' was lowered from the vaulting, the office of None was sung *tarde et solenniter* (slowly and ceremoniously); the slowness is a traditional way of marking the solemnity of a liturgical occasion.[28] On the other hand, in a *Visitatio Sepulchri* from Bamberg, again very late (sixteenth-century), the angels of the Sepulchre, inviting the Marys to inspect the empty tomb, were to sing *alacri voce* (in a quick? brisk? eager? lively? manner).[29] This suggests dramatic rather than merely liturgical fitness. *Alacer* is one of several words of which it is

---

[26] Young (1933), 1.385: Lectionary, Benedictine Abbey of Rheinau. In this and in the subsequent notes I have checked matters of provenance, date, MS function and types of dramatic ceremony from the 'Handschriftenverzeichnis' in Lipphardt (1975), VI, noting any disagreements that occur. Lipphardt does not print any texts but those for the Easter season, but his list of MSS is often useful beyond this.

[27] Young, 1.505–6: Breviary (Lipphardt (1975), VI.343), Regensburg Cathedral. The directions as to speed belong to the liturgical close of the ceremony, not to the *planctus* itself.

[28] Young, 1.490–1: Breviary (Lipphardt, VI.218), collegiate church at Halle. On this solemn occasion of late date (1532) the *tubicines et fistulatores civitatis* took part.

[29] Young, 1.324: *Agenda Bambergensia* (Ingolstadt 1587).

sometimes impossible to say whether they describe the desired musical effect objectively in physical terms, or subjectively through the feelings of the performer.

Loudness and pitch. A far larger number of rubrics – the largest single category, certainly – employ terms such as *altus, mediocris, modicus, humilis, excelsus, elatus, remissus, submissus, suppressus,* to indicate singing styles. Again, the terms are in their root meanings physical and normally bear this interpretation. The occasions on which the 'Quem queritis' dialogue opens with the priest singing *alta voce* are too numerous to mention individually. The point is simply that something new and important is about to happen. It must be signalized. Provided the priest's question was boldly put, I do not suppose it mattered whether it was actually sung at a high pitch or not.[30] Rather more rarely the adjective *excelsus* is used in the same position – *Angeli excelsa voce cantent versum* 'Quem queritis' (Clermont-Ferrand, fourteenth-century).[31] In this instance the Marys reply *humili voce.* The fact that the second phrase lies at the same pitch as the first would seem to make nonsense of a pitch interpretation of *excelsa* and *humili.* But it could be relevant, since the Angels are sung by two choirboys in the higher octave, the Marys by three men (*presbyteri*, priests) an octave lower. One suspects, however, that the terms have some emotional overtones at least.

There are some contexts in which words like *altus* come in groups of three. In these instances they seem certainly to indicate pitch. At the church of St Martin in Tours (date uncertain) the 'Quem queritis' was followed by a thrice-repeated exchange between two boys, one singing 'Accendite', the other 'Psallite fratres', *exaltando vocem* (raising the pitch of his voice?).[32] And at an *Elevatio Crucis* ceremony from Bamberg (in a late source – 1587) we find that priest and choir together announce the Resurrection in a shared antiphon 'Surrexit dominus de sepulcro' – *tribus vicibus*, three times, each time at a higher pitch (*voce semper altius elevata*).[33] A mid-point – of pitch, intensity or whatever it may be – is normally indicated, if at all, by *mediocris* or similar term. A 'Quem queritis' at Trier (1389) was sung *mediocriter*, to be followed by

---

[30] What does matter is the pitch of the 'final', which in the case of the 'Quem queritis' is often *g*, and its relation to the other items which form the context of the dialogue (I thank Susan Rankin for comment on this point). The pitch actually chosen for performance would, of course, be related to practical concerns, relative not absolute. In a twelfth-century *Visitatio* from the abbey of Remiremont (Young (1933), I.248) the first of three Resurrection antiphons is to be sung 'secretly' (*clam*), the second (it appears) similarly, the third 'openly and in a high/loud voice' (*manifeste et alta voce*); this seems to indicate a climactic intention.

[31] Young, I.244: Breviary, Clermont Cathedral (Lipphardt (1975), VI.376, dated to the second half of the fifteenth century). It is sung by two boys, *ornati sicut angeli.*

[32] Young, I.224 (from a MS presumed lost). An Ordinal from the collegiate church of canons and canonesses at Essen (fourteenth-century) is even clearer – the cry 'Christus dominus surrexit' was sung by an Apostle: first, *in gravibus*; then, *altius*; then *bene alte* (Young, I.333–5).

[33] *Ibid.*, I.172–5: *Agenda Bambergensia* (Ingolstadt 1587); connected with the Mass of the Presanctified, but other details not known.

the display by the celebrants of the *sudarium* (the empty shroud) and their singing *alta voce* 'Surrexit dominus'.[34]

Unless the context makes it clear, none of these terms I have mentioned as referring to pitch or loudness in an objective physical way is free from ambiguity. The use of *alta voce* with important new movements or announcements (sometimes preceded or followed by an Alleluia or two) meant inevitably that the word took on an emotional colouring; similarly with the words at the other extreme, *humilis* etc. It may be, in fact, a desire to state, and not merely imply, these emotional colourings that leads to the use of so strong a phrase as *multum suppressa voce* (in a very subdued voice) for the utterance of the three Marys as they approach the tomb, '[O Deus]! Quis revolvet nobis ab hostio lapidem . . .?'[35] (traditional introductory antiphon).

Timbre or texture. Another important but small group of words is more easily defined, though finer shades of meaning are bound to elude us. They describe the type of singing required in physical terms – *sonorus, clamosus, clarus, suavis, dulcisonus, blandus, apertus* – and they have to be carefully distinguished from the 'emotional' words, such as *lacrimabilis* (tearful), which describe not the sound directly but the state of mind that should produce it. There are of course borderline cases. In the *Carmina Burana* Christmas play (thirteenth century)[36] Augustine has to answer in a voice *sobria et discreta*; the term *discretus* is presumably physical and means 'clear, clearly articulated', whilst *sobrius* indicates restraint in either a physical or an 'emotional' sense (though at this point such a distinction is not perhaps very meaningful). Such indications are rare in the liturgy itself; but, for example, the Sarum Ordinal requires that at Matins on Maundy Thursday a boy (*unus puerulus*) shall sing 'Mortem autem crucis' *sincera voce* (with a pure-sounding voice – a physical term).[37]

In a *Visitatio* from the monastery of St Lambrecht (twelfth century or later), a clear (ringing?) voice (*clara voce*) is to be used by one of the three Marys to answer the question 'Tell us, Mary, what did you see on the way?' – 'I saw the tomb of the risen Christ and the glory of his resurrection [*gloriam resurgentis*]'.[38] A sonorous voice (*sonora voce*) is used by the three Marys when they lift the cross on high and sing the antiphon *Surrexit Dominus de sepulchro*. Such directions, I think, extend the use which underlies the introduction of words indicating pitch and loudness. That is to say, they draw attention to the

---

[34] Young, 1.252: Ordinal, monastery of St Maximin (Lipphardt (1975), VI.446, revising Young's date).

[35] Young, 1.266: Gradual and Sequentiary, monastery of Zwiefalten, mid-twelfth-century (Lipphardt, VI.433).

[36] Young, II.177: the weight of scholarly opinion seems to favour a date in the first half or third of the thirteenth century (Lipphardt, VI.332).

[37] Frere, *Use of Sarum* (1898), II.67.

[38] Young, 1.363: *Directorium*, Benedictine (Lipphardt, VI.281, dating *c.* 1200). By contrast a *remissa vox* is to be used for the Marys' first question, 'Quis revolvet nobis ab hostio lapidem . . .?'

most important utterances, they magnify them in such a way that their significance cannot be missed. In a dramatic form so little dependent on realism and character-portrayal, it would be quite wrong to assume without question that such stylistic directions refer to supposed interior experience.

The particular necessity for other words in this group is less easy to determine. Why, for instance, should the *Regularis Concordia* (965–75), containing the famous early detailed description of the *Visitatio Sepulchri*, specifically require that the Angel's question 'Quem queritis' should be sung *dulcisone* (with a sweet sound)?[39] Similarly, in the 'Quem queritis' dialogue as performed at Compostela five hundred years later, why is it twice stated that the singing should be rendered *blande* (pleasingly? smoothly?)?[40]

So much for the physical categories of speed, pitch, loudness and timbre; turning now to the other main group of terms which may help to answer the problem of 'expressiveness', the question is in what sense the devisers or arrangers of medieval liturgical plays thought of their music as denoting, embodying, representing, or expressing feeling. I shall call the terms generically 'emotional', since they all concern the emotions in some way, and I hope this will not prejudge the question I am trying to answer.

In the simpler dialogues and dramatic ceremonies (they are not necessarily the earliest) the singers are scarcely actors in any real sense; the male clerics do not pretend to be wailing women on the way to the sepulchre. While in some sense *representing* them they do not *impersonate* them. In some, not necessarily the most elaborate, ceremonies and plays it appears as if a kind of dramatic illusion is aimed at. Phrases like *ad similitudinem querentium, ad imitationem angeli, in persona mulierum*, occur, and often *vice mulierum, vice angeli*.[41] The apparent implication 'Let's pretend' is applied occasionally to singing directions. So we have, for instance, in the Dublin *Visitatio* (fourteenth-century) the instruction to the 'first Mary' *quasi lamentando dicat* (the other two Marys are to imitate 'her'); later, all three rejoice in the empty sepulchre, *alta voce quasi gaudentes et admirantes et parum a sepulchro recedentes* ('in a high/loud voice, as if rejoicing and marvelling and withdrawing a little from the sepulchre').[42] In the Fleury play of Emmaus (*Peregrinus*) the unrecognized wayfarer, Christ, 'shall begin to sing' *gravi voce, quasi eos increpando* (in a low? solemn? earnest? voice, as if reproaching them) 'O foolish and slow of heart to believe . . .'[43] In

---

[39] Young, I.249. Perhaps in this and the following example there is a consciousness of sexual differentiation between roles?

[40] Donovan, 54. Donovan comments that 'the text possesses all the simple charm' of St Ethelwold's version (*Regularis Concordia*) written five hundred years earlier; 'in many churches the liturgical plays remained the same for centuries'. This naturally does not mean that the ceremonies were necessarily sung in the same style.

[41] See Young (1933), I.249 (twice), 325, 241, and 364 (with 241) for details. One could, of course, interpret even these phrases as merely supporting a 'representational' theory.

[42] Young, I.347: Processional, Church of St John the Evangelist. Facsimile of *Visitatio* in Chambers, II, frontispiece.

[43] Young, I.471.

the Fleury *Visitatio* Mary Magdalene 'goes quickly' to Peter and John: 'and standing before them, as if sad, let her say, "They have taken away my Lord" . . .' (*stansque ante eos quasi tristis dicat*: . . .).[44]

On the face of it these directions call for an *emotional modification* of the actor's, performer's, voice. He is to express lamentation or rejoicing as the case may be. It may seem, therefore, somewhat perverse to question it. But there is, I believe, ground for being sceptical about a thoroughgoing naturalistic interpretation even of these more explicit rubrics. The ground is the general style of 'acting', in so far as it is known.

A remarkable document of the fourteenth century throws some light on this question of physical presentation and gesture. It is a *Planctus Marie* which was sung in the Cathedral of Cividale del Friuli on Good Friday.[45]

Ex. 163

---

[44] *Ibid.*, I.394.

[45] *Ibid.*, I.506–12, and with facsimile of opening page as pl. xii (Cividale, Reale Museo Archeologico MS CI, fol. 74). The *planctus* is ed. Coussemaker (1860), 285–91; Yearley (1983), III.144 (no. 50), without the rubrics (for which see II.348; performing edn W. L. Smoldon, *Planctus Mariae* (Oxford 1965). See also Lipphardt (1975), VI.248: the MS is a Processional apparently from the Benedictine Monasterio Maggiore of Cividale, *c.* 1400.

MAGDALENE: O brothers (*Here let her turn to the men with arms extended*) and sisters
(*Here to the women*), where is my hope, where is my consolation (*Here let her strike her
breast*)? where is absolute salvation (*Here let her raise her hands*), O my Master (*Here let
her bow her head and prostrate herself at Christ's feet*)? MARY SALOME: O grief (*Here let her
strike her hands together*), O grief! For why, my dear son (*Here let her point to Christ with
open hands*), do you hang here when you are life itself abiding throughout all ages (*Here
let her strike her breast*)? JOHN: Heavenly King, on behalf of sinners (*Here with hands
stretched out let him point to Christ*) you make expiation which belongs to others (*Here let
him indicate the people throwing himself forward*), you a lamb without spot. MARY [the
mother of James]: Pure flesh, dear to the world (*Here let her point to the cross with open
hands*), why do you thirst on the altar of the cross, a sacrificial victim for sins (*Here let
her strike her breast*)? JOHN: Let mothers' inward parts weep (*Here let him turn to Mary
pointing to her tears*) for the wounds of Mary.

The problem with this text is to know what acting style is implied. Young
assumes that it is 'realistic'; but the sentence in which he does so is revealing –
'The care with which the rhetoric is here supported by realistic stage-
movements could hardly be exceeded.'[46] *Rhetoric* is indeed the keyword – this
elaborate, formal system for teaching the craft of speech (based on the ancient
art of oratory) produced the witty sound-and-meaning play of these lines

⁴⁶ Young (1933), I.512.

> Cur in ara crucis ares,
> caro que peccato cares,
> caro culpe nescia?   (115–17)

Why do you thirst on the altar of the cross, you whose flesh knows no sin, whose flesh is ignorant of guilt?

Surely, to go with this, gestures of an equally formal, equally oratorical kind are required? The branch of rhetoric known as *actio* (delivery, the orator's performance) existed to codify and teach them.[47] What was taught was an art of conventions – not subtle, human, infinitely shaded self-expressive movements, but immediately recognizable, deliberately impressive, even histrionic gestures.

How does the music fit with such a stylized interpretation? It also is patterned; a short and neat melodic rhyme such as is contrived for 'O dolor, proh dolor' (stave 2) occurs comparatively rarely in traditional plainsong. This phrase, incidentally, contains one of the melodic germs of the piece (A).

Ex. 164

This germ, especially the central rise and fall (B), occurs about ten times on the single page quoted, and three times it is preceded by an 'intonation' (C).

Small repeated phrases are not unknown in the traditional Gregorian repertory, but the continual harping on the same motif, especially a 'tuneful' one, by strict or modified repetition, is much more like the procedures we have seen at work in *lai* or free sequence.[48] Space forbids analysis of the whole of this massive *planctus* which, incomplete at the end, runs to some 120 lines. The melodic resources of the composer are in fact much more varied than this opening suggests. It could be described as an extended free composition; new material is constantly introduced. But at the same time there is a sort of refrain-melody which appears a number of times.

Ex. 165

---

[47] On rhetoric as an 'emotive' not an 'expressive' art, see chapter 8:VII above.

[48] 'While, on the whole, Gregorian melody is highly variable and un-predictable, exhibiting a tendency towards constant change of design, it is not entirely devoid of the opposite principle of melodic construction, that is, repetition in one form or another' (Apel (1958), 258). The repetitive principle is certainly seen in the double, triple and fourfold Alleluias which are, for example, a feature of the Easter liturgy (see *LU*, 765–84 *passim*, Dominica Resurrectionis), but even here the relative freedom and inventiveness of liturgical chant is evident.

There are then *lai*-like features, but the composition as a whole is far too *un*patterned for it to be categorized as a *lai*. Nor is it 'narrative' melody; the material is too rich and complex for that. What it does have is figures of musical rhetoric of a kind that occur with less insistence in other *planctus*. They take the form of affective melismas, on emotive words, especially when those words denote sounds and are themselves probably onomatopoeic in origin – e.g. *fleant*, *flete*; for exclamations – O *dolor*, proh *dolor*!; or on apostrophes – O Maria Mag*da*lena / dul*cis*sima Mag*da*lena / Mater Jhesu cruci*fi*xi. Such devices seem to me quite in keeping with the stylized verbal rhetoric and the stylized gestures. They are affective, and effective, ornaments, with a basis in the sounds of speech.

I suggest, then, that in interpreting these phrases of 'emotional' description quoted earlier, such as *quasi lamentando dicat* and *alta voce gaudentes*, we should allow for other possibilities than psychological naturalism. In some cases the 'emotion' of the 'character' may have been represented by stylized gestures *accompanying* the singing rather than expressed *in* the singing itself. In other cases, clearly defined and formally distinguished vocal styles may have been adopted, analogous to the straightforward categories of *alta voce* and *humili voce* previously discussed, but refining on them. But this is conjecture.

That no organic, 'human', connection between the 'emotion' of a particular chant, a particular speech, and the 'emotion' of the performer was necessarily demanded, we have by way of summary the striking evidence of a group of dramatic ceremonies attaching to the Harrowing of Hell. The ceremony celebrates Christ's descent to Satan's kingdom, his overthrowing of it and his triumphal return with the liberated prophets (from Adam onward); it is essentially triumphant. Why then should the canons of Zurich in the thirteenth century sing 'Cum rex glorie' 'in a subdued voice' (*remisse*)?[49] This antiphon is generally known as *Canticum triumphale*. Even odder, why should the priest representing Christ (Mainz, fourteenth-century) knock at the doors of the church singing *Tollite portas . . .*! (Lift up your heads, ye everlasting gates . . .!) again 'in a subdued manner' (*submissa voce*)?[50] The fact is that, in Young's words, 'from the very outset the *Depositio* and *Elevatio* were committed to a close dependence upon the text and mood of the authorized liturgy of Holy Week . . . the *Elevatio* was often performed almost privately . . . and behind closed doors'.[51] The style of singing, too, conforms to the demands of liturgical propriety, not to the demands of a dramatic situation humanly conceived. The paradox is striking and informative.

There is a final small category of words of an overtly 'emotional' kind, mostly occurring with *voce* – i.e. directly describing the voice. In a thirteenth-

[49] Young (1933), I.153–4: Breviary of a collegiate church, 1260 (Lipphardt (1975), VI.476). At Mainz (see following note) the *Canticum triumphale* was sung *sub silencio*, i.e. 'in a low voice', again.
[50] Young, I.161–2: Rituale-Agendum of Mainz; no specific institution (Lipphardt, VI.408).
[51] Young, I.177, stressing 'the subdued tone which usually pervades the *Elevatio*'.

century *Visitatio* from Nuremberg, the risen Christ addresses Mary Magdalene *auctorabili voce* (in the voice of authority).[52] Elsewhere, boys singing the roles of the three Marys (Bamberg, sixteenth-century) sing *querula voce* (in a complaining? plaintive? voice) 'Quis revolvet?'[53] Other adjectives include: *flebili voce et submissa* (weeping and subdued); *plangendo* (lamenting); *letabunda* (joyful, happy) – all these from Barking *Visitatio* (fourteenth-century).[54] Such terms as these are rare and some are admittedly late; but used in such a way they must indicate, I think, a directly emotional style of performance in which dramatic expressiveness (i.e. trying to produce in performance the effects of emotions felt by the 'characters') has, in the final analysis, a place. Such an admission must open our minds to the possibility also that other early melody, including monophonic songs, could have *in performance* an 'expressive' aspect.

[52] Young, 1.399: Antiphoner of Augustinian Canons, Chiemsee, early-thirteenth-century (Lipphardt (1975), VI.353).

[53] Young, 1.232–4: *Agenda Bambergensia* (1587). This very late printed source characterizes the Marys as *anxie*.

[54] Young, 1.381–5. See further, concerning Barking ceremonies, pp. 317–18 above.

II

MUSIC AND MEANING: THE PROBLEM OF EXPRESSIVENESS

Trying to feel one's way into the musical experience of our remote ancestors has all 'the fascination of what's difficult'. It is in all conscience hard enough to tell a friend what we have just experienced in listening to a piece of music, or to understand what it is he is trying to tell us. However, the difficulty is also a challenge and one that at this stage in our enquiry must be taken up. The preceding chapters have sketched various ways in which words and melody were related during the early Middle Ages – in number, in movement, in dramatic action, through the sounds of speech, and in other ways. It is possible to go a long way in describing their relations, in fact, without ever becoming more than lightly involved in questions of meaning.

I hope that for the purposes of this discussion we can take a broad, commonsense view of 'meaning', using it to cover that whole area of experience which is not the music itself but something other, something describable, even though not precisely, in non-musical terms. This describable thing which is not the musical sound–construct itself can be the effect music has on the listener, or the presumed feelings (actual or recollected) of the composer as he wrote, or the experience referred to in the words of the text. This is a very simple set of categories; each one is capable of and may need refinement. Thus, the first – the 'effect' music has – may be as varied as an incitement to action, a moral restraint, a nostalgic recollection, a visual association, a state of contemplative withdrawal, a metaphysical enlightenment.

The evidence that one might assemble to present a view of musical experience in this period is bewilderingly diverse. It could include the views of musical and literary theorists, of writers on education, of philosophers and theologians and moralists; it could take into account not only the statements of poets and preachers and chroniclers but also the *assumptions* about music which underlie their more casual references and descriptions. This is to mention only written evidence. Those who devised or copied images in wood or stone or paint sometimes, indeed not seldom, depict musicians, musical instruments, musical activity. However, because of the extreme difficulty of interpreting visual evidence and my own lack of expertise in it, I shall not attempt to use it. I believe that in any case visual depictions of the musical art could only be of the most limited use in determining the central question of this chapter: To what extent, if at all, did medieval listeners regard a relationship of *meaning* between words and music as an important part of their experience of song? In the first part of this chapter I shall use the evidence of the musical and literary theorists as a frame for the argument since it is in theory, naturally, that one finds the most systematic and comprehensive attempts to formulate questions about music. But just as it is misleading to think of musical theory as being a closed and neatly defined field of study, so also with literary theory. Many of the most interesting statements come, in fact, from speculative writers who deal not only with words and with music but with other subjects as well. The evidence of these other writers will be adduced where it comes in most aptly.[1]

There is no such thing as a typical medieval musical treatise. Even though their authors pillage each other's works and deferentially copy large portions out of the Great Authors of an earlier age, Boethius (*c*. 480–*c*. 524), Cassiodorus (*c*. 485–*c*. 580) and Isidore of Seville (*c*. 559–636), they nearly all have their individual and particular interests. However, many of them have at least one common problem and common function. The function is to teach. Guido of Arezzo writes in his Epistle to Bishop Theodaldus, prefacing the *Micrologus* (*c*. 1025): 'I offer to your most sagacious and fatherly self the precepts of the science of music [*musice artis regulas*] . . . endeavoring only that

---

[1] It is not practicable to provide a comprehensive bibliographical note for the main subject of this chapter since the material is so diverse, but some comments on approaches to the Latin theorists may be of use. The older collections of musical texts by Gerbert (1784) and Coussemaker (1864) are gradually being superseded by modern scholarly editions and translations. The principal theorists are entered by name in the Bibliography below; the entry refers the reader to editions and translations. The *New Grove* article 'Theory, Theorists', sects 5–6 (Palisca) surveys medieval theory, which deals at first principally with speculative matters, with practical plainsong, and only later with polyphony; numerous individual articles in *New Grove* summarize theoretical treatises, including the valuable but easily overlooked article by Gushee, 'Anonymous theoretical writings'. See also Gallo's bibliographical report (1972). Extracts from the main writers are in O. Strunk, *Source Readings in Music History* (London 1952); a convenient chronological list, in Smits van Waesberghe's book on musical education in the Middle Ages (1969), p. 195; RISM (series B/III, in progress) is devoted to cataloguing all medieval theoretical works.

The best general introduction to the multitude of Latin writers (philosophers, rhetoricians etc) is perhaps still that of de Bruyne whose voluminous study of medieval aesthetics (1946) contains a wealth of quotation from late classical authors (Boethius, Cassiodorus, Martianus Capella etc.) as well as from medieval authors; its especial value is that it deals with *all* the arts, not just with music, and covers writers whose main concerns were non-musical. But as a survey of the whole field which at the same time deeply questions the assumptions we bring to our reading of the treatises Gushee's 68-page article, 'Questions of Genre in Medieval Treatises on Music' (1973) is unrivalled. The essay raises many questions about the 'intellectual style' of individual authors which go beyond the concerns of the present chapter; but Gushee's central thesis is distinctly relevant: 'the conventional categories of classification over-accentuate the stability of the components of medieval musical thought.' Despite the 'durability' of certain attitudes and definitions we must see individual features in the treatises as 'responses to changes in musical style, institutional needs, or intellectual fashions affecting all branches of culture' (433). The writings of rhetoricians are described, historically placed, and edited by J. J. Murphy in his several books (1971, 1974, 1978). Medieval discussions of metre and rhythm are dealt with in chapter 12 below.

I am indebted to Richard Luckett for reading this chapter and commenting upon it.

it should help both the cause of the church and our little ones.'[2] Guido's purpose is practical. He is dismayed by the standard of singing and 'extremely sorry for our singers who, though they should persevere a hundred years in the study of singing, can never perform even the tiniest antiphon on their own'.[3]

If the authors' common function is to teach the performance of the chant, their common problem and endeavour is how to reconcile to this practical purpose the body of theoretical material which they had inherited. As Richard Crocker has written,

the medieval theorist stands at the juncture of two quite different traditions. On the one hand he inherits from classical Antiquity a set of terms, methods and ideas which were originally created in connection with Greek classical culture. On the other, he must deal with a legacy of song, the sacred chant of the Church, which seems to have its roots in quite a different culture . . . The history of early medieval theory may be seen as the working-out of a relationship between these two elements, a rationalization of the sounding art work – the sacred chant – according to the intellectual methods of Greek theory.[4]

It is this effort at rationalization which makes many of the technicalities of medieval theory so uncommonly difficult to understand. They seem to the modern reader to be so many ingenious but inept answers to questions which indeed were real enough – such as how to establish the intervals between notes – but which could be, and eventually were, solved much more simply.

By way of entry we may take the treatise of Aurelian of Réôme. His *Musica disciplina*, the earliest surviving medieval treatise on music, was written in the mid ninth century and retained its popularity at least until *c.* 1100; fourteen manuscripts (not all of the complete text) have been traced.[5] After a dedication to his former Abbot, Bernard, 'arch singer . . . of the entire Holy Church', Aurelian opens with a 'praise' of music ranging from the myth of Orpheus to the Apocalypse. The following chapters, II to VII, deal with: the name 'music', and music's inventors and its proportions; the three 'kinds' of music (of the universe, of man, of instruments); the parts of music (harmonics, rhythmics and metrics); the names of sounds (of voice, wind instruments and

[2] Guido, *Micrologus*, ed. Smits van Waesberghe (1955), 84; transl. Babb and Palisca (1978), 58.
[3] 'Maxime itaque dolui de nostris cantoribus qui etsi centum annis in canendi studio perseverent, numquam tamen vel minimam antiphonam per se valent efferre.' Guido claims that within a month his boys can sing chants which they have never seen or heard before (*invisos et inauditos cantus*) without any hesitation (*indubitantes*). Transl. Babb and Palisca, 58; ed. Smits van Waesberghe, 85.
[4] Crocker (1958a), 2. My thoughts on *musica* and its significance for the understanding of the relations of music and poetry are greatly indebted to the stimulus of this article.
[5] The treatise is ed. Gushee (1975); transl. Ponte (1968) from his own text. Gushee comments (introd., 13) on the generally dependable nature of the late source used by Gerbert (1784) and the competence of the transcription. A much longer summary of *Musica disciplina* is in Gushee, 'Aurelian' in *New Grove*. Gushee also comments helpfully on the nature of the 'compilation', as he essentially regards it, both in *New Grove* and more extensively in his (1973) essay, 388–93.

strings); music and mathematics; and the difference between a musician and a singer. The material for these chapters is taken from the *auctores* – Boethius, Cassiodorus, St Augustine, Isidore and Bede. The bulk of the remainder of the treatise, chapters VIII to XX, is more practical and less derivative; it describes the eight ecclesiastical modes with much detailed reference to actual chants, especially the psalms, and their performance; 'these eight modes govern all the sweetness of music'. A final chapter of some length contains general definitions of the principal chants of the Mass and the Office.

This jumble of speculative theory and practical comment does not seem on the face of it likely to help us much. However, it does give immediate prominence to one or two questions that we shall have to be concerned with, as well as to a number of the main issues of musical theory between the ninth and the thirteenth centuries. One particularly thorny question is that of terminology. Innocent-looking words like *harmonicus, rhythmus, modulatio, simfonia, modus, tropus,* and indeed *musica* itself turn out to have meanings quite different from the expected and, furthermore, are not used consistently in the period. *Musica*, for example, may mean in one context the organized sound of modern terminology; in another it may refer to the discipline, i.e. to musical theory. In yet another context, *musica* may signify a metaphorical harmony (metaphysical to them, metaphorical only to us) which describes both an aesthetic and a theological order.

I The concept of *musica*

It will not, I think, be easy to discover whether there was felt to be a 'relationship of meaning' between words and music without some prior consideration of *musica* in its various aspects. Although Music was only one of the seven liberal arts, with Grammar, Rhetoric and Dialectic (the *trivium*) and Geometry, Astronomy and Arithmetic (the other subjects of the *quadrivium*), it was regarded in its widest sense as fundamental:

Musica enim generaliter sumpta obiective quasi ad omnia extendit, ad deum et creaturas, incorporeas et corporeas, celestes et humanas, ad sciencias theoricas et practicas.[6]

For Music in the most general sense encompasses in reality practically everything – God and his creatures spiritual and corporeal, heavenly and human, and also knowledge in its theoretical and practical aspects.

It is, of course, in a way misleading to say that *music* is fundamental. We have at once come up against the difficulty of the term. One could paraphrase the idea behind this quotation as follows: the universe itself is a manifestation of perfect ratios, proportions, measures ('Thou hast ordered all things in

[6] Jacques de Liège (Jacobus Leodiensis), *Speculum Musice,* I,i. His dates are *c.* 1260 – after 1330 (*New Grove*).

measure, and number, and weight': *omnia in mensura et numero et pondere disposuisti*;[7] no one, therefore, can expect to understand it unless he has thoroughly mastered the disciplines of number. Amongst the number systems to which the human reason and human senses have access, music, realizing numbers in sounds, is prominent. It seems as if in many writers and many contexts *arithmetica*, or another term, could be substituted for *musica* without changing the sense.[8] The reason why *musica* is so much more commonly used as an image is, perhaps, that unlike arithmetic and geometry it exists, as man does, in time – and, unlike astronomy, its temporal movements are readily apparent to the human senses. Not that every musical person is capable *ipso facto* of penetrating the secrets of the universe. The theorists maintain adamantly that it is quite possible to enjoy music simply as an animal; *qui facit, quod non sapit, diffinitur bestia* (Guido). They are never tired of quoting and amplifying Boethius's distinction between a musician (*musicus*) and a singer (*cantor*). Aurelian writes that there is as large a difference between a musician and a singer as between a grammarian and the man who reads the lesson. Elsewhere a singer is likened to a drunken man reeling home (he hopes) along a road he does not know.[9]

Dante in a characteristically individual passage defined the place of Music among the seven liberal arts in such a way as to bring out its essential nature – the study of relation and proportion. This striking section of the *Convivio* establishes an elaborate parallel between the seven arts and the seven planets in their spheres: heaven, allegorically interpreted, signifies knowledge, and 'the heavens' are the branches of knowledge.[10] The heaven of the Moon resembles Grammar; the heaven of Mercury may be compared to Dialectic; the heaven of Venus, to Rhetoric; and so forth. The planet chosen to represent Music is Mars. The heaven of Mars has two properties, of which the first is 'the perfect beauty of its relation to the rest' (*la sua più bella relazione*). The beauty of its 'relation' consists in the fact that it is the fifth heaven of nine and occupies a central position with four heavens disposed symmetrically on either side of it.[11] At this point, and in this context, one expects Dante to rehearse the traditional commonplaces – about the heavenly harmony, the *musica mundana*, the beauty of numbers and so forth. Instead, he argues that the proportional essence of music is seen in two things – in words according well together (*ne le parole armonizzate*) and in songs (*ne li canti*)

---

[7] Vulgate, *Liber Sapientiae*, xi.21.

[8] See above chapter 1, introduction. Cf. Dante, *Convivio*, II.xiii.15–16: *Arismetrica* is like the heaven of the Sun, *ché del suo lume tutte s'illuminano le scienze* ('because by its light all branches of knowledge are illuminated').

[9] Aurelian, ch. VII, p. 77. Johannes Afflighemensis, ch. 11 (ed. Smits van Waesberghe, p. 52): *Cui ergo cantorem melius comparaverim quam ebrio.* . . . . The attempted medieval rapprochement between *musicus* and *cantor* is discussed by E. Reimer in *AMw* 35 (1978) 1–32; the question is one of the main themes of Gushee (1973).

[10] For translations of the *Convivio*, see chapter 1, note 25 above.

[11] See Stevens (1968a), 1ff, on which the present discussion is based.

de' quali tanto più dolce armonia resulta, quanto più la relazione è bella: la quale in essa scienza massimamente è bella, perché massimamente in ella s'intende. (II. xiii. 23)

. . . of which the more beautiful the proportions, the sweeter the resultant harmoniousness; and the proportions are most beautiful in the art of music because in music they are most aimed at.

Dante is clearly defining music in a wide sense: it is the music of *words* as well as the music of instruments and voices. This brings out one aspect of poetry, verse, which in a moment we must examine in some detail: it is itself a branch, or, it would be more accurate to say, a manifestation of *musica*. Literature, as we today understand the term, was not one of the medieval *artes liberales*: one of its aspects, effective verbal communication, was dealt with under Rhetoric, whilst the rhythmical craft of verse belonged to Music in most cases, though sometimes to Grammar.

Before we embark on the problem of music's relation to language in general, and poetry in particular, as it was seen by the thinkers of the early Middle Ages, it is important to realize how small a part this problem had in the whole body of speculation and practical advice current at the time. My brief summary of Aurelian of Réôme's *Musica disciplina* will have given an idea of the situation. Only his chapter on the parts of music (harmonics, rhythmics and metrics) seems immediately relevant. A later treatise by Johannes Afflighemensis, *De musica* (c. 1100–21), leaves an only slightly different impression.[12] He has the same end in view as his model. Guido of Arezzo (c. 991–1033+), to instruct the young and ignorant in the understanding and proper performance of the chant. With them in mind he even dares to say (of the interval-ratios *sesquioctava* [8:9], *sesquitertia* [3:4] etc.),

Since a discussion of such matters would tax the young and less learned, and since we are addressing boys and those not yet mature, we leave this topic to the acumen of the arithmeticians [*arithmeticorum hoc subtilitati relinquimus*].[13]

He has chapters on most of the expected topics (the 'invention' of music and the etymology of the word; the measurement and use of the monochord; the modes, their 'tenors', finals and ranges). His seemingly most original chapters – on melodic composition – are based on Guido. They do, in fact, contain remarks on words and music which are of great interest (see below); but the bulk of the treatise is fairly strictly concerned with matters of practical importance to monastic singers. This is, indeed, the secret of his attraction; he has a pragmatic approach.[14] Johannes is particularly enthusiastic about the new method of notating pitches which was invented by his master, Guido. It

---

[12] Johannes Afflighemensis (John of Afflighem, near Brussels), formerly identified as an Englishman, John Cotton. The problem of his identity, still not finally solved, is discussed by Gallo (1972), 84; by N. E. Smith in *New Grove*; by Palisca (in Babb and Palisca) rejecting the Flanders ascription of Smits van Waesberghe in favour of south Germany.

[13] Transl., 111; text, Smits van Waesberghe, 68.

[14] 'When he tries to be systematic, he blunders': see Babb and Palisca, 96–7.

is in all essentials the system of staff notation still in use today. The *f*-line was written in red at this stage and the *c*-line in yellow, but the principle of lines and spaces had been established; and, as Johannes proudly says, 'musical neumes with lines [*musicis et regularibus neumis*] . . . lead the singer by a path so true and easy that even if he wished to he could not go astray'.[15] Johannes also has fresh things to say on the perennial and centrally important subject of the eight modes (ecclesiastical 'scales', as it were). His discussion reminds us, finally, that even the traditional and hoary concerns of the theorists are capable of re-interpretation in a way that makes for interest.

One topic discussed by Aurelian of Réôme which does not appear in Johannes Afflighemensis some 250 years later is that of the three divisions of *musica* – that is, of music theory – into *harmonica*, *rhythmica* and *metrica*. The categories go back at least to Cassiodorus whose *Institutiones* (sixth century A.D.) provided the Middle Ages with one of their basic texts.[16] Unlike Boethius, Cassiodorus is not deeply concerned with the mathematics of music – not at least with the detail of Greek theory. He believes, of course, in the reality of the metaphysics of number; *numerus est qui cuncta disponit*, and *musica est scientia que de numeris loquitur*. But his interests, and the weight of his discourse, fall in more readily with a feeling for music as sound. It would be true to say, in fact, that what interests him is 'significant sound'. Speech is a kind of music, too. So of the three divisions he writes:[17]

armonica est scientia musica quae discernit in sonis acutum et gravem. *rhithmica* est quae requirit in concursione verborum, utrum bene sonus, an male cohaereat. *metrica* est, que mensuras diversorum metrorum probabili ratione cognoscit ut verbi gratia. heroicon, iambicon, elegiacon et cetera.

The science of harmonics is that branch of musical theory which distinguishes between high and low sounds; rhythmics investigates the way words move in conjunction – whether the sound of them fits well or not; metrics examines by the process of reason the measured patterns of the various metres – as for instance heroic, iambic, elegiac etc.

These theoretical divisions apply to natural as opposed to artificial music, music of the human voice not of instruments. Vocal music is found both in song (sung poetry) and in speech; it obeys, in both kinds, the laws of pitches, rests, accents, 'the melody of feet', and the composition of the phrase. To

[15] Transl., 150, from *De Musica*, ch. 21: 'Of what use the neumes are that Guido invented'.
[16] The standard edition of Cassiodorus (*c*. 485–*c*. 580) is by Mynors (1937). The influential account of the seven liberal arts is in the second book of the *Institutiones divinarum et humanarum litterarum* (after 540).
[17] Ed. Mynors, 144 (Mynors reads: *inconcursionem*; *mensuram*). De Bruyne, I, ch. 2, discusses Cassiodorus's attitude to *musica* as one of the liberal arts and his eloquent 'Christianizing' of Greek sentiment. He is, however, wrong in glossing *rhithmica* as if it referred to the relationship between words and music. The distinction is not made. See further Crocker (1958a), 3.

Cassiodorus the metres are like the 'modes' of instrumental music; each has its peculiar character and individual effect:[18]

ut in organis toni, ita in humana voce varias animi affectiones gravida metra pepererunt.

In the same way as the 'modes' in instrumental music, so the pregnant metres manifested by the human voice have given birth to diverse emotional states in the mind.

The threefold division of vocal music theory undergoes an interesting development in the first post-classical author to take up the theme, the Venerable Bede (*c.* 673–735). He is particularly interested in the type of organized sound called *rhythmus, rithimus, ritmus*.[19]

videtur autem rhythmus metris esse consimilis, quae est verborum modulata compositio, non metrica ratione, sed numero syllabarum ad iudicium aurium examinata, ut sunt carmina vulgarium poetarum. et quidem rhythmus per se sine metro esse potest, metrum vero sine rhythmo esse non potest . . .

It is evident that a 'rhythm' [i.e. words arranged in the 'rhythmical' style] is similar to 'metres' for it is a patterned structure [*modulata compositio*] of words without metrical system but deliberately arranged to please the ear through the number [which includes the rhythmical disposition] of syllables, as are the songs of vernacular poets. And, indeed, a *ritmus* can exist without metre but not a *metrum* without rhythm . . .

This passage will be of importance in chapter 12 as early recognition of the fundamental distinction between a 'rhythmic' tradition in early medieval song, based on a syllable-counting system, and a 'metrical', i.e. quantitative, writing in 'feet'. It signifies less in the present argument; it does, however, at least remind us again that the chief concern of those who theorize about song – music and verse – is with sounds, the temporal organization of sounds in time.

Crocker warns against the temptation to read too much into the classical (and medieval) procedure of including rhythmics and metrics under 'music'. We should not assume that reference is being made to the relation between text and music in composition nor, however, on the other hand that 'rhythmics and metrics are included solely for the sake of an analysis of poetry'.[20] The discussion is a general one about the 'theory of proportions in sound'; music and poetry are considered primarily as manifesting in their different media fundamental common laws. However, when Crocker suggests that the following passage in Aurelian of Réôme may be a unique

[18] De Bruyne, 1.63, from the *Letter to Boethius*.
[19] Bede, *De arte metrica*, XXIV (ed. Keil, 258). And see Murphy (1974), 78. *Modulata compositio* is difficult to translate; Murphy evades it with 'modulation'. The passage is of particular interest as associating a 'non-metrical' syllable-counting system with vernacular songs. But, as Klopsch and others have pointed out, the even earlier *Ars Palaemonis* makes the same association.
 (When not quoting from other authors, I shall use the spelling *ritmus* to refer to a poem or song written in the syllable-counting tradition in order to distinguish it from 'rhythm' in the wider modern sense. Similarly, *metrum* is distinguished from 'metre'.)
[20] Crocker (1958a), 8.

reference to the relationship between text and melody, he is a less sure guide. Aurelian speaks here of plainchant; he writes:[21]

In rithmica autem provisio manet ut cum verbis modulatio apte concurrat, ne scilicet contra rationem verborum cantilenae vox inepte formetur.

In 'rhythmic' music one must take care that the melody [? melodic structure] shall agree properly with the words, lest the sound of the melody be improperly shaped at variance with their *ratio*.

The difficulty in interpretation has arisen from translating the word *ratio* as 'meaning' (Joseph Ponte) or 'rhythm of the text' (Crocker).[22] I believe that 'structure' or 'syntactic ordering' might be better translations of what Aurelian has in mind, and that the explanation is to be sought in later chapters of his treatise. For instance in chapter x (on the first mode, authentic) he says that the singer should know[23]

ut noverit cantor propriam perfectamque in esse debere responsorio litteraturam. Versum autem eiusdem ita debere aptari quatenus iunctus repetitioni integrum littere servet sensum.

that the proper and complete text ought to be present in the response, and that the verse of the same ought to be fitted to it in such a way that, joined to the refrain, it may preserve the complete sense of the response.

In the next chapter he says that, in order to make sense,[24]

licentiam cantor habet [quam libet responsorii in repetitione eiusdem] mutare syllabam, etiam et verba si necessitas exiget . . .

the singer has a licence to change any syllable or even the words [of the response] itself, if necessity demands . . .

It is evident that Aurelian has a well-developed sense of the proper structural or phrasal relationship between the text and the music. I think he had this particular type of grammatical/syntactical alteration in mind when he wrote the sentence about the melody agreeing properly with the words; these recommendations to singers seem to show how his mind works. So far from having 'no very clear notion of what rhythmics might have to do with singing', he is saying surely that melody should respect verbal structure, in a line or in a larger unit, as we have seen it generally does in plainchant.[25] It is an attempt on his part to make sense of a traditional definition in a way that relates it to practical concerns of the time.

[21] Aurelian, ch. vi (ed. Gushee, p. 71); my transl.
[22] Transl. Ponte, 28; Crocker (1958a), 11.
[23] Ed. Gushee, 88; transl. Ponte, 28. The translation 'sense' is perfectly correct here. And it is clear that the point of preserving the *ratio* is in order not to obscure the words; but the *ratio* is not itself the words.
[24] Ed. Gushee, 99 (the brackets are his); transl. Ponte, 29.
[25] Crocker (1958a), 11. And see chapter 8:iv above.

11 Text and music

The topic of the three categories of musical theory has led to consideration of
the way the theorists thought about the relationship of text and music. The
first generalization to emerge is that they are often working with a definition
of *musica* which is broad enough to include them both and which indeed does
not always distinguish between them, since music and speech are both arts
which measure sounds in time. This is, I think, the moment to mention two
other currents in the broad stream of tradition which led to the songs of the
Middle Ages: they are the association of song with oratory, and the tendency
to regard the perfect art as a triple one – poetry that is sung and danced, *que
cuncta . . . tria . . . sociata perfectam faciunt cantilenam.*[26]

The necessity of music in the training of an orator is worked out in detail by
Quintilian, to take the matter back no further. Quintilian's *Institutio oratoria*
(written A.D. *c.* 92) expounds a complete system for the education of the ideal
orator.[27] His general education, which begins in the cradle, will include music
because many wise men, including Plato, thought it worth study and because
the art of letters and the art of music were once united. What are the advan-
tages the orator will derive from the study of music (which incidentally
includes dancing, as in the culture of the Greeks)?[28]

Numeros musice duplices habet in vocibus et in corpore, utriusque enim rei aptus
quidam modus desideratur. Vocis rationem Aristoxenus musicus dividit in *rhuthmon*
et *melos*, quorum alterum modulatione, alterum canore ac sonis constat. Num igitur
non haec omnia oratori necessaria? quorum unum ad gestum, alterum ad colloca-
tionem verborum, tertium ad flexus vocis, qui sunt in agendo quoque plurimi,
pertinet.

(The orator) has in his voice and in his physique 'musical numbers' of two kinds, for in
both a certain style [measure?] is required which is suited to the matter in hand.
Aristoxenus, the musician, divided the ordering of the voice into *rhythmos* and *melos*,
of which the first consists of proportions, the other of tone [?timbre] and sounds
[?pitches]. Are not, then, all these things necessary in a speaker? Of them, one deals
with gesture, the second with the arrangement of words, the third with modulations
of the voice, of which indeed a large number are required in pleading.

It is from the *De nuptiis* of Martianus Capella (?early-fifth-century) that
Remy of Auxerre (late-ninth-century) develops the doctrine of a perfect song

---

[26] See note 33 below.
[27] Quintilian: see Murphy (1974), 22 and n. 42 (basic short bibliography). Ed. and transl.
Butler (1920). On Quintilian's attitude to '*musice* as the handmaiden of *rhetorice*', see Warren
Anderson 'Quintilian', in *New Grove*. Quintilian was especially popular in the schools of
twelfth-century France (Murphy, 125–30). For a more extended account of Quintilian in the
Middle Ages, see Colson's edn (1924), introduction, pp. xiii ff.
[28] Book I.x.22 (Butler, I.170). Shortly afterwards (I.x.27) Quintilian relates how Gaius Grac-
chus used to have a musician standing behind him during his speeches, who gave him the
appropriate notes on a pitch-pipe.

uniting the arts of word, melody and dance.[29] 'For Martianus perfect music manifests itself in the form of a poem which is sung and mimed: it is at the same time poetry, melody and dance.'[30] The concept is, of course, a Greek one. Remy, who has been described as the most comprehensive theorist of rhythm in the period, divides music into three main categories relating respectively to its formal analysis as melody, its performance as an art, and its interpretation.[31] Each category has three subdivisions. Those of melodic theory have a familiar look:

(a) *in sonis*   : *harmonica (melos)*
(b) *in numeris* : *rhythmica (rhythmus)*
(c) *in verbis*   : *metrica (metrum)*[32]

The relevant comments occur in the discussion of *musica rhythmica*. Rhythm is perceived in three ways: through sight, hearing, and touch. The eye perceives rhythm in the bodily movements of the dance; the ear, in instrumental or vocal music; the touch ('and this is the business of doctors') – in the human body.[33] Rhythms of sight and sound find their perfect expression in danced song.

In tria . . . genera dividentur: in corporis motum id est gestum, in sonorum modulandique rationem atque in verba . . . quae cuncta id est haec tria, socia pro sociata, perfectam faciunt cantilenam.

It is divided into three kinds: movement of the body, i.e. gesture; orderly arrangement of pitches and temporal measurements [?]; and words . . . all of which, i.e. these three, in association make a perfect song.[34]

Although they appear rather different, these further extensions of the concept *musica* to include matters within the sphere of the orator, as well as poetry which is sung and danced to (not to mention the art of healing), are related.

Many connections were established between words and music in the speculative writers of the age – and it is a long 'age' indeed from Bede to Roger

---

[29] Martianus Capella, *De nuptiis Philologiae et Mercurii*, ed. Dick (1925). Book 9 deals with music (*harmonia*). Study and transl.: Stahl, Johnson and Burge (1971). Martianus's discussion is derived for the most part directly from the Greek of Aristides Quintilianus. Remy of Auxerre: see note 31 below.

[30] De Bruyne, I.319.

[31] Remy of Auxerre: he wrote many commentaries including a liturgical 'essay on the ceremonies of the Mass' (Gushee in *New Grove*). His widely circulating Commentary on Martianus Capella is ed. Lutz (1962); the old text by Gerbert (1784), 1.63 ff, is very incomplete. See also de Bruyne, I.319ff: 'La rythmique de Rémi d'Auxerre.'

[32] Ed. Lutz, gloss no. 499.7.

[33] Ed. Lutz, gloss no. 516.17: '*Omnis igitur numerus triplici ratione id est tribus modis, discernitur: visu audituque vel tactu. Visu, sicut sunt ea, quae motu corporis colliguntur id est gestus corporis et saltationes; auditu, cum ad iudicium modulationis intendimus* scilicet in organicis sive humanis vocibus; *tactu haec species ad medicos pertinet . . .*' (Martianus's text is in italics, Remy's gloss in roman). See also Adank (1978), 43, for discussion of Bacon's 'visible music' of *saltus, plausus, chorus*, etc; and H. Müller's basic study of Bacon in 'Zur Musikauffassung des 13. Jahrhunderts' in *AfMw* 4 (1922), 405–12.

[34] Ed. Lutz, gloss no. 517.8.

Bacon.[35] Some of these connections were of a light analogical variety: thus, there are eight musical modes *because* there are eight parts of speech, just as there are seven intervals *because* there are seven gifts of the spirit, seven planets in heaven, seven days in the week.[36] (The 'lightness' of the analogy is, naturally, a modern way of looking at it. Grocheo is fully serious when he says, as his reason for supporting this figure seven, that since man is a microcosmos, an epitome in himself of the great Whole, 'his laws and operations ought to imitate divine law completely, as far as possible'.)[37] Other connections are a matter of observation – as, for instance, of the way Gregorian chant works and the structural parallelism between text and music. It is a feature of the chant which we have already noted in chapter 8, 'Speech and melody'. Guido of Arezzo works up a quite detailed parallel:[38]

Igitur quemadmodum in metris sunt litterae et syllabae, partes et pedes ac versus, ita in harmonia sunt phtongi, id est soni, quorum unus, duo vel tres aptantur in syllabas; ipsaeque sole vel duplicatae neumam, id est partem constituunt cantilenae; et pars una vel plures distinctionem faciunt, id est congruum respirationis locum.

Just as in verse there are letters and syllables, units and feet and lines, so in music there are *phthongi*, that is sounds, of which one, two or three are grouped as syllables; one or two of these constitute a neume, that is the unit of music; and one or more of these parts make up a period, that is a suitable place to breathe.

This is the opening sentence of the controversial and often-discussed chapter xv of the *Micrologus* (*c.* 1025). Later in the chapter he refers to a number of techniques which appear to derive from rhetoric. The question of music and rhetoric is a large one and bears directly on the central concern of this chapter, sound and meaning, to which we shall come shortly. Before we do so I will mention one further words–music connection of the oddest kind: it is a method which Guido claimed to have devised, and Johannes Afflighemensis adopted, for composing new chants more or less by rule of thumb out of the vowels of the literary text.[39] Bizarre as it may sound coming from a musician, and a great practical musician at that, the method consists of placing the five vowels (a-e-i-o-u) in repeated succession under the letters of the monochord (i.e. the great scale, or gamut, ranging from G up to *a'*) and then allowing

---

[35] The conception of an 'age' is not a meaningless one, in this respect: the reverence for authority, the *auctores*, from the Greeks to the most recent past, combined with an almost total unawareness of any author's *historical* context, produced an intellectual situation in which all were felt to be in an important sense contemporary.

[36] Grocheo relates the eight modes to the eight Beatitudes and to the smallest cube number, 2^3 (ed. Rohloff, 154); Aurelian of Réôme relates them to the celestial motions (ed. Gushee, 79); Aribo sees plagal and authentic modes as poor and rich, female and male ('Aribo' in *New Grove*). On the seven concords, see Grocheo (ed. Rohloff), 118.

[37] Grocheo (ed. Rohloff), 118; (transl. Seay), 7.

[38] Guido (ed. Smits van Waesberghe), 162–3; my transl. Cf the differing translations of this crucial chapter by Crocker (1958a), 12; by Babb, 70; by Smits van Waesberghe (1951), p. xx; by Vollaerts, *Rhythmic Proportions* (1958), 169.

[39] Johannes Afflighemensis, ch. xx, after Guido, ch. xvii.

your text to write the melody for you. His example 'Sancte Johannes meritorum' generates the melody.[40]

Ex. 166

(In the Renaissance a melody derived by this technique is known as *soggetto cavato*.) Realizing doubtless how restrictive this method is to a would-be composer if applied in its primitive simplicity, Guido allows a second rank of notes, established on the same principle, to extend the range of choice.

The interesting thing is, first, that Guido really does seem to believe in the validity of the method and, secondly, that the reasons he gives for doing so are based on analogies between melody and speech:[41]

1. Perpende igitur quia sicut scribitur omne quod dicitur, ita ad cantum redigitur omne quod scribitur. Canitur igitur omne quod dicitur, scriptura autem litteris figuratur . . .
2. . . . forsitan cum tantum concordiae tribuunt verbis, non minus concinentiae praestabunt et neumis . . .
3. quia cum his quinque litteris omnis locutio moveatur, moveri quoque et quinque voces ad se invicem ut diximus, non negetur.

1. Consider, then, that just as everything which is spoken can be written, so everything that is written can be made into song. Thus everything that is spoken can be sung; now, in writing it is denoted by letters . . . 2. . . . perhaps since they bring such euphony to words, they will offer no less 'harmony' to the neumes . . . 3. for since all speech is activated by these five letters [the five vowels], it should not be denied that five notes also may be set in motion amongst themselves in turn, as we have said.

I said earlier (p. 381) that one generalization about music and speech to emerge from a consideration of musical theory is that the theorists, who are often philosophers and thinkers on a much wider scale, work with 'a definition of *musica* large enough to include them both' – and much else besides. The theorists sometimes, indeed, do not trouble themselves to distinguish between them, since music and speech (not just verse) are both arts which measure sound in time. We can now add, in further summary, that this general position gave rise to the discussion of a number of connections between text and music, between speaker and musician – some obvious, some odd. The connections rest on comparisons between speech and music ranging

---

[40] Guido (ed. Smits van Waesberghe), 187–9; see Babb, 75 and fig. 5.
[41] Guido, *ed. cit.* 187–9.

from the establishment of analogies and the demonstration of similarities to the assumption of virtual identity. In the chapter by Guido of Arezzo just discussed he makes a statement which puts one basic medieval attitude in the clearest possible terms. For our purposes it is perhaps the single most important practical and aesthetic insight to be derived from the overall concept of *musica*:[42]

sicut persaepe videmus tam consonos et sibimet alterutrum respondentes versus in metris, ut quamdam quasi symphoniam grammaticae admireris. Cui si musica simili responsione iungatur, *duplici modulatione dupliciter delecteris.*

Thus in verse we often see such concordant and mutually congruous lines that you wonder, as it were, at a certain harmony of language. And if music were added to this, with a similar internal congruity, *you would be doubly charmed by a twofold melody.*

Guido wrote this probably sometime in the 1020s. What he is saying is Dante's theme some three centuries later: music and poetry are governed by the same laws, and the pleasure each gives is the pleasure of proportional sound.

Quella cosa dice l'uomo essere bella, cui le parti debitamente si rispondono, per che de la loro armonia resulta piacimento. Onde pare l'uomo essere bello, quando le sue membra debitamente si rispondono; e dicemo bello lo canto, quando le voci di quello, secondo debito de l'arte, sono intra sé rispondenti. Dunque quello sermone è più bello, ne lo quale più debitamente si rispondono [le parole] . . .   (*Conv.* I. v. 13)

One says a thing is beautiful when its parts duly 'answer' one another, because pleasure results from their harmoniousness. Further, a man appears beautiful when his limbs duly answer one another; and we say a song is beautiful when its sounds [? notes] are responsive to one another according to the requirements of art. So that speech is the more beautiful in which the words more properly answer one another . . .

The concept of *armonia*, harmoniousness, could certainly be said to be one of 'significant sound'; but the significance of the words and the significance of the music are the same – they both manifest *musica*, 'realize' its truth in sounds. Important though this is, and fundamental for our general understanding of words and music, it does not immediately provide a straight answer to the question framed at the beginning of this chapter: 'To what extent, if at all, did medieval listeners regard a relationship of *meaning* between words and music as an important part of their experience of song?' In considering this question, as we shall now do, different approaches will be necessary. But the truths of *musica* provide a touchstone on which to try them.

---

[42] Guido, ch. xvii (edn, 186ff): *Quod ad cantum redigitur omne quod dicitur* (the emphasis is mine). The transl. is from Babb, 74; I have, however, replaced his 'with a similar interrelationship' (for *simili responsione*) by 'with a similar internal congruity' to make it absolutely clear that Guido is not speaking about a direct relationship between the two arts. The term *metrum* is usually opposed to *ritmus* (see chapter 12:1 below); here, however, it may refer to poetry in general. The context does not elucidate.

III The emotive effects of music

In the following discussion I shall, as hitherto, observe a strict distinction between 'emotive' and 'expressive'. 'Emotive' will refer to the effects music has on those who hear it; 'expressive' will refer only to antecedent experiences which lie behind the music, as it were, and are thought to be made manifest in it. Amongst the *emotive* effects attributed to music are experiences of ethical insight, moral activity (behaviour), devotional fervour, spiritual ecstasy, amorous delight or simply pleasure. Many of these figure amongst the commonplaces of medieval thinking. References to *expression*, the mimesis of internal states, are on the other hand rare. I shall consider first the emotive effects, and then what one might call the experiential (the emotions associated in various contexts with the hearing, performing, creating of music). From the discussion as a whole it may be possible to draw some conclusions about expression, and other forms of mimesis if any, in medieval song.

The fundamental emotive effect of music is pleasure. Cassiodorus, together with a host of others, affirms it as self-evident, speaking as he does of the *suavitas* of instrumental music – *instrumenta dulcisona . . . que mulcent aurium delectabiliter sensum* ('sweet-sounding instruments . . . which caress with delight the sense of hearing').[43] Pleasure for Cassiodorus may be directed towards good or bad ends; but that is not the point for the moment. A sense of well-being arising through the senses is what music produces, and 'sweet' (in various languages) is the word most often chosen to describe it. For Dante, *dolcezza* is the quality of Casella's song (*Purg.* ii. 14); *dolce* describes the song of those who mount up after the Grifon (xxxii.88); and, when the divine Pageant is approaching,

> E una melodia dolce correva
>   per l'aere luminoso.   (*Purg.* xxix. 22)

And a sweet melody ran through the bright air.

The pleasure may be intensely emotional. When Dante hears the song of the angels after his meeting with Beatrice, he is melted by their *dolci tempre*, 'sweet harmonies', like Apennine snow in the warm south wind, or a wax candle in the fire (*Purg.* xxx. 82). And many writers recalled the famous passage in which St Augustine records his response to music:[44]

quantum flevi in hymnis et canticis tuis, suave sonantis ecclesiae tuae vocibus conmotus acriter! voces illae influebant auribus meis et eliquabatur veritas in cor meum et exaestuabat inde affectus pietatis, et currebant lacrimae, et bene mihi erat cum eis.

How greatly did I weep in thy hymns and canticles, deeply moved by the voices of thy sweet-speaking Church! Those voices flowed into mine ears, and the truth was

---

[43] Cited de Bruyne, 1.65, without precise reference. I have not been able to trace it.
[44] *Confessions*, ed. J. Gibb and W. Montgomery (Cambridge 1908), 248–9.

poured into my heart, whence the agitation of my piety overflowed, and my tears ran over, and blessed was I therein.

It is almost impossible even for quite simple people to record an experience of musical pleasure without putting an interpretation upon it. How much more so for men like Dante and Augustine with their supreme genius for articulation. The endlessly repeated stories about the power of music are a testimony to the naiveté which attended most interpretations. Johannes Afflighemensis, who will serve as an example, opens his chapter on this topic with an impressive, but far from original, list of claims:[45]

It should not pass unmentioned that singing [*musicus cantus*] has great power of stirring the souls of its hearers [*commovendi . . . animos*], in that it delights the ears, uplifts the mind, arouses fighters to warfare, revives the prostrate and despairing, strengthens wayfarers, disarms bandits, assuages the wrathful, gladdens the sorrowful and distressed, pacifies those at strife, dispels idle thoughts, and allays the frenzy of the demented.

Johannes goes on to tell how King Saul was affected by David's singing to the harp; how the Greek physician Asclepiades cured the insanity of a mad patient by singing to him; how Pythagoras 'recalled a certain licentious youth from his passion' through music. All these stories are in Guido of Arezzo, his master, and in other authorities (the story of Asclepiades, for instance, in Isidore, Cassiodorus, Martianus Capella and Censorinus).[46]

At the end of our period Petrarch, in a little known Dialogue from his *De remediis utriusque fortune* (1366) providing 'a fairly superficial summary of the kind of encyclopedic information so dear to the medieval arts curriculum', makes Reason (*Ratio*) reply to Joy (*Gaudium*) as follows:[47]

Joy: I am charmed by songs and sounds [*cantibus et sonis*].
Reason: Wild animals, too, and birds are tricked by song. More remarkable yet, even the fish are touched by the sweetness of music [*musica dulcedine*]. You know the story of Arion and the dolphins . . . It is attested by the bronze statues which stand where after such great danger the harper was first brought to shore unharmed, sitting on the back of the swimming fish. The Sirens, too, are believed to deceive through song. Not believed but known by experience is the fact that man daily deceives man with smooth words and, to be short, that there is nothing more suited for deceit than the voice.

Whereas Johannes Afflighemensis chose his comments and examples to form part of a conventional 'praise' of music, Petrarch has chosen his to form part of an equally conventional 'dispraise'. Oscillation between these two extremes in response to the powerful and often unsettling experience of music was a

---

[45] Transl. after Babb, 136, who however translates *musicus cantus* as 'chant'; Latin text (ed. Smits van Waesberghe), 114. Similar passages are in Aurelian of Réôme (ed. Gushee, 132; transl. Ponte, 56) and in Aribo (ed. Smits van Waesberghe, 47), and others.
[46] References in Babb, 136, n. 2. Censorinus was a third-century Roman grammarian.
[47] C. H. Rawski, 'Petrarch's Dialogue on Music', *Speculum* 46 (1971) 302ff, with edition of the text, serves as a historical index to all these *topoi*.

typical medieval ambivalence; they found themselves 'caught in this sensual music' and feared the consequences.

It was a world where dichotomies flourished – Heaven was opposed to Hell, the *eternum* to the *seculum*, *caritas* to *cupiditas*. Inevitably music could not remain metaphysically or morally neutral. The twelfth-century philosopher Adélard of Bath, in a treatise entitled *De eodem et diverso*, symbolized his two metaphysical principles (the One and the Many) in two ladies called respectively Philocosmia (lover of the world) and Philosophia (lover of wisdom, truth).[48] The former stands for the pleasures of sense, in this all-too-beautiful, transient world; the latter for the love of the invisible world. The sensibility of Philocosmia takes pleasure in the *musica practica pura* of minstrels and uninstructed singers; her experience is characterized by *voluptas*. Philosophia delights in a more intellectual music, created and understood only by true *musici*; this is *letitia*, joy. The contrast is not a traditional black-and-white one. Both kinds of music are to be heard and enjoyed.

Once again it is Dante who, combining praise and dispraise, can finely articulate, and make us believe in, the dangers.[49] His Casella episode hints with delicacy and firmness that the experience of music, however beautiful, can induce spiritual inattention and weakness. The pervasive sanity and sympathy of Dante's utterances on this subject are in marked contrast to the tirades of some medieval moralists.[50] It is like his treatment of sex – tender, touching, and yet inexorably true. The most outspoken passage about the effects of musical experience is the one in which Dante dreams of the Siren. When first seen, she is a stuttering, squinting woman, distorted and maimed. But as Dante gazes at her she seems to lose her ugliness, and her pallid face takes the colour that love wishes to give it:

> e lo smarrito volto
> com' amor vuol, così le colorava.   (*Purg.* xix. 14)
>
> . . . and her pallid face even as love wills did colour.

Then she sings a song, seductive in itself and telling of her earlier seductions, of how she led Ulysses and other sailors astray.

> 'Io son,' cantava, 'io son dolce serena,
>   che i marinari in mezzo mar dismago;
>   tanto son di piacere a sentir piena!
>
> Io volsi Ulisse del suo cammin vago
>   al canto mio; e qual meco si ausa
>   rado sen parte; sì tutto l'appago!'   (xix. 19)

[48] On Adélard's 'musical psychology', see de Bruyne, II.130–2. The treatise is ed. H. Willner,
    Beiträge zur Geschichte der Philosophie des Mittelalters IV.1 (Münster 1903).
[49] Stevens (1968a), 7–8.
[50] See Robertson, 127–9, who discusses iconographic representations of the Old Song and the
    New.

'I am,' she sang, 'I am the sweet Siren, who leads mariners astray in mid-sea, so full am I of pleasantness to hear. / I turned Ulysses from his wandering way with my song; and whoso liveth with me rarely departs, so wholly do I satisfy him.'[51]

The Siren, as Dorothy Sayers observed, 'is the projection upon the outer world of something in the mind'; there is a kind of absorption in music, in sex – the two are here inextricably twined – which is a self-absorption, a destructive egotistical fantasy.

Dante was also deeply moved by liturgical as well as secular music, and there are many references in the *Commedia* such as that to the Negligent Rulers (*Purg.* viii. 13) who at the hour of sunset sang the Compline hymn 'Te lucis ante terminum' so sweetly that he was taken out of himself (*fece me a me uscir di mente*). An interesting and rather unusual description of the desired emotive effects of liturgical chant occurs in Aurelian of Réôme (see above, p. 374). In general one should be cautious in applying criteria of devotionally affective power to medieval liturgical music – or, to be more precise, cautious in attributing such criteria to its makers. Such a concern is commonly a sign of Reformation thinking. The chant is, first and foremost, an utterance of prayer and praise; it is part of the *opus Dei*. Aurelian would certainly have taken that for granted. He writes in this passage about the secondary effect – the discipline, purification, direction of the emotions. The Alleluia[52]

congrue ante evangelium canitur ut per hoc canticum mentes fidelium quodammodo ad audiendum salutis verbum suscipiant purificationis initium.

is fittingly sung before the Gospel, so that by this chant the minds of the faithful may in some way begin to be purified for hearing the word of salvation.

His remarks on the Agnus Dei, sung before the communion in the order of the Mass, suggest a rather more complex sort of emotive effect:[53]

Communicantibus etiam primum canitur canticum 'Agnus Dei . . .' ut fideles quique corpori et sanguini Domini communicantes, quem percipiunt ore, hauriant vocis modulatione ut scilicet quem gustant . . . recolant ex se crucifixum et mortuum atque sepultum . . .

For the communicants the first chant that is sung is: Agnus Dei . . . so that all the faithful communicating on the body and blood of the Lord may drink with the melody of the singing Him whom they receive by mouth; that is to say, within themselves may contemplate, crucified, dead and buried, Him whom they taste . . .

Is some metaphor of liquefaction implied here in the experience of the music? The Communion itself is simply explained: it is sung that the minds of the

---

[51] Transl.: Temple Classics edn (London 1901), 231.

[52] Ed. Gushee, 130; transl. Ponte, 55. Aurelian would have had an earlier repertoire in mind, but in view of his continued popularity and the basic nature of the ideas involved, the early date seems not to affect the issue.

[53] Ed. Gushee, 131 (my transl.).

faithful 'may be drawn by the sweet melody and elevated into sublime contemplation' (*dulcissima modulatione mens eius trahatur et suspendatur in sublimissimam contemplationem*).[54]

Johannes de Grocheo takes the question of emotive chanting one step further when he says that the Kyrie eleyson, the first part of the Ordinary of the Mass, should be sung in a particular manner *in order to* achieve a particular effect – i.e. it should be sung slowly in 'perfect longs' in the same style as *cantus coronatus* in order to move the hearts of the congregation to devotion.[55] Connections such as this between style of performance and emotive effect are very rarely made.

Medieval writers about music clearly did not need the Greeks to tell them that different kinds of music must, emotively, produce different results. They were, however, fascinated by one particular aspect of Greek theory, the character of the different modes. The theory of the modes was one of those areas, like interval theory, in which it seemed imperative to effect the reconciliation of which I spoke at the beginning of this chapter, between inherited classical theory and the day-to-day practical experience of the chant. It was in essence a problem of melodic analysis and classification.

In their final medieval form the modes were eight in number, grouped in four pairs, the pairs having their finals on *d, e, f* and *g* respectively, and each pair existing in two forms, a higher (authentic) and a lower (plagal); but this neat formulation was not achieved until the early eleventh century.[56] Compared to the central intellectual endeavour involved in this effort to categorize melodic structures, the ethical issue was a small and peripheral affair. However, a number of theorists do take it up. Guido says that the diverse characters of the modes fit in with the diversity of men's minds: one man is pleased by the 'intermittent leaps' (*fractis saltibus*) of the *e*-mode (authentic), another by the 'volubility' (*garrulitas*) of the *g*-mode (authentic).[57] But Guido does not differentiate between the diverse pleasures aroused. Nor indeed does Johannes Afflighemensis. But the latter, whilst basing his discussion on Guido, lets his

---

[54] Ed. Gushee, 131.

[55] 'Isti autem cantus cantantur tractim et ex longis et perfectis ad modum cantus coronati, ut corda audientium ad devote orandum promoveantur et ad devote audiendum promoveantur . . .' (ed. Rohloff, 162, who takes the plural as referring to Kyrie and Gloria). Grocheo goes on to speak in similar terms about the 'Responsory of the Mass' (i.e. the Gradual), the Alleluia and the Offertory.

[56] The classic statement of the importance of the 'final' is that of the *Dialogus de musica* (anon., formerly attributed to 'Odo'; the standard edn is still that of Gerbert (I.251–64)): 'A tone or mode is a rule which distinguishes every chant by its final' (*Tonus vel modus est regula, quae de omni cantu in fine diiudicat*; 257). Shortly afterwards (c. 1026) Guido of Arezzo defined the *ambitus* (*Micrologus*, ch. xiii). For an exposition of this and other matters related to the concept(s) of mode, see Harold S. Powers's major article 'Mode' in *New Grove* (especially sect. II, 'Medieval Modal Theory'). The *Dialogus* is transl. almost entire in Strunk (1950), 103–16.

[57] Guido, *Micrologus*, ch. xiv (ed. Smits van Waesberghe, 159; transl. Babb, 69).

imagination run riot; it is almost as if he were inventing the modern programme-note:[58]

Alios namque morosa et curialis vagatio primi [modi] delectat, alios rauca secundi gravitas capit, alios severa et quasi indignans tertii persultatio iuvat, alios adulatorius quarti sonus attrahit, alii modesta quinti petulantia ac subitaneo ad finalem casu moventur, alii lacrimosa sexti voce mulcentur, alii mimicos septimi saltus libenter audiunt, alii decentem et quasi matronalem octavi canorem diligunt.

Some are pleased by the slow and ceremonious peregrinations of the first [mode], some are taken by the hoarse profundity of the second, some are delighted by the austere and almost haughty prancing of the third, some are attracted by the ingratiating sound of the fourth, some are stirred by the well-bred high spirits and the sudden fall to the final of the fifth, some are soothed by the tearful voice of the sixth, some like to hear the spectacular leaps of the seventh, some favor the staid and almost matronly strains of the eighth.

It is not easy to know quite what to make of this 'romantic' description, which seems to bear the imprint of an imaginative mind, if not one merely fanciful to the point of whimsy. We shall return to it later. For the moment it is sufficient to remark that the *emotive* effects are, as I said, not spelt out, though some are certainly implied – by the words 'taken', 'delighted', 'stirred', 'melted'.

IV   The experience of music

It would be convenient if a neat distinction could be maintained between the emotive and other 'experiential' aspects of music. Certainly the theorists do not make it. They seem in fact to be talking, often at the same time, about three different things which we must try to keep separate:

(i)   characteristics of the music itself (e.g. 'spectacular leaps', 'matronly strains' mentioned by Johannes);

(ii)   the feelings it arouses in the listener – i.e. his experience of the music as it happens (e.g. the sense of *suavitas*, the feeling of being 'melted');

(iii)   the resultant actions, behaviour and *non*-musical feelings (e.g. devotion, well-being, lust, powerlessness).

None of these three aspects, it must be stressed, opens a view into music's 'expressive' or mimetic relations nor implies that they necessarily exist.

As is already obvious, some of the most revealing comments about the experience of music come from the writings of those not professionally concerned with the theory of music at all. One reason for this is that practically all medieval theorists are most actively concerned with the ecclesiastical chant and its proper performance in the liturgy. They find room for some speculative theory, usually of a routine kind, but not for musing on the experience of hearing music. It is especially difficult to acquire an

---

[58] Johannes Afflighemensis, ch. XVI (ed. Smits van Waesberghe, 109; transl. Babb, 133), but see the discussion of the difficulties, p. 404 below (I have substituted 'soothed' for 'melted'). The passage is taken up by Jerome of Moravia (fl. 1272–1304).

understanding of the way medieval listeners or musicians of various types responded to secular (i.e. non-liturgical) music, the music associated for example with courtliness and with personal devotion. Johannes de Grocheo is the only theorist who specifically attempts to establish categories of secular music and to describe them in some detail. He is conscious of music's emotive effects and social uses, though his moralizations are somewhat stiff and second-hand. He says, for example, about the *chanson de geste* (*cantus gestualis*) as a social force: it 'ought to be sung to old people and working citizens and the lower classes (*mediocribus*) . . . so that hearing the miseries and calamities of others they will more easily sustain their own and return to their work with more alacrity'.[59] But his remarks on the experience of the music do not take us very far.

Secular musical experience was associated with the two loves of which Adélard of Bath, and many other writers, treated – the love of this world and the love of God. The love of this world is epitomized in the literature and art of *courtoisie*, courtliness. The manifestations of the phenomenon usually known today as courtly love – though 'courteous love' might be a better term – are immensely diverse. It is the central and most frequently recurring idealism in that huge body of medieval literature which we call 'romance', ranging from the anonymous 'classical' romances of the mid twelfth century through three centuries to Malory and beyond. It permeates the visual arts, tapestries, illumination and ivories, those 'silent forms' that can still 'tease us out of thought'. It must also have pervaded the conventions, ceremonies, acts and graces of social life in a thousand ways now lost to us. What is now to be discussed is the way in which the experience of music became amalgamated with this complex of courtly forms.

We may begin from the private experience, or what purports to be the private experience, of the poet–lover. First, he chooses song as the natural medium for his thoughts and feelings. Then, as is evident from hundreds of examples, he refers specifically to the connection between his singing and his love. So, Jaufré Rudel from the mid twelfth century:[60]

> Quan lo rius de la fontana
> s'esclarzis, si cum far sol,
> e par la flors aiglentina,
> e'l rossinholetz el ram
> volf e refranh ez aplana
> son dous chantar e l'afina,
> dreitz es qu'ieu lo mieu refranha . . .

[59] See above, note 55 for Grocheo's remarks on the chants of the Mass. On the *cantus gestualis*, see Rohloff, 130 (he translates *mediocribus* as *niedriggestellten*). Grocheo's remarks seem to bear little relation to the actualities of *chanson de geste* performance (see chapter 6:IV above) and smack rather of Plato's theories: *Et ideo iste cantus valet ad conservationem totius civitatis* (Rohloff, 130; see also his commentary, 24, 26–8).

[60] Text ed. Goldin, no. 19 (p. 102). For line 5 Goldin gives 'turns, modulates, softens'; Press (p. 31) 'turns, softens and smooths'; de la Cuesta (p. 56) 'utters . . . and polishes'. De la Cuesta prints the melody from BN MS fr.22543 (Source 32).

When the water of the fountain runs clear, as it is wont to do, and the eglantine flower appears, and the nightingale on the bough repeats and modulates and smooths out his sweet song and refines it, right it is that I should modulate mine.

and Adam de la Halle a century or more later:[61]

> Puis ke je sui de l'amourouse loi,
> bien doi Amors en cantant essauchier;
> encore i a milleur raison pour coi
> jou doi canter d'amoureus desirier:

Since I follow the religion of love, it is incumbent on me to exalt Love in my singing. There is, moreover, a better reason why I should sing of amorous desire.

Bernart de Ventadorn (*fl.* 1150–80) clarifies the relation in his 'Tant ai mo cor ple de joya'. He says his heart is so full of joy that it 'disnatures' him, and he doesn't feel the ice and the snow of winter; 'the ice I see is a flower, the snow is green things that grow' –

> per que mos chans mont' e poya
> e mos pretz melhura.[62]

so that my song mounts and rises up, and my worth increases.

There is an integral connection here and elsewhere between the joyful experience of love, the lover's sense of his *pretz* (the English 'worth' hardly gives it full weight) and his song, itself a creative surge, like spring. As Bernart says in another poem, 'De totas partz soi de joi claus', 'I am surrounded by joys on every side; but the joy which comes from her exceeds all others'.[63] *Joia, joie*, is a central concept in courtly experience; *joi* is what the song talks about and embodies.

As a commentary on the emotional, or imaginative, experience of music this does not unfortunately get us far. One reference to the equation 'love–joy–song' is very much like another. However, there is one feature of them which has a particular interest: for these poet–musicians music is more or less confined, in theory at least, to positive experiences of joy; there should be no music of melancholy, and the counterpart to joyful song is silence. So writes the Châtelain de Coucy (d. 1203):[64]

> Tout sunt parti de moi joieuz talent
> et quant joie me faut, bien est raisons
> qu'avec ma joie faillent mes chançons.

I am altogether deprived of joyous desires; and, when joy is wanting, there is good reason that with my joy my songs cease too.

Song is essentially the concomitant of *douz panser*. The sorrows of love may be consoled by music, but no kind of music provides a natural response to them

---

[61] Ed. Marshall, no. xvi (p. 69).
[62] Goldin, no. 22 (p. 128).
[63] See above chapter 1:11 (Ex. 1): 'Can l'erba fresch''.
[64] Goldin, no. 9 (p. 358).

in the way that it does to the joys of love. This points to a repetition on the secular plane of the underlying concept of music as a manifestation of order, proportion, *armonia*, from which arise pleasure, well-being and a sense of being 'in tune', humanly speaking. The courtly *joie* is a species of *musica humana*, and heard music is one of its symptoms. If your *musica humana* is not properly tuned because of unhappiness, you should keep silent. Needless to say they did not – the paradox of *li dous maus* was too attractive; but their 'unhappiness' seems never to find direct expression in their music.

   The love of God is a theme so fundamental and universal in the writings of the Middle Ages that it is difficult to know where not to look for evidence about the nature and power of music. In its essential quality the non-liturgical, private devotional experience does not differ greatly from the liturgical and communal. The fundamental experience of sacred music is one of praise. 'Singing together' was both actuality and metaphor in the communion of the saints. This famous Alleluiatic sequence of the tenth century epitomizes the universal chorus of praise in which the whole creation joins:[65]

1   Cantemus cuncti melodum
     nunc *Alleluia.*

2a   in laudibus aeterni regis   2b   hoc denique caelestes chori
     haec plebs resultet   cantant in altum
     Alleluia.   *Alleluia . . .*

4a   nubium cursus,   4b   fluctus et undae
     ventorum volatus,   imber et procellae,
     fulgurum coruscatio   tempestas et serenitas,
     et tonitruum sonitus   cauma, gelu, nix, pruinae,
     dulce consonent simul   saltus, nemora pangant
     Alleluia.   *Alleluia.*

Let us all now sing the melody Alleluia / 2a. Let this people resound Alleluia in praise of the eternal king. / 2b. At last the heavenly choirs sing this on high, Alleluia . . . / 4a. Let the passage of the clouds, the flight of the winds, the flashing of lightning and the rumbling of thunder sweetly sound together Alleluia / 4b. Waters and waves, rain and storms, tempest and calm, heat, cold, snow and frosts, woodlands and groves, let them all record Alleluia.

Just as *joie* is the keyword to associate with musical experience in the literature of romance, so *gaudium* in the religious sphere:[66]

          Favent igitur
          resurgenti Christo cuncti gaudiis –
          flores, segetes
          redivivo fructu vernant,
          et volucres
          gelu tristi terso dulce jubilant.

[65] Raby (1953), 216. See von den Steinen, 132, 186; and Kusch, 144, with German transl; Schaller–Könsgen, no. 1894 (early-tenth-century).
[66] Cited Chailley (1955b), 215.

All therefore show favour with their joys to Christ as he rises – the flowers, the crops, flourish with their new fruit, and the birds, now the sad frost is melted away, carol sweetly.

The context of this *gaudium*, a spring-scene linked with the Resurrection of Christ, is interesting (and not in the least unusual); it reminds us of the close interconnection between songs of the two joys, the two loves. This interconnection is deliberately established (and is not merely unconscious permeation) in the *chanson pieuse* and in popular songs of the Franciscans.

The number of *chansons pieuses* is small in the total repertoire of troubadour and trouvère songs but constitutes a distinctive genre. Gautier de Coinci (*c.* 1177–1236) incorporated some twenty or more songs into his *Les Miracles de Nostre Dame*.[67] The *topos* of song arising from the joy of love is common indeed and is simply transferred from his secular models; the only difference is that the love which inspires him is the love of Our Lady:[68]

> Quant ces flouretes florir voi
> et chanter oi ces chanteeurs
> por la fleur chant qui a en soi
> toutes biautez, toutes valeurs.
> Ele est et mere et fille a roy,
> roses des roses, fleurs des fleurs.
> Certes molt l'aim: Diex doinst qu'aint moi
> et qu'ele y mete bonnes meurs.

When I see the flowers blooming and hear the singers singing, I sing for the flower who has in herself all beauties, all dignities. She is the mother and the daughter of a king, rose of roses, flower of flowers. Indeed I love her greatly: God grant that she love me and that she should implant good qualities in me.

The two loves, in their association with music, are beautifully blended by Dante in the *Commedia*. Music is, of course, only one aspect of the great synthesis of courtly and divine.[69] Invited by St John to discourse on love, Dante says that 'God, the "good" which contents this court [of heaven], is the Alpha and Omega of all the scripture which Love reads to me.'

> Lo ben che fa contenta questa corte,
>   Alfa ed O è di quanta scrittura
>   mi legge Amore o lievemente o forte.   (*Par.* xxvi. 16)

In this stanza the blend of courtly and religious feeling is so deep that it cannot be broken down except artificially. The circling, singing lights of the blessed are also courtiers in the court of Heaven; the burning of romantic passion is also the burning desire for the highest of all loves; and the 'lectures' which the

[67] Ed. Chailley (1959) with full musical commentary.
[68] R1677; ed. Chailley, 171 (no. 6). The song is a *contrafactum* of 'De chanter me semont Amors' (R2030) by Vielart de Corbie.
[69] See Stevens (1968a), 6–7.

God of Love reads to his servants are the lessons also of St John's Gospel. The synthesis is complete.

The blending of courtly-amorous and religious meanings of love-music is achieved in two of the ladies of the *Purgatorio*. Matilda, blessing those whose sins are forgiven them, sings *come donna innamorata*, 'like a woman in love'; the phrase seems to come straight out of an erotic *pastourelle* by Cavalcanti. Leah, Rachel's sister, of whom Dante dreams on the ascent to the Earthly Paradise, provides music of spiritual consolation. She is a young, courtly lady wandering through a plain, gathering flowers and singing;

> giovane e bella in sogno mi parea
> > donna vedere andar per una landa
> > cogliendo fiori; e cantando dicea . . .   (*Purg.* xxvii. 97)

Such identification of the two loves was not confined to Dante or to fourteenth-century Italy. The English poet of *Pearl* achieved a comparable synthesis on a smaller scale.[70] The central figure in his dream is a courtly pearl-maiden, herself a queen in the court of Heaven, presided over by Mary, 'quene of cortaysye'. Music is not prominent, but the climax of the poem, the dreamer's vision of the New Jerusalem, includes the procession of virgins (the queens) singing before the Lamb.

> Then glory and gle watz nwe abroched;
> Al songe to love that gay juelle.
> The steven moght stryke thurgh the urthe to helle
> that the Vertues of heven of joye endyte.   (1123–6)

nwe abroched: newly given vent to / *to love*: in praise of / *gay juelle*: i.e. Christ / *steven*: voice / *moght stryke*: must have pierced / *of joye endyte*: out of joy utter (in song)

The *Pearl*-poet would certainly have understood Dante.

The music of religious praise not only stands for order (*relazione, armonia*) but is bound up, then, with the experience of love. It is perhaps for the latter reason (as well as because the divine order can never be fully understood by man) that the experience of music can be represented as itself a mysterious thing and be used also as a metaphor for the ineffable states of mystic contemplation. The anonymous author of the *Musica Enchiriadis* (? *c.* 900) is struck by the irrationality of musical delight: the meaning of music is one of the things which in this life we see through a glass, darkly.[71] Both this author and Regino of Prüm (*c.* 842–915) tell the moving myth of Orpheus and

---

[70] Late-fourteenth-century; ed. E. V. Gordon (Oxford 1953). I have modernized the orthography of the quotation.

[71] The date of *Musica Enchiriadis* is disputed; see Gushee 'Musica enchiriadis' in *New Grove*, sect. 4. The text pr. Gerbert, I. 152–73 (wrongly attributed to Hucbald), is reasonably sound according to Gushee; it is the basis of L. Rosensthiel's transl. (1976). The edn of H. Schmid (1981) replaces it; the reference is to p. 57.

Eurydice to explain the mysterious and irrational character of music.[72] According to their etymology, Orpheus means *optima vox*; Eurydice, true judgement (*profunda dijudicatio*). According to Regino, Orpheus wants to recall Eurydice from the depths of hell with his *cithara*. He fails because the intellect of man is incapable of penetrating the inner secrets of 'harmony' and reducing them to scientific rules. When man starts to exercise the full light of his reason on music, it vanishes into the darkness. To quote the *Musica Enchiriadis*,[73]

Sed dum rursus per Orpheum, id est, per optimum cantilenae sonum, a secretis suis ac si ab inferis evocatur, imaginarie perducitur usque in auras huius vitae, dumque videri videtur, amittitur. Scilicet quia inter caetera, quae adhuc ex parte et in aenigmate cernimus, haec etiam disciplina haud ad plenum habet rationem in hac vita penetrabilem.

But whilst it [the true understanding of music] is being summoned from its secret places, as if from the underworld by Orpheus, – that is, by 'the best sound of song' – and being brought in mental images up into the clear air of this present life and at that moment seems to be seen [for what it is], it is lost. This is evidently because, amongst other things which in the present we see only in part and darkly, this knowledge too has a basis to which in this life our minds can hardly penetrate to the full.

I said above that music, because it is ultimately inaccessible to human reason, could be used as a metaphor for the inexpressible religious experiences of the higher contemplatives and mystics. Whether 'metaphor' is the correct term I am not sure. The relation of music to spiritual experience is a complex one. First, the sounds of actual music induce a joy, a *gaudium*, which as Cassiodorus says 'raises our senses to divine realities and charms our ears with its measure[?]' (*sensum nostrum ad superna erigit et aures modulatione permulcet*).[74] But the reason why this works, so to speak, is that these divine realities are themselves a music; and in the 'heavenly habitations', to quote Abélard, angels and saints 'in the ineffable sweetness of harmonic modulation render eternal praise to God'.[75] The idea of an angelic liturgy is natural and commonplace; the devotions of a Christian on this earth enable him to share in it.[76] If this heavenly music is indeed 'real', then to share in it is not a metaphoric experience; it is rather our earthly music that is the metaphor.

The deep interpenetration of the literal and metaphorical is to be seen in the

---

[72] See de Bruyne, 1.337–8. Regino, *Epistola de armonica institutione*, ed. Gerbert, 1.246. No modern edn is published, but see Y. Chartier's diss. 'L'Epistola de armonica institutione de Reginon de Prüm' (Ottawa 1965).

[73] Gerbert, 1.172.

[74] Ed. Mynors, Book II.v.10 (p. 149).

[75] Cited von Simson, 37.

[76] Hammerstein, *Musik der Engel* (1962), 127–8, with supporting patristic quotation. Of the Church Fathers, it is said that *quidam hunc modum cantandi ab Angelis didicerunt* (some of them learnt this manner of singing, i.e. plainchant, from the angels): Gerbert, 1.8, from *Instituta patrum de modo psallendi* (?*c.* 1000); see chapter 8, note 69, above.

mystical writings of Hildegard of Bingen (1098–1179), who was herself a musician of talent.[77] The very title of her song-collection which she made in the mid twelfth century shows the nature of her preoccupation: *Symphonia armonie celestium revelationum* ('symphony of the harmony of heavenly revelations'). Whether God himself or his Creation is the focus of meditation matters little, because everything has meaning as *musica*. As Schmidt-Görg has written,

The whole cosmos, animal and human, the qualities of body and mind, the Church, the saints, the angels and evil spirits, the Mother of God, the three persons of the Trinity: everything is conceived as symbolic sound and is consummated in the heavenly harmony.[78]

In one striking passage of a sequence on St Rupert, Hildegard contrasts the heavenly with a devilish dance. 'In you', she says to the holy Rupert, 'the Holy Spirit makes music'.[79]

> . . . O vas nobile   quod non est pollutum
> nec devoratum   in saltatione
> antique spelunce,   et quod non est maceratum
> in vulneribus   antiqui perditoris
>
> In te symphonizat spiritus sanctus
> quia angelicis choris   associaris . . .

. . . noble urn, that remains untarnished, not drunk to the dregs in the dance in the ancient cave, nor destroyed in the attacks of the ancient ravager –
The Holy Spirit makes music over you, for you belong to the dances of angels . . .
(Dronke)

The dance is an image often used for the harmony of the heavenly host. And with a synaesthetic image common in the *Divina Commedia*, Hildegard elsewhere several times equates the experience of music with light, fire and burning:[80]

Ita et tu, o homo, quae es paupercula et fragilis natura, audis in symphonia sonum de igneo ardore virginalis pudoris . . . et sonum de acumine viventium luminum in superna civitate lucentium . . .

Thus, O man, being of a poor and weak nature, you hear in the music a sound drawn from the fiery heat of virgin modesty [i.e. Mary's] . . . and sound drawn from the sharpness of the living lights which are resplendent in the heavenly city.

---

[77] Hildegard: see Barth (edn 1969); Dronke (1970), ch. 5; and Ian Bent's concise article in *New Grove*.

[78] Ed. Barth *et al.*, 9.

[79] *Ibid.*, 254–5, with German transl.; see also Dronke (1970), 167–8, from whom I quote the English translation.

[80] Hammerstein (1962), 56–7. The term *symphonia* meant for Aristotle a mixture of high and low notes, and this definition persists into the Middle Ages (see H. J. Marx, *IMS Report 1972*, 541–7).

Elsewhere in her visions Hildegard recounts how she saw 'in the height of the celestial secrets two ranks of heavenly spirits shining with great brightness'; they surrounded five other rows, and these all together surrounded another two, like a crown, making nine angel-choirs.[81]

Et hae acies omnes in omni genere musicalium organorum mirificis vocibus mirabilia illa resonabant.

And all these ranks [of angels] were re-echoing those marvels with every kind of musical instrument in wonderful voices [? sounds].

As I have said, it is virtually impossible to separate the literal from the metaphorical. Certainly Hildegard must have believed in the reality of the heavenly music; the continuous, heard singing of monks in choir (*non cessantes ullis horis cantando cum sonitu*) performs the liturgy of the angels (*angelicum ordinem exercent*).[82] But to say 'reality' is perhaps only to shift the question on to a semantic level. The point, surely, is that the experience of spiritual truth and joy and the experience of 'music' are so closely linked in her imagination as to be indistinguishable.

To sum up, the experience of music, which in the Middle Ages was obviously as intense as in any other period of history, is one which for them inevitably calls up words like *suavitas*, *dulcedo*, *gaudium*, and their vernacular equivalents. When further explanation or rationalization was required, what could be more natural than that they should fall back on the *ratio* which lay behind every *sensus*, every manifestation of the *sensus*? This *ratio* was Number, *musica* itself, order, proportion, consonance. No further explanation was necessary. The question now, for us, is whether this experience of music left room for any special words-and-music relationship other than the principal one – of analogical harmony – already described. Or, to put the question rather more particularly, when medieval writers discussed the expressive aspect of song, was this conceived as being something in which the *verbal text*, with its densely specific meanings, was important?

v Expressiveness

For clarity's sake, I revert once more to my working definition of the term 'expressive'. I do not intend the term to cover the whole range of relations which in the broadest sense could be called 'mimetic', but only to the group of relations which link music with the moods, feelings, emotions of human beings. Other kinds of musical mimesis have already been discussed in the preceding chapters, especially in chapter 8, where I argued that Gregorian chant 'imitates' the sounds of speech, if often in a highly stylized form. It must

[81] Hammerstein, 55.
[82] *Ibid.*, 55.

also be abundantly clear that no consideration of *musica* can avoid being a discussion of the 'metaphysical mimesis' which underlies the whole ramifying concept. Within this frame of meaning both sounding music and sounding words are validated as manifestations of that *harmonia* which is *ordinatio coeli et terre*, 'the ordering of all things in heaven and in earth'. It may, however, be diluting the meaning of 'mimesis' to make it cover the universal analogy which *musica* is. As symbol, sacrament, *speculum* or *umbra*, whichever word is chosen, music can be said only in the most general sense to 'imitate' a truth, the reality which is forever unknowable and inaccessible. Curiously enough, this grand metaphysical mimesis at the back of musical aesthetics may well have worked *against* the more limited expressiveness which we are now to consider. Otto von Simson makes the point tellingly with reference to the visual arts:[83]

We should by no means overlook the positive aspects of this aesthetics: its underlying distrust and depreciation of the imitative in art, and indeed of all imagery, kept alive sensibility for the 'non-objective' values in artistic design and thus constituted a powerful counterweight to the overwhelming pictorial and illustrative concerns of medieval art.

Musical expressiveness gets some attention in the early Middle Ages – from theorists, moralists, poets, the writers of liturgical and dramatic rubrics, and others. Their remarks fall into three main categories, referring to:

(i)   an expressiveness *of the performer*, deriving from style of singing;
(ii)   an expressiveness *in the music itself* (independent of any words), related to what the singer may be feeling, or pretending as an actor to feel – i.e. to his non-musical experience;
(iii) an expressiveness specifically *related to the verbal content* of a song, or of chant.

These categories are not watertight but will serve, I hope, as a basis for discussion.

First, expressiveness of the performer. Evidence about performers and what they should or should not do is not easy to come by. In chapter 10:III I quoted rubrics from various ceremonies and plays, some of which indicated the sort of emotional colour which a singer might be directed to apply to his or her performance.[84] I did not quote there rubrics from the pseudo-dramatic eighth-century *Harrowing of Hell* – such as *Tunc Adam lugubri et miserabili voce clamabat . . .* ('Then Adam cried out in a mournful and miserable voice') – as the text seemed not to be evidence of what actually happened in the live performance of drama. But it does apparently represent what someone in the

[83] Von Simson, 23.
[84] The evidence could be amplified from other sources: see for instance Johannes Afflighemensis on the suprascript 'letters' in neumed chant MSS. He is critical of their ambiguity: 'L', for example, might stand not only for *leva* (raise) but for *leniter, lascive* or *lugubriter* (smoothly; playfully or wantonly?; mournfully); see ch. 21 (Latin text, p. 139; transl. Babb, 150). See also chapter 8, notes 12 and 27 above.

eighth century imagined a performer might do with his voice, emotionally.[85] The question remains whether these emotions were felt to be latent, or embodied, *in the music itself* or whether they were seen as performers' *additions to* the music, a way of rendering it. If the latter, it would not be surprising. The formulas of everyday speech in every age have a similar neutrality and flexibility.

That ecclesiastical singers, the despised *cantores* of medieval theory, did on occasion display unseemly and extravagant emotions is known from the censures of moralists. In his *Speculum charitatis*, Ailred of Rievaulx (1109–67), the great Cistercian abbot, lambastes theatrical choirmen:[86]

Ad quid, rogo, terribilis ille follium flatus, tonitrui potius fragorem, quam vocis exprimens suavitatem? Ad quid illa vocis contractio et infractio? Hic succinit, ille discinit; alter medias quasdam notas dividit et incidit. Nunc vox stringitur, nunc frangitur, nunc impingitur, nunc diffusiori sonitu dilatatur. Aliquando, quod pudet dicere, in equinos hinnitus cogitur; aliquando virili vigore deposito, in femineae vocis gracilitates acuitur, nonnunquam artificiosa quadam circumvolutione torquetur et retorquetur. Videas aliquando hominem aperto ore quasi intercluso halitu exspirare, non cantare, ac ridiculosa quadam vocis interceptione quasi minitari silentium; nunc agones morientium, vel exstasim patientium imitari. Interim histrionicis quibusdam gestis totum corpus agitatur, torquentur labia, rotant, ludunt humeri; et ad singulas quasque notas digitorum flexus respondet.

What is the purpose, I ask, of that appalling blasting of bellows, which conveys the crashing of thunder rather than the sweetness of a human voice? And what of the constriction and 'breaking' of the note? There's one man singing in unison whilst another sings a *discantus* part; yet another sings 'divisions' on certain medial notes and chops them up. Now the voice is strangled, now broken off, now forced, now broadened with a fuller sound. Sometimes – I blush to say it – they force from their voices the sound of horses neighing; at other times manliness is abandoned and thin womanish noises are produced, occasionally by a kind of artificial distortion [falsetto?] switching from one to the other and back again.

Sometimes you can see a man with his mouth open not singing but breathing out almost with held breath and by a sort of ridiculous suspension of the sound threatening, as it were, silence. And now he imitates the agonies of the dying or of those experiencing ecstasy. All the time his whole body is in movement with the kinds of gesture used by actors – his lips twist and turn, his shoulders work up and down, and with the flexing of his fingers he marks every single note.

Emotional self-indulgence is a malady incident to singers in all ages. It can be distinguished both from the true 'expressiveness of the performer' just discussed, which is not *self*-centred but disciplined by the text, the rubric (if

[85] D. N. Dumville, 'Liturgical drama and panegyric responsory from the eighth century', *Journal of Theological Studies* n.s. 23 (1972) 374–406, argues that this text is the earliest surviving liturgical drama. C. Clifford Flanigan, 'The liturgical drama and its tradition: a review of scholarship 1965–75', *Research Opportunities in Renaissance Drama* 18 (1975) 92, describes it more plausibly as 'a private non-liturgical devotion'.

[86] Cited Young (1933), I.548, from *PL* 195:571 (1855).

any) and the occasion. It can be distinguished also from the second main category – expressiveness in the music itself. The idea that there was a type of melody, the *jubilus*, which expressed the inner yearnings of the soul when they got beyond words was of long standing. Amalarius of Metz (*c.* 775 – *c.* 850) writes of it in connection with the sequence:[87]

Haec iubilatio, quem cantores sequentiam vocant, illum statum ad mentem nostram ducit, quando non erit necessaria locutio verborum, sed sola cogitatione mens menti monstrabit quod retinet in se.

This *jubilatio*, which singers call a *sequentia*, induces in us a mental state when the utterance of words will not be necessary but by thought alone mind will show to mind what it has within itself.

This passage is admittedly slanted more towards the emotive effect than to the expressive origin of wordless music, but the phrase *mens menti monstrabit* (mind will show to mind) implies a content, as it were, in the music which not being the music itself can yet be communicated *through* the music. The conception seems to go back at least to St Augustine:[88]

Qui jubilat, verbat non dicit; sed sonus quidam est laetitiae sine verbis. Vox est enim animi diffusi laetitia, quantum potest, exprimentis affectum, non sensum comprehendentis. Gaudens homo in exsultatione sua ex verbis quibusdam quae non possunt dici et intelligi, erumpit in vocem quadam exsultatione sine verbis, ita ut appareat cum ipsa voce gaudere quidem sed quasi repletum nimio gaudio non posse exprimere quid gaudet.

He who jubilates does not utter words; rather, it is a sort of sound of gladness without words. The voice comes from a mind diffused with gladness which is expressing feeling to the highest degree possible [but] not understanding its meaning. A man delighting in his exultation breaks away from any words whatever, since they cannot be spoken nor understood, into a vocal sound of, as it were, exultation without words. The result is that he seems to be rejoicing indeed in his very voice but not to be able to express what rejoices him [because it is] as it were filled with too great joy.

This makes the expressive basis of the *jubilus* clear. 'To sing is to utter the words in the mouth [*verba ore proferre*] . . . to jubilate, however, is to rejoice.' So writes Cassiodorus, following on from St Augustine.[89] Jubilation, is what *non articulatis verbis sed confusa voce proferimus* (we bring out not with distinctly uttered words but in an unarticulated voice). The idea is not lost during the Middle Ages and the term *jubilus* appears much later, in the *Diffinitorium* of Tinctoris (fifteenth-century), for example, as *cantus cum excellenti quadam laetitia pronuntiatus* (a song uttered with a certain supreme happiness); he does

---

[87] Amalarius, *Liber Officialis* (*c.* 823), III.16.3 (ed. J. M. Hanssens, *Studi e Testi*, vol. 139 (Rome, 1949), 304.

[88] Augustine, commentary on Ps. 99; cited de Bruyne, 1.66, no. 2, in discussion of Cassiodorus's distinction between song and 'jubilation': *Cantare est verba (Domini) ore proferre . . . jubilare vero gaudere est.*

[89] Cited de Bruyne, 1.66, n. 2.

not, however, specify the absence of words.[90] The compatibility of this conception of jubilant song, bursting spontaneously from a full heart, with love-joy associated with troubadour and trouvère song is obvious – even though the latter poets never allow joy to condemn them to wordlessness. In both cases a surge of musical creativity arises (or is assumed to arise) from the personal experience of intense happiness.

So much for *jubilatio*, expressiveness without words. We come now to the third category, in which musical expressiveness is related to the content, even if not always to the particular words, of a song or chant. The author of the *Musica enchiriadis* (c. 900) ponders in this passage on the 'meaning' of music and the expressive relations between music and emotion:[91]

Quomodo vero tantam cum animis nostris musica commutationem et societatem habeat? Etsi scimus quadam nos similitudine cum illa compactos [esse], edicere ad liquidum non valemus, nec solum diiudicare melos possumus ex propria naturalitate sonorum, sed etiam rerum. Nam affectus rerum quae canuntur oportet ut imitetur cantionis affectus, ut in tranquillis rebus tranquillae sunt neumae, laetisonae in jucundis, moerentes in tristibus, quae dure sunt dicta vel facta, duris neumis ex-primi . . . In talibus cum iudicatio nostra esse possit, plura sunt tamen quae nos sub causis occultioribus lateant.

But how may music to such an extent have intercourse and union with our minds? Even though we know that we ourselves are joined by a certain similarity with music, we have not the power to enunciate it clearly; nor can we come to a judgement of a melody considered on its own on the basis of the individual nature of its sounds or even of its content. For it is necessary that the emotional characteristics of the song should imitate the emotional characteristics of the things which are being sung about: thus in peaceful matters the neumes are peaceful; in pleasant matters, they are glad-sounding; in sad, they are mournful; those things which have been harshly spoken or done [should be] expressed in harsh notes . . . [But] while in such cases we can exercise judgement, there are many things which lie hid from us in darker origins.

Although he does not know completely how music works, the author argues that a partial key to the understanding of music's effect is in the way the *affectus* (emotional characteristics) of the melody imitates the *affectus* of the things the music is about. As we shall see in a moment, this is an idea which will be taken up by Guido of Arezzo and by Johannes Afflighemensis some centuries later in similar terms.

However, before we look at those passages it will be worth while examining the genesis of the idea. It appears to go back to the ancient rhetoricians. Quintilian had from the Greeks a threefold view of 'music': it consisted, as we already know, of dance, melody, and words. The threefold skills of the orator – gesture, voice-modulation and verbal arrangement – correspond to these. The orator, he goes on to argue, in order to be fully

[90] Tinctoris, *Terminorum musicae diffinitorium* (ed. Coussemaker (1864), IV.177–91), 184.
[91] Gerbert, I.172; *affectus* (normally of human feelings): 'disposition, state of mind, mood' (see Lewis and Short).

'affective' must conform his voice to the *affectus* (emotional characteristics?) of what is being said. Lofty things will be delivered (*canere*, to sing or sound) in an elevated manner, joyful things sweetly, things indifferent in a light style.[92] To put the matter in a nutshell, a theory of expressive sound – expressive in order to be fully affective – deriving from traditional rhetoric finds itself juxtaposed somewhat awkwardly with a dominant, mathematical theory of sound as *musica*. Whether medieval authors over the long period we are considering recognized any incompatibility between the two equally respectable, equally authoritative traditions I do not know. Since all Truth was indisputably One, it is unlikely that they admitted any ultimate incompatibility at all.

I wish now to return to the passage quoted earlier (p. 391) in which Johannes Afflighemensis characterized the different modes. He described them as having qualities such as *morosa et curialis vagatio* ('slow and ceremonious peregrinations'), *severa et quasi indignans . . . persultatio* ('stern and almost haughty prancing'), *adulatorius . . . sonus* ('ingratiating sound'), *modesta . . . petulantia* ('well-bred high spirits'). The context of this passage is a discussion of musical taste; the chapter is headed 'How different people take pleasure in different modes' (*Quod diversi diversis delectentur modis*). Just as not everyone likes the same food, so not everyone likes the same kind of music. So a sensible and wise composer (*bene cautus musicus*) will pay attention to the audience he writes for and try to please them. Johannes is, then, not addressing himself to the 'problem of expressiveness'; he is more concerned with the resultant musical experiences, the *emotive* effects which we considered earlier. At the same time, an expressive view of music appears to underlie the language of this passage. 'Appears', certainly. Even though some of the details of the translation are dubious – e.g. it is not clear whether *persultatio* should be translated as 'leaping', 'prancing', or (in its less common meaning) 'resounding' – nevertheless adjectives such as *curialis* are metaphoric not literal. The author is saying that the characteristic movements of the first mode are *curialis*, 'courtly', 'ceremonious'; that something in the fourth is reminiscent of a flatterer; something in the eighth of a matron. The implications of these seemingly fanciful epithets, metaphors, are never drawn out; they do not seem to correspond to anything commonly experienced in the various modes. One is simply left guessing.

If these passages were all we had to go on as evidence of a consciously held view of song as an expressive art, they would not take us very far. The theorists seem to combine a respectful feeling about what was due to the theory of the Greek modes with an equally respectful attitude to some of the precepts of ancient rhetoric. One consequence is this whimsical rigmarole of Johannes Afflighemensis. However, this same Johannes was also one of the

---

[92] Quintilian, *Institutes*, I.x.24: 'Namque et voce et modulatione grandia elate, iucunda dulciter, moderata leniter canit, totaque arte consentit cum eorum quae dicuntur adfectibus.' See also section II above and note 27.

most practical and down-to-earth of the medieval theorists, and in chapter
xviii of his *De musica* he gives advice about how to compose *cantus* which is
both specific and relevant to our inquiry. Claude Palisca has described Johannes's treatise as 'the most readable and comprehensible of the medieval introductions to the chant repertory';[93] but what gives this chapter even wider
interest for us is that Johannes brings to an end his previous chapter by saying,
'Even if new compositions are now not needed for the Church, still we can
exercise our talents in putting to music the "rhythms" [i.e. syllable-based
verses] and threnodic verses of the poets' (*in rhythmis et lugubribus poetarum
versibus decantandis ingenia nostra exercere*).[94] Despite the reference to *musica
ritmica*, it is nevertheless plainchant that he seems to have most in mind and
from which all his actual musical examples are taken.

The whole chapter is not long; the first paragraph is worth quoting in full.[95]

Praecepta de cantu componendo

Primum igitur praeceptum modulandi subnectimus, ut secundum sensum verborum cantus varietur. Quis autem canendi modus cuilibet materiae conveniat, prius
docuimus, cum diversos diversis delectari diximus: quosdam enim curialitati, quosdam lasciviae, quosdam etiam tristitiae aptos monstravimus. Sicut autem laudem
desideranti poetae studendum est ut facta dictis exaequet neve eius, quem describit,
fortunis absona dicat, sic laudis avido modulatori annitendum est uti ita proprie
cantum componat, ut quod verba sonant cantus exprimere videatur. Itaque si iuve-
num rogatu cantum componere volueris, iuvenilis sit ille et lascivus; sin vero senum,
morosus sit et severitatem exprimens. Quemadmodum enim comoediarum scriptor,
si partes iuvenis seni vel luxuriosi avaro mandaverit, derisui subiacet, quales apud
Flaccum Plautus et Dorsennus inducuntur, ita reprehendi potest modulator, si in tristi
materia salientem modum adduxerit, vel in laeta lacrimabilem. Providendum igitur
est musico, ut ita cantum moderetur, ut in adversis deprimatur et in prosperis
exaltetur. Hoc autem non adeo praecipimus ut semper necesse sit fieri, sed quando fit,
ornatui esse dicimus. Habemus tamen de his quae diximus aliqua exempla. Siquidem
antiphonae in Resurrectione Domini exultationem in ipso sono praetendere videntur,
ut sunt hae: *Sedit Angelus, Cum Rex Gloriae, Christus resurgens*. Ista autem ant. *Rex
autem David* non tantum in verbis sed etiam in cantu moerorem sonare videtur. Sed et
in auctoribus quaerimoniae per hypolydium, quia is miserabilem sonum habet,
frequentissime decantantur.

Advice about composing a song

Therefore the first piece of advice we offer about making a melody is that the music
shall be varied according to the sense of the words. Moreover, we gave instructions
earlier as to which mode is appropriate to which matter, when we stated that different
people take pleasure in different modes: we showed that some modes were appropriate to courtliness, some to jollity, and some too to sadness. Just as a poet who is

---

[93] Babb and Palisca, 100.
[94] Latin text (ed. Smits van Waesberghe), 116; transl. Babb, 137; 'in putting to music':
  decantando, literally 'in singing, chanting'.
[95] *Ibid.*, 117–18; my transl.

desirous of praise must study aptly to relate deeds to words and not say things which are incongruous with the fortunes of the character described, so the praise-loving composer must take pains to put together a melody with such decorum that the melody is seen to express what the words declare. Thus if you are willing to write a song at the request of young people, it must be youthful and frolicsome. But if it is for old men, then it must be slow-moving and express austerity. For just as a writer of comedies opens himself to derision if he gives the part of a youth to an old man or the part of pleasure-lover to a miser, as Plautus and Dorsennus are represented as doing in the writings of Horace, in the same way a composer can be criticized if he introduces a sprightly mode when the subject is sad, or a tearful mode when it is happy. So the musician has to take care to manage his melody so that in dealing with adversity it runs at a low pitch [*literally* is pressed down] and with prosperous circumstances it runs high [*literally* is exalted]. We do not, however, insist that this must always be done; but when it is done, it is in our view an added beauty. We have some examples of what we have been saying: for instance antiphons for Easter Day seem to simulate exultation in their very sound, as these do: 'Sedit angelus', 'Cum rex glorie', 'Christus resurgens'. Moreover the antiphon called 'Rex autem David' not only in its words but even in its melody seems to sound forth sorrow. And even by the earliest composers [i.e. the 'authorities'] complaints are most often sung in the hypolydian mode [the lower of the two modes on *f*] because it has a plaintive sound.

This interesting and unusually detailed passage makes several distinct statements about words and music:

(i)   that the melody should be varied according to the sense of the words;
(ii) that, in consequence, the melody should seem to express what the words 'sound' (*sonare*);
(iii) that the desired congruity may be a matter of high and low pitch, or dependent on more elusive musical qualities, indicated but hardly illuminated by such adjectives as *lascivus, morosus*;[96]
(iv) that we can actually observe this congruity at work in certain specific chants.

Johannes's remarks and suggestions are so out of keeping with the general aesthetic tenor of medieval musical discussion that we have to enquire rather closely what has prompted him to think about chant in this way. The answer, in a single word, is again rhetoric. Johannes's treatise as a whole is based on Guido of Arezzo's *Micrologus*, the fifteenth chapter of which contains a single sentence which may have been Johannes's starting-point. Guido, too, is giving precepts about composing:[97]

Item ut rerum eventus sic cantionis imitetur effectus ut in tristibus rebus graves sint *neume*, in tranquillis jocunde, in prosperis exultantes, et reliqua.

Item: the effect of the song should imitate the course of events [as set forth in the text], so that in sad affairs the neumes should be low [? harsh ? grave], in peaceful affairs pleasant, in prosperous affairs exulting [? leaping about], and so on.

[96] There are two Latin words: *mōrosus*, peevish, fretful, captious; and the rarer *mŏrosus*, slow, delaying. In the context the latter seems more likely.
[97] See note 38 above.

This in its turn is extremely like the passage from the *Musica enchiriadis* of some two centuries earlier, quoted above, and both resemble Quintilian's requirements of the orator. What Johannes Afflighemensis does, I think, is to bring out more clearly than the earlier writers the rhetorical nature of his position and to relate the *affectus* of music not just generally to the subject of the song (the vague *in rebus*) but to the meaning of the words themselves (*sensus verborum*).

The rhetorical concepts of aptness (usually termed *decorum*) and persuasiveness are the twin threads which run through Johannes's discussion. The idea that a written work (poem, sermon, letter) must like an oration be apt to the occasion, the audience, the subject and the speaker was basic to the *ars rhetorica*. Johannes actually draws the parallels between the demands made on a writer and on a composer. The poet must take care not to write things which are *absona* (inharmonious, incongruous) with the circumstances; and so must the musician. A dramatist must observe *decorum* when he creates a character; and so must a song-writer when he creates a melody. When writing verses the poet avoids *homoioptoton*; similarly the composer must not too often repeat the same melodic figure (Johannes gives two examples to prove this point). It is wholly clear in this chapter on what lines the author is arguing.

The most interesting single feature of Johannes' discussion of musical *decorum* is his naming of actual chants which he regards as examples of expressiveness. The chants are extant in medieval service-books and we are fortunate, therefore, to be able to check what he means. The antiphon 'Rex autem David', to which he draws especial attention, survives in both the Worcester and the Sarum Antiphonaries; the texts differ only in the smallest details. I give the Sarum version.[98]

Ex. 167

Rex au- tem Da- - vid, co-o- per- to ca- pi- te, in- ce- dens lu-ge- bat
fi- li- um di-cens: Ab-sa- lon, fi-li mi, fi-li mi_ Ab- sa- lon, quis mi-chi
det ut e- go mo- ri- ar pro te, fi-li mi_ Ab- sa- lon?

But King David, going with his head covered, mourned his son saying 'Absalon my son, my son Absalon, would God I might die for you, O my son Absalon?'

---

[98] *Sarum Antiphonal*, 297. Stave 2, the first *fili mi*: MS *filium* (I thank Peter Dronke for this emendation). Antiphon at First Vespers for the First Sunday after Trinity (*Sarum Breviary*, col. mclxxii).

The text of the famous lament of David for his slain son Absalon is found in the Vulgate (*Liber II Regum*, xviii. 33, xix. 4). The text of the antiphon differs slightly from it, omitting for instance that David 'cried out in a loud voice' (*clamabat voce magna*).

This antiphon, Johannes says, 'seems to sound forth sorrow not only in its words but even in its melody'. If it 'expresses sorrow' – and his *videtur* ('seems') introduces a frankly subjective note – it is sorrow of an extraordinarily restrained and undemonstrative kind. The antiphon appears in fact to have a typical eighth-mode antiphon melody. Antiphons for the Magnificat at Vespers are rather longer than the normal psalm-antiphons and are melodically a little more elaborate, less syllabic.[99] 'Rex autem David' is well within the conventional limits and makes less use of short melismas than it might. The eighth mode (described, we remember, earlier by Johannes as 'staid and matronly')[100] has like other modes a 'character' which could be defined in purely musical terms; the antiphons have long been known to be highly formulaic. One does not in fact need to be deeply versed in the chant to hear affinities, for example, between 'Rex autem' and this eighth-mode antiphon for the Benedictus.[101]

Ex. 168

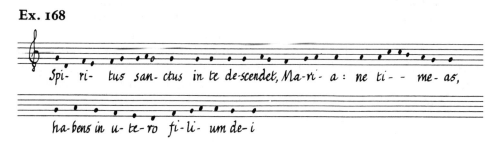

Spi- ri- tus san- ctus in te de-scendet, Ma-ri- a : ne ti - - me- as,

ha-bens in u- te-ro fi-li- um de-i

The Holy Spirit will descend upon you, Mary. Do not be afraid; you will hold in your womb the son of God. Alleluia.

This joyful message for Lauds of Advent Sunday is presented in the same restrained, unmelismatic, conjunct style as David's lament and uses some of the same melodic formulae. It is hard to avoid the conclusion that Johannes Afflighemensis does what many musicians since have done – he reads into the melody of 'Rex autem David' his own emotional response to a highly emotional text. (Then, as so often in recent centuries, it is *words* that specify the emotion in a song, not the music.) But Johannes does this not in the name of romanticism but in allegiance to the principles of rhetoric; he wishes to see music working as if it were literature and analyses it in the only terms which he has at his command.

I do not wish to seem eager to discredit the attempt of Johannes

[99] Apel (1958), 393.
[100] Perhaps, therefore, not obviously appropriate to a dramatic, royal lament.
[101] *Sarum Antiphonal*, 420; see also *ibid.*, 14.

Afflighemensis to make contemporary sense of an implied relationship between words and music which he inherited in a very rudimentary shape from
his predecessors. That he should want to make sense is a striking fact in itself.
However unconvincing his argument, there seems to be behind it something
felt and personal. Expressive reactions to the experience of music – the idea
that music, especially song, has something to 'say', something to convey
which is not summed up by the all-embracing concept of *musica* – must be
allowed to have existed. Johannes felt this, even though his actual argument
does not persuade. Perhaps there is some element of the 'applied' in his
discussion. He has inherited ideas about the modes as ethical entities and other
ideas about the analogy between speech and music, the orator and the composer. He tries to work out the significance of these ideas by applying them,
rather loosely, to a repertoire of traditional chant which needs another set of
concepts altogether if it is going to be understood.

vi Conclusion

By way of summary, we may say that the early Middle Ages had a strong, it
sometimes seems an overwhelming, sense of the metaphysical importance of
organized sound. *Musica* is their central concept and it is resonant, one may
justly say, with theological and philosophical echoes. There can never, surely,
have been a time in which the idea of music, often scarcely distinguished from
the other arts of number, had a greater intellectual and imaginative role. A
large part of the energy of the theorists goes into working out the detailed
applications of *musica* to the practical art of music – in this early period
essentially the art of melody, 'harmonics'. The practical art with which they
were mostly concerned was Gregorian chant.

Poetry is traditionally seen – and we must not think this a light or superficial
idea – as a branch of music or, better, as another manifestation in sound of
musica. When words and music come together they have to agree, certainly,
but this agreement is primarily a matter of parallel 'harmonies', agreements of
phrase and structure, of balance and 'number', so that in song the mind and ear
may be 'doubly charmed by a double melody'. Such a view does not exclude
from the effects of music emotional experiences of great power (romantic or
mystical or any other); indeed it is often invoked to explain them. It does,
however, seem to exclude – or, at least, patently and consistently neglects –
the close and detailed expressive relations between words and music which we
find in the songs of later periods. For this reason a theory of expressive sound
closely related to subject-matter, a theory apparently derived from antique
rhetoric, has only a limited place in 'the medieval experience of music'. It
remains marginal and never finds a comfortable place in the Great Synthesis.

PART III

MELODY, RHYTHM AND METRE

12

THE THEORISTS

Amongst the writings of the Archipoeta there occurs this striking couplet:

> Poeta conposuit racionem rithmicam,
> at Yrus inposuit melodiam musicam.[1]

Whatever the precise sense of the adjective *rithmicam*, the meaning must be that the poet composed, put together, a 'rhythmical' *ratio*, a pattern, and the musician wrote a melody which fitted the pattern. I have argued in previous chapters that number – in its literal sense of counting syllables and lines, and in its wider sense of proportion, pattern, balance – provides the key to an understanding of the courtly and clerical art of song and to the relationship between music and text. It is not the only key we need, as I hope my discussions of narrative, dance-song, plainchant and drama have shown. But it is the most important and in its implications the most neglected. It was very difficult for our grandfathers, because of their upbringing in the last decades of classical romanticism, and is still not easy for us, despite Schoenberg, Berg and others, to take the medieval obsession with number seriously. Their rapt attention to it – if 'obsession' seems too strong a word – needs to be taken very seriously indeed. It is not merely a metaphysical exercise but an abiding and controlling aesthetic concern, with important practical results – *poeta conposuit racionem rithmicam*. The aim of the remaining chapters is, as promised earlier, to consider the practical relevance of the aesthetic of number to the vexed and vexing problem of rhythm in monophonic, non-liturgical song.

These chapters, which emerged as a by-product of my main enquiry, cannot within the space available set out an absolutely comprehensive case for the acceptance of the isosyllabic interpretation as a basis for the scholarly understanding of monophonic song and, incidentally, for its adoption by performers as a basis for practical interpretation. I hope, nevertheless, to set out in sufficient fullness the main reasons for a decisive rejection of the 'modal rhythm' theory and to lay down, I believe for the first time, the main lines of argument on which an extended positive case for the isosyllabic interpretation might rest other than the (in my view) mistaken ground of hegemony of the

---

[1] H. Krefeld, ed., *Die Gedichte des Archipoeta* (Heidelberg 1958), no. 7, stanza 11. The M S reads *atyrus*; the editors have variously suggested *Tityrus, syllabis, at Irus* etc. Klopsch, 50, states that this couplet implies the primacy of the text; I think it more clearly implies the primacy of the *ratio* to which words and music may independently be fitted. See, however, chapter 15 note 19 below.

verbal text.[2] The case is based on medieval rhythmic theory, on palaeography, on the analysis of genres and finally on the implications of the aesthetic of words-and-music as sketched in the chapters above. The repertoire I have used most is the northern French, consisting of thousands of notated melodies – of trouvère songs in all their diversity, dance-songs in both popular and courtly-popular modes, and vernacular motets. But I also take into account the repertoire of Latin songs (*conductus*, sequence, *planctus* and *lai*) described in earlier chapters and, of necessity, polyphonic pieces which are contemporary with the songs (1150–1300) and apparently related to them. It scarcely needs saying at this stage that the French language is at the centre of European courtly culture and that conclusions reached about French song will have a substantial validity. However, the repertoire of Latin songs is no less important; here the increasing, though not universal, use of regular verbal accent raises special problems which will require some special consideration.

None of the solutions so far proposed to the rhythmic problem is in my view wholly satisfactory, and some are very unsatisfactory indeed. Even the flexible transcriptions proposed by Monterosso, close as they may seem in practical terms to what I am proposing, are misleading in as much as they rest upon a questionable conception of the relationship of the words to the melody. It is in this relationship that a tenable view satisfying to the scholar and to the practical musician – the *musicus* and the *cantor* – must be grounded.

A convincing solution will be, first, one which is supported by the assumptions, and the rare overt statements, made by medieval philosophers, encyclopedists and theorists of music and poetry about the art of song, and by the hints and occasional comments to be gleaned from other writings of the period. Secondly, it will be palaeographically sound and will take into account

---

[2] The only consistent proponents of isosyllabic interpretation have been the Italians, though they are far from being in perfect agreement one with another. The principal statements are: Sesini (1942) in the introduction to his edition of the troubadour chansonnier of Milan (Bibliotheca Ambrosiana R71 sup.); Paganuzzi's critique (1955) of Sesini; and Monterosso's study of the rhythmic problem (1956). To which should be added by way of complement: F. Liuzzi, ed., *La lauda e i primordi della melodia italiana* (Rome 1934) and Vecchi's anthology (1958) of Latin songs, sequences etc. The most substantial case is made by Sesini, who in a brief account (pp. 66–9) uses the important passage cited below (text to note 6) from Aurelian of Réôme and grasps the essential significance of the distinction between *metrum* and *ritmus*. He errs, however, in my view, by insisting on ternary metre and by using the terminology of metrical feet – indeed, of the modal theory itself ('Nella misura ternaria ogni tipo di verso trova la sua sistemazione', p. 47). Having caught a glimpse of freedom he then erects a systemic prison. Paganuzzi (1955) proposes a 'free rhythm'; it is to be based on the approximately equal-note rhythms of Gregorian chant, as interpreted by the scholars of Solesmes, in transcriptions 'fondate sulla isochronicità dei valori temporali e l'assenza della misura (metrica)'. Isochronism is not the same as isosyllabism. To judge from the examples given in his article the method results, however, in iso-*syllabic* transcriptions, without the regular barring he objects to in Sesini but with slight rhythmic lengthenings dependent on the text (pp. 42, 46). Monterosso (1956) advocates a flexible isosyllabic interpretation in which each stanza of a song is rhythmically moulded by the words (see further chapter 15:1 below). He gives a transcription (pp. 120–1) of part of Marcabru's 'L'autrier, just'una sebissa'.

the details of the notations used, as well as the visual presentation of the songs in the sources. Thirdly, the solution will be one that makes sense in the whole musical scene, and especially makes sense of the relations of the different genres to one another. Finally, it must show how the general aesthetic, as I have called it, of number can be realized in a practical, satisfying and balanced relationship between the words and the melody.

It may be helpful if, before I embark on the detail of the argument, I state as succinctly as possible the main line the enquiry will take and how I hope to meet the requirements I have just stated.

(i)   Theoretical sources in the early Middle Ages oppose the two main traditions of rhythm in song: one, known as *musica metrica*, describes sounds which are measured in longs and shorts and grouped in 'feet'; the other, *musica ritmica*, specifically excludes durational values and deals with the organization of strictly counted syllables, unmeasured, into harmonious and balanced wholes. The first tradition is eventually associated with, if it does not directly generate, the 'rhythmic modes' of early polyphony. By contrast, it is in the context of the second tradition, that of syllable-counting, that the theorists discuss vernacular song.

(ii)   The presentation of the songs in the manuscripts is generally in keeping with this, in that the huge majority of monophonic songs with poetic texts are found written out in a non-mensural notation. Whether their texts are in French or Latin, Italian or Spanish, they are evidently composed and as evidently presented in a syllabic style – that is to say, the natural unit of melody is the syllable, to which a single note, or a small group of notes in ligature, is fitted.[3] The palaeographical evidence is not explicit but is seldom at odds with an isosyllabic rendering. This means that in most songs each syllable, whether accompanied by a note or a note-group, is a visual unit of approximately the same length as its neighbours. The unit of notation is the syllabic unit; the rhythm – that is, the overall temporal pattern – is established by the 'number' (in every sense) of these units, their length, balance, and combination into lines and sections and strophes. It is here also that problems of chronology (we are dealing with a wide span) and of the gradual emergence of a written tradition from an oral one have to be taken into account. The significance of variant versions of the same melody is often baffling.

(iii)   The question of genre is also of prime importance. A theoretical distinction between *cantilena* and *cantus* in the treatise of Johannes de Grocheo is paralleled by a rhythmic distinction between measured *rondeau* and *refrain* on

---

[3]   The problem of the adaptation of the syllabic style to the different linguistic circumstances of stress-languages such as German and English is not one for the present study. H.-H. Räkel considers it in an interesting article, 'Metrik und Rhythmus in der deutschen und französischen Lyrik am Ende des 12. Jahrhunderts', *Jahrbuch für internationale Germanistik*, ser. A vol. 2 (Bern 1976) 340; for him the comparatively free accent-grouping in German contrafacts confirms that the French originals can have had no melodically autonomous rhythm (*keinen autonomen Melodierhythmus*). See also Jammers (1963), introduction, 35 ff.

the one hand and unmeasured courtly *chanson* on the other. The various genres require various rhythmical interpretations; the whole so-called trouvère repertoire cannot be treated as if it were a seamless unity. Especially problematic are mixed genres such as *pastourelle* and *lai*, in which different rhythmic traditions combine and, sometimes, conflict. Moreover, the intermingling of monophonic and polyphonic repertoires (in *conductus* and motet, particularly) poses questions of historical interpretation which may be accentuated by genre distinctions.

(iv)   Finally, the relationship of words and music has to be considered. Any proposed interpretation of the rhythm of medieval song is bound, consciously or otherwise, to rest upon assumptions about this. The previous chapters of this study have shown, I hope, how deeply imbued medieval thinkers, poets and musicians were with the aesthetic of 'number' including form, shape, balance and proportion, and how this seems to have put a blind around their conceptions of other ways music and poetry might respond to each other – not a complete blind, it is true (we have found several chinks in it). It is in *chanson* and *cantio* that 'number' is most positively present; and it is 'number' more than anything else that forms the working link between verse and melody. I shall argue that the harmonious balance between them which is implicit in the concept of *musica* can be most fully realized in isosyllabic interpretation and that this is a positive reason for preferring it.

I   Theory of *ritmus* and *metrum*

At the risk of seeming repetitive, I must reaffirm at the start of the argument the known and agreed importance of syllable-counting in the Latin as well as the vernacular songs of the Middle Ages. Ewald Jammers, who draws very different conclusions from my own about rhythm, writes:

Syllable-counting verse, in the realm of Latin poetry called simply 'rhythm', or *ritmus*, is the basis of medieval poetry. In the course of time the sequence adapts itself to this principle and the hymn . . . It is the verse of poetry in the romance languages and, in so far as it was combined with accentual verse, also of German poetry.[4]

The earliest post-classical statement about syllable-counting song is, as mentioned earlier, that made by the Venerable Bede (*c.* 673–735) in his treatise *De Arte Metrica*:

videtur autem rhythmus metris esse consimilis, quae est verborum modulata compositio, non metrica ratione, sed numero syllabarum ad iudicium aurium examinata, ut sunt carmina vulgarium poetarum.

This statement by Bede (translated on p. 379 above) makes one of the fundamental medieval distinctions – between *ritmus* and *metrum* – a distinction

[4] Jammers (1975), 32; see also Husmann (1953a), and W. Meyer (1909), *passim*, but especially I.136ff, 'Der *Ludus de Antichristo* und über die lateinischen Rhythmen'.

which as late as the fourteenth century was still thought essential.[5] A triple division of speech into *prosa, ars metrica* and *ars rhythmica* is common from the ninth to the fourteenth centuries; but more usually the straight contrast is worked out between the two traditions of verse – which means, in effect, of song. In chapter 1 of this book I tried to show the practical results for musicians of a belief in number, *numerus*, especially in the vernacular courtly chanson with its syllable-counting, its precisely 'numbered' lines, its strophic invariability. What this achieved, in the outcome, was a description of the *ritmus* tradition as it manifested itself in the high style of the vernacular. The task now is to put this into a wider historical context and to assess the relevance of the two traditions to a consideration of our central problem, the rhythmic interpretation of monophonic song.

The theorists of *musica* throughout this long period, I must emphasize, are not discussing simply music as such, nor verse; they are interested in 'significant sound' however it is produced. The terms they use could apply to either art. Despite varying individual interests, they are generally talking about *both* without distinguishing between them; they are talking, that is, about song as a single unified art.

Aurelian of Réôme, writing in the middle of the ninth century and repeating much of Bede's definition almost verbatim, spells out one issue of great importance. *Ritmus*, he says,[6]

nullam tamen habet pedum rationem sed tantum contentus est rithmica modulatione.

has no system of feet but is simply held together by rhythmical 'modulation'.

[5] A distinction of terms goes back some ten centuries, at least, to the Greeks (Crocker (1958a), 4; Seidel, 16 col. 1). However, as Crocker makes clear (5–7), classical writers on 'rhythmics' and St Augustine are theorizing entirely about poetry which has measured feet, longs and shorts. It is not until the time of Bede that a 'relatively new kind of poetry' (syllable-counting) is brought into discussion and the medieval distinction becomes central and essential. The existence of the two major rhythmical traditions has long been known and is well documented in the books and articles referred to. No one, however, to my knowledge has attempted to define their essential relevance to medieval vernacular song and the problem in hand, except Sesini and his compatriots (see note 2 above). Indeed, Smits van Waesberghe, in his comprehensive *Musikerziehung* (1969), 150, states that the distinction between *musica rhythmica* and *musica metrica* is 'completely superfluous' (*vollkommen über-flüssig*). Even Seidel (article, section 11) somewhat misleads when he heads a section: *In der Musiktheorie des Mittelalters sind die Termini Rhythmus und Metrum peripher*. This is only true of the technical musical theorists, and true because their subjects were plainsong and polyphony. Monterosso (1956), 103, is close to stating the main issue; but his correct insistence on the *valori tutti equali* of all syllables as a basis is combined with the unhelpful notion of rhythmical 'feet' as a universal organizing concept; this is expressly excluded in the contrast between *metrica* and *rhythmica*.

[6] Ed. Gushee, 67. The text continues: '. . . metrum est ratio cum modulatione, rithmus vero est modulatio sine ratione et per sillabarum discernitur numerum'. (Both kinds of verse have *modulatio*, but only 'metrical' verse has the regular pattern of feet.) So also Remy of Auxerre (late-ninth-century): 'Hoc interest inter rhythmum et metrum quod rhythmus est sola verborum consonantia . . . nulla lege constrictus, nullis certis pedibus compositus' (ed. Lutz, II.335).

Ratio seems reasonably clear: it means a regular scheme, the metrical system. *Modulatio* is more difficult to translate: it describes the quality of pattern and proportion which all songs have to have whether in the 'metrical' or in the 'rhythmical' tradition, the quality which I earlier called 'a balanced structural accord'. The important issue is that a *ritmus* is an unmeasured song.

Four hundred years later the English philosopher Roger Bacon (*c.* 1219–94) confirms the major distinction. In his *Opus maius* he writes:[7]

Et metrica docet omnes rationes et causas pedum et metrorum. Et rhythmica de omni modulatione et proportione suavi rhythmorum docet.

And 'metrical' theory teaches the schemes and principles of feet and of the metres [which they make up]. And 'rhythmical' theory teaches us about all 'modulation' and sweet proportion in *ritmi*.

The fundamental difference between the two traditions is that 'metrical' theory is concerned with durational values in the sort of poems and songs, i.e. *metra*, which are scanned by feet in long and short syllables, while 'rhythmical' theory is concerned with another principle of organizing sound, found in the sort of poems and song, i.e. *ritmi*, which are not scanned in feet. *Metrica* describes and analyses such lines as these – from Boethius's *De consolatione philosophiae* (bk iii, metre 9)

$$\bar{\text{O}} \text{ qu}\bar{\text{i}} \text{ perpet}\breve{\text{u}}\text{a m}\bar{\text{u}}\text{nd}\bar{\text{u}}\text{m r}\bar{\text{a}}\text{ti}\bar{\text{o}}\text{n}\breve{\text{e}} \text{ gub}\bar{\text{e}}\text{rn}\bar{\text{a}}\text{s}$$
$$\text{T}\bar{\text{e}}\text{rr}\bar{\text{a}}\text{r}\bar{\text{u}}\text{m c}\bar{\text{e}}\text{li}\breve{\text{q}}\text{ue s}\breve{\text{a}}\text{t}\bar{\text{o}}\text{r qu}\bar{\text{i}} \text{ t}\bar{\text{e}}\text{mp}\breve{\text{u}}\text{s }\breve{\text{a}}\text{b }\bar{\text{e}}\text{v}\bar{\text{o}}$$

The poem is in hexameters of the Virgilian type, in which the number of syllables may vary from line to line. *Ritmica* deals with poems like, at the other extreme, this hymn by a tenth-century Spanish monk in honour of St Gregory:[8]

Celebs monachus   fit abbas largifluus,
Strenuus rector   pauperumque dilector,
Dat ut naufrago   argenteam angelo
scutellam marcis   ceteris erogatis . . .

The author seems here to be attending solely to the number of syllables in each line: 5 + 7. There is neither rhyme nor regular accent nor, certainly, the slightest regard for quantity. One popular definition of *ritmus* verse is *consonans paritas syllabarum certo numero comprehensarum* – 'a harmonious equality of syllables assembled together in a predetermined number' (Antonio da Tempo, whose further comments in context make it seem certain that

---

[7] *Opus maius*, 1.100, ed. J. H. Bridges, 2 vols. (Oxford 1897); Bacon returns to the distinction in a later section where he discusses the importance of music to theology (1.237).

[8] *AH* xix.250, cited Norberg (1958), 128, who observes, 'il ne reste plus que le nombre de syllabes', the poet writes lines of 5 + 7 syllables 'sans tenir compte d'une structure quelconque'.

numerus here has its simple literal meaning).[9] *Consonans* is clear enough – 'consonance', sounds that agree. Inevitably, *consonantia* becomes, in a more restricted meaning, one of the terms for 'rhyme'. But, interestingly enough, another term for 'rhyme' in Latin is *rhythmus* (*ritmus*) itself; and this is in fact the origin of our word 'rhyme'.[10] Rhyme became in due course an almost invariable feature of *ritmus* verse, but it was not the essence of the matter any more than accent was. Indeed Dante specifically says that it is inessential: *de rithimo vero mentionem non facimus, quia de propria cantionis arte non est* ('we make no mention of rhyme because it does not properly belong to the art of song').[11]

A final definition of *ritmus* from a Latin treatise of the first half of the thirteenth century will draw the various threads together. It comes from the abbey library of Admont and is entitled *Regule de rithmis:*[12]

Rithmus enim est congrua diccionum ordinatio, consona, continenter sillabarum æqualitate prolata. Dicitur autem *rithmus* a græco *rithmos*, idest numero, quoniam certa lege numerorum constituendus est. Numerus ergo in ipso notandus est, primo quidem in *distinccionibus*, postmodum vero in *sillabis* et *consonanciis*.

A poem written in the *ritmus* style is a congruent structure of words, harmonious in itself, extended by a progression of equal syllables. It is called a *ritmus* from Greek *rhuthmos* that is 'number', because it is to be constituted [com-posed] according to fixed numerical rule. Number has to be observed in a *ritmus*, first in regard to the lines, and after that in regard to the syllables and the rhymes.

To this theorist rhyme *is* an essential part of a *ritmus* poem. It is interesting, however, that he says nothing about accent, even though his (all Latin) examples, both sacred and secular, use accent for the most part regularly and clearly. For example:[13]

> Lúx illústris ángelórum,
> álme páter séculórum . . .

Here, however, there may be some ambivalence: absolutely regular accent pattern, except at line-endings and caesuras, is not demanded.

The division into two categories corresponds, of course, to the major historical development in Latin verse technique during the first millennium A.D. The quantitative, durationally measured verse of classical Latin (the *ars*

---

[9] Antonio da Tempo, ed. Grion, p. 71. On *paritas*, see MS Admont 759, cited Klopsch, 35.
[10] On the extension of meaning from 'rhythm' to rhyme in the twelfth and thirteenth centuries, see Seidel. The whole article 'Rhythmus/Numerus' is of the greatest interest and relevance. On the original meaning of *rhythmus*, see W. Meyer (1909), III.140ff: 'Die Testimonia der alten Grammatiker über "Rhythmus"', with numerous quotations.
[11] See chapter 1, note 30 above.
[12] Mari, *Trattati medievali* (1899), treatise iv, p. 28.
[13] Mari, 29.

metrica of the theorists) was gradually edged to the side though never totally replaced by a system which is often, but somewhat misleadingly, called 'accentual'.[14] Accent became important, as the Admont examples show, in much of the verse written in the non-quantitative styles; and, indeed, in some poems an accentual organization reproduces in its own terms the familiar patterns of the old classical metres.[15] The classical alcaic

Quīs pŏssĭt amplō   fāmĭnĕ prǣpŏtēns

is imitated accentually as

Laúdes Déo   dícam per sécula
Qui mé plasmávit   in manu déxtera
Et reformávit   crúce purpúrea.[16]

Norberg gives the ordinary scheme of the accentual alcaic as: . . . / . . . . / . . with the possibility of variants at the beginning of each hemistich. The openness and freedom of such an arrangement, in which nothing is really fixed except the cadence of each hemistich, itself suggests that 'accentual' is not the ideal term. The one thing that binds and unites the non-quantitative verse is not accent but, as I have already stressed, number. 'Rhythmical' verse is in essence syllable-counting verse.

The features of this poetic tradition, apart from the emphasis on the numbering of un-measured syllables, are: attention to the proper and parallel marking of the line-*ending* by accent (paroxytone and proparoxytone in Latin verse, 'strong' and 'weak' endings in the vernaculars); and the development of elaborate strophic patterns in which the principle of 'balanced structural accord' (Aurelian's *rhythmica modulatio*, Bacon's *proportio suavis*, Dante's *armonia*) can be worked out. From a combination of these two features, it seems, emerges rhyme, for rhyme both confirms the importance of the line-ending as a determining structural feature and through its linking of sounds helps to build 'sweet proportions'.

The theoretical writers are, to sum up, almost of one mind in distinguishing, at least up to the early fourteenth century, between two contrasting rhythmical systems:[17] *ars metrica*, which has 'feet' made up of long and short syllables; and *ars ritmica*, which requires precisely numbered

---

[14] Amongst recent discussions, those of Norberg (1958) and Klopsch (1972) are particularly helpful.

[15] Norberg, ch. 6, especially 94ff, 'Imitation de la structure'.

[16] Norberg, 101. Both quantitative and accentual forms are somewhat rare in medieval practice.

[17] As one might expect, the terminology is not used with perfect consistency by medieval writers (no terminology is), and one has to expect the occasional contradictory statement such as Odington (fl. 1298–1316) makes in his *De Speculatione Musice*, part 4: 'Rhythmus non est certo fine moderatus; sed tamen rationabiliter ordinatis pedibus currit.' This appears to be based on Augustine, to whom of course the post-Bede distinction was not meaningful (ed. Hammond, p. 89, n. 2). Part 4 of the treatise, significantly, is entitled 'De Inaequalitate Temporum in Pedibus'.

syllables, 'modulation and sweet proportion', and concentrates on pattern and consonance. Of particular importance in the present discussion is the fact that the *ritmus* tradition seems also to rely on the temporal equality of these numbered syllables. The explicit statements of the theorists in support of this are both positive and negative. On the positive side we have had, for instance, in the quotations above:

consonans paritas syllabarum – 'a harmonious equality of syllables' (Antonio da Tempo)
ordinatio . . . sillabarum aequalitate prolata – 'a structure extended by a progression of equal syllables' (Admont MS)

On the negative, we are told insistently that *ars ritmica* is, by definition, an art which

nullam habet pedum rationem – 'has no system of feet' (Aurelianus of Réôme)

John of Garland (early-thirteenth-century) makes an explicit contrast:

sine metricis pedibus ponitur ad differentiam artis metrice – 'is put together without metrical feet, thus being distinguished from the *ars metrica*'[18]

These diverse testimonies build a strong case for believing that compositions in the *ritmus* style are not only numerically constructed and by definition unmeasured but put their constructions together from *units of equal temporal value*. The system is an isosyllabic one.[19]

At this point the reader might well ask how we can be sure of the relevance of the foregoing discussion to the solution of the rhythmic problems of monophonic song. There is, as I see it, a straightforward answer to this: 'non-liturgical' song belongs to the *musica ritmica* tradition.[19a] The songs of the troubadours and trouvères and their 'Latin' contemporaries are palpably syllable-counting artefacts and, as a concomitant, are not measured in feet; they are *ritmi*. The concerns of the theorists, if rarely musical in a strict and exclusive sense, are not simply an aspect of the literary and verbal. To repeat, the relevance of the two rhythmical traditions, *musica ritmica* and *musica metrica*, is precisely that they are rhythmical traditions, *concerned with the phenomenon of sound in general*, and therefore with song as a unified art, not with poetry or with music alone.

It is true that occasionally in the theorists one will come across a statement that seems to categorize the two arts in such a way as to undermine the general position I wish to establish – which is, that pronouncements about rhythm and metre are pronouncements about both the arts, even if in a particular

[18] Mari, treatise v (John of Garland), p. 36. The identification of John of Garland, poet and grammarian (*c.* 1190–*c.* 1272), an Englishman working in Paris, with Johannes de Garlandia (fl. *c.* 1240) the musical theorist, is rejected by most scholars (see Baltzer, 'Johannes de Garlandia' in *New Grove*).
[19] This conclusion is totally independent of the question whether the poems and the melodies are separable or inseparable.
[19a] The inadequacy of the term 'non-liturgical' is painfully obvious in relation to the sequence repertoire in particular (see chapter 3 above).

context only one seems to be at issue. Thus Roger Bacon distinguishes between *musica melica* which *in cantu consistit* (exists in song) and the three other kinds of 'human sound' – prose, metre and 'rhythm' which are *in sermone* (speech).[20] However, as we see from elsewhere, *melica* seems to correspond to the more usual term *harmonica*; the traditional categories are left undisturbed, and it is unlikely that Bacon specifically wished to exclude music from the others. The theorist Lambertus, writing at the same time (before 1279), spells out the applicability of *ritmica* to song as well as to poetry:[21]

Rhytmica vero est illa que in scansione verborum requirit, utrum bene vel male cohereant dictiones; *quia cantando utendum est, tanquam legendo* [my italics]

'Rhythmical' theory is that which in the matter of verbal 'scansion' [i.e. a reading of the words as verse] seeks to know whether the words cohere well or badly; for this coherence must be observed in singing as well as in reading.

Putting the discussion in the wider context of *musica*, meaning the 'order, proportion, *harmonia*' etc. which is theorized about (for *musica* certainly also refers to the phenomenon itself and not simply to the methods of analysing it), it may be helpful to recall the conclusion reached in chapter 11:

The concept of *armonia*, harmoniousness, could certainly be said to be one of 'significant sound'; but the significance of the words and the significance of the music are the same – they both manifest *musica*, 'realize' its truth in sounds.

Most attempts at the rhythmic interpretation of early monophonic songs have been based on theories (sometimes merely on unexamined assumptions) about the relationship between two separate entities – words and music. There are very few explicit medieval statements on the topic, and they mostly deal with structure; it is not surprising, therefore, that investigators have been baffled.[22] When I first started to think about the problem I found it very hard to explain. Indifference might be the reason; but, given the huge output of song-making, this seemed unconvincing. Was it more likely that the answer to the problem of words-and-music was so obvious and so incontrovertible that it did not need stating? I now believe so. The answer is implicit in the concept of *musica*: there is no need for fundamental discussion of the relationship between the two arts because, as already stressed, fundamentally they are not two but one – the art of ordered sound. When, rarely, their relationship

[20] Cited Seidel, 16, from *Opus tertium* (completed 1279), ed. J. S. Brewer, Rolls Series (London 1859), 230. On Bacon's conception of music, see Adank, 33.

[21] Coussemaker (1864), 1.252, who reads *vitandum*; the emendation *utendum* is Seidel's (p. 16). The definition requiring 'coherence' is found in Cassiodorus (see Crocker (1958a), 3; Seidel, 16); but the necessary gloss equating song and speech appears to be Lambertus's addition. By *scansio* is meant not the process of intellectual analysis but, evidently, the rhythmical movement of the words as they are read out loud. See Lewis and Short, s.v. 'scansio', quoting Bede.

[22] The category of explicit statements about musical–verbal structures has already been discussed (see above, chapter 8:IV). To this should be added the rare statements about 'mood' and ethos (chapter 11:V).

is discussed it is in these terms, as the striking passage from Guido of Arezzo quoted earlier (p. 385) makes clear: song is 'twofold melody'.[23] The essential unity of the two arts cannot be over-stressed. Melody and poem existed in a state of the closest symbiosis, obeying the same laws and striving in their different media for the same sound-ideal – *armonia*. In this fundamental respect, in which they are both manifestations of *musica*, it is misleading to talk about a direct relationship between the two arts, and it is wrong to be surprised, or puzzled, that medieval writers do not discuss it.

The apparent gap in medieval theory has of course been filled, with modern theories. And one of these has been so influential and so long-lived that it inevitably calls for examination and refutation. Although never completely unchallenged, its dominance has been such that a common response to any expression of scepticism is still – 'Why do you not accept the modal theory?'

II   Modal rhythm and *musica metrica*

The system of transcription known as 'modal rhythm' (which has, of course, no connection whatsoever with the 'modes' or scales of tonal analysis) was formulated in the first decade of this century by three Continental scholars – Friedrich Ludwig, Jean Beck, and Pierre Aubry.[24] It is so called from another meaning of the term *modus*; Anonymus VII (*c.* 1260–80) defines it thus:[25]

Modus in musica est debita mensuratio temporis, scilicet per longas et breves; vel aliter, modus est quidquid currit per debitam mensuram longarum notarum et brevium.

Mode in music is the orderly measuring of time in long and short [notes]; or, to put it another way, mode is whatever proceeds in an appropriate measurement of long and short notes.

The musical theorists of the period usually distinguish six schemes of longs and shorts, all of which produce triple-time metres:

[23] Guido uses the term *metrum*, but not, it appears, in its strictest meaning. In the early twelfth century the theorist Hugo of Bologna uses the term *metricum carmen* generically to cover three kinds of composition, but makes the essential distinction, nevertheless: (i) measured in feet (*cum pedum mensura*) called *carmen*; (ii) numbered in syllables, with rhyme (? *consonantia vocum*), called *riddimus* (i.e. *ritmus*); (iii) mixture of both called *prosimetrum* (the term is clearly not used in the normal sense of prose interspersed with verse). See Klopsch, 48, who cites this passage from L. Rockinger, *Briefstelle und Formelbücher* (Munich 1863–4), I.54. However, even if Guido does use *metrum* in the strict sense my argument is not affected, since from the beginnings it is stated that *metrum*, like *ritmus*, must have *modulatio* (the 'balanced structural accord').

[24] See Jammers (1975), 38 n.1.

[25] Coussemaker (1864), I.378 (an unreliable text); transl. Waite, *The Rhythm of Twelfth-Century Polyphony* (1954), 13. The earliest exposition of the modes is said to be that of Johannes de Garlandia (fl. *c.* 1240), *De Mensurabili Musica*, ch. 1 (ed. Reimer, p. 36); the most extensive discussion is by Anonymus IV (ed. Reckow). Amongst the numerous modern expositions, see especially Waite; Frobenius, 'Modus' in *HMT*; and Ian Bent, 'Rhythmic Modes' in *New Grove*.

(1)	— u	♩ ♩	trochaic
(2)	u —	♩ ♩	iambic
(3)	— u u	♩. ♩ ♩	dactylic
(4)	u u —	♩ ♩ ♩.	anapaestic
(5)	— —	♩ ♩	spondaic
(6)	u u u	♩ ♩ ♩	tribrachic

All such definitions and schemes come from writers whose concern is solely with polyphonic music. It was through studying these treatises and the Notre Dame polyphonic repertoire notated in ligature patterns that Ludwig discovered the key to the rhythmic interpretation of the polyphonic motets, *clausulae* etc. His conclusions marked a permanent and incontrovertible advance in understanding.[26] It was from Ludwig, too, that the suggestion first originated that the key to the rhythm of secular songs, at least the French ones, might be the very same. The idea was worked out in enthusiastic detail by his pupils Aubry and Beck, both of whom claimed it as their own.

The application of the rhythmic modes to melismatic *polyphony* is certain (if not clear in every detail) because the choice of mode was determined by the configurations of the notation – i.e. the ligature patterns.[27] But monophonic songs with words and notes syllabically organized offer no such clue. Aubry and Beck suggested that the rhythm of the words provided the missing link in the procedure. All that one needed to do was to deduce the metre of the poem from the rhythm of the words, discover which of the six modes was the appropriate one, and transcribe the melody in the rhythm of that mode. The result is, in effect, a 'prosodized' music, a *musique mesurée* born before its time.[28]

[26] Ludwig (1910), Exkurs II. See also Apel, *Polyphonic Notation* (1961), and Hiley, 'Notation' in *New Grove*, sect. III.2(ii). It has to be remembered that the thirteenth-century theory 'is a mental abstraction from flexible practice' (Hiley), a developed system whose application even to polyphony before c. 1225 is uncertain.

[27] As an example of the method at its most simple, a ligature-pattern consisting of a three-note ligature followed by a succession of two-note ligatures is transcribed Long Short Long Short Long Short Long Short Long . . . (1st Mode, trochaic).

[28] The history of the modal theory as applied to secular monophony over half a century is summarized in detail by Kippenberg, *Der Rhythmus im Minnesang* (1962); see also Monterosso (1956). There is no necessity to repeat it here. Among the staunchest adherents of strict modalism (or metricalism) in recent years have been Friedrich Gennrich, Lipphardt, and Tischler ('the musical clues all favour a metric–rhythmic interpretation of trouvère song in general' (Rosenberg and Tischler (1981), p. xxii)). The hypothesis has, however, been sceptically viewed over many years (e.g. by Appel (1934); Handschin (1935); Machabey (1957); Monterosso (1956); Sesini in *Studi Medievali* n.s. 11 (1938) 210; van der Werf (1972)). More cautious modalists (introducing chronological and other modifications) have been Beck (1927), Husmann (five articles 1952–3), and Jammers (1975). Generally speaking recent scholars, such as Stäblein (1975) and Räkel (1977), have adopted an open and neutral

Thus the first rhythmic mode (trochaic) applied to 'Quant li rossignols s'escrie' (R1149) produced this interpretation:[29]

Ex. 169

1 Qant li ros- si- gnols s'es- cri- e, Qui nos des- duit de son chant,
2 Por ma bel- le 'dol- ce a- mi- e, Vois mon cuer ros- si- gno- lant.

3 Join- tes mains mer- ci li cri- e, Car on- ques rien n'a- mai tant,
4 Et bien sai, s'el- le m'o- bli- e, Que joi- e me va fi- nant.

When the nightingale calls, delighting us with his song, I go with my heart echoing its song for my beautiful sweet friend. With hands joined I cry her mercy for I never loved anything so much. And I know well, that if she forgets me joy is at an end.

The third mode (dactylic) worked out as follows for 'Li chastelain de Coucy' (R358):[30]

Ex. 170

1. Li chaste - lain de Cou- ci a- ma tant
3. por ce fe- rai ma con- plainte en son chant

2. qu'ainz por a- mor nus n'en ot do- lor grain- dre;
4. que ne cuit pas que la moi- e soit main- dre. [etc.]

The châtelain of Coucy loved so extremely that no one ever for love had greater grief. For this reason I will make my plaint to [the pattern of] his song, for I do not think my grief can be any less than his . . .

(Both songs are anonymous.) I shall examine in the final chapter the aesthetic assumptions about the relations of poem and melody which underlie this method of transcription and which I find quite unacceptable. At present I give the songs simply as examples of the method.

[29] Beck, *La musique des troubadours* (1910), 83, with facsimile (pl. viii) from the Chansonnier St Germain, fol. 39v.
[30] Rosenberg and Tischler, no. 81 (p. 157); the song is a contrafact of *A vous, amant* (R679). Tischler inserts some eighteen editorial *b* flats, but the weight of the sources tells against this. Parallel variant melodies of both chansons in van der Werf (1977), 224ff.

approach, represented in their transcriptions by rhythmically undifferentiated note-heads. But editions of medieval song continue to appear in which, without argument, modal rhythm is assumed to be acceptable (e.g. Maillard (1967); Wilkins (1967); *Oxford Anthology* (1977) for the trouvère songs).

There are many arguments which may be advanced against the modal
theory (as well as some which may be used to support it). They are of a
palaeographical (notational) and of a historical kind (concerned with the facts
of genres and styles and taste), and they will be considered later. For the
moment I am concerned only to enquire whether there are any statements in
medieval theory, musical or otherwise, to justify the application of the
rhythmic modes to monophonic song. To the best of my belief there are not.
The practical discussions of the musical theorists almost all engage either with
plainsong or with polyphony (see chapter 11). The writers on polyphony are
interested, as they have to be for practical reasons, in measure, precisely
measured musical time which allows the easy synchronization of different
voices. The more literary theorists, on the other hand, are interested in general
problems of rhythm and metre. For reasons which I have explained, they do
not talk explicitly about monophony as such; but they make a fundamental
distinction between measured verse/song (*ars metrica*) and 'numbered',
'sweetly proportioned' verse/song (*ars ritmica*). To the latter category belongs
the huge bulk of troubadour and trouvère songs and Latin songs written in
syllabic style. The key question then arises: where does the medieval
description of the 'rhythmic modes' fit into this general theoretical picture?
The answer is, I believe, clear: the modes of the theorists, in so far as they
relate to medieval rhythmic theory, are a manifestation of *musica metrica*, and
so far from providing a key to troubadour and trouvère melody they are *on
theoretical grounds entirely inappropriate*. The so-called 'rhythmic modes' can
have nothing to do with *musica ritmica*. They would more properly be termed
the 'metrical modes'; they are *ipso facto* inapplicable to syllable-counting
monody, for they describe a style traditionally opposed to it.[31]

---

[31] It is natural to enquire whether the *ars metrica* has left any positive evidence of its existence as a
monophonic style in the Middle Ages, which might provide, by contrast, confirmation of the
nature of syllable-counting song in the *ritmus* tradition. Such evidence is elusive for obvious
reasons: the earliest notated quantitative Latin texts (tenth to twelfth centuries) are no less
ambiguous in their rhythm than the syllabic ones; they do not use the mensural symbols later
devised for polyphony. Even the long notational history of the *Song of the Sibyl* (see chapter 9
above, Ex. 138 and note 44), in 27 hexameter lines, casts no light on the problem. The
increasing tendency for quantitative *patterns* (hexameter, sapphic, alcaic etc.) to be represented verbally in accentual terms (Norberg (1958) ch. 6) helps not at all: it could mean that
for practical purposes all sense of classical durational values had lapsed, or that (at any rate
when sung) accent itself indicated duration (see chapter 14:VI, note 57 and related text), an
accented syllable being twice as long as an unaccented. E. Jammers, 'Der Vortrag des
lateinischen Hexameters im frühen Mittelalter', *Quadrivium* 2 (1958) 16–31, states that the
surviving neumed passages from Virgil and other epic writers cannot have been performed
metrically (i.e. in a measured style) because of their abundant melismas on short syllables.
Jammers suggests a pervasive influence from liturgical psalmody leading to a mixed style in
which word-accent, half-line caesura (in the hexameter) and metre all play a part. In his book
on notation (1975), ch. 2, Jammers argues that in the Carolingian Renaissance all quantitative
secular verse was performed with long and short notes for 'long' and 'short' values. Among
the classical texts found set in the early Middle Ages are in addition to Virgil, passages from
Statius, Juvenal and Martianus Capella, several odes of Horace, verses ('metres') from
Boethius etc. The whole field is surveyed in detail and densely annotated by G. Wille in his

What historical warrant (it may now be asked) is there for associating the modes with *musica metrica*, the traditional theory of rhythm measured like classical poetry in feet consisting of longs and shorts? The *prima facie* practical case could hardly be stronger. The six modes, expounded with remarkable consistency from the thirteenth century onwards, consist of recurrent patterns made up of long and short notes;[32] the metres established by these patterns are the six common classical metres named in the table above. For reasons sometimes explained by reference to theological–metaphysical potency of the number three, the proportions between long and short notes in the modes are always adjusted to produce a triple metre;[33] this was not so with the classical metres, but the discrepancy hardly affects the general strength of the case, which rests on the simple fact that both *musica metrica* and the theory of the 'rhythmic modes' are theories of temporal measurement involving proportional values which are susceptible of description as falling into recurrent units or 'feet'.[34]

It would be satisfying if, in addition, a direct link could be established between the two theories. This linking has been claimed for Walter Odington, whose *De speculatione musice* is usually dated around 1300. Odington's short fourth part is, in fact, a discussion of the metrical foot as a unit of temporal organization:[35]

---

[32] One inconsistency, however, concerns the number of the modes: see G. Anderson, 'Magister Lambertus (*c.* 1270) and nine rhythmic modes', *AcM* 45 (1973) 57–73; Anderson argues that the increase reflects new compositional techniques and the 'breakdown of the outworn modal system'. Grocheo refers to Lambert's and other classifications in his treatise (ed. Rohloff, p. 140: lines 29ff).

[33] Triple effects in the main metre may be avoided in practice, e.g. by the adoption of the fifth, spondaic, mode which results in a series of equal notes (usually transcribed as dotted minims with triple division only *within* the syllabic unit). See Husmann (1953a), 13, in regard to the melodies of the earlier troubadours. A second way of avoiding triple-time effects is to adopt the sixth, tribrachic, mode. The equal-syllable units (in this case normally transcribed as crotchets) may then be arranged in larger duple patterns (see for example Beck's transcription of 'Je suis espris doucement' (R656) in (1927), II, no. 159), though triple pattern (3/4) is still available (see 'Joie d'amours que j'ai tant desiree' (R506), *ibid.*, II, no. 158). In his Cangé transcriptions (1927) Beck makes liberal use of modes 5 and 6 and produces what are in effect isosyllabic transcriptions described in modal terms.

[34] Strictly speaking, the modal theory is concerned solely with durational values and not with stress. The question whether each metrical foot is a modern 'bar' with an initial stress is much debated in relation to early polyphony (see B. A. Antley in an unpublished diss., Florida State Univ. 1977: summarized *RILM* 12/1 (1978) no. 279).

[35] Ed. Hammond, 89.

---

magisterial study *Musica romana* (Amsterdam 1967) ch. 6, with full reference to the secondary literature of the last hundred years and more. The recent recovery of a lost leaf belonging to the Cambridge Songs (Source 9) is of especial interest, as adding to the number of neumed Boethian texts (see M. T. Gibson, M. Lapidge and C. Page, 'Neumed Boethian metres' in *Anglo-Saxon England* 12 (1983) 141–52). The tradition of singing classical texts, which Wille believes was continuous from antiquity, appears to lapse after the 'twelfth-century Renaissance' to be resuscitated in the sixteenth century with humanistic fervour.

Pedes sunt qui certis syllabarum temporibus insistunt, et tempus quidem est mensura motus syllabae, ut cum selectum pulsum habeat syllaba dicatur longa et duorum temporum. Accidit autem unicuique pedi arsis et thesis, id est elevatio et depositio, quae sunt tempore mensuratae.

Feet proceed by fixed 'times' [temporal values] of syllables. And a 'time' indeed is the measure of the movement of a syllable, so that when a syllable has a separate beat it should be called a long and has two 'times'. To each foot belongs an *arsis* and a *thesis*, that is a raising and a lowering, which are measured in temporal value.

Much of the discussion has a faintly pedantic air, describing metrical feet of some rarity (e.g. the *procelleusmaticus* (four shorts)) and giving them distinctly unhelpful glosses (the *celeusma* is a song sung by vine-dressers when they get to the end of the row). Odington concludes by saying, 'So much, then, on the subject of metric' (*haec de hac parte, scilicet metrica, sufficiant*).[36] There is no reference in these chapters to the rhythmic modes as such, nor to triple-time organization. I cannot see, much as I would like to, that the theoretical link is here established.[37]

William Waite, whose book *The Rhythm of Twelfth-Century Polyphony* (1954) contains the most extensive discussion of the matter, was concerned to argue that 'modal rhythm was created [I would rather say 'formulated as a theory'] with metrical considerations in mind'. He quotes two further passages, neither of which on closer reading appear to be relevant.[38] A more persuasive piece of evidence, tiny though it is, comes from a single sentence elsewhere in Odington's treatise, where he writes that 'The *longa* with the first

[36] Ed. Hammond, 90 (celeusma), 91 (conclusion).

[37] Treitler (1979), 524ff, discussing metre and rhythm in early polyphony, draws attention to another aspect of the problem: he asks whether 'the ancient metres could provide practical models for the rhythmic performance of music' and considers the testimony of plainchant-treatises. Guido of Arezzo (*Micrologus*, ch. xv; see chapter 11 n. 38, above) describes the relation between feet and neumes: 'Non autem parva similitudo est metris et cantibus, cum et neumae loco sint pedum et distinctiones loco sint versuum, utpote ista neuma dactylico, illa vera spondaico, alia iambico more decurrit . . .' (ed. Smits van Waesberghe, 172–3). (For further references to metrical singing of chant, see A. Angie in *KJb* 29 (1934).) Treitler is properly sceptical about the relevance of this; first, because 'the actual rhythmic practices', the lapse of which was lamented in the eleventh century, 'must have been forgotten' by the time the rhythmic modes were fashionable (late twelfth century); secondly, because we are 'completely unenlightened' as to the precise practical meaning of Guido's remarks – which are introduced, incidentally, in a phrase Treitler does not quote, with the qualifying remark 'we *often* sing in such a way that we *appear almost* to scan verses by feet' (*saepe ita canimus, ut quasi versus pedibus scandere videamur*, p. 171). Nevertheless, Treitler's general observation that 'the explanations of the modal system bear the conceptual stamp of the tradition of metrics', even if metric theory was in detail inadequate, supports for my argument the essential point. He, however, omits to mention the existence of traditional *musica metrica* theory, which would further strengthen his case.

[38] Waite, 25. The first passage, from Odington (ed. Hammond, 44), relates music, number and not metrics but arithmetic (*arsmetrica*, which Waite reads as *ars metrica*); the second, from a compendium, *Introductio musice*, based on the *De plana musica* of Johannes de Garlandia (ed. Coussemaker (1864), 1.157–75), similarly relates music and arithmetic and is similarly misunderstood.

composers of *organum* had two *tempora* as in meters [*sicut in metris*].'[39] This looks like a firm parallel between the two metrical systems, one polyphonic and the other of vernacular song. To this may be added the evidence of Alexander de Villa-Dei, one of the most widely read medieval grammarians, who refers in his *Doctrinale* (*c.* 1199) to six quantitative metres which precisely parallel those of contemporary modal composition in choice, number and nomenclature. Moreover, Alexander was a firm adherent of the Paris 'school', as a centre of antique studies. Rudolf Flotzinger, who first pointed out the relevance of this text,[40] sums up by observing that 'a connection between the development of the modal system and the (manifestly Parisian) metrical theory seems to exist beyond question'.[41] It is hard to believe that educated men would not have recognized the parallel.

III Johannes de Grocheo

It would be unsatisfactory to conduct a discussion on the theory of rhythm and metre in medieval song without considering the oft-quoted treatise of Johannes de Grocheo with its unique discussion of contemporary secular music. Grocheo seems to have lived and worked in Paris in the latter part of the twelfth century; the earliest text of his treatise survives in a manuscript copied some hundred years or so later.[42] In it he describes music as it was practised in Paris in his own day. He gives some thought as to the proper categories to adopt. The traditional threefold Boethian categories arouse his scepticism: of the *musica humana* he scathingly asks, 'Quis enim audivit complexionem sonare?' (Who ever heard the human temperament produce sounds?).[43] Nor do the Greek *genera* (diatonic, chromatic and enharmonic) spur him to enthusiasm; the Greeks neglected vocal music, he says. He then toys with a proposed division of music into *plana sive immensurabilis* (i.e. ecclesiastical plainchant) and *mensurabilis* (i.e. measured polyphony).[44] This he

---

[39] Waite, 24, from Coussemaker, I.235 (see ed. Hammond, 127–8).

[40] R. Flotzinger, 'Zur Frage der Modalrhythmik als Antike-Rezeption', *A Mw* 29 (1972) 203.

[41] Flotzinger, 208; he stresses, as Treitler does (note 37 above), the importance of the 'metric-concept' for theoretical exposition even more than for their actual development. My argument does not depend on any theory of origins, only on the idea of a conscious parallel, a parallel arising from *need* since they had no other terminology of temporal measurement.

[42] The studies of Grocheo by E. Rohloff (1930; 1943) culminate in his edition, *Die Quellenhandschriften zum Musiktraktat des Johannes de Grocheio* [*sic*] (Leipzig 1972), with facsimiles of two MS sources, translation, commentary, and glossarial index. The long-standard text and translation of Wolf (1899–1900) are still worth consulting. The English translation by Seay (1967) often merely anglicizes the Latin ambiguities of the original. See also Anderson 'Johannes de Grocheo' in *New Grove*. Virtually nothing is known of Grocheo's life; he seems to have been active *c.* 1300. The attribution to Grocheo rests on one MS (Darmstadt 2663).

[43] Rohloff (1972), 122: line 35. The significance of Grocheo's categories is discussed by practically everyone who has written on the problem of rhythm in secular monophony.

[44] *Ibid.*, 124: 8–19. The reference to polyphony is clear: '*per mensurabilem intellegunt illam* [*musicam*], *quae ex diversis sonis* simul mensuratis et sonantibus *efficitur*, sicut in conductibus et motetis' (my emphasis).

dislikes too. If those who propose it mean by *immensurabilis* 'completely *ad libitum*', they are forgetting that every art must be measured by its own rules (*debet illius artis regulis mensurari*). If they mean *non ita precise mensurata*, 'not so precisely measured', then in his view the categories do not hold. In the end Grocheo settles on three categories which genuinely reflect, he says, the music of his own age and place.[45] He will discourse analytically

(1)   *de simplici musica vel civili quam vulgarem musicam appellamus* (concerning melodic, non-ecclesiastical music which we call vernacular music);

(2)   *de musica composita vel regulari vel canonica quam appellant musicam mensuratam* (concerning composed music – i.e. according to rules and canons – which they call measured music);

(3)   about a third kind, the *genus ecclesiasticum*, which (in a somewhat mysterious way) results from the first two and crowns their efforts (*ad quod ista duo tamquam ad melius ordinantur*) – i.e. liturgical music.[46]

Musical historians searching for clues about secular monody have gone over Grocheo's first category minutely and found much to puzzle them, especially in the detailed descriptions. By the adjective *simplex* Grocheo appears to mean, as others do, 'melodic', 'monophonic' (not 'simple');[47] he never mentions a polyphonic form in this long section, which is divided into vocal and instrumental.[48] The vocal forms are subdivided as follows into song proper and dance-song:

(a)	*cantus*	(b)	*cantilena*
	gestualis		*rotunda*
	coronatus		*stantipes*
	versiculatus/versualis		*ductia*

Civilis could have a range of meanings and does not perhaps exclude chansons with pious texts, since the *cantus coronatus* deals with *caritas* as well as *amicitia*. 'Non-ecclesiastical' or 'secular' might be the nearest general equivalent.[49]

[45]   *Ibid.*, 124: 29–41, 'musica qua utuntur homines Parisiis'.

[46]   There is an excellent brief account of Grocheo's treatise and elucidation of his categories by Gallo (English edn), 10–13. The (German) rendering of this passage by Rohloff, 23, is not entirely satisfactory.

[47]   Rohloff, 125, translates as *einfach*, which leaves the matter open. But the meaning 'melodic', i.e. for one voice, is well attested. Stäblein (1975), 74 and n. 753, cites Anonymus IV, who when he refers to *simplices conductus* is clearly defining their monophonic quality. The passage (ed. Reckow, 1.46) specifies *triplices*, *duplices* and *simplices conductus*. See also Ludwig (1910), 123–4.

[48]   Rohloff, 130: line 21. It so happens that the surviving *stantipes* (*estampies*, *istampite*) are wordless; they are for that reason assumed to be instrumental. But Grocheo makes it clear that they, with the *cantilena rotunda* (the dance-song, *rondeau*, *rondellus*), can be performed in *voce humana*. In a later paragraph (Rohloff, 136: 12ff) he discusses the instrumental performance of *ductia* and *stantipes*, not of *cantilena rotunda* (though he observes that a good vielle-player (*bonus autem artifex in viella*) can play every kind of music). See further n. 64 below.

[49]   *Civilis*: 'to do with citizens, with the *civitas*, the city or state'. It is interesting and noteworthy that Grocheo does not use the term *curialis*, 'courtly'; he is not speaking of an exclusively aristocratic art. By the late thirteenth century, as we know for example from the abundant

The term *vulgaris*, translated by some commentators as 'popular', may well embrace in this context its very common medieval meaning of 'vernacular' (cf. Dante's title *De vulgari eloquentia*).[50] None of Grocheo's examples in this section are in Latin; all are French. The emphasis is certainly on the highest aristocratic art and ideals, especially in the *cantus coronatus*, which Grocheo describes as follows:[51]

Cantus coronatus ab aliquibus simpliciter conductus dictus est. Qui propter eius bonitatem in dictamine et cantu a magistris et studentibus circa sonos coronatur, sicut gallice *Ausi com l'unicorne* vel *Quant li roussignol*. Qui etiam a regibus et nobilibus solet componi et etiam coram regibus et principibus terrae decantari, ut eorum animos ad audaciam et fortitudinem, magnanimitatem et liberalitatem commoveat, quae omnia faciunt ad bonum regimen. Est enim cantus iste de delectabili materia et ardua, sicut de amicitia et caritate, et ex omnibus longis et perfectis efficitur.

The 'crowned song' is called by some simply *conductus*. It is crowned for its sounds [i.e. most highly rated ?] by the masters and students of this science because of its excellence in words and melody: for example, the French songs 'Ausi com l'unicorne' and 'Quant li roussignol'. It is, too, customarily composed by kings and nobles and moreover sung in the presence of kings and secular princes to incite their minds to boldness and courage, magnanimity and generosity, all of which make for good government. For that kind of song is constructed from matter which is delightful as well as difficult – friendship and love, for instance – and is formed entirely of perfect 'longs'.

The meaning of *cantus coronatus* has been much discussed.[52] It can hardly mean only songs which have been declared as winners, 'crowned' in artistic

---

[50] Grocheo also uses the word *vulgaris* in the wider sense (e.g. to describe his whole first category (Rohloff, 130: line 16)) but here also the translation 'popular' would have some misleading associations.

[51] *Ibid.*, 30: lines 36–43.

[52] The *cantus coronatus* is recently discussed by: Rohloff (1972); van der Werf (1972), 'Glossary' 153–5, and his article in *New Grove*. See also Reckow, 'Conductus' in *HMT*. Three things are clear: (i) at *puys* and similar gatherings songs which won contests were 'crowned', *chansons couronnées*; (ii) in certain MSS trouvère chansons are presented with a crown drawn above them (see van der Werf, 'Cantus coronatus' in *New Grove*); (iii) Grocheo describes *cantus coronatus* as evidently the highest type of secular song. These three attested facts are complicated by further references in Grocheo associating *cantus coronatus* with instrumental performance on the *viella* (Rohloff, 136: lines 7–11) and with the singing of liturgical chant (Rohloff, 162: 12–23) 'in a drawn-out manner'? 'in a leisurely style'? (*tractim et ex longis et perfectis ad modum cantus coronati*). Charles W. Warren, 'Punctus organi and cantus coronatus in the music of Dufay', *Dufay Quincentenary Conference*, ed. A. W. Atlas (Brooklyn 1976), argues that *circa sonos coronatur* (literally "it is crowned around the sounds") refers to 'a practice of improvisation', the addition of melismas, or 'divisions'. I thank Margaret Bent for drawing my attention to this article.

---

records of civic life in Arras, the erstwhile noble and courtly art had been taken up by the bourgeoisie (see Marie Ungureanu, *La bourgeoisie naissante: société et littérature bourgeoises d'Arras* (Arras 1955) and the corrective notice by H. Roussel in *Revue des sciences humaines*, n.s. fasc. 87 (1957) 249–86). Hence the growth of the *puys* at Arras and elsewhere.

contests, the *chansons couronnées* of the *puys*;[53] the social milieu seems too
aristocratic (*coram regibus et principibus terrae*) for the *puy* to have figured. The
description and the examples are of the highest form of trouvère art. One
could not in fact wish for a better general specification for *la grande chanson
courtoise* than this that Grocheo offers; and his named examples confirm this
precisely.[54]

The rhythmic features of this 'melodic, secular, vernacular' art are never
explicitly described, except in the phrase about the *cantus coronatus* – which has
proved so puzzling – *ex omnibus longis et perfectis efficitur*. 'Longs' cannot in this
context be a palaeographical description (and *efficitur* does not in any case
mean 'copied, written' but 'accomplished, formed'), unless Grocheo is referring to a version of the melody quite different from the one which
survives for 'Ausi com l'unicorne sui' (R2075) in some dozen manuscripts,
because the known melody always contains a number of note-groups in
ligature as well as single notes.[55] It must therefore, I think, be a temporal
indication and must mean that the unit of rhythm (the *tactus*) is the long
'without imperfection' (which in mensural terms would mean 'not shortened,
not reduced in length by one-third'). In this case, each numbered unit would
have the duration of a long whether it was written as a single note or as a group
of notes in ligature – that is to say, the rhythm would be based on isosyllabic
movement. Grocheo's phrase, it seems to me, is puzzling chiefly if one is
intent on a measured, metrical interpretation.

However, whether this is a correct interpretation or not, the most interesting thing is the nature of the main categories themselves and what can be
inferred from them. The general contrast remains between a first category of
music which is *simplex*, *civilis* and *vulgaris* ('melodic, secular, vernacular') and
a second, music which is *composita*, *regularis* and *canonica*. This latter is essentially polyphony – *discantus* and *organum* – and 'they [the theorists] have
devised many rules for it' (*de hoc plures regulas invenerunt*).[56] The rules (*canoni-
cus*, from Greek, means 'according to rule') deal in part with 'vertical' consonances; they also deal, most importantly, with measure:

alii ad tres consonantias attendentes cantum ex tribus compositum, uniformi mensura
regulatum invenerunt, quem *cantum praecise mensuratum* vocaverunt.[57]

---

[53] To the list may now be added the long lost 'Si tost c'amis entant a bien amer' (R758a), first
printed by T. Wright, *Anecdota literaria* (1844), and recently rediscovered in the Public
Record Office (London) by Andrew Wathey, who kindly allows me to refer to his find.

[54] Beck (1927), II.51, agrees; there he argues that Grocheo's reference to *longae* shows the
predominant use of Mode 5 (spondaic). See also my comment on this procedure at the end of
note 33 above.

[55] See van der Werf (1979), 290. In this connection the eccentric notation of 'Amours m'ont si
doucement' (R658, by Adam de la Halle) should be mentioned; it is notated in MS *W* (Source
34), though not in its other source (MS *P*), entirely in longs. The song, however, is not a
typical *grand chant* (see Stevens (1974), 39).

[56] Rohloff, 138: line 11.

[57] Rohloff, 138: 17–19.

others, following the idea of the *three* consonances [octave, fifth and fourth], have devised a *three*-part song controlled by a regular measure, and this they have entitled 'precisely measured song'.

The essential difference, then, is between *musica composita* (all the examples are polyphonic), which is precisely measured and regular, and *musica simplex* (all examples are monophonic), of which the song-forms, dance excepted, are unmeasured.[58] In vernacular melodies one looks for *concordantia* (harmonious proportion), a special requirement of the art of melody, as we can see from Grocheo's description of the *cantus coronatus* as *concordantiis ad se invicem harmoniam facientibus* ('creating, with balanced sounds, a mutual harmoniousness').[59] In the polyphonic music, *consonantia* is needed, and a procedure for temporal measurement. And this procedure Grocheo goes on at once to discuss fully – a course of action which significantly he had not found it necessary to adopt in the section about *simplex musica*.[60] The smallest ordinary unit is the *tempus*, though it is he says capable of 'infinite' subdivision. Three *tempora* make a *perfectio*, which is the measure constantly in use in 'modern' music. There follows immediately on this an exposition of the modal system, as outlined above.[61] Grocheo's examples of 'precisely measured' genres are motet (an aristocratic form), *organum* and hocket.

In assessing Grocheo's contribution to an understanding of the rhythmic problem, it is not I think helpful to concentrate too exclusively on the single phrase *non ita precise mensurata*, as has sometimes been done. The phrase comes, as said above, in a categorization rejected by Grocheo himself, and it refers in its context to plainchant. Grocheo's main contribution is implicit in the whole way he handles his two non-liturgical categories. At the end of his discussion of polyphony he reiterates twice that this is the end of the section about *measured* musical forms (*mensuratis . . . musica precise mensurabili*) implying a clear contrast with the previous section.[62] Moreover, his placing of the exposition of the 'rhythmic' modes in the polyphonic section is clearly significant; and so is the careful use and definition of terms associated with melodic analysis. Grocheo, to be sure, does not employ the categories so common in some other writers, who explicitly distinguish *musica ritmica*

---

[58] Rohloff, 138: 5–7. 'In quo propositum de simplici seu vulgari musica terminatur. De musica igitur composita et regulari sermonem perquiramus' (With which the exposition relating to melodic, vernacular music is concluded; let us now enquire carefully into the teaching about composed and rule-directed music).

[59] Rohloff, 132: 46–7. 'Versus vero in cantu coronato est, qui ex pluribus punctis et concordantiis ad se invicem harmoniam facientibus efficitur'. *Concordantia* may in some contexts refer exclusively to the rhyme-sound; here it includes rhyme and assonance (?) as part of a bigger *harmonia* – harmoniousness, euphonious proportion. It is significant that Grocheo does not mention metre or metrical feet.

[60] Rohloff, 138: 24ff, deals with *mensurari et modus mensurandi*.

[61] Rohloff, 140: 14ff. Grocheo prefers Johannes de Garlandia's six to Lambert's nine and characteristically observes in passing that six is the first perfect number (140: 16).

[62] Rohloff, 148: 25–7.

from *musica metrica*;[63] and this is an omission one would like to be able to account for. However, the implicit agreement between his exposition and theirs is quite striking. In brief, an awareness of the two contrasting traditions of medieval rhythmic theory gives strong support to the fundamental contrast implied throughout Grocheo's treatise between unmeasured (but harmoniously proportioned) monophonic song and strictly measured, 'modal', mensurally notated polyphonic art.[64]

[63] According to Rohloff's comprehensive glossarial index, Grocheo nowhere uses either term.
[64] There is, of course, one respect not to be overlooked in which the plain contrast of the two traditions is blurred. The monophonic category also contains the dance-forms (*cantilena*: see p. 430 above and n. 48). These I have assumed in ch. 5 and argue in ch. 13 and ch. 14 must have been measured music. The fact of the matter seems to be that Grocheo is trying to make his categories do somewhat more for him than they can – i.e. enforce at the same time distinctions between practice and 'art', vernacular and Latin, melodic and polyphonic, etc.

13
PALAEOGRAPHY, NOTATION AND PRESENTATION

One of the surprising features of scholarship in this field over the last eighty years has been a lack of attention to the actual notation of non-liturgical monophonic music.[1] This has been partly due, I believe, to the extraordinary and uncritical haste with which in the early years of this century the 'modal' interpretation was adopted – a haste not so extraordinary, perhaps, when one recalls the names and fine talents of the scholars who fought for the honour of having invented it. The lack of attention has arisen primarily from a basic assumption behind the 'modal' system – that the original notations are inadequate to represent the intentions of those who composed the songs. This used to be coupled with the extraordinary idea that musicians lacked the capacity to devise a method of distinguishing long and short notes. In this section of the chapter I shall try first to get inside the 'intellectual mechanism', as it has been called, of the scribe and to establish whether the manuscript presentation and notation of the songs supports an interpretation of them as isosyllabic, or not. I ought to say at the outset that the notational evidence is in many respects ambiguous, baffling and inconclusive, and that I do not pretend to have found a new clue with which to unravel it. What I hope to do, however, is to look at the notation positively, as a possible system for presenting songs isosyllabically, to see how satisfactorily it could meet that end and what objections can be made to this interpretation.

[1] The French musicologist Armand Machabey, in a series of studies, mostly on Latin song, published during the late 1950s and early 1960s is a distinguished exception (see Bibliography). Higinio Anglès is another; see his studies and tabulation of notational forms in *La Música de las Cantigas* (1943–64). Jammers (1975) is to my knowledge the only book-length study devoted ostensibly to the notation of the non-liturgical monophonic music of the Middle Ages, but it is disappointingly thin in actual palaeographical observation; it is more a study of rhythmic problems in the wider sense. On the other hand, although devoted mainly to the polyphonic repertory, Roesner's dissertation (1974) contains much detailed and suggestive information about the ways a non-mensural notation may convey meaning. (I thank Daniel Leech-Wilkinson for drawing my attention to this.) See also Roesner's article in *EM* 7 (1979) 174, concentrating on notational modifications as they affect performance. More generally on the issues involved in the study of old notations, which cannot be conceived as a mechanical exercise, see Arlt's essay 'Aspekte der musikalischen Paläographie', introductory to the series Palaeographie der Musik, vol. 1; and Treitler, 'Music Writing' (1982). Another valuable contribution is Parker (1979), concentrating on the Chansonnier St Germain (Source 31); see also note 61 below.

1 Notation and layout

The symbols used in the chansonniers are those of square notation;[2] they are analogous to, and clearly derive in their essentials from, plainsong notation in its earlier neumed and later square forms. Moreover, they are the notational symbols of early polyphonic music as well.[3] These three broadly distinguishable systems, then, use the same symbols, just as different languages may all be written in Roman letters but obviously do not use them in the same way. This would scarcely be worth saying, were it not for the persisting tendency to deny the secular monophonic notations a *notational* validity of their own. The long-standing tradition of interpretation in accordance with the principles of 'modal rhythm' is of its very nature external. Whether applied rigidly, as in some transcriptions, or flexibly and musically, as in others, it remains external – a way of deciding what the notation 'means' by a kind of *ex cathedra* pronouncement derived from the poetic metre. This method of interpretation has done scholarship a disservice by distracting attention from the notation itself, which is long overdue for a thoroughgoing and searching analysis such as scholars have devoted to the palaeography of the chant and of early polyphony.[4]

To see a medieval monophonic song only in a modern transcription is to risk getting quite a false impression of it. Modern notation is comparatively *explicit*; it means what it says, and what it says is in general outline unambiguous – pitches and durations are clear. Not so with medieval notations, at least with monophonic notations up to about 1300. To transcribe a song into modern staff notation is comparable to the process of editing a medieval literary text. Both processes may lead to over-simplification. The modern editor who punctuates a medieval text subjects it, for instance, to rules of modern syntactical punctuation with its clear principles of logical subordination and sequence. These may sometimes be appropriate but, for instance in the long alliterative paragraphs of *Piers Plowman*, often are not.[5]

It will be convenient to start with a troubadour song, Bernart de Ventadorn's 'Can l'erba fresch' e.lh folha par', which was discussed from a

---

[2] The only major exception is the Chansonnier St Germain, which is written in Messine neumes.

[3] Tischler states the opposite: 'The fact is that in the late twelfth and early thirteenth centuries this notation derived from the very first one [i.e. polyphonic] to indicate rhythm', referring to the modal notation of Leonin and Perotin (Rosenberg and Tischler, p. xxii). I know of no warrant for so dogmatic a statement; it seems likely that the *three* traditions were at that time mutually influential.

[4] For chant, see chapter 8:III above. For early polyphony, see Calvin M. Bower and others, 'A Bibliography of Early Organum (*c.* 850–1150)', *Current Musicology* 21 (1976) 16–45. For the later, including Notre-Dame, polyphony an army of scholars have built on the pioneering work of Ludwig's monumental *Repertorium* (1910 etc.); bibliography in A. Hughes (1974) (nos. 1335–1494).

[5] See N. F. Blake, *The English Language in Medieval Literature* (London 1977), ch. 3, 'The Editorial Process'; and A. G. Rigg, ed., *Editing Medieval Texts* (New York 1977).

different point of view in chapter I (Ex. I). It is laid out on a single page of the troubadour chansonnier *R* (BN MS fr. 22543) with five other *cansos* complete and the beginning of a sixth; they are all by Bernart.[6] The manuscript presentation is typical of strophic songs in Provençal, French and other languages. The first verse is written in full with its melody; the other verses follow written as prose (presumably to save space, and parchment, and to make the page look good – which it does). There is punctuation in the text, but it consists only of full points whose function is to mark the end of the line of verse. Sometimes a vertical stroke appears in the music at the same place (in stave 3 after *chan*, for instance); it shows the end of the musical phrase which, as we know, always coincides with the poetic line. The normal procedure was for a text scribe to write in the words first, without regard for the 'proper' layout (i.e. the formal structure) of the stanza, under the empty, previously ruled staves. The music scribe (who may, of course, have been the same man) then filled in the melody above the text, syllable by syllable. Sometimes (this *canso* may be an example) the order of copying can be proved by an examination of the palaeographical detail.[7] In the case of this chansonnier, and indeed of this particular page, this is not necessary: the left-hand column contains a song with words only beneath an empty stave – Bernart's 'En avril can vei verdeiar'.[8] This state of affairs is, alas, all too common in this and some other manuscripts. The text scribe, clearly an educated man, notes at one point the reason for it: *deficit quod deficiebat in exemplari* ('missing, because it was not in the original'). This is interesting, also, as an explicit reference to a previous written tradition at this date (late-thirteenth-century); but it does not prove that the whole tradition and transmission of the songs was a written one.[9]

One reason for writing the words first was that a verbal syllable takes up more lateral space than a single note (and sixty of the seventy-two syllables in this song have single notes) or a small note-group. If the scribe wanted the underlay (perhaps better called 'overlay') to be precise, and he did, it was safer to have the text in place before the melody. His concern brings us immediately to the most striking single fact about this song as a *visual* object – a fact that is equally true of the huge majority of songs from the troubadour, trouvère and Latin repertoires. I refer to the absolutely clear and unambiguous relationship between note and syllable, or between note-group and syllable. The note-groups are 'bound' together in ligatures. This particular music scribe (or the scribe of his exemplar if he copies closely) seems to have had a particular fondness for the oblique forms of ligatures (see stave I, symbol 4) in which

---

[6] Facsimile of whole page in Stäblein (1975), pl. 47 (from BN fr. 22543 (Source 32)); see also Appel, pl. xix (Pillet–Carstens, p. 78, no. 39).

[7] For instance, the tails of the *virgae*/longs are adjusted in length so as not to get mixed up with the already written text (see the last stave of 'Can l'erba' in col. 2, where the lowest notes are tailless *puncta*/breves).

[8] BN fr. 22543 (Source 32) lacks music for all but 160 out of 1165 songs.

[9] Oral and written traditions are discussed in the Afterword to this chapter.

higher and lower notes are made by a single broad stroke of the pen. This peculiarity has, it is virtually certain, no stylistic significance whatsoever; *glissandi* or *portamenti* are not in question. Generally speaking, the notation of this *canso* is a comparatively straightforward one; it does not hint at stylistical subtleties.[10]

It is a paradox of musical history that not only this, the largest of the Provençal chansonniers, but all the troubadour and trouvère chansonniers are of late date – from the second half of the thirteenth century and the early fourteenth century.[11] Bernart de Ventadorn was in his prime *c.* 1150, a century or more earlier. If, as in the parallel case of chant manuscripts, we also had sources of an earlier date, written in neumes, we might be able to put the two together and reconstruct the melodies in subtler and truer forms. There are, it is a sad fact, no twelfth- or early thirteenth-century collections of either southern or northern French songs. The earliest surviving chansonnier dates from sometime after the middle of the thirteenth: it is the Chansonnier St Germain (B N fr. 20050) and contains a number of troubadour songs as well as a large trouvère repertory.[12] Unlike all the other main chansonniers, which were compiled over the next fifty years, the Chansonnier St Germain is written not in square (quadratic) notation but in Messine neumes. The syllabic presentation, however, is just as clear as in the later manuscript mentioned above, as the following diplomatic transcription will show:[13]

Ex. 171

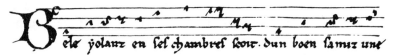

But clear syllabic neuming goes back over the centuries and is indeed a constant and inalienable feature of Latin as well as of vernacular song. Here is the opening of the *planctus cigni* (see ch. 4: 1 and Ex. 38 above) from one of the Winchester Tropers (*c.* 1050):[14]

[10] The principal means of conveying such subtleties elsewhere is in various forms of the *plica*, the only liquescent neume widely used in secular monophonic notation. See note below. The *plica* is further discussed by Roesner (1979), 189 and n. 28. On liquescents generally, see chapter 8:III above.

[11] The chansonniers are briefly described by Raynaud (1884) and Jeanroy (1918). For a concise, up-to-date summary, see 'Sources' in *New Grove*, sect. III.4 (pp. 639–43, with plates). Jammers (1975) 2–15, gives a succinct over-view of all the main sources of non-liturgical monophony (including the French chansonniers), with much detailed bibliography and well-reproduced plates.

[12] See notes 1 and 2 above.

[13] 'Bele Yolanz' (R1847) is a *chanson de toile*.

[14] Reproduced in Stäblein (1975), pl. 7, from Oxford, Bodleian M S Bodley 775, fol. 176v. Stäblein, 114, n. 3, gives a long list of facsimile reproductions from the M S.

Ex. 172

P lángamt filii plóranone una·A lrmf
  cingui quictanf freraunt aequora·O qua

A final example from the Later Cambridge Songs (? thirteenth-century) shows that even in a more informal style of presentation – not to say slapdash – the syllabic principle still holds and makes the problem of underlay (the precise physical relation of the words to the notes) easy to solve. The fact that the melody is more melismatic does not complicate the issue; even when the visual placing is imprecise, the system of ligatures ensures that normally no ambiguity is possible.[15]

Ex. 173

The theory – not just *a* modern but *the* medieval theory, as earlier discussion has shown – that song in the *ritmus* tradition rests essentially on the practice of *number*, syllable-and-note-group-counting, gets strong visual support from the manuscripts over three centuries or more.[16] Most sources (there are of course some rare exceptions) exercise a care so precise and so successful that it is scarcely ever necessary to discuss how the melodies are related to the texts. What we see before us is a visually striking, unwaveringly *unitary*, syllable-by-syllable presentation of the melody. That this suggests approximately equal units more strongly than any precisely measured combination and supports isosyllabism rather than modal rhythm is, I think, temptingly obvious. Temptingly, because we must not expect or deduce too much from notation; there are too many 'lost traditions' for that. It does not, naturally, amount to proof in itself, but visual evidence *is* evidence; it is not negligible, though it has been neglected. Certainly, if one had to invent a notation in which the importance of numbered and equal syllables should be clear and uncumbered, one could hardly do better. The syllables control the spacing of the notes – and perhaps their *aural* dimensions in the flow of musical time.

[15] 'Diastematica vocis armonia' (Walther 4342), reproduced from the Later Cambridge Songs (Source 8), fol. 1v, in Fenlon (1982), opp. p. 43.

[16] The discussion of visual evidence is based in part, with some modifications, on pp. 52–3 of Stevens (1981b).

This way of putting it might suggest that the words were primary and directive not only in process of copying out a song but also in its creation. This was not, I believe, so. It was pattern – a purely numerical structure of stanzas, lines and syllables – which preceded, or at least took precedence over, both the melody and the poem. The 'numbers' of a monophonic song of the period, whether chanson or *cantio*, can be worked out quite simply and directly from the melody without reference to the text. The degree of concurrence between the manuscripts is impressive.[17] In contrast to most melismatic chants, where the allocation of syllables is liable to variation, the melody of a 'secular' song is a stable, unit-based construction. The inner detail of the unit may change – that is to say, for instance, that a descending *clivis* in one source may be paralleled in another by a *nota plicata* or a *climacus* – but except in minor instances the melody retains its distinct recognizable units.[18]

Ex. 174

[17] See the comparative melodic versions in the two published volumes of trouvère chansons in van der Werf (1977) and (1979).

[18] The comparatively simple music example (based on van der Werf (1977), 270) gives lines 3–4 of a chanson, 'A la douçour dou tens' (R1754), probably by the Chastelain de Coucy. A fifth source, trouvère MS *V*, transmits a different melody, which I have omitted. (On the oddities of this MS see F. McAlpine, 'Un chansonnier médiéval: édition et étude de ms 24406 de la Bibliothèque Nationale', unpublished diss., University of Paris, Sorbonne 1974.) Van der Werf gives further minor variations from the *KNPX* group. MS *T* (Chansonnier de Noailles) is notated a fourth higher in the original. A more extended example of a whole chanson (Adam de Halle's 'Jou n'ay autre retenance') is reproduced in Stevens (1981b), chart x.

The melody is not simply a labile and malleable series of single notes to be disposed of according to the will, or whim, of the individual copyist; and it allows very few opportunities for arbitrary re-arrangement. It is a 'numerical–musical' object in its own right, as the nature of the numerous *contrafacta* also demonstrates.[19]

Not all the palaeographical evidence points in the same direction, and we shall have to consider later certain chansons, for instance, which are in a mensural or quasi-mensural notation. But before we do so I should like to dispel the idea, if it has arisen, that melody without 'measure' and without the adornments of instrumental accompaniment is necessarily simple and probably dull. The answer to this must in the end be a musical answer. The point, however, that I wish to make here is notational. The diversity of symbols available to the medieval music scribe was greater than a modern editor conventionally has at his command. That the scribes wished to make use of this diversity surely tells us something about musical style, something about what they or their predecessors were 'hearing in their heads' as they copied their songs.[20] To judge from the notation, what they heard cannot have been simple.

From a close examination of the notational practices of the different scribes (and they *are* all different) there emerges a positive picture of diversity, versatility and inventiveness, carried sometimes to the point of eccentricity. It is by no means unusual for a single scribe to employ 40 or 50 distinguishable symbols; a modern editor will use perhaps a dozen. This versatility, which it is difficult, if not impossible, to represent in a modern edition, conveys more vividly than anything else the sense of a melodic style *très nuancée*, flexible, elusive, not easy to pin down in a precisely conceived scheme of consistent note values.[21]

These comments were originally framed as part of a study of the notation and presentation of the chansons of a single trouvère, Adam de la Halle

[19] *Contrafacta* are assembled and studied in the standard works by: Spanke, *Beziehungen* (1936); Gennrich, 'Internationale Melodien' (1928–9), 'Lateinische Kontrafakta' (1930), *Formenlehre* (1932); Chailley, *Gautier* (1959); Räkel (1977). It is of the essence of monophonic *contrafacta* in the Romance languages, that the unit-count remains constant: it is established in the notation by ligature-grouping and in the text by precise syllabization. The position in regard to stress-languages (German and English) is less predictable.

[20] Whatever one may conclude about the musicality of any particular scribe, who may have been a mere mechanical copyist, somewhere along the line of oral/written transmission someone wished to use more than the simplest symbols to convey what he had in his mind.

[21] Stevens (1981b), 53. The number of available symbols in the different manuscripts can be gauged from *ibid.*, charts I–IX; the variety of compound *plicas* is often astonishing.

(?1245–1288?) but I believe they have a general validity for the monophonic repertory. The conclusion rests on a detailed examination and charting of notational forms, of a kind which still needs to be done for the whole huge repertory.

By way of example we may take for analysis the Paris manuscript BN fr. 847 (trouvère MS *P*), an important source for Adam de la Halle studies and the one used by J. H. Marshall as the base text for his edition of the poems. The manuscript is a composite, and the 'Adam de la Halle chansonnier', consisting of two quires with two added pages (fols. 211–228v), may not originally have had anything to do with the rest of the manuscript.[22] There is, however, a close melodic correspondence between it and another separable miniature chansonnier (trouvère MS *Wx*), which is part of the so-called Adam de la Halle Manuscript (MS *W*).

The hand [of MS *P*] is clear and not unattractive but . . . will not stand up to comparison with that of *W*. In its wealth of *plica*-symbols, this scribe rivals the scribe of *Wx*. Admittedly we have the evidence of 33 songs as against 14 from *Wx*. Both manuscripts contain between 25 and 30 identifiable types of single, double and compound *plica*; MS *P* slightly fewer than *Wx*. But the *P*-scribe makes up for it in variety of *conjunctura* and *climacus* forms. Like *Wx*, *P* has several ingenious combinations of *plica* and *conjunctura*. It looks sometimes as if the scribes act on the principle that a *plica* or *plica*-stroke may be inserted anywhere into a ligature. And there are certainly grounds for thinking that, at least in *P*, some *plicas* were added later, in a lighter browner ink.[23]

The scribe's apparent inventiveness may sometimes result as much from graphic uncertainty as from melodic subtlety. Nevertheless, both manuscripts testify, I suggest, to the survival of a notational code especially suited to the needs of a melodic musical tradition – a code more diverse, more flexible, and perhaps more susceptible to personal manipulation than the necessarily more formal and rigid mensural notations which modern editors are accustomed to use.[24] The great notational diversity acts in the interests of suggestiveness rather than of prescription, and we have perhaps been wrong in searching so diligently over the years for a key which would unlock the code with the same mechanical ease and precision with which one might unlock a door.

It might be thought that Adam de la Halle is a rather late and special case on which to be basing an important argument:[25] namely, that the diversity of

[22] *Ibid.*, 41.

[23] *Ibid.*, 41 (I omit here the references to the notational charts and the *RISM sigla* for MSS).

[24] It would be quite misleading to give the impression that 'melodic' and 'monophonic' are synonymous terms. What I have said about monophonic notations applies with equal force to early polyphonic sources, i.e. to the *melody* of polyphony. The opposite may also be true: see, especially, Roesner (1979). He also discusses briefly the ornamentation of plainchant (p. 177), referring to Jerome of Moravia's terms *reverberatio, flos harmonicus, nota procellaris* etc.

[25] Adam is special only in the sense that he alone amongst the trouvères is known to have been a polyphonic composer, of *rondeaux* and motets (ed. Wilkins (1967)), a poet, and a dramatist.

trouvère notations represents a style of singing which, grafted on to the *apparent* bleakness of a single line of melody, would have given it imaginative life and subtle creativeness. But, so far from weakening the case, Adam's late position in the long succession strengthens it. By those who valued the trouvère art Adam was held in high esteem; his courtly chansons survive with musical texts in ten chansonniers of the late thirteenth and early fourteenth century.[26] The fact that the sources are closer to the original poet–composer in this case than in many others assures us that what we have may well be presented in the style which he himself envisaged. The lateness of the sources themselves (a characteristic of the *whole* repertory, not just of Adam's chansons) may also give added significance to the choice of this notation over others which were then available and widely used. The word 'choice', however, may seem to beg an important question; I return later to this issue.

In the absence of systematic notational studies one is obliged to cast about somewhat randomly for other examples. But, coming nearer home (though not much nearer, since Arras is only some sixty miles from the Channel) we can find in the history of one 'English' song, a diversity of presentation which will serve to fill out the picture. 'Angelus ad virginem' is an English song at least in the sense that its principal musical sources are English (or British) and that it was popular enough to have two English *contrafacta* and to have been mentioned by Chaucer.[27] We need not for the moment concern ourselves with the well-known polyphonic versions of the song, but only with the two monophonic. They occur in the Arundel Songs (Source 12) and in the Dublin Troper (Source 7) respectively; the Dublin Troper was compiled *c.* 1360, the Arundel Songs probably rather earlier in the century.

Both Arundel and Dublin present the standard melody as a song for one voice; yet it is obvious at a glance that the Arundel version (version (a) in the music example below) implies a different rendering from the Dublin version (II). The latter presents the song in a straightforward square notation on a four-line stave. The notational symbols used are: the *virga* (the square or squarish note-head has a tail down to the right varying in length from the barely visible to $\frac{3}{16}''$); the *punctum* (normally a square note-head without tail, but in this and other British sources often rhomboid in shape – see line 1, symbol 2 'angelus'); the descending and ascending two-note neumes, *clivis* (3.7 'formidinem') and *podatus* (8.4 'paries'); and the *plica* (a liquescent neume the simplest form of which, (4.2 'demulcens' and 4.4 'inquit'), consists of a note-head with two downward tails – the main note has a written pitch, the *plica*'d note which follows it is lighter and of indeterminate pitch and often goes with an *n, l, r,* or other sounded consonant.) Although the *virga* and the

[26] Listed and described in Stevens (1981b).
[27] The discussion which follows is based on my article 'Angelus ad virginem' (1981a) listing and describing all the known versions. (On p. 310, line 22, *syllables* is an error for *stresses*.) Since its publication Page has noted another reference to the song: '*Angelus ad virginem*: a new work by Philippe the Chancellor?', *EM* 11 (1983) 69.

punctum may resemble the long and the breve of mensural notation, there is no sign in the manuscript that they have mensural significance; they are undifferentiated as temporal symbols.

The Arundel version of the same melody is more complicated. The notation, on a five-line stave, is of the same basic type – a square notation – but in this case the comparative variety of symbols used suggests a greater flexibility of melodic style. In the Arundel song *virga* and *punctum* are again undifferentiated, and there are the same basic ligatures. Variety is achieved mainly through the use of *plica* combinations. The downward *plica* is normally attached to a double main note (1.1 'Angelus', 1.6 'virginem'), perhaps suggesting the lengthening of the main note; this is supplemented by an upward *plica* (1.2 'Angelus', 3.2 'virginis', 5.1 'Ave', etc.) on a single note and by *plicas* attached to two- and three-note neumes (9.1 'intacta', 11.5 'celi').

Ex. 175a

An-	ge-	lus	ad	vir-	gi-	nem

| 2 | sub- | in- | trans | in | con- | cla- | ve, |

| 3 | vir- | gi- | nis | for- | mi- | di- | nem |

| 4 | de- | mul- | cens | in- | quit: | A- | ve, |

| 5 | A- | ve, | re- | gi- | na | vir- | gi- | num, |

| 6 | ce- | li | ter- | re- | que | do- | mi- | num |

| 7 | con- | ci- | pi- | es | 8. et | pa- | ri- | es | 9. in- | ta- | cta, |

| 10 | sa- | lu- | tem | ho- | mi- | num; |

| 11 | tu | por- | ta | ce- | li | fa- | cta, |

12 me- de- la cri- mi- num.

Ex. 175b

An- ge- lus ad vir- gi- nem

2 sub- in- trans in con- cla- ve,

3 vir- gi- nis for- mi- di- nem

4 de- mul- cens in- quit: A- ve,

5 A- ve, re- gi- na vir- gi- num,

6 ce- li ter- re- que do- mi- num

7 con- ci- pi- es 8. et pa- ri- es 9. in- ta- cta,

10 sa- lu- tem ho- mi- num;

11 tu por- ta ce- li fa- cta,

12 me- de- la cri- mi- num.

The angel, entering secretly the Virgin's chamber, calmed her fear and said, 'Hail, hail, O queen of virgins, you shall conceive and bear the Lord of heaven and earth, the salvation of men, whilst remaining a virgin. You are made the doorway to heaven, the remedy for sin.

What can we deduce from the existence of two very differently notated monophonic versions? From the known late date of the Dublin version we

could deduce that by the middle of the fourteenth century a simpler style of
notating non-liturgical songs had become the rule.[28] The three other songs
copied with 'Angelus ad virginem' are equally straightforward in their notation; and this little group follows on from a series of Marian sequences with
the same notational characteristics.[29] Alternatively, we could suppose that, as
so often in the history of music for centuries to come, the notated melody was
only a skeletal frame for the performer to clothe with the 'garment of style'. It
is impossible to decide. Certainly, if the performer wished to sing the song in a
measured style (the familiar triple metre), it would be easier to do so from the
Dublin than from the Arundel copy. If, on the other hand, a more fluid
rendering was *à la mode*, then the Arundel notation with its abundance of
liquescent notes and little 'flowers' of melodic ornament (see, especially, lines
9 and 11) is more suggestive.[30] The notation, on a five-line stave, appears
closer to the neume-systems from which it derives – systems which, as the
history of Gregorian chant notation shows, *lost* subtlety, sophistication, and
nuance at the same time as they developed clarity in pitch indications.

I have dwelt on the technicalities of the notation in order to dispel the
all-too-easy assumption, to which I referred earlier, that monophonic means
musically 'primitive' and simple, and in order to question, as one must, the
still-predominant view that the notation was inadequate to express what was
meant. It is only if we think that all monophonic songs of this period were
sung in clearly measured long and short notes like late-thirteenth-century
polyphony that we shall regard the notation as hopelessly wanting in precision. Of course, all musical notations are inadequate to some degree or other,
not least our own modern system; but almost all older systems have something to tell us that a modern transcription cannot convey.

II Mensural and non-mensural notation

Notation is – the obvious will bear repeating – a *visual* system; it is a way
of representing sounds to the eye. Moreover, in the earliest centuries (ninth
to thirteenth) it would not be taken for granted that the rhythm would
be indicated purely by symbolic (i.e. non-representational, arbitrary,
conventional) signs, such as today's semibreve, minim, crotchet etc. The
opposite could, admittedly, have been taken for granted – that notation had no
durational significance whatsoever. But another possibility, that the placing
and spacing of notational signs had a directly iconic (i.e. representational,

---

[28] 'Angelus' was certainly in liturgical use by the fifteenth century (Stevens (1981a), 322–3),
and it could be that the Dublin version was also. But 'non-liturgical' seems justified by the
group as a whole (listed in note 29 below).

[29] They are: the Latin *lai* 'Omnis caro' (see Walther 13348; transcr. chapter 4, Ex. 55 above);
'Scribere proposui' (Walther 17394); 'In ecclesiis celi gloria' (Anderson L190; not in Walther),
facsimile in Hesbert (1966).

[30] The ornaments seem to have no obvious relation to verbal accent, witness the 'double plicas'
in 5.4 and 5.7, 6.4, and 6.7 etc.

visually positive) function is also possible.[31] Nevertheless, there are considerable difficulties, weighty objections to the particular, if tentative, hypothesis that the visual presentation of monophonic music as a syllabic system gives support to an isosyllabic interpretation; and these difficulties we must now consider.

We may start with the simple question: does non-mensural notation imply unmeasured music? Certainly not always, as the history of polyphony in the twelfth and thirteenth centuries clearly shows. But it is difficult to frame the right questions. The positive claim I have been putting forward, that non-mensural secular notations have a validity of their own, does not *ipso facto* exclude measured interpretation. The stylistic nuances might be compatible with a regular pattern of longs and shorts. But there are two objections to this, which may be illustrated from the Arundel version of 'Angelus'. One is musical. The usual 'trochaic' 3/4 rendering of the tune, attested by the polyphonic settings, pushes some note-groups on to shorter (and in 3/4 time markedly weaker) beats, especially here the second syllable of 'vir*gi*nem'.

Ex. 176

Not that there is any *prima facie* objection to melismas or ornaments or (as here) stylistic graces being on light beats.[32] But they are less natural and easy if their relaxed performance is constrained by the demands of regular metre. In this particular case the issue is complicated by doubts about the meaning of the double-*plica* and *pressus* type symbols (shown in Ex. 175a). Both look as if they indicate weight or emphasis by means of slight lengthening or double articulation; but one cannot be sure. (If the first of these symbols is merely this scribe's way of writing a normal *plica*'d note, then the problem does not arise.)

A second objection to reading metrical patterns into non-mensural notation is that it perpetually requires the interpretation of identical symbols in different ways. Again, the objection cannot be sustained in simple logic. If a sign-system works, it works; and that is good enough. But there is something distinctly untidy, intellectually, in having the same notational symbol perform different functions, sometimes on adjacent notes, for reasons *outside*

---

[31] I borrow the convenient distinction which Treitler ((1982b) 238ff) has introduced into the discussion from C. S. Peirce, *Collected Papers* (Cambridge, Mass., 8 vols. 1931–58).

[32] But the opposite view is often taken by 'modalists', namely that compound neumes (i.e. short melismas notated in a single ligature) by their very nature indicate long notes. For a recent example, see Rosenberg and Tischler, introd., pp. xxiv–xxv.

the system itself (e.g. the metre of the words). A telling example is the last phrase of Blondel's 'Amour dont sui espris' (RI545).[33]

Ex. 177

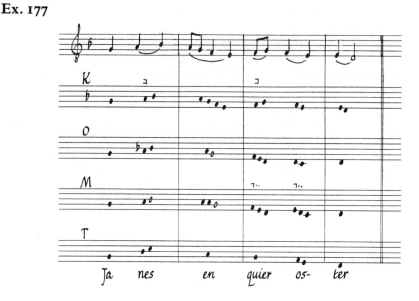

However one interprets this song modally, there are bound to be inconsistencies of the type described – as for example the *podatus* in version K, note-groups 2 and 4; and the *climacus* in M, groups 4 and 5. Such discrepancies are different in kind from strictly *notational* ambivalences, as for instance in later mensural notation when a *longa* may be 'imperfected' (losing one-third of its value) by a following *brevis*, or a *brevis* 'altered' (doubling its value) by a following *longa*. Are there any examples in the period 1000–1500 of the *text* determining the durational value of the notation, apart from those which the hypothetical system of 'modal rhythm' in secular song would provide?[34] (We have to remember that modal rhythms in polyphony are either notated or inferred on *musical* grounds.)

The problem of notational 'inconsistencies' was taken up at length by the French musicologist Armand Machabey, who, evidently worried by the

[33] Van der Werf (1977), 103. I omit the melody of M S *V*, which is wholly different throughout (see note 18 above); the metric-modal version is taken from van der Werf (1972), 102. He discusses the song at length and observes that the sources show a 'remarkable uniformity' in the distribution of melismas – which is true, even though this last line is not a good example of it. It does not to my mind follow that such stability indicates measured melody; nor can one assume that a melisma requires a long syllable.

Blondel's song was evidently popular: there are two Latin *contrafacta* and a pious version by Gautier de Coinci. See Introduction above, text to note 4.

[34] An exception (to date, entirely unsubstantiated) to this observation could be the 'measuring' of non-mensural neumes by quantitative Latin classical texts belonging to the *musica metrica* tradition. (See chapter 12, n. 31 above.)

intellectual untidiness to which I have referred, devoted a series of studies to notational equivalences.[35] He showed in detail that the only way to avoid blatant inconsistencies of notational meaning in such songs as 'Licet eger', 'Clauso cronos' and 'Fas et nefas' (all from the *Carmina Burana*) was to assume temporal equality of syllables (*l'isochronisme*). The unit is the long; and all ligatures (note-groups) occupy the same space of time as a single long (the *virga* or *punctum* of non-mensural terminology).[36] The principle applies to non-mensural songs in whatever language. In his *Notations musicales non modales* (1959 edn) Machabey discussed Aubry's transcription of the chanson 'A la doucor d'este qui reverdoie' (R1754: variously attributed) and on the same grounds came down in favour of isochronous interpretation, 'the same signs or groups [i.e. ligatures] receiving always the same transcription'.[37]

One further notational observation is relevant here, since scribal attitudes may be involved. It has been well observed by van der Werf that

the least-used source of information about rhythm and meter lies in the differences and similarities among the various readings of chansons with multiple versions . . . If . . . all chansons were meant to be performed in modal rhythm or in any other kind of regular alternation of long and short syllables, or accented and unaccented tones, most of these performers and notators must have known about it.

Consequently, if a certain chanson was always performed in the same meter, one would expect not only that the variations would have remained within the same meter but also that the meter must have prompted the performer to make certain types of variants in certain places.[38]

In practical terms this means that the distribution of notes and note-groups (short melismas) could be expected to follow a coherent and rational *metrical* pattern. But this is very rarely the case. So, to take a particular instance, the principle of isosyllabic transcription makes better sense of melodic variants such as we see in the musical illustration just given. In the 'modal' transcription which heads the table the third syllable occupies a whole bar; this is because it has four notes. But in fact, as sources *O*, *M* and *T* show, the ligature is only decorative of a single note (with or without *plica*).[39]

---

[35] Machabey, 'Licet eger', in *La Musique et les Musiciens en Normandie*, Etudes Normandes, ed. René Etienne, no. 83 (Rouen 1957), 229–32; and his study of goliardic songs (1962). This article takes the form of a critique of the reconstructions of songs from the *Carmina Burana* by Lipphardt (1955) and (1961), all of which are in measured (modal) transcriptions; the first of these (1955) contains useful facsimiles.

[36] Notational 'equivalences' can be established either within a single song, if melodic material is repeated, or by comparison between songs. The process applies both to neumed and to quadratic notation.

[37] See his Annexe II, 'Monodie', especially p. iii.

[38] Van der Werf (1972), 41–2.

[39] Modal transcribers tend to produce four-bar phrases (e.g. by the stretching out of ligatures, as here) to accord, perhaps unconsciously, with the conventional melodic structures of a later era. The double-*plica* of *M* (note 3) could, of course, indicate a lengthening, though not necessarily a doubling.

Before we leave the question of the interpretation of non-mensural notation, two further categories must be mentioned: *rondeaux* and motets. *Rondeaux*, *rondelli* and the *refrains* from which they are constituted are normally in mensural (or at least semi-mensural) notation. There is no ambiguity about this *refrain* from *Robin et Marion*.[40]

Ex. 178

Ber- ge- ron- ne- te sui mais t'ai   a- mi bel et coin- te et gai

In the chapter on dance-song I gave a number of these *refrains* and described their essential relation to dance. There is no doubt of their genre, in fact – which incidentally has nothing to do with the theoretical category of *metrum*. We shall return in the next chapter to the importance of genre in rhythmical interpretation. For the moment it is necessary to say only that when occasionally *refrains* are found in non-mensural notation, they should nevertheless be transcribed metrically. (See Exx. 63–65 pp. 187 ff above: *rondeaux* by Guillaume d'Amiens from the Vatican Chansonnier.) This is only to state again in particular terms one of the main themes of the present chapter, that notation in this period is not an intellectual code that has to be cracked but a complex set of signs which has to be interpreted. To every system of signs one has to bring a context of understanding; it is no use approaching a French poem with the instruments of the German language. The context of understanding needed for the interpretation of dance-song is fairly clear and obvious.[41] The context needed for the courtly chanson is something very different: it has to do with 'number' and *armonia* and syllabic movement, and remains still to be fully defined.

But to return to the practicalities of the notation: motets also are found in non-mensural notation, most significantly for instance in the Chansonnier de Noailles, a principal trouvère manuscript. Many of the eighty-seven motets are found elsewhere, notated mensurally, as in the Las Huelgas Manuscript.[42] But there are many other good reasons for the accepted view that their non-mensural presentation in Noailles is to be interpreted as measured music. The first reason is that they are polyphonic but not written in score. This

[40] By 'semi-mensural' is meant notation in which the main features (e.g. alternation of long and breve) are clear but the details are ambiguous. The *refrain* given (Boogaard, no. 251) is thoroughly 'modern' in using the two-semibreve ligature (a–*mi*). See facsimile in Varty, opp. p. 80, from the Adam de la Halle MS (Source 34).

[41] See chapter 5:IV above, where I have taken it as 'axiomatic that all choral dance-songs, dances sung and performed in company, must have a metrical base, an underlying regular rhythm', duple or triple.

[42] Gennrich (1958) lists eighty-nine motets; Reaney, in RISM B.IV[1], 381–93, lists eighty-seven concordances with Montpellier, Bamberg, Las Huelgas and other motet collections; also with the Chansonnier du Roi.

means that there are no visual aids to help the performers synchronize their parts; but synchronization is essential. Secondly, their 'worded' voice-part(s), *motetus* and *triplum*, all of which are supplied with French texts, have the strongest associations with, and often derive directly from, *refrain* and *rondeau* – i.e. dance-type, measured music.[43] Thirdly, the main tradition of the thirteenth-century motet, as it is known from major and minor sources, is of measured polyphony indicated by mensural or semi-mensural notation. And, lastly, the Noailles pieces make no kind of sense musically unless they are made to conform to the genre and conventions of early motet.[44]

The Noailles Chansonnier provides a clear example of the need, already mentioned, to posit that a musician could recognize the genre of a piece written in non-mensural notation and apply its conventions in performance.[45] In the case of this particular MS he would also have to know the conventions of singing a *lai* (the manuscript is a principal source for the French *lai*) and various types of *chanson*, if they differed the one from the other.

The well-documented use of non-mensural notations for the recording of various types of measured music means, then, that there is no simple equation to be drawn up between non-mensural notations and the isosyllabic, numbered style. But this general conclusion does not in itself constitute a valid objection to the isosyllabic hypothesis. It simply reminds us again of the certainty that 'a context of understanding' has to be brought to every sign-system, including chanson-notation, and alerts us to the further possibility that different monophonic notations, having different contexts, may require different 'solutions'.

A seemingly more cogent objection is based on the fact that in some sources of monody, French and Latin songs are found in mensural or semi-mensural versions, or have been mensuralized by notational alterations. In the trouvère repertoire, the Chansonnier Cangé and the Chansonnier du Roi contain chansons with mensural indications which elsewhere appear without them.[46]

---

[43] For example: fol. 179 'Onques n'amai tant' (Gennrich (1958), no. 820) = Boogaard 1427; fol. 179 'Qui loiaument sert s'amie' (Gennrich no. 819) = Boogaard 1605; fols. 179–179v 'D'amor trop lointaigne' (Gennrich no. 82) = Boogaard 454 (but omitting the cross-reference); and so on.

[44] Motets agreed to have been measured in performance are not fully mensural in notation until late in the century. The mid-thirteenth-century sources move towards this. Clear, graphic distinction between long and breve is associated with Franco of Cologne (*Ars cantus mensurabilis*, ? between 1250 and 1280).

[45] The Noailles motets, however, seem to present a particular problem. They are exceedingly difficult to transcribe, and it is difficult to see how in their surviving written form they could ever have served for performance.

[46] The position is variously stated. Tischler (Rosenberg and Tischler, p. xxi) writes, 'some manuscripts employ a notation that clearly indicates the rhythm'. This is seriously mislead-ing. Of the seventeen 'major' chansonniers (see 'Sources' in *New Grove*, 'MSS', xvII.639–43, 'Secular monophony, French') only two merit consideration, the Chansonnier Cangé and the Chansonnier du Roi. In Roi (Source 28), the songs in mensural notation are a late addition; their notation is 'advanced'. In Cangé (Source 29), the position is more compli-cated: 'at one extreme there are many melodies in the same non-mensural notation as is used

The chanson 'De bone amour' (R1102) by Gace Brulé (late-twelfth-century) is a case in point.[47] The mensural version opens as follows.

Ex. 179

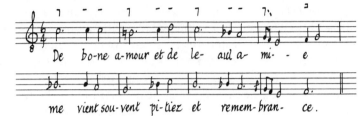

De bo-ne a-mour et de le- aul a- mi- - e

me vient sou-vent pi-tiez et remem-bran- ce.

From good love and a loyal friend there comes to me often pity and remembrance . . .

I have transcribed it in the third (dactylic) mode in accordance with the accepted conventions of early mensural notation, by which the *longa* consists of three *breves*. Jean Beck, however, in his transcription of the whole manuscript (1927) often used duple measure for this mode. This notation is in any case best described as 'semi-mensural' since only *longae* and *breves* are clearly distinguished; the ligatures have no agreed mensural meaning.[48] In measure 4 the first group could equally well be ♩ ♩ ♩ or ♩. ♪♩. The first important fact to note about 'De bone amour' is that,

---

[47] Two differing versions are reproduced by Parrish, *Notation* (1957), on facing plates xiv and xv (the fol. no. for the non-mensural version, from B N n.a.fr.1050, trouvère MS X (pl. xiv), should read fol. 58v). Van der Werf (1977), 447ff, gives parallel transcriptions from eight MSS plus two *contrafacta*; the mensural version of O (Chansonnier Cangé) is misleadingly not given a measured transcription, though this is noted (p. 588); the editor regards the O versions in general as of dubious value. Räkel, 180–2, discusses the melodic variants.

[48] In transcriptions of 'pre-Franconian' notated polyphony and in transcriptions of monophony by 'modalist' editors, the smaller notes within the ligature group are usually measured. In the case of polyphony the interpretation is disputable; in the case of monophony it must, additionally, be subjective. If, however, the relative flexibility and fluidity of isosyllabic interpretation are taken as a stylistic basis for transcription and performance, then it is reasonable, even if not strictly necessary in logic, to assume that the constituent parts of the note-group (the musical syllable) are also not measured.

---

in the other sources, and at the other extreme there are a very few melodies in a semi-mensural notation which clearly and faultlessly indicates modal rhythm' (van der Werf (1972), 40). In between the two extremes are chansons in an intermittently mensural notation which does not consistently stem, or not stem, the note-heads to produce convincing metrical patterns. In addition, Frankfurt, Stadtbibl. MS *olim* 29 (now without signature) contains four songs in semi-mensural notation; and the MSS of Gautier de Coinci, some others (see Chailley (1959)). The total number of clearly mensurated vernacular songs is very small indeed.

In regard to the Latin repertory, the monophonic *conductus* and *cantiones* are non-mensural in the principal sources (e.g. the Beauvais MS; the Florence MS; the Later Cambridge Songs); it goes without saying that this is also the case with the earlier sources (e.g. the Aquitanian MSS associated with St Martial; see chapter 2, note 3 above).

being evidently popular, it survives in some eleven other versions, two of which are contrafacts.[49] None of the other versions contains mensural symbols. This is in itself telling evidence for the truly overwhelming weight of the monophonic notational tradition.

One of the principal arguments repeated over the years by the advocates of metrical, measured, interpretation has been that the mensural songs show us clearly what was obscure in the rhythm of the others. But, as sceptics have from time to time observed, it is only a minutely small proportion of the many hundreds, indeed thousands, of melodies surviving which have mensural indications. One quite possible alternative reason for their existence is that by the end of the thirteenth century the 'rhythmic modes' had become so popular that musicians (scribes, performers) decided to try the effect of them on some of the older melodies that they knew.[50] The French motet was the fashionable form in the thirteenth century. Its appeal to an élite is well described by Grocheo:[51]

Cantus autem iste non debet coram vulgaribus propinari, eo quod eius subtilitatem non animadvertunt nec in eius auditu delectantur, sed coram litteratis et illis qui subtilitates artium sunt querentes.

But that type of song ought not to be set before the common people, because they do not heed its subtlety nor take pleasure in hearing it. It ought rather [to be performed] to educated people who are looking for the subtleties of the arts.

Part of the *subtilitas* of the motet, setting aside its being polyphonic, may have been the apparently new, and newly complex, style of its metrical melodies.[52]

Ex. 180

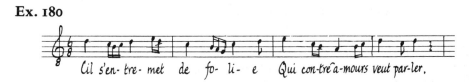

Cil s'en-tre-met de fo-li-e Qui con-tre'a-mours veut par-ler.

[49] There is, in fact, evidence that by the late thirteenth century the modes may have been losing their popularity amongst the more 'advanced' composers and theorists, if indeed they were ever flexible enough to cope with the actualities of music. The whole relationship between theory and practice is disputable and much disputed (see, especially, Roesner's detailed survey (1974), 162ff: 'the system of modal notation underwent considerable expansion to accommodate it to the requirements of actual practice' (190)).

[50] Machabey (1959) states a similar, more general, conclusion: 'les *modi* et la ternarité générale furent des engouements, des styles passagers, quoique très puissants', etc. See also Räkel, 181, on the mensural version of 'De bone amours' (note 47 above): 'the mensuration of O covers over the melody with the abstract scheme of a later conception'. The assumption that later sources define earlier rhythmic tradition is adopted in the case of the sequence by B. Gillingham in *ML* 61 (1980) 50, and in the case of *conductus/cantio* by Anderson (1978d).

[51] Rohloff, 144: lines 23–6. Grocheo goes on to observe that the motet should be sung to grace the festivities of those who can appreciate it (*in eorum festis decantari ad eorum decorationem*).

[52] Montpellier Codex, fol. 223v; see also Bamberg Codex, fol. 46. This triple motet is conveniently available in *Oxford Anthology*, no. 46: 'Cil s'entremet' / 'Nus hom' / 'Victime paschali', Gennrich (1958), 596, 597. Ed. Rokseth (1935), II.301.

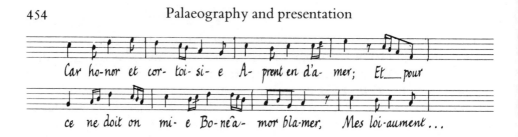

Car ho-nor et cor- toi- si- e A- prent en d'a- mer; Et pour

ce ne doit on mi- e Bo-n'e'a- mor bla-mer, Mes loi-aument . . .

The man who is willing to speak against Love is meddling with madness, for honour and courtesy are learnt from Love; and therefore one should never cast blame on good love, but loyally . . .

A sophisticated taste may well have preferred this sort of 'metricalized' melody – and not only when it was combined in interesting rhythmic counterpoint with one, or more often two, others. Motets from the principal collections, the Montpellier and the Bamberg Codices, date in their composition from the middle of the century, and the fashion for their music (music *à la mode* in more than one sense) would be strongly formative in the period *c.* 1250–1300, when the major chansonniers of troubadour and trouvère song were being compiled.[53] In broad social terms, it can be said that by this time the formerly aristocratic art of the courtly makers was falling increasingly into the hands of the bourgeois, the citizenry, who in the *puys* of Arras and Toulouse and elsewhere were regulating, codifying and finally ossifying it, whilst the 'real' aristocracy were pursuing a new thing.[54] This is a simplification and also to some extent speculative. The activities of Charles d'Anjou both lend specific colour to it and, through the Arras connection, show how complicated the situation was.

Modal theory was known at least in a restricted circle centred about the court of the trouvère Charles d'Anjou, whose patronage extended to such figures as Perrin d'Angicourt, Rutebeuf and Adam de la Halle. The lai *Ki de bons est, souëf flaire*, attributable perhaps to Charles, provides a systematic exposition of modal theory, each of its strophes developing a different mode . . . The work, however, appears only as a late addition to the Manuscrit de Roi and thus stands only at the periphery of the repertory.[55]

The vogue of the French motet is symptomatic of a new fashion of metrical melody; it reached another fine flowering of intricacy in the monophonic art

[53] See Sources for dates of *compilation* of the principal motet collections.
[54] Concerning the Arras *puy* and its significance see chapter 12, note 49 above. There is no full study of the *puys*; see 'Puy' in *New Grove* (Harris-Matthews), with bibliography. The activities of the patently bourgeois London *puy* are well documented (H. T. Riley, ed., Munimenta Gildhallae Londiniensis, II.1, Rolls Series (1860a)); it is possible that R758, the 'crowned' song referred to in chapter 12, note 53 above, may have been associated with it. Räkel (263, 337 and *passim*) bases the social aspect of his study on the generalization here broadly stated, though he does not bring further historical–social evidence to support it.
[55] Karp, section III.4 of the article 'Troubadours and Trouvères' in *New Grove*.

of the fourteenth century, especially in the *lais* of Machaut.[56] In many ways, then, the motet may represent some sort of reaction against the art of the trouvères. The fact that there are a number of mensurally notated trouvère songs should not be in the least surprising. If it were not for the evidently conservative (conservative in two senses) nature of the huge recording enterprise of the late-thirteenth- and early-fourteenth-century chansonnier-makers, we might have lost not only virtually the whole troubadour–trouvère repertory as we know it but also the bulky (if baffling) testimony that its 'old-fashioned' notation gives as to the nature of traditional monophonic song.[57] We might then have been less surprised than, I think, we should be by songs adapted to the new metrical taste.

The same general questions and observations apply to the *mensuralized* pieces from the same period – that is, songs in French and Latin whose original notation has been revised in order to produce clearly measured music.[58] The Reading Abbey Manuscript, one of the most important English sources, contains several instances of this notational bringing-up-to-date, amongst them the well-known 'Summer Canon'.[59] A less-known example is the Latin *lai* 'Samson, dux fortissime', whose popularity was not confined to England. About the notational history of this dramatic *planctus* we are well informed.[60] The earliest version, in a Stuttgart manuscript from south-west Germany or German Switzerland, is written in slightly heighted neumes of the first half of the thirteenth century. Another has recently been discovered in a late-thirteenth-century troper from Palermo, written in square notation which is rhythmically undifferentiated (the *virga* and *punctum*, which will become the

[56] The thirty-three monophonic songs of Jehan (Jehannot) de Lescurel (d. 1304) represent a midway point; they form a section of the *Roman de Fauvel* MS and are written in pre-Ars-Nova mensural notation. Ed. Wilkins (1966).

[57] Concerning the conservators of the southern, Provençal tradition, see the discussion of *Las Leys d'Amors* (Toulouse), at the end of chapter 1 above.

[58] In addition to the Reading Abbey MS (Harl. 978), the Egerton Chansonnier (Egerton 274) contains reformed, 'modernized', notation. The 'mensuralizer' (?c. 1330: Ludwig, 1.152) altered the notation to produce not longs and breves as in Harley but breves and semibreves and double minims. One of the Harley sequences, the well-known 'Ave gloriosa virginum regina' (see chapter 3:111, Ex. 36 above), is mensoralized again in Egerton.

[59] 'Sumer is icumen in': Besseler–Gülke, pl. 12 (one of the best of innumerable facsimile reproductions), fairly clearly shows the alterations. The matter is discussed by M. F. Bukofzer, '*Sumer is icumen in*': a revision, University of California Publications in Music (Berkeley 1944), especially 86–88: his argument that 'the original form of the rota was written in duple meter' (i.e. mensurally notated in an 'English' style, two equal breves to a long) has not been generally accepted. See also Dobson and Harrison, no. 9.

[60] Walther 17193; Anderson L42. The sources are: (i) Stuttgart, Landesbibliothek, MS Asc. 1.95 fols. 30–31v, Cantionarium (see W. Irtenkauf in *Codices Manuscripti*, 3 (1977) 22); (ii) Palermo, Bibl. Naz. MS I.B.16, fols. 193–195 (incomplete), a late-thirteenth-century Dominican troper (I am grateful to David Hiley for drawing this previously unknown source to my attention and for giving me information about it); (iii) the Reading Abbey MS, fols. 2–4v (see especially Hohler (1978)); (iv) Karlsruhe, Badische Landesbibliothek, MS St Georgen 38 (no music), fol. 117. Facsimiles of (iii) are reproduced in *EEH*, pl. 12–17 (some notational alterations are clearly visible, e.g. pl. 20, stave 7, notes 5–6).

longa and *brevis* of mensural notation, are indistinguishable; sometimes the notehead is lightly tailed, sometimes not). The Harley version is notated in a system which in normal photographic reproduction looks clearly mensural – for the most part notes with and without tails alternate. The manuscript shows, however, that this has been achieved by the alteration, not quite consistent, of the original by a later scribe. Some tails have been added, some erased, some crossed through. The slightly rhomboid forms of the *punctum* which look like semibreves (a note not found at this date as a simple symbol with mensural meaning) are in the mensuralized version to be read as breves. It is an early type of mensuration without Franconian subtleties such as internal ligature distinctions. The usual question arises: for what purpose were the emendations introduced? To clarify an existing interpretation? or to introduce a new, more up-to-date one? Certainly, the *notation* is being brought up to date, but this does not necessarily tell us anything about the original performance of the *lai* – i.e. whether it was measured or not. That depends, to repeat, on the 'context of understanding' one brings to the piece; and that in its turn depends, I shall argue in the next chapter, on the genre to which the piece belongs and on its musical characteristics; the *lai*, in fact, presents particular problems (see ch. 14:IV).

In conclusion, I hope in this chapter to have restored some sense of the genuine validity of various monophonic notations – a task which in the absence of the necessary specialized studies is not easy. The notational styles are not simply to be regarded as crude, and at the same time needlessly elaborate, ways of indicating pitches. It is, of course, easier to assert the idea of inherent notational validity than to define wherein the validity lies. But some provisional generalizations may be made. The notations seen in their manuscript and general historical context give apparently clear indication that the chansonnier scribes were for the most part positively avoiding clear mensural patterns and metrical schemes composed of long and short notes measured in strict proportion. Even though they show knowledge of and occasionally use symbols which may in some contexts have a rhythmic, even a durational suggestiveness – some longs and breves, ligatures denoting two semibreves, double *plica*s, and a few extensive ligatures forming melismas to a single syllable – it by no means follows that they always use the new mensural symbols with a mensural meaning, as a recent study of a song from the Chansonnier St Germain has shown.[61] All the big chansonniers are palpably late in the courtly monophonic tradition, and many of the scribes are evidently acquainted with some form of mensural notation. One's sense of a consciously adopted or at least consciously retained notational style receives the strongest confirmation of all from the Adam de la Halle Chansonnier, containing his 'complete works'. It juxtaposes in a carefully planned,

[61] See Beate R. Suchla, 'Zu Notation, Metrum u. Rhythmus des altfranzösischen Liedes', *A Mw* 36 (1979), 159–82; a detailed study of the notational background to the chansonnier and the song 'Pour le tens qui verdoie' (R1768), added *c.* 1300.

homogeneous collection non-mensural courtly chansons with mensurally notated *monophonic* music (the *refrains* of *Robin et Marion* and of *Renart le nouvel*), to say nothing of the polyphonic pieces. The main contrast is clear: there was a notation traditionally appropriate to the numbered syllabic style of *musica ritmica* and another (then still in the process of being worked out) appropriate to the measured style of *musica metrica*. The big question is: what meaning should we attach to this juxtaposition and to the obstinate survival of the traditional monophonic notation? Did the scribes deliberately choose the non-mensural notation and deliberately eschew more precise formulations that were open to them? There are certainly other possibilities. The scribes of the trouvère chansonniers may have been a specialized breed accustomed to their own style. Indeed, if it is true that the once courtly art had now in the late thirteenth century acquired chiefly bourgeois (civic, municipal) guardians, they could well have been, as scribes, not only uninterested but incompetent and out of touch. The manuscripts are, unfortunately, singularly devoid of the interesting particularities which, in determining provenance and function, might throw light on this. However, even if the copyists were widely skilled and notationally versatile, they were essentially *copyists*. They had exemplars before them, an obvious task to perform and doubtless a living to make. Why should they exert themselves? Inertia is a mighty force. The surviving chansonniers do not at all give the impression of being near a live centre of creativity. Their innumerable variants testify indeed to a process of improvisation, ornamentation, 're-creation' even (not to mention lapses of memory), but one's impression is that all this may have been some way back along the line of transmission, not in the here and now.

Whatever we make of the juxtaposition of notational styles – and in my view it is conscious, deliberate and meaningful – the numbered, syllabic style could still, palaeographically, be interpreted as measured melody. However – and this is the main point – the traditional secular notations must be studied for themselves, and when they are so studied they yield other possibilities. What have we learnt so far?

(i)   That the music is as clearly and consistently 'syllabic' in its presentation as the text, and that very precise care is taken over this;

(ii) that although 'syllabic' is not the same thing as 'isosyllabic', no apter representation of *iso*syllabic melody could be desired;

(iii) That the melodic style as presented is evidently flexible, subtle, *nuancée* – a style for which, even at this late stage in the development of neumatic notation, a great diversity of notational signs was thought, by some scribes at least, to be appropriate;

(iv) that, as the palaeographically or melodically variant versions of the same song may show, the tradition is closely allied to an oral art, with all the flexibility that that implies.

Through studying this notation in all its diversity, and not by-passing it, we can glimpse the nature of the gap between written record and living performance and gain insights into the rhythmic traditions of secular monody. It is, I believe, naive and unhistorical to assume that there is here simply either an abstruse puzzle of which the solution has eluded us, or on the other hand mere 'primitive' notational inadequacy. 'Le style, c'est la notation.'

Afterword

Much has been written in recent years on the relation between oral and written traditions in early Western music, following on the intense activity of literary scholars with its starting point in the classic work of Milman Parry and A. B. Lord. See especially the studies of Leo Treitler: 'Oral, written and literate process' (1981), examining *inter alia* the way that writing did not in the first instance 'displace' oral traditions but 'assumed a role within them' (p. 485); 'Homer & Gregory' (1974), theory and practice of oral transmission in oral poetry and plainchant (see chapter 9 note 49 above); 'Music Writing' (1982) developing a semiotic approach to early notation, which gives proper attention to 'the context and function' of written musical signs (see ch. 9 note 16). See also Hucke, 'Historical View of Gregorian Chant' (1980), and Huglo, 'Tradition orale' (1973).

The problem as it relates to the tradition of secular song has been less studied, and the materials for its study are much more limited. Above all we do not have the long *historical* record of notations spread over a wide geographical area. The evidence to be considered is of two kinds: (i) that of comparative versions of melodies in the big chansonniers, and also in *conductus/cantio* (all these sources are of late date, i.e. several centuries later than the earliest chant M S S); and (ii) that of *contrafacta*. The earlier editors and commentators did not greatly concern themselves with the problem, though realizing that the existence of so many variants raised questions such as 'Did the scribe work from copy or from memory? How did he envisage his task?' (Beck (1927), ii.9). Beck, at least, had come to realize that the phenomenon of multiple melodies and the nature of the innumerable variants made an *Ur*-text approach inappropriate as well as quite impractical (see also Bédier and Aubry, 28–30, on the repertoire of Crusade songs; no surviving M S was a copy of any other surviving M S); we should 'trust the scribe' and accept, with the obvious reservations about scribal error, the authenticity of the versions before us. The relationship of oral and written tradition has been taken up more critically and profitably in two recent books, van der Werf (1972) and Räkel (1977); and material for the detailed study of variants is now published in the former's editions, (1977) and (1979). Van der Werf (1972: ch. 2) discusses the problem of transmission: we can choose 'a scribal tradition, an oral tradition, or some combination of the two'. He concludes, sensibly, that after a period of exclusively oral tradition there was (*c.* 1250 onwards) 'a dissemination in writing parallel to the continuing oral tradition'. Räkel also argues that 'trouvère song was first cultivated by the feudal nobility as an oral, improvisational medium of social communication, therefore existing in ever new variants, but that later in the thirteenth century the art was chiefly practised by the upper bourgeoisie, where it became a sophisticated entertainment with melodies fixed by a written tradition and "corrected", i.e. made more regular in form, meter and melody' (see summary in Tischler's review in *JAMS* 32 (1979) 335). Räkel, 135–7, sums up the significance of his detailed study of *contrafacta* in French (e.g. Gautier de Coinci) and in Latin (*conductus*-repertoire). The earlier *contrafacta* represent the state of the melodies at that time (as well as providing dates for some melodies by reference to historical events); interestingly, the earlier, 'aristocratic' melodies are often, though not always, more embellished, less standardized.

It is evident that the chant material provides the evidence for answering many fascinating basic questions about oral and written traditions at the historical moment when the writing of music began to emerge. The 'secular' material, on the other hand, testifies chiefly to the continued existence during the thirteenth century of oral transmission still interacting with the written records. By the later thirteenth century, written affiliations of a secure and recognizable kind are apparent for trouvère song between the various big chansonniers. The pioneer work of Schwan, *Die altfranzösischen Liederhandschriften* (1886), was based entirely on literary evidence. However, his hypothesis of three main MS traditions or 'families' is on the whole borne out by more recent work on musical MSS. (In van der Werf (1977) and (1979), for instance, the group KLNPX is satisfactorily represented by a single melodic line; see (1977), introd. p. xi). However, Parker, 'La tradition manuscrite' (1978), introduces certain necessary qualifications; he also argues that 'the more the melodic variants for one song run contrary to the general pattern of MS filiation, the more likely it is to have been a late arrival into the *written* tradition' (p. 194).

14
RHYTHM AND GENRE

We shall not be concerned in this chapter with the relation between words and music as such; that is reserved for the next and final section of the argument. It is the lack of distinction amongst the various musical–poetical genres in many discussions of rhythm which first needs to be rectified.[1]

. . . an important clue to the metric character of trouvère songs comes from the hundreds of passages from such songs, textual, musical, or both, that are included in thirteenth-century motets, where the metric–rhythmic character is certain; and the text scansion of such passages fits naturally into their musical rhythm. In fact, a number of complete trouvère songs are incorporated in motets and some even set to new Latin texts in conductus, and all of them are treated in strict meter. Finally, there are many dance and dance-related songs, rondeaux and virelais, in the repertory, which are clearly metric.

Thus, the musical clues all favor a metric–rhythmic interpretation of trouvère songs in general, even where the notation does not indicate relative note values.[2]

Faced with the huge variety of monophonic songs, it would be absurd for us to believe that we ought to be looking for a single rhythmic solution, and equally absurd to believe that because the same melodies are found in French motets, Latin *conductus*, dance-songs, and the wide range of trouvère songs they necessarily had the same rhythmic meaning in every context. The re-creation of old material in new forms is of the very essence of medieval art. To take a story and make it new is, for instance, what the great romance

---

[1] The concept of genre has recently been much in question; but in the repertoires under discussion there is nothing problematical in the concept itself. In the French and Provençal repertoires in particular much use was made of it historically, for practical disposition (the Lorraine Chansonnier, Source 26) and for theoretical instruction (*Las Leys d'Amors*: see chapter 1:1 above). Difficulties arise only in the practical application of the concept. In the huge area of medieval Latin song, including sequence, *lai*, etc., terms, as we have seen (chapter 2), are used less precisely. For my immediate purposes, the authenticated medieval categories (chanson, *jeu-parti*, *pastourelle*, *lai* etc.) form a good starting-point, though certain formal distinctions related to the use of the *refrain*/refrain are also necessary. For a thorough-going literary typology, see Bec, *La lyrique* (1977). Musicologists have traditionally concentrated on formal categorization: e.g. Spanke, *Beziehungen* (1936), and Gennrich, *Formenlehre* (1932).

[2] Tischler (1981), p. xxii; he names the two main genres – chansons and dance-songs – but assumes they are both part of one repertoire, the implication being that there can be no rhythmic distinction between them. Tischler's views on the rhythmic problem are expounded in more detail in three articles: *Studies in Medieval Culture* 8–9 (1976) 49; *Orbis Musicae* 3 (1976) 3; *Mf* 32 (1979) 17.

writers were doing from Chrétien to Chaucer and beyond. One aspect of 'making new' has already been glimpsed in the way monophonic songs in French and Latin were re-*notated* in the late thirteenth and early fourteenth centuries. Another is the way they could be incorporated into polyphonic forms, where they might or might not retain their original rhythms. A third is in the widespread practice of *contrafactum* – the writing of new words, sometimes whole sets of new words, to an existing tune.

1 Monophonic melodies and the French motet

The incorporation of melodies into polyphonic forms may be taken first. Hans Tischler states that 'hundreds of passages' from the repertoire of the trouvères are 'included in thirteenth-century motets'. This is most misleading.[3] Hundreds of melodies with French words indeed make up the *motetus* (and *duplum*) parts of motets. Most of them are freely composed, of course, and their texts are in an individual style distinct from that of *grand chant*. Of the rest, far and away the largest number come from the repertoire not of trouvère song properly so called but of dance-song. This introduces a fundamental distinction of rhythmic genre which has to be reckoned with – between the metrical tradition of anonymous dance and dance-song (*refrain*, carole, *rondeau, estampie* etc.) and the numerical tradition of monophonic *conductus*, chanson, sequence and *lai*.[4] It may be better, in fact, to speak of

---

[3] A somewhat truer picture can be gained from Gennrich, 'Trouvèrelieder und Motetten-repertoire' (1926–7), who lists thirteen (but no more than thirteen) out of a total number of some 1500 trouvère chansons as appearing in motets. What is especially significant is that most even of these thirteen have *refrain* connections: for example (1) R759 incorporates Boogaard *refr.* no. 948; (2) R498 incorporates Boogaard 1427; (3) R33: Boogaard 665, 1447; (4) R19 (*pastourelle*): Boogaard 1154, 1632, 1715, 1877; (5) R1485: Boogaard 1149, 1580; (6) R1510, 'Main s'est levee Aelis': no *refrains* quoted, but the dance-song connection is established. And so one might continue. Apart from the songs with identifiable *refrains* listed by Boogaard there are a number which are not strictly to be described as trouvère songs 'included in motets' but the opposite, motet-parts which have found their way into the trouvère chansonniers, such as R558 (single-stanza *pastourelle* text; no motet version survives (see Raynaud, *Recueil de Motets* (1881) – the standard collection of motet-*texts* – II.126)), R1663, R1877 (single eighteen-line stanza), etc. The trouvère chansonniers most involved are Roi and Noailles. This group have the characteristics, in fact, of *motetus* melodies not of trouvère chansons; they are identifiable textually by exceedingly long and complex metrical forms worked out *for one stanza only* (see discussion in Rokseth (1935), IV.239ff). There appears, however, to be at least one genuine example of a trouvère chanson used in the composition of a motet: 'Orendroit plus' (R197) in Turin, Reale Bibl. MSS vari. 42, fol. 21, as a *tenor*. The tenuousness of the link between *grand chant* and motet is in stark contrast to the firmness of the links between dance-song and motet; Boogaard lists some five hundred *refrains* in the motet repertoire.

[4] This distinction between the basic genres has, of course, been remarked before, notably by Handschin in his review-article 'Modaltheorie' (1935); see especially p. 79: 'However, the main fact is that interchange between motets and monody practically concerns only one special class of monody – that is, the French rondeau and the refrain-forms related to it . . .' See also, more recently, Räkel (p. 136): 'The melodic style of the dance is perpetually in a close relationship with polyphony; the result is a lively give and take . . . observable principally between dance-lyric, *conductus*, and motet repertoire.'

dance-song simply as 'measured', to avoid any confusion with the *musica metrica* discussed earlier as a theoretical category.[5] It is 'measured' for obvious good physical reasons. We do not have to subscribe to the 'modal' theory, or to any other, to believe that there has always been music associated with physical movement (dancing, marching, heaving on ropes) which was measured, and music associated with non-physical things (celebration, praise, sorrow, amorous sentiment) which need not be measured.

The early medieval repertoire of dance-songs in French and Latin was described in chapter 5. As an example of their use in polyphony we may consider a short motet.[6]

Ex. 181

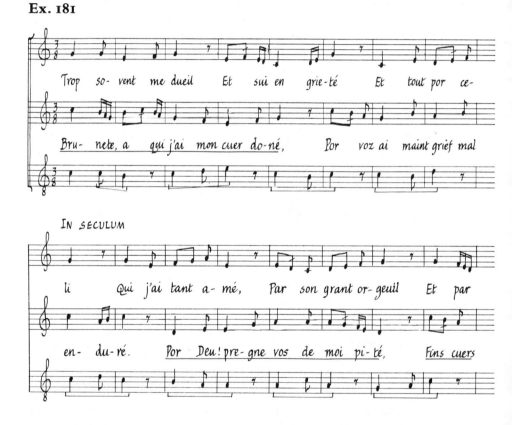

---

[5] Dance-song belongs to the category of *usus* (practical music), not *ars* (speculative thinking); see Engelbert of Admont, *De Musica* (ed. Gerbert, II.287–369) ch. III, p. 289.

[6] Transcribed Rokseth (1935), II. 177 (no. 85), from the Montpellier Codex, fols. 124v–125 (facsimile in vol. I). The most recent edn is by Tischler (1978), no. 86 (part II, p. 85). The motet is also available in the *Historical Anthology*, I, no. 32(d) (Rokseth's and Tischler's transcriptions avoid *HAM*'s irregular penultimate bar).

sa fier-té. A ma dame ai mis mon cuer et mon pen-sé
a- mo- rous! De de- bon- ai- re- té Vient a- - mors.

VOICE I: I am too often miserable and in sorrow, and all for her whom I have loved so much – because of her great pride and her haughtiness. *In my lady I have set heart and thought.*
VOICE II: *Brunete, to whom I have given my heart,* for you I have painfully suffered many a sorrow. *For God's sake, take pity on me, gentle loving heart! / It is from sweet behaviour that love comes* VOICE III: . . . for ever.

This three-part motet is based on a favourite tenor, taken from the Easter Gradual 'Hec dies', a long and elaborate chant for soloists and choir. The relevant phrase is:[7]

Ex. 182

...in se- cu-
lum

(Was it chosen for its words – 'for ever' – or for its melody?) The chant is segmented into a short repeated pattern on a purely numerical basis; melodic sense has nothing to do with it. The upper parts incorporate a number of fragments from dance-songs.[8] The last phrase of the *motetus* is a *refrain*, 'En ma dame ai mis / mon cuer et mon panser', which appears as a *rondeau* in BN fr. 12786; as a *refrain* in the trouvère song 'Chanter vueil pour fine Amour' (R1957, Jakemin de la Vante; no surviving music) and the *ballete* 'Je me dueil, amie' (anon., no music); and in two other motets besides the one above. Boogaard lists three other *refrains* in the upper parts of this short motet: two of them are not found elsewhere; one, 'De debounerete / vient amors', is found

[7] *LU*, 799.
[8] For detailed references to the *refrains* described below, see Boogaard. *Triplex* m.19, Boogaard 662 (five other occurrences); *motetus* m.1, Boogaard 295 (*unicum*); m.11, Boogaard 1505 (*unicum*); m.19, Boogaard 468 (three other occurrences).

in a *chanson-avec-des-refrains*, 'Quant je voi este' (Perrot de Douai), and is
quoted in two courtly poems (the anonymous *Salut d'Amours*, which has a
refrain in each of its forty stanzas, and Philippe de Remi's *Salut a refrains*). The
amount of quotation in this motet is by no means unusual. For the extreme
case we might turn to the motet 'La bele m'ocit; Dieus, qui m'en garira', in
which there are no fewer than thirteen *refrains*.[9] The social phenomenon is a
fascinating one; it shows how deep was the interpenetration of the
sophisticated motet with the French courtly world.[10] The present question is
more practical. The vernacular motet uses widely a certain type of metrical
melody which is epitomized in the borrowed *refrains* but is not confined to
them.[11] For instance, the top part of our example, 'Trop sovent me dueil'
contains only one *refrain*, but the whole style of the melody seems designed
to introduce or 'frame' it. The melody is strongly triadic on *c*; every single
phrase (snippets of five units/syllables) begins and ends on a note of the major
triad. The very simple metrical scheme produces a neatly and consistently
balanced melody of six identical units leading into the final *refrain*, which is
differently constructed. This melody is in light rhythmic counterpoint at
some points with the other parts – for example, at the entry in measure
10.[12]

This style of melody is evidently in sharp contrast to that of the trouvère
chanson as we have seen it. The light, tuneful, balanced melodies of the
dance-song tradition contrast sharply with the rather stately, elegant, far less
'obvious' melodies of the trouvères. Why then have scholars over the years
claimed that we can gain clues about the trouvère chanson from the motet? It
is, of course, partly a question of terminology. If you call every monophonic
song with a French text a trouvère song, then you may logically make such a
claim. But there are two objections to this. The first is that this definition of
trouvère song is unsatisfactory; the term best defines itself for us from the
contents of the major chansonniers with their huge repertoire of mostly
attributed, mostly high courtly, chansons. The trouvère chansonniers,
properly so called, do not contain collections of *rondeaux* and *refrains*, though

[9] Gennrich (1958), no. 166: Montpellier, fol. 231 (2 voc.), transcribed Rokseth (1935), III.1
(no. 178). Boogaard, p. 301.

[10] The popularity or fashionable attractiveness of the motet-style *as melody* is shown by the
occurrence of motet-parts without their *tenors* as monophonic songs, even if rarely, in
trouvère chansonniers. See note 3 above; also the remarks of the theorist Jacques de Liège
(*c.* 1260–1330+) *Speculum Musicae*, lib. 7, ch. 3: 'cum aliquis per se cantat motetum aliquem
triplum vel quadruplum sine tenore et tunc absolute' (Coussemaker (1864), II.386, attributed to Johannes de Muris).

[11] Rokseth, IV.209, observes that the idea of including *refrain*-texts led to the inclusion of
text-plus-melody, but that *refrains* may have different melodies in different places. Whatever
the origin of the *refrains*, they do not contrast musically with the rest of the motet; there is
'perfect homogeneity'. Boogaard lists over five hundred motets containing *refrains*.

[12] The bar-lines are, of course, editorial; but the 'measures' thus indicated are real – they
correspond to something objective in the music.

some trouvères in their own special, highly self-conscious way incorporate material from the rich store of popular and courtly–popular melody.[13] The second point is that if the term 'trouvère' is, somewhat inappropriately, going to be used for the whole vernacular repertoire, then it becomes even more necessary to make distinctions of genre within it.

The principal distinction of genre is between dance-songs of the courtly–popular tradition and chansons in a high style. This distinction corresponds to one between the two main rhythmical traditions, *musica metrica* (measured) and *musica ritmica* (numbered–syllabic). This being so, it is incumbent to explain what the presence of a large number of *refrains* signifies within the trouvère repertoire proper, i.e. within the chansons themselves. If they have their metrical melodies with them, does not this cast doubt on an isosyllabic interpretation of those songs at least? *Raynauds Bibliographie* does not list *refrains* as such, yet from this bibliography of over 2100 items Boogaard has culled several hundred which use *refrains*. The categories include the following more substantial ones, all of which are distinct from the *grands chants* which constitute the bulk of the repertoire:

    (i)   *balletes, estampies* (all from the Lorraine Chansonnier)
    (ii)   refrain-songs
    (iii)   *chansons-avec-des-refrains*
    (iv)   *pastourelles*

These account for about nine-tenths of the items listed. In the remaining tenth are a number of courtly–popular songs (*chansons d'histoire* etc.), religious songs (especially of Gautier de Coinci), and motet texts, but very few 'straight' chansons – *grans chans*, as the Lorraine copyist calls them. Of the main categories, the first are 'dance-poems'; they have no music in the Lorraine Chansonnier and few concordances, and may be discounted for present purposes.[14] This leaves us with refrain-songs (that is, chansons which use their *refrains* (tags) as refrains in the formal sense), *pastourelles*, and *chansons-avec-des-refrains*. It will be convenient to take the latter first; the purpose in each case will be to see whether the basic contrast between the two rhythmic traditions – measured dance-songs and unmeasured courtly chansons – is brought into question or confirmed.

[13] The essential nature of the main trouvère repertoire is further discussed by van der Werf in his review of Rosenberg and Tischler (*J A M S* 35 (1982) 539–40). Two apparent exceptions are: the Adam de la Halle M S (Source 34), which includes *rondeaux* and motets in separate sections (all polyphonic in this case); and the Lorraine Chansonnier (Source 26), numerous types of songs arranged by genre (no music).

[14] *Ballete, balette*: the Lorraine Chansonnier contains some 155 poems with refrain under this heading. They show 'in varying combinations . . . the characteristics of either the *ballade* or the *virelai*, but not all of them correspond to the (strict) description of either one' (van der Werf (1972), 159). Outside this music-less chansonnier there are very few examples of these types.

II *Chansons-avec-des-refrains*

The cumbersome but conventional term *chansons-avec-des-refrains* stresses the difference between these and the straightforward refrain-songs. Van der Werf anglicizes it as 'chansons–with–multiple–refrains', which usefully draws attention to the fact that a chanson of this type has not one *refrain* but a whole set – a different one for each stanza.[15] This anonymous example from the Chansonnier Cangé shows how this arrangement worked:[16]

Ex. 183

[15] Van der Werf (1972), 23. *Chansons-avec-des-refrains* are lucidly discussed by Gérold, *La Musique au moyen âge* (1932), 139, who inclines to believe that the reason for not copying out the music for the *refrains* of subsequent verses was in order not to disturb the well-established neat-looking procedure for copying chansons. He distinguishes between those chansons with the same *refrain* in each stanza and those which have *refrains* varying in length, rhythm, subject and melody, and he gives examples of both. Rosenberg and Tischler, no. 6, evidently worried by the principle of contrast, print in their text *refrains* for subsequent verses of a *chanson-avec-des-refrains* (a *pastourelle*) 'conjectured by analogy [my italics] to the end of st. 1' whilst providing in a note the two actual surviving manuscript *refrains* (to strophes 2 and 3) with their *different* melodies. This procedure betrays a strange incomprehension of the object and lacks any MS authority. Gérold, 142–5, cites Jean de Neuville's *pastourelle* (R962) 'L'autrier par un matinet', with all its *refrains*.

[16] 'Quant la flor de l'espinete' (R979) is in three MSS. The *refrains* are stanza 1: Boogaard 683 *unicum*; stanza 2, Boogaard 952, also in motet 11; stanza 3, Boogaard 811, also in *Li confrere d'Amours*; stanza 4, Boogaard 1287, also in two other *chansons-avec-des-refrains*, a motet *enté* (Gennrich M160) and Mathieu le Poirier, *La Cour d'Amour*; stanza 5, Boogaard 1406, *unicum*. Ex. 183 is Cangé fol. 120, which gives the melody for the stanza 1 *refrain* only; the notation is semi-mensuralized but has puzzling inconsistencies.

si di- rai con fins a- mis:

En sim- ple plai- sant bru- ne- te

ai tot mon cuer mis.

When I see the flower on the hawthorn becoming white like a lily, and the grass putting on its green again, and all the other delights, then I choose to compose a little song. And I will say as a courtly lover should: *Refrain:* 'On an innocent and attractive brown-haired girl I have set my whole heart.'

A recurrent characteristic in songs of this type is that the *refrain* is not assimilated into the musical–metrical structure. Whether it occurs at the end, as here, or in the middle of the stanza, as in some other chansons, it remains to a varying degree a metrical and musical excrescence. The *refrain* in stanza 3, for instance, is of two lines counted $5^{v} + 5$, but in stanza 4 of two lines counted $11^{v} + 11$.[17] Quite apart from the fact that *refrains* generally come supplied with their own tunes,[18] there is no way in which two *refrains* of such different length could possibly be sung, in the same style, to the same musical phrase. This brings one to the problem of interpretation.

It is obvious, I believe, that there is an element of deliberate play in these chansons, a disingenuousness, an assumed naiveté. The *refrains* are *in contrast* to the rest of the chanson. Even though the general style of the 'Quant la flor' is comparatively light, less ceremonious than in a *grand chant* proper, nevertheless there is at least a conventional poetic contrast between the leisurely, unfolding syntax and meditative sentiments of, for instance, stanza 2:

> Puisque g'i ai mon corage
> mis en li et mon pansé
> et que fait li ai homage
> et mon cuer vers li torné
> bien doi de sa grant beauté
> faire chançon . . .

Since I have set my whole mind on her and my thought and have done homage to her and directed my heart towards her, it is my duty to compose a song about her great beauty . . .

and its taut, extravert *refrain*:

> *J'aing le bele, la blonde, la sage;*
> *Tot mon cuer li ai donné.*

I love the beautiful, the fair, the wise; I have given her my whole heart.

[17] Stanza 3: *Ma leaux pansee / Tient mon cuer joli.* Stanza 4: *He Dex, donez moi mes fins amors joie / Ausi veraiement con grant mestier en ai.* Stanza 5: *Nuns n'i a pooir fors ma douce amie / a ma dolour alegier.*

[18] When not supplied in the *chansonniers*, they can often be traced elsewhere.

This contrast reinforces, in this case, the meaning of the poem. The musical question now is not whether there is a generic contrast in the repertoire between the melodic styles of courtly chanson and 'popular' *refrain* (that much we can take as established), but what we can infer from it to help us with the problem of rhythmic interpretation in this particular song. It would be convenient for my argument if I could simply say that there was a clear contrast in every case between the two rhythmical styles and that this implied a playful use of 'measure' in an otherwise conventionally isosyllabic song. Unfortunately the case is not simple, chiefly because the melody of the first *refrain* is used earlier in the course of the first stanza (lines 5 and 8). Nor is the example an isolated one: the two *chansons-avec-des-refrains* following immediately in this *chansonnier* both have a similar sort of musical link.[19] There are two possibilities of rhythmic interpretation. Either the measured metre of the *refrain* sets the pattern for the whole song; or there is a rhythmic contrast intended, in addition to the other contrasts, between the chanson and its *refrains*. We ought not, I think, to discard the second possibility simply because of its oddity. It may indeed seem to us odd to have the same succession of notes sung in different rhythms (isosyllabic and then measured) in the same stanza; but on the other hand this applies *to the first stanza only*, since subsequent stanzas will have a different *refrain*-tune.[20]

III   Refrain-songs

Besides these curious *chansons-avec-des-refrains* there are also in the trouvère chansonniers a number of refrain-songs – that is to say chansons of the type in which a repeated line or lines forms an invariable refrain in the normal sense of the term. They are diverse in character: most are rather light, like Thibaut's 'Por conforter ma pesance' (R237), with its six-line stanza, its short line, and its vocalized refrain '*E, e, e*'; some are more serious, like his 'Nus hon ne puet ami reconforter' (R884) with the following refrain[21]

Ex. 184

8 Da- me, mer-ci, do- nez- moi es- pe- ran- ce 9 de joie a- voir.

[19] In 'Quant florist la pree' (R548) the line before the *refrain* uses the *refrain* melody; in 'Quant la saisons est passee' (R536) the opening uses the *refrain* melody and line 8 'rhymes' with it. Cf. also 'L'autrier par un matinet / Erroie' (R962); the chanson was probably composed out of the *refrain* melody to strophe 1 (Gérold, 142).

[20] A *chanson-avec-des-refrains* with particularly rich associations is 'Main se leva la bien faite Aelis' (R1509) by the trouvère Baude de la Kakerie (Quarière) (see chapter 5, note 54, above). T. H. Newcombe studies Ernoul Caupain's 'Entre Godefroi et Robin' (R1377), a *pastourelle-avec-des-refrains*, in *Festschrift Wolfgang Boetticher*, ed. H. Hüschen et al. (Berlin 1974), with particular reference to the use of the same *refrains* elsewhere.

[21] Van der Werf (1979), 131–2 (five melodies; my transcription is from Chansonnier de l'Arsenal (trouvère MS K: Source 26).

Lady, for pity, give me hope of having joy.

The refrain is not found elsewhere, so there is no way of knowing whether it had currency as a *refrain* or not; there is only internal evidence. The words have the required aphoristic, detached quality (Boogaard lists two others that begin 'Dame merci'). The melody points slightly but inconclusively in the other direction with its retarding ornamental neumes at the end of each phrase.[22] It seems in any case that the refrain-song is a somewhat peripheral form in the trouvère repertoire. There are only around thirty among the 350 songs in the large Chansonnier Cangé. Blondel de Nesle has only one refrain-song, doubtfully attributed; Adam de la Halle has none.[23] If the form is peripheral, then it is on the popular periphery (or courtly–popular, since we have to remain on our guard against imagining that any of these songs are really 'of the people'). The problem of rhythmic interpretation is, then, different perhaps from that presented by the *chanson-avec-des-refrains* with its more deliberate courtliness and its evident contrast, in both metre and tone, between courtly and mock-popular styles. The refrain-song is more of one piece. The problem, nevertheless, is still to estimate to what extent the metrical styles associated with the *refrain* and dance-song had been taken up, assimilated into, an aristocratic art – an art, that is, dominated by aristocratic ideals. Are the two genres, *grand chant* and refrain–chanson, genuinely competing to decide the overall rhythmic interpretation of a particular song? Or are they playfully juxtaposed? Should refrain-songs be measured or not?

Thibaut's 'Pour conforter ma pesance', just mentioned, presents the problem clearly. It enjoyed considerable popularity, surviving in eight manuscripts, all main chansonniers; in all except one the notation is non-mensural, but in the Chansonnier de Noailles the chanson (the first and only one with a notated melody in a section devoted entirely to Thibaut and headed *Li Rois de Navarre fist ces chancons . . .*) is written clearly in longs and breves.[24]

Ex. 185

---

[22] But see some of the identified *refrains* quoted in ch. 5:IV above.

[23] Leo Wiese, ed., *Die Lieder des Blondel de Nesle, Kritische Ausgabe nach allen Handschriften* (Dresden 1904), attributes thirty-one songs to Blondel, some doubtfully. Karp ('Blondel' in *New Grove*) lists twenty-three as genuine.

[24] The first twenty folios of the Chansonnier de Noailles are ruled for music, but only four melodies are filled in (out of fifty-seven in all). The transcription is from fol. 4. See ch. 1, Ex. 3 for an unmeasured transcription.

(For translation, see p. 42.)

The question is whether the measured rendering indicated in Noailles is the 'correct' one (i.e. traditional, accepted (Thibaut died in 1253)) or a fashionable re-writing of the kind considered above (this chansonnier also includes a fascicle of motets: Source 30). I incline to the view that the measured rendering is traditional *because of the genre*: the song belongs, or so it seems, to a genre related in stylistic simplicity to the world of the *refrain* and dance-song.[25] In actual fact there is some slight palaeographical support for this, because the next notated song in the manuscript is in the usual undifferentiated notation appropriate to a *grand chant*.

The concept of genre as a rhythmical determinant is, as we see, not always easy to apply. There is no genre, however (except perhaps the *lai*), which is more puzzling than the *pastourelle*, and to this we must now turn. Before doing so, however, I should emphasize again that these lighter song-types are greatly in the minority. Roughly three out of every four songs of this huge and dominating European repertoire are chansons of the standard type and tone – that is, more or less solemn and ceremonious, parading their polished art rather than disguising it. It is necessary to say this because many histories and anthologies give the opposite impression.[26] Songs of a quasi-popular nature

[25] The mensural version unambiguously brings out the triadic structure of the melody (especially in lines 1 and 3). Other relevant characteristics are: the shortness of the strophe; its construction from short lines (7ˇ 37ˇ377ˇ5); the tonal stability; the obvious musical rhyme in the *cauda* (5.4–7; 7.4–7), which also recalls the 'open' form of 2.1–3 and 4.1–3; and the very high proportion of single notes to melismas (42 to 3). 'Single-noting', however, is not uncommon in Thibaut's chansons (see R273, R324, R529 (*pastourelle*)). For interesting variants, especially to the refrain-line, see van der Werf (1979), 237.

[26] Most recently Rosenberg and Tischler; but even Gérold may be criticized on this score.

are more immediately attractive to modern ears: for this reason, if for no other, they have won a disproportionate share of attention.

IV   The *pastourelle*

It will be convenient, and not misleading, to consider with the *pastourelle* various other songs of similar kind purporting to deal with the 'bergier de ville champestre' or 'bele Yolanz en chambre koie'.[27] They are mostly *chansons d'histoire* in the exact sense, for they usually tell a story.[28] As an example of the *pastourelle* proper I take 'A une ajornée / chevauchai l'autrier' (R492) by Moniot de Paris:[29]

Ex. 186

A u-ne a-jor-ne-e   2 che-vau-chai l'autrier;
3 en u-ne val-le-e   4 pres de mon sen-tier
5 pas-tore ai trou-ve-e   6 qui fet a proi-sier.
7 Ma-tin s'iert le-ve-e   8 pour es-ba-noi-er.
Refr. Bel ert et se-ne-e,   10 je l'ai sa-lu-e-e;
11 plus ert co-lo-re-e   12 que flor de ro-sier.

I was riding out at dawn one day and, in a valley near my path, I came upon a shepherdess, a maiden of worth. She had got up in the morning to enjoy herself.

---

[27] For a recent bibliography of the *pastourelle*, see Bec, I.119ff. The collection of texts by Bartsch, *Romanzen und Pastourellen* (1870), long standard, has now been replaced (for *pastourelles*) by Rivière, *Pastourelles* (1974–6). See also M. Zink, *La pastourelle, poésie et folklore au moyen-âge* (Paris 1972); and, for a general literary survey, Helen Cooper, *Pastoral: Medieval into Renaissance* (Woodbridge 1977). The only recent musical study devoted to the *pastourelle* (1100–1300) is that of Pascale (1976); the musical observations and transcriptions in Rivière, III, are tentative and out of date. Rosenberg and Tischler, however, print eleven *pastourelles*, eight of which have melodies, with full commentary.

[28] On the genre see chapter 6, note 81, above.

[29] Chansonnier de l'Arsenal, p. 191. See also van der Werf (1979) 405. Gérold, 131. Text in Bartsch (1870), 297–8.

Refrain: She was beautiful and intelligent – I greeted her; she was fresher in colour than the flower on a rose-bush.

The story of this *pastourelle* is the usual, in one of its expected variants. A knight rides out on his charger and sees an attractive shepherdess (*plus ert colorée / que flor de rosier*). She calls to her sweetheart Robin to come to her aid. The knight says, in effect, 'Don't bother with Robin, who has no money. I'll give you horse and saddle if you'll do what I wish.' But she is a wise girl and replies 'I'd be foolish to lose my virginity – and my chances of a good marriage'. To some extent this story, or rather its basic situation (the knight–shepherdess encounter), defines the genre. But other features of the genre are regularly recurrent and for our present purposes more important. They include: elegant contrivance in the making of the verse; the use of short lines and economically patterned rhymes, with varied weak and strong endings; precisely numbered syllables as in *la grande chanson*; the common use of refrains and *refrains*. It is important to realize how disingenuous the literary style is; Robin and Marion may be innocent but the poet certainly is not. The following stanza from an anonymous *pastourelle* demonstrates light verbal ingenuity at least in its concatenations.[30]

> Bergier de ville cham*pestre*
> *pestre*   ses aignoiax me*not*.
> et *n'ot*   fors un sien chienet en d*estre*;
> *estre*   vousist par *senblant*
> en *enblant*
> la ou Robins flajo*lot*,
> et *ot*   la voiz qui *respont*
> et *espont*
> la note du dorenlot

A shepherd from a country hamlet led his lambs out to pasture; he had nothing with him except his dog he led on his right hand. He would have wished, it seemed, as he ambled along, to be where Robin was playing his flute; he hears the voice answering and performing the melody of the little song.

The poet observes the canons of aristocratic poetry – he counts his syllables and observes his rhymes – and more.

Musically speaking, the short lines mean short phrases, and short phrases encourage a balanced neatness – melodic effects which are telling but not especially subtle. The telling short phrases are easy to put into a tonal frame similar (though not identical) to one we observed in some Latin sequences and *lais*; and, unless we discard all the evidence of our modern ears, it is right to hear Ex. 186 in some such way.[31] The existence, and clear notation, of 'open' and 'closed' cadences elsewhere encourages us to hear them also in 'A une ajornée'. The phrases ending on *b* (1, 3, 5, 7, 11) are 'open'; those ending on *c* (2, 4, 8, 12) are 'closed'. The sense of an embryonic *c*-major tonality is

---

[30] Bartsch, 195.
[31] For further comment, see chapter 4, note 40, above.

enhanced by the suggestion of a *g* triad in phrases 2 and 4. These comparatively simple tonal effects (my account slightly over-simplifies them) are characteristic of this group of quasi-popular chansons as a whole and distinguish them from *grands chants*. The effects are enhanced by predominantly single-note style (no ligatures, only the occasional liquescent (1.2, 3.2, 5.3 etc.)), again in general contrast to the more florid high courtly melodies.[32] These stylistic features, all rhythmic considerations apart, are the features of medieval French and Latin dance-song (see chapter 4 above) as we can reconstruct it from the large repertoire of surviving *rondeaux* and *refrains*. The connection also extends to matters of form, especially to the principle of phrase-repetition. In form as in style the *pastourelle* 'A une ajornée' is an example of what one might call *la petite chanson courtoise*. That is to say, it starts off like a standard chanson with a *frons* of two parts, AB-AB (1–4); but then, instead of the usual complex and unpredictable *cauda*, it has two identical quatrains of melody both of which open with A, slightly modified, and end with a phrase (8) which is not so very far removed from B. The second quatrain forms a refrain. Technically speaking, the song is a *chanson-avec-des-refrains* in so far as the refrain alters after stanza 2 and again for the last stanza, 5. But so closely are these refrains related to the main text, the unfolding story, that it is impossible to see them as *refrains* in the special sense (none of them is recorded elsewhere).[33] The close poetic link between refrain and stanza is, as we have seen, a musical link as well. The melody, I suggest, was conceived as a single whole, but a more obviously balanced and superficially patterned whole than we find in *la grande chanson courtoise*.

The *pastourelle*, with related small genres such as the *aube* and the *reverdie*, is the meeting-place of two traditions: the courtly chanson and dance-song. This fact is even more obvious in some *pastourelles* than in the one I have just analysed. Of 109 or so surviving *pastourelles* 58 have music, and 33 of those use refrains/*refrains*.[34] There are, in fact, over a dozen *pastourelles-avec-des-refrains*, of which 'L'autrier par un matinet' (R962) is a good example. As Gérold has observed, 'a piece of this kind clearly shows that these *pastourelles* had become the game of a refined society. In order to give spice to a some-what banal tale, the poet borrowed fragments of known songs.'[35] Three of the six *refrains* are known from elsewhere: one in a motet, one in *La Court de Paradis* and one in another *pastourelle*.[36] At the other extreme we find the melodic simplicity of 'L'autrier quant je chevauchoie' (R1698a), from a single

---

[32] See note 25 above.

[33] Boogaard (no. 241) lists the refrain of stanzas 1–2 as a *refrain* unique to this chanson, but does not list the subsequent refrains.

[34] Pascale, 585.

[35] Gérold, 144. As will be evident from the earlier discussion (chapter 5:11 above), 'fragment' is probably not the right word; the *refrains* seem to have been independent entities. Gérold, 142–4, gives all the music including the *refrains* for the subsequent verses and for the *envoi*. Text: Bartsch (1870), 194–5; Rivière, II no. 57.

[36] The *refrains* are listed in Boogaard: nos. 1626, 1275, 1105 (all *unica*); 652 (motet); 1788 (*Paradis*); 559 (*pastourelle-avec-des-refrains*).

chansonnier.[37] (It is rather striking that half the surviving *pastourelles*, in the strict sense, have each only a single manuscript source – a sign, perhaps, of the lower artistic esteem in which they were held.)

The problem of rhythmic interpretation is at first sight more or less the same for the *pastourelle* group as it was for the refrain-songs. That is to say, some of the basic requirements of the chanson in high style are still very much present – precise syllabic counting, matching of phrases of melody with phrases of syntax, strophic form – but they encounter the requirements of another perhaps older, certainly more rootedly physical, tradition, that of the dance-song with its clearly defined measure, repeated melodies, clear phrasal balance, and so on. However, there is a further complication in the songs of this group which must be expounded before the case can be judged. They are, as I said, mostly 'stories', and many have the characteristics of narrative music.[38]

Ex. 187

[37] Rosenberg and Tischler, no. 20.
[38] RI583: trouvère MS *K*, fol. 170 (four other sources); Bartsch (1870), 242–3; Rivière, III no. 88; Pascale, 601–2 (facs. of *K*).

The other day I was riding out near Paris and found a shepherdess looking after her sheep. I got off my horse and sat down next to her and asked her for her love. She replied 'By St Denis, I love one more handsome than you, fair sir, and much better brought up. I never knew or saw such a man as he is, ever; I shall not love another, I swear it, for he is handsome, courteous and clever. Heavens, I am young and attractive and I love one who is young and attractive and very wise.'

This *pastourelle*, 'L'autrier chevauchoie deles Paris', is not an exciting musical event. It consists, in effect, of three melodies, the first two of which are very closely related; they are the vehicle for eight monorhymed lines of ten syllables, such as might constitute a short *laisse* in a narrative poem. In the first stanza of the song (it happens to be one with multiple *refrains*) the last three lines are set to a melody of similar type – i.e. with small range and limited melodic movement. The song combines this static quality with an elusive tonality. Other *pastourelles* have narrative melodies also – indeed, virtual recitation-tones:[39]

I was riding the other day in the morning beside a wood very near to the entrance . . .

And some pieces have long stanzas, much longer than that of a *grand chant*. 'L'autrier par un matinet' (R965) has seventeen lines; it was quoted earlier, (ch. 6, Ex. 92) as narrative music, and that is where it also belongs. It would be possible to 'measure' this *pastourelle* throughout, as Gérold does;[40] but if the principle of *contrasting* rhythmical styles within a song is accepted, as I have suggested it should be in certain *chansons-avec-des-refrains*, then a contrast is possible here as shown in the transcription (pp. 231–2).

The rhythmic interpretation of the *pastourelle* depends on the weight one puts upon the different traditions which are undoubtedly present in it. The first tradition is that of the courtly chanson. The same author–composers were responsible for writing the *pastourelles*; there are, however, a comparatively high proportion of anonymous *pastourelles*. The second tradition is that of dance-song, very strongly present in the ubiquitous *refrains*; no other genre (the motet apart) uses them to this extent. The third is that of narrative song, which manifests itself occasionally in the form of static

---

[39] R527 by Richart de Semilli (five sources). The recitation feature is found, of course, in other types of chanson; see chapter 6:IV above.
[40] Gérold, 126–7.

melodies, quatrain-structure, monorhymes. As a working rule one should, I think, first regard a *pastourelle* as special type of courtly–popular dance-song. On this basis it calls for measured transcription in triple time – triple, because surviving mensurally notated *refrains* are always in triple metre (see ch. 5: 1 v above). *Pastourelles-avec-des-refrains*, however, may invite rhythmical contrast between the song as a whole and the *refrains* embedded in it. Other *pastourelles*, because of their likeness to *grands chants* or to narrative music, may seem to call for isosyllabic transcription – though one should avoid the too easy assumption that all narrative music must be unmeasured, non-metrical. It is, then, doubtful whether one can or should suggest a single 'right' interpretation which will fit all *pastourelles*. Rather, each case must be judged on its merits. We ought not necessarily to look for the most straightforward and obvious solutions. The *pastourelle* is a sophisticated genre where several traditions meet; it is an imaginative literary and musical plaything. The same may be true also of the *lai*.

v The *lai*

In the hands of a master poet–musician, a true *Meister*singer, the *lai* was without doubt the most impressive, indeed magnificent, of all non-liturgical lyric forms; it has been called the 'parade-piece' of medieval song.[41] In an earlier chapter I surveyed the genre, briefly, and some of the Latin pieces in more detail (ch. 4: 1 v); for the present purpose I will use the vernacular. Vernacular *lais* were, at least from the early twelfth century, associated with the Latin. It is not agreed whether Abelard's *Planctus virginum Israel* was the model for the French *Lai des Pucelles* (R1012) or vice versa; but the closeness of the two is indisputable. Hans Spanke used the pair to demonstrate the 'general similarity of the French *lais* with the Latin'.[42] Certainly most of the general conclusions established earlier will be valid also for these: the *lai* 'hovers between the requirements of "narrative music" – speed, fluidity, repetition, open-endedness – and the requirements of an artefact – pattern, variety, fixity, structure'.

It is necessary for our purposes to emphasize the narrative element in the independent, so-called 'lyrical *lais*'. It has sometimes been overlooked or denied; Gérold, however, in his perceptive little volume, wrote of the late-thirteenth-century *Lai de Notre Dame* (R1017) by Ernoul le vielle,[43]

---

[41] For bibliography see chapter 4, note 49.

[42] Spanke (1938: repr. 1977), 163. Text and music of *Lai des Pucelles* in Jeanroy et al. (1901), no. xxiii; emended, in Maillard (1963), 262–71, with provisional transcription of Abelard's *planctus*. On Abelard, see chapter 4, note 31 above. On the French–Latin connection, see Bertau, *Sangverslyrik* (1964), 157ff.

[43] Gérold, 211. The *lai* is printed with heavy editorial emendations in Jeanroy et al. (1901), no. x v ii; see also Maillard (1964), 25. I have retained in Exx. 189 and 190 all the small melodic variants of the M S. Some may indeed be scribal errors, but most of them seem to demonstrate a continuously improvisatory style of performance. Ernoul's name 'le vielle' (see *New Grove*) is traditionally modernized as 'le vieux' but could, it is thought, mean 'the vielle-player'.

In this *lai* the author, with evident intention, approaches the style of liturgical psalmody; but, on the other hand, we will recall that epic poems too were sung with constant repetition of the same melodic phrases, and it could well be that this procedure, which we recognize in the lyrical *lais*, recalls something of the ancient narrative *lais* [i.e. the lost Breton tradition].

It is good to have this testimony, especially as it is not linked to any thesis about rhythmic interpretation. Indeed, quite the opposite. Gérold's transcriptions are all modal; his argument would be strengthened if they were not. I quote the following passage from another *lai*, attributed to Ernoul, in a neutral transcription; it is the opening of the *Lai de l'Ancien et du Nouveau Testament* (R1642) from the Chansonnier de Noailles.[44]

Ex. 189

NOTE: 7.6: MS e̲ d̲ not in ligature

---

[44] Chansonnier de Noailles, fols. 63v–64; printed in full in Jeanroy et al. (1901), no. XVIII; Maillard (1964), 14.

If there's any man in this place who might wish to hear a good *lai*, so good a *lai* was never made as this one is to listen to. It is all about Jesus Christ, who made the Lord's Prayer and who spoke the words which John the Evangelist wrote down. At his death everyone was sad, for many days and many years after. To young people and to their elders may this song be profitable in such a way that sin may not oppose any of them that hear.

Ernoul's *lai* is immensely long: 265 lines arranged in twenty-three strophes. This is exceptional, even for a courtly *lai*, and most are shorter. 'Flours ne glais' has 196 lines; the *Lai de la Rose*, 225; the *Lai des Pucelles*, 222. For convenience sake I give the full text of a much shorter one, 'La doce pensee' (R539) by Gautier de Dargies (*c.* 1165–1236+), from the same chansonnier; it has only forty-seven lines.[45]

Ex. 190

---

[45] Chansonnier de Noailles, fol. 147. Also in Chansonnier du Roi, fol. 90. I have transcribed from Noailles. See also Jeanroy *et al.* (1901), no. ii: emended analysis in Spanke (1938: repr. 1977), 184.

5 je lor par-doins, car tant m'ont fait d'o-nor,

6 ke la mil-lor del mont ai en-a-me-e.

3 Qui voit sa cri-ne bloi-e   2 ki sam-ble ke soit d'or,

3 et son col ki blan-çoi-e   4 de-seur som bel chief sor,

5 c'est ma da-me, ma joi-e   6 et mon ri-ce tre-sor;

7 cer-tes, je ne vau-roi-e   8 sans li va-loir He-ctor.

4 De si bel-le dame a-mer   2 ne se por-roit nus def-fen-dre;

3 puis k'a-mors m'i fait pen-ser,   4 el m'i de-vroit bien a-pren-dre

5 co-ment por-roie a-chie-ver,   6 puis k'ail-lors ne puis en-ten-dre.

5 Se je li di-soi-e   2 ke s'a-mors fust moi-e,

3 grant or-guell fe-roi-e,   4 nis se le pen-soi-e.

6 Ains sos-fer-rai mon mar-ti-re;   2 ja ne sav-ra mon pen-se,

3 se par pi-tie ne re-mi-re   4 les maus que me fait por-ter;

5 car tant re-doc l'es-con-di-re   6 de sa tres grant vo-len-te,

7 tel co-se por-roi-e di-re   8 dont el me sa-roit mal gre.

7 La ou diex a as-sam-ble   2 pris et va-lor et bon-te,

3 t'en va, des-cors, sans plus di-re,   4 fors i-tant, pour l'a-mor de,

5 c'om puet bien par toi es-li-re   6 ke ne je chant fors por le

7 dont diex me doinst es-tre a-me.

(1) The sweet thought that comes to me from love has entered into my heart for always, without any going back. So much have I desired the sweet pain that nothing on earth has such a savour for me.

(2) Sweet lady, before this I never told you my great sorrow at any time, but rather have always kept it hid. My eyes have killed me, by leading me into error; the pain they have caused will never end. I pardon them, because they have conferred such honour on me, that I have fallen in love with the best lady in the world.

(3) Whoever sees her blonde hair which seems as if made of gold and her neck white beneath her fair golden head [will know that] it is my lady, my joy and my precious treasure. Indeed, if I did not have her, I would not care to be as worthy a man as Hector.

(4) No one could help loving so beautiful a lady. Since love makes me think thus, she ought to teach me how I might succeed, for I have no thoughts for anyone else.

(5) If I said to her that her love was mine, I would be acting very arrogantly even if I thought it [was true].

(6) Rather, I will endure my pain; she shall never know my thoughts, if she does not in pity look on the sufferings she causes me to bear. For I fear so greatly the withdrawal of her abundant good will [that] I would be in danger of saying something which would displease her greatly.

(7) There, where God has brought together reputation, personal worth and goodness – go there, my *descort*, and say no more to her than this, for the love of God: that one may well perceive by means of you that I do not sing except for her by whom may it please God to grant that I am loved.

At first sight – sight on the page – 'La doce pensee' may appear to be a courtly chanson writ large. There is certainly nothing in the words to counteract this impression. In the accumulated clichés of

> Qui voit sa crine bloie
> ki samble ke soit d'or,

et con col ki blançoie
deseur som bel chief sor,
c'est ma dame, ma joie,
et mon rice tresor

we are invited to re-live the high courtly generalities of the garden of the Rose, invoked by Gautier himself in a *grand chant*, 'Humilitez et franchise, doucours, deboneretez' (R1626). Musically, too, the melody looks rather chanson-like. In some strophes (the third, for example) there is a larger sprinkling of note-groups than in Ernoul le vielle at least. However, the ear should soon pick up the insistent *lai*-tonality, based on the *g*-triad but with the constant shadow of an *f*-triad behind it, as for instance in strophes 1.4 and 2.2, with the traditional cadence in the former.[46]

Ex. 191

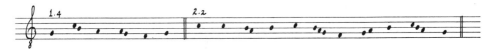

Another un-chanson-like feature of this *lai* is the wide sweep of the melody, especially in strophes 3 (*d* to *g'*) and 7 (*f* to *g'*).[47] More typical in fact of *lai*-conventions are the pithier, more restricted, idioms of strophes 4, 5 and 6. It is interesting, and surely the sign of an artist's endeavour to make something of inherited materials, that in the second half of the song the *f*-triad drops into the background as, beginning modestly in strophe 5, formulas centred on *c* take its place. The *lai* moves to a fine climax in strophe 7 (phrases 1 and 2) before descending to more familiar statements. The end (final on *c*) still seems somewhat unexpected (Aubry emended it to end on *g*). The composer seems to have a firm sense of a musical structure, of a kind, if not of a refinement, that Guillaume de Machaut was to perfect over a century later.[48]

The *lais* by named composers, Ernoul excepted, seem on the whole to be more elaborate and ambitious than the anonymous *lais*. What appears to be a more traditional common style (it is full of melodic commonplaces) is to be heard in the anonymous compositions. In *Lai d'Aélis*, for instance, the following phrase is used sixteen times in a row.[49]

[46] Strophes 1, 2, 3, 4, 7 have *g* final.
[47] While this is true of the contrast between chansons and *lais* as a whole, Gautier's own chanson melodies are characterized by wide range, as Karp observes ('Gautier de Dargies' in *New Grove*). Gautier's chansons are now available in van der Werf (1977), 123–85.
[48] The *lais* of Machaut are ed. Ludwig and Besseler, vol. IV (1954), and ed. Schrade, *PMFC* II (1956).
[49] Jeanroy et al. (1901), no. xxv (p. 143, stave 11); see the emended analysis in Spanke (1938: repr. 1977), 178. Some editorial reconstruction is necessary since Noailles does not notate the melody fully through long 'narrative' passages but writes the words as prose. Exx. 192–3 are taken from the MS. Ex. 193 is from *Lai d'Aélis*.

Ex. 192

The anonymous style is more predominantly single-note; and there are certain passages of sequential melody such as are extremely rare in the courtly chanson.[50]

Ex. 193

Finally, as in the case of the Adam of St Victor sequences and the Latin *lais* we can see clear evidence of a melodic 'treasury' on which all composers could draw:[51]

> The poverty of most of the melodic motifs, the frequent repetition of the same phrases during the course of one or more stanzas, the appearance of the same motif in various *lais*, encourage the supposition that the authors of the anonymous *lais* drew on old stock.

The rhythmic interpretation of the French *lai*, as of the Latin, is extremely problematic. Like the *pastourelle*, the *lai* is where traditions meet; and the traditions are, if not quite the same, very similar. The *lai* is courtly art-song; it

[50] The anonymous *lai* 'Puis qu'en chantant covient que me deport' (Jeanroy et al. (1901), no. XXVI) is somewhat of an exception to the single-note generalization.
[51] Gérold, 215. On pp. 214–15 he quotes specific examples of stock motifs.

is associated with dance (the *lai* is formally related to *estampie* and *ductia*);[52] and it is 'narrative melody'. But the balance is different. Whereas in the *pastourelle* we are continually conscious of dance-song and its demands – are in fact continually meeting scraps of dance-song in the form of *refrains* – in the *lai* we are not. To my knowledge no surviving *lai* makes use of a *refrain* or refers musically to the dance-*song* repertoire. The *Lai de la Pastourelle*, in which of all *lais* one might most have expected to find the dance-song immanent, since it is full of the literary clichés of the *pastourelle*, is decisively not orientated towards dance-song: it contains no *refrains*, and its music is that of the popular Latin sequence 'Ave gloriosa virginum regina', which served for other French *lais* also (see p. 106).[53] The *lai* is much more of a narrative form, as we have seen. Even though the vernacular *lais* do not often tell a story, they retain marked traces in their music of narrative procedures.

However, the substantial narrative presence gets us no further with the rhythmic problems of the *lai* than the shadowy link with dance-form, since it cannot be established that medieval narrative melody was necessarily un-measured; some types may well have had 'measure'. We are left with the third element, which links the *lai* with the *grands chants* of the troubadour and trouvère tradition. The *lai* is obviously rooted, with the sequence, in the syllabic and syllable-counting tradition of *musica ritmica* and shares with the courtly chanson many obvious features which need no reiteration here. Rhythmically, this means that the reasons in favour (and in disfavour) of isosyllabic interpretation are roughly the same, theoretically and palaeo-graphically, as in the case of the courtly chanson. The question at this stage of the argument is whether the 'aesthetic' of the genre – and the *lai* is a genre with quite distinct features – supports or militates against this interpretation.

At the end of chapter 4, I summed up this aesthetic as 'a sort of aural geometry'. The elaborate sense of pattern, which is absent from the courtly chanson, derives in part from verbal factors: a continuously displayed rhyth-mic contrast between strophes; not infrequent ambivalence in the stresses of the individual line; the play of rhyme. Parallel to these verbal patterns, and coinciding with them in their main structure, are musical patterns: 'they have their own relations, echoes, contrasts, building up into a "net" of sounds that fits perfectly over the "net" of words but has a different mesh'. This conspi-

---

[52] The Lorraine Chansonnier (Source 25) contains nineteen poems without music labelled *estampies* (ed. Streng-Renkonen). Bec (1977), I.241, characterizes the poetic form and gives three examples (II.181). Some *estampies* contain double-versicles and could have been sung to melodies similar to those which survive in musical sources, the oldest probably being the Chansonnier du Roi (eight monophonic textless pieces, each entitled *estampie royal* or *real*). English sources of (untitled) *estampies* are the Reading Abbey MS (facsimile in Besseler–Gülke, pl. 13) and Oxford, Bodleian Douce 139. See the basic articles of Handschin (1929) and Spanke (1931b: repr. 1977), and the comprehensive summary of research by van der Werf, 'Estampie' in *New Grove*. It has to be added that relations between *lai* and dance are much clearer in the instrumental *estampie* (*stantipes* (Grocheo), *istampita* (Ital.)) than in the poetic form (Bec finds the formal criteria not greatly significant).

[53] *Lai de la Pastourelle*, pr. Jeanroy *et al.* (1901), no. XXIV, and see Ex. 36 above.

cuous and obtruded sense of pattern is *the* generic feature of *lai*-melody. It is reinforced in the *lai*, as in the 'intermediate' and later sequence, by the fairly regular verbal accent and by the special kind of lively, angular, single-note melody described in the earlier chapter. These traits introduce a *direct* relationship between individual words and notes, though of a severely limited kind; and this direct relationship must have some bearing, one would think, on the rhythmical interpretation. Conclusions are bound to be tentative; but what fits best, in my view, with the 'aesthetic' of the *lai* is a *metrical but not a measured rhythm,* in transcription and for performance. It must be admitted, on the other hand, that an assortment of measured patterns with longs and shorts could also well display the kaleidoscopically varied schemata of the *lai*. However – and this is the point that needs stressing – durational values are not essential. If I am right, the crucial 'meaning' of a *lai*, the thing which distinguishes it as a genre from *la grande chanson* on the one hand and the dance-song on the other, resides in its 'aural geometry'. To convey this, accentual patterns are required but need not be durational; metres are required but not necessarily measure.

VI   *Conductus* and *cantio*

The *lai* is a genre in which many traditions meet; it is also one in which clear distinctions between Latin and French forms cannot be made. The links between these two languages are evident throughout the monophonic repertory. Many of the genre boundaries are similarly drawn and many of the same problems of rhythmic interpretation arise, as indeed we have already seen. However the huge repertoire of Latin song raises particular problems of its own as well as presenting the familiar conundrums in a new guise.

I attempted in chapter 2 to give some idea of the range and variety of Latin strophic song – hymn, *versus*, *conductus*, *cantio*. In the present section discussion will be confined to the sources most nearly contemporary with the written tradition of trouvère song, i.e. of the thirteenth century, such as the Beauvais MS (Source 15) and the Florence MS (Source 10). The songs themselves are in many cases demonstrably twelfth-century in origin, as indeed are many of the troubadour and trouvère chansons also.

The first question to be considered is whether genre distinctions are a necessary element in the rhythmical interpretation of the Latin songs discussed in earlier chapters 2 and 5 under the headings, *conductus*, *cantio* and *rondellus*. These headings were chosen mainly to indicate broad divisions of function and milieu: *conductus* was limited 'for the most part to songs associated with the liturgy and with its extended "secular" festivities, especially at Christmas and New Year', whilst *cantio* referred 'generally to art-songs of a less obviously functional' kind. The dance-song (*rondellus*) was described in chapter 5, where it found a place because of its obvious links in form and style with the vernacular dance-song (*carole*, *rondeau*) based on the *refrain*. But when one comes to ask what precisely its function was, or what purpose was served (for instance) by the songs collected in the eleventh fascicle of the Florence MS, then the only answer one can give is vague: dance-song is related to *conductus* and to the wider milieu of clerical celebration and festivity (see ch. 2: 11).

So we have to return to the idea of genre as formally and stylistically determined. On formal grounds the main distinctions correspond, in fact, to those of vernacular song: they are *conductus* and *cantio* (generally strophic song like the *chanson*); *rondellus* (refrain-type, like the *carole* and *rondeau*) and *lai* (sequence-type). In each case the parallel is confirmed by surviving *contrafacta*. *Rondellus* and Latin *lai* both conform closely in form and style to their vernacular partners: *conductus* and *cantio*, however, raise problems which require separate consideration.

It will be convenient to discuss rhythmic interpretation under the two headings *conductus* and *cantio*. The broad division by function and milieu already referred to is reflected in an equally broad temporal division. The *conductus* as an ecclesiastical phenomenon belongs mainly to the twelfth century, even though some of its main documents (the New Year Offices of Beauvais, Sens and Laon) belong to the thirteenth. The evidently non-liturgical, though still often festive, *cantio* overlaps somewhat in time (*c.* 1160–*c.* 1240+) with the *conductus*, but very little in a purely musical way; concordances between the two repertoires (which Janet Knapp designates as 'Aquitaine and related areas' and 'Notre Dame of Paris' respectively) are rare.[54]

The pertinent questions are whether these two fairly distinct repertoires constitute, from the rhythmic point of view, two distinct genres; and whether the second (Notre Dame) category, which embraces both monophonic and polyphonic pieces, does even in itself constitute a *single* genre. May there not be more essential distinctions between polyphonic *conductus* and monophonic *cantio* than the number of voices involved?

I shall continue to use the term *cantio* rather than *conductus* for the Latin songs of the Notre Dame and associated repertoires, even though (as stated earlier, p. 50) medieval usage would suggest *conductus* as the generic term during the twelfth and thirteenth centuries. Such is the power of a name that in our thinking we have, it seems to me, too easily fallen into the assumption that all the compositions normally designated *conductus* must have more in common with each other than they have with other genres. I hope that my adoption of the term *cantio* will at the least open up the question in a fresh way.

Wulf Arlt, in the introductory remarks to his transcriptions of the liturgical and paraliturgical *conductus* from the New Year Office of Beauvais Cathedral, sets out three possibilities:[55] that the rhythm was musically autonomous (this

---

[54] Knapp, 'Conductus' in *New Grove*. The repertoires may of course overlap in the sources (e.g. in the Later Cambridge Songs: Source 8).

[55] Arlt (1970), II, pp. xvii ff.

would lead in his view to an equal-*note* transcription, as in plainchant of this period); that it was determined by the text; or that a combination of music and text together established rhythmic form. Put in these general terms the problems seem more or less identical to those we have already confronted in trouvère song. But there is one essential differentiating factor which Arlt goes on to discuss. Latin verse in the twelfth and thirteenth centuries is frequently governed (or at least supported) by accent. This accent, we have seen, is not always in the strictest sense regular,[56] but it is generally patterned and predictable, and in the later sources certainly not 'free'. The question is how this feature is to be realized, if it is to be realized, in a musical interpretation. Following Arlt's second postulation (rhythm determined by text) the verbal accent could transfer itself to an isosyllabic melody purely as accent, forming rhythmic groups of variable length and shape; alternatively, the strong and weak accents could be translated into long and short syllables.[57] A *conductus* presented above (Ex. 14 with translation) in a neutral interpretation represented by undifferentiated note-heads is given here in two metrical transcriptions (one of which is also measured).

Ex. 194

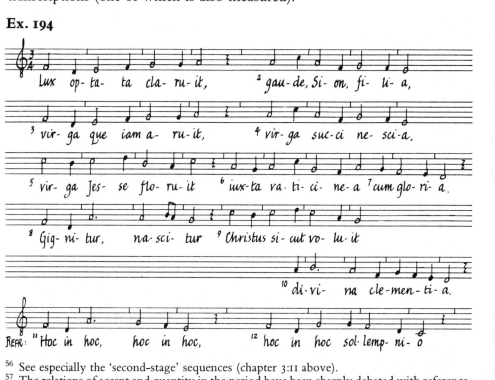

[56] See especially the 'second-stage' sequences (chapter 3:11 above).
[57] The relations of accent and quantity in the period have been sharply debated with reference to polyphonic conductus by Treitler (1979) and Sanders in *JAMS* 33 (1980), 601–7 (with a reply from Treitler, 607–11). See also Knapp (1979), and Tischler (1980). Ex. 194 is based on Arlt (1970) II, p. xix, who comments on how unforced such a triple-metre interpretation is. It may be observed, however, that the *duple*-metre version is similarly unforced and completely apt.

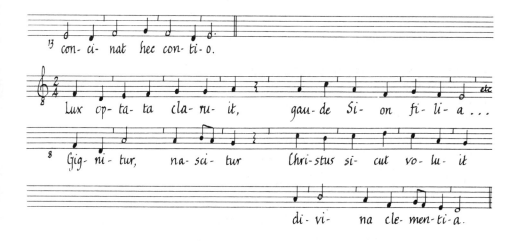

Arlt's three choices do not perhaps cover all the possible solutions of the problem. As I have argued earlier, pattern as a manifestation of number is in itself 'certain good' and its own justification. Thus it is open to us to postulate a musical autonomy which is not an equal-*note* construct but an equal-*unit* one based on the syllable and its music – i.e. isosyllabic. A melody so conceived may be flexible enough to 'collaborate' with an accentual text without either subduing or being subdued by it. This is near to Arlt's third alternative but differently conceived; it depends, as in the case of the vernacular chanson, on the concept of a *ratio*, a *numerus*, a pattern, which is basic both to the words and to the music, validating them both as separate entities, but allowing neither to predominate.

The main source for the *cantio* is the Florence MS. In this manuscript are collected polyphonic settings of liturgical texts, commonly incorporating chant melodies, 'extra-liturgical' compositions with verse texts, polyphonic songs, and two fascicles of monophonic songs – one of *cantiones*, the other of *rondelli*. The notation of the polyphony is modal, except for two mensural additions to the sixth fascicle; but this, of course, does not apply to the *cantiones*, which having, as a rule, text throughout cannot employ the 'patterned ligature' system of modal notation.[58] The *cantiones* of the Florence manuscript are non-mensural. Some fourteen Notre Dame songs are found in a species of mensural notation in the Las Huelgas MS (*c.* 1300) and, variously

[58] Knapp (1979) argues that in a group of the polyphonic *conductus* in the Florence MS the undifferentiated notation of the texted passages may represent the natural and accepted way of writing a fifth-mode rhythm (spondaic: i.e. equal longs): 'it is precisely the simple forms [of notation] which are needed to indicate the fifth mode regardless of whether the music is syllabic or melismatic' (p. 406). Husmann (1952a) came to the same conclusion about the melismatic *conductus* in general. See my comment on Beck's similar 'covert isosyllabism', chapter 12: II, note 33, above.

garbed or garbled, in the *Roman de Fauvel* (compiled 1316).[59] In addition, Gordon Anderson reports,[60] there are two songs

based on *clausulae* whose rhythms are clear, another one is found as a motet in La Clayette [BN fr. 13521], while Santa Sabina [Rome, Convent of S. Sabina, XIV L.3], a source with some mensural properties, gives an indication of the basic rhythms of four more works . . . Three Notre-Dame monophonic conductus have concordances among French chansons notated in mensural sources, and one prosa also occurs in a mensural transmission.

The precise value of these various concordances can be established only by individual examination.[61] Anderson, however, prefers to proceed on the simple, general hypothesis that 'later mensural sources represent very accurately the intentions of the scribes as transmitted in earlier sources'. This hypothesis rests on a dubious historical assumption which he does not appear to question. It is the same as that held by the 'modalists' of vernacular song (see ch. 12:11), namely that there could be no significant changes of taste or fashion in the performance of monophonic melody between *c.* 1200 and 1350. The hypothesis also takes it for granted that polyphonic and monophonic compositions belonged to a single unified rhythmic tradition, whereas the opposite is at least as arguable: that polyphony, itself a relative novelty, was distinguished by novel rhythmic procedures.

If these novel procedures are applied to the grandly conceived *cantio* by Philip the Chancellor, 'Veritas veritatum', quoted earlier (Ex. 22), it takes on a quite different complexion. The rhythmic modes, however they have come to be used by modern scholars in the interpretation of other songs, were origin-

---

[59] Anderson, in his article on the rhythm of the monophonic conductus (1978d), relies without question on these two later sources and does not assuage the doubts raised by other scholars, e.g. Steiner (1966), 64, who writes that although the notation of the Las Huelgas MS is 'generally regarded as mensural', the single fact that it contains 'the graphic modifications affecting propriety and perfection that are characteristic of mensural notation' does not prove it, given such oddities as the total absence of single-note breves. Anglès, the major editor of the MS, also concluded that the notation was not mensural. As for the *Roman de Fauvel*, 'of the seven monophonic compositions from *F* [Florence MS] fasc. x that are found in *Fauv* with essentially the same melodies, only two can be said to have their rhythm clearly indicated in the late source' (Steiner, 64–5). The worth of *Las Huelgas* and *Fauvel* remains questionable. Falck does not discuss the rhythmic problem in his *Notre Dame Conductus* (1981); he gives it as his opinion that 'any rhythmic transcription of a conductus can never be more than a theory, but a theory about the music itself not about the notation' (Introd., p. ii).

[60] Anderson (1978d), 480–1.

[61] Anderson does not examine them. Briefly, the motet concordance cannot illuminate the rhythmic problem for reasons already explained (ch. 14:1); Santa Sabina (Rome) MS does indeed have 'mensural properties' but they are not wholly consistent (see H. Husmann, 'Ein Faszikel Notre-Dame-Kompositionen auf Texte des Pariser Kanzlers Philipp in einer Domi-nikanerhandschrift' in *A Mw* 24 (1967), 1–23, with one facsimile); the chanson concordances (unspecified) can of their very nature have only a questionable validity; the 'prosa' is presumably 'Ave gloriosa virginum regina' (fol. 447), for which the sources are manifold – some are mensural, more are not (see ch. 3, Ex. 36: it is a quite different genre of song in any case, and not evidence for *conductus* interpretation).

ally a polyphonic musical system pure and simple. They find their most
certain application to long melismatic passages without words in which the
configuration of the ligatures is totally untrammelled by a different, and
incompatible, use of them in 'syllabizing' a text. The result of applying modal
formulas to a complex Latin song like 'Veritas veritatum' is, in Gordon
Anderson's transcription, as follows.[62]

Ex. 195

This, it should be noted, is not a modal transcription in the Aubry–Beck sense
– that is to say, the editor has not applied a strictly regular, abstract verbal
metre to the melody. The notation is agreed to be non-mensural; the editor
has given his own individual sense of what the melody would have been like if
it had been mensurally notated in the style of the polyphonic *conductus* as he
conceives it.[63]

There are good reasons to think, however, that the polyphonic *conductus*
and the monophonic *cantio* were indeed regarded as separate genres. There is,
to begin with, no great degree of musical connection between them – no
greater than between any other two separate genres.[64] Of the eighty-three
monophonic songs assembled in the tenth fascicle of the Florence MS only
five have polyphonic connections and several of these are tenuous. 'Concordance patterns suggest that the polyphonic repertories are a unified tradition,
whilst the sources which transmit the monophonic repertory are largely

---

[62] Anderson (1978b), p. 30 (K19).

[63] See Anderson (1973).

[64] See the useful tables of concordances in Falck, *Notre Dame Conductus* (1981), and the
information in Anderson (1972), K1–K83; also note 54 above.

different ones' (Falck).[65] Most of the other important sources of *cantiones* are, in fact, collections of texts with no music (the Bekyngton Miscellany, for example).

More authors' names, too, are known, such as those of Philip the Chancellor and Walter of Châtillon. These facts have led Falck to conclude that 'for the latter thirteenth century at least, the monophonic conductus [*cantio*] was more a literary than a musical genre'. This is a sound observation if it means that there are many important surviving manuscripts without music. But what precisely is meant by a 'literary' genre? Certainly the term will not do if it implies that the music was subsidiary in interest. If on the other hand we would be equally prepared to call the troubadour and trouvère chanson a 'literary' genre, the term may stand. There is a genuine balance of interest between words and music in both.

There could, further, be evidence in theoretical writings for the distinction of genres. As Janet Knapp has written, 'three large treatises of the thirteenth century which relate quite particularly to the Notre Dame school refer to the conductus as a species of discant or modally ordered *polyphony* . . . The theoretical support for a modal reading of the [polyphonic] conductus is incontrovertible.'[66] The English theorist Anonymus IV does, unusually, refer to the existence of monophonic song (*conductus simplex*); but no theorist speaks of its rhythmic interpretation. The notation is 'even more ambiguous than that of the polyphonic pieces, and the failure of the theorists to include them in the discussions on rhythm raises serious doubts as to whether they were modally conceived'.[67] The precise nature of a rhythmic contrast between polyphonic and monophonic songs in the Florence manuscript is not easy to formulate, partly because the problem of transcribing the polyphonic *conductus* modally has not been solved, and partly because of puzzling interrelations such as the following.

At the end of the Florence MS collection there is a through-composed *cantio* in a single twenty-nine-line stanza about the Prodigal Son, 'Minor natu filius'; it occurs also in the Egerton Chansonnier (Source 14), the second largest source of Notre Dame songs. 'Minor natu' is based on the final melisma (*cauda*) of a two-part song 'Austro terris influente'; the author, Philip the Chancellor, has apparently taken its last words to begin his new poem, which fits the melody syllable by syllable.[68] Most interestingly, as Robert Falck has

[65] Falck, 129. The full details are available in Anderson (1972). Some of the *cantiones* have a dozen or more text sources without music: e.g. 'Dum medium silentium tenerent' (K15); 'Quisquis cordis' (K52).

[66] Knapp (1979), 383, 385 (my italics).

[67] Knapp, 'Conductus' in *New Grove,* IV, 655.

[68] 'Minor natu', Florence MS, fols. 450v–451; 'Austro terris', fols. 299–300v (Anderson K82 and G1). See Falck's catalogue of individual compositions (1981), no. 208, discussed pp. 114–15 and transcribed as Ex. 25. It is, of course, possible that Philip wrote the song first as a completely separate item and that the composer of 'Austro' borrowed the melody (see Knapp (1979) 386, n. 17). The Egerton Chansonnier (Source 14) is discussed by Falck, 110ff; it is 'the only collection of the works of Philippe the Chancellor with notation'.

observed, the Egerton song breaks into a rough mensural notation at the precise point where the *cauda* of the Florence version begins, in modal notation (indicated by ligature patterns). A natural interpretation of this phenomenon is that Philip liked the new style of metrical melody (the 'modes') and decided to make use of it; this is not an isolated example.[69]

That the generic affinities of monophonic Latin song of the *cantio* type may be more with vernacular chanson than with the polyphonic *conductus* itself is allowed, though not of course established, by the comparative paucity of concordances between the monophonic and polyphonic repertoires and their inconclusive nature. In this respect the *cantio* could be similar to the chanson; the trouvères wrote no polyphonic *grands chants*. On the other hand there are *contrafactum* links between the two types of monophonic song. In the Florence manuscript half a dozen songs have their parallel French versions; and in the Egerton Chansonnier there are, though no new *contrafacta*, a sizeable group of trouvère chansons.[70] Most striking of all is the remark by Johannes de Grocheo (ch. 12: 111): introducing his description of *cantus coronatus*, in which he names two trouvère chansons, he says *cantus coronatus ab aliquibus simplex conductus dictus est* ('some call the "crowned" song a *conductus* for single voice'). Interestingly enough, one of his examples, 'Quant li rossignols' (R1559), is a contrafact (or *vice versa*) of the Latin song 'Nitimur in vetitum' from the Florence manuscript.[71]

On the evidence it looks as if the polyphonic conductus was certainly modal and should be transcribed in measured rhythms, whilst the monophonic *cantio* (*conductus simplex*) was not. This would correspond to the main contrast of the earlier theorists between *musica metrica* and *musica ritmica* and would confirm the supposition that the long-standing contrast of rhythmical traditions had at least by the later thirteenth century been translated into an opposition between polyphonic and monophonic music. On the one hand we have measured motet and polyphonic *conductus*; on the other, predominantly isosyllabic chanson, monophonic *conductus* and *cantio*.

---

[69] See Falck, 114; Knapp, 385–6.

[70] On the *contrafacta* between Latin songs and trouvère chansons, see: Spanke (1936), 150–4 (twenty-three examples chosen principally on metrical grounds); Gennrich, 'Internationale Melodien' (1928); and, more recently, Räkel, especially pp. 75–107, discussing Walter of Châtillon and Philip the Chancellor, together with Gace Brulé, Thibaut de Blaison, Blondel de Nesle and other trouvères.

[71] Fol. 438; Falck (1981), no. 219; and see his article on two of Philip the Chancellor's songs (1967).

15
WORDS AND MUSIC: A BALANCED RELATIONSHIP

'The historical study of words and music is bound to show, if nothing else, how manifold the possible relationships are between the two. Each age has its own characteristic notions of how they should be joined in song; and it requires a genuine effort of the historical imagination to shake off the assumptions of our own, or of another, age and to engage with the object as it really is.'[1] I have tried in the present study to bring out some of the 'characteristic notions' of the Middle Ages; above all, to show how the aesthetic of 'number' predominated not only in the theory but in the practice of many types of song. In this final chapter I shall try to show how this predominance bears directly upon the relationship of music and poetry and, through this, upon the problem of rhythmic interpretation. The hypothesis of isosyllabic interpretation for the central and major part of the repertoire – the serious, high-style chanson of the troubadours and trouvères, and the *cantio* of the Latin song-writers – is well supported, in my view, by combined arguments of a theoretical, palaeographical and musical–historical kind. It must now be subjected to a final test: will it properly represent the relations between words and music in so far as we have been able to understand and to reconstruct them?

1 Assumptions and theories

Most, perhaps all, theories of rhythmic interpretation for medieval song rest on assumptions about the relations of words and music. One such theory supports the system of *Vierhebigkeit* or *Viertaktigkeit* propounded by Hugo Riemann and others around the turn of the century: every melody is arranged to form a phrase of four regularly spaced beats, and the text is manhandled into submission to it, with bizarre results especially if the song is at all melismatic.[2] The theory was a natural one for an educated musician to hold a hundred years ago. The assumptions behind it – of 'classical' balance of phrase – seem, if unformulated, to have influenced Coussemaker's transcriptions published some forty years earlier.[3]

---

[1] Stevens (1974), 26.
[2] The system is discussed by Kippenberg, 78–83, who quotes an astonishing example from Johannes Wolf, *Handbuch der Notationskunde* (Leipzig 1913), 1.176. See also the characteristically lucid comments of Gérold, 92ff, with exx. (p. 102).
[3] Ex. 196 is from Coussemaker (1852), 'Monuments', pp. iv–v.

Ex. 196

From the rising of the sun to the western shores of the sea lamentation strikes every breast. Beyond the seas a huge sadness has touched the multitudes with excessive grief. Alas, my misery – I lament!

Another theory of music's dominance still has currency today. It proposes an equal-*note* transcription; that is to say, the melody is transcribed according to traditional plainchant interpretation.[4]

Ex. 197

The happiness of this world does not last for any time; it wends away soon.

With both these theories, and some others, there is at least the negative assumption that a proper *balance* between the demands of music and poetry is not one that need be insisted upon. I assume the opposite and shall argue later that the assumption is historically grounded: a proper balance seems to me an absolute requirement for an acceptable solution of the rhythmic problem.

My first task in this chapter will be to examine some of the deeply held, if not always deeply questioned, beliefs which are current about words-and-music in medieval song. The assumption that it is the words which substantially determine the rhythm of a song is shared not only by convinced adherents of the 'modal' theory but by its strongest opponents, such as Appel (1934), Monterosso (1956) and van der Werf (1967). The practical results they

[4] Ex. 197 is from Dobson and Harrison, p. 244 (no. 7). Another theory which works on the principle of music's dominance over the text is that of Sesini (1942); he transcribes isosyllabically, but his rhythmic schemes are strictly regular (i.e. in ternary metre, though not measured) in subservience to the fundamental demands of the music ('Verso è anzitutto un ritmo musicale, per sè stante: le parole vi si adattano', p. 76).

come to are very different; but at root they do have certain beliefs in common. Appel says that we should pay regard to the division of the line (*Versgliederung*) and word-accent and sing the chansons in a 'free rhythm'.[5] Monterosso distinguishes (subtly but not with absolute clarity) between a musical rhythm which is 'identified with the rhythm of the words' and one which 'can be revealed' by it; this latter, which he believes was obvious to medieval poet–musicians, could be 'very easily recognized following the analysis of the metre and the rhythm of the words' (*dopo l'analisi della metrica e della ritmica testuale*).[6] Van der Werf is more ready to subordinate the melodies to the exigencies of the text: 'the rhythm in which one might *declaim* the poem without the music' will shape the musical interpretation.[7] David Hughes, finally, commenting recently on the Notre Dame *conductus* (twelfth-century), writes: 'The Notre Dame *conductus* did not need symbols for long and short notes – the singer could *read the rhythmic values directly out of the poetry*.'[8]

Those who believe that 'rhythmic values' may be 'read directly out of the poetry' belong, we see, to two camps: the first holds that the scansion of the verse-line gives the clue from which a regular pattern may be derived; the second holds that it is the sound of the individual words themselves which establishes the rhythm of the melody. Attention to the scansion produced the theory of 'modal rhythm', the application of the rhythmic modes of polyphony to monophonic song. The various modifications and limitations suggested by scholars over the years to make the theory more workable without abandoning the concept behind it are all equally irrelevant if one cannot accept the concept in the first place; I shall not discuss them here.[9] The 'prosodized music' produced by the modalists, I have argued, goes contrary to the categories established by traditional theories of *musica*, pays little regard to the general nature or the detail of the musical notation and manuscript presentation, and blurs over necessary distinctions of genre and style. We must now add that it distorts the balance between the text and the melody. The distortions are cumulative.

First of all, the rhythm of the text is distorted. The idea of regular patterns of iambs or trochees or dactyls was never one to cause comfort to philologists. If the Romance languages used regular schemes of accentuation at this period, the modern ear – even the trained ear of a philologist – cannot reliably detect them, as the analyses by Carl Appel of Bernart de Ventadorn's poems showed many years ago.[10] The comments of Jean Beck on the troubadour and

---

[5] Appel (1934) 1–43.

[6] Monterosso (1956), 87, 98–9.

[7] Van der Werf (1972), 44 (his italics).

[8] Hughes, 'Music and Meter in Liturgical Poetry' (1976), 44 (his italics).

[9] For the various refinements and qualifications of modal theory, see the summaries in Kippenberg, ch. 4.

[10] Appel (1934). I am most grateful to the late Leslie Topsfield for advice and discussion on this point. There is, of course, no perfect unanimity even among philologists; but Roger Dragonetti, despite the acknowledged importance and comprehensiveness of his *La technique poétique des trouvères dans la chanson courtoise* (1960), is in a minority when he argues for the

trouvère repertoire, coming as they do from one of the 'inventors' of modalism, are even more striking:[11]

amongst more than ten thousand Provençal and French chansons which I have examined with this point in mind . . . I have not found a single one in which the tonic, or etymological, accents of the words fall in the same position throughout all the stanzas.

(Small wonder that Beck had come by 1927, the date of his edition of the Chansonnier Cangé, to believe that the fundamental rhythmic mode of monophonic music was the fifth, the spondaic, consisting entirely of equal notes. This mode Beck identified with Grocheo's description of the *cantus coronatus* as *ex omnibus longis et perfectis*, thus enabling himself to propose what is in effect an isosyllabic interpretation (*'la valeur isochrone de toutes les syllabes'*) whilst still calling it a modal one.)[12] To the initial textual distortion, of accent, modal rhythm adds a second, that of duration. Since all 'feet' in the polyphonic system are triple, accented syllables are made twice as long as unaccented. (In the unhappy third, dactylic, mode things are even worse: the accented syllable is three times the length of the first, and one and one-half times the length of the second, short syllable – see table, p. 424 above). This compounded distortion is then applied to the melody, the inner, organic, musical life of which has to be made subservient to the distorted text. Those who have made these 'applications' most sensitively have tried and often

[11] Beck (1927), II.43–4.
[12] *Cantus coronatus*: see above, chapter 12, note 52; Beck (1927), 43. Beck, however, did not allow himself the rhythmic freedom which the covert isosyllabism of the fifth mode opened up; he saw it essentially as a means of introducing duple metres in place of triple (p. 45). See chapter 14, note 58.

---

existence of underlying regular metrical pattern in Old French verse. In fact, it is only in the decasyllabic strophe that he finds a clearly marked predominance of *rythme métrique ou carré*, i.e. with alternate weak and strong syllables (p. 512). Elsewhere the metre (i.e. the given *external* controls) seems to consist, as the theorists said it should, in precisely numbered syllables, in the observance of the caesura in lines of eight or ten syllables, and in accenting the rhyme-word (see above, ch. 1:1, text to note 35). But in any case the examples assembled by Dragonetti himself (pp. 504ff, 'Les schemes composites') do not seem to me to establish his point. He further argues that the poems rely on *rythme de tension* (i.e. between a *mesure iambique* and a *rythme trochaique*, for example in 'Doúce dáme', (p. 506)); such a conception – though familiar to us in English verse from *c.* 1550 onwards – contributes nothing, to my ear, towards an understanding of the fluid *armonia* of such a stanza as this from Thibaut de Champagne (R1476), which Dragonetti takes for particular analysis (p. 512); the markings and groupings are my own:

Je vous di bien une riens sanz mentir:	2 2 3 3
Qu'ens Amors a eür et grant cheance.	3 3 2 2
Se je de li me poïsse partir,	1 3 3 3
Melz me venist qu'estre sires de France	1 3 3 3
Ore ai je dit com fous desesperez:	1 3 2 2
Melz aim morir recordant ses biautez	1 3 3 3
Et son grant sens et la douce acointance	4 3 3
Qu'estre sires de tout le mont clamez.	3 3 2 2

succeeded in making musical accommodations between the chosen metre and the melody, as for instance in the matter of ligatures. They have suggested, however, in this latter case two incompatible solutions: one, that note-groups should fall on short, rhythmically weak, beats because the musical sense of the melody seems to require it (rather as in later music the last note *before* the cadence may be elaborately ornamented); the other, that note-groups should occur on long, often rhythmically strong, beats because this gives them time to be spread out without disturbing the smooth flow of the measured melody.[13]

Ex. 198

I have spoken about 'distorting the balance' between the text and the melody, and by doing so I may seem to be begging the question. Despite the evident distortions of the text (one only has to look at example (b) above) and the concomitant straitening of the melody, it could be held that the result is at least a working rapport between the two. What is now evidently incumbent on anyone who believes, as I do, that this 'working rapport' is a makeshift and inadequate affair is to define the ideal balance between words and music in such a way as to show clearly how it meets the aesthetic requirements of the age in practical terms. To do this it will be useful to recapitulate some earlier arguments.

II   Balance: the 'double melody' and the numerical Idea

One generalization which emerged in chapter 11, 'Music and meaning', was that the theorists, who were often philosophers and thinkers on a large scale, worked with a definition of *musica* broad enough to include both music and words; that, indeed, the theorists sometimes do not trouble themselves to distinguish between music and speech, since both are arts which measure sound in time. This position led, however, in some rare instances when the two were separately identified, to striking formulations implying a relationship between them of (as it might seem to us) an unusual kind. One

---

[13] The first example, by Pèire d'Alvernha, is from troubadour MS *R* (Source 32), fol. 6, transcr. Gérold, 159 (see de la Cuesta, pp. 103–4, for comparative transcription from *R* and troubadour MS *X* (= the trouvère Chansonnier St Germain)). The second example is the refrain-line of 'Bien doit chanter' (R169) by Guillaume le Vinier, transcr. Rosenberg and Tischler, p. 327 (no. 136).

statement by Guido d'Arezzo is particularly revealing, and for the practical and aesthetic insight it gives us is worth quoting again:[14]

sicut persaepe videmus tam consonos et sibimet alterutrum respondentes versus in metris, ut quamdam quasi symphoniam grammaticae admireris. Cui si musica simili responsione iungatur, *duplici modulatione dupliciter delecteris*.

Thus in verse we often see such concordant and mutually congruous lines that you wonder, as it were, at a certain harmony of language. And if music were added to this, with a similar internal congruity, you would be doubly charmed by a twofold melody.

This is what *musica* means in relation to song – that the ear will be 'doubly charmed by a twofold melody', both musical and verbal. Nothing in Guido's statement appears to conflict with what Dante will be saying three centuries later at the end of the great creative period of melodic art. Where Guido talks of a *symphonia grammaticae* and a *modulatio*, Dante speaks of an *armonia*. It is one of his favourite words to describe not only the proportions of music and of words but of anything – the parts of the human body, for instance.[15] Significantly neither Guido nor Dante, nor anyone else to my knowledge, says in specific terms how the text and the melody relate to one another except structurally.[16] Their answer to the question – what is the relationship between words and music in song? – is never explicit, because it need not be. The key to the answer (and, as argued above, pp. 422–3, the reason for the apparent conspiracy of silence about it) is in this all-pervading concept of *armonia*.

On this issue, the most revealing single passage in Dante comes not from a treatise but from canto xxviii of the *Paradiso*.[17] Dante, gazing upon the eyes of Beatrice, suddenly becomes aware of something which was not previously in his sight or thought. It is as if a man were looking into a mirror and someone lit a taper behind him:

> a sé rivolge, per veder se 'l vetro
>   li dice il vero, e vede ch'el s'accorda
>   con esso come note con suo metro . . .   (*Par.* xxviii.4)

He turns back to himself to see if the mirror tells him the truth, and he sees the reality agreeing with the image as music to its verse.

If the term *metro* means the words of a song, as seems necessary for the contrast here, then we have a most revealing analogy for the relationship between words and music as Dante conceived it. The music is as intimately and sensitively bound up with words as an object to its reflection in a mirror, or as

---

[14] Guido speaks of *metra*, and not of *ritmi* (see ch. 11:11, text to note 42 above). This does not, I think, affect the present argument.

[15] The pleasures of *consonantia*, *armonia* – ordered and balanced sound – are described by Dante in a passage of the *Convivio* quoted p. 385 above.

[16] The structural concords between grammatical–syntactical units and musical units are discussed in chapter 8:iv above.

[17] The paragraphs that follow are rephrased from Stevens (1968a), 13–14.

a shadow to the body that casts it. The sounds of the music and the sounds of words are not indivisible; but when they are together, they are closely analogous, or parallel.

The point is made again in the *De Vulgari Eloquentia*. In this passage Dante defines a song as follows:

cantio nil aliud esse videtur quam actio completa dictantis verba modulationi armonizzata. (II.viii.5)

He has just said that those who 'harmonize' words (*armonizantes verba*), in his sense, make songs, whether they have music with them or not; poems are musical constructs in words. A song in the fullest sense is 'the completed action of one who artistically puts words together into a harmonious whole' . . . or, perhaps better, 'puts words together, harmonizing them into a rhythmical accord' (*modulationi*). *Modulatio* can also mean 'melody', a musical phrase (e.g. II.x.2). But here the logic seems to forbid it; Dante is not speaking of a direct relationship between the words and the music. The word *modulatio*, or rather the way he uses it here, suggests something other than the text itself and perhaps prior to it – a *ratio rhythmica* (rhythmic pattern), in fact. At any rate, both the mirror-image and the marriage-image suggest the closest physical union. The reflection in the mirror can be blotted out, but if restored it inevitably takes the same shape as before.

The relationship between poem and melody is to be close, physical, and (I think we may infer) equal. As Ewald Jammers has written, the task of the music is 'to create form in common with the text' (*mit dem Text gemeinsam Form zu schaffen*).[18] The enterprise is a joint one, and we should beware of any interpretation which exalts one art over the other. We must allow neither the dominance of the poem over the melody nor the opposite, the dominance of the melody over the poem. We can, of course, admit sometimes the chronological precedence of the words, as for instance when a chanson-text is found in multiple settings, or when a poet–composer is praised for writing 'new melodies to all his *sirventes*'.[19] But mention of the *sirventes* is a reminder that on the other hand the melody often came first in time; the *sirventes*, typically on a political or moral theme, was normally written to fit a pre-existent melody: it was, in a word, a contrafact.[20] Many *chansons pieuses* were contrafacts of secular chansons. The point need not be laboured, since the

[18] Jammers (1963), 13. His sub-chapter 'Die Einheit von Musik und Dichtung' (pp. 10–16) contains some of the most perceptive comments on the medieval relations of music and poetry that I have read.

[19] Guilhen Rainol: see Beck (1908), 102. Salimbene's chronicle (cited Ludwig (1910) 247–9) recounts how Henry of Pisa composed: e.g. 'he made a song to the text of Philip the Chancellor' (*cantum fecit in illa littera* . . .) etc. See also Grocheo on *modus componendi*; he says that someone (*unus*) prepares the words by way of 'matter' (*dictamina loco materiae*) and then a melody apt by way of 'form' (*cantus . . . proportionalis loco formae*) is put to it (*introducitur*); Rohloff, 134.

[20] See Stevens and Karp 'Troubadours and trouvères' in *New Grove*.

whole activity of making contrafacts was so widespread.[21] I mention it again here simply to remind how often in medieval monody the music came first in time, before the words. The convenient phrase 'setting words to music', which slips out so easily in the discussion of song in all periods, does in a normal modern context mean, curiously, precisely the opposite of what it says. In relation to medieval song it can often be construed literally – the words are 'set' to music which is already there.

I have stressed the word 'physical' because it is of the first importance to know, and to know imaginatively, that *sounds* are the matter of medieval song and the basis for the union between the text and the melody. What the writer of a contrafact is doing is to take one set of numbered sounds and to replace them with another. But if sounds are the *materia*, 'number' is the *forma* – or, to use another of their favourite antitheses, the *ratio* behind the *sensus*. So it may be that the relationship between words and music in serious art-song (chanson and *cantio*)[22] should be regarded as *metaphysical* rather than physical – it goes beyond the 'musical potential of the poem' into the realm of the Ideal. In plain language, the musician did not set the words of the poem to music; he set its pattern. It was this pattern, a purely numerical structure of stanzas, lines and syllables, which preceded both the melody and the poem. The pattern had to be realized in two media – the medium of words and the medium of notes – and it did not matter in the least which was realized first.

I have spoken in temporal terms. But it might be better to say that the *numeri*, the rhythmic proportions and relations, took precedence over the melody and the poem rather than that they necessarily preceded them both in time – the *armonia* of the song thus exists in ideal form, as a numerical reality waiting to be incarnated, as it were, either as music or as poetry (verbal music) or both. To talk, therefore, about a direct relationship between music and poetry is misleading. The notes and the words are not so much related to one another as related both to a single numerical Idea.

This hypothesis is not put forward merely as a possible *philosophical* basis for the aesthetic of courtly song. It is intended as a practical suggestion about the way trouvère songs in the high style came into being and about the way we should both study and hear them.[23] One practical result, if the hypothesis is true, could be that we should cease to be as preoccupied as we have been about a referential relationship directly between the words and the notes and begin to study the implications of having two parallel synchronous shapes.

[21] Amongst the contrafacts in English sources alone that have been mentioned in this study are 'Bien doit chanter', 'Angelus ad virginem', 'Ave gloriosa virginum regina', 'Letabundus', and 'Flos pudicitie'.

[22] The paragraphs which follow are based on Stevens (1974–5), 27–8.

[23] See ch. 12, opening quotation: 'Poeta conposuit rationem ritmicam. . .'.

III   A balanced relationship: rhythmic implications

It now remains to draw out from the conception of words-and-music formulated above the implications for rhythmic interpretation. I believe that the aesthetic ideal embodied in the conception of 'two parallel synchronous shapes' does indeed have implications which support isosyllabic interpretation. It would be foolish indeed to claim that they prove its truth; but combined with the other kinds of evidence that have been put forward in the last three chapters they constitute, I believe, a strong positive case.

The first advantage of isosyllabic transcription and performance – performance, since an interpretation that cannot be realized in sound is not worth arguing for – is that it allows both elements of the double melody to flow *naturally*. The concept of what is 'natural' may be difficult, we shall see, to apply to music, but as applied to words it is reasonably straightforward. The ordinary movement of formal speech – that is, of the slightly stylized speech used for the recitation of verse – is certainly closer to the isosyllabic than it is to the measured (quantitative). This is perhaps even truer of the Romance languages, such as French and Latin, than it is of the Teutonic, in which strong and weak syllables are more contrasted. The syllables when sung isosyllabically will, of course, be slightly elongated and more clearly articulated but without the uncomfortable distortions of speech-movement which other transcriptions impose.

An enquiry into what is 'natural' in melody could take us into very deep waters. One could well argue that it was perfectly 'natural', for instance, to give every one of a succession of *notes* an equal time-value. But there is another possible view, I think, of what most 'naturally' might be made of melodies consisting, as they so often do, in the courtly chanson and *cantio*, of an irregular mixture of single notes and short note-groups. If there is a musical reason for this feature of the original melodies, it is likely to be found in the contrast between the two, a contrast which a 'modal' transcription modifies or disguises and which an equal-note transcription magnifies at the expense of the words.[24] One of the musical effects of the contrast in an isosyllabic interpretation is a slight 'stretching out' of the melody at cadences, where small melismas are most characteristically found, as for example in this chanson by Blondel de Nesle (R1227).[25]

Ex. 199

²⁴ This argument does not, of course, apply to the simplest types of sequence, *lai*, chanson and *conductus*, all of which are composed on the single-note-to-syllable principle.
²⁵ Van der Werf (1977), 78–84; ten musical versions of the chanson survive. The variants are numerous and interesting especially at cadences but, except in the eccentric trouvère M S R, rarely of structural import.

12 je   ne   m'en   doi   plain- dre   mi-   e;

13 com- ment   qu'ai-e   es-   té   i-   riez,

14 dou- ce-   ment   sui   en-   gi-   gniez.

Since I am deprived of joy through my own fault, I must not complain at all; however wretched I may have been, I am most sweetly duped.

These are the last four lines of the first stanza of 'Quant je plus sui', an ambitiously designed strophe of 115 syllables disposed in fourteen lines. The equality of the syllables in an isosyllabic rendering must – to repeat – be approximate, sensitively judged, not metronomic; the *rubato* required, however, at the close of such lines should not disturb the basic syllabic pulse, nor the organic shape of the melody as a whole (phrase 13, for example, needs to keep sufficient rhythmic momentum to flow into phrase 14). The opposite effect – of foreshortening, with a slight quickening of the syllabic pulse – seems to be called for when (as often happens in the course of a song) a phrase, or a long succession, of single notes breaks into the 'mixed style'.[26] Clearly it cannot be logically proved that the effects I have described are the only natural interpretation of, or reason for, the style as we encounter it in its mixture of single notes and note-groups; but, equally, that they are *one* natural interpretation cannot be denied, since they allow the contrast to be clearly heard.

The second way in which the isosyllabic style realizes the aesthetic ideal embodied in the concept of a 'double melody' is by enabling a balance and equality between the words and the music. In various other kinds of song which we have considered, *im*balance and *in*equality are the rule. In the singing of narrative, for example, the story is what matters: the melody is simply a vehicle for it. On the other hand, dance-song and related forms exist primarily to realize a rhythm; even pitches are not absolutely essential, and words are little more than pretty appurtenances except in so far as they articulate the rhythm, the regular pulse, of the dance. However, nothing we have seen in the manifold utterances of poets and theorists encourages us to think that in the serious art-songs which constitute the great bulk of the surviving repertoire either the words or the music should be allowed to predominate. Indeed, the concept that has emerged of a *ratio rhythmica* awaiting its double realization in words and music positively leads to the belief in an equal alliance.

[26] See examples quoted Stevens (1974–5), 20–1.

Balance and equality are the ideal to be aimed at. But they can be completely upset, even in an isosyllabic rendering, if the relationship between the poem and the melody is wrongly conceived. Such a wrong conception vitiates, to my way of thinking, van der Werf's interpretation in his influential book of 1972.[27] In his account of 'Versification and Melody' he writes:

One cannot deny that there existed a preferred form for the poem as well as a preferred form for the melody. Neither can one deny that both forms are combined very often, but it is obvious that the authors worried very little about agreement or lack of it between the two. It is equally obvious that, in general, the melodies as they appear in the manuscripts *do not do justice to the refinements of the poem*. However, this is irrelevant because it was not the music per se but rather the performer who had to do justice to these refinements. And it is more important to conclude that with this type of melody, *performed in a declamatory rhythm*, the chansons could be performed in such a way that the melody would fit the poems perfectly.

There are three respects in which I believe this attitude to be deficient. The first is that the author evidently underrates the melodies as such (this point was discussed above, p. 40). The second is that he is too eager to find a direct relationship between melody and text; I hope my remarks above about the absence of such a relationship will have shown that such inclinations are in most instances misdirected. The third is particularly relevant in the present argument. Van der Werf says that by subordinating the melody to the declamation of the text it can be made to 'fit the poems perfectly'. He appeals to the concept of 'free rhythm':[28]

. . . we have found an abundance of reasons for assuming that the vast majority of the chansons were performed in what may be called a *free rhythm* largely dictated by the flow and meaning of the text. Somewhat more specific might be the term '*declamatory rhythm*' indicating that these songs were sung, or *recited*, in the rhythm in which one might declaim the poem without the music.

Van der Werf recommends that 'one should study first and foremost the text . . . one should develop a rendition designed not so much to sing a song but rather to recite, or declaim a poem [these, incidentally, are somewhat different procedures in themselves] to an audience while freely making many nuances in stress and duration'. An editor should not choose a style of presentation which '*risks directing too much attention towards the melody*'.[29]

---

[27] First proposed in his article 'Deklamatorischer Rhythmus' (1967), and developed in his book (1972), from which my quotation is taken (p. 68; my italics). I understand from the author that he would now wish to withdraw the term 'declamatory', whilst not abandoning his general position.

[28] Van der Werf (1972), 44 (his italics). It should be observed that he nowhere proposes an isosyllabic interpretation as such. He has in mind a 'free rhythm', which is not the same thing. He speaks of the concept of 'approximate equality' as applying only to syllabic (i.e. single-note) progression, and then 'very freely'; the question 'whether notes in a group were sung faster or more slowly than single notes' is for him a completely open one.

[29] Van der Werf (1972), 44–5 (my italics).

I have expounded this theory at some length (even though it is not entirely new) because it is an attractive one and has already found many supporters.[30] One might say it has the fatal seductiveness of the modal theory itself. It panders too easily to modern tastes; there is something here that every musical person can get hold of.[31] For myself, I am convinced that it is misconceived. It has no medieval authority; it belittles the music as such; and it upsets the balance and equality which should exist between the poem and the melody – *dox est li cans, biax est li dis* (Sweet is the melody, beautiful the verse). Of course the *dis* is important, but its importance should not be asserted at the expense of the *cans* which has its own 'sweetness'. I know of no contemporary evidence to support the idea that courtly melody was a thin, pliable, plastic medium with no personality of its own. This is certainly not the impression we get from Dante (for instance) when in Ante-purgatory he asks his friend Casella for an *amoroso canto*. The company were *tutti fissi ed attenti / a le sue note* (held in rapt attention to his music), so much so that they had to be rudely awakened – yet still, Dante says, *la dolcezza ancor dentro mi suona* (the sweetness still sounds within me).

A 'declamatory' theory not only upsets the balance but, it should be noted, makes the words prominent in the wrong way, even if their prominence were admissible. It emphasizes the speech element at the expense of the 'musical' element *in the poems themselves*, their *armonia*. In the foregoing pages I have made rather frequent appeal to this concept; I can only plead its previous neglect, not of course as a general aesthetic idea, but as an important key to the problems of words-and-music and, thence, to rhythmic interpretation. It is what at root medieval people themselves seem to have assumed song was 'about', and they use the idea not with the air of esoteric discovery or pride of philosophic speculation but, as Eloise does in this letter to Abelard, with perfect naturalness:[32]

pleraque amatoria metro vel rhythmo composita reliquisti carmina, que *ex nimia suavitate tam dictaminis quam cantus* sepius frequentata tuum in ore omnium nomen incessanter tenebant ut etiam illiteratos melodie dulcedo tui non sineret immemores esse.

You left many love-songs, written in the measured or in the syllabic style, which, being widespread *because of their great verbal and musical sweetness*, kept your name in

---

[30] E.g., Stäblein in his discussion of rhythm (p. 88–9) has lent it the authority of his approval, though this does not seem wholly consistent with his observation that only highly wrought individual melodies could keep their identity over the years as these mostly do (p. 84).

[31] Van der Werf perhaps exposes his 'expressive' assumptions when he remarks temptingly that 'performance in a really free rhythm gives an able singer the opportunity to make exclamations of joy as well as outcries of despair to any type of melody' ((1972), 69). However, there may indeed have been what one could call 'an expressiveness of the performer' (see chapter 10:III above in relation to drama) which did not manifest itself at all in basic musical terms.

[32] Ed. Monfrid (1962) p. 115, lines 198ff.

everyone's mouth, so that the mellifluousness of your melody should not allow even the uneducated to be ignorant of who you were.

The aptness, in sum, of an isosyllabic (but not inflexible, rigid or metronomic) movement to present a balanced and equal relationship between the poem and the melody cannot, surely, be doubted. The movement is near enough to formal speech not to distort the rhythmic patterns inherent in the verse and at the same time sufficiently ordered and measured to allow the melody its independent, self-directing life. No other rhythmic interpretation, as I see it, can so satisfactorily meet the just claims of the two separate arts, and so naturally represent the aesthetic of number that makes them one.

GLOSSARY

This glossary contains musical and literary terms used with some frequency in the course of the book. In selecting the musical terms to be glossed, I have had the needs of literary readers mostly in mind and *vice versa*. I have also included several common terms, such as 'mensural', 'measured', 'metrical', 'tonality', 'modality', etc., which the argument has required me to use in precisely defined senses to avoid confusion. Other terms, less in need of glossing, are given in the General Index. Fuller and more refined definitions of the musical terms will be found in Apel's *Harvard Dictionary of Music* (*HDM*) in *New Grove* etc.

accentus   A term used to describe the simplest type of chant (*see* recitation and tone below) contrasted with *concentus* which describes chants with distinctive melodies of their own.

Alleluia   Liturgically, the third chant of the Proper of the Mass. See Table, chapter 8, p. 270. Replaced in Lent by the Tract.

amice   'A linen cloth, square or oblong in shape, with strings attached' (*ODCC*) worn liturgically.

antiphon   (a) In its principal meaning a short chant sung before and after a psalm or canticle. (b) The term was, and is, used for other chants, notably for the four elaborate Marian antiphons sung at Compline (e.g. 'Alma redemptoris mater').

Antiphonal, antiphoner, antiphonary   Service-book containing the music for the Office; complementary to the Breviary which often had only the texts.

antistrophe   A repetition of a strophe, in precisely the same metrical form.

aube (Prov. *alba*)   Dawn-song.

authentic   See mode.

ballade   A term used in the fourteenth century to designate one of the three *formes fixes*. The *ballade* is characterized by high style, A A B form, and a final refrain-line. It normally has three stanzas and an envoy.

ballette, balete   The name given by the compiler of the Lorraine Chansonnier (Source 25) to a large group of songs (without music), distinct from the category of *grans chans* (*grands chants*). They have refrains but no clear single defining form.

bergerie ('sheepfold')   A pastoral poem or dramatic scene.

canticle ('little song')   A liturgical song with a Biblical text (other than a psalm), e.g. the Magnificat (the Song of the Blessed Virgin Mary).

cantio   In later medieval usage, a song on a religious subject. In the present study, a Latin song comparable in style and scope to *canso* and chanson, with no evident liturgical connection, and in this respect contrasted with *conductus* (see below).

cantus coronatus ('crowned song')   This term, used by Johannes de Grocheo to refer to a sophisticated kind of trouvère song, perhaps simply a *grand chant*, is much disputed (see chapter 12: III and note 52).

carole   A generic term for a type of dance-song characterized by a refrain or refrains and by division between chorus and soloist. The term is not used in the Middle Ages to denote a particular form, but variations on *rondeau* form occur frequently as texts.

cauda ('tail')   (a) The B section, having no fixed length or pattern, of a chanson stanza in A A B form (see also *frons* and *pes*).

(b) A textless, melismatic passage in a *conductus*, usually found at the beginning and/or at the end.

chanson-avec-des-refrains   'Chanson-with-multiple-refrains' (van der Werf): a type of *trouvère* chanson in which each stanza, though perfectly regular and conventional in other respects, has a different *refrain* (in the thirteenth-century sense – see below), which may not conform, either musically, or metrically, or logically, to the rest of the stanza.

chanson de toile ('song of weaving')   A genre of trouvère chanson (monorhymed with refrain) in which a lady sits at her loom bemoaning the absence of her sweetheart. Sometimes called *chanson d'histoire*.

chanson d'histoire   See *chanson de toile*.

climacus   A descending three- or four-note neume.

clivis   A descending two-note neume.

Communion (*communio*)   The fifth and last chant of the Proper of the Mass. See Table, chapter 8, p. 270.

Compline (*completorium*)   The last Office in the liturgical day.

concentus   See *accentus*.

conductus (plur. *conductūs* or *conducti*)   A song with a Latin text, usually to a freely composed tenor, for one, two or three voices moving chordally. In the Middle Ages and by many modern scholars the term is often used generically to mean Latin song. I restrict its use to the large corpus of songs connected with the liturgy, with festive ceremony, drama and entertainment, where its original meaning of a song connected with 'leading' (escorting) is to some extent retained, and distinguish it from *cantio* (see above).

conjunct   Of a melodic line, proceeding by steps of a tone or semitone, not by leaps.

conjunctura   A descending ligature in square notation of at least three conjunct notes; related to the neume *climacus* (see above).

contrafactum, contrafact   A song, or vocal part, to which a new set of words has been fitted – normally, in this period, with precise syllabic equivalence.

dalmatic   A liturgical garment in the form of an over-tunic reaching down to the knees.

descort   A disputed term which seems to allude to a 'discordance' of some kind (e.g. lack of predictable repetition in the *lai*; use of different languages) in the song so described.

discantus (discant)   In the oldest and simplest sense, a second voice-part composed to a *cantus* (song, normally a plainsong). The term soon came to denote the two-part composition itself.

dominant   See tenor (a), below.

double-cursus   A sequence with double-cursus is one in which a series of strophes (metrical–melodic units) is precisely repeated.

ductia   An instrumental, or at least word-less, form related to the sequence; shorter than the *stantipes* (estampie).

duplum   In early polyphony (*organum* and clausula) the voice above the tenor. In the thirteenth-century motet, when words were added to it, called the *motetus*.

episema   A short dash attached to a note or neume in early chant notation, indicating a lengthening.

estampie (Lat. *stantipes*; Prov. *estampita*)   A poetic and musical genre related in form to the sequence; it is sometimes found without words and is presumed to have been danced.

farse ('stuffing')   Vernacular term for trope (see below) and used particularly of tropes in the vernacular.

final (noun)   The last note of a melody, often used quite arbitrarily to determine 'mode'.

florilegium   An anthology.

forme fixe   The term used by modern scholars to denote a 'fixed form' in fourteenth-century lyric and song. Those normally included are *rondeau*, *virelai* and *ballade*.

frons   The first section (AA) of a chanson in AAB form; the repeated unit A is the *pes*.

goliardic metre   A line of 13 syllables with a caesura after the seventh (7pp + 6p: e.g. *Meum est propósitum/in taberna móri*).

Gradual   (a) Service-book containing the music for the Mass; complementary to the Missal, which normally had only the texts.
(b) The second chant of the Proper of the Mass. See Table, chapter 8, p. 270.

gran(d) chan(t)   The term used by trouvère-chansonnier scribes and others to refer to the courtly chanson (e.g. in the Lorraine Chansonnier). It differs from the *ballette* and the *ballade* in having five stanzas, normally, and no refrain.

hemistich   A half-line unit of verse.

heterophony   The combination together of different forms of a single melody, as in many types of Oriental music. It is sometimes argued that the accompaniment of medieval song may have taken this form of ornamental doubling.

historia   A term frequently used for the 'rhymed Office', which told the story of a saint.

homophonic   'Sounding together'; used of a composition in which the different voices move at the same time, i.e. chordally.

intonation   (a) The 'melody' of speech, its pitch contour.
(b) The opening notes (the *incipit*) of a chant melody, e.g. for the recitation of a psalm.

Introit   The first chant of the Proper of the Mass. See Table, chapter 8, p. 270.

Invitatory psalm   Psalm 94 (Vulgate) which as the first chant of Matins opens the liturgical day.

isosyllabic   Of a song, consisting of melodic units of approximately equal length, each corresponding to a single syllable of the text.

jeu-parti (Prov. *joc-partit*)   A debate-song, usually on an amorous or courtly theme, shared between two, real or imaginary, troubadours or trouvères.

jubilus   Jubilant song, characteristically without words, expressing spiritual joy; in Gregorian use, the wordless melody sung on the last syllable of the Alleluia.

lai (Ger. *Leich*)   (a) The 'lyrical' *lai*, with French or Latin text, is an extended composition with a 'free sequence' structure – that is to say, the versicles within the strophe may vary from an unrepeated single to three or four.
(b) The narrative *lai* is a short narrative poem (usually of a few hundred lines) on a romance subject.

laisse   The verse-unit of the Old French *chanson de geste*; itnnsists of an indeterminate number of lines, linked by assonance or, later, rhyme. It may incorporate a refrain.

Lauds   The second of the Office Hours. See chapter 8, list on p. 269.

lectio   Reading; lesson.

ligature   A notational symbol (in neumatic or square notation) containing two or more notes 'bound' together. The most common function of the ligature in twelfth- and thirteenth-century monophonic secular music is to indicate notes which are to be sung to the same syllable (similar to the modern slur). In the earliest neumatic notations the ligatures may have a rhythmic significance; in mensural polyphony, a metrical significance.

liquescent   A special category of modified neume indicating not only pitch (or pitch direction) but also apparently a special manner of performance. Liquescents and other neumes which ornament the melodic line are generally found in connection with diphthongs and double consonants – i.e. they are closely linked to word-sound. See *plica* below.

Matins   The first of the Office Hours. See chapter 8, list on p. 269.

measured   Of music, consisting of notes of different lengths in fixed proportion. Measured music is not necessarily written in mensural notation, nor is it necessarily metrical.

melisma; melismatic   An extensive group of notes to a single syllable of text. The most florid
types of chant are referred to as 'melismatic'.

mensural   Of musical notation, written in symbols which clearly distinguish between notes of
different lengths in fixed proportions.

metrical   Of words or of music, based on a regular time-scheme, or pattern, whether indicated
by varying duration (quantitative) or by stress/accent.
Note: I use the noun 'metre' in the general and accepted sense of the imagined abstract
pattern behind the words of a poem or the melody of a song, whether marked by
recurrence or not.

metrum   A poem or song written according to the principles of *musica metrica* – i.e. based on the
durational (quantitative) system of classical prosody; contrasted with *ritmus*. Such are the
'metres' of Boethius.

modality   See tonality below.

mode   As a melodic or harmonic term, the scale in which a piece is written. Medieval theorists
from *c.* 1000 categorize chant in eight modes, two cadencing on each of the notes *c, d, e* and
f. Each mode has in theory two forms. The 'authentic' ranges from the final to an octave
above; the 'plagal' ranges one fourth lower than the 'authentic'.

mode, rhythmic   A recurrent metrical pattern of long and short notes. The standard system of
six rhythmic modes was devised by theorists in the thirteenth century for the notation and
analysis of polyphony. The application of 'modal rhythm' to monophony is a twentieth-
century invention.

motetus   The worded (Fr. *mot*) upper voice of a polyphonic motet as distinct from its *tenor*
(normally with Latin *incipit* only). See *duplum* above.

neuma   An extended melody of a melismatic nature, often with internal repetitions; it has no
words but may be vocalized to a single vowel.

neumatic   Used by scholars of plainchant to describe a style of melody which is neither
elaborately melismatic nor purely syllabic. Most secular melodies fall into this category.
Their compound neumes normally consist of two, three or four notes.

neume   An early notational symbol used for the writing of plainchant and secular melodies. A
neume may be 'simple' (single-note) or 'compound' (formed of several notes). Most
neumes indicate pitches only directionally and not precisely; they are mnemonic rather
than fully explicit. Neumes are described as 'unheighted' ('non-diastematic') when they
lack pitch-lines or stave and are not distinguished vertically from each other.

Nocturn   One of the three sections, almost identical in form, into which the Office of Matins
is divided.

Offertory   The fourth chant of the Proper of the Mass. See Table, chapter 8, p. 270.

Office (*officium*)   A service of the 'hours' (*horae*); the eight Offices follow each other at
approximately three-hourly intervals from Matins (before dawn) to Compline (before
the night's rest). They are distinct and separate from the Mass. See chapter 8, list on
p. 269.

Officium   (a) See Office above.
            (b) Ceremony (or *ordo*).
            (c) Alternative term for Introit.

Ordinal   A liturgical service-book which gives details of the ceremonial (from Lat. *ordo,*
ceremony).

Ordinary   See Proper below.

ordo   Ceremony.

ouvert/clos   'Open/shut'. Of cadences, or phrase-ends, *ouvert* describes an 'open' ending that
implies a continuation of the melody, *clos* a 'closed' ending satisfying in itself.

para-liturgical   A term used to describe items which are 'alongside' the liturgy but not in regular, prescribed use. (The variations in 'use' between liturgical centres make the term difficult to use with precision.)

pastourelle   A type of medieval song, in Latin or a vernacular, which tells of an encounter between a knight on horseback and a shepherdess.

pes ('foot')   (a) An ascending two-note neume, also called *podatus*.

(b) Initial phrase of an A A B-chanson (see *frons* above).

plagal   See mode above.

planctus (Fr. *plainte*; Prov. *planh*)   A formal lament for the death of a historical or fictional personage. The *planctus* has no fixed form.

plica   The only liquescent sign regularly used in square notation of twelfth- and thirteenth-century secular monophony. It always follows a main note and appears to indicate a lighter note of unspecified pitch with a different timbre. It is also used in polyphonic notation.

porrectus   A three-note neume in which the middle note is the lowest.

pressus   An ornamental neume: the first reduplicated note is followed by one of lower pitch.

Proper   Collective term for those items in the Mass (beginning with the Introit) which are 'proper' to the particular occasion, as opposed to the Ordinary which consists of the invariable portions (Kyrie, Gloria, etc.).

prose, *prosa*   A verbal text for a sequence; hence, a term for the sequence itself (Fr. *prose*).

punctum ('point')   (a) The simplest neume form: a dot or short dash. It developed into the breve of mensural notation.

(b) A mark of punctuation.

puy (derivation uncertain)   A society formed to promote the writing and performance of vernacular songs (in Provençal or French); a meeting of such a society. *Puys* held regular competitions and awarded prizes.

quadratic notation   Square notation; a development from neumatic notation, in which most of the notes (liquescents excluded) are written in square form. It became standard for the copying of liturgical books throughout Europe, except in Germany.

quantitative   Of verse, measured by the duration of syllables (long and short), as distinct from 'accentual'.

quilisma   An ornamental neume, normally the second in a three-note ascending group.

razo (Prov.)   The 'reason', i.e. theme or argument, of a troubadour poem.

recitation (adj.)   I use this term to describe melodies having the general characteristic of psalmody – i.e. sung mostly at a single pitch, with intonation and cadence figures – in order to avoid the anachronistic connotations of the term 'recitative'.

refrain/*refrain* (Fr.)   (a) Usual meaning: a line or lines repeated unchanged, or slightly modified, throughout the stanzas of a strophic song.

(b) When italicized it has a special medieval meaning: a short aphorism, proverb or maxim of an amorous, courtly nature, often accompanied by a dance-like tune.

response   See versicle below.

responsion, *responsio*   A term occasionally used by musical scholars to describe the technique of melodic echo, repetition and cross-reference within a song.

Responsory (*responsorium*)   A chant, often of great complexity, sung after a lesson during an Office. Abbreviated lessons ('chapters') in certain services are however followed by short responsories.

reverdie   A song which has as its theme the renewal of the earth (and feelings of love) in spring.

rhymed Office   A type of Office especially popular *c.* 1100–1300 in which almost all the musical items (antiphons, responsories etc.) were supplied with metrical texts.

rhythm   In a general sense, the total temporal organization of a musical or verbal entity, including the effects of metre, accentuation and duration. To be distinguished from *ritmus* (*rhythmus*), below.

ritmus (rhythmus)   A poem or song written according to the principles of *musica ritmica* in which the counting of syllables predominates; contrasted with *metrum*.

romance (Ger. *Romanz*; Fr. *romance*)   The term is sometimes used to denote a short narrative lyric such as the *aube* or *chanson de toile*.

rondeau (rondel)   A variety of dance-song (see *carole* above) characterized in its simplest form by the repeat in mid-stanza of the first phrase (text and music) of a two-line refrain (A B aA ab A B).

rondellus   (a) A *rondeau* with Latin text; the form in the twelfth and thirteenth centuries is not fixed, but refrain-lines are an essential feature.

(b) A type of 3-voice polyphony, cultivated by English composers, similar to a round.

scandicus   An ascending three-note neume.

sequence   A composition based, in its so-called standard form, on 'progressive repetition': this means, musically as well as metrically, A(A) B B C C D D EE FF. . . . Each strophe (A B C etc.) may take a different metrical pattern and have a different melody. In the 'standard' sequence here designated each strophe has two versicles ('little verses').

sequentia   Strictly, a sequence melody without text. Sometimes called by the modern term *sequela*.

sirventes   A troubadour song in which the words (usually satirical, political or moral) are written to a borrowed melody.

square notation   See quadratic notation above.

stichic   Of verse, or song, consisting of single-line units.

stole   A long strip of silk worn round the neck on various liturgical occasions, especially by deacons.

strophe   In classical use, the first section of an ode, which is repeated. In the present study I use the term to refer to a metrical–musical unit, especially in relation to sequence and *lai*; these forms consist of a number of varying strophes each of which may be repeated once or more. See versicle (b) below.

strophic   Of a poem or song, consisting of identical stanzas which are repeated. (The hymn and the trouvère-chanson are both strophic forms.)

syllabic   Of a song, either (a) having a relationship of one note to a syllable, a 'single-noted' text; or (b) comprised of a mixture of single notes and short note-groups each of which is attached to a single syllable of text. A syllabic melody may or may not be isosyllabic (see above).

Tenebrae ('darkness')   Service sung on the evenings preceding the last three days of Holy Week. As the service proceeds the lights in the Church are gradually extinguished; the final psalm is sung in complete darkness.

tenor   (a) The reciting pitch of a psalm-tone and thence, by extension, the dominating note, or 'dominant', of a modal melody apart from the final. The tenor constitutes as it were a 'secondary tonal centre' (*HDM*).

(b) The lowest part in a polyphonic composition; often a borrowed melody or at least the first composed.

through-composed   A song, set to music, which does not use the device of repetition. A strophic poem may have 'through-composed' music even though its metrical shape suggests stanzaic repetition. A single stanza may also be described as 'through-composed' (Dante's *oda continuata*) if repetition is avoided.

tonality   By modern writers normally used to describe the 'classical' system of harmonic organization based on major and minor scales, and opposed to modality (a musical system based on the modes). In the present study I use a broad definition of tonality which 'includes all tonal relationships whether "tonal" or "modal"' (*HDM*).

tone   A melody used for recitation, centring on a single note, e.g. lesson-tone, psalm-tone.

tonic (adj.)   (a) Relating to verbal pitch or stress (e.g. tonic accent).

(b) The principal note in the tonal organization of a piece. In the 'classical' period identified with the tonic of the major or minor scale in which the piece is written; in medieval monophonic music usually identified with the 'final' (the last note) – an identification which is sometimes unsatisfactory.

torculus   A three-note neume in which the middle note is the highest.

Tract   See Alleluia above.

triadic   Formed of the notes of the common chord (e.g. in *c* major the notes *c e g*). The harmonic use of the triad is scarcely recognized by medieval theorists (but see *HDM*).

triplum   The third voice-part of a polyphonic motet above the *duplum* (see *motetus* above).

tritone   An interval of three tones – e.g. from *B* to *f*, or *c* to *f* sharp.

trope   (a) Literary: a figure of speech.

(b) Musical: an interpolation, textual or musical, into an already existing composition.

troper   A liturgical book containing tropes; often combined with a sequentiary.

undifferentiated   As applied to notation, a type of notation, neumatic or square, which is not designed to give clear and unambiguous indications of durational values, even though it may suggest rhythmical nuances.

Use   The term denotes the whole system of liturgical observances (texts, music and ritual) obtaining in a particular area or religious organization (e.g. the Use of Sarum; Cistercian Use).

versicle   A 'little verse': (a) liturgically, a short text answered by a response, such as – Versicle: *Tu autem, domine, miserere nobis*; Response: *Deo gracias*; (b) The repeated unit within the strophe of sequence or *lai*.

versus (*vers*)   A term of wide meaning. Apart from its more limited metrical applications (e.g. a line of verse) it was widely used, especially before *c*. 1200, to designate a new style of song principally in Latin but also in Provençal based on syllable-counting and rhyme.

Vespers, First   At some principal feasts (e.g. the Annunciation) the liturgical celebrations begin with Vespers of the preceding day, hence called First Vespers.

vida   A short 'life', i.e. biography, of a troubadour, derived for the most part from his poems.

virga ('rod')   A neume consisting at its simplest of a single vertical or oblique stroke; it developed into the long of mensural notation.

SOURCES

For the sake of clarity and memorability I have generally referred in the text and notes to the principal manuscripts which I have used by title rather than by library and shelf-number or by RISM *siglum*. Many titles are well known (e.g. The Cambridge Songs); others are, I think, fairly obvious choices (e.g. The Adam de la Halle Manuscript). The alphabetical index following this note enables the reader to find the manuscripts in the main list where they are ordered, with others, by city or town of present location.

The manuscripts are described in the main list with select bibliography; but the descriptions and bibliography are kept short since most of the information is available in fuller form elsewhere, particularly in the major *New Grove* article 'Sources, MS' (see Bibliography under Fallows). Longer lists of sources are in *Raynauds Bibliographie* (rev. Spanke 1955), in Jammers (1975) and in Stäblein (1975) to name no others. The length of the entry and the selection of references are governed not by intrinsic interest but by relevance to the present study.

1

Amiens: Bibliothèque Municipale de la Ville MS 573   fourteenth century

Lectionary from Saint-Remy d'Amiens. (See *Catalogue Général des MSS des Bibliothèques Publiques de France: Départements*, vol. XIX (Paris 1893).) The MS contains *inter alia* noted offices of Christmas and Epiphany and (fol. 193ff) 'farsed' epistles of St Stephen, St John and the Holy Innocents. The epistle for the Innocents is printed in Aubry (1906) 34–40.

2

Arras: Bibliothèque Municipale M S 657 (trouvère M S *A*)   late thirteenth century

The Chansonnier d'Arras

Three unrelated M S S bound up together. The second of these (fols. 129–60) is the chansonnier, itself an assemblage of fragments. Gennrich (*ZfrP* 46 (1926) 325) demonstrated a connection with the Chansonnier du Vatican.

Edited: Jeanroy (1925a) complete facsimile, restoring original order of M S; no transcription.

Described: *New Grove*, 'Sources M S', 639; Stevens (1981b) 33–4.

3

Bamberg, Staatliche Bibliothek, M S Lit. 115   ? late thirteenth century

The Bamberg Codex

An important source (80 fols.) of French thirteenth-century motets; also contains the *Practica artis musice* (1271) by Amerus. Provenance unknown; ? 'centre west of the Rhine' (*New Grove*).

Edited: Aubry (1908) with facsimile of whole M S and transcription.

Described: *New Grove* 'Sources', 656; R I S M (1966) 56ff. See also under Montpellier Codex (Source 19).

4

Burgos: Monasterio de Las Huelgas   *c.* 1300–*c.* 1325

The Las Huelgas M S

Large M S of mainly polyphonic music, with 45 monophonic pieces, written for the Cistercian convent of Las Huelgas.

Edited: Anglès (1931) with facsimiles and commentary.

Described: *New Grove* 'Sources', 656; R I S M (1966) 210ff.

5

Cambridge: Corpus Christi M S 473   *c.* 1000

The Winchester Troper

The earliest surviving M S of polyphony for practical use. 'Compiled mainly between *c.* 996 and 1006 for use at Winchester Cathedral, it contains music for a single singer, the cantor . . .' In this first state of the M S 'the plainchant which supplied the other voice [was] supplied from elsewhere or, more probably, from memory' (Leech-Wilkinson in Fenlon (1982) 15). Oxford, Bodleian, M S Bodley 775 (mid-eleventh century), a troped Gradual, complements the Winchester Troper.

Edited: Frere (1894) partial edn with many facsimiles.

Described: *New Grove*, 'Sources', 651, lists the numerous studies and facsimile reproductions.

6

Cambridge, Trinity College M S B.14.39   mid-thirteenth century

The Trinity Miscellany

A miscellany of English, Latin and Anglo-Norman materials, copied *c.* 1255–60 for a Franciscan community in Worcestershire (Reichl). The lyrics have no music.

Edited: With introduction and commentary, Reichl (1973).

7

Cambridge: U L Add. 710   mid-fourteenth century

The Dublin Troper

Consuetudinary (Sarum); Troper and Sequentiary; small group of mainly monophonic Latin songs; documents. The M S was in use at the cathedral of St Patrick in Dublin *c.* 1360.

Edited: Hesbert (1970), complete facsimile, introduction, incipit index etc.

Described: Hohler (1978) 35–6, n. 19 comments on Hesbert; *New Grove*, 'Sources', 632; R I S M (1964) sequences; R I S M (1966) 488–9, 'Angelus ad virginem' only; Stevens in Fenlon (1982) 79–81. Unpublished description, based on notes by R. A. B. Mynors, in Cambridge University Library (Manuscript Room).

8

Cambridge, U L M S Ff.i.17(1)   early thirteenth century

The Later Cambridge Songs

Eight leaves, possibly forming in the first instance a self-contained little songbook, but used in the fourteenth century to bind another M S (now C U L M S Ff.i.17(2)). Thirty-five Latin, including two macaronic, compositions, of which nos. 1–22 are monophonic (nine have empty staves), no. 28 is for three voices, the rest for two. Provenance: (?) Leicestershire.

Edited: *E E H* I (1897) plates 25–30, facsimile of polyphony; Lipphardt, 'Unbekannte Weisen' (1961), four facsimiles; Schumann, *Liedersammlung* (1943–50), edition of literary texts, description of M S etc.

Described: Ludwig (1910) 326; M. Lütolf, *Die mehrstimmigen Ordinarium Missae-Sätze* (Bern 1970) 46ff, gives account of M S with comments on notation and provenance; *New Grove*, 'Sources', 652; R I S M (1966) 485, polyphony; Stevens in Fenlon (1982), 40.

9

Cambridge: U L M S Gg.v.35   mid-eleventh century

The Cambridge Songs

A school-book of graded reading-matter, enlarged by one of the original scribes with, *inter alia*, the so-called 'Cambridge Songs' copied in Canterbury from a German exemplar (Lower Rhine). Two neumed songs. (A further single leaf from the M S was discovered in Frankfurt (Stadt- und Universitätsbibliothek, Fragm. lat. 1 56) by Margaret Gibson in 1981. It has since been presented to Cambridge University Library.)

Edited: Breul (1915), with facsimiles; Bulst (1950); Strecker (1926), standard text.

Described: *New Grove*, 'Sources', 637; Rigg and Wieland (1975), full description, list of contents; Stevens in Fenlon (1982) 20, with special reference to notation.

10

Florence: Biblioteca Mediceo-Laurenziana, Plut. 29.1   mid-thirteenth century

The Florence MS

This Parisian manuscript of 441 fols (originally more) is the largest single source of Notre Dame polyphony; it is also the major source for two types of Latin song. Fascicle x contains 83 monophonic *cantiones* (*conductus*); and fascicle xi, 60 monophonic *rondelli* (dance-songs).

Edited: Anderson (1978b) and (1978c), monophonic music (*cantiones* and *rondelli*) with separate literary texts and translations; Dittmer (1966–7), facsimile of whole MS; Rokseth (1947), transcribing *rondelli* only; Steiner (1964), partial edition.

Described: Anderson K1–83 and M1–60, list with bibliography for each song; Gennrich (1958), motets; Ludwig (1910), detailed listing with concordances; *New Grove*, 'Sources', 652; RISM (1966) 610ff, incipits of polyphonic items, bibliography; Steiner (1966), detailed description of milieu, authors and musical problems.

11

Kilkenny (Republic of Ireland), Episcopal Palace MS (without shelf-mark)

mid-fourteenth century

The Red Book of Ossory

The MS [*Liber Ruber Ossoriensis*] contains: diocesan documents of the See of Ossory; political documents, statutes, ordinances; and miscellaneous texts including 60 Latin poems, some with marginal jottings in English or French. Compiled at Kilkenny, 1360–5 (Stemmler).

See chapter 5: III above for editions, further description, the preface to the songs, and bibliography.

12

London: BL MS Arundel 248   early fourteenth century

The Arundel Songs

A miscellaneous manuscript containing many items of a theological, devotional and academic nature, such as Hugo de Sancto Charo on the symbolism of the Mass, a Tree of the Virtues and Vices, and an *oratio academica de modis docendi et disputandi*. Thirteen songs in English, French and Latin, in various hands. Provenance unknown.

Edited: EEH1, plates xxxii–xxxvi, eleven items in facsimile; Sanders, *PMFC* xiv (1979), four items.

Describbed: *Arundel MSS Catalogue* (1834) 73, itemization; RISM (1966) 491, with bibliography for polyphonic pieces; Stevens (1981a), notation.

13

London: BL MS Arundel 384   fourteenth century, 2nd half

The Arundel Latin Lyrics

'Written in England. Homiletic and ethical writings, ps-Ovid, *De vetula*; after the songs, excerpts of Cicero, an essay on the astrolabe, and an index to Boethius' *Consolatio*' (Dronke, 1965a). No music for the 28 poems, which belong to the period 1150–1250, but they have musical concordances.

Edited: W. Meyer (1909) full introduction and commentary.

Described: *Arundel MSS Catalogue* (1834) 112; Dronke (1965a) II.557, lists love-poems; Raby (1957) II.247, with extracts.

14

London: BL MS Egerton 274 (trouvère MS *F*)   *c.* 1250 onwards

The Egerton Chansonnier

A large assemblage of mixed material including: Latin songs and *rondelli*; tropes and sequences; the French 'chansonnier' (fols. 98–118); two longer Latin poems; miscellany of compositions with sacred Latin texts. The MS was much revised (including its notation) and corrected over a long period of years: e.g. ten chansons have French text erased and Latin responsories supplied in stanza 1. A Picard scribe wrote the chansons (Gennrich). Anselm Hughes suggests Norman–French origin (*NOHM* II.313).

Edited: Gennrich (1925) 402, description of MS, edition of French songs, one facsimile.

Described: *New Grove*, 'Sources', 639; Raynaud (1884) I.35, lists chansons; RISM (1966) 496ff.

15

London: BL MS Egerton 2615   mid-thirteenth century

The Beauvais MS

Contains the Mass and Office, much elaborated, for the Circumcision (New Year's Day) at Beauvais; and the *Ludus Danielis*. The MS was compiled *c.* 1230 but contains much earlier material.

Edited: Arlt (1970), complete edition of Circumcision Office (including all the *conductus*), study and commentary.

Described: RISM (1966), 501ff, polyphony; *New Grove*, 'Sources', 652.

16

London: BL MS Harley 978   mid-thirteenth century

The Reading Abbey MS

The well-known manuscript containing the *rota* 'Sumer is icumen in'. Although written in several sections, it was probably 'the work of a single mind' (Hohler); it contains Latin songs and textless pieces of the sequence-*lai-estampie* genre, calendar of Reading, the fables and *lais* of Marie de France, Goliardic verse, an important index of polyphony, and other items. Provenance: Reading Abbey, but reflecting wider (?University) not purely local interests.

Edited: Besseler and Gülke (1973) 44, plates 12, 13, 15, selected facsimiles. *EEH* I, plates xii–xxii, selected facsimiles.

Described: Bukofzer (1944), date, notation etc.; Handschin (1949, 1951) with discussion of all the music; Hohler (1978), extended study of provenance of MS and contents; *New Grove*, 'Sources', 658; RISM (1966) 505; Schofield, B. 'The provenance and date of "Sumer is icumen in"', *MR* 9 (1949) 81.

17

London: BL MS Harley 2253   *c.* 1330–40

The Harley Lyrics

A large collection of English and Anglo-Norman verse and prose texts, including many of the best known Middle English lyrics. The MS has no music. Provenance: Herefordshire (Ker).

Edited: N. R. Ker, *Facsimile of British Museum MS Harley 2253*, EETS (1965): facsimile of the greater part of the MS, list of contents, detailed description; Brook (1964), edition of English lyrics.

18

London: BL MS Royal 2.B.IV   ? late twelfth/thirteenth century

The St Albans Troper

Troper–sequencer. See RISM (1964), 156; Frere (1894), xxxi. Facsimiles from the MS in *Paléographie Musicale* III (1892) plate 196; Stäblein (1975) plate 42 ('Laudes crucis').

19

Montpellier: Faculté de Médecine, H196   *c.* 1270–*c.* 1300+

The Montpellier Codex

A MS of 400 fols., the major source for the French thirteenth-century motet (and thence of *refrains*); compiled over a period, possibly in Paris.

Edited: Rokseth (1935–9) facsimile of whole MS, complete edition, extensive introduction and commentary; Tischler (1978), complete edition.

Described: Boogaard (1969) index of motet-*refrains*; Gennrich (1957), bibliography of motets; (*New Grove* 'Sources', 656; RISM (1966) 272ff, list of incipits etc.

20

Montserrat: Monasterio de S. Maria   fourteenth century

The *Llibre Vermell*

The MS belonged, and still belongs, to the monastery of Montserrat near Barcelona, an important place of Marian pilgrimage; it records, amongst other details of pilgrim life at the shrine, ten songs, of which five are monophonic. See *New Grove*, 'Montserrat', and 'Spain', 784. Detailed studies listed in chapter 5 note 69 above.

21

Munich: Staatsbibliothek, MS clm 4660   thirteenth century, 1st half

The *Carmina Burana*

The most important source for medieval Latin secular lyric of the twelfth century. The manuscript also contains some German songs, Latin plays for Christmas and Easter etc. A few items have unheighted neumes. The MS presents the material more or less thematically. Provenance: ?Tyrol (Bischoff). Date: *c.* 1220–30 (Dronke).

Edited: Bischoff (1967), facsimile of whole MS with introduction; standard edition by Hilka, Schumann and Bischoff (1930–70). Parallel text edition by Fischer, Kuhn and Bernt (1979) with German translation. Musical reconstructions by Lipphardt (1955, 1961) and Machabey (1962).

Described: Dronke (1962); Dronke (1965a), list of love-poems; Raby (1953; 1957); Young (1933),the plays.

22

Orléans: Bibliothèque Municipale MS 201   twelfth/early thirteenth centuries

The Fleury Playbook

The MS is a miscellany containing homilies, other religious items, a hymn and a prose and ten 'plays'. The 'playbook' (with cursive neumes) consists of four quires (pp. 176–243) forming a separable unit that has no demonstrable connection with the rest of the manuscript. Provenance uncertain; the traditional ascription to Fleury and the recent ascription to nearby St Lhomer-de-Blois (Corbin) are both questioned.

Edited: Coussemaker (1860), transcription in modern square notation: Tintori and Monterosso (1958), facsimile of whole 'playbook', poorly reproduced, with transcriptions in contested measured notation; Young (1933) vols. I and II *passim*, prints all the texts.

Described: Albrecht (1935) ch. 6, Corbin (1953), provenance; Donovan (1970), provenance; Lipphardt, VI (1981), description (see also v.770); Rankin (1981a) II.69ff, description; Rankin (1981b), selected transcriptions, commentary.

23

Oxford: Bodleian MS Add. A.44   late-twelfth/early-thirteenth centuries

The Bekyngton Miscellany

A large *florilegium* of medieval Latin prose and verse containing amongst its 113 items extracts from, for example, Jerome; the epistle *Valerii ad Rufinum*; Walter Map; also pieces labelled *carmen metricum, carmen ritmicum, dialogus, planctus, disputatio*. No music; but over 30 concordances with the Florence MS and 15 with the *Carmina Burana*. Several items bear the name 'Eraclius'. Provenance: perhaps the Victorine house of Wigmore, W. Herefordshire. The MS belonged in the fifteenth century to Thomas Bekyngton, Bishop of Bath and Wells.

Edited: Wilmart (1941, 1956) lists contents in detail and prints selection principally of inedited poems; Raby (1957) II 356–9 (Appendix III) prints small selection.

Described: Dronke (1965a), II 568, lists love-poems; Rigg (1984), full and detailed description.

24

Oxford: Bodleian MS Douce 139   thirteenth century, 2nd half

Statutes, other legal matter, items relating to Coventry; verses; the music is not an integral part of the MS: 'Foweles in the frith' (2 voc.); textless dances (1 voc.); one motet. Provenance: ?Coventry.

Edited: *EBM* I (1901) facsimile 6; *EEH* I (1897) plate 7. See also Dobson and Harrison (1979) no. 8.

Described: RISM (1966) 535ff.

25

Oxford: Bodleian, MS Douce 308 (trouvère MS I)   early fourteenth century

The Lorraine Chansonnier

Four related MSS bound up together. The last section of the MS (fols. 147–297) contains poems without music or provision for music, arranged by genres (*grans chans*, *estampies* etc.). Still in possession of a Lorraine family in the fifteenth century (Pächt and Alexander I 46).

Edited: Steffens (1896, 1900), diplomatic edition.

Described: Raynaud (1884) I 40ff.

26
Paris: Bibliothèque de l'Arsenal, MS 5198 (trouvère MS *K*)   late thirteenth century

The Chansonnier de l'Arsenal

The MS, paginated 1–420, contains more than 500 notated songs written uniformly throughout. As a source it is closely related textually and musically to trouvère MSS *L*, *N*, *P* and *X* (see Schwan (1886); van der Werf (1977) introduction p. xi).

Edited: Aubry and Jeanroy (1909–10): facsimile of pp. 1–384 only; the transcriptions (modal) are also incomplete.

Described: *New Grove*, 'Sources', 639; Raynaud (1884), 1.54–73, list of songs.

27
Paris: BN MS fr. 146   early fourteenth century

The *Roman de Fauvel* MS

Contains the *Roman de Fauvel*, a satirical and anti-clerical romance, with musical interpolations; *dits* by Geoffroi de Paris; over 30 compositions by Jehannot de L'Escurel (*d.* 1302), all monophonic except one, an early sixteenth-century rhymed chronicle. The *Roman* was completed in 1314; the musical compositions by Chaillou de Pesstain, *c.* 1316 or slightly later. Provenance, Paris.

Edited: Aubry (1907b) facsimile of *Fauvel*; Schrade (1956) edition of polyphony from *Fauvel*; Wilkins (1966) edition of J. de L'Escurel.

Described: Boogaard (1969) lists 50 *refrains*; Gennrich *RVB* (1921) I 290ff, II 230ff; Harrison (1963), study of the monophonic music (96 items); *New Grove*, 'Fauvel' (Sanders); *New Grove*, 'Sources', 657; RISM (1969) 163ff, polyphonic items.

28
Paris: BN MS fr. 844 (trouvère MS *M* incorporating *t*)   thirteenth century

The Chansonnier du Roi

Over 550 songs, including some two-part motets, *lais* (two are in Provençal), some 50 troubadour songs, and a later section of 60 chansons by Thibaut. According to Beck, it was compiled *c.* 1250 for Charles d'Anjou, but most scholars date later. Some mensural songs amongst the later additions to the MS. The MS has been mutilated by removal of illuminations.

Edited: Beck (1938), facsimile of MS in reconstructed original order, edition and study.

Described: *New Grove*, 'Sources', 639; Raynaud (1884) 1.78ff, list of songs; RISM (1966), 374ff.

29
Paris: BN MS fr. 846 (trouvère MS O)   late thirteenth century

The Chansonnier Cangé

The MS contains about 400 songs, mostly with their music, arranged alphabetically in groups. The only trouvère chansonnier other than *Roi* to contain a number of chansons in some sort of mensural notation (see ch. 13: 11 and note 46).

Edited: Beck (1927), facsimile, edition, study.

Described: *New Grove*, 'Sources', 641; Raynaud (1884) 1 110ff; RISM (1966) 379ff.

30
Paris: BN MS fr. 12615 (trouvère MS *T*)   late thirteenth/fourteenth centuries

The Chansonnier de Noailles

The main MS contains 481 songs. Added matter includes 87 polyphonic motets, songs of Adam de la Halle and Jean de Renti, poems. Provenance unknown, but poems refer to Arras, the writing is described as of that district, Artois (Jeanroy), and Adam de la Halle was from Arras.

Edited: There is no facsimile or complete edition of the MS.

Described: Gennrich (1958), motets; *New Grove*, 'Sources', 641; Raynaud (1884) 1 153ff, lists songs; RISM (1966) 381ff, polyphony; Schwan (1896) 20ff; Stevens (1981b) 42–3.

31
Paris: BN MS fr. 20050 (trouvère MS *U*)   thirteenth century, 2nd half

The Chansonnier St Germain

The MS contains some 350 chansons (all anonymous), many with empty staves and some without provision for music; unusually among trouvère chansonniers, it has a handful of Provençal songs. Provenance unknown, but notated in Messine neumes (district of Lorraine).

Edited: Meyer and Raynaud (1892), complete facsimile; plates in Stäblein (65a, 65b) and in Jammers (10, 12).

Described: *New Grove*, 'Sources', 641; Parker (1979), with special reference to notation; Raynaud (1884) 1 172ff, lists songs; Schwan (1886) 174ff.

32
Paris: BN MS fr. 22543 (troubadour MS *R*)   *c.* 1300

The principal source of troubadour songs. Contains also *vidas*. Of the 1165 texts 696 have staves drawn for the melodies, but only 160 melodies were written in. Provenance: S. France.

Edited: de la Cuesta (1979): includes complete edition of melodies in an unmeasured transcription with diplomatic reproduction of neumes but standardized texts; Gennrich, *Nachlass*, III, IV, and XV (1958–65), diplomatic reproduction of neumes without texts; van der Werf (1984), includes complete edition of melodies in an unmeasured transcription.

Described: Beck, *Melodien* (1908), 8–14, description of MS, list of songs; de la Cuesta (1979), 35, with bibliography; *New Grove*, 'Sources', 638; Stäblein, 168 and plate 47.

33

Paris: BN MS fr. 25408   mid-thirteenth century

A miscellany written in England in 1267 containing Latin and French prose and verse. The music is added, fols. 116–120v. Three polyphonic pieces (see RISM (1966) 393) are interspersed with monophony. MS described, M. Sepet in *Bibliothèque de l'Ecole des Chartes*, 36 (1875) 139, with edition of 'Omnis caro' (text only). Music: see especially Machabey, *Notations* (1957, 1959), with transcriptions.

34

Paris: BN MS fr. 25566 (trouvère MS *W*)   late thirteenth century

The Adam de la Halle MS

Comprises two different and originally separate entities: (i) *Wx*: eight leaves containing chansons of Adam de la Halle from a lost chansonnier; (ii) *W*: a large MS containing his 'works', musical (monophonic and polyphonic) dramatic and literary, as well as much other material (an illuminated bestiary, Bodel's *St Nicholas*, the *Renart le nouvel*, etc.). Some authorities wrongly state that Adam's chansons are in 'pre-Franconian' or 'semi-mensural' notation; this cannot simply be inferred from the fact that some notes are tailed and others not.

Edited: Coussemaker (1872) and Wilkins (1967) editions of Adam's music; Marshall (1971), text edition of chansons.

Described: *New Grove*, 'Sources', 641; Raynaud (1884) I 198; RISM (1966) 395, with bibliography for polyphonic pieces; Stevens (1981b), notation.

35

Paris: BN MS lat. 1139   *c.* 1100+

A celebrated 'St Martial MS', containing in addition to liturgical items (tropes and sequences), the *Sponsus* drama, Procession of Prophets, Lament of Rachel, *conductus, versus*, Song of the Sibyl. From the region of Limoges; 1096–1100 with thirteenth-century additions. Late Aquitanian unmeasured notation.
   There is no edition of the MS, but many individual items are edited.

Described: Chailley (1960) 109ff, in detail (as MS *U*); *New Grove*, 'St Martial' and 'Sources', 625; Spanke (1930, 1932), lists contents (1930: 287–304).

36

Paris: BN MS lat. 1154   ninth/tenth centuries

The earliest of the so-called St Martial MSS. Probably from the abbey of St Martin, Limoges. For details of the 'song-section' (fols. 98v–142), see chapter 2, above, introductory section and note 3.

37

Paris: BN MS lat. 15131   late thirteenth century

A miscellany of educational, philosophical and other material compiled perhaps by a clerk teaching in the monastery of St Victor. The last two gatherings (fols. 177ff) contain a small collection of Latin *rondelli* and similar verses, some with French *refrains* attached to them. See chapter 5: III above and note 66.

38

Rome: Vatican MS Reg. lat. 1490 (trouvère MS *a*)   ? early fourteenth century

The Chansonnier du Vatican

Songs arranged by genre, including motets; the monophonic *rondeaux* of Guillaume d'Amiens; *chancons de Nostre Dame*; etc. Mutilated. See Chansonnier d'Arras (Source 2).

Edited: Monaci, *Facsimili di antichi manuscritti* (Rome 1881), *Facsimili di documenti* (Rome 1911), some facsimiles.

Described: *New Grove*, 'Sources', 643; Raynaud (1884) 1 219ff; RISM (1966) Stevens (1981b) 34–6.

39

Siena: Biblioteca Comunale H.x.36 (trouvère MS *Z*)   *?c.* 1300

The Siena Chansonnier

Contains 100 songs with music and one without. No other contents. Provenance unknown.

Edited: Spaziani (1957), text and translation; Steffens (1892), diplomatic edition of text.

Described: Raynaud (1884) 1 237; *New Grove*, 'Sources', 642.

40

Wolfenbüttel: Herzog-August-Bibliothek, Helmstedt 628   mid-thirteenth century

The Wolfenbüttel MS (W₁)

Large collection of *organa*, clausulas, polyphonic *conductus* and tropes; three monophonic *conductus*. A principal source of early polyphony, but not of monophony. ?St Andrews (Scotland).

Edited: Baxter (1931), facsimile; Waite (1954), partial edition.

Described: Ludwig (1910); *New Grove*, 'Sources', 653; RISM (1966) 97ff; Roesner (1974), detailed study and bibliography.

Manuscripts also referred to

Admont, Abbey Lib. MS 759: p. 418 n. 9; p. 419. **Aix-en-Provence**, Bibl. Méjanes MS 572: p. 176 n. 49; p. 224 n. 68. **Aix-la-Chapelle** MS 13: p. 100 n. 31. **Amiens**, Bibl. de la Ville MS 573 (Source 1: p. 245 n. 20. **Angers**, Bibl. Mun. MS 477: p. 51 n. 11. **Cambridge**, Gonville and Caius College MS 11: p. 174 n. 38. Gonville and Caius College MS 54: p. 174 n. 39. Gonville and Caius College MS 240: p. 144 n. 60. Trinity College MS B. 11. 13: p. 321 n. 36. Trinity College MS O. 3. 58: p. 198 n. 107. UL MS I. i. 3: p. 18 n. 21. UL MS Dd. 1. 15: p. 322 n. 38.

Chartres MS 520 (destroyed): p. 239; p. 240 n. 12. **Cividale**, Reale Museo Archeologico MS CI: p. 367 n. 45. **Clermont-Ferrand** MS 240: p. 238 n. 9; p. 239. **Darmstadt** MS 2663: p. 429 n. 42. **Evreux**, Bibl. Mun. MS 2: p. 130 n. 40. **Frankfurt**, Stadt. Bibl. MS olim 29: p. 451 n. 46. **Graz**, UB MS 807: p. 293 n. 60. **Hereford**, Cathedral Close MS P. 3. 3: p. 173 n. 36. **Karlsruhe**, Badische Landesbibliothek MS St Georgen 38: p. 455 n. 60. Badische Landesbibliothek MS Lichenthal 60: p. 89 n. 8. **Laon**, Bibl. Mun. MS 239: p. 301 n. 77. Bibl. Mun. MS 263: p. 91 n. 23.

BIBLIOGRAPHY

The bibliography is intended principally as a finding list for works referred to in the course of the book by author or by author and date. It does not attempt to be comprehensive. I have, however, included a number of other books and articles which I have found helpful, especially works of reference and editions. Dictionary articles are listed only when they are both substantial and central to the concerns of this book.

Aarburg, U. (1957) 'Muster für die Edition mittelalterlicher Liedmelodien', *Mf* 10 (1957) 209–217

——— (1958) 'Ein Beispiel zur mittelalterlicher Kompositionstechnik', *AMw* 15 (1958) 20–40

Adank, T. 'Roger Bacons Auffassung der Musica', *AMw* 35 (1978) 33–56

Adler, G., ed. *Handbuch der Musikgeschichte*, Frankfurt 1924, revised edn 1930

Albrecht, O. E. *Four Latin Plays of St Nicholas from the 12th-century Fleury Playbook.* Philadelphia 1935

Analecta Hymnica medii aevi, ed. G. M. Dreves, C. Blume, H. M. Bannister, 58 vols. Leipzig 1886–1922

——— *Analecta hymnica medii aevi – Register*, ed. M. Lütolf with D. Baumann, 2 vols. in 3. Bern 1978

Anderson, G. A. 'Notre-Dame and related conductus: a catalogue raisonné', *Miscellanea Musicologica* 6 (1972) 153–229; 7 (1975) 1–81 [cited in the text and notes (without date) as 'Anderson K79', etc.]

——— (1973) 'The rhythm of *cum littera* sections of polyphonic conductus in mensural sources', *JAMS* 26 (1973) 288–304

——— ed. (1976) *The Compositions of the Bamberg Manuscript.* CMM 75. 1976

——— (1978a) *The Las Huelgas Manuscript: Burgos, Monasterios de las Huelgas.* CMM 69: II, Motetti et Conductus. 1978

——— ed. (1978b) *Notre-Dame and related conductus: Opera Omnia,* VI: 1 pt. *Conductus – Transmitted in fascicule X of the Florence Manuscript.* Institute of Medieval Music [1978]

——— ed. (1978c) *Notre-Dame and related conductus: Opera Omnia,* VIII: 1 pt. *Conductus – The Latin Rondeau Repertoire.* Institute of Medieval Music [1978]

——— (1978d) 'The rhythm of the monophonic conductus in the Florence MS as indicated in parallel sources in mensural notation', *JAMS* 31 (1978) 480–9

Anglès, H., ed. (1931) *El Codex musical de Las Huelgas. (Música a Veus dels Segles XIII–XIV)*, 3 vols. Barcelona 1931 [facs.]

——— (1935) *La Música a Catalunya fins al segle XIII.* Barcelona 1935

——— ed. (1943–58) *La música de las Cantigas de Santa María del Rey Don Alfonso el Sabio,* 3 vols. Barcelona 1943–58 [facs.]

——— (1955) 'El *Llibre Vermell* de Montserrat y los cantos y la danza sacra de los peregrinos durante el siglo xiv', *Anuario Musical* 10 (1955) 45–78

——— (1975) *Scripta Musicologica*, ed. I. López-Calo, 3 vols. Rome 1975

Anonymus IV: see Reckow

Antiphonale Monasticum pro diurnis horis. Rome 1934

Antonio da Tempo   *Delle rime volgari*, ed. G. Grion. Bologna 1869

Apel, W. (1961)   *The Notation of Polyphonic Music: 900–1600.* Cambridge, Mass., 1942; 5th edn (rev.) 1961

——— (1954)   'Rondeaux, Virelais and Ballades in French 13th-century Song', *JAMS* 7 (1954) 121–30

——— (1958)   *Gregorian Chant.* Bloomington, Ind., 1958

Appel, C. ed. (1915)   *Bernart von Ventadorn, seine Lieder mit Einleitung und Glossar.* Halle 1915

——— (1934)   'Die Singweisen Bernarts von Ventadorn', *Beihefte zur ZfrP* 81 (1934) 1–43

Aribo: see Smits van Waesberghe (1951)

Arlt, W. (1970)   *Ein Festoffizium des Mittelalters aus Beauvais in seiner liturgischen und musikalischen Bedeutung*, 2 vols. Cologne 1970

——— (1978)   'Einstimmige Lieder des 12. Jahrhunderts und Mehrstimmiges in französischen Handschriften des 16. Jahrhunderts aus Le Puy', *Schweizer Beiträge zur Musikwissenschaft* 3 (1978) 7–47

Aubry, P., ed. (1905)   *Les plus anciens monuments de la musique française.* Mélanges de Musicologie critique IV Paris 1905 [facs.]

——— (1906)   *La musique et les musiciens de l'église en Normandie au XIIIe siècle.* Paris 1906

——— ed. (1907a)   *Estampies et danses royales: Les plus anciens textes de musique instrumentale au moyen-âge.* Paris 1907

——— ed. (1907b)   *Le Roman de Fauvel.* Paris 1907

——— ed. (1908)   *Cent motets du XIIIe siècle.* Paris 1908 [facs. of Bamberg Codex]

——— (1909)   *Trouvères et Troubadours.* Paris 1909, 2nd edn (rev.) 1910. Engl. transln 1914

Aubry, P. and Jeanroy, A. ed.   *Le chansonnier de l'Arsenal: reproduction phototypique: transcription du texte musical en notation moderne.* Paris 1909–10

Aucassin et Nicolette: see Bourdillon; Roques; Matarasso [transl.]

Augustine, St.   *De Musica libri sex (Oeuvres de Saint Augustin, VII)*, ed. G. Finaert and F.-J. Thonard. Bruges 1947

Aurelian of Réôme: see Gushee; Ponte [transl.]

Axton, R.   *European Drama of the Early Middle Ages.* London 1974

Axton, R., and Stevens, J., transl.   *Medieval French Plays.* Oxford 1971

Babb, W., transl., and Palisca, C. V., ed.   *Hucbald, Guido, and John on Music: Three Medieval Treatises.* New Haven 1978

Baldwin, C. S.   *Medieval Rhetoric and Poetic (to 1400).* London 1928; repr. 1959

Barth, P. M., Ritscher, M. Immaculata, and Schmidt-Görg, J., ed.   *Hildegard von Bingen. Lieder.* Salzburg 1969

Bartsch, K. (1868)   *Die lateinischen Sequenzen des Mittelalters.* Rostock 1868; repr. 1968

——— ed. (1870)   *Altfranzösische Romanzen und Pastourellen.* Leipzig 1870

Basler Jahrbuch für historische Musikpraxis, ed. W. Arlt. Winterthur 1978

Baum, R.   'Le descort ou l'anti-chanson', in *Mélanges de philologie romane, dédiés à la mémoire de Jean Boutière*, ed. I. Cluzel and F. Pirot, 2 vols. (Liège 1971) I. 75

Baxter, J. H., ed.   *An Old St Andrew's Music Book*, Cod. Helmst. 624 [W₁]. Oxford 1931 [facs.]

Bec, P. (1961)   *Petite anthologie de la lyrique occitane du moyen âge: initiation à la langue et à la poésie des troubadours.* Avignon 1961

——— (1977–8)   *La lyrique française au moyen âge (xiie–xiiie siècles). Contribution à une typologie des genres poétiques médiévaux*, 2 vols. Paris 1977–8

Beck, J. B. (1908)   *Die Melodien der Troubadours.* Strasbourg 1908

——— (1910)   *La musique des troubadours.* Paris 1910

—— ed. (1927) *Le Chansonnier Cangé*. Corpus Cantilenarum Medii Aevi, ser. I. 2 vols. Paris 1927 [facs.]

—— and Beck, L., ed. *Le manuscrit du Roi*, Corpus Cantilenarum Medii Aevi, ser. II. 2 vols. Paris 1938

Bede. *De arte metrica*, ed. H. Keil, in *Grammatici latini* VII (Leipzig 1880), pp. 227–60

Bédier, J. (1896) 'Les fêtes du mai', *Revue des Deux Mondes* 135 (1896) 146–72

—— (1906) 'Les plus anciennes danses françaises', *Revue des Deux Mondes* 76 (1906) 398–424

—— ed. (1912, 1938) *Les chansons de Colin Muset*, avec la transcription des mélodies par Jean Beck. CFMA, Paris 1912; 2nd edn 1938 [(enlarged), without music]

—— and Aubry, P. *Les chansons de croisade*. Paris 1909

Beowulf and The Fight at Finnsburg, ed. Fr. Klaeber, 3rd edn (with supplements), London 1950

Bergin, T. G. *Anthology of the Provençal Troubadours*. 2nd edn (rev. and enlarged), New Haven 1974

Bernhard, M. *Studien zur Epistola de armonica institutione des Regino von Prüm*. Munich 1979

Bertau, K. H. (1964) *Sangverslyrik. Über Gestalt und Geschicklichkeit mittelhochdeutscher Lyrik am Beispiel des Leichs*. Göttingen 1964

—— (1965) 'Epenrezitation im deutschen Mittelalter', *Etudes germaniques* 20 (1965) 1–17

—— and Stephan, R. 'Zum sanglichen Vortrag mittelhochdeutscher strophischer Epen', *ZfdA* 87 (1957) 253–70

Besseler, H., and Gülke, P. *Schriftbild der mehrstimmigen Musik*. Musikgeschichte in Bildern, ed. W. Bachmann, III: 5. Leipzig 1973

Biber, W. *Das Problem der Melodieformeln in der einstimmigen Musik des Mittelalters*. Bern 1951

Bielitz, Mathias. *Musik und Grammatik*. Munich 1977

Birnbaum, S. H., transl. *Johannes de Garlandia: Concerning Measured Music*. Colorado Springs 1978

Bischoff, B. (1960) 'Gottschalks Lied für den Reichenauer Freund', in *Medium Aevum vivum. Festschrift für Walther Bulst*, ed. H. R. Jauss and D. Schaller (Heidelberg 1960), pp. 61–8

—— ed. (1967) *Carmina burana: Faksimile-Ausgabe der Hs. Clm 4660 und Clm 4660a*. Brooklyn, NY 1967

Boogaard, N. H. J. van den *Rondeaux et refrains du XIIᵉ au début du XIVᵉ siècle*. Paris 1969

de Boor, H. A. W. *Die Textgeschichte der lateinischen Osterfeiern*. Tübingen 1967

Boorman, S., ed. *Studies in the Performance of Late Medieval Music*. Cambridge 1983

Bosworth, J. and Toller, T. N. *An Anglo-Saxon Dictionary*. London 1898; Suppl. 1921

Bourdillon, F. W., ed. *C'est d'Aucasin et de Nicolete*. Oxford 1896 [facs.]

Bragard, R. ed. *Speculum Musice*, books 1–5, CSM, III (Rome, 1955–68)

Brault, G. J., ed. *The Song of Roland: An Analytical Edition*, University Park, PA, 1978

Breul, K. H., ed. *The Cambridge Songs: A Goliard's Songbook of the Eleventh Century*. Cambridge 1915 [with facs.]

Bronarski, L. *Die Lieder der hl. Hildegard: Ein Beitrag zur Geschichte der geistlichen Musik des Mittelalters*. Leipzig 1922; repr. 1973

Brook, G. L., ed. *The Harley Lyrics*. Manchester 1948, 3rd edn 1964

Brunetto Latini *Li Livres dou Tresor*, ed. F. J. Carmody. Berkeley and Los Angeles 1948

Brunner, H. 'Epenmelodien', in *Formen mittelalterlicher Literatur* [Festschrift. Siegfried Beyschlag] (Göppingen 1970), pp. 149–78

Bruyne, E. de *Etudes d'esthétique médiévale*, 3 pts. Bruges 1946

Bukofzer, M. F. (1944) '"Sumer is icumen in", A Revision', in *University of California Publications in Music* 11.2 (Berkeley and Los Angeles 1944), pp. 79–114

—— (1953) 'Interrelations between Conductus and Clausula', *AnnM* 1 (1953) 65–103

Bullock-Davies, C. (1973) 'The Form of the Breton Lay', *MÆ* 42 (1973) 18–31

——— (1978) *Menestrallorum Multitudo: Minstrels at a Royal Feast*. Cardiff 1978

Bulst, W., ed. *Carmina Cantabrigiensa*. Heidelberg 1950

Butler, C. *Number Symbolism*. London 1970

Butler, H. E., ed. and transl. *Quintilian: Institutionis oratoriae libri xii*. 6th edn, Cambridge, Mass., 1965

Cable, T. *The Meter and Melody of Beowulf*. Urbana, Illinois 1974

Caldwell, J. *Medieval Music*. London 1978

Carmina Burana: see Hilka, Schumann and Bischoff [all references are to this edition]

Cardine, Dom E. *Sémiologie grégorienne*. Rome 1968; French transl. 1970

Carter, H. H. *A Dictionary of Middle English Musical Terms*. Bloomington, Ind., 1961

Cassiodorus: see Mynors

Cattin, G. *Il Medioevo I*. Storia della Musica I. Turin 1979. English edn: *Music of the Middle Ages I*, transl. S. Botterill. Cambridge 1984

Chadwick, H. *Boethius: the Consolations of Music, Logic, Theology and Philosophy*. Oxford 1981

Chailley, J. (1948) 'Etudes musicales sur la chanson de geste et ses origines', *RdM* 17 (1948) 1–27

——— (1950a, 1969) *Histoire musicale du Moyen Age*. Paris 1950; 2nd edn 1969

——— (1950b) 'La nature musicale du *Jeu de Robin et Marion*', in *Mélanges . . . G. Cohen* (Paris 1950), pp. 111–17

——— (1955a) 'Autour de la chanson de geste', *AcM* 27 (1955) 1–12

——— (1955b) 'Les premiers troubadours et les *versus* de l'école d'Aquitaine', *Romania* 76 (1955) 212–39

——— (1959) *Les chansons à la vierge de Gautier de Coinci*. Paris 1959

——— (1960) *L'Ecole musicale de Saint Martial de Limoges jusqu'à la fin du XIe siècle*. Paris 1960

Chambers, E. K. *The Medieval Stage*. Oxford 1903

Chartier, Y. 'L'Epistola de armonica institutione de Réginon de Prüm', diss., University of Ottawa 1965

Chaucer: see Robinson

Chaytor, H. J. *The Troubadours and England*. Cambridge 1923

Chevalier, C. U. J. *Repertorium Hymnologicum*, 6 vols. Louvain 1892–1920

Clemoes, P. 'Liturgical influence on punctuation in late Old English and early Middle English M S S'. Cambridge University Department of Anglo-Saxon *Occasional Papers* no. 1. Cambridge 1952

Colson, F. H., ed. *M. Fabii Quintiliani Institutionis Oratoriae Liber I*. Cambridge 1924

Corbin, S. (1953) 'Le ms 201 d'Orléans: drames liturgiques dits de Fleury', *Romania* 74 (1953) 1–43

——— (1977) *Die Neumen. Palaeographie der Musik*, ed. W. Arlt, I: 3. Cologne 1977

Coussemaker, E. de (1852) *Histoire de l'harmonie au moyen âge*. Paris 1852

——— (1860) *Drames liturgiques du moyen-âge*. Rennes 1860; repr. 1964

——— ed. (1864–76) *Scriptores de musica medii aevi*, 4 vols. Paris 1864–76

——— ed. (1872) *Oeuvres complètes du trouvère Adam de la Halle: poésies et musique*. Paris 1872; repr. 1965

Crocker, R. L. (1958a) 'Musica Rhythmica and Musica Metrica in antique and medieval theory', *JMT* 2 (1958) 2–23

——— (1958b) 'The repertory of proses at St Martial de Limoges in the 10th century', *JAMS* 11 (1958) 149–64

——— (1966a) *A History of Musical Style*. New York 1966

——— (1966b) 'The Troping Hypothesis', *MQ* 52 (1966) 183–203

——— (1973) 'The Sequence', in *Gattungen* (q.v.), pp. 269–322

——— (1977) *The Early Medieval Sequence*. Berkeley and London 1977

Cuesta, I. F. de la, and Lafont, R. ed. *Las cançons dels trobadors*. Institut d'estudis occitans. Toulouse 1979

Curtius, E. R. *European Literature and the Latin Middle Ages*, transl. W. R. Trask. London 1953

Dante. *Le opere di Dante*, ed. M. Barbi et al. Testo critico dell Società Dantesca Italiana. 2nd edn, Florence 1960

——— see also Marigo

Davenson, H. [pseud. of Henri Marrou]. *Les Troubadours*. Paris 1961; rev. 1971

Dick, A., ed. *Martianus Capella. De nuptiis Philologiae et Mercurii*. Leipzig 1925; rev. edn 1969

Dictionnaire des lettres françaises: Le Moyen Age, ed. R. Bossuat, L. Pichard, G. Raynaud de Lage. Paris (1964)

Dittmer, L., ed. *Faksimile-Ausgabe der Hs Firenze, Biblioteca Mediceo-Laurenziana Pluteo 29, 1*. Institute of Medieval Music. Brooklyn n.d. 1966–67

Dobson, E. J., and Harrison, F. Ll., ed. *Medieval English Songs*. London 1979

Dolan, D. *Le drame liturgique de Pâques en Normandie et en Angleterre au moyen âge*. Paris 1975

Donovan, R. B. *The Liturgical Drama in Medieval Spain*. Toronto 1958

Dragonetti, R. *La technique poétique des trouvères dans la chanson courtoise*. Bruges 1960

Dronke, P. (1962) 'A critical note on Schumann's dating of the Codex Buranus', *Beiträge zur Geschichte der deutschen Sprache und Literatur* 84 (1962) 173

——— (1965a) *Medieval Latin and the Rise of the European Love-Lyric*, 2 vols. Oxford 1965; 2nd (corr.) edn 1968

——— (1965b) 'The beginnings of the sequence', *Beiträge zur Geschichte der deutschen Sprache und Literatur* 87 (1965) 43–73

——— (1968) *The Medieval Lyric*. London 1968; 2nd edn 1978 [with extended bibliography]

——— (1970) *Poetic Individuality in the Middle Ages*. Oxford 1970

——— (1973) 'The Rise of the Medieval Fabliau', *Romanische Forschungen* 85 (1973) 275–97

——— (1979) 'The Song of Songs and Medieval Love-Lyric', in *The Bible and Medieval Culture*, ed. W. Lourdaux and D. Verhelst (Leyden 1979), 236–62

EBM Early Bodleian Music, ed. J. Stainer (with J. F. R. and E. C. Stainer). London 1901 [facs.]

EEH Early English Harmony from the 10th to the 15th Century, ed. H. E. Wooldridge, 2 vols. PMMS. London 1897 and 1913

Ellinwood, L. 'The conductus', *MQ* 27 (1941) 165–204

Falck, R. (1967) 'Zwei Lieder Philipps des Kanzlers und ihre Vorbilder: neue Aspekte musikalischer Entlehnung in der mittelalterlichen Monodie', *AMw* 24 (1967) 81–98

——— (1981) *The Notre Dame Conductus: A Study of the Repertory*. MSD xxxiii. Institute of Medieval Music. 1983

Fallows, D. 'Lai' in *New Grove* (1980) [list of *lais* in French, German and Provençal]

——— 'Sources, MS', sect. III, *New Grove* (1980) [lists and describes sources in Latin and six vernaculars]

Faral, E. (1910) *Les Jongleurs en France au moyen âge*. Paris 1910

——— (1958) *Les arts poétiques du XIIe et du XIIIe Siècles*. Paris 1958

Farmer, D. H. *The Oxford Dictionary of Saints*. Oxford 1978

Fenlon, I., ed. (1982) *Cambridge Music Manuscripts 900–1700*. Cambridge 1982

Ferretti, P. *Esthétique Grégorienne*. Tournai 1938

Finnegan, R. *Oral Poetry: Its Nature, Significance and Social Context*. Cambridge 1977

Fischer, C., Kuhn, H., and Bernt, G. ed. *Carmina Burana: Die Lieder der Benediktbeurer Handschrift. Zweisprachige Ausgabe*. Munich 1979

Fischer, K., von 'Die Passion von ihren Anfängen bis ins 16. Jahrhundert', in *Gattungen* [q.v.]

Flotzinger, R. 'Zur Frage der Modal-rhythmik als Antike-Rezeption', *AMw* 29 (1972) 203–8

Foster, K., and Boyde, P. ed. *Dante's Lyric Poetry*, 2 vols. Oxford 1966

Frank, I. *Repertoire Métrique de la Poésie des Troubadours*. Bibliothèque de l'Ecole des Hautes Etudes, 303 and 308. Paris 1953 and 1957

Frere, W. H., ed. (1894) *The Winchester Troper, from MSS of the Xth and XIth Centuries*. Henry Bradshaw Society VIII. London 1894

———— (1898–1901) *The Use of Sarum*, 2 vols. Cambridge 1898 and 1901

Gallo, F. A. (1972) 'Philological Works on Music Treatises of the Middle Ages', *AcM* 44 (1972) 78–101

———— (1977) *Il Medioevo II*. Storia della Musica II. Turin 1977. English edn: *Music of the Middle Ages II*. transl. K. Eales. Cambridge 1985

Gatien-Arnoult, A. F., ed. *Las Flors del gay saber, estier dichas Las Leys d'amors*, 4 pts. Monuments de la littérature romane I–III. Toulouse 1841–3

Gattungen der Musik in Einzeldarstellungen: Gedenkschrift Leo Schrade, ed. W. Arlt and others. Bern 1973

Gennrich, F. ed. (1921, 1927, 1963) *Rondeaux, Virelais und Balladen*, 3 vols. Dresden 1921, Göttingen 1927, Langen 1963

———— (1923) *Der musikalische Vortrag der altfranzösischen Chansons de geste*. Halle 1923

———— (1926) 'Die altfranzösische Liederhandschrift, London British Museum Egerton 274', *ZfrP* 45 (1926) 402–44

———— (1926–7) 'Trouvèrelieder und Motettenrepertoire', *ZMw* 9 (1926–7) 8–39, 65–85

———— (1928–9) 'Internationale mittelalterliche Melodien', *ZMw* 11 (1928–9) 259–96, 321–48

———— (1930) 'Lateinische Kontrafakta altfranzösischer Lieder', *ZfrP* 50 (1930) 187–207

———— (1932) *Grundriss einer Formenlehre des mittelalterlichen Liedes als Grundlage einer musikalischen Formenlehre des Liedes*. Halle (Saale) 1932

———— (1955) 'Ist der mittelalterliche Liedvers arhythmisch?' *Cultura neolatina* 15 (1955) 109

———— (1956) *Lateinische Liedkontrafaktur*. Studien-Bibliothek XI. Darmstadt 1956

———— (1958) *Bibliographie der ältesten französischen und lateinischen Motetten*. Darmstadt 1958

———— ed. (1958–65) *Der musikalische Nachlass der Troubadours*. Summa Musicae Medii Aevi III, IV, XV. Darmstadt 1958–65

———— ed. (1962) *Le Jeu de Robin et de Marion. Li Rondel Adam*. Studien-Bibliothek XX. Langen 1962

Gerbert, M. ed. *Scriptores ecclesiastici de musica sacra*, 3 vols. St Blasien 1784; repr. Milan 1931

Gérold, T. *La Musique au moyen âge*. CFMA. Paris 1932

Gmelch, J., ed. *Die Kompositionen der heiligen Hildegard*. Düsseldorf 1913 [facs.]

Goede, N. de, ed. *The Utrecht Prosarium*. Monumenta musica Neerlandica. Amsterdam 1965

Goldin, F., transl. *Lyrics of the Troubadours and Trouvères* [with original texts]. New York 1973

Gordon, R. K., transl. *Anglo-Saxon Poetry*. rev. edn, London 1954

Gougaud, L. 'La danse dans les églises', *Revue Historique Écclésiastique* 15 (1914) 5–22; 229–45

Graduale Triplex. Solesmes 1979 [the *Graduale Romanum* (Solesmes 1974) augmented with the neumes of Laon 239 and other early MSS]

Graduel Neumé, ed. Dom E. Cardine. Solesmes 1972 [based on *Graduale sacrosanctæ Romanæ ecclesiæ* (Rome 1908)]

Greene, R. L., ed. (1974) *The Lyrics of the Red Book of Ossory*. Medium Ævum Monographs n.s. V. Oxford 1974

———— ed. (1977) *The Early English Carols*. 2nd edn (rev. and enlarged), Oxford 1977

Grion: see Antonio da Tempo

Gröninger, E. *Repertoire-Untersuchungen zum mehrstimmigen Notre Dame Conductus*. Kölner Beiträge zur Musikforschung II. Regensburg 1939

Guido of Arezzo: see Smits van Waesberghe (1955); Babb and Palisca [transl.]

Gushee, L. A. 'Questions of Genre in Medieval Treatises on Music', in *Gattungen* (q.v.), p. 365–433

——— ed. *Aurelianus Reomensis: Musica Disciplina.* CSM xxi (1975)

Hammerstein, R.   *Die Musik der Engel: Untersuchungen zur Musikanschauung des Mittelalters.* Bern 1962

Hammond, F. F., ed.   *Walteri Odington De Speculatione Musicae.* CSM xiv. n.p. 1970

Handschin, J. (1929–30, 1930–1) 'Über Estampie und Sequenz', *ZMw* 12 (1929–30) 11, 13 (1930–1) 113

——— (1935) 'Die Modaltheorie und Carl Appels Ausgabe der Gesänge von Bernart de Ventadorn', *MÆ* 4 (1935) 69–82 [see also *AcM* 20 (1948) 62]

——— (1949, 1951)   'The Summer Canon and its Background', *MD* 3 (1949) 55–94, 5 (1951) 65–113

——— (1952)   'Conductus-Spicilegien', *AMw* 9 (1952) 101–119

——— (1954) 'Trope, Sequence and Conductus' in *NOHM* ii. 128–74

Hardison, O. B., jr.   *Christian Rite and Christian Drama in the Middle Ages.* Baltimore 1965

Harley Lyrics: see Brook

Harrison, F. Ll. (1958)   *Music in Medieval Britain.* London 1958

——— (1979): see Dobson and Harrison

Harrison, G. A.   'The Monophonic Music in the *Roman de Fauvel*', diss. Stanford University 1963

HDM   *Harvard Dictionary of Music*, ed. W. Apel, 2nd edn (rev.), London 1970

Hesbert, R. J. (1963–75)   *Corpus antiphonalium officii*, 6 vols. Rome 1963–79

——— ed. (1966)   *Le Tropaire-Prosaire de Dublin: MS Add. 710 de l'Université de Cambridge (vers 1360).* Monumenta Musicae Sacrae iv. Rouen 1970

Hildegard von Bingen: see Barth, P. M., *et al.*

Hilka, A., Schumann, O., and Bischoff, B., ed.   *Carmina Burana.* 3 vols Heidelberg 1930–70

Historical Anthology of Music, i: *Oriental, Medieval and Renaissance Music*, ed. A. T. Davison and W. Apel. Oxford 1947; rev. edn Cambridge, Mass. 1948

HMT   *Handwörterbuch der musikalischen Terminologie*, ed. H. H. Eggebrecht with F. Reckow. Wiesbaden 1972

Hoepffner, E., and Alfaric, P. ed.   *La Chanson de Sainte Foy*, 2 vols. Paris 1926

Hohler, C.   'Reflections on some manuscripts containing 13th-century polyphony', *JPMMS* 1 (1978) 2–38

Holschneider, A.   *Die Organa von Winchester: Studien zum ältesten Repertoire polyphoner Musik.* Hildesheim 1968

Hopper, V. F.   *Medieval Number Symbolism.* New York 1938

Hoppin, R. H.   *Medieval Music.* New York 1978

——— ed.   *Anthology of Medieval Music.* New York 1978

Hucke, H.   'Toward a new historical view of Gregorian chant', *JAMS* 33 (1980) 437–67

Huff, J. A.   transl. *Walter Odington 'De Speculatione Musicae' Part IV* MSD 31 Rome 1973

Hughes, Andrew (1970) 'The *Ludus super Anti-claudianum* of Adam de la Bassée', *JAMS* 23 (1970) 1–25

——— (1974)   *Medieval Music: The Sixth Liberal Art.* Toronto Medieval Bibliographies iv. Toronto 1974

Hughes, Dom Anselm. 'In hoc anni circulo', *MQ* 60 (1974) 37–45

Hughes, D. G. (1972)   'Music for St Stephen at Laon', in *Words and Music: the Scholar's View: a medley of problems and solutions compiled in honour of A. Tillman Merritt.* ed. L. Berman (Cambridge, Mass., 1972), pp. 137–59

——— (1976)   'Music and Meter in Liturgical Poetry', *Medievalia et Humanistica* n.s. vii ed. P. M. Clogan (Cambridge, 1976): *Medieval Poetics*, pp. 29–43

Huglo, M.   'Tradition orale et tradition écrite dans la transmission des mélodies grégoriennes', in *Studien zur Tradition in der Musik* [Festschrift Kurt von Fischer], ed. H. H. Eggebrecht and M. Lütolf (Munich 1973), pp. 31–42

Husmann, H. (1952a) 'Zur Grundlegung der musikalischen Rhythmik des mittellateinischen Liedes'. *A Mw* 9 (1952) 3–26

—— (1952b) 'Zur Rhythmik des Trouvère-gesanges', *Mf* 5 (1952) 110–31

—— (1953) 'Das Prinzip der Silbenzählung im Lied des zentralen Mittelalters', *Mf* 6 (1953) 8–23

—— (1954) 'Das System der modalen Rhythmik', *A Mw* 11 (1954) 1–38

—— (1964) *Tropen- und Sequenzenhandschriften*. RISM B. v. 1 (Munich 1964)

—— (1967) 'Ein Faszikel Notre Dame Kompositionen auf Texte des Pariser Kanzlers in einer Dominikaner-handschrift' [Santa Sabina MS], *A Mw* 24 (1967) 1–23

The Index of Middle English Verse ed. C. Brown and R. H. Robbins, New York 1943; and Robbins, R. H., and Cutler, J. L. *Supplement*. Lexington, Kentucky, 1965

Irtenkauf, W. Der *Computus ecclesiasticus* in der Einstimmigkeit des Mittelalters', *A Mw* 14 (1957) 1–15

Jacques de Liège *Speculum Musicae*: see Bragard; Coussemaker (1864), II. 193–433 [Books 6–7]

James, M. R. *The Apocryphal New Testament*. Oxford 1924; corr. edn 1953 [transl.]

Jammers, E. (1957) 'Das mittelalterliche deutsche Epos und die Musik', *Heidelberger Jahrbücher* 1 (1957) 31–90

—— (1959) 'Der musikalische Vortrag des altdeutschen Epos', *Der Deutschunterricht* 11 (1959) 98–116

—— (1963) *Ausgewählte Melodien des Minnesangs*. Tübingen 1963

—— (1964) 'Der Vortrag des altgermanischen Stabreimverses in musikwissenschaftlicher Sicht', *ZfdA* 93 (1964) 1–13

—— (1965a) *Tafeln zur Neumenschrift*. Tutzing 1965

—— (1965b) 'Studien zu Neumenschriften, Neumenhandschriften und neumierter Musik', *Bibliothek und Wissenschaft* 2 (1965) 85–105

—— (1969) *Schrift Ordnung Gestalt: Gesammelte Aufsätze zur älteren Musikgeschichte*, ed. E. Hammerstein. Bern 1969

—— (1975) *Aufzeichnungsweisen der einstimmigen ausserliturgischen Musik des Mittelalters. Palaeographie der Musik*, ed. W. Arlt, I: 4. Cologne 1975

Jeanroy, A. (1918) *Bibliographie sommaire des chansonniers français du moyen âge*. CFMA. Paris 1918; repr. 1965

—— ed. (1925a) *Le chansonnier d'Arras: reproduction en phototypie*. Paris 1925

Jeanroy, A., Brandin, L., and Aubry, P. ed. (1901) *Lais et descorts français du xiiie siècle; texte et musique*. Paris 1901; repr. New York 1969 [cited in the notes as 'Jeanroy et al. (1901)']

—— (1925b) *Les Origines de la poésie lyrique en France au moyen âge*. 3rd edn, Paris 1925

Jehan de l'Escurel: see Wilkins

Jerome of Moravia. *Tractatus de Musica*, ed. S. M. Cserba. Regensburg 1935

Johannes Afflighemensis: see Smits van Waesberghe; Babb and Palisca

Johannes de Garlandia *De mensurabili musica*, ed. E. Reimer. Beihefte zum *A Mw*. Wiesbaden 1972

Johannes de Grocheo: see Rohloff; Seay; Wolf

Johner, D. *Wort und Ton im Choral; ein Beitrag zur Aesthetik des gregorianischen Gesanges*. 2nd edn, Leipzig 1953

Jones, C. W. (1963) *The St Nicholas Liturgy and its Literary Relationships ninth to twelfth centuries*, Berkeley, California 1963 [with essay on music by G. Reaney]

—— (1975) 'Carolingian Aesthetics: why modular verse?' *Viator* 6 (1975) 309

Jonsson, R. and Treitler, L. 'Medieval music and language: a reconsideration of the relationship', in *Studies in the History of Music I: Music and Language*. New York 1983

Jusserand, J. J. *English Wayfaring Life in the Middle Ages*, transl. L. Toulmin Smith. 4th edn, London 1950

Kehrein, J., ed.   *Lateinische Sequenzen des Mittelalters aus Handschriften und Drucken*. Mainz 1873

Kippenberg, B.   *Der Rhythmus im Minnesang*. Munich 1962

Klopsch, P.   *Einführung in die mittellateinische Verslehre*. Darmstadt 1972

Knapp, J. ed. (1965)   *Thirty-Five Conductus*. Collegium Musicum VI. New Haven 1965

——— (1979)   'Musical declamation and poetic rhythm in an early layer of Notre Dame conductus', *JAMS* 32 (1979) 383–407

Korth, M., *et al.*, ed.   *Carmina Burana: lateinisch–deutsch. Gesamtausgabe der mittelalterlichen Melodien mit der dazughörigen Texten*. Munich 1979

Krieg, E.   *Das lateinische Osterspiel von Tours*. Würzburg 1956

Kusch, H.   *Einführung in das lateinische Mittelalter, I: Dichtung*. Darmstadt 1957

Långfors, A., Jeanroy, A., and Brandin, L. ed.   *Recueil général des jeux-partis français*. Paris 1926

Las Leys: see Gatien-Arnoult

Legge, M. D.   *Anglo-Norman Literature and its Background*. Oxford 1963

Lewis, C. T., and Short, C.   *A Latin Dictionary*. Oxford 1879

Liber Usualis missae et officii. Rome 1950 [cited in the notes as '*LU*']

Linker, R. W.   *A Bibliography of Old French Lyrics*. Romance Monographs, 31. University of Mississippi 1979

Lipphardt, W. (1955)   'Unbekannte Weisen zu den *Carmina Burana*', *AMw* 12 (1955) 122–42 [3 facs.]

——— (1960)   'Liturgische Dramen', *MGG* VIII (1960)

——— (1961)   'Einige unbekannte Weisen zu den *Carmina Burana* aus der zweiten Hälfte des 12. Jahrhunderts', in *Festschrift Heinrich Besseler zum 60. Geburtstag* (Leipzig 1961), pp. 101–25 [7 facs.]

——— ed. (1975–6, 1981)   *Lateinische Osterfeiern und Osterspiele*, vols. 1–5 (Berlin 1975–6); vol. 6 (1981)

Loriquet, H., Pothier, J., and Collette, A., ed.   *Le Graduel de l'église cathédrale de Rouen au xiiie siècle*, 2 vols. Rouen 1907

LU: see *Liber Usualis*

Ludwig, F. (1910)   *Repertorium organorum recentioris et motetorum vetustissimi stili*, I, pt 1. Halle 1910

——— ed. (1926–54)   *Guillaume de Machaut: Musikalische Werke*, I–IV; vol. IV with H. Besseler. Leipzig 1926–54

——— (1930)   'Die geistliche nichtliturgische, weltliche, einstimmige und die mehrstimmige Musik des Mittelalters bis zum Anfang des 15. Jahrhunderts', in *Adlers Handbuch*, I. 2nd edn, Berlin 1930

McAlpine, F.   'Un chansonnier médiéval: édition et étude du MS 24406 de la Bibliothèque Nationale' [trouvère MS *V*]. Diss. University of Paris Sorbonne 1974

Machabey, A. (1957, 1959)   *Notations musicales non modales des XIIe et XIIIe siècles*. Paris 1957; enlarged edn, 1959

——— 'Introduction à la lyrique musicale romane', *Cahiers de Civilisation Médiévale* 2 (1959) 203–11, 283–93

——— (1961)   'Les planctus d'Abélard, remarques sur le rythme musical du xiie siècle', *Romania* 82 (1961) 71–95

——— (1962)   'Etude de quelques chansons goliardiques', *Romania* 83 (1962) 323–347

——— (1964)   'Remarques sur les mélodies goliardiques', *CCM* 7 (1964) 257–78

Maillard, J. (1959)   'Coutumes musicales au Moyen-Age d'après le Tristan en prose', *CCM* 2 (1959) 341–53

——— (1963)   *Evolution et esthétique du lai lyrique des origines à la fin du XIVème siècle*. Paris 1963

——— ed. (1964)   *Lais et chansons d'Ernoul de Gastinois*. MSD. Rome 1964

——— ed. (1967a)   *Anthologie de chants de troubadours*. Nice 1967

——— ed. (1967b)   *Anthologie de chants des trouvères*, with J. Chailley. Paris 1967

—— ed. (1967c)   Roi-trouvère du XIIIᵉ siècle, Charles d'Anjou. Musicological Studies and
    Documents 18. Rome 1967
Mari, G., ed. 'I trattati medievali di ritmica latina', Memoire del Reale Istituto Lombardo di
    Scienze a Lettere: Classe di lettere vol. 20 (Milan 1899) 373–496
Marigo, A., ed.   Dante: De vulgari eloquentia. 3rd edn, rev. P. G. Ricci. Florence 1957
Marrocco, W. T., and Sandon, N., ed.   Medieval Music. Oxford Anthology of Music. Oxford
    1977
Marshall, J. H., ed.   The chansons of Adam de la Halle. Manchester 1971
—— see also Razos de Trobar
Martianus Capella: see Dick; Stahl et al. [transl.]
Matarasso, P.   Aucassin et Nicolette and Other Tales. Harmondsworth 1971
Mengaldo, P. V., ed. [Dante:] De vulgari eloquentia. Vulgares Eloquentes III. Padua 1968
M[eyer], P.   'Mélanges anglo-normands', Romania, 38 (1909) 434–41
—— and Raynaud, G. Le Chansonnier de Saint-Germain-des-Prés (Bibl. nat. fr. 20050). Paris
    1892 [facs.]
Meyer, R., Bédier, J., and Aubry, P., ed.   La chanson de Bele Aalis par le trouvère Baude de la
    Quarière. Paris 1904
Meyer, W. (1905–36)   Gesammelte Abhandlungen zur mittellateinischen Rhythmik, 3 vols. Berlin
    1905–36
—— (1909) 'Die Arundel-Sammlung mittellateinischer Lieder', Abhandlungen der König-
    lichen Gesellschaft der Wissenschaften zur Göttingen 11 (1909) 3–52
Misset, E., and Aubry, P., ed.   Les proses d'Adam de Saint-Victor. Paris 1900; repr. New York
    1969
Moberg, C. A.   Über die schwedischen Sequenzen. Eine musikgeschichtliche Studie, 2 vols. Uppsala
    1927
Mölk, U., and Wolfzettel, F.   Répertoire métrique de la poésie lyrique française des origines à 1350.
    Munich 1972
Mone, F. J., ed.   Lateinische Hymnen des Mittelalters, 3 vols. Freiburg 1853–5
Monterosso, R. (1956)   Musica e ritmica dei trovatori. Milan 1956
—— (1965) 'Musica e poesia nel De Vulgari Eloquentia', in Dante: giornata internazionale di
    studio per il VII centenario: Ravenna 1965, Faenza 1965, p. 83
Murphy (1971)   Medieval Rhetoric: a select bibliography. Toronto 1971
—— (1974)   Rhetoric in the Middle Ages: a history of rhetorical theory from St Augustine to the
    Renaissance. Berkeley 1974
—— (1978)   Medieval Eloquence: Studies in the theory and practice of medieval rhetoric. Berkeley
    1978
Musica Enchiriadis: see Schmid; Rosenstiel [transl.]
Mynors, R. A. B., ed.   Cassiodori Senatoris Institutiones. Oxford 1937
Nicoll, A.   Masks, Mimes and Miracles: Studies in the Popular Theatre. New York 1931
The New Grove Dictionary of Music and Musicians, ed. S. Sadie, 20 vols. London 1980
The New Oxford History of Music II: Early Medieval Music up to 1300, ed. Dom A. Hughes.
    London 1954; rev. 1955, repr. 1961
Nichols, S. G., and Galm, J. A., ed.   The songs of Bernart de Ventadorn. Chapel Hill, N.C., 1962
Norberg, D. (1954)   La poésie latine rythmique du haut moyen âge. Stockholm 1954
—— (1958)   Introduction à l'étude de la versification latine médiévale. Stockholm 1958
—— (1968)   Manuel pratique de latin médiéval. Paris 1968
—— (1984)   L'accentuation des mots dans le vers latin du moyen âge. Paris 1984
Odenkirchen, C. J.   The Life of St Alexius in the Old French Version of the Hildesheim Manuscript.
    Brookline, Mass., 1978

Odington: see Hammond; Huff [transl.]

Opland, J. *Anglo-Saxon Oral Poetry: A Study of the Traditions*. New Haven 1980

Oxford Anthology: see Marrocco and Sandon

Oxford Book of Medieval Latin Verse, ed. F. J. E. Raby. Oxford 1959

Oxford Dictionary of the Christian Church, ed. F. L. Cross. London 1957

Pächt, O., and Alexander, J. J. G. *Illuminated Manuscripts in the Bodleian Library, Oxford*, 3 vols. Oxford 1966–73

Paganuzzi, E. 'Sulla notazione neumatica della monodia trobadorica', *RMI* 57 (1955) 23–47

Page, C. 'Anglo-Saxon Hearpan: their terminology, technique, tuning and repertory of verse, 850–1066'. Diss. York 1981

Palaeographie der Musik, nach den Planen Leo Schrades, ed. W. Arlt, 3 vols. Cologne 1975–

Paléographie Musicale: les principaux manuscrits du chant grégorien [etc.], ed. A. Mocquereau and J. Gajard. Solesmes, Tournai, etc. 21 vols 1889–1974

Parker, I. (1977) 'Troubadours and trouvère song: problems in modal analysis', *RBM* 31 (1977) 28–37

——— (1978) 'A propos de la tradition manuscrite des chansons de trouvères', *RdM* 64 (1978) 181–202

——— (1979) 'Notes on the Chansonnier St Germain des Prés', *ML* 60 (1979) 261–80

Parkes, M. B. 'Punctuation, or pause and effect', in Murphy (1978), 127–42

Parrish, C. *The Notation of Medieval Music*. New York 1957

Pascale, M. 'Le musiche nelle pastourelles francesi del XII e XIII secolo', *Annali della Facoltà di lettere e filosofia, Università degli studi di Perugia* 13 (1976) 575–631

Pearsall, D. *Old English and Middle English Poetry*. London 1977

Pillet, A., and Carstens, H. *Bibliographie der Troubadours*. Schriften der Königsberger Gelehrten Gesellschaft, Sonderreihe III. Halle 1933

Polyphonic Music of the Fourteenth Century, ed. L. Schrade. Monaco 1956–

Ponte, J., transl. *The Discipline of Music (ca. 483) by Aurelian of Réôme*. Colorado 1968

Pope, J. C. *The Rhythm of Beowulf*. New Haven 1942; rev. edn 1966

Press, A. R. *Anthology of Troubadour Lyric Poetry*. Edinburgh 1971 [texts and trans.]

Quintilian: see Butler, H. E.; Colson

Raby, F. J. E. (1953) *A History of Christian-Latin Poetry from the Beginnings to the Close of the Middle Ages*. 2nd edn, Oxford 1953

——— (1957) *A History of Secular Latin Poetry in the Middle Ages*, 2 vols. 2nd edn, Oxford 1957

——— (1959) *The Oxford Book of Medieval Latin Verse*, ed. F. J. E. Raby. Oxford 1959

Räkel, H.-H. *Die musikalische Erscheinungsform der Trouvèrepoesie*. Bern 1977

Rankin, S. K. (1981a) 'The Music of the Medieval Liturgical Drama in France and in England', Ph.D. diss. Cambridge (1981), 2 vols.

——— (1981b) 'Les drames du manuscrit 201 de la Bibliothèque municipale d'Orléans', in *Les Sources en Musicologie* Editions du Centre National de la Recherche Scientifique. (Paris 1981), pp. 67–78

Raynaud, G. *Bibliographie des chansonniers français des XIIIᵉ et XIVᵉ siècles*, 2 vols. Paris 1881

——— *Recueil de motets français des xiiᵉ et xiiiᵉ siècles*, 2 vols. Paris 1881

R: *Raynauds Bibliographie des altfranzösischen Liedes*. Rev. edn (enlarged by Hans Spanke), Leiden 1955; repr. (with alphabetical index; unrevised) 1980 [cited in the notes and text above as 'R0000']

The Razos de Trobar of Raimon Vidal and Associated Texts, ed. J. H. Marshall. London 1972

Reckow, F. (1967) *Der Musiktraktat des Anonymus IV*, 2 pts. Wiesbaden 1967

——— (1972) 'Conductus', in *HMT* (q.v.)

Reese, G. *Music in the Middle Ages*. New York 1940

Regino of Prüm: *Epistola de armonia institutione*: [Gerbert, i. 230–47]

Reichl, K.   *Religiöse Dichtung im englischen Hochmittelalter*. Munich 1973 [edn of Cambridge, Trinity Coll. MS B 14.39]

Reiss, E.   'Number Symbolism and Medieval Literature', in *Medievalia et Humanistica* n.s. 1 (1970) 161–174

Remy of Auxerre.   *Remigius Autissiodorensis Commentum in Martianum Capellam*, ed. Cora E. Lutz, 2 vols. Leiden 1962 and 1965

Renart le Nouvel by Jacquemart Gielée, ed. H. Roussel. SATF. Paris 1961

Richter, L.   'Die beiden ältesten Liederbücher des lateinischen Mittelalters', *Philologus* 123 (1979) 63–8

Rigg, A. G. (1978)   'Medieval Latin Poetic Anthologies II', *Medieval Studies* 40 (1978) 387–407

——— (1984)   'Eraclius Archipoeta: Bekyngton Anthology nos. 14, 15, 20, 77.' *MÆ* 53 (1984) 1–9

——— and Wieland, G. R.   'A Canterbury classbook of the mid-eleventh century' [the Cambridge Songs manuscript], in *Anglo-Saxon England* IV, ed. P. Clemoes (Cambridge 1975), pp. 113–30

de Riquer, M.   *Los trovadores: historia literaria y textos*, 3 vols. Barcelona 1975

RISM (1964)   H. Husmann, *Tropen- und Sequenzenhandschriften* (Munich 1964)

RISM (1966)   G. Reaney, *Manuscripts of Polyphonic Music: 11th–Early 14th Century* (Munich 1966)

RISM (1969)   G. Reaney, *Manuscripts of Polyphonic Music (c. 1320–1400)*. (Munich 1969)

Rivière, J.-C., ed.   *Pastourelles*. TLF, 3 vols. Geneva 1974–6

Robbins, R. H., ed.   *Secular Lyrics of the XIVth and XVth Centuries*. Oxford 1952

Robertson, D. W.   *Preface to Chaucer: Studies in Medieval Perspectives*. Princeton 1963

Robin et Marion: see Gennrich (1962); Varty; Axton and Stevens

Robinson, F. N., ed.   *The Works of Geoffrey Chaucer*. 2nd (rev.) edn, Oxford 1957

Roesner, E. (1974)   'The Manuscript Wolfenbüttel, Herzog-August-Bibliothek, 628. Helmstadiensis: A study of its origins and of its eleventh fascicle', Ph.D. diss. New York University 1974

——— (1979)   'The performance of Parisian organum', *EM* 7 (1979) 174–89

Rohloff, E.   *Die Quellenhandschriften zum Musiktraktat des Johannes de Grocheio*. Leipzig 1972 [facs.; Latin text; German transl.]

Rokseth, Y., ed. (1935–9)   *Polyphonies du xiiie siècle. Le MS H.196 de la Faculté de Médecine de Montpellier*, 4 vols. Paris 1935–9 [facs.]

——— (1947)   'Danses cléricales du XIIIe siècle', in *Publications de la Faculté des Lettres de l'Université de Strasbourg* Fasc. 106 (Paris 1947), pp. 93–126

Roques, M., ed. (1925, 1962)   *Aucassin et Nicolette*. CFMA. Paris 1925; 2nd edn (rev.) 1962

Rosenberg, S. N., and Tischler, H., eds.   *Chanter m'estuet: Songs of the trouvères*. London 1981

Rosenstiel, L., transl.   *Music Handbook* [*Musica Enchiriadis*]. Colorado Springs 1976

Sachs, C.   *World History of the Dance*. New York 1963

Sahlin, M.   *Etude sur la carole médiévale*. Uppsala 1940

Salmen, W.   *Der fahrende Musiker im europäischen Mittelalter*. Kassel 1960

Sanders, E. H., ed.   *English Music of the Thirteenth and Early Fourteenth Centuries*. PMFC XIV. Monaco 1979

Sarum Antiphonal   Frere, W. H. ed. *Antiphonale Sarisburiense: a reproduction in facsimile*. PMMS. London 1901–24; repr. 1966

Sarum Breviary   Proctor, F., and Wordsworth, C., ed. *Brevarium ad usum insignis ecclesiae Sarum*, 3 vols. Cambridge 1879–86

Sarum Gradual   Frere, W. H., ed., *Graduale Sarisburiense*. PMMS. London 1894; repr. 1966

Sarum Missal   Legg, J. W. *The Sarum Missal*. Oxford 1916; repr. 1969

Schaller, D., and Könsgen, E. *Initia carminum Latinorum saeculo undecimo antiquiorum: Bibliographisches Repertorium für die lateinische Dichtung der Antike und des früheren Mittelalters.* Göttingen 1977

Schlager, K.-H. 'Cantiones', 'Hymnen' etc., in *Geschichte der Katholischen Kirchenmusik*, I, ed. K. G. Fellerer. Kassel 1972

Schmid, H., ed. *Musica et scolica enchiriadis una cum aliquibus tractatulis adiunctis.* Munich 1981

Schrade, L. (1953) 'Political Compositions in French music of the 12th and 13th centuries', *AnnM* I (1953) 56–

—— ed. (1956) *The Roman de Fauvel.* PMFC I. Monaco 1956

—— ed. *The Works of Guillaume de Machaut.* Polyphonic Music of the Fourteenth Century, I–III. Monaco 1956–7

Schumann, O. 'Die jüngere Cambridger Liedersammlung', *Studi Medievali* n.s. 16 (1943–50) 48–85 [the Later Cambridge Songs]

Schwan, E. *Die altfranzösischen Liederhandschriften: ihr Verhältnis, ihre Entstehung und ihre Bestimmung.* Berlin 1886

Seay, A., transl. *Johannes de Grocheo: Concerning Music.* Colorado Springs 1967

Seidel, W. 'Rhythmus/Numerus', in *HMT*

Sesini, U. (1942) *Le melodie trobadoriche nel Canzoniere provenzale della Biblioteca Ambrosiana (R. 71 sup).* Turin 1942

—— (1949) *Poesia e musica nella latinatà cristiana dal III al X secolo*, ed. G. Vecchi. Nuova Biblioteca Italiana VI. Turin 1949

Smits van Waesberghe, J., ed. (1950) *Johannes Afflighemensis: De musica cum tonario.* CSM I. Rome 1950

—— ed. (1951) *Aribonis de musica.* CSM II. Rome 1951

—— ed. (1955) *Guido of Arezzo: Micrologus.* CSM IV. Rome 1955

—— (1961) *The Theory of Music from the Carolingian Era up to 1400.* RISM B. III.1. Kassel 1961

—— (1969) *Musikerziehung: Lehre und Theorie im Mittelalter.* Musikgeschichte in Bildern, ed. W. Bachmann, III.3. Leipzig 1969

Smoldon, W. L. ed. (1960) *The Play of Daniel: a medieval liturgical drama.* PMMS. London 1960

—— (1980) *The Music of the Medieval Church Dramas*, ed. C. Bourgeault. Oxford 1980

Spanke, H. (1928) 'Das öftere Auftreten von Strophenformen und Melodien in der altfranzösischen Lyrik', *ZffSL* 51 (1928) 73–117

—— (1929) 'Das Corpus der ältesten französischen Tanzlyrik', *ZfrP* 49 (1929) 287

—— (1930a) 'Das lateinische Rondeau', *ZffSL* 53 (1930) 113–48

—— (1930b, 1932a) 'St Martial-Studien. Ein Beitrag zur frühromanischen Metrik', *ZffSL* 54 (1930) 282–317, 385–422; 56 (1932) 450–78

—— (1930c) 'Tanzmusik in der Kirche des Mittelalters', *Neuphilologische Mitteilungen* 31 (1930) 143–70

—— (1930–1) 'Der Codex Buranus als Liederbuch', *ZMw* 13 (1930–1) 241–51

—— (1931a) 'Rhythmen- und Sequenzstudien', *Studi Medievali* n.s. 4 (1931) 286–320; repr. *Studien* (1977), pp. 1–35

—— (1931b) 'Über das Fortleben der Sequenzenform in den romanischen Sprachen', *ZfRP* 51 (1931) 309–34; repr. *Studien* (1977), pp. 36–61

—— (1932b) 'Zur Geschichte der lateinischen nichtliturgischen Sequenz', *Speculum* 7 (1932) 367–82; repr. *Studien* (1977), pp. 91–106

—— (1934) 'Aus der Vorgeschichte und Frühgeschichte der Sequenz', *Zeitschrift für deutsches Altertum und deutsche Literatur*, 71 (1934) 1–39; repr. *Studien* (1977), pp. 107–45

——— (1936) *Beziehungen zwischen romanischer und mittellateinischer Lyrik mit besonderer Berücksichtigung der Metrik und Musik.* Berlin 1936

——— (1938) 'Sequenz und Lai', *Studi Medievali,* 11 (1938) 12–68; repr. *Studien* (1977), pp. 146–202

——— (1941) 'Die Kompositionskunst der Sequenzen Adams von St Victor', *Studi Medievali,* n.s. 14 (1941) 1–29; repr. *Studien* (1977), pp. 203–31

——— (1942) 'Ein lateinisches Liederbuch des 11 Jahrhunderts', *Studi Medievali* n.s. 15 (1942) 111–42 [the Cambridge Songs]

——— (1977) *Studien zu Sequenz, Lai und Leich,* selected by U. Aarburg. Darmstadt 1977

Spaziani, M. *Il canzoniere francese di Siena – Biblioteca Comunale,* H.X.36. *Introduzione, testo critico e traduzione.* Florence 1957

Stäblein, B. (1956) *Hymnen I: Die mittelalterlichen Hymnenmelodien des Abendlandes.* MMMA 1. Kassel 1956

——— (1962) 'Die Schwanenklage. Zum Problem Lai-Planctus-Sequenz', in *Festschrift Karl Gustav Fellerer zum sechzigsten Geburtstag,* ed. H. Hüschen (Regensburg 1962), pp. 491–502

——— (1965) 'Sequenz', in *MGG* XII (1965) 522–49

——— (1966) 'Zur Musik des Ludus de Antichristo', in *Zum 70. Geburtstag von J. Müller-Blattau,* ed. C.-H. Mahling (Kassel 1966), pp. 312–27

——— (1975) *Schriftbild der einstimmigen Musik.* Musikgeschichte in Bildern, ed. W. Bachmann, III: 4. Leipzig 1975

Stahl, W. H., and Johnson, R. (with E. L. Burge). *Martianus Capella and the Seven Liberal Arts,* 2 vols. New York 1971 [vol. II contains transl. of *De Nuptiis*]

Steffens, G., ed. (1892) 'Die altfranzösische Liederhandschrift von Siena', *Archiv* 88 (1892) 301–60

——— ed. (1896–7, 1900) 'Die altfranzösische Liederhandschrift der Bodleiana in Oxford, Douce 308', *Archiv* 97, 98, 99, 104 (1896–7; 1900)

Steinen, W. von den *Notker der Dichter.* Bern 1948

Steiner, R. (1964) 'Some monophonic Latin songs'. Diss. Catholic University of America 1964

——— (1966) 'Some monophonic Latin songs composed around 1200', *MQ* 52 (1966) 56–70

——— (1974) 'La musique des lais', in G. Fotitch and R. Steiner, ed. *Les lais du roman en prose d'après le manuscrit de Vienne 2542.* Munich 1974

Stephan, R. 'Über sangbare Dichtung in althochdeutscher Zeit', *Bericht über den internationalen musikwissenschaftlichen Kongress,* ed. W. Gerstenberg *et al.* (Kassel 1977), pp. 225–9

Stevens, D. W. 'Music in honor of St Thomas of Canterbury', *MQ* 56 (1970) 311–48

Stevens, J. ed. (1952) *Medieval Carols.* Musica Britannica IV. London 1952: rev. edn, 1958

——— (1961) *Music and Poetry in the Early Tudor Court.* London 1961; repr. Cambridge 1979

——— (1968a) 'Dante and music', *Italian Studies* 23 (1968) 1–18

——— (1968b) 'Music in some early medieval plays' in *Studies in the Arts,* ed. F. Warner (Oxford 1968), pp. 21–40

——— (1973) *Medieval Romance: Themes and Approaches.* London 1973

——— (1974–5) ' "La grande chanson courtoise": the songs of Adam de la Halle', *PRMA* 101 (1974–5) 11–30

——— (1980) 'Medieval Drama', *New Grove* XII (1980)

——— and Karp, T. (1980) 'Troubadours and Trouvères', in *New Grove* XIX (1980)

——— (1981a) '*Angelus ad virginem*: the history of a medieval song', in *Medieval Studies for J. A. W. Bennett,* ed. P. L. Heyworth (Oxford 1981), pp. 297–328

——— (1981b) 'The Manuscript Presentation and Notation of Adam de la Halle's Courtly Chansons', in *Source Materials and the Interpretation of Music: a Memorial Volume to Thurston Dart,* ed. I. Bent (London 1981), pp. 29–84

—— (1982) *The Old Sound and the New: an inaugural lecture.* Cambridge 1982

Storey, C. ed. *La Vie de Saint Alexis.* Oxford 1946

Strecker, K., ed. *Die Cambridger Lieder.* Monumenta Germaniae Historica. Berlin 1926 [the Cambridge Songs]

Streng-Renkonen, W. O. *Les Estampies françaises.* CFMA. Paris 1931

Strunk, O., ed. *Source Readings in Music History.* London 1952

Studien: see Spanke (1977)

Suñol, G. (Dom) 'Els Cants dels Romeus (segle xivᵉ)', *Analecta Montserratensia* 1 (1918) 100–92 [*Llibre Vermell*]

Szövérffy, J. *Weltliche Dichtungen des lateinischen Mittelalters: Ein Handbuch,* 1. Berlin 1970

Tintori, G., and Monterosso, R., ed. *Sacre rappresentazioni nel manoscritto 201 della Biblioteca Municipale di Orléans.* Cremona 1958 [Fleury Playbook]

Tischler, H., ed. (1978) *The Montpellier Codex.* Recent Researches in the Music of the Middle Ages and Early Renaissance, II–VII, 3 ps (8 fasc.). Madison, Wisconsin, 1978

—— (1980) 'Versmass und musikalischer Rhythmus in Notre Dame Conductus', *A Mw* 37 (1980) 292–304

—— (1982a) 'A propos meter and rhythm in the Ars Antiqua', *JMT* 26 (1982) 313

Topsfield, L. T. *Troubadours and Love.* Cambridge 1975

Treitler, L. (1974) 'Homer and Gregory: the transmission of epic poetry and plainchant', *MQ* 60 (1974) 333–72

—— (1979) 'Regarding meter and rhythm in the Ars Antiqua', *MQ* 65 (1979) 524–558

—— (1981) 'Oral, written and literate process in the transmission of medieval music', *Speculum* 56 (1981) 471–91

—— (1982b) 'The early history of music writing in the West', *JAMS* 35 (1982) 237–79

—— (1984) 'Reading and singing: On the genesis of occidental music-writing.' *Early Music History* 4 (1984) 135–208

Van Deusen, N. 'The medieval Latin sequence: a complete catalogue of the sources and edition of the texts and melodies', *JPMMS* 5 (1982) 56–60

Varty, K., ed. *Le Jeu de Robin et de Marion par Adam de la Halle.* London 1960 [musical transcriptions by Eric Hill]

Vecchi, G., ed. (1951) *Pietro Abelardo: i planctus.* Modena 1951

—— (1954) *Uffici drammatichi padovani.* Florence 1954

—— (1958) *Poesia Latina Medievale.* Parma 1958 [texts; Italian translations; 34 music examples; 14 plates]

Veen, J. van der 'Les aspects musicaux des chansons de geste', *Neophilologus* 41 (1957) 82–100

Villetard, H., ed. *Office de Pierre de Corbeil.* Bibliothèque musicologique IV. Paris 1907

Vollaerts, J. W. A. *Rhythmic Proportions in Early Medieval Ecclesiastical Chant.* Leiden 1958

Von Simson, O. *The Gothic Cathedral: Origins of Gothic Architecture and the Medieval Concept of Order.* Princeton 1974

Wagenaar-Nolthenius, Hélène 'Estampie/stantipes/stampita', in *L'ars nova italiana del trecento II, Certaldo 1969,* ed. F. A. Gallo (Certaldo 1970), pp. 399–409

Wagner, P. (1907) *Introduction to the Gregorian melodies: a handbook of plainsong.* 2nd edn (rev. and enlarged), pt 1, transl. A. Orme and E. G. P. Wyatt [from *Einführung,* 1]. PMMS. London (1907)

—— (1911–21) *Einführung in die gregorianischen Melodien,* 3 vols. 3rd edn, Leipzig 1911–21

Waite, W. *The Rhythm of Twelfth-Century Polyphony.* New Haven 1954

Wallensköld, A., ed. *Les chansons de Thibaut de Champagne, roi de Navarre.* Paris 1925

Walpole, A. S. ed. *Early Latin Hymns.* Cambridge 1922

Walther, H. *Initia carminum ac versuum medii aevi posterioris latinorum. Alphabetisches Verzeichnis der Versanfänge,* 2 vols. Göttingen 1959 and 1969

Weinrich, L. (1968) 'Dolorum solatium: Text und Musik von Abelards Planctus David', *Mittellateinisches Jahrbuch* 5 (1968) 59

—— (1969) 'Peter Abelard as Musician', *MQ* 55 (1969) 295ff, 464ff

Werf, H. van der (1965) 'The Trouvère Chansons as Creations of a Notationless Musical Culture', *Current Musicology* 1 (1965) 61–68

—— (1967a) 'Deklamatorischer Rhythmus in den Chansons der Trouvères', *Mf* 20 (1967) 122–44

—— (1967b) 'Recitative melodies in trouvère chansons', in *Festschrift für Walter Wiora*, ed. L. Finscher and C.-H. Mahling (Kassel 1967), pp. 231–40

—— (1972) *The Chansons of the Troubadours and Trouvères: A Study of the Melodies and Their Relation to the Poems*. Utrecht 1972

—— ed. (1977) (1979) *Trouvères-Melodien* I and II. Monumenta Monodica Medii Aevi XI and XII. London 1977 and 1979

—— and G. A. Bond, ed. (1984) *The Extant Troubadour Melodies: Transcriptions and Essays for Performers and Scholars* (Rochester, NY 1984)[1]

Werlich, E. *Der westgermanische Skop. Der Aufbau seiner Dichtung und sein Vortrag*. Münster 1964

Westrup, J. A. 'Medieval Song' in *NOHM* II. 220–69

Widsith, ed. K. Malone. London 1936; rev. edn, Copenhagen 1962

Wilkins, N., ed. (1966) *The Works of Jehan de l'Escurel*. CMM 30 (1966)

—— (1967) *The Lyric Works of Adam de la Hale*. CMM 44 (1967)

Wilmart, Dom A. 'Le florilège mixte de Thomas Bekyngton', *Medieval and Renaissance Studies* 1 (1941) 41–84; 4 (1956) 35–90

Wolf, J. 'Die Musiklehre des Johannes de Grocheo', *SIMG* 1 (1899–1900) 65–130 [Latin text and German transl.]

Worcester Antiphonary. Antiphonale Missarum XIIIᵉ siècle: codex F160 de la Bibliothèque de la Cathédrale de Worcester, ed. A. Mocquereau. Paléographie Musicale 1st series, vol. XII. Solesmes 1922

Yearley, J. (1981) 'A bibliography of planctus', *JPMMS* 4 (1981) 12–52

—— (1983) 'The medieval Latin planctus as a genre'. Diss. 3 vols. York 1983

Young, K. (1908–9) 'A contribution to the history of liturgical drama at Rouen', *MP* 6 (1908–9) 201–27

—— (1933) *The Drama of the Medieval Church*, 2 vols. Oxford 1933

Zumthor, P. *Langues et techniques poétiques à l'époque romane (xi–xiiiᵉ s.)*. Paris 1963

---

[1] This important edition of the complete troubadour repertoire, with introduction and commentary, was not available in time for me to make use of it.

GENERAL INDEX

Bold page numbers indicate the more important references. A page number prefixed by 'G' indicates a reference to the Glossary. Medieval names are given as in *New Grove*. In cross-references **IFL** means Index of First lines, to which the reader is generally referred for individual songs and song-titles.

Aaliz (Alice), *see* 'Bele Aaliz' **(IFL)**
Abelard, Peter, 120–30, 135–7, 397, 476, 503
accent, 419–20, 486, 494–5
  in *cantio*, 70
  in chanson, 46
  in chant, 280–3, 286, 291–2
  in *conductus*, 58
  conventions for describing, xv
  of duration and of pitch, 280–3 *passim*, 291, 495
  and *ictus*, 97
  in *lai*, 154
  of Latin: classical, 280, 426n.31; medieval, 68, 97, 99, 151, 152
  in named sources: Admont MS, 419; Cambridge Songs, 116, 117; 'Dolorum solatium', 127; *Las Leys*, 25n.43; 'Pange, lingua', 54; 'Planctus ante nescia', 138; *Song of the Flood*, 151–2
  in sequence, 97–9, 100, 105
  shift of, in 'proclitic pronouns', 54n.19
  'tonic' (pitch), 280–3 *passim*, 291, 292, G510 (*s.v.* tonic (a))
accent-signs, 211, 214, 273
accentus, 200, 273, 297n.69, G505
Accentus Moguntinus, 213
accompaniment, instrumental
  in chanson, 35, 43n.82
  for dance, 161
  in dance-song, 159n.1
  for German narrative, 222
  in *lai*, 118n.25, 141
  for Old English verse, 206, 208
  for Saints' Lives, 265
  for Uzbek epic, 266
  see also instruments
Adam de la Bassée: *Ludus super*

Anticlaudianum, 193–4
Adam de la Halle, 34–6, 175, 44–3
  and courtly love, 393
  his *jeux-partis*, 315
  notation of chansons, 441–3
  number in, 35–6, 38–40
  and *refrains*, 177
  and refrain-songs, 469
  Robin et Marion, 175–7 (Ex. 62), 224 (Ex. 83), 315, 450 (Ex. 178), 457
Adam de la Halle MS (Source 34), 224n.68, 441–3, 456–7, 465n.13, 521
Adam de St Victor, 91, 101–8 *passim*, 126
Adélard of Bath: *De eodem et diverso*, 388
Adoration of the Cross, 318–19
affectus, 403, 404
  see also emotive effects
Ailred of Rievaulx: *Speculum charitatis*, 401
Alanus de Insulis (Alain of Lille): *Anticlaudianus*, 193
alba, see *aube*
Albrecht von Scharfenberg, 216: *jüngere Titurel, Der*, 215–17 (Ex. 77), 217
Alexander de Villa–Dei: *Doctrinale*, 429
Alleluia, G505
  in Mass and sequence, 83–4, 86n.12, 113, 270, 394
  as single word, 303–4 (Exx. 128, 129)
Amalarius of Metz, 402
Amerus: *Practica artis musice*, 513
Anderson, Gordon A., 48n.2; 56n.23, 73n.66, 427n.32, 488–9
Anglès, Higinio, 435n.1, 488n.59
Anonymus I, 284n.44

Anonymus IV, 423n.25, 430n.47, 490
Anonymus VII, 423
Antichristus, play of, 59, 314
antiphon, *antiphona*, 179, 252–4, 408, G505
Antonio da Tempo: *Delle rime volgari trattato*, 23, 418–19
Apel, W. C., 171n.31, 273–6, 282, 289–91, 295, 301
Appel, Carl, 494
Archipoeta, 413
Aribo, 383n.36
  De Musica, 276–7
Aristoxenus, 381
arithmetic, *see* number: disposition
Arlt, Wulf, 48n.2, 56, 58, 485–7
armonia (*harmonia*, harmoniousness), 14, 20–1, 22, 385, 400, 422–3, 433, 497, 503
  in chanson, 32–3, 38–40
  in Latin song, 68, 79
  in 'Planctus ante nescia', 137–8
Arras, 24, 175, 430n.49, 454, 520
  see also Chansonnier d'Arras
ars metrica, see *metrum*
ars nova, 8–9
ars ritmica, see *ritmus*
artes liberales, 375, 377
Arundel Latin Lyrics (Source 13), 515
Arundel Songs (Source 12), 64n.46, 80, 83, 100n.31, 153, 178n.54, 443, 515
aube, 314–15, G505
Aubry, Pierre, 423, 424, 449
Aucassin et Nicolette, 202, 225–6 (Ex. 86), 227, 257
Aurelian of Réôme: *Musica disciplina*, 374–80 *passim*, 383n.36, 389–90, 417–18
'authenticity', 273n.13
Axton, Richard, 166–7, 308n.1

General index

549

French, 186, 219
German, 215
'Romanus' letters, *see littere
significative*
rondeau, 162–3, 170–1, 172, 181,
185, 186–98 *passim*, G510
relationship between words
and music in, 196–8
see also dance-song
rondellus, **178–86**, 191–7 *passim*,
484–5, G510
bibliography of, 178n.55
relationship between words
and music in, 196–8
see also dance-song
Rouen Ceremony of the
Shepherds, 336–47
rubrics in dramatic texts, 362–71

Sachs, Hans, 218
Sahlin, Margit, 166, 179
St Albans Troper (Source 18), 93,
95, 100n.31, 102n.37, 517
St Alexis of Rome, Life of, 236–7,
263, 264
St Augustine, 161, 375, 402,
417n.5
Confessions, 386–7
De Musica, 13, 14–15
St Augustine's, Canterbury, 114
St Basil, Life of, 114
St Dunstan, 205
St Eulalie, sequence, 237
St Eustace (Placidus), Office of,
250–1
St Foi d'Agen, Chanson de, 233–4
St John the Evangelist, feast of,
180, 241
St Leger, Life of, 237–8
St Martial, feast of, 179–80
St Martial MS: BN lat. 1139
(Source 35); BN lat. 1154
(Source 36): *see* Manuscripts
(p. 523)
St Martin, abbey of, 49, 111, 521
St Nicholas, 181
Fleury plays on, 255–61
St Stephen, 236, 241
feast of, 179, 180, 240
epistle of, 239–44 (Exx. 94,
95), 263–4
St Thomas of Canterbury
(Thomas Becket), 68, 264
feast of, 241
Life of, 264–5
Office of, 251–5 (Exx. 99–
101)
St Victor, monastery of, 181, 521
see also Adam of St Victor
Saints' Lives, 201, 233–4, **235–9**,
263–5

in epistles, 239–49
in Offices, 249–55
see also individual saints
Salimbene, 498n.19
Salut d'Amours, 175, 464
Salisbury, 270–1
Sarum Use, 270, 321–3
scansion, 494; *see also* accent: of
duration; *metrum*
Schwan, E., 459
scop, 204–5, 210n.34
Seidel, W., 417n.5
Sens Cathedral ceremonies, 58,
61, 180
sequela, 110n.3, G510 (*s.v.
sequentia*)
sequence, **82–109**, G510
accent in, 96–7
bibliography of, 83n.7
'double-cursus', 110, 135
form (in *lai* and *planctus*), 119,
126, 129–42 *passim*, 149,
153–5 *passim*
parallelism in, 87, 90, 113
relationship between words
and music in, 90–1, 96, 99–
100, 108–9, 154–5
in the rhymed Office, 254–5
secular, **110–14**, 114–19
(Cambridge Songs)
sequentia, 84, 86, 90, 110n.3,
G510
Sesini, Ugo, 8, 414n.2, 493n.4
sestina, 31
Shippey, T. A., 207n.24
Siena Chansonnier (Source 39),
522
simile (musical), 302
von Simson, Otto, 400
sirventes, 223, 498, G510
Smoldon, W. L., 257n.43,
261n.50, 309n.3, 329
social context and milieu
civic, *see* bourgeoisie;
oral/written tradition; *puy*
courtly, *see* chansonniers (and
under individual
chansonniers); dance-song
ecclesiastical, *see* liturgy; para-
liturgical repertoire and
under individual towns,
festivals (e.g. Beauvais
cathedral; Palm Sunday),
and items (e.g. *rondelli*)
popular, *see* dance-song;
minstrels
sonnet, 23
sound(s), 499
expressive, 78, 323, 361
of individual words, 22, 23,
45–6, 78, 90, 154, 280, 494

and meaning in chant, **291–
307**
metaphorical, 301–02
onomatopoeic, 301, 303
patterns of, 21–2, 31, 127; *see
also: jubilus*; rhyme
see also chansonniers;
manuscripts; notation: in
named sources
Spanke, Hans, 6, 44, 104, 108,
116n.17, 180n.63, 182n.69,
185n.84, 476
speech, 199, 268
and chant, 272–83, (notation)
299 (sounds)
in isosyllabic performance,
500, 504
in medieval theory, 381–5,
417, 496
see also rhetoric; sound(s);
Spruchdichtung, 221n.61
Stäblein, Bruno, 7, 52, 54, 63,
84, 110–14 *passim*, 142, 148,
186n.86, 254, 503n.30
Steiner, Ruth, 76, 488n.59
Stevens, Denis, 255n.38
stress, *see* accent
'structural' note (tenor), 286, 292
see also recitation-tone
syllabic style (of chant), 277–8,
G510
syllabism; syllable-counting, 23,
25, 415, 416, 420, G510 (*s.v.*
syllabic)
in the Cambridge Songs, 115–
16, 119
in chanson, 31–47 *passim*
in Latin song, 54, 55, 59–63
passim, 67, 75, 77
palaeographical evidence of,
437–40, 457
in *planctus cigni*, 113
in poetic theory, 21–5 *passim*
in *refrain*, 195
in sequence, 82, 90, 97, 104,
109
see also isosyllabic hypothesis;
number; *ritmus*
symbolism
poetic, 92, 113, 148, 311
of number, *see under* number
symphonia, 398n.80

Tam Lin, 203 (Ex. 73)
Tenebrae (service of), 279, G510
tenor, *see* recitation-tone;
'structural' note
theorists (medieval), 19–25, **373–
409**, **413–34**
bibliography of, 373n.1

INDEX OF FIRST LINES

The index includes the first lines of songs, song-titles, poems, *refrains*, dramatic and liturgical items and musical examples. Attributions, where known, are given in parentheses. Variant spellings are not noted. Bold page numbers indicate the important references.

'A la doucor d'este qui reverdoie', 449
'A la doucour dou tens' (? Châtelain de Coucy), 440–1 (Ex. 174)
'A ma dame ai mis mon cuer et mon pensé', 193 (Ex. 68)
'A solis ortu usque ad occidua', 52, **493** (Ex. 196)
'A une ajornée/chevauchai l'autrier' (Moniot de Paris), 471–3 (Ex. 186)
'A vous amant', 425n.30
'Ad mortem festinamus', 182
'Advertite, omnes populi', 116–18
'Alleluia', *see* Alleluia **in General Index**
'Alleluia . . . Iam vere scimus', 343–4 (Ex. 152)
'Alto consilio divina ratio', 59–60 (Exx. 12, 13), 154
'Amour dont sui espris' (Blondel de Nesle), 2, 448 (Ex. 177)
'Amours m'ont si doucement' (Adam de la Halle), 432n.55
'Angelus ad virginem', 443–6 (Ex. 175), 447 (Ex. 176)
'Angelus Domini descendit', 302 (Ex. 126)
'Anglia, planctus itera', 78
'Ar ne kuthe', 130n.40
'Arce summa', 114n.11
'Argumenta faluntur fisice', 70–1 (Exx. 19a, 19b)
'As enfants et as grans' (Ernoul le vieux/vieil), 228 (Ex. 88)
'Au tems pascor', 231
'Au vert bois deporter m'irai', 172–3
'Aucassins ot du baisier', 226 (Ex. 86)
'Audigier, dist Raimberge', 224 (Ex. 83)
'Audite quid dixerit', 312, 326–7 (Ex. 138), 327n.49, 521
'Ausi com l'unicorne sui' (Thibaut de Champagne), 37–8, 431, 432
'Austro terris influente', 490
'Ave gloriosa mater salvatoris', 82–3
'Ave gloriosa virginum regina' (Philip the Chancellor), 82, 106–8 (Ex. 36), 455n.58, 483, 488n.61
'Ave Maria' (antiphon), 308 (Ex. 132), 310n.5
'Aveuc tele compaignie', 175

'Beata viscera', 337 (Ex. 144)
Bele Aaliz (Alice), 80, 162, 177–8

'Bele Alis matyn se leva', 178
'Bele Doette', 230
'Bele Yolanz', 438 (Ex. 171)
'Ben deu hoi mais', 247, 248
'Benedicta tu', 309 (Ex. 133), 310n.5
'Benedicto gratias deo' (Notker), 110
'Bergeronnete sui mais t'ai', 450 (Ex. 178)
Berta vetula, see 'Arce summa'
'Biaus doz amis', 173
'Bien doit chanter' (Guillame le Vinier), 496n.13

'Can l'erba fresch' e.lh folha par' (Bernart de Ventadorn), 27–33 (Ex. 1), 393, 436–7
'Cantemus cuncti melodum nunc *Alleluia*', 394
'Cara michi pignora', 257 (Ex. 103)
'C'est la fins' (Guillame d'Amiens), 187–8 (Ex. 63)
'Chanter vueil pour fine Amour' (Jakemin de la Vante), 463
Christliche Schifflein, Das, see 'Matheus schreibt am achten'
'Cil s'entremet', 453–4 (Ex. 180)
'Clangam (Clangant), filii', 110–14 (Ex. 38), 136 (Ex. 47), 438–9 (Ex. 172)
'Clangat pastor', 254–5 (Ex. 101)
'Collegerunt pontifices', 289–92 (Ex. 122)
'Concelebremus', 49, 98 (Ex. 31)
'Cultor agri domini', 253 (Ex. 100)
'Cum appropinquaret Dominus', 278 (Ex. 112)

'Dame, merci', 468–9 (Ex. 184)
'Dame, t'amor requier', 482 (Ex. 193)
'D'amourous cuer voel canter' (Adam de la Halle), 34–6, 38–40 (Ex. 2)
'De bone amour' (Gace Brulé), 452–3 (Ex. 179)
'De chanter me semont Amors' (Vielart de Corbie), 395n.68
'De debounerete', 463–4
'De profundis ad te', 138–40 (Exx. 50–3)
'Dejost als breus jorns' (Pèire d'Alvernha), 496 (Ex. 198a)
'. . . descendit', 302–3 (Ex. 126)
'Deus, Deus meus, respice in me', 279, 304–6 (Ex. 131)
'Di nous, marchans tres bons', 261–2 (Ex. 108)
'Diastematica vocis armonia', 439 (Ex. 173)

551

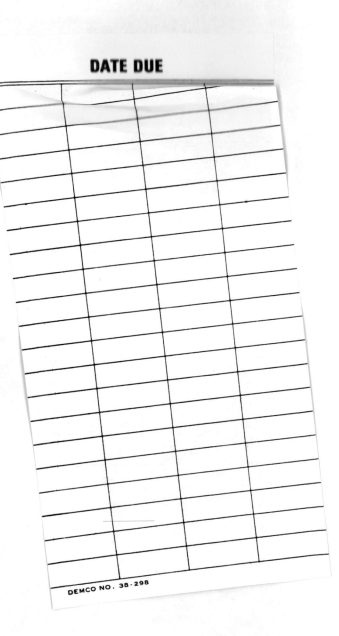

DATE DUE

DEMCO NO. 38-298